THE OXFORD
HISTORY OF ENGLISH MUSIC

VOLUME I

FRONTISPIECE. British Library, MS Add. 57950, fo. 81^r
(early 15th century: see Ex. 47)

THE OXFORD HISTORY OF ENGLISH MUSIC

VOLUME I

FROM THE BEGINNINGS TO *c*.1715

JOHN CALDWELL

CLARENDON PRESS · OXFORD

1991

Oxford University Press, Walton Street, Oxford OX2 6DP
Oxford New York Toronto
Delhi Bombay Calcutta Madras Karachi
Petaling Jaya Singapore Hong Kong Tokyo
Nairobi Dar es Salaam Cape Town
Melbourne Auckland
and associated companies in
Berlin Ibadan

Oxford is a trade mark of Oxford University Press

Published in the United States
by Oxford University Press, New York

British Library Cataloguing in Publication Data
The Oxford history of English music. / Caldwell, John
Vol. 1. From the beginnings to c. 1715
1. England. Music, history
I. Title 780.942
ISBN 0–19–816129–8

Library of Congress Cataloging-in-Publication Data
The Oxford history of English music. / John Caldwell.
Includes bibliographical references and index.
Contents: v. 1. From the beginnings to c. 1715.
1. Music—England—History and criticism. I. Title.
ML286.C28 1991 780'.942—dc20 90–14229
ISBN 0–19–816129–8

Typeset by BP Integraphics Ltd, Bath, Avon
Printed in Great Britain by
Bookcraft (Bath) Ltd., Midsomer Norton

To Janet, Peter, and Sarah

not forgetting

Dorabella and Fiordiligi,
whose constant need for personal services
during the decade of this book's composition
has considerably delayed its eventual completion

Preface

❦

THIS book owes its inception to a suggestion made many years ago that I might write a replacement for Ernest Walker's *History of Music in England*, the third edition of which appeared, substantially revised by J. A. Westrup, in 1952. I say 'inception' advisedly, since neither I nor the publisher foresaw the extent to which the project would have to grow in order to attain even a modest degree of comprehensiveness. In the event the new work, now entitled *The Oxford History of English Music*, has been divided into two volumes, a decision that has solved some problems and created others.

My definition of 'English Music' is inevitably wide and flexible. England absorbed a great deal of French culture in the Middle Ages, and it is not always easy to say whether a piece of music in an 'English' manuscript is English or not, even in a narrow geographical sense. The difference in nationhood was nevertheless apparent to contemporaries, even to the majority of the educated and well-to-do who wrote Latin and spoke French; and we should endeavour as far as possible to maintain and recognize the distinction as regards musical origins. Nearer to home, the word 'English' may grate upon the sensibilities of those from outside English borders who notice that Scottish and, in the next volume, Welsh and Irish matters are touched upon now and again. But 'British' would have been equally unsatisfactory, and I wanted to avoid giving the impression by the use of still more inclusive language that an account of music throughout these islands was being attempted. The intention, rather, is to discuss only those aspects of music outside England that can be illuminated by the comparison or that embody a substantial English element.

The division into two volumes, though forced on me by circumstances, has enabled me to make a small historiographical point. The date *c.*1715 may look odd in view of the change of dynasty in 1714, but the latter does not have quite the significance for musical history as it does for political. At the same time it is not unconnected with the profound changes that one can observe during the years 1711–20. At the beginning of that decade, Handel arrived in London to participate in a lively if somewhat decadent musical culture; by the end of it he had established himself as the major figure on the English musical scene. English music had ceased to be post-Purcellian; it had become thoroughly Italianate, and it was Handel who rescued the idiom from its potential for triviality. The consequences of that coup are matter for my second volume; in the meantime it is pleasant to reflect on the historical irony that brought to the English throne the very employer from whom Handel had overstayed his leave. The guarantee of stability provided by the Act of Succession was paralleled by the teutonic solidity offered by Handel, in its own way a guarantee of musical continuity in this country.

I am grateful to the Leverhulme Trust for the award of a Fellowship that facilitated the profitable use of a sabbatical year while the research for this volume was at a crucial stage. My personal debts to individuals during what has become a very long haul are too numerous to mention in full, but I wish particularly to thank those who read substantial parts of the typescript and by whose comments I have been saved from many a blunder and omission: Professor Brian Trowell, Dr Christopher Page, Dr Andrew Wathey, Dr John Milsom, and Dr Harry Johnstone. Dr F. W. Sternfeld has given invaluable advice and encouragement from the inception of the book onwards. I need hardly add they are not responsible for errors and inadequacies remaining; for these, I alone must take the blame. I also acknowledge with pleasure the encouragement and assistance of the staff of Oxford University Press, in particular Bruce Phillips and David Blackwell. My greatest debt, however, is to my wife, Janet, who has transformed a chaotic bundle of manuscript and typed material into a series of immaculately word-processed files, always with the greatest tact and efficiency; the index in particular is as much her work as mine. My dedication reflects my obligation not only to her, but to a family whose growing pains have largely coincided with those of this book, and whose members have put more into it than they know.

Oxford
1991

Acknowledgements

❧

THE author and publisher are grateful to the following for permission to reproduce photographs of materials in their possession: the Trustees of the British Museum (Frontispiece, and plates XIV and XV); the Bodleian Library, Oxford (plates II, III, XII, XIII, and XVI); the Master and Fellows of Corpus Christi College, Cambridge (plate I); the Biblioteca estense, Modena (plates IV and V), the Dean and Chapter, Durham Cathedral (plate VI); the Warden and Fellows of All Souls' College, Oxford (plate VII (a)); the Bate Collection of Historical Instruments (plate VII (b)); the Welsh Folk Museum, St Fagans, Cardiff (plate VIII); the National Portrait Gallery, London (plate IX); the Faculty of Music, Oxford University (plates X and XI).

They are additionally grateful to the following publishers for permission to quote extracts from their publications: Messrs Stainer and Bell Ltd (Exx. 131–4, 141–5, 174–5, 148–58); Messrs Stainer and Bell and the Musica Britannica Trust (Exx. 75–83, 123, 125, 127, 129, 137, 176, 178–9, 184, 189–192, 200–3); the British Academy (Exx. 92–5, 100–2, 121–2, 117–18, 135, 139); Friedrich Hänssler KG and the American Institute of Musicology (Exx. 84–8, 89–91, 99); Professor David Wulstan (Exx. 110, 114, 116, 136); Messrs. Faber and Faber (Exx. 180–1, 198–9); and Messrs Novello and Co. Ltd. (Exx. 204–5, 212–13, 216–17).

Contents

List of Plates

❧

between pp. 334–5

Tables

Abbreviations

THE following, in addition to those in common use, are employed in the footnotes and bibliography. Where full details are given here the item is not repeated in the bibliography; nor are details given of easily found journals and some other series.

AcM   *Acta Musicologica*

AH   Analecta hymnica medii aevi, ed. G. M. Dreves, C. Blume, and H. M. Bannister, 55 vols. (Leipzig, 1886–1922). *Register*, ed. M. Lütolf, 2 vols. in 3 (Berne and Munich, 1978)

AIM   American Institute of Musicology

AMw   *Archiv für Musikwissenschaft*

AnnM   *Annales Musicologiques*

AS   *Antiphonale Sarisburiense* (fac.), ed. W. H. Frere, 6 vols. (London: PMMS, 1901–25; repr. Farnborough: Gregg, 1966)

BGPM   *Beiträge zur Geschichte der Philosophie des Mittelalters*

BUCEM   *British Union Catalogue of Early Music*, ed. E. Schnapper, 2 vols. (London, 1957)

CEKM   Corpus of Early Keyboard Music, ed. W. Apel and others (AIM, 1963–)

CMM   Corpus Mensurabilis Musicae, ed. A. Carapetyan and others (Rome, etc.: AIM, 1947–)

CNRS   (Éditions du) Centre National de la Recherche Scientifique

CS   Scriptorum de Musica ... Nova Series, ed. E. H. de Coussemaker, 4 vols. (Paris, 1864–76; repr. Milan, 1931; Hildesheim, 1966)

CSM   Corpus Scriptorum de Musica, ed. A. Carapetyan (Rome, etc.: AIM, 1950–)

DPL   Documenta Polyphoniae Liturgicae Sanctae Ecclesiae Romanae, ed. L. Feininger, 13 vols. (Rome and Trent: Societas Universalis Sanctae Ceciliae, 1947–52)

DTO   Denkmäler der Tonkunst in Österreich, ed. G. Adler and others (Vienna and Graz: Artaria, 1894–)

EBM   *Early Bodleian Music*, 3 vols., ed. Sir J. Stainer (vols. 1–2) and E. W. B. Nicholson (vol. 3) (London: Novello, 1901–13)

EECM   Early English Church Music, ed. F. Ll. Harrison and others (London: Stainer and Bell, 1963–)

EEH	*Early English Harmony*, vol. i, ed. H. E. Wooldridge (fac.) (London: PMMS, 1897)
EETS	Early English Text Society
ELS	The English Lute-Songs (= The English School of Lutenist Song Writers, ed. E. H. Fellowes, 32 vols. in 2 series (London: Stainer and Bell, 1920–32); rev. R. T. Dart and others, 1959–)
ELS (fac.)	English Lute Songs, 1597–1632: A Collection of Facsimile Reprints, ed. F. W. Sternfeld (Menston: Scolar Press, 1967–9)
EM	The English Madrigalists (= The English Madrigal School, ed. E. H. Fellowes (London: Stainer and Bell, 1914–24); rev. R. T. Dart and others, 1958–)
EMH	*Early Music History*, ed. I. Fenlon (Cambridge, 1981–)
EMV	*English Madrigal Verse 1588–1632*, ed. E. H. Fellowes (Oxford, 1920; 3rd rev. edn. by F. W. Sternfeld and D. Greer, 1967). References are to the 3rd edition
ESLS	English School of Lutenist Song Writers (see ELS)
ESPHT	*English and Scottish Psalm and Hymn Tunes c.1543–1677*, ed. M. Frost (London: SPCK and OUP, 1953)
GS	*Graduale Sarisburiense* (fac.), ed. W. H. Frere, 2 vols. (London: PMMS, 1894; repr. in 1 vol., Farnborough: Gregg, 1966)
GSJ	*Galpin Society Journal*
HBS	Henry Bradshaw Society, Publications of (London, etc., 1891–)
IMM	Institute of Medieval Music
JAMS	*Journal of the American Musicological Society*
JPMMS	*Journal of the Plainsong and Medieval Musical Society*
JRMA	*Journal of the Royal Musical Association*
LSJ	*Lute Society Journal*
MB	Musica Britannica (London: Stainer and Bell for the Royal Musical Association, 1951–)
MC	Musica da Camera, ed. J. Caldwell (London: OUP, 1972–)
MD	*Musica Disciplina*
MGG	*Die Musik in Geschichte und Gegenwart*, ed. F. Blume, 16 vols. (Kassel and Basel, 1949–79)
ML	*Music and Letters*
MLE	Music for London Entertainment 1660–1800 (Tunbridge Wells: Richard Macnutt, 1983–7; London: Stainer and Bell, 1988–)
MMMLF	Monuments of Music and Music Literature in Facsimile (New York: Broude Bros.)
MQ	*Musical Quarterly*
MR	*Music Review*
MSD	Musicological Studies and Documents
MT	*Musical Times*

NGD	*The New Grove Dictionary of Music and Musicians*, ed. S. Sadie, 20 vols. (London, 1981)
NOHM	*The New Oxford History of Music*, ed. J. A. Westrup and others, 10 vols. (London and Oxford, 1954–90)
PMA	*Proceedings of the Musical Association*
PMFC	Polyphonic Music of the Fourteenth Century, ed. L. Schrade and others (Monaco: Éditions de l'Oiseau-lyre, 1956–85)
PMMS	Plainsong and Medieval Music Society
PRMA	*Proceedings of the Royal Musical Association*
PS	*The Works of Henry Purcell* (Purcell Society)
RBMAS	Rerum Britannicarum Medii Aevi Scriptores (Rolls Series), 99 vols. (London, 1858–96)
RISM	*Répertoire International des Sources Musicales* (Munich and Duisberg, 1960–)
RMARC	*Royal Musical Association Research Chronicle*
RRMBE	Recent Researches in Music of the Baroque Era
RRMR	Recent Researches in Music of the Renaissance
SBK	Stainer and Bell, Keyboard Series
SS	Surtees Society, Publications of
STC	*A Short-Title Catalogue of Books Printed in England, Scotland, and Ireland . . . 1475–1640*, 2nd edn. by W. A. Jackson, F. S. Ferguson, and K. F. Pantzer, 3 vols. (London, 1976–90)
TCM	Tudor Church Music, ed. E. H. Fellowes and others, 10 vols. (London: OUP, 1922–9); Appendix (London, 1948)
TVNM	*Tijdschrift der Vereeniging voor Nederlands Musikgeschiedenis*

Author's Note

❧

SMALL roman numerals refer to volumes, arabic numerals to pages, except that arabic numerals are used for volumes of journals and, following an oblique stroke, for parts of a volume. Large roman numerals refer to a series within a collection. In the books of the Bible, small roman numerals indicate the chapter or psalm number in the Vulgate Latin, arabic numerals those of the Authorized Version (which in the Old Testament follows the Hebrew). In both cases the verse, if cited, follows in arabic after a colon. For example, Ps. cxviii: 1 (Latin) = Ps. 119: 1 (English), though the verses are not always identical.

References to musical pitches are to the Helmholtz system (*C* = cello C; *c* = viola C; *c′* = middle C, etc.). The anachronistic but convenient convention *a 2*, *a 3*, and so on, refers to polyphonic music in two, three (etc.) strict parts. In the musical examples, time-values are generally reduced (by the amount stated) in Chapters 1–5; but not thereafter, although some examples are transposed if the written pitch is seriously misleading. Small accidentals are implied by but not stated in the source, while those above the staff or in square brackets are purely editorial. English texts set to music are given in the original orthography in Chapters 1–4; thereafter, except where stated, they are modernized (to avoid inconsistencies between part-books or different editions), although titles (but not first lines) and literary quotations retain the original spelling wherever possible. Medieval Latin texts are given a medieval orthography, later ones that of the source used.

In the first four chapters, part-names, including *tenor*, are treated as Latin technical terms referring primarily to polyphonic function rather than to vocal range, and are given in italic type; thereafter they are treated as voice-parts in the modern sense and are given in roman type, even if in Latin. In Anglican music the terms 'decani' ('of the dean') and 'cantoris' ('of the cantor') are used of the south and north sides of the choir respectively and are sometimes abbreviated in the examples to 'Dec' and 'Can'. Other abbreviations used in some of the examples are Tr (triplex or treble), M (medius or mean), Ct (contratenor or countertenor,) T (tenor), and B (bass or bassus).

References to the calendar year are adjusted to begin on 1 January; dates refer to the Julian calendar throughout the period covered by this book. Thus Charles I was executed on 30 January (not 10 February) 1649 (not 1648). There are no references to Continental dates after 1581.

1

FROM THE BEGINNINGS TO
THE MIDDLE OF THE
THIRTEENTH CENTURY

WHEN during the course of the fifth century Britain was first colonized by Germanic peoples in appreciable numbers, they brought with them a long-standing tradition of sung narrative poetry, which according to Tacitus was their only record of the past.[1] Although similar traditions no doubt already belonged both to the Celtic peoples whom they eventually supplanted in most parts of Britain, and to the Scandinavians who invaded and settled in large numbers from the end of the eighth century, it was in the context of the Anglo-Saxon language and culture that the genre first made a noticeable impact on the artistic life of the country. The great monument of this tradition is *Beowulf*, a poem of over 3,000 lines and the oldest epic in any Germanic language. Neither its date nor its place of origin is known for certain, but an eighth-century Midlands or Northern milieu is generally assumed. The single manuscript in which it has come down to us, however, was written in Wessex in the tenth century, and it is uncertain how closely the extant version resembles chanted heroic poetry, orally composed and orally handed down from singer to singer. Nor do we know to what extent the poem, even if faithfully recorded in the first instance from an authoritative branch of the oral tradition, was subsequently modified on the basis of written copies. In all probability a poet of genius has at some point refined and polished a rougher original, perhaps arranging a number of distinct lays into a single cohesive narrative. That, after all, is a plausible view of the Homeric poems, or, in a period long after that of *Beowulf*, such European masterpieces as the *Chanson de Roland* and the *Nibelungenlied*.

The musical nature of the *Beowulf* poem or its unwritten ancestor is also a matter that has occasioned a good deal of speculation. But while

---

[1] *Germania*, ch. 2.

the structure of alliterative verse may lead to certain conclusions, the precise rhythms and the melodic contours, the nature of the accompaniment and its relation to the vocal line, can only be conjectural.[2]

The main interest of *Beowulf* in musical history is as a source for the social context of singing and 'harping' in heroic terms. As in the *Iliad*, music-making is as likely to be by the aristocrat as by the professional. After the defeat of the monster Grendel 'a fellow of the king's . . . wrought a new lay made in the measure'.[3] Improvised as it was on horseback during the journey home, no mention is made of any musical content: but this is surely the kind of thing which, recollected in the tranquillity of the king's hall, would have been given a musical setting either by the versifier himself or by a professional singer. The discovery of a hoard of treasure, and the reflection that the men who amassed it have wholly disappeared, gives rise to the comment 'there's no joy from harp-play, gleewood's gladness'.[4] The word 'harp' (as verb or noun) must refer in this poem not to the triangular or quadrangular instrument later so called, but to a form of lyre known from a number of survivals and representations from the ancient Germanic world. The most spectacular of these survivals, and one which is lent an added significance by its discovery in a ship-burial analogous to that described at the beginning of *Beowulf*,[5] is the extensive remains of a musical instrument found at the Sutton Hoo site in 1939. Though originally reconstructed as a quadrangular harp, it has more recently been appreciated that it must have been a 'round lyre' of the Germanic, and more specifically Anglo-Saxon, type, and it is now displayed as such, side by side with the original fragments and much else of great historical interest, in the British Museum.[6] We shall never know the exact nature of the music played on such an instrument; but the small number of its strings (six) suggests a gapped tuning suitable for the accompaniment of song, while its quiet tone would have been appropriate both to the performance of a professional singer before a hushed audience and to the private amusement of an aristocrat.

Singing to such an instrument must have been an accomplishment which permeated several layers of Anglo-Saxon society. Apart from the hints in

---

[2] For a recent thorough discussion of the issues involved, with reference to earlier writers, see J. Stevens, *Words and Music in the Middle Ages: Song, Narrative, Dance and Drama, 1050–1350* (Cambridge, 1986), 204–12.

[3] ll. 867–71. This quotation and the next are from the translation of extracts from *Beowulf* in M. Alexander, *The Earliest English Poems* (Harmondsworth, 1966). Cf. *Beowulf*, ed. with an intro., notes, and prose transl., by M. Swanton (Manchester, 1978), the most useful edition for the general reader.

[4] ll. 2262–3.

[5] ll. 26–52; Alexander, *Earliest English Poems*, 49.

[6] Cf. Plate VI. For the details of this and other Germanic lyres see R. and M. Bruce-Mitford, 'The Sutton Hoo Lyre, *Beowulf*, and the Origins of the Frame Harp', *Antiquity*, 44 (1970), 7–13.

Beowulf, the representation in more than one psalter of King David playing the lyre suggests an aristocratic use, while the well-known story of St Aldhelm retaining his congregation for the sermon after Mass by addressing them in the manner of a minstrel[7] is scarcely less apposite. Bede's account of Cædmon's shame at being unable to play when the 'cithara' was handed round after a meal gives a vivid picture of the level of accomplishment expected at a lower social level,[8] while *Widsith*, which is believed to incorporate some of the oldest poems in the English language, is the story of a widely travelled minstrel, or *scop*, and his repertory of ancient Germanic legend.[9] Much of this evidence illustrates the adaptation of a heathen practice to the purposes of the church—Cædmon's inspiration, when it came, was of a wholly religious kind—and it prompts the conjecture that the singing of alliterative verse may have resembled, or become assimilated to, the idioms of Christian psalmody.

The lyre was eventually superseded in England as the minstrel's instrument *par excellence* by the true harp, although it survived for several centuries in a modified form both as a plucked instrument and, as the *chorus* or *crowd* (from the Welsh word *crwth*) as a bowed instrument. The origin of the harp in medieval Europe is in many ways a mystery. The large triangular form, as tall as the player, is already found carved on Scottish standing stones of the ninth and tenth centuries, which tends to confirm an insular origin; while in subsequent epochs a wide variety of sizes and shapes can be seen. The Junius XI manuscript in the Bodleian Library, of the tenth or early eleventh century, already shows the smaller triangular form, resting on the player's knee, perhaps the most characteristic type of the Middle Ages.[10] The word *hearpe* eventually came to denote this instrument alone, though for a time it must have referred to both lyre and harp. The newer instrument may have owed its popularity in England to its suitability for a wide repertory and a more brilliant manner of performance, perhaps as much in solo instrumental music as in accompanying the voice. A passage in the poem known as *The Fortunes of Men* seems to illustrate this type of virtuoso music, the province of the skilled, if indigent, professional:

Another shall sit with his harp at his lord's feet, and shall receive payment; and

---

[7] 'quasi artem cantitandi professum'. William of Malmesbury, *Gesta Pontificum*, ed. N.E.S.A. Hamilton, RBMAS, lii (1870), 336. The story is derived from King Alfred's lost *Handboc*. Cf. Aldhelm, *De virginitate*, ll. 67–74.

[8] *Historia ecclesiastica*, iv, ch. 22.

[9] Alexander, *Earliest English Poems*, 38–42.

[10] R. and M. Bruce-Mitford, 'The Sutton Hoo Lyre', 11–12. A small quadrangular type also existed, though this is sometimes hard to distinguish, especially when carved on standing stones, from the Celtic *cruit* (or *crot*; Lat. *rotta* etc., Welsh *crwth*), which is a form of lyre.

ever the leaping shackle, the joyfully sounding nail, shall quickly pull the strings, causing them to make a shrill noise; his need is great.[11]

Such passages as this, and the Riddle of the Song-Thrush, with its references to changing (*wrixlan*), 'head-tone' (*heafodwoþe*), 'tunes' (*wisan*), and so on,[12] provide our nearest approach to an Old English musical terminology. Though in the specialized idiom of verse, they offer a more vivid picture than the bald equivalents of Latin terms provided by prose documents such as translations of Bede or the Bible. Nor are we any better informed as to the overall character of musical life, other than in the Church, during the Anglo-Saxon period. It is hardly conceivable that a considerable proportion of sung poetry was not lyrical rather than narrative in content and form. Such poems as *Deor* and the fragmentary *Wulf and Eadwacer*,[13] with their haunting refrains, may point to the character of a lost body of sung lyrical poetry, though here again it may be that the written form represents a stylized modification of vocal idioms. No doubt the ample documentation from the later Middle Ages for the widespread use of dance and popular song at every social level, with its concomitant abundance of musical instruments, can be extrapolated into the Anglo-Saxon period; but beyond some scraps of evidence from a scanty iconography the details remain obscure.

There is, however, one class of document that does shed a feeble light on the cultivation of music outside the liturgy, though not beyond the Church's sphere of influence. There do exist two or three English pre-Conquest manuscripts of Latin verse in which some of the poems, or parts of poems, are surmounted by 'unheighted neumes', those aggravatingly imprecise guides to melodic contour that are the remote ancestor of modern musical notation. Some of the poems in Boethius' *Consolation of Philosophy* are found treated in this way, as well as some of the non-liturgical hymns of Prudentius, a Spanish writer of the fourth century.[14] Such material was eminently suited to the medieval classroom, where these poems may indeed have been chanted; but the actual tunes are irrecoverable unless any of them turn out to be identical (as is the case with one or two Continental examples) to liturgical hymn-tunes preserved in later manuscripts.

[11] 'Sum sceal mid hearpan · æt his hlafordes | fotum sittan, · feoh þicgan; | ond a snellice · snere wræstan, | lætan scralletan · sceacol, se þe hleapeð, | nægl neomegende; · biþ him neod micel', ll. 80–4. The interpretation and text are doubtful; see C. Page, 'Anglo-Saxon Hearpan', D. Phil. diss. (York, 1981), 179 seqq.; J. Stevens, *Words and Music*, 206.

[12] No. 8 in the edition of the Riddles published in *The Anglo-Saxon Poetic Records*, iii (New York, 1936), 185. There is a literal translation, with a discussion of the correct solution of the riddle, in P. F. Baum, *Anglo-Saxon Riddles of the Exeter Book* (Durham, NC, 1963), p. xv.

[13] Alexander, *Earliest English Poems*, 43, 85.

[14] For neumes in a liturgical context see Plate I. For Boethius, see Page in *Boethius: His Life, Thought and Influence*, ed. M. Gibson (Oxford, 1981), 306–11, with a facsimile from Oxford, Bod. Lib., Auct. F. I. 15, from Canterbury. Neumed hymns by Prudentius are found in another Bodleian MS, Auct. F. 3. 6, from the later 11th cent.

The most interesting of these documents is a collection of songs preserved in a manuscript now in the Cambridge University Library and generally known as the 'Cambridge Songbook'.[15] The songbook proper is but a small part of a collection of materials brought together for use in the school attached to the abbey of St Augustine's, Canterbury; the manuscript includes amongst other things Hucbald of St Amand's famous musical treatise *De harmonica institutione*. The songbook itself is believed to have been copied from a German exemplar. Of the songs with neumes only one, an erotically worded farewell of a schoolmaster to a favourite pupil and entitled 'O admirabile Veneris idolum', has a melody that can be reconstructed. This is because it was also used for a Christian song in the same metre, 'O Roma nobilis', the music of which has been recorded in a readable notation. In this case the tune and both poems are probably all Italian. All but one of the remaining songs with neumes are on a single leaf of the songbook: they are further examples of poems (*metra*) from *The Consolation of Philosophy*. A few other poems with neumes are found elsewhere in the manuscript, but these too cannot be transcribed.[16]

The significance of all this for English music is sociological rather than musical. It is quite possible that the neumes (and hence the actual tunes) for the Boethian *metra* at least were invented by the English scribe himself; but there are difficulties in allocating the notated phrases to the complete poems, and in any case the melodies are indecipherable. But we may perhaps legitimately imagine the spectacle of a class of boys and youths, destined to become monks or clerks, improving their Latin with the aid of verse that is mostly decorous (and philosophically quite demanding) even when pagan, some of it at least being sung to melodies that might be either universally known or of purely local origin.[17]

The Church and its sacred chant was naturally a dominant feature of the musical life of the emergent English nation. Although Gregory the Great had allowed St Augustine considerable freedom in the choice of liturgical (and hence musical) practice in his newly founded Church,[18] there was a tendency to prefer things Roman in contra-distinction to the older practices favoured by the existing British Church and by Celtic Christians generally.

[15] Cambridge, Univ. Lib., MS Gg. v. 35; ed. with fac. by K. Breul, *The Cambridge Songs* (Cambridge, 1915); song texts ed. K. Strecker (Berlin, 1926). On the MS as a whole, see A. R. Rigg and G. R. Wealand, 'A Canterbury Classbook of the Mid-Eleventh Century', in *Anglo-Saxon England*, 4 (1975), 113–30.

[16] See M. Gibson, M. Lapidge and C. Page, 'Neumed Boethian *metra* from Canterbury', in *Anglo-Saxon England*, 12(1983), 141–52; I. Fenlon (ed.), *Cambridge Music Manuscripts 900–1700* (Cambridge, 1982), 20–4.

[17] A whole repertory of neumed verse by such authors as Virgil, Horace, Statius, and Juvenal survives in Continental and English MSS. Horace's ode 'Est mihi nonum' (I. xi) is set to the tune of 'Ut queant laxis' in MS Montpellier 425, the tune on which Guido of Arezzo based his solmization symbols *ut re mi fa sol la*.

[18] *Hist. eccl.* i, ch. 27.

The British Church was wrong, so it seemed to romanized Christians, in its method of computing the date of Easter and in its form of tonsure. Such points may seem trivial today, but they were symptomatic of larger things—in particular the attitude to centralized authority—and they led to a sharp polarization of the differences between the Churches and the eventual disappearance of the Celtic Church in England.[19] This could not but be reflected in liturgical and musical practice; and when the music of the newer and ultimately dominant Church required reform (as seems to have been not infrequently the case), it was the Roman methods that were chosen as a model. Thus we read in Bede's *Historia ecclesiastica* of the activities of James the Deacon in the diocese of York during the second quarter of the seventh century: 'He had a wide knowledge of church music; and when peace was at length restored to the province and the number of believers increased, he began to teach many people to sing the music of the Church after the Uses of Rome and Canterbury.'[20] A successor to James in Northumbria was Æddi, known as Stephen, the biographer of St Wilfrid, who had invited him north from Kent; and at about the same time, in the year 669, Putta, 'a most skilled exponent of Roman chant, which he had learnt from pupils of blessed Pope Gregory', was consecrated Bishop of Rochester.[21] The best-known of Bede's references to the teaching of Roman chant in England is his circumstantial account of the visit of John, arch-cantor of St Peter's and abbot of St Martin's monastery in Rome, to teach the chant for the liturgical year according to the Use of St Peter's to the monks at Wearmouth and elsewhere (680).[22] The same episode is referred to in Bede's *Historia abbatum*, where it is mentioned that John's teaching on ecclesiastical matters was conveyed both viva voce and in writing. This is a modified version of the account in a slightly earlier and anonymous *Historia abbatum* from the same centre, namely Wearmouth or Jarrow: here the wording suggests that it was the

[19] The British Church had accepted the decision of general councils up to that of Arles in 455, where the method of computing Easter proposed by Leo I was adopted in a modified form. Subsequent events, however, had isolated it from Continental catholicism; and while liturgical uniformity was not at that time a great issue, its ignorance of developments on the Easter question, together with its failure to convert the invaders, helped to create the situation of conflict which followed the arrival of St Augustine. At the Synod of Whitby in 663 the question of the date of Easter was argued with the Irish Church, which had played a much more positive role in the conversion and was to continue to do so; and with the victory of the Roman side the way was paved towards a more uniform liturgical observance throughout the country.

[20] *Hist. eccl.* ii, ch. 20. The translation used in this and the following quotations is that of L. Sherley-Price (Harmondsworth, 1955).

[21] *Hist. eccl.* iv, ch. 2. After the destruction of Rochester in 676, Putta settled in Mercia and taught the chant there (ibid., ch. 12). The Northumbrians subsequently needed further instruction, since under bishop Acca of Hexham (himself a skilled singer) Maban, who had been taught by successors of the disciples of Gregory in Kent, was retained for twelve years to teach ecclesiastical chant. Ibid. v, ch. 20.

[22] *Hist. eccl.* iv, ch. 16.

singing itself that was so taught.[23] This, taken in conjunction with the well-known thirteenth canon of the Council of 'Clofeshoe' (perhaps Brixworth, 747), which specified the singing of the services 'in accordance with the written exemplar received from Rome',[24] has sometimes been taken as indicating some form of musical notation; but in default of any certain indication of the existence of written music at this date, and indeed in the face of a certain amount of evidence to the contrary, it seems best to regard these phrases as referring to copies of the verbal texts only, like the antiphonal and 'missal' which Egbert, Archbishop of York in the eighth century, reports as having been sent with St Augustine to England.[25]

A related question is that of the form of Roman chant actually transmitted to England, and whether any very authoritative version of the melodies can have been preserved under such circumstances. Written Continental sources of chants for the Roman rite, which do not begin to appear until about 900, preserve two distinct types, the so-called Gregorian and the Old Roman, the earliest manuscript of the latter being dated 1071. Without entering into the controversy over the relation between the two, and their places and dates of origin, it may be stated with some confidence that whatever was heard in Rome in the seventh century is unlikely to have resembled either of them in detail. Quite possibly it was a form of chant in which, had it survived, we should recognize the parent of both. What should be made clear, however, is that despite the apparently musical terminology employed by Bede and others, the prime concern of all these reformers was the establishment of an authorized Roman liturgical framework and a dependable version of the texts. In a period when the improvisation of solo chants from stock materials was still an important method of composition, nothing very stable in the way of a melodic tradition is to be expected; and in all probability it was not aimed at.

What is certain is that when the earliest English manuscripts of chant begin to appear in the early eleventh century it is the 'Gregorian' repertoire, enhanced by tropes and Sequences (see n. 31 below), that they preserve. It was Alcuin, once a pupil at the school founded at York by Egbert, who was responsible at least to some extent for making the arrangements consequent upon the substitution of the Roman for the Old Gallican rite in the Frankish kingdom under Pepin III and Charlemagne, though some of the details formerly attributed to Alcuin are now thought to be the

---

[23] 'qui nos abundantur ordinem cantandi per ordinem et uiua uoce simul et litteris edocuit', *Venerabilis Baedae Opera historica*, ed. C. Plummer (Oxford, 1896), i. 391; cf. ibid. 369.

[24] 'in cantilenae modo celebrentur, iuxta exemplum videlicet, quod scriptum de Romana habemus ecclesia.' Gerbert, *De cantu et musica sacra* (St Blaise, 1774), i. 262, cited P. Wagner, *Einführung in die gregorianischen Melodien*, i (3rd edn., Leipzig, 1911), 231.

[25] Egbert, *De institutione catholica*, cited Wagner, *Einführung*, 192. A certain amount of additional information on church music in England at this time is given by Wagner, pp. 197–8, 228–32.

work of St Benedict of Aniane. One of the consequences was the adoption or indeed to some extent the creation of 'Gregorian' chant in this part of the world. The new rite and the Frankish version of the chant were to become generally adopted in Rome during the eleventh century, supplanting the Old Roman forms in many of their strongholds, ultimately to drive them out altogether. In the meantime, with the aid of musical notation and the universal applicability of Alcuin's version of the Roman liturgy, 'Gregorian' chant had triumphed almost everywhere including England itself.[26]

It is in the aftermath of the monastic revival of the tenth century that the first signs of a distinctively English contribution to liturgical music can be discerned. The Viking attacks on Lindisfarne in 793 and on Iona in 795 may be taken as the symbolic beginning of a century and a half of decline in the English Church, particularly in the sphere of its monastic life. Invasion and battle bred illiteracy and a decline in religious vocation, and these in turn must have affected the music of the Church, its most fragile possession and the one which the monasteries were most active in preserving. The brief revival under Alfred, who saw only too plainly the trend and undertook heroic measures to reverse it, was followed by the even stronger decline of the later ninth and early tenth centuries. By 900 monastic life had virtually disappeared, the monasteries themselves being peopled by secular clerks. The political stability of England under Eadwig (955–9) and Edgar (959–75) set the scene for the remarkable change of emphasis in the latter part of the century,[27] during which not only were old monasteries reformed and new ones founded, but even in cathedral churches such as Winchester and Worcester the secular clergy were replaced by monks. Of the three principal figures in the reform, two—St Dunstan (c.909–88) and Æthelwold (d. 984)—are significant figures in musical history. Æthelwold is said to have built an organ at his abbey of Abingdon 'with his own hands';[28] and as bishop of Winchester (from 963, the year before the expulsion of the clerks) he was presumably responsible for the instrument in use before the construction of a much larger one during the episcopacy of Ælfeah II (984–1005). As for St Dunstan, his genius took many forms. He was a metal-worker and a painter as well as a musician. He donated an organ to Malmesbury abbey, played several instruments,

[26] The main exceptions were Milan, where the Ambrosian liturgy still held sway, and Mozarabic Spain, where the Roman rite and chant were not introduced until the 11th cent.

[27] It was, however, preceded by St Dunstan's 15-year rule as abbot of Glastonbury from 940 under Edmund (939–46) and Eadred (946–55). Dunstan was exiled by Eadwig, to return on the accession of Edgar.

[28] *Chronicon monasterii de Abingdon*, ed. J. Stevenson (London, 1858), ii. 278. It was under Æthelwold at Abingdon that monks were sent from Corbie to revive the chant there. Ibid. i, ch. 129.

and more importantly is credited with an actual composition, the very beautiful Kyrie 'Rex splendens'.[29]

It was not, however, at Canterbury, where St Dunstan became archbishop in 960, but at Winchester that monastic reform and the revival of church music seem to have been centred. The organ set up by Ælfeah and described so fully, if in somewhat exaggerated terms, by Wulfstan the cantor,[30] was but the outward sign of a genuinely flourishing musical culture, already established by Æthelwold on becoming bishop. This is symbolized by the two tropers from Winchester, the earliest complete English liturgical manuscripts with musical notation to have survived. The earlier and smaller of the two, now MS 473 at Corpus Christi College in Cambridge, has been dated between 996 and 1006 so far as its original contents are concerned.[31] It is to be described technically as a *cantatorium*, in the sense that it is a small book destined for the cantor's own use; unlike some *cantatoria*, however, its contents are not confined to those parts of the chants sung by the cantor alone, and it must have been used by him as an *aide-mémoire* for teaching the choir as well as for singing from. It is not at all improbable that this was Wulfstan's own book and that his is one of the two principal early hands to be discerned in it. Its most distinctive feature, however, is its inclusion of a large number of polyphonic parts to various kinds of chant. This is the earliest practical source of polyphonic music to have come down to us from anywhere, which makes this manuscript a document

[29] Eadmer (d. 1124) in his *Life* of St Dunstan tells the story of the communication of a Kyrie to Dunstan in a dream, and adds that it was sung at Mass in many places in his day. It was later identified with 'Rex splendens', sung in the Salisbury rite on the feasts of St Michael and St Dunstan. Eadmer's words seem to refer to the melody itself rather than to any added prose; and the tune does occur, without the text 'Rex splendens', in the Bodleian troper shortly to be described. *Memorials of St Dunstan*, ed. W. Stubbs, RBMAS, lxiii (London, 1874), pp. cxiv–cxv, 207, 357; A. Planchart, *The Repertory of Tropes at Winchester* (Princeton, NJ, 1977), i. 259–60. For the melody see Ex. 1 below.

[30] *Narratio metrica de Sancto Swithuno*, preface, ll. 141–72; discussed A. Holschneider, *Die Organa von Winchester* (Hildesheim, 1968), 139–44; J. W. McKinnon in *The Organ Yearbook*, 5 (1974), 4–19.

[31] Planchart, *The Repertory of Tropes*, i. 32. This is not too discordant with the earlier estimate of A. Holschneider, *Die Organa*, 19–20, who places the manuscript in the first quarter of the 11th cent. It is to be noted that while the manuscript was written before the Bodleian troper described below, it was copied from a later archetype, and to a certain extent (particularly with regard to its polyphonic music, discussed below) may well represent the original written form of the music which it contains. The two manuscripts are known as tropers from the presence in them of tropes, or accretions to the liturgy, in this case the Mass. Tropes may consist of purely musical additions to the existing chant, of verbal additions with newly composed music (the usual medieval sense), or of intercalated words set to existing melismatic music (yielding the *prosa* or *prosula*). The Sequence (*sequentia*) was at first a lengthy melismatic setting of the word 'Alleluia' when this was repeated after the verse in the Alleluia of the Mass (the complete form being Alleluia, verse, Alleluia and/or Sequence). Sequences with additional text seem originally to have been modelled on the melismatic versions—hence their commonly used name *prosa*—though opinion is divided as to whether this was invariably the case. The Winchester tropers contain examples of both melismatic and texted (syllabic) Sequences, with monophonic and polyphonic examples of each. Later Sequences, which nearly always have a rhythmical text, were either given fresh musical settings or were adapted to a melody previously furnished for a similar text.

of the first importance in the history of Western music. The notation of these parts, like the rest of the manuscript, is in unheighted neumes, making accurate transcription impossible; yet, the chant melodies themselves being recoverable from later sources and the polyphonic parts being annotated with abbreviations (the so-called *litterae significativae*) indicating variations of speed and of pitch, some sort of attempt is not only possible but obligatory for the serious investigator.

The other manuscript from Winchester, sometimes called the 'troper of Ethelred', is in the Bodleian Library at Oxford.[32] It is larger than the other and somewhat later; its original contents were copied around 1050, although they derive from an archetype going back to between 978 and 980. It too has its own special distinction, since it is the earliest surviving manuscript to contain the music for a genuinely dramatic version of the Easter dialogue 'Quem quaeritis in sepulchro'.[33] Two other pre-Conquest manuscripts of ecclesiastical chant may be referred to here: the incomplete troper Cotton Caligula A. XIV in the British Library (c.1050), probably from Canterbury, and the 'Portiforium Wulstani' at Cambridge, Corpus Christi College, MS 391. The latter is a breviary with music which once belonged not to the cantor of Winchester but to his namesake, bishop of Worcester from 1062 until his death in 1095.

It is a difficult matter to assess with any precision the indigenous element in these pre-Conquest liturgical manuscripts. All of them are closely related to French sources in repertory and notation, though they are not exclusively French in content. The section of the Bodleian manuscript devoted to proses (Sequences with texts), for example, contains both French and German ('Notkerian') proses. Music for the feasts of English Saints, for example Swithun and Æthelwold at Winchester, might be supposed to embody original composition by native musicians; yet so far as the 'standard' liturgical forms are concerned—antiphons and responds of the Mass and Office—the new texts were generally adapted to older music in a fashion universal throughout western Europe. It is true that tropes fall into a different category: a total of thirty-seven certain and fifty-eight probable tropes of English origin has been identified, though some of these are also adaptations.[34] Unfortunately, the bulk of this material is indecipherable, being in unheighted neumes and without parallels in later sources; only the melodies of some of the adaptations can be recovered.

Of course we have St Dunstan's Kyrie 'Rex splendens', mentioned above; and it may be that one or two of the other items of the Ordinary of the Mass in the rich collection of melodies used in the English Church, both before and after the Conquest, might prove to be the work of Englishmen.

---

[32] MS Bod. 775 (shelved as Arch. F. d. 7).
[33] See W. Smoldon, 'The Easter Sepulchre Music Drama', *ML*, 27 (1946), 1–17.
[34] Planchart, *The Repertory of Tropes*, i. 145–66.

The magnificent Kyrie known as 'Rex summe' is possibly one such.[35] But by and large the 'English' element in the plainsong books of the Middle Ages is represented by a process of adaptation, both in connection with the fitting of new words and for its own sake. This latter is particularly true of the hymn-melodies in the later Middle Ages, where there seems to have been a conscious process of refashioning in order to meet a highly sophisticated conception of melodic beauty.

In much the same way, the liturgical dramas which were actively cultivated in England and elsewhere in the British Isles contain little in the way of original composition. The Bodleian sepulchre drama is an important historical document, but there is nothing to suggest that it was not taken over in its entirety from a French archetype. It is very close in its form to what is prescribed in the rubrics of the *Regularis Concordia*, Æthelwold's monastic customary for English houses; but the *Regularis Concordia* itself was based on existing and widespread Continental practice. The brief *officium* simply adds four short antiphons to the dialogue 'Quem quaeritis in sepulchro', widely known as a separate piece in several Continental centres. It has to be remembered in considering this form of liturgical music that it originated in monasticism and that its context was the night Office. Its function, nevertheless, was the instruction of the assembled laity; and in England as on the Continent it was natural that it should be incorporated into the customs of the secular cathedrals. But it never achieved the degree of artistic independence, as exemplified both in the choice of subject-matter and its treatment, that it had in France: this was to be the province rather of the vernacular mystery play which succeeded it in this country. The most frequently found liturgical plays are the Easter sepulchre play, the *peregrinus* play performed on Easter Monday, and the Shepherds' play performed between Matins and the midnight Mass of Christmas. Amidst a mass of documents testifying to their widespread use there is a surprising paucity of musical or even verbal texts. The plays were not included in antiphonals or graduals, whether monastic or secular, as they sometimes were in France; with the decline of troping in the twelfth century a convenient context for their copying all but disappeared; their next home was the processional, but even so there are surprisingly few survivals. Two fourteenth-century processionals of Salisbury Use from Dublin[36] preserve what is possibly the most extended form achieved by the Easter play within a liturgical framework in these islands. Here too there is little or nothing

[35] *The Use of Salisbury: The Ordinary of the Mass*, i, ed. N. Sandon (Newton Abbot, 1984), 64 (Kyrie XVII).

[36] Oxford, Bod. Lib., Rawl. lit. d. 4; Dublin, Marsh's Lib., Z4. 2. 20. A transcription and facsimile of the Easter play in these manuscripts is given in M. Egan-Buffet and A. J. Fletcher, 'The Dublin *Visitatio Sepulcri* Play', *Proceedings of the Royal Irish Academy*, C/90 (1990), no. 7 (pp. 159–241); see also D. Dolan, *Le Drame liturgique de Pâques* (Paris, 1975) 141–72.

in the music attributable to an insular origin. The opening lament for the
three Marys, for instance, derives both verbally and musically from the
version found in the Fleury play-book,[37] while the adaptation of the Easter
Sequence 'Victimae paschali laudes' as a dramatic confrontation between
the women and the two apostles was by then a commonplace of this drama.

If little individuality is to be found in the monophonic music of the English
medieval church, it is quite otherwise so far as polyphony is concerned.
There is no evidence to show that the polyphony of the 'Cambridge' Winchester troper is anything but insular in origin. It is true that there is no
contemporary collection of Continental music with which the Winchester
polyphony can be compared; but some Continental fragments of slightly
later date[38] yield no concordances with it, a situation which contrasts with
the rather surprising appearance of an early twelfth-century piece in both
France and England, in a repertory of which the survivals are much less
numerous.[39] It has even been argued that Wulfstan himself may have composed most of this music. Wulfstan was certainly an outstanding figure
at Winchester in the early eleventh century, though his documented
achievements are literary rather than musical. He must, however, have
been a skilled singer and instructor, if the tropers are to be accepted as
a genuine record of the Winchester repertory in his day. William of Malmesbury believed him to have written a musical treatise 'de tonorum armonia'.[40]
On the other hand the enormous size of the polyphonic repertory, though
not the apparent uniformity of the idiom, does weigh somewhat against
the theory of single authorship. Nevertheless, Wulfstan must have been
actively engaged in the teaching and performance of the repertory; all but
a few of the *organa* were copied in the same hand, which may possibly
be that of Wulfstan himself; and it is precisely in the sphere of polyphonic
elaboration that we should expect the individuality of a cantor to be exerted.
At the very least, we might legitimately think of Wulfstan as compiler,
arranger, and in part composer of the repertory.[41]

[37] Orléans, Bibl. de la ville, 201 (13th cent.).
[38] Chartres, Bibl. mun., 4, flyleaf (destroyed); Rome, Bibl. vat., Reg. lat. 586 and 592 (both from
Fleury).
[39] Chartres, Bibl. mun., 109 and 130 (destroyed), of the late 11th and early 12th cents. respectively.
All these sources are described in Holschneider, *Die Organa*, 63–7. The concordance with the insular
source is discussed below, p. 18.
[40] *Gesta regum Anglorum*, ed. W. Stubbs, in RBMAS, xc. (London, 1887–9), 166 seqq.
[41] The case for Wulfstan's authorship of most of the *organa* is argued in detail by Holschneider,
Die Organa, 76–81, and Planchart, *The Repertory of Tropes*, i. 32. The term *organum* (plural *organa*)
referred originally to all polyphonic performance and composition; and it remained a generic term
for liturgical polyphony (*organum duplum, triplum, quadruplum*, in two, three, and four parts respectively)
until the early 14th cent. More narrowly, following the adoption of the 'sustained-note' style (see
below), the word, sometimes qualified by the adjective *purum*, came to refer to that style in contra-
distinction to *discantus*, a rhythmical descendant of the note-against-note style (below, p. 24).

The bulk of the *organa* are Tracts, Alleluias, and Office responds. A cycle of Sequences, wordless except for the initial Alleluia, was begun but not completed. There are also twelve troped and untroped Kyries, eight Glorias (including one in Greek), and various processional and other antiphons. The notation, in unheighted neumes, is unhelpful to the modern transcriber but perfectly adequate for the cantor, who needed only a reminder of what he already knew. The difficulty of transmitting such a repertory in this way from one centre to another is a powerful argument for a wholly English, if not exclusively Wintonian, origin: the essentials of the music can have been conveyed only by oral tradition. The music is neither in score nor with the parts displayed separately on the same page: the chant melodies on which the polyphony is based must be sought elsewhere in the manuscript or, failing that, from a comparable source such as the Bodleian troper. One or two have failed to materialize altogether. The notation, however, has its positive aspects. The neumes incorporate a wealth of nuance, and a brief examination suffices to show that this music is far removed from the dry concoctions of the theorists of *organum*, who are usually satisfied with letters or symbols which indicate specific pitches but not the manner of performance. The music is written in a note-against-note fashion, but the severity is mitigated by what must have been a highly expressive vocal style. A modern transcription can and should exhibit these nuances, even if their interpretation, like that of pitches themselves, is not always certain. The large amount of contrary motion (another point of distinction from the *organum* of the theorists) resolves many of the difficulties, as does the reasonable assumption that the *vox organalis* lies beneath the plainchant for much of the time. The transcription in Ex. I of the polyphonic setting of St Dunstan's Kyrie 'Rex splendens' in its untroped form is offered with every reservation (see overleaf).[42]

We know that polyphony was cultivated elsewhere than at Winchester before the Conquest. A valuable account of the dedication of Ramsey Abbey in 991 helps to explain the function of the organ and the conventions of the vocal performance. The organ, it seems, served to introduce the singing with its 'thunderous' sound; after which the singers performed in groups of five, one on each side of the choir, one side singing the plainsong

---

[42] See Plate I. Cambridge, Corpus Christi College, MS 473, fo. 137ʳ (*vox organalis* and part of the plainsong); ibid., fo. 57ʳ, and Oxford, Bod. Lib., Bod. 775, fo. 63ʳ (plainsong). In the transcription, ↶, ∿, and ∿ represent the *oriscus* (perhaps signifying a portamento-like anticipation of the following note) and ⋀ the *quilisma* (probably an ascent to the following note through the intermediate diatonic or chromatic pitches). The capital letters in the top part represent a pitch-notation (A = *c*) used by Hucbald and other early theorists; in the lower part the symbols (known as 'Notkerian letters') have the following meanings: iv = *iusum* (a lower pitch); l = *levatur* (a higher pitch); e = *equaliter* (the same pitch); m = *mediocriter* (a small change of pitch); t = *tenere* (a slight prolongation).

Ex. 1

Lord have mercy. Christ have mercy. Lord have mercy.

while the other 'sweated' at the *organum* part.[43] The Winchester music, it is true, gives the impression of a refined and sophisticated art. But it is clear, from the portions of the chants set, that both 'solo' and choral performance was envisaged; and the idiom cannot have been an easy one for the monastic choir to master. We would give much to know more precisely how the Winchester organ, with its own capacity for polyphony, functioned in relation to the singers, and what it played when it sounded alone.[44]

The Norman Conquest, when it came, affected every layer of English society profoundly and in many ways. The severity and aloofness of the Anglo-Norman monarchy, the replacement of Englishmen in the highest offices of Church and State by Norman Frenchmen, and the consequent division between the French-speaking ruling classes and the English-speaking populace, are some of its best-known consequences. Yet it would not do to exaggerate. The Conqueror could claim a kinship with the Old English monarchy, and had resolved to preserve its laws and institutions. The English language matured during the centuries of its cultural submersion, and there is no stage in its development that is not recorded by the clerks, whether in prose or in verse: annals, devotional literature, biblical paraphrase, moral fable, licentious farce, and amorous lyric are some of the genres in evidence between 1100 and 1250.

The early Norman court retained many of the trappings of its Anglo-Saxon predecessor. William, however, introduced the practice of periodic 'crown-wearings' in different parts of his new kingdom, whereby his power and his authority might be demonstrated. They were held on the great religious feasts, and the Mass on these occasions, as at William's coronation proper, always included the so-called *Laudes regiae*, a series of acclamations and petitions beginning 'Christus vincit', addressed to Christ as king and to the Saints.[45] The crown-wearings and associated *Laudes* were a novelty for England; yet even here, the selection and distribution of the invocations

---

[43] 'Namque magister organorum cum agmine ascendit populorum in altis sedibus, quo tonitruali sonitu excitavit mentes fidelium laudare nomen Domini. . . . Cum dextera pars sonum melodum personaret inclytis vocibus, tum sinister iubilando organicis desudabat laudibus. Alternantibus sic quinis vocibus inter se fratribus, pulchrum spectaculum praebuit illa vespera cunctis audientibus.' Byrhtferth of Ramsey, *Vita Sancti Oswaldi*, ed. J. Raine, RBMAS, lxxi. 1, 464 seqq., cited by Holschneider, *Die Organa*, 136–7.

[44] Some kind of accompaniment, with or without alternation, is suggested by the use of the instrumental letter-notation mentioned above (n. 42) in conjunction with neumes, for the proses of the Corpus Christi MS. The letters appear only in alternate verses, but that may be only because the musical repetition makes the duplication unnecessary. There is no proof, of course, that the letters amount to a genuine 'tablature' or organ part. Holschneider, *Die Organa*, 89–91.

[45] E. H. Kantorowicz, *Laudes Regiae* (Berkeley, Calif., 1946); I. Bent, 'The English Chapel Royal before 1300', *PRMA*, 90 (1963–4), 77–95, esp. 82–4, 91–3; H. Cowdrey, 'The Anglo-Norman Laudes Regiae', *Viator*, 12 (1981), 37–78. The term *Laudes regiae* is not contemporary, and they were not (in theory at least) sung 'to' the monarch but in his presence.

demonstrates a close connection with the Litany of the Saints as sung in England before the Conquest. The *Laudes*, though not addressed to the king himself, tended (and were intended) to add to his glory by association, thus obscuring both their origin in the Litany and the fact that they were frequently used on non-royal occasions.[46]

The public worship of the monarch was assisted in the first instance by a monastic or secular foundation in the place concerned. There were also special payments to 'clerks' (*clerici*, usually educated men in minor orders) for singing 'Christus vincit'. It is likely, too, that the clerks of the household took part as singers in his private worship as he moved around the country. Under Henry I even the crown-wearings were often performed in small chapels, and this may have reflected a growing tendency towards self-sufficiency in the royal worship. In the thirteenth century the chaplains and clerks of the king's *capella* developed as a regular institution for its maintenance, and eventually the term was applied to the institution itself.[47] Of course the notion of a private ecclesiastical establishment is much older,[48] but it is the development of the royal chapel as an institution, with its provision for potentially elaborate music, that is of particular significance.

In the same way, the secular entertainment of the royal household, including music as we understand it, would at first have been provided much as in Saxon times. There is no evidence to begin with of a regular salaried staff, but there was presumably a plentiful supply of performers willing and able to amuse the court in its hours of leisure. The Conquest bequeathed a new word for such people, 'minstrel', from the French *menestrel*, itself from the Latin *ministerialis*, a craftsman. This was initially a word of wide general significance, those with specific talents (whether they were purely musical or more akin to those of the modern variety artist) being designated according to their skill: *harpour*, *sautreour*, *vigilator* (literally 'watchman'), and

---

[46] The *Laudes* as sung at the coronation of William's Queen, Matilda, in 1068, preserved with neumes in the British Library, MS Cotton Vitellius E. XII, fo. 160ᵛ, are discussed at length by Cowdrey, 'Laudes Regiae'. The other musical sources from England are the late 11th-cent. Durham Gradual, Durham University Library, Cosin V. V. 6 (see K. Hartzell, 'An Unknown English Benedictine Gradual of the Eleventh Century', *Anglo-Saxon England*, 4 (1975), 131–44); and the 13th-cent. Worcester Gradual and Antiphoner, Worcester Cathedral MS F. 160, fos. 100ᵛ–101ʳ, 351ʳ–352ʳ (fac. of the former in *Antiphonaire monastique XIIIᵉ siècle: Codex F. 160 de la bibliothèque de la cathédrale de Worcester*, 2 vols. (Tournai, 1922–5, = Paléographie musicale, I/xii), pls. 201–2).

[47] The term *capellanus* (chaplain) originally referred to the person in charge of the cloak or *cappa* of St Martin of Tours as it accompanied the Frankish monarchs on their peregrinations. The word *capella* was adopted to mean the whole collection of movables required for the performance of the liturgy; it also came to refer to the buildings or rooms in which it was celebrated. It was used in England in both senses during the Norman and Plantagenet periods, while a 'chaplain', usually in priests' orders, might be in charge of either movables or buildings or indeed hold some other administrative office. Bent, 'The English Chapel Royal', 77–82.

[48] Edward the Confessor might hear the Office sung in his own *oratorium*: *Vita Eadwardi Regis*, ed. F. Barlow (London, 1962), 63; and the concept can be traced back in England to the ménage of Bertha, the Frankish wife of Æthelbert of Kent, *c.*594 (Bede, *Hist. eccl.* i, Ch. 25; ed. Plummer, i. 45).

so on. Later, minstrels came to be thought of more particularly as instrumentalists, or at least as musical entertainers whose songs would be instrumentally accompanied; they were frequently the subject of clerical attack on account of the scurrilous reputation of the lower sort, and they came eventually to be organized under royal, noble, or municipal patronage. Questions of their status and organization were a preoccupation of eighteenth- and nineteenth-century antiquaries, such as Percy and Ritson, but the topic is best approached from a wide view without too much attention being given to arguments based on terminology. In this period, there is no evidence of regular service or of protective organization for secular musicians, and only the feeblest hints, towards the end, of what their music may have been like; but the literary sources in both French and English provide ample justification for the opinion that professional entertainment penetrated to all levels of society.[49]

One of the strongest forces for continuity within the Church was the retention of monastic chapters in cathedrals which already had them (such as Winchester and Canterbury), and their extension to others (such as Durham) which at the time of the Conquest did not. In this respect the ideals of the Conqueror and those whom he chose for the highest ecclesiastical offices—above all Lanfranc of Bec, who replaced the deposed Stigand at Canterbury—coincided with those of the tenth-century English reformers. Lanfranc's monastic *Consuetudines* were within the spirit of the earlier *Regularis Concordia*,[50] and many characteristics of the English monastic liturgy, modelled as it was on that of such French Benedictine houses as Fleury, Tours, and Corbie, were retained.[51] Nevertheless, the Conquest encouraged the planting of houses of Continental orders—Cluniac, Cistercian, and others—and, quite apart from the social consequences in terms of landholding, ownership of benefices, and the like, the effects on church music were far from negligible. The Cluniac concern for liturgical order and enrichment, and the reaction against over-elaboration which characterized the Cistercian rule, permeated the English monastic scene and left their imprint on the religious and musical life of the nation in many less direct ways.

The Normans also reformed the constitutions of those cathedrals that retained secular chapters, giving more independence to the canons than they had enjoyed hitherto either in cathedrals or in the collegiate establishments that were the greater 'minsters' (Old English 'mynster') of the Anglo-Saxon period.[52] Rural and isolated sees were moved close to new centres

---

[49] For a stimulating discussion of the social and moral status of musical minstrels in medieval society see C. Page, *The Owl and the Nightingale: Musical Life and Ideas in France, 1100–1300* (London, 1989).

[50] F. M. Stenton, *Anglo-Saxon England* (3rd edn., Oxford, 1971), 672.

[51] Hartzell, 'An Unknown English Benedictine Gradual'.

[52] Stenton, *Anglo-Saxon England*, 148–9, and map on p. 454.

of population, as for example Sherborne to Salisbury or rather (in the first instance) to the fort later known as 'Old Sarum'. Here one of William's nominees, Osmund, composed the constitutions and ordinances that make him the father of the English medieval liturgy. They were to be the model for the secular cathedrals of the southern English province, though all had their local usages to a greater or lesser extent. There are few reliable documents of the secular liturgy in England before the Conquest, and even fewer scraps of evidence for its music, but it is reasonable to suspect that it was in poor shape.[53] Whatever its condition, a fresh start was now made on the basis of northern French models, and in due course the Use of Salisbury came to be the accepted criterion for both liturgy and chant.

Only small fragments of liturgical polyphony have come down to us from the long period between the Norman Conquest and the middle of the thirteenth century. One of these is the piece already mentioned as having a concordance in a French course, a setting of the verse 'Dicant nunc Iudaei' from the Easter antiphon 'Christus resurgens'. In the now destroyed Chartres MS 109 this was the fifth in a set of eight *organa* for the Easter season.[54] The interesting point about this collection, like the similar group of six pieces in the former Chartres 130, is that the choice of texts clearly indicates that polyphony had by now become a matter for the cantors alone, that is to say for trained solo singers: this was to be the norm until in the early fifteenth century the first signs of a reinstatement of choral polyphony can be discerned. Another significant point is that these manuscripts are in score, the words being written beneath the lowest part, which is the plainsong. The plainsong is not yet necessarily the lower part in pitch, but it is no longer so consistently above the added part, and the way was now open for the development which would ultimately place it decisively in the lowest position. The insular source of 'Dicant nunc Iudaei' is a Benedictine Gradual from Ireland, where it occurs in its proper liturgical place;[55] the notation, both of the polyphony and of the plainsong melodies which form the bulk of the manuscript, suggests a date in the second half of the twelfth century, though the Chartres source is probably earlier and the style of the music, which is still exclusively note-against-note, suggests the early part of the century. The Bodleian manuscript usefully

[53] The Leofric Missal, Bodley 579, a sacramentary written in the diocese of Arras/Cambrai, to which much else has been added, was brought to England and given to Exeter by bishop Leofric; it may possibly contain elements of the pre-Conquest Exeter use. Two 11th-cent. fragments of noted missals, possibly from Exeter, are in Oxford, Bod. Lib., lat. lit. e. 38. Further on Exeter MSS see S. Rankin, 'From Memory to Record', *Anglo-Saxon England*, 13 (1984), 97–112.

[54] Holschneider, *Die Organa*, 64–5 (description); 180 (transcription).

[55] Oxford, Bod. Lib., Rawl. c. 892, fos. 67ᵛ–68ʳ; Holschneider, *Die Organa*, 180–1 (transcription); F. Harrison, *Music in Medieval Britain* (London, 1958), 116–17.

supplements the fragmentary Chartres version, though unfortunately the binder has snipped off the upper part at the end.

A somewhat similar piece is the verse 'Ut tuo propitiatus' from the respond 'Sancte Dei pretiose' for St Stephen's day. This occurs on a page of random jottings added at St Augustine's, Canterbury, to a volume of Latin writings from Cornwall.[56] The piece, in alphabetical notation, has been dated nearly a century earlier than 'Dicant nunc Iudaei'; but it is virtually indistinguishable from it in style, and the date of composition of both is probably early twelfth century. The lack of a Continental concordance might encourage us to think of the music as of English origin in this instance at least.

Much more important than either of these fragments is a collection now in Cambridge.[57] Here too, though the music is damaged and hard to read, we can detect the influence of comparatively recent developments in France. In the south of the country, and perhaps more particularly at the great Benedictine abbey of St Martial near Limoges, a type of polyphonic composition had emerged, as early as 1100, which enabled composers to break away from the confines of note-against-note writing. Two new techniques arose: in one, the number of neumes or ligatures in each part corresponded even though the precise number of notes might not; in the other, several notes might be sung to just one in the *tenor* or lower part, a style nowadays known as 'melismatic' or 'sustained-note' *organum*. A further important development was in the choice of texts for polyphony. Hitherto nothing had ever been set which did not have a prior existence as a liturgical plainsong form. At St Martial, however, polyphony was applied to a new type of Latin text known as *versus* or *conductus*: a sacred poem in uniform stanzas, sometimes a processional piece for 'conducting' ministers in the liturgy and often set in monophony. A polyphonic *conductus* might set an already existing *conductus* melody; more often, however, the *tenor* was newly composed. Still more startlingly, the upper part might 'trope' a liturgical text while the lower part sang the original to its own plainsong. This is the principle of the medieval motet, a form which did not fully emerge until the thirteenth century. The earliest St Martial manuscript[58] contains one piece of the latter type, together with three *conducti* in score and some other pieces of 'hidden' polyphony: in these the parts are written out as alternating sections of monophony, but can be coalesced to make two-part

[56] Oxford, Bod. Lib., Bodley 572, fo. 49ᵛ. The piece has been transcribed many times: it can be found for example in *NOHM*, ii. 308–9 and in A. T. Davison and W. Apel, *Historical Anthology of Music* (Cambridge, Mass., 1946), i, no. 26b; and there are facsimiles in *EBM*, iii, pl. xvi, *EEH*, i, pl. i, and W. Apel, *The Notation of Polyphonic Music 900–1600* (Cambridge, Mass., 1953).

[57] University Library, Ff. i. 17 (1), described in Ludwig, *Repertorium organorum recentioris et motetorum vetustissimi stili* (Halle, 1910, and reprints), i. 326–9; O. Schumann, 'Die jungere Cambridger Liedersammlung', *Studi medievali*, NS, 16 (1943–50), 48–85; J. Stevens in I. Fenlon (ed.), *Cambridge Music Manuscripts*, 40–4; facsimile of most of the polyphonic music in *EEH*, i, pls. 25–30.

[58] Paris, Bibliothèque nationale, fonds lat. 1139. See *RISM*, B IV¹, pp. 402–4.

music. The later codices exhibiting the same style contain a much larger repertory but are not connected specifically with St Martial. One of them is an appendix to a manuscript containing the office of St James for use at Santiago de Compostela in Northern Spain:[59] it includes liturgical *organa* in sustained-note style as well as *conducti*.

The Cambridge manuscript consists of a single quaternio (four double leaves): a little booklet of optional extras, as it were, for the liturgy. Neither its small format nor its subsequent use as flyleaves for a volume of theological tracts have been conducive to a good state of preservation. Nevertheless, it appears that none of the leaves has actually been lost, though some of them are damaged at the edges and badly rubbed. As reconstructed the manuscript begins with twenty-two monophonic *conducti*, not all of them provided with music, though for the most part the staves were ruled. There follow thirteen polyphonic pieces, one of which, 'Verbum Patris umanatur', is in three parts.[60] Originally placed in the thirteenth century by Ludwig and Wooldridge, the manuscript is now generally regarded as a twelfth-century source, though it may well be from towards the end of that century. Its musical script is nearer to that of the Compostela manuscript than to that of the French sources just cited; and nearer still in its general character, though probably several decades earlier, to an *organum*-treatise now in the Vatican.[61] The provenance of the Cambridge manuscript is quite unknown, though an English origin can be inferred from its script and from its use in the binding of an English codex. Much of the music is quite 'international' in character. An extract from the third piece, 'Ad honorem salvatoris', illustrates two aspects of melismatic writing in the style then current: the use of melismas in the *tenor* part, when the upper part normally follows suit in note-against-note style; and the use of melismas in the upper part against a held note in the *tenor* ('sustained-note' style). This stylistic dichotomy was to be an important factor in the development of thirteenth-century music. As yet it is impossible to transcribe most of this music into specific note-values, and the alignment of the two parts, which in performance must have been somewhat haphazard, is largely a matter of guesswork (Ex. 2).[62]

The manuscript includes one motet, based on the 'Benedicamus Domino'

[59] Still in the cathedral archive at Compostela. Its music was fully transcribed by Wagner, *Die Gesänge der Jakobusliturgie zu Santiago de Compostela* (Fribourg, 1931); a facsimile was published in Compostela in 1944, ed. Dom G. Prado and W. M. Whitehill, under the title *Liber Sancti Jacobi: Codex Calixtinus*.

[60] There are several concordances with Continental sources, all listed in Schumann, 'Cambridger Liedersammlung'.

[61] Ottoboni lat. 3025, fos. 46ʳ–50ᵛ, 13th cent.; ed. with facsimile in F. Zaminer, *Der Vatikanische Organum-Traktat* (Tutzing, 1959).

[62] fo. 8ᵛ, formerly 299ᵛ; *EEH*, pl. 26. The small notes represent the *plica*, apparently to be performed lightly and quickly. The text in the original is under the lowest voice, but is clearly intended to be sung by both. Various details of the underlay, and of the vertical alignment of the two voices, are editorial. The text probably refers to St Thomas of Canterbury.

Ex. 2

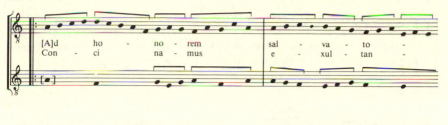

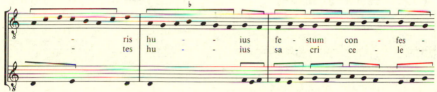

In honour of the saviour the church observes the feast of this confessor [St Thomas of Canterbury]. Let us sing together in exultation as we celebrate the solemnities of this holy man.

like those of the 'St Martial' sources; but it is a curiosity in that the upper part is a kind of quodlibet built up of the words and music of several snatches of liturgical plainsong.[63] The scribe seems to have had difficulty in grasping the nature of the piece and his copy is almost impossible to transcribe with any certainty. The last piece in the manuscript, 'Ad cantus leticie', is the earliest known version of a song which became extremely widely known in the later Middle Ages and retained its popularity in the Renaissance and down to modern times. It is short enough to be quoted complete, and its style is sufficiently simple to encourage a transcription in specific rhythmic values (Ex. 3 overleaf).[64]

[63] 'Amborum sacrum spiramen', fo. 4ᵛ (EEH, pl. 30). The extracts are identified by Ludwig, Repertorium, 329, and Harrison, Music in Medieval Britain, 129.

[64] fo. 3ᵛ (EEH, pl. 28). The solutions adopted here as to the problem of rhythm and alignment are largely those of Jacques Handschin, who printed the piece in the version of Cambridge, Bamberg (MS P. VI. 19) and Piae cantiones (1582, repr. G. R. Woodward in 1910) in Schweizerisches Jahrbuch für Musikwissenschaft, 3 (1928), pp. 22–3 of the Notenbeilage. The piece may not necessarily be English, though the Cambridge MS is the earliest source. The manuscript gives the first three stanzas (with variants) of the four-stanza poem printed in AH, xx. 80.

Ex. 3

Hope, and love of the heavenly kingdom, invite us today to songs of joy.

The remaining polyphonic items are tropes of 'Benedicamus Domino' (in the sense that their texts incorporate, or conclude with, those words) and *conducti* designed to precede a lesson. 'Verbum Patris umanatur' is probably also a substitute for the 'Benedicamus Domino', though it does not include those words.[65] It is, as Harrison says, 'particularly joyful'; although there are not many full triads, the piece could be regarded as early evidence of the English love of fullness of sound. It is, in any case, the earliest piece of English three-part writing that we have (though there is a French concordance in two parts only); and unless our chronological assumptions are hopelessly astray, only the second such piece known to us altogether (the earliest being 'Congaudeant catholici' from the Compostela manuscript). It is given here in Anselm Hughes's rhythmic reconstruction (Ex. 4).[66]

Pieces of the same general type as the two-part *conducti* in the Cambridge manuscript are found in MS Burney 357 of the British Library (a lengthy

[65] Harrison, *Music in Medieval Britain*, 129, where it is suggested that 'Verbum Patris umanatur' might have replaced the second 'Benedicamus' at Lauds on Christmas Day, when 'Verbum Patris hodie' was sung as a substitute for the first 'Benedicamus'.

[66] fo. 4ʳ (*EEH*, pl. 29) as given in *NOHM*, ii. 304. In bar 10, the second note in the second voice is *g* in the manuscript. The triplet groups in bar 11 could be interpreted as equal notes (as by Hughes) or in iambic rhythm. The manuscript gives the first, second, fourth, and fifth stanzas of the five-stanza poem printed in AH, xx. 104.

Ex. 4

Ver - bum Pa - tris u - ma - na - tur, o, o, dum pu - el - la sa - lu - ta - tur,

o, o, Sa - lu - ta - ta fe - cun - da - tur vi - ri ne - sci - a.

He - i, he - i, no - va gau - di - a.

The word of the Father is made flesh, O, O, as the young virgin is hailed, O, O; as she is hailed she is made fruitful, knowing not a man. Ah, ah, new joys.

'Amor patris et filii', ending with the words 'Benedicamus Domino': the musical script appears to be of the twelfth century);[67] and in Harley 524 (a short *conductus* entitled 'Veri floris sub figura': here the manuscript appears to be of the thirteenth century, though the musical style is of the twelfth).[68]

The next stage in the history of church music in the British Isles is represented not by a fragment but by an extensive collection of liturgical polyphony of the type associated with the cathedral of Notre-Dame in Paris. Now in the Ducal Library of Wolfenbüttel,[69] it belonged in the fourteenth century to the Augustinian cathedral priory of St Andrews in Scotland, and was transported to the Continent in the sixteenth century by the Protestant humanist Flacius Illyricus in his search for pre-Reformation anti-clerical

[67] fos. 15ᵛ–16ʳ; *EEH*, pls. 9–10. The 'Benedicamus Domino' does not seem to be a separate piece.
[68] *EEH*, pl. 31.
[69] Codex Helmstadensis 628 (Cat. no. 677). Fac. ed. J. H. Baxter, *An Old St Andrews Music Book* (London and Paris, 1931); Ludwig, *Repertorium*, 7–57.

literature.[70] It is probable that it originated in Scotland; but before the difficult questions of its provenance and date can be discussed, something must be said of the Parisian repertory that it contains and its significance for the later history of music in England.

During the later twelfth and early thirteenth centuries a notable school of polyphonic music had arisen in Paris, centred around the newly constructed cathedral of Notre-Dame.[71] Its main achievement was the establishment of a new type of purely liturgical *organum*, for which the untroped texts of the cantors' portions of the responsorial chants of the Mass and Office were used (Gradual and Alleluia of the Mass, Great Respond of Vespers and Matins), together with the untroped 'Benedicamus Domino'. The complete collection of these two-part *organa* was known as the *Magnus Liber*. Two aspects of this new repertory demand consideration. In the first place, its creators (of whom the most important appears to have been a certain Magister Leo or Leoninus) made an even stronger distinction than hitherto between passages in sustained-note style, which was used for syllabic or nearly syllabic portions of the original chant being set, and those in note-against-note style, which was reserved for passages which in the chant were melismatic. Secondly, a new idiom was evolved for this latter style, which came to be known as *discantus*, based on rhythms which we should now recognize as compound duple, 6/8 in modern transcription. It was rarely in the strict sense note-against-note; but, to use present-day note-values, the *tenor* might be laid out in a rhythm based on dotted minims or dotted crotchets, or both, while the upper part moved largely in crotchets and quavers. Its descent from the 'neume-against-neume' system mentioned above is clear. A system of notation was evolved in which the rhythms were indicated, not by the shape of the signs but by the way in which the ligatures (groups of notes written as a single symbol) were arranged. The general rhythmic character of thirteenth-century music, which was largely conditioned by or derived from this compound duple style, may be summed up by the word *modus* (mode), which was used both as a generic term meaning, broadly, 'rhythm', and also to indicate specific rhythmic patterns. Similarly the term 'modal' has been coined in modern times to indicate the method of notation just referred to. To take an actual example, the first rhythmic mode, consisting of alternating long and short notes (crotchets and quavers), was indicated in modal notation by a three-note ligature followed by as many two-note ligatures as were required to complete the musical phrase. Although modal notation, which

[70] Baxter, *An Old St Andrews Music Book*, pp. VIII–XII. There is no evidence, however, that the companion volume also acquired by Flacius Illyricus (Wolfenbüttel, Cod. Helmstad. 1099, cat. 1206) also came from St Andrews.

[71] For the literature, which is exceedingly extensive, see *NGD*, s.v. 'Organum and Discant', Bibliography sect. VI; C. Wright, *Music and Ceremony of Notre Dame of Paris 500–1550* (Cambridge, 1989).

was unsuited to syllabic word-setting and suffered from various other disadvantages, was eventually superseded by 'mensural' notation, in which the shape of the notes and ligatures defined their meaning, a large body of thirteenth-century music, both English and Continental, is wholly or partly written according to the modal system.

Apart from liturgical *organa*, the Parisian repertory of this period included *conducti*, separate *clausulae*, or short passages of *discantus*, and motets. The polyphonic *conductus* was by now invariably in *discantus* style throughout, that is to say without passages in sustained-note style, with or without lengthy melismas in which all the parts moved together (these were known as *caudae*, even when they occurred in the middle of a piece). *Discantus* style was also present throughout liturgical *organa* in three or four parts, since although there might be lengthy sustained notes in the *tenor*, the upper parts still moved in similar rhythms against each other. *Organa* of three and four parts were the special province of Magister Perotinus Magnus, the 'optimus discantor' who succeeded Leoninus, the 'optimus organista', at Notre-Dame. He is also said to have composed many *conducti*, to have 'abbreviated' the *Magnus Liber*, and to have composed many new and better *clausulae* or *puncta*.[72] It is probable that many of the numerous short passages of *discantus*, settings of melismas taken from responsorial chants, are sections composed by Perotinus and his associates for the purpose of improving the *Magnus Liber*. But this cannot be true of all of them—frequently several are grouped together like sets of variations on the same theme, while others are three- or four-part works—and one is led to suppose that many of them were composed as independent items, related to but not belonging to the liturgy.

The motet, in the narrow sense of the term, arose from the practice of adding texts to the upper parts of *clausulae*, both independent and otherwise.[73] Although, as we have seen, the motet-principle of simultaneous troping was in operation as early as about 1100, the result in that case, and in others like it, cannot be said to be a motet in the accepted sense. The same is true of texted adaptations of passages in the four-part *organa* of Perotinus—'tropical organa', as they have rather inelegantly been called. The motet—with or without a parent *clausula*—may be defined as a piece based upon a melisma from a chant, with a separate text or texts in the upper part or parts. In a two-part motet, of course, there will be only one such text; but in motets of three and four parts there was a choice

---

[72] 'Et nota, quod magister Leoninus, secundum quod dicebatur, fuit optimus organista, qui fecit magnum librum organi de gradali et antifonario pro servitio divino multiplicando. Et fuit in usu usque ad tempus Perotini magni, qui abbreviavit eundem et fecit clausulas sive puncta plurima meliora, quoniam optimus discantor erat, et melior quam Leoninus erat.' F. Reckow (ed.), *Der Musiktraktat des Anonymus IV* (Wiesbaden, 1967), i. 46.

[73] The most complete edition, though hard to use, is *The Earliest Motets*, ed. H. Tischler, 3 vols. (Yale, 1982).

of methods: either a single text could be shared between the upper parts (the so-called *conductus*-motet); or each upper part could have its own text (the double or triple motet, according to the number of texts employed). In the later thirteenth century in France the motet became largely secularized, the vernacular being normally used for profane texts; not infrequently a combination of sacred and secular texts is found in the same work. English composers do not seem to have adapted the model to profane purposes, though they did adopt another French innovation, the employment of a secular song as *tenor*.[74]

A further feature of *discantus*-sections, *clausulae*, and motets was the layout of the *tenor* part in short rhythmic patterns or *ordines* (sing. *ordo*), repeated as many times as was required by the melodic phrase (cf. Ex. 6 below). Sometimes the entire *tenor* melody (known as *color*) might be repeated with the identical rhythms, a procedure nowadays called 'double-cursus' structure. The repeat of a melody in different rhythms, usually quicker ('irregular diminution') is also to be met with. These techniques were not much used by insular composers of this period (though some singers must already have been familiar with them from the Notre-Dame repertory), but they are of considerable importance for the subsequent development of English music.

The St Andrews manuscript is generally considered to incorporate the earliest extant version of Leoninus' *Magnus Liber*,[75] together with a supporting repertory which is by far the most conservative of the various selections of pieces contained in the three principal sources of Notre-Dame music. At the same time it contains two responds of St Andrew, similar to though not identical in style with that of the main corpus, and a whole section of music of a quite different character universally recognized as being of 'insular' (English or Scottish) origin. The date and ultimate provenance of the manuscript are far from certain, but it now seems clear that it must be assigned to the earlier part of the thirteenth century, perhaps around 1240. An insular provenance is most probable, although the main scribe may have received his training in Paris.[76] If the manuscript was indeed written in Great Britain, there is no good reason to believe that this was in a centre in England rather than Scotland. Scotland enjoyed its own direct links with Europe during most of the Middle Ages, and there is no problem about access to a French exemplar for the copying of the main repertory; nor is it impossible that the actual copying was done at St Andrews. As

---

[74] See ch. 2, pp. 76–9.

[75] Ed. from this source in W. G. Waite, *The Rhythm of Twelfth-Century Polyphony: Its Theory and Practice* (New Haven, Conn., 1954).

[76] The most recent contributions to the study of this manuscript are by E. Roesner, 'The Origins of W1', *JAMS*, 27 (1976), and by J. Brown, S. Patterson, and D. Hiley, 'Further Observations on W1', *JPMMS*, 4 (1981), 53–80.

for the music itself, the pieces on St Andrew come at the end of the section of Office responds and must have been copied from a source other than that of the main repertory. If they are by an English or Scottish composer then they are by an insular master of the Parisian style of whom no other evidence exists; but this is by no means an impossibility. Rather more certainty attaches to the troped Sanctus and Agnus settings from the main body of the manuscript—five are for three voices, two are for two, and twelve are monophonic. These have no counterpart in the Notre-Dame repertory, but there are parallels with other insular sources,[77] and the conclusion must be that they are by English or Scottish composers.

The most consistently insular part of the manuscript, however, is its eleventh and last section (or 'fascicle'), which is devoted to music for Marian Masses: troped Kyries, a troped Gloria, Alleluias, a Tract, Offertories, and troped settings of the Sanctus and Agnus. Even here, passages from the standard Notre-Dame repertory have been found embedded in the music, although the fascicle as a whole is markedly insular in character.[78] All the music is in two parts and in *discantus* style, though its rhythmic structure is not always regular. At one time the music was considered to be archaic compared with that of Notre-Dame; it is in many ways much less accomplished, but the exclusion of sustained-note style in the Alleluias suggests on the contrary a more up-to-date idiom. It is of course possible that the sustained-note style was never widely cultivated by native composers, and that the restriction to *discantus* style in the St Andrews source is due to long-standing tradition and lack of adventurousness rather than to a conscious modernism. In all probability the truth lies between these extremes: here perhaps is an early instance of a typically insular characteristic, the countering of an inherent conservatism by putting old techniques to new uses. Several extracts from this section of the manuscript have already appeared in print.[79] The opening of the Offertory 'Felix namque es' illustrates the setting of a plainsong melody frequently used by English composers in the later Middle Ages (Ex. 5 overleaf).[80]

The opening of a three-part Sanctus-trope from the body of the manuscript shows a degree of accomplishment approaching that of contemporary Parisian *organum triplum*, remarkable indeed if by a British composer (Ex. 6, p. 29).[81]

---

[77] e.g. Cambridge, Univ. Lib., Ff. ii. 29, which also includes part of the Notre-Dame three-part Alleluia 'Dies sanctificatus': *EEH*, pls. 37–8; Ludwig, *Repertorium*, p. 228.

[78] Discussed by Harrison, *Music in Medieval Britain*, 130–1.

[79] Complete pieces in *Historical Anthology of Music* (above, n. 56), no. 37 (Kyrie 'Rex virginum'); Harrison, *Music in Medieval Britain*, 131 (Alleluia 'Post partum').

[80] Wolfenbüttel, Codex Helmstad. 628, fo. 193^v (modern foliation). The rhythms are highly conjectural, but a transcription in a style approaching that of contemporary French music seems preferable to one in free rhythm.

[81] Ibid., fo. 82^v.

Ex. 5

Fe - - - - - lix nam - -
- - - - que es
sa - cra vir - go

Happy are you, holy virgin . . .

The St Andrews manuscript, fascinating and important though it is, lies off the main course of English thirteenth-century music in so far as this can be discerned from the surviving material. It may be that an Augustinian house singing a predominantly French repertory was by no means unique at the time; but this is not the picture suggested to us by the evidence of the period immediately following. This, on the contrary, indicates that the main centres of interest were Benedictine houses and that their repertory, while related to contemporary French methods, developed on indigenous lines.[82] It is surprising that the great secular cathedrals, such as Salisbury, which was already noted for its music, should not have been prominent in the cultivation of polyphony, since in France the secular cathedrals had largely replaced the Benedictine abbeys as leaders in this field; but our fragments, until about the middle of the fourteenth century, are from such places as Worcester, Reading, Peterborough, and Bury St Edmunds, while the customaries of Westminster, St Augustine's at Canterbury, and Norwich refer specifically to polyphonic music.

[82] See, however, n. 77. It may be that the Notre-Dame repertory was more widely cultivated in England than the evidence indicates. Augustinian houses adopted the local usage, normally that of Salisbury (Harrison, *Music in Medieval Britain*, 48), and the Wolfenbüttel MS may therefore represent the normal usage of a secular cathedral. See also Ch. 2, n. 7.

Ex. 6

San - ctus. Per - pe - tu - o nu - mi - ne cun - cta re - - - - - - - - gens.

Holy. Ruling all things with everlasting power . . .

The remains of the secular and non-liturgical repertory between the Conquest and about 1250 are exceedingly scanty. No doubt one of the prime duties of a 'harper' was, as previously, the recitation of narrative poetry;[83] but our previous caveat against regarding any extant literary document as an example of verse for singing remains fully in force. There is not much evidence for regarding the romances of the twelfth and thirteenth centuries as having been sung in anything like that form;[84] while in the case of the shorter 'lays', whatever their value in throwing light on the conventions of courtly minstrelsy, there is positive reason to consider them as a self-conscious literary adaptation of an older musical tradition of which the remains have vanished.[85]

Rather less caution is needed in viewing the lyrical poetry of the twelfth and thirteenth centuries as texts for singing, if only because much of its versification can only be explained by an immediately musical inspiration. Most of what we possess in written form, both literary and musical, owes its preservation to the interest of the clergy, who still enjoyed a virtual monopoly of literacy and who were acutely conscious of the value of popular idioms in promoting Christian doctrine. Our very first examples of the setting of English words, the three songs attributed to St Godric (d. 1170), are religious in character, though they can hardly be thought of as a means of popularization, their musical idiom resembling that of plainchant. It is difficult to know what part if any St Godric played in the musical part of these strange effusions (assuming that the attribution has any factual basis whatsoever), and they must remain on the periphery of the normal run of early medieval English music.[86]

The establishment of the Plantagenet dynasty, and the subsequent marriage of Henry II to Eleanor of Aquitaine, brought the English court within the domain of troubadour culture, though this was insufficient to displace the French language, in its Anglo-Norman form, as the main medium of aristocratic communication. Songs in French became a normal accompaniment of courtly life at all times—Richard I himself is cited as author

---

[83] Above, pp. 2–3.

[84] It may be, however, that the Northern French tradition of sung epic poetry (cf. E. Rohloff, *Die Quellenhandschriften des Johannes de Grocheio* (Leipzig, 1972), p. 130) found some echo in England; if so, the Anglo-Norman copy of the *Chanson de Roland* (Oxford, Bod. Lib., Digby 23), the oldest surviving MS, may be a kind of 'libretto' for such a performance.

[85] Marie de France: *Lais*, ed. A. Ewert (Oxford, 1978), pp. x–xii, where the evidence is clearly summarized.

[86] See J. B. Trend, 'The First English Songs', *ML*, 9 (1928), 111–28, with facsimile and transcriptions; Fenlon, *Cambridge Music Manuscripts*, 36–9 (with fac. of Univ. Lib. MS Mm. iv. 28, fo. 149ʳ); *Medieval English Songs*, ed. Dobson and Harrison (London and Boston, 1979), 103–9, 228–9, 295–6; C. Page, 'A Catalogue and Bibliography of English Song from its Beginnings to *c*.1300', *RMARC*, 13 (1976). Page's article is an invaluable and fully-referenced inventory of all settings of English texts to 1300. (References to *Medieval English Songs* will normally be to the sections entitled 'Texts and Textual Commentary', 'Music', and 'Musical Commentary' in turn.)

of two songs with extant melodies—and a few have come down to us in English sources;[87] but the material is insufficient to permit us to identify a national style in this area. French influence is clearly evident in several of the monophonic songs with English words which have survived. One especially interesting fragment of the early thirteenth century[88] permits us to assume that French and English songs might rub shoulders in a songbook of the kind familiar from French sources, mostly of a later date. Though it consists of only a single leaf, it gives us two songs with French texts, the first incomplete, and the tune and first stanza of an English song. As in many French chansonniers the music and text are laid out in two columns on each page, the text of the second and subsequent stanzas written as prose following the tune with its first stanza. The first song begins half-way through the tune at the words 'chant ai entendu', followed by three further stanzas; the second, 'Mult saprisme li termines', has five stanzas in all. The English song, for all its fragmentary nature, communicates its sense of weary desolation across the centuries with surprising force (Ex. 7).

Ex. 7

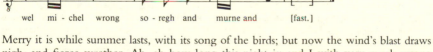

Merry it is while summer lasts, with its song of the birds; but now the wind's blast draws nigh, and fierce weather. Ah, ah how long this night is; and I with very much wrong sorrow and mourn and [fast].

---

[87] e.g. the crusaders' song 'Parti de mal', Brit. Lib., Harl. 1717 (*EEH*, pl. 8); 'Bien deust chanter ky eust leale amie' from Brit. Lib., Arundel 248 (*EEH*, pl. 36); 'De ma dame vull chanter' from Oxford, Bod. Lib., Ashmole 1285 (*EBM*, i, pl. 1), as well as others referred to below.

[88] See Plate II. Oxford, Bod. Lib., Rawl. g. 22, fo. 1ʳ⁻ᵛ. Fac. in *EBM*, i, pls. ii–iii. The English song is in *Medieval English Songs*, 121–2, 241, 297–8; text only in *English Lyrics of the XIIIth Century*, ed. C. Brown (Oxford, 1932), 14.

Most of the surviving material relating to secular song, however, dates from the end of the thirteenth century or the beginning of the fourteenth. Even that most famous and most controversial of all medieval English compositions, the canonic 'Sumer is icumen in', whatever its true date may be, is best considered in relation to that new self-confidence and individuality that is so characteristic of the second half of the century, in its music as in so much else. The same applies to writings about music. The monastic revival of the tenth century had opened the way for an influx of post-Carolingian musical theory, in particular the writings of Hucbald and the anonymous *Musica* and *Scolica enchiriadis*. Practical treatises were compiled by Wulfstan of Winchester and, after the Conquest, by Osbern of Canterbury and Theinred of Dover.[89] In the twelfth century a series of writers, of whom Aelred of Rievaulx and John of Salisbury were the chief, expressed their views on the place of music in the Church and in society.[90] Aelred's uncompromising opposition to polyphonic elaboration attracted Puritan attention in the seventeenth century and has become widely known in William Prynne's translation. But it represents only one side of a picture of which the musical documents, however scattered, form the other. Aelred's views must have been a response to a flourishing culture that threatened the purity of his own Cistercian worship. Before they found an echo in Wyclif and the Lollards in the fourteenth century, there had arisen the much more positive standpoint associated with some of the chief figures of the mendicant orders and with the Oxford University of their day. Here again the currents of thought arising in the first part of the thirteenth century found issue in the second and are matter for the following chapter.

Gerald of Wales, a chaplain to Henry II and later archdeacon of St Davids, provides us with our most vivid glimpses of musical life in the British Isles during the twelfth century. He praises the instrumental music of the Irish as being their only worthwhile skill, mentioning their rapid execution and intricate yet sweet-sounding polyphony.[91] Some of the detail is devalued

---

[89] *Musica et Scolica enchiriadis una cum aliquibus tractatulis adiunctis*, ed. H. Schmid (Munich, 1981): the work is preserved, with others, in Cambridge, Corpus Christi College, MS 260 (Fenlon, *Cambridge Music Manuscripts*, 6–10, incl. fac.). Cf. the copy of Hucbald in the 'Cambridge Songbook' MS (cf. n. 15: ed. M. Gebert, *Scriptores de Musica sacra potissimum*, 3 vols. (Sankt Blasien, 1784), i. 103–21; trans. in *Hucbald, Guido and John on Music*, ed. C. Palisca, (New Haven, Conn., 1978)). For Osbern, see Bibliography; the treatise of Wulfstan is lost (cf. Holschneider, *Die Organa*, 76–7); that of Theinred has not been published: see J. L. Snyder, 'The *De legitimis ordinibus pentachordorum et tetrachordorum* of Theinred of Dover' (Ph.D. diss., Indiana, 1982), and his article 'A Road Not Taken: Theinred of Dover's Theory of Species', *JRMA*, 115 (1990), 145–81.

[90] *Aelredi Rievallensis opera omnia*, ed. A. Hoste and C. H. Talbot, i (Turnhout, 1971), 97–9; *Patrologia Latina*, cxcv (n.d.), cols. 571–2 (from the *Speculum caritatis*, ii, ch. 23); *Ioannis Sarisberiensis episcopi Carnotensis Policratici . . . Libri viii*, ed. C. C. J. Webb (Oxford, 1909), i. 39–44; *Patrologia Latina*, cxcix (1855), cols. 401–4 (from i, ch. 6). Their position is well summarized, with further bibliography, in *NGD*, s.v. 'Aelred of Rievaulx', 'John of Salisbury'.

[91] *Giraldi Cambrensis Opera*, v, ed. J. F. Dimock (London, 1867); RBMAS, xxi, vol. 5, 153 seqq.

by its being repeated verbatim in the later *Descriptio Kambriae*; but in the latter he adds his famous description of Welsh part-singing, in which there are 'as many parts as there are singers'.[92] For good measure he throws in an account of two-part song in northern Britain, which he conjectures to be of Scandinavian origin. Gerald cannot be relied on for technical detail, but the broad tenor of his account is perfectly plausible and serves as a reminder of how unrepresentative are the written documents of non-liturgical music. In particular there is no purely instrumental music extant from anywhere in Europe until the later thirteenth century: a whole world of early medieval music is destined to remain a closed book to us.

Music was cultivated as widely in the British Isles as elsewhere during the long period covered by this chapter. But progress towards the development of an English national style had hardly yet begun. It is not necessary to view this in a wholly negative light, for example by citing the Conquest as an inhibiting factor. The dominions of Henry II included the whole of the western side of modern France from the Channel to the Pyrenees, giving access to a broad range of Continental culture including the music associated with Limoges and the pilgrimage to Compostela.[93] England was politically dominant in the Angevin empire, and the connection gave her the broadest of bases on which to build a national culture in the centuries of retrenchment that followed. If Paris provided the most exciting intellectual stimuli of the twelfth and thirteenth centuries, it was the wider range of the English dominions overseas that yielded the soil in which the exotic and the native could combine to produce a recognizably English music.

[92] Ibid. vi. 189–90; cf. also p. 183 (on music in the home), 186–7; trans. by L. Thorpe: *Gerald of Wales, The Journey through Wales/ Description of Wales* (Harmondsworth, 1978), 242–3, 236, 239; and other passages of musical interest in both books.

[93] See above, p. 20 and n. 59. On the pilgrimage to Santiago see J. S. Stone, *The Cult of Santiago* (New York, 1927).

2

THE LATER THIRTEENTH AND THE FOURTEENTH CENTURIES

DURING this period English music acquired a distinctive national voice. In one sense the whole epoch can be seen as a preparation for the great outburst of creative energy associated with the age of the Lancastrian kings, which found material expression in the compilation of the 'Old Hall' manuscript, the first great monument of English music.[1] But it would be wrong to see the era of the later Plantagenets as merely preparatory. It was one great artistic achievement in its own right, symbolized in music by such collections as the 'Worcester' repertory of polyphonic music, in literature by the writings of Chaucer and Langland and a whole series of devotional writers, in architecture by a host of fine churches, and in art, at the end of the period, by so splendid an artefact—if it is indeed the work of an Englishman—as the Wilton diptych.

Certainly it is a period of developing and changing musical style, and there is no hard-and-fast boundary between it and the one following. Yet although this chapter begins irrationally enough in the middle of Henry III's long reign, the end of that of Richard II is such a watershed in English history as to compel its adoption in this context too.

The loss of Normandy and the adjacent provinces under King John in 1203–4 had ushered in a new era in the relationship with France. Anglo-Norman became an insular dialect, cut off from linguistic development abroad.[2] Politically, much more now hinged upon the English possessions south of the Loire, until Edward III (reigned 1327–77), following the confiscation of Gascony, laid claim to the throne of France itself,[3] and the

---

[1] Cf. Ch. 3.

[2] I. K. Pope, *From Latin to Modern French* (2nd edn., Manchester, 1952), 421.

[3] This claim was not formally abandoned until 1814. Gascony was finally lost in 1453, Calais (by then the last bit of 'English' France) in 1558.

whole basis of Anglo–French relations was irrevocably changed once more. The resulting Hundred Years War (1337–1453) cuts across the dynastic boundary on which we have settled. Nevertheless the prosecution of the war under Henry V differed sharply from its conduct under Edward III by virtue of its intensely nationalistic, as opposed to a primarily feudal, spirit. The final outcome, so wounding to that emergent nationalism, was in the long run the best possible one from the point of view of the growing nation-state, and hence from the point of view of a distinctive quality in its music as in all other aspects of its culture.

This is to look far ahead. In the thirteenth and early fourteenth centuries, England was still formally united to a large part of France, and bound by ties of intellectual interest to its expanding nucleus. English students flocked to the University of Paris, and their seniors contributed to its lustre; Oxford University was modelled on it.[4] French in some form was the first language of every monarch before Henry IV, of the nobility, and of most of the higher clergy. The French-born and the French-educated filled the major offices of Church and State. Though the great age of monastic penetration from France, most notably in the plantation of houses of the Cluniac, Premonstratensian, and Cistercian orders, was by now over, its influence long remained. At the same time a transformation in the intellectual and religious balance of the country was initiated by the arrival of the Dominicans (Order of Preachers) in 1221 and of the Franciscans (Order of Friars Minor) in 1224.[5] The English language came to be more widely used, giving rise to a substantial body of lyric poetry (much of it devotional), and in the fourteenth century to the impressive achievements to which allusion has been made. Gradually, and in diverse ways, the context for a truly English music was being created.

The major centres for the cultivation of polyphonic music at this time were the larger monasteries, and in particular the cathedral priories such as Worcester, Canterbury, and Durham. Towards the end of the period the contribution of the 'secular' establishments—cathedrals, collegiate churches, and the household chapels of the royalty and nobility—comes more clearly into focus, although it is only rarely that the cultivation of

[4] One of these was John of Garland (Johannes de Garlandia), born in Oxford around 1180 or 1190; his *Morale Scolium* contains a discussion of music, though the musical theorist of the same name was probably a younger man. The identification was maintained by William Waite ('Johannes de Garlandia', *Speculum*, 35 (1960), 179 seqq.) but rejected by Reimer (ed., *Johannes de Garlandia: De mensurabili musica*, 2 vols., Wiesbaden, 1972). On the early history of Oxford see *History of the University of Oxford*, i (Oxford, 1985); vol. ii. will contain a substantial chapter on music.

[5] D. Knowles, *The Religious Orders in England*, i. (Cambridge, 1948), 127–45, 163–253.

polyphony can be ascribed to any of them with certainty.[6] The Chapel Royal was emerging as the best equipped of these, and with its staff of chaplains and clerks (six each from the time of Edward I until the end of the fourteenth century) provided the model for a new generation of musically orientated foundations in the fifteenth century. Polyphonic music of the Notre-Dame type was sung by it from the middle of the thirteenth century at least,[7] and the Chapel may well have been at the forefront of musical developments throughout the fourteenth century.[8]

The first tantalizing hints of a truly indigenous repertory are found in a lengthy list of polyphonic pieces at the end of a manuscript written in (or having close links with) Reading Abbey.[9] It appears to be the index to an otherwise lost collection, and only later bound in to the manuscript; but there is internal evidence of the connection with Reading. The list gives the name of two composers, R. de Burg[ate], who was Abbot of Reading from 1268 to 1298, and W. de Wicumbe (i.e. William of Winch-combe), a monk of Reading who also spent four years at Leominster Priory, where he acted as precentor and copied several manuscripts.[10] The rather similar name of W. de Winton, also a monk of both Leominster and Reading, appears at the head of the list, with what precise significance it is hard to say since Burgate's name appears in connection with the first piece. The first group of pieces consists of three Gloria-tropes and five troped Alleluias, the second (headed by Winchcombe's name) of thirty-seven Alleluias, presumably untroped. It is possible that most of these were Notre-Dame compositions (except for the last eight, which are Marian and have no Continental concordances), and that Winchcombe was merely the

---

[6] The statutes and ordinals of Exeter and Lincoln make clear reference to polyphonic music, while inventories from Exeter, St George's, Windsor (refounded as a collegiate church in 1348), Lichfield, and St Paul's reveal a polyphonic repertory in those places. Harrison, *Music in Medieval Britain*, 109–113; see further Bowers, 'Choral Establishments', 2062 seqq.

[7] The English theorist known as 'Anonymus IV' (see Bibliography) refers to the excellent singing of 'Master Johannes Filius Dei, Makeblite at Winchester, and Blaksmit at the court of the last King Henry' (Henry III, d. 1272), of whom the first is mentioned in the St Paul's inventory of 1295 and the third in a royal 'Liberate' roll of 1260/1 as one of the three 'clerks of the king's *capella*'. The five surviving Wardrobe inventories from 1296/7 to 1305/6 each refer to two books of *cantus organi*, one beginning 'Viderunt' and the other 'Alleluia'. Harrison, *Music in Medieval Britain*, 132–3; I. Bent in *PRMA*, 90 (1963–4), 93–5, where it is suggested that the two books would have been kept with the materials of the *capella* before being consigned to the Wardrobe.

[8] For a sketch of the earlier development of this institution see Ch. I, p. 16.

[9] London, Brit. Lib., Harley 978, fos. 160ᵛ–161ʳ. At the beginning of the manuscript is a small musical collection including the famous 'Sumer is icumen in'; there follow a calendar of Reading Abbey, medical treatises, and a substantial collection of Latin and French verse including the *lais* of Marie de France. *Catalogue of Harleian MSS* (1808), i. 488–9; Ludwig, *Repertorium*, 267–78; B. Schofield, 'The Provenance and Date of "Sumer is Icumen in"', *MR*, 9 (1948), 81–6.

[10] Ludwig, *Repertorium*, 270–71 (with the names mistranscribed); Schofield, 'Provenance', 83–4; Harrison, *Music in Medieval Britain*, 135–6.

copyist.[11] The remaining items are *conducti* and motets with little or no identifiable connection with the contemporary French repertory.

The repertory associated with the Benedictine Cathedral Priory of Worcester in many ways illustrates the implications of the Reading index. Although fragmentary, the collection is of considerable bulk when transcribed *in extenso*.[12] Some caution is needed, however, in assessing the role of Worcester in its compilation. The fragments have mostly been recovered from the bindings of later books from the Chapter Library; it may be a fair inference that the manuscripts from which they were torn were copied in the Winchester scriptorium, but it is going too far to deduce from this a Worcester 'school' of composers as was once assumed. Several pieces also occur in other manuscripts, and in some cases (such as the motet 'Thomas gemma Cantuarie/Thomas cesus in Doveria' in honour of St Thomas of Canterbury and St Thomas of Dover)[13] the locale of origin is obviously different. With these reservations, however, we may plausibly speak of a Worcester repertory. Fragments of several codices have been recovered. One of these was evidently a large volume, for its folios were numbered and ran to 136 at least. The others contain no visible numbering and are mostly even more exiguously preserved; but they too may once have been extensive documents.[14]

The intelligent study of the Worcester fragments, and of others like them, presents problems of the most appalling complexity. Apart from the great number of unattached bits and pieces, the leaves which can be shown to belong to the single large volume already referred to are the work of several different scribes; and in addition some pieces have been erased, or partially erased, to make way for new material. Thus we have evidence for changing fashions even within a single codex. The notation, which is of considerable refinement, is nevertheless not free from ambiguity; and many pieces have been subjected to a process of notational 'reform' which may or may not conceal changes in the method of performance. The music,

[11] Three of the Marian Alleluias have counterparts in the insular fascicle of the St Andrews MS (see Ch. 1). The collecting of Alleluias separately was an English phenomenon: cf. n. 7 above, and the fragmentary and incomplete MS Oxford, Bod. Lib., Rawl. c. 400* described by L. Dittmer, 'An English Discantuum Volumen', *MD*, 8 (1954), 20–58.

[12] There are editions by Dom A. Hughes (*Worcester Mediaeval Harmony* (London, 1928)) and L. Dittmer (*The Worcester Fragments* (AIM, 1957)); the complete pieces are also given, with other material, in *English Music of the Thirteenth and Early Fourteenth Centuries*, ed. E. Sanders (Monaco, 1979) (cited below as *English Music*).

[13] *Worcester Fragments*, no. 67, from Oxford, Bod. Lib., lat. liturg. d. 20, fo. 35ʳ, and two other MSS; *English Music*, no. 61.

[14] The principal MS is Oxford, Bod. Lib., lat. liturg. d. 20, made up of materials from several Bodleian MSS and including photostats of others that are comparable. Other fragments are still kept in the Chapter Library at Worcester (MS 68), and a few more are in the British Library (Add. 25031). Parts of the Worcester MS are included as photostat copies in lat. liturg. d. 20, and are incorporated within Dittmer's new foliation for the latter.

which is generally in three but occasionally in four parts, was normally written out in separate parts on facing pages of the open book; and since not many consecutive leaves have survived, a great proportion of what has come down to us consists of single voice-parts, or pairs of parts, the remainder being irretrievably lost. A little, but not much, can be reconstructed on the basis of a known plainsong or a repetitive technique such as *rondellus*.[15] In the circumstances, it is surprising how much can be gathered from the fragments that remain.

The repertory at Worcester, as elsewhere, consisted partly of liturgical music, usually troped, and partly of *conducti* and motets. In due course motets came to supersede the more significant types of liturgical music, as the erasures just mentioned clearly show. Unlike the similar development on the Continent, however, English motets remained invariably sacred in subject. In its general character the Worcester repertory is a little later than that represented by the Reading list (which is itself an advance on the contents of the St Andrews manuscript), but there are nevertheless some apparent concordances with it.

Although the distinction between liturgical and non-liturgical music is in some ways fundamental it is not quite so hard-and-fast as might be imagined. Certain types of liturgical music habitually made use of motet or *conductus* techniques, while a motet based on a *tenor* extracted from a liturgical plainsong might in some cases be regarded as a troping substitute for that extract, or even for the whole of the liturgical item from which it is taken. If we begin our tour of the repertory with the Ordinary of the Mass, we shall immediately find examples of this blurring of distinctions. The first two extant pieces of the Worcester repertory are settings of Kyrie melodies, untroped in the *tenor* but carrying two different troping texts in the upper parts in the manner of a 'double' motet. The beginning of the second piece, which is virtually complete for two-thirds of its length, will illustrate the method and the style, which, however, is not that of the earliest layer of 'Worcester' polyphony. The *tenor* is the plainsong Kyrie 'Lux et origo' in its untroped form, and the ninefold Kyrie is set in full without the need for the alternation of sections in plainsong. Though the trope 'Lux et origo' itself is absent, it is nevertheless this text which the upper parts elaborate and comment upon (Ex. 8, pp. 40–1).[16]

In contrast to this, a Gloria from a different section of the fragments[17] is in three-part *conductus* style, even to the extent that its *tenor* part, as far as can be ascertained, is newly composed. The Credo was apparently

---

[15] See below, p. 47.

[16] *Worcester Fragments*, no. 2, from Oxford, Bod, Lib., lat. liturg. d. 20, fos. 1ᵛ–2ʳ (photostats of Worcester, Chapter Lib., MS 68, fragment x); cf. *English Music*, Appendix no. 21.

[17] *Worcester Fragments*, no. 88, from Worcester, fragment xix, fos. c2ᵛ and b2ʳ; Oxford, Bod. Lib., Mus. c. 60, fos. 82ᵛ–83ᵛ (adapted); *English Music*, no. 44.

not set polyphonically at this period; but a series of Sanctus settings from the second of the two principal manuscripts that can be recognized in the surviving fragments is of interest in belonging to the oldest layer of the repertory (nos. 58–62). Though none of them is complete, it can be deduced that so far as the texts are concerned the method employed was exactly that of the Kyries discussed above; the difference is that these pieces bound along in the compound duple rhythm which had characterized French music in the earlier part of the century and which was still a lively element in English music towards its end. A short passage at the end of one of these works can be completed from another fragment from elsewhere in the Worcester survivals (Ex. 9, p. 42).[18]

The only Agnus Dei from Worcester is in *conductus* style with the plainchant in the middle voice, one of a series of such pieces from a fragment belonging to the later fourteenth century.[19] From the Proper of the Mass are preserved two settings of the Marian Introit, 'Salve sancta parens', the first as a *conductus*-motet in three parts, the second as a four-part motet with three troping texts in the upper parts;[20] two sections of a Tract, 'Gaude Maria virgo', in which the sole surviving upper part is also troped;[21] and the Marian Offertory 'Felix namque', of which the same is true.[22] But by far the largest contribution to the Proper of the Mass is represented by settings of Alleluias.

English untroped three-part Alleluias are rarely found at this period,[23] although they may be represented in the Reading index referred to above. In this form, polyphony was provided for the opening phrase (the word 'Alleluia' being then repeated in plainchant by the choir from the beginning to the end of the melisma) and for the verse up to the final melisma, which was sung by the choir in plainchant. In the repetition, the soloists would again begin the Alleluia (either in plainchant or by repeating the polyphonic opening section) and the choir would then continue to the end of the melisma in plainchant. The partial troping of the verse in such a scheme may be illustrated by a setting of the Alleluia with the verse

[18] *Worcester Fragments*, no. 61, from Worcester, fragment xxxv, fo. d^v (photostat in Oxford, Bod. Lib., lat. liturg. d. 20, fo. 32^v); extract completed from no. 77, lat. liturg. d. 20, fo. 39^v, a two-part fragment from a different source.

[19] *Worcester Fragments*, no. 84, from Worcester, fragment xix. There are a few more in contemporary sources: *English Music*, nos. 11, 13, 14, 20 (all *a 2*, troped).

[20] *Worcester Fragments*, nos. 9 (Worcester, fragment xxxi^r; photostat in Oxford, Bod. Lib., lat. liturg. d. 20, fo. 7^r; variant concordance ibid., Mus. c. 60, fo. 79^r), 64 (Worcester, fragment xxxv, fo. 6 (b); photostat in Oxford, Bod. Lib., lat. liturg. d. 20, fo. 33^r); *English Music*, nos. 67, 74.

[21] *Worcester Fragments*, no. 35, from Worcester, fragment ix, fo. 1^v; photostat in Oxford, Bod. Lib., lat. liturg. d. 20, fo. 20^v.

[22] *Worcester Fragments*, no. 4, from London, Brit. Lib., Add. 25031, fo. 2c^r; photostat in Oxford, Bod. Lib., lat. liturg. d. 20, fo. 20^v.

[23] For an example see *English Music*, no. 63.

Ex. 8

Ex. 8, continued

Triplum. A shining golden light is made within the vast heavens, from which light glory comes. Mary, mother of the king most high, in whose everlasting life all things rejoice, help us with thy holy prayer and have mercy on your servants.
Duplum. Light and glory of the heavenly King, Mary, mistress of the world, full of grace, in whose worship all that praise you rejoice: you, Mary, who can help us after the trials of this world, have mercy.

'Nativitas gloriose virginis Marie', from one of the more damaged and exiguous of the Worcester fragments.[24]

    This example of English *organum triplum* may be usefully compared with the great setting of the same text, also in three parts, composed earlier in the century by Magister Perotinus.[25] The quite exceptional feature of the English work, however, is the literal quotation of a portion of Perotinus' original composition, at the words 'ex semine Abrahae'. What is more, the upper parts are here provided with a troping text in the manner of a *conductus*-motet, corresponding to the word 'Abrahe' and beginning

---

[24] *Worcester Fragments*, no. 8, from Worcester, fragment xviii, fos. 1ᵛ–2ʳ; *English Music*, Appendix no. 16. The Alleluia is preceded in the fragment by the Marian Gradual 'Benedicta et venerabilis', no. 80a on fo. 1ʳ.
[25] *The Works of Perotin*, ed. E. Thurston (New York, 1970), 71–83.

Ex. 9

Triplum. Hosanna: in celestial glory let the heavenly hosts sound 'holy' three times in the highest.

Duplum. Hosanna: in the heavenly hierarchy let the harmony of the angels' song sound sweetly: 'holy, holy, holy' in the highest.

Tenor. Hosanna in the highest.

'Abrahe, divino moderamine'.[26] Although this extract does not appear in quite this form in any Continental source—it is found separately as a two-part work (without the top part), and as a three-part work, with various texts and combinations of texts—it is possible that the English composer took this version of the text and music directly from a Continental model.[27] Our example shows first the setting of the word 'Nativitas' by Perotinus and the English composer, and secondly the beginning of the section 'ex semine' in both versions (Ex. 10, pp. 44–6).

A later stage in the development of the English polyphonic Alleluia is represented by two works in the principal Worcester codex—the Alleluias 'Pascha nostrum' and 'Per te Dei genitrix'[28] in double-motet style throughout. In another variant of the genre, the liturgical form is extended by means of a free prelude before the beginning of the Alleluia, a melismatic interlude before the verse, and sometimes by an alternative setting for the repetition of the soloists' intonation of 'Alleluia'. These features are present, to varying degrees, in a series of ten Alleluias from the second Worcester codex[29] and in those of the Bodleian manuscript already mentioned.[30] None of these works is complete in the sources, but whole sections can be reconstructed. The variety of techniques represented is bewildering. *Rondellus* or interchange of parts (described more fully below) is frequent, either between two upper parts or between all three. Every opportunity for varying the principle of troping is made use of. The prelude to the Alleluia 'Post partum', from another part of the manuscript, is a sophisticated example of *rondellus* which occurs in the Montpellier codex to a different text, 'Alle psallite cum luya'.[31] In the Worcester source a text beginning 'Ave magnifica Maria' is shared between the upper parts against the progressively elaborated

[26] The text in the Worcester piece, which like its model is written in score, is written below the lowest voice even during the trope, though at that point it fits only the rhythm of the upper parts, at least as notated. The English composer omitted from his *tenor* the notes which in the chant are set to the word 'Abrahe', this having already been accounted for in the trope.

[27] For the surviving Continental motet-versions see *The Works of Perotin*, 84–8.

[28] *Worcester Fragments*, nos. 27, 28, from Oxford, Bod. Lib., lat. liturg. d. 20, fos. 14ᵛ–16ʳ; *English Music*, nos. 71, 72. In this edition the identity of the verse of the first of these is said to be unknown, but it appears to be a version of 'Pascha nostrum' for Easter Day as indicated by Dittmer. Another example of a fully troped Alleluia in *conductus*-motet style will be found in *English Music*, no. 69.

[29] *Worcester Fragments*, nos. 45–6, 49–52, 54–7, from Oxford, Bod. Lib., lat. liturg. d. 20, fos. 25ᵛ–30ᵛ, partly photostatted from Worcester fragments xxxv, ix; some are in *English Music*, Appendix nos. 17, 18b–21. The gaps in the series are caused by later additions made over erasures.

[30] Rawl. c. 400* (see n. 11); the prelude of one such fragment, notated with words only but corresponding to *Worcester Fragments*, no. 19, also in *English Music*, Appendix no. 18a; another, fully restorable, ibid., no. 70.

[31] *Worcester Fragments*, no. 19 (cf. n. 30): Worcester, fragment xxviii, f. a2ᵛ, photostat in Oxford, Bod. Lib., lat. liturg. d. 20, fo. 11ʳ⁻ᵛ; Montpellier, Fac. de Médecine, H 196, fos. 392ʳ⁻ᵛ; cf. *Polyphonies du XIIIᵉ siècle*, ed. Y. Rokseth, 4 vols. (Paris, 1936), no. 339; *The Montpellier Codex*, ed. H. Tischler, 4 vols. (Madison, Wis., 1978–85), no. 339. (Future references to this MS will be by number and refer to either edition.)

Ex. 10

Perotinus

Ex. 10, continued

Anon.

continued

free *tenor*.[32] An abbreviated quotation will illustrate the technique and also
the relationship of this section with the continuation which, being fragmentary and without concordances, cannot alas be reconstructed (Ex. 11, pp.
48–9).

A rather similar prelude and intonation, apparently to the Marian verse

---

[32] Its prelude is a transposition of that of no. 56 (*English Music*, no. 18b), where the verse is 'Dulce
lignum'. The middle voice is missing in both cases, but may be restored from Montpellier no. 339;
the complete words are in Rawl. c. 400★ (see n. 11).

Ex. 10, continued

Perotinus

(b) (i)

Anon.

(a) The Nativity ... (b) (i) from the seed ... (ii) from the seed of Abraham by divine intervention ...

'Virga Iesse', survives without significant lacunae[33] and illustrates the addition of a troping text to the *tenor* against a more usual application of *rondellus* technique in the upper parts. This can be represented concisely as shown in Ex. 12 (pp. 50–1).

Such a process of liturgical elaboration could not be continued indefinitely, and the impulse which had led to this kind of extension, like the troping of upper voices, was more significantly realized in the already widely cultivated forms of *conductus* and independent motet. The Reading index had listed a series of thirty-eight *conducti*, and the surviving sources provide additions to, and a few possible concordances with, this list.[34]

English *conducti* of the later thirteenth and early fourteenth centuries often employed the device of the *rondellus*, a formalized interchange of voices according to some such scheme as the following:

A	B	C	*D*	E	F
C	*A*	B	F	*D*	E
B	C	*A*	E	F	*D*

In this, the italicized letters represent a section of music carrying text (usually the same one for the same letters of the diagram), the others being melismatic. But *rondellus* was never adopted for an entire piece, and Ex. 13, from a lengthy *conductus*, 'Flos regalis', will illustrate both the technique and something of its context (see p. 52).[35]

There are not a great many *conducti* extant in English sources, and by no means all of them employ *rondellus* technique. A short piece entitled 'Beata viscera' (no. 19) is illustrative of the simpler type to be found in the Worcester repertory. One aspect in particular may be noted, namely the tendency for the music to proceed in 6–3 chords. This is of some significance in view of later developments, and it is found at this period both in association with an elaborated plainchant in one of the voices, and, when the music is freely composed, as in Ex. 14 (p. 53).[36]

Rondellus is also frequently found in English motets of this period and slightly later, up to about the middle of the fourteenth century. In such cases it is confined to a pair of parts above the *tenor*, though in four-part motets there may also be exchange between the *tenor* and a fourth part

[33] *Worcester Fragments*, no. 46, from Oxford, Bod. Lib., lat. liturg. d. 20, fo. 25ᵛ; middle part on fo. 26ʳ, photostatted from Worcester, fragment xxxv, fo. iʳ; *English Music*, no. 20. The verse itself is completely missing.

[34] e.g. the entry 'Virgo pudicitie' may refer to the second of three *conducti* in Oxford, Bod. Lib., Rawl. liturg. d. 3, fo. 71ʳ.

[35] Oxford, Bod. Lib., Corpus Christi College 489, fragment 22, fo. iʳ; *English Music*, no. 28.

[36] *Worcester Fragments*, no. 91, from Worcester, fragment xix, fo. a2ʳ, one of a series of liturgical items and *conductus* written in score. It is given in a more satisfactory rhythmic interpretation in *The Oxford Anthology: Medieval Music*, ed. W. T. Marrocco and N. Sandon (London and New York, 1977), no. 55, and again in *English Music*, no. 43.

Ex. II

Ex. 11, continued

[Interlude]

Post   et   in   pu - er - pe - ri -   o

[Tenor missing]

Post]

Hail, most mighty Mary.   Hail, saving bearer of God, Mary.
Hail, most wonderful Mary. Hail, cleansing, child-bearing Mary.
Hail, grace-giving Mary, bearing salvation to the world.
Hail, glorious Mary, shining with heavenly light†
Hail, Mary, Alleluia. After and in childbirth . . .

* In each repeat exchange upper two parts, using second text in each voice. Revert to original voice and upper text in following section. In the lowest voice, substitute the bracketed rests for the final note in the repeat of each section.
† A reference to the hymn 'O quam glorifica luce coruscas'.

in the same range. English motets with a *primus* and *secundus pes*, or with *tenor* and *quartus cantus* (the equivalent of *tenor* and *contratenor* in Continental music) are not uncommon, and the procedure may have developed independently of Continental influence. There are also a few examples of the older type of four-part motet, with three texted parts and a *tenor*.

The Reading list had included motets both with a single text and with two texts; it is not clear whether the former were two-part works or three-part 'conductus-motets' (see p. 26), though the latter interpretation seems the more probable.[37] A *rondellus*-motet might be the equivalent of either a *conductus*-motet or a double-motet, depending on whether the texted voices do or do not draw on the same poem. An example of the former is 'Quam admirabilis' (no. 16), in which the underlying metre must necessarily be binary (Ex. 15, pp. 54–5).[38]

A good example of *rondellus* in the upper parts against two lower parts is provided by 'Rota versatilis', a lengthy motet in praise of St Katherine of Alexandria. It survives only in scattered fragments (none of them from Worcester), but they have been painstakingly assembled, and one section

[37] Ludwig (p. 274) and Harrison (p. 136), however, reach the opposite conclusion.
[38] *Worcester Fragments*, no. 16, from Worcester, fragment xxviii, fos. b1ᵛ–b2ʳ (photostat in Oxford, Bod. Lib., lat. liturg. d. 20, fos. 9ᵛ–10ʳ); *English Music*, no. 53 (values reduced to one-eighth only).

Ex. 12

Al - - - - - - - -

Al - le-lu - ya psal - lat hec fa - mi - li - a.

Al - (Al) - le-lu - ya con - ci - nat hec fa - mi - li - a.

hec fa - mi - li - a.

Al - le-lu - ya tim - pa - ni - zet, al - le - lu - ya

hec fa - mi - li - a. [Al - le-lu - ya] tim - pa - ni - zet, al - le - lu - ya

psal - lat le - tus ce - tus cum ar - mo - ni - a.

ci - tha - ri - zet le - tus ce - tus cum ar - mo - ni - a

Al - le - lu - ya psal - lat De - o lau - dum et pre - co - ni - a.

Al - le-lu - ya con - ci - nat De - o lau - dum et pre - co - ni - a.

Ex. 12, continued

[continuation lost]

Middle part. Alleluia, let this family sing praise. Alleluia, let it strike the drum; alleluia, let the joyful crowd sing praise with harmony. Alleluia, let it sing joyful songs of praise to God. Alleluia.

Lowest part. Alleluia, let this family sing together. Alleluia, let it strike the drum; alleluia let the joyful crowd play the cithara. Alleluia, let it sing together joyful songs of praise to God. Alleluia.

    * Exchange upper parts in each repeat; revert to original part in continuation.
    † This note omitted (in error?) in repeat.

Ex. 13

Fragrant rose, springtime primrose, free your servants from evil.

Ex. 14

Be - - - - - - - [Be -]

a - ta vi - sce - ra Ma - ri - e vir - gi - nis,

Blessed is the womb of the virgin Mary.

survives intact to give an idea of the character of this elaborate composition (Ex. 16, p. 56).[39]

When *rondellus* in the upper parts is combined with an ostinato in the *pes*, as in 'Virgo regalis' (no. 12),[40] the result can be particularly attractive. The ostinato technique was also employed in double-motets. The *pes* in such cases was often constructed of irregular phrase-lengths, as in 'Puellare gremium' (no. 76)[41] or in Ex. 17, in which the phrases are of nine bars (double longs) each (see pp. 58–9).[42]

One further technique may be mentioned here: that of the *rota* or perpetual canon. The most famous of all *rote* is the 'Sumer' canon discussed below. Ex. 18 resembles a modern round in that the interval of entry is commensurate with the total combined musical content; once the third voice has entered, the effect is of a *rondellus* with a continuous text. The resulting combination is heard fourteen times in different scorings (see p. 60).[43]

The 'Sumer' canon itself—a six-part setting of the text 'Sumer is icumen in'—demands consideration here, partly because of its technical affinity

---

[39] M. Bent, 'Rota Versatilis', *Source Materials and the Interpretation of Music* (London, 1981), 65–98, where the sources are listed.

[40] Cf. *English Music*, no. 51.

[41] Ibid., no. 49.

[42] *Worcester Fragments*, no. 6, from London, Brit. Lib., Add. 25031, fos. 3r, 1r (photostat in Oxford, Bod. Lib., lat. liturg. d. 20, fos. 4v–5r); *English Music*, no. 54.

[43] *Worcester Fragments*, no. 21, from Oxford, Bod. Lib., lat. liturg. d. 20, fos. 12r–v; *English Music*, no. 35.

Ex. 15

Ex. 15, continued

How admirable and venerable you are, royal virgin. Hail, giver of solace, gracious to the just, illustrious mother. Radiant in appearance and in the sweetness of your unborn child, O Mary, cause us to be placed in the summit of heaven and to enjoy glory in place of guilt.

★ Exchange upper parts in repeat; revert to original part in continuation.

with the kind of music just discussed, and partly because the Reading manuscript in which it occurs also gives a sacred text, 'Perspice, christicola'. The music is in the form of a four-part canon at the unison, superimposed on to a two-part *rondellus*. The canonic voices enter at two-bar intervals, and as this is also the interval at which the other two voices exchange

Ex. 16

The wheel of Katherine is made most cruel, a punishing wheel in a world of double deceit. Its hidden parts are brought to light in a hideous outcome; its ruins are scattered by a superhuman force. (NB the interpretation of this stanza is far from certain, but it appears to refer to Katherine's escape from the wheel to which she was bound and the damage which it did to the onlookers. See the article cited in n. 39 and the rather different interpretation put forward there on pp. 86–9.)

★ Upper parts exchange in repeat.

their parts, the music is in effect a set of variations on a two-bar ground. (Fundamentally it is even simpler, as the two bars are virtually identical in harmonic content.) In the accompanying presentation, the entire musical material is shown as concisely as is compatible with readability. The singers of the canon simply enter at two-bar intervals as shown (for convenience there are two parts to a staff and the even-numbered entries, though fully written out as to the music, are not as regards the text), following the staves down the page and observing the repeat as marked. The lowest staff, the two-part *pes*, is repeated indefinitely. The score-reader must imagine the top staff alone against the *pes* to begin with, followed by every possible combination of two adjacent staves over the *pes* after that. The scheme may be continued indefinitely as indicated by the figures: no mechanism for a conclusion is given in the manuscript (Ex. 19, p. 61).[44]

The date of composition has been a subject of controversy, but *c*.1280 seems to be justified both by the style of the music and such palaeographical considerations as are relevant.[45] The music has, however, been subject to revision, both as to the actual melodic line and in the notation of its rhythm, the latter being now unequivocally trochaic.[46] It has also been suggested that the Latin text, a poem appropriate to the Easter season, is the one for which the music was originally composed.[47] But it is difficult to ignore, first, the primacy of the relationship between the English text and the music in the manuscript (the English text appears above the Latin text and has a better correspondence with the notes above), and, second, the obvious musical references to the song of the cuckoo. The work may perhaps be thought of as a monastic *jeu d'esprit* given respectability by the later addition of a sacred poem.

The creative joy evident in these exuberant displays of technical skill is one aspect of English late thirteenth-century style. The other side is represented by a thoughtful pursuit of more recent Continental ideas. Though this took various forms, one of its clearest manifestations is in the sphere of rhythm. Exx. 8, 15, and 16 already illustrate a gradual tendency,

---

[44] London, Brit. Lib., Harley 978, f. 11ᵛ, restoring the original readings as far as possible but interpreting undifferentiated lozenges (breves) trochaically (cf. E. H. Sanders, 'Duple Rhythm and Alternate Third Mode in the 13th Century', *JAMS*, 15 (1962), 249–91. A 'binary' (i.e. simple 2/4) rhythm would nevertheless be possible, as in Ex. 15 above. Cf. *Medieval English Songs*, no. 9; *English Music*, nos. 4a, 4b.

[45] M. Bukofzer, '"Sumer is icumen in": A Revision', *University of California Publications in Music*, 2 (1944), 79–114, proposed *c*.1310 against the *c*.1240 of earlier palaeographers. Schofield in *MR*, 9 (1948), 81–6, restated the grounds for the earlier date, though extending the possibilities by implication to *c*.1260.

[46] For a recent study, with full references and facsimile, see W. Obst, '"Sumer is icumen in": A Contrafactum?', *ML*, 64 (1983), 151–61, qualified by correspondence from R. Wibberley, ibid., 65 (1984), 332–3.

[47] Harrison, *Music in Medieval Britain*, 142–4, supported (on dubious metrical grounds) by Obst, *ML*, 64.

Ex. 17

Ex. 17, continued

Triplum. The father of the eternally begotten, speaking of the Son by the prophets in diverse utterance, now that the chariot of the seasons had run its course, sent the only-begotten one from the throne of heaven … (reading 'a prophetis' for 'et prophetis' in the MS).

Duplum. Let the mother of grace sing praises; the church rejoices in her through whom the court of heaven rejoices in the newly born; glory is sung to God in the highest, to which the angelic voice resoundingly bears witness …

evident throughout the Middle Ages and the Renaissance and in all countries, for the speed of the music to slow down and for smaller note-values to be introduced to fill the 'vacuum' created by the loss of speed. Though this tendency is far from uniform in pace, it is a useful guide to stylistic development, and as a means of comparison between the music of different countries or cultural centres. The examples of mensurable music in this chapter hitherto have reduced the notes to one-sixteenth of their original value, a long being represented by a crotchet or dotted crotchet, a breve by a quaver, and so on, a scale of reduction nowadays generally considered suitable for Continental music of the late twelfth and early thirteenth centuries. It is a measure of English conservatism that such a scale should still seem appropriate for a substantial body of late thirteenth-century music; but for the next group of works to be discussed in this chapter a reduction to one-eighth gives a more readable result (the breve becoming a crotchet, and so on). This change of rhythmic character, which is felt principally as an increase in dignity and breadth, is the basis of the observations made above as to stylistic development within the Worcester repertory. It brings English music within the realm of the later thirteenth-century motet style in France, and ultimately to the proliferation and rhythmic organization of the smallest note-value then known, the semibreve, a development associated in France with the names of a series of innovators from Petrus de Cruce to Philippe de Vitry.[48]

The slowing down of tempo was often combined with the introduction

[48] For these later developments see below, pp. 75–6.

Ex. 18

Pure Mary, mother of hosts, force of life, guide to mariners, truly a vessel of strength; Jeremiah calls you a rod of purity; Elijah proclaims you as a light of great substance. By this prophecy you bear a mighty progeny, by the highest Wisdom you shelter the sum of justice. O high priestess, in the presence of the royal mercy, save us because you remain the giver of grace. By you Messiah weeping was bound to sadness; give to your servants the holy reward of joy (reading 'prefert Helya' for 'presit Helyam').

* The singers enter one by one, and each sings the melody five times; except that the first singer to enter sings the first phrase a sixth time, and the third to enter ends with the second phrase of the fifth time.

of a fourth part, either of the *quartus cantus* type or (less commonly) as a *quadruplum* in the older Parisian fashion.[49] But this was by no means invariable, and there are (quite apart from such a *tour de force* as the 'Sumer' canon) a number of pieces in which the presence of a fourth part proves compatible with the older rhythms. Ex. 16 above provides an example, though the tempo here is much gentler than that of (say) Ex. 12. Another interesting case is that of 'Thomas gemma Cantuarie', already referred to.

[49] Cf. Ch. 1, p. 26. There are English examples of this texture in Westminster Abbey, MS 33327 (EECM, xxvi, pl. 175); *Worcester Fragments*, ed. L. Dittmer, fac. and transcription, nos. 1 and 2 from this MS; and in the New College MS (see below, pp. 76–8).

Ex. 19

Summer has arrived, loudly sing 'cuckoo'. The seed grows and the meadow blooms, and now the trees put forth shoots. The ewe bleats after the lamb, the cow lows after the calf. The bullock leaps, the buck farts, merrily sing 'cuckoo'. Cuckoo, cuckoo! You sing well, cuckoo, never stop now.

★ wde = uude, i.e. 'wood'.

The three versions in which this fascinatingly subtle set of ostinato variations survives exhibit successive degrees of elaboration, and hence of tempo reduction. Although only one of them is reasonably complete, any of them could be restored by comparison with the other two.[50]

The final phase of development within the Worcester repertory is represented by 'Candens crescit lilium' (no. 53), written over part of the original set of Alleluias in the second codex.[51] The structure of this work is a mosaic of no more than six four-bar sections, repeated apparently at random but making in reality a sophisticated refrain-form. The opening will convey the essence of the style (Ex. 20, pp. 64–5). The overall form may be expressed as follows:

A	a	b	a	c		
B	d	e	b	d	e	c
A	a	b	a	c		
B'	f	e	b	f	e	c
A	a	b	a	c		

Since, however, as can be seen, c is merely a 'second-time' variant of b, and since also f e is a variant of d e, the degree of unity is much greater than appears at first sight.

Such works as this illustrate a growing tendency towards the use of structures which can be described as 'isoperiodic'. The use of regular phrase-lengths might be applicable to the entire structure, as here, or to individual parts, in which case two or more of them might be overlapping. When an entire structure can be sectionalized, of course, the sections might not be of identical length but related to each other according to simple ratios. The larger plan of 'Candens crescit', for example, might be described as 2:3:2:3:2, while that of 'Rota versatilis' (see above, Ex. 16), literally 27:19:9:20:9, is very close to 3:2:1:2:1.

It will be convenient at this point to break into the continuous history of English sacred polyphony in order to review developments in other areas during the later thirteenth and early fourteenth centuries. The thirteenth century, at first sight a somewhat barren field in terms of actual survivals, is in reality astonishingly rich once the boundaries have been determined and the significance of the more striking artefacts properly

---

[50] Cf. n. 13. Apart from the Worcester source (no. 67), the piece survives in Cambridge, Gonville and Caius College, MS 512/543 (the only complete version) and Princeton, University Library, MS Garrett 119 (the most elaborate version). In *The Worcester Fragments*, all three versions are given in vertical alignment.

[51] Oxford, Bod. Lib., lat. liturg. d. 20, fo. 28ᵛ, completable from Cambridge, Pembroke Coll., MS 228, fo. 11ᵛ, *English Music*, no. 60.

assessed. One must begin with the plainchant of the period, since although it is in many respects a continuation of the older tradition, it was subject to a constant process of revision, clarification, and expansion. A full account would be out of place here, but mention should be made of the progress towards a standard and clearly legible form of the chant conformable to the Use of Salisbury.[52] The chant of the York Use was similarly provided for, as well as the variants appropriate to Exeter and other 'secular' establishments. The monastic versions are also well represented at this period, the Worcester Antiphonal and Gradual being outstanding.[53]

The repertory of traditional chants was greatly increased by the composition of new melodies for the Ordinary of the Mass, and by the writing of hymns, Sequences, and *conducti*. In many cases the chants were not new but adapted from older English or Continental sources, sometimes with new texts added or substituted. But in a curious way the earliest phase of fully legible notation coincides in England with a flowering of melodic beauty so intense as to create the impression of a new and indigenous art. Can anything be more perfect than the chant for the hymn 'Sancte Dei pretiose' in its 'English' form (Ex. 21, p. 65)?[54]

The Sequences and *conducti* of this era are virtually indistinguishable in form, with their predominantly trochaic rhyming verse, though even the later Sequences preserve something of the character of the older examples through an accumulation of tiny details. The majority of the melodies seem to require a free rhythmic interpretation, but occasionally the notation implies performance in ternary metre. The two examples given in Ex. 22 are from roughly contemporary (late thirteenth-century) manuscripts, and each illustrates the typical shorter Marian devotional *cantio* in 'Sequence' or double-versicle form (see pp. 66–7).[55]

One group of Sequence-like chants, of which the 'Stabat mater dolorosa' is the best known, helps to illustrate the link between formal and popular devotion at this period. A number of thirteenth-century English poems are based on one or other of these, and in most cases there is a musical setting, polyphonic or monophonic, extant. One of these is a direct

---

[52] See esp. the early 13th-cent. MSS used for the facsimiles of the *Antiphonale Sarisburiense* (*AS*) (Cambridge, Univ. Lib., Mm. ii. 9, known as the Barnwell Antiphoner) and *Graduale Sarisburiense* (*GS*) (London, Brit. Lib., Add. 12194). Cf. *The Use of Salisbury*, ed. N. Sandon, in progress.

[53] *Paléographie musicale*, I/ xii (2 vols., 1922–5: antiphonal only).

[54] *Hymnorum cum notis opusculum* (Antwerp, 1525), fo. 9ᵛ. Two earlier Continental versions are given in *Monumenta Monodica Medii Aevi*, i. *Die Hymnen* (I), ed. Bruno Stäblein (Kassel and Basle, 1956), 82, 227–8. The melody is a *cento*, derived in part from the secular Sequence 'Aurea personet lyra': ibid. 540.

[55] (a) Cambridge, Univ. Lib., Add. MS 710, fo. 120ʳ: facsimile in *Le Tropaire-prosaire de Dublin*, ed. R.-J. Hesbert (Rouen, 1966), pl. 172; (b) Oxford, Bod. Lib., Rawl. liturg. d. 3, fo. 70ᵛ. The text of the latter was also set as a two-part *conductus* in the Notre-Dame style: e.g. in Wolfenbüttel, Helmstadt 628, fo. 128ᵛ.

Ex. 20

Ex. 20, continued

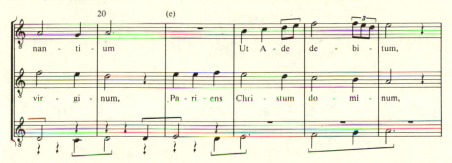

Triplum. White grows the lily; the virgin womb brings forth the Son to the world, creator of all things, ruler of rulers, so that Adam's debt . . . [might be redeemed].
Duplum. White lily, dove-like fount of our race, rose growing without a thorn, you are acknowledged as mother. Hail, queen of virgins, bearing Christ the lord.

translation of the poem 'Stabat iuxta Christi crucem', unfortunately fragmentary, from St Werburgh's Abbey in Chester.[56] The same Latin poem, with the English poem 'Stond wel moder under rode' written below, is given with music in another manuscript, again incomplete. Here, however, the English poem, which survives elsewhere in full, is not a direct translation

Ex. 21

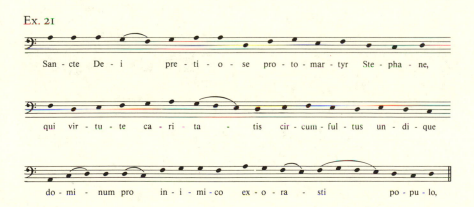

Precious saint of God, Stephen protomartyr, who suffused with charity called upon the lord on behalf of your enemy the people, . . .

[56] Oxford, Bod. Lib., Tanner 169*, p. 175; fac. in *EBM*, i, pl. 5; *Medieval English Songs*, no. 10; the poem printed in *English Lyrics of the XIIIth Century*, 9–10.

Ex. 22

(a)

Gau - de Ga - bri - e - lis o - re virgo De - o gra - vi - da.
Gau - de par - tu gau - dens flo - re vir - gi - na - li can - di - da.

Gau - de gau - dens sur - re - xis - se fi - li - um a fu - ne - re.
Gau - de gau - dens te vi - dis - se ce - los hinc a - scen - de - re.

Gau - de quam as - sum - psit ve - re fi - li - us ad gau - di - a.
Gau - de gau - dens; fac gau - de - re nos te - cum in glo - ri - a.

O dul - cis - si - ma, O be - ni - gnis - si - ma, O vir - go Ma - ri - a.
O pi - is - si - ma,

(b)

Be - a - ta vir - gi - nis fe - cun - dat vi - sce - ra vis
Ca - rens o - ri - gi - nis la - be pu - er - pe - ra De -

san - cti spi - ri - tus, non car - nis o - pe - ra.
i et ho - mi - nis dat no - va fe - de - ra.

Ar - de - re cer - ni - tur ar - den - ti ra - di - o ru -
Sic nec cor - rum - pi - tur con - ce - pto fi - li - o vir -

bus nec u - ri - tur i - gnis in - cen - di - o.
go nec le - di - tur in pu - er - pe - ri - o.

Ex. 22, continued

Mi - ra - tur ra - ci - o   De - um   in   ho - mi - ne   sus -
Nec fi - et que - sti - o   de   tan - to   lu - mi - ne   sit

ce - pto   fi - li - o   de   ma - tre   vir - gi - ne.
fi - des   ra - ci - o   vir - tus   pro   se - mi - ne.

(*a*) Rejoice to God, virgin with child by the word of Gabriel. Rejoice, rejoicing in childbirth, shining with the flower of virginity. Rejoice, rejoicing that your son has risen from the grave. Rejoice whom your son truly assumed to [heavenly] joys. Rejoice, rejoicing; make us to rejoice with you in glory. O most sweet, most devout, most merciful virgin Mary.

(*b*) The power of the holy Spirit, not the works of the flesh, makes fruitful the blessed womb of the virgin; lacking the stain of a [carnal] origin the birth of God and man gives us a new covenant. The berry is seen to burn in a burning circle, but is not consumed in the heat of the flame; so neither is the virgin corrupted by the conception of her son, nor is she wounded in giving birth. Reason is abashed that God should be born as man of a virgin mother; nor should there be any question concerning such a revelation that faith, reason, and virtue should serve for [human] seed.

* = ■first time.
† = ■second time.

Ex. 23

(or: ♩ ♫♩ ♩ ♩ ♩ ♩ ♩ *etc.*)

Je - su   Cri - stes   mil - de   mo - der   stud, bi - held hire sone o
þe sone   heng, þe   mo - der   stud ___   and   bi - held hire chil - des

ro - de   þat   he   was   i - pi - ned   on.
blud ___   wu   it   of   hise   wun - des   ran.

Jesus Christ's mild mother stood, beheld her son on the cross on which he was nailed. The son hung, the mother stood, and beheld her child's blood, where it ran from his wounds.

but a newly composed dialogue between Christ and his Mother at the crucifixion.[57]

Examples such as these seem to show that English versions of such poems could be sung in the liturgy, or at least in popular devotional services such as might be organized either by monks or, perhaps more commonly, by friars. There are also two polyphonic compositions of a similar type, 'Edi beo thu, hevene quene',[58] and 'Jesu Cristes milde moder', a portion of which may be quoted (Ex. 23, p. 67).[59] Two-part writing of this kind, with its emphasis on the interval of a third and much crossing of parts, has been claimed as characteristic of popular English part-singing,[60] which it probably is, although very little of the kind has survived.

The manuscript in which this setting has come down to us contains a particularly rich and varied selection of the more informal type of religious music cultivated in the later thirteenth century. There is the familiar 'Angelus ad virginem', with an English version 'Gabriel from evene king', in a monophonic version;[61] a number of other Latin and French songs, monophonic and polyphonic; and two purely English monophonic songs. 'Worldes blis ne last no throwe', a pious reminder of the transitoriness of earthly joys, has a finely organized melody,[62] while 'The milde lomb', another Sequence-like poem on the Passion, has a more restrained but scarcely less fine setting (Ex. 24).[63]

The Latin and French repertory should not be neglected, though its Englishness may be harder to determine. Even 'Angelus ad virginem' was widely known on the Continent, and the poem itself has been attributed to no less a personage than Philippe, Chancellor of the University of Paris in the early thirteenth century.[64] The same problem confronts us in relation

[57] Complete with music in London, Brit. Lib., Roy. 12 E. 1, fo. 193[r]; incomplete, with Latin and English texts, in Cambridge, St John's Coll., E 8 (olim 111), fo. 106[v]. Facsimile of the latter in C. Page, 'A Catalogue and Bibliography of English Song from its Beginnings to c. 1300', RMARC, 13 (1976), 82; Medieval English Songs, no. 11; the poem in English Lyrics, 89–91, and from the Cambridge MS on pp. 203–4.

[58] Oxford, Corpus Christi College, 59, fo. 113[v]; Oxford Anthology, no. 57; Medieval English Songs, no. 13; English Music, no. 2; English Lyrics, 116–18.

[59] London, Brit. Lib., Arundel 248, fos. 154[v]–155[r]; Medieval English Songs, no. 12; English Music, no. 1; English Lyrics, 83–5. There are facsimiles of all the Arundel pieces in EEH, i, pls. 32–6.

[60] G. Reese, Music in the Middle Ages (New York, 1940), 389. There is no justification, however, for the application of the term gymel to this kind of polyphony.

[61] London, Brit. Lib., Arundel 248, fo. 154[r]; Medieval English Songs, no. 15; English Lyrics, 75–6. There is a two-part version in the British Library, Cotton fragment 29, fo. 36[v]; and two three-part settings in Cambridge, Univ. Lib., Add. 710 (see n. 55). For the monophonic version see below, Ex. 46.

[62] London, Brit. Lib., Arundel 248, fo. 154[r]; also in Oxford, Bod. Lib., Rawl. g. 18, fos. 105[v]–106[r] (EBM, pl. 4); text only ibid., Digby 86, fos. 163[v]–164[r]. Medieval English Songs, no. 7; English Lyrics, 78–82.

[63] London, Brit. Lib., Arundel 248, fo. 154[r]; cf. Medieval English Songs, no. 14; English Lyrics, 77–8.

[64] See C. Page, 'Angelus ad virginem: A new work by Philippe the Chancellor?', Early Music, 11 (1983), 69–70.

Ex. 24

(with freedom, approximately one temporal unit for each syllable)

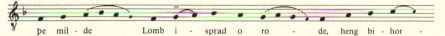

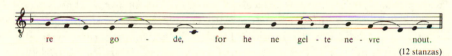

(12 stanzas)

The mild lamb, spread on the cross, hung overrun with blood for our guilt, for our good; for he was never guilty of anything.

Ex. 25

(3 stanzas; the last line is a refrain)

Hail, virgin of virgins, parent of the begetter; hail, light of lights, orb of splendour; hail, flower of the dales, distillation of the righteous dew, Mary, hope of our life.

to the monophonic Sequences and similar pieces from other manuscripts, such as Harley 978 (from Reading, discussed above) and the additions to a Salisbury Gradual now in the Bodleian Library, MS Rawl. lit. d. 3. Where the music is polyphonic, style is a more reliable guide. The sonorities of a piece like 'Salve virgo virginum', from the Arundel manuscript, with its full triads and crossing of the two lower parts (analogous to those of Ex. 23) are good evidence of English origin (Ex. 25, p. 69).[65]

The same music is set to a French poem immediately afterwards in the manuscript. Latin and French are also combined in the monophonic 'Flos pudicicie/ Flur de virginité' (fo. 153[r]), which bears the title 'Cantus de domina post cantum Aaliz'. This is a lively little piece in *lai* form; that is, it is analogous to the Sequence in its repetitive structure and its progression from one melodic unit to another. It is to be confused neither with the popular strophic song 'Bele Alis matyn se leva' nor with the *Lai d'Aélis* from the Noailles chansonnier.[66] There is an apparent reference to it, however, in the anonymous literary *Lai de L'Espine*, where a 'lai … d'Aelis' is said to have been sung by an Irishman to his *rote*. The context suggests that this was a narrative poem, which the original version of 'Flos pudicicie' may very well have been (Ex. 26).[67]

The purely secular lyric is less well represented. 'Bien deust chanter', at the end of the same collection (fo. 155[r]), is a religious contrafactum of a song by Blondel de Nesle, but it serves to remind us that trouvère song was assiduously cultivated at this period. London had its own *pui*, a gild of merchants devoted to charity, and to the cultivation of music and poetry like those at Arras and other French cities. It had a chapel in the Guildhall (from 1299), a chaplain, and a set of statutes (in French) governing amongst other things the contests in music and poetry that were a feature of its gatherings. The music was considered to be as important as the verse, and a contest was held annually to determine the winning 'chanson reale courounée'.[68] Despite the Continental origin of the melody it may not be too far-fetched to think of 'Bien deust chanter' as an entry in such a contest (Ex. 27, p. 72).

A song in both French and English, the so-called Prisoner's Prayer 'Eyns ne soy ke pleinte fu/ Ar ne kuthe ich sorghe non' (i.e. 'Formerly I knew not how to sorrow'), is even more closely connected, since it survives

---

[65] Arundel 248, fo. 155[r]; *English Music*, no. 19a.

[66] *Lais et descorts du treizième siècle*, ed. A. Jeanroy, L. Brandin, and P. Aubry (Paris, 1901), 142–5; 'Flos pudicicie', ibid. 160–2, with its French text only. On the strophic 'Bele Alis' see *Early English Carols*, ed. R. Green (Oxford, 1977), pp. cxlv, cxlvii; J. Stevens, *Words and Music*, 178–9.

[67] Arundel 248, fo. 153[v]; cf. Stevens, *Words and Music*, 80–2 and, for a discussion of the *lai* and its narrative aspects, 140–55. The *Lai de l'Espine* is edited by R. Zenker, 'Der Lai de l'Epine', *Zeitschrift für Romanische Philologie*, 17 (1893), 233–55.

[68] *Munimenta Gildhallae Londiniensis: Liber Custumarum*, ed. H. Riley (London, 1859–62), ii. 216–28. For other French songs in English MSS see Ch. 1, n. 87.

Ex. 26

Flos pu - di - ci - ci - e, au - la mun - di - ci - e, ma - ter mi - se - ri - cor -
di - e: sal - ve vir - go se - re - na, vi - te ve - na, lux a - me - na,
ro - re ple - na, se - pti - for - mis spi - ri - tus vir - tu - ti - bus, or - nan - ti - bus
ac mo - ri - bus ver - nan - ti - bus.

Flower of modesty, temple of purity, mother of mercy; hail, serene virgin, vein of life,
pleasing light, filled with dew, with the virtues of the sevenfold Spirit, and with his adorning,
flowering merit.

in the Guildhall's own *Liber de Antiquis Legibus* (fos. 160ᵛ–161ʳ). But it is
again a religious poem, this time based on an earlier Latin composition,
the widely distributed 'Planctus ante nescia'.[69] 'Man mei longe him lives
wene', with its rather unadventurous tune,[70] is again on the subject of
'dethis wither-clench', so that for an English song on an amorous subject
we must turn to an early fourteenth-century fragment, 'Bryd on bere',
the tune and text of which are terribly mangled.[71] A blank staff in the
manuscript suggests that the composition was originally in two parts; but
a melody is all that survives, and, however imperfectly preserved, it is a
precious remnant of an all too rare genre (Ex. 28, p. 73).

The purely secular motet was evidently cultivated in performance, since
we have at any rate one copy of such a piece, 'Au queer ay un maus',

[69] Both in *Medieval English Songs*, no. 4; *Chanter m'estuet*, ed. S. Rosenberg and H. Tischler (London,
1981), 143–6; *English Lyrics*, 10–13; fac. in Page, *RMARC*, 13 (1976), 83. A song even more clearly
related to the *pui* has been recently been discovered, 'Si tost c'amis entant a ben amer' by Renaus
de Hoiland: London, Public Record Office, E163/22/1/2. Discussed, and the first stanza with its music
printed, by C. Page, 'Secular Music', *Cambridge Guide to the Arts in Britain*, ii (Cambridge, 1988),
237.
[70] Maidstone, Kent County Record Office, A. 13, fo. 93ᵛ; poem alone also in Oxford, Bod. Lib.,
Laud misc. 471, fo. 65ʳ; *Medieval English Songs*, no. 6a; *English Lyrics*, 15–18; fac. in Page, *RMARC*
(1976), 82.
[71] Cambridge, King's Coll., Muniment Roll 2 W, 32ᵛ; fac. in N. Wilkins, *Music in the Age of Chaucer*,
(Cambridge, 1979), 98. There is a full discussion of the problems in *Medieval English Songs*, no. 16a,
but some of the emendations to the words (which may indeed restore the poem to something like
its original form) are contrary to the needs of the melody and are unlikely to reflect what the composer
actually set. Earlier discussions and transcriptions in *NOHM*, iii. 113, and P. Dronke, *The Medieval
Lyric* (2nd edn., London, 1978), 145–6, 245.

Ex. 27

Well should he sing who would have a loyal friend; he would be well protected who knew how to choose her. To love is natural, but the important thing is to love well and to abandon foolish love. For he who pursues his desire foolishly will be deceived by it when he thinks better to enjoy it; since foolish love makes soul and body perish. But whoever relies on sweet Mary with true heart cannot repent of it.

Ex. 28

Bryd o - ne bre - re,   brid, brid o - ne tre - we,* kynd is   co - me of
Lo -ve, lo -ve to   cra —   ve.   Blid – ful   bi – ryd, on   me   þu
re — we, or greid lef greid þu me   my   gra — ve.

Bird on briar, bird on twig, Nature has come from Love to beg for love. Happy bird, have pity on me, or prepare, dear one, my grave for me.

* MS 'brere'.

Ex. 29

based on a popular rondeau, 'Joliettement my teent li maus'.[72] This survives
in the Parisian repertory as 'Au cuer ay un mal',[73] so it is evidently not
an indigenous composition. However, on another leaf in the same manuscript (fo. 5ʳ) is a two-part setting of a highly pessimistic fragment, 'Foweles
in the frith',[74] and on the reverse a lively dance-like instrumental piece,
a practically unique example of the contemporary minstrel's art, possibly
for a stringed instrument but breaking into three-part harmony at the end
(Ex. 29, p. 73).[75]

There are also three two-part instrumental works, possibly to be identified
with the type defined by Johannes de Grocheio as the *ductia*, in the Harley
manuscript.[76] Further evidence of the interactions between the popular
and the learned is to be found in the earliest known motet with an English
text in the upper part, 'Worldes blisce have god day' with the *tenor*
'Domino',[77] and by the use of a secular song, 'Dou way Robin' as the
tenor of a Latin motet, 'Sancta mater gracie' (Ex. 30).[78]

The next stage in the development of English music may be conveniently
illustrated from a collection of leaves now belonging to New College,
Oxford (and housed in the Bodleian Library), MS 362, section XXVI.[79]
There is no clue, however, as to its ultimate origin. The fragments, which
are relatively undamaged, were once part of a large volume consisting of
over 90 leaves—perhaps many more. Although there is one concordance
with the Worcester repertory amongst the twenty or so pieces (complete
or fragmentary) in the manuscript, and one or two others in the old-
fashioned compound duple rhythm (e.g. the *rondellus*-motet 'Excelsus in
numine/Benedictus dominus'),[80] the general impression is of a later stage
than even the final layer of the Worcester music (one or two specimens
of *ars nova* in the latter apart). The date of copying seems to be about

[72] Oxford, Bod. Lib., Douce 139, fo. 179ᵛ; *EBM*, i, pl. 8 (fac.); ii. 16–19 (transcription).

[73] Montpellier Codex, no. 260.

[74] *EBM*, i, pl. 6; *Medieval English Songs*, no. 8; *English Music*, no. 3; *English Lyrics*, 14.

[75] Oxford, Bod. Lib., Douce 139, fo. 5ᵛ (*EBM*, i, pl. 7).

[76] London, Brit. Lib., Harley 978, fos. 8ᵛ–9ʳ (*EEH*, i, pls. 18–19); *English Music*, nos. 16–18. For Johannes de Grocheio, a regent master of Paris University in the late 13th or early 14th cent., see the important discussion in J. Stevens, *Words and Music*, 429–34; the treatise itself ed. E. Rohloff, *Die Quellenhandschriften des Johannes de Grocheio* (Leipzig, 1972).

[77] Cambridge, Corpus Christi College, MS 8, flyleaf; cf. *English Lyrics*, 114; M. Bukofzer, 'The First Motet with English Words', *ML*, 17 (1936), 225–33; *Medieval English Songs*, no. 17; *English Music for Mass and Offices*, ed. Harrison, Sanders, and Lefferts (Monaco, 1983), ii, no. 53.

[78] Princeton, University Library, Garrett 119 (*tenor*); London, Brit. Lib., Cotton frag. 29, fo. 36ʳ (upper part); *Medieval English Songs*, no. 18; *English Music for Mass and Offices*, ii, no. 52, with text incipit read as 'Veni mater gracie'.

[79] Facsimile in *Manuscripts of Fourteenth-Century English Polyphony*, ed. F. Ll. Harrison and R. Wibberley (London, 1981); all the complete motets are in *Motets of English Provenance*, ed. F. Ll. Harrison (Monaco, 1980).

[80] New College 362, fos. 86ᵛ–87ʳ; *The Oxford Anthology*, no. 48; *English Music for Mass and Offices* i, no. 99.

Ex. 30

Upper part. Holy mother of grace, star of brightness, visit us this day, full of piety. Come source of mercy, come soon to us prisoners, solace of those in need, fount of sweetness.
Tenor. Be off with you, Robin, the child will weep; be off with you, Robin.

1320 or a little later, and the provenance is probably monastic although this cannot be proved. There is a complete absence of specifically liturgical items, and the sequence of marginal ascriptions of certain motets to particular feasts—'de sancto Thome Cant', 'de sancto Laurencio', and so on—do not suggest any kind of ordering according to the calendar. Nor can the order have been alphabetical. It is possible, of course, that the survivals are part of an appendix to a predominantly liturgical collection; but their general character suggests that the decline in the composition of strictly liturgical music evident from the Worcester source was by now complete.

Some of the New College motets exhibit a still further degree of experiment with smaller note-values than we have yet encountered. Bearing in mind that the breve of the manuscripts is a crotchet in our transcriptions, and that the semibreve was the smallest value then theoretically recognized, we shall find that (somewhat surprisingly to the modern musician) it was considered possible to set two, three, four, five, and even larger numbers of semibreves against a single breve. It must not be thought, however, that the constituent notes of such groups were necessarily or even usually performed equally. During the later part of the thirteenth century in France there had emerged a tendency to assimilate groups of two semibreves to a prevailing triple subdivision of the beat: in other words to perform them as in iambic (♪♩) or trochaic (♩♪) rhythm. Though the iambic rhythm, favoured by Franco of Cologne, had a wider theoretical acceptance, the interpretation seems to have been largely a matter of taste; and there is a strong case to be made out for preferring a trochaic interpretation in a good deal of early fourteenth-century music. When the permissible number of semibreves to the breve was increased beyond three (an innovation attributed to Petrus de Cruce at the end of the thirteenth century), the problem of their rhythmic organization was intensified. While an equal-note performance of these larger groups of short notes cannot be entirely ruled out—there is some ambiguously worded support for it by Jacobus of Liège—it seems certain that a basic principle of assimilating them to a triple, and later to a duple, subdivision of the beat, with the short notes last, was generally preferred. Not until the body of teaching associated with the name of Philippe de Vitry and known collectively as the *Ars nova* was promulgated around 1320 was the matter finally resolved. According to this doctrine, the minim or *semibrevis minima* (literally the shortest kind of semibreve) was made the yardstick by which the longer note-values were measured. But the full impact of the *ars nova* was somewhat delayed in England, and for the interpretation of English music in the first half of the fourteenth century we have to be satisfied with the vague notions of a transitional period which on the Continent lasted for little more than twenty years (from about 1300 to 1320).

The more advanced type of rhythmical experiment was normally carried out in the context of three-part writing, while works in four parts maintained their dignified motion. The distinction can be seen in a pair of works in the New College manuscript based on the same *cantus firmus*, a song entitled 'Mariounette douche'. In the first of these, 'Caligo terre scinditur/ Virgo mater et filia/ Tenor', the *cantus firmus* is not the *tenor*, which is freely composed, but the second voice, with its added text 'Virgo mater'. In Ex. 31 the smaller note-values have been interpreted in accordance with the principles already enunciated.[81]

In contrast its companion, a motet on the mission to England, moves sedately: this is not, however, a motet with *quartus cantus* but a work in which three upper voices, each with text, move against the *tenor*, 'Mariounette douche' (Ex. 32, p. 78).[82]

The use of a secular song as *tenor* is somewhat unusual, though it is matched in a number of works including the New College motet 'Ade

[81] New College 362, fo. 88ᵛ; *The Oxford Anthology*, no. 49; *Motets of English Provenance*, no. 5.
[82] New College 362, fo. 89ʳ; *Motets of English Provenance*, no. 6.

Ex. 31

Triplum. The earthly mist is pierced, hit by a shaft from the sun, when the sun is born of a star in the dawn of faith.

Duplum. The virgin, mother and daughter of the highest king, is become a remedy for those who mourn.

Note: The *triplum* text is related to Prudentius, *Cathemiron*, ii. 5–8.

Ex. 32

Quadruplum. The sunny warmth of Romulus [i.e. Rome] melts the ice of Britain, and the worldly hearts of the people [are loosed from the filth of madness].

Triplum. Gregory, the sun of the world, sent Jove from the Cancer of Rome to the Libra of England.

Duplum. Peter, your little boat sometimes wanders, but it usually gets back on course after many dangers.

Tenor. Sweet Marionette ...

finit perpete/Ade finit misere/A definement desté lerray'.[83] Here the texts
of the upper parts are a sort of trope of the beginning of the French song,
a reversal of the Continental practice of relating a secular text in an upper
voice to a Latin *tenor*. The justification for this procedure is hard to fathom;
but if as the manuscripts suggest the text of the French song was not sung,
there would have been no impropriety.

The variety of approach to be found in the New College manuscript
is impressive. 'Ianuam quam clauserat' has not only a 'Quartus cantus' to
complement its liturgical *tenor*, 'Iacet granum', but an alternative 'Tenor
per se de Iacet granum', a single part that could act as a substitute for
the original two—the earliest example of this procedure known in England.[84]
This work is constructed as a series of fourteen eight-bar phrases,
the regularity of which is disguised, first by the constant overlapping of
the second voice, which has a similar structure at a distance of four bars,
modified at the beginning and at the end, and secondly by the irregularity
of the overlapping *quartus cantus* and *tenor*. It is in fact somewhat rare for
a liturgical *tenor* to be laid out with complete regularity, even when the
technique approaches that of Continental isorhythm. In the very fine three-
part 'Virgo sancta Katerina/De spineto rosa crescit', based on the relatively
often used *tenor* 'Agmina', the initial strictness is substantially modified during
the course of its five statements, through which an impressive increase
of rhythmic tension is gradually built up (Ex. 33, pp. 80–2).[85]

A number of other sources, all fragmentary, complement the New College manuscript and give depth to our view of English music up to the
middle of the fourteenth century. Two motets in honour of St Edmund,
from leaves which once belonged to the abbey of Bury St Edmunds,[86]
exhibit a contrast similar to that demonstrated in Exx. 31–2. This source
was once dated to around 1375; but it is not entirely uniform in character
and the portion containing these motets can hardly be later than 1350,
the music itself being very probably rather earlier still. Some of this music
is of considerable ingenuity in its construction, 'isoperiodic' techniques being

[83] New College 362, fo. 87ᵛ; *Motets of English Provenance*, no. 4. The poem associated with the
tenor melody has survived in Oxford, Bod. Lib., Douce 308, printed in *Chanter m'estuet*, 168–70. This
motet, with four others based on secular tunes (one has the English incipit 'Wynter') is also in Tours,
Bibl. mun., 925; cf. *English Music for Mass and Offices*, ii, 224–38.

[84] New College 362, fos. 84ᵛ–85ʳ; *Motets of English Provenance*, no. 1. Two of Philippe de Vitry's
motets carry a *solus tenor* (ed. L. Schrade in PMFC, i, nos. 7, 11).

[85] New College 362, fos. 89ᵛ, 82ʳ; *Motets of English Provenance*, no. 7. The example of motet-
composition given by Walter Odington (CSM, xiv. 143), a Continental motet with an added *triplum*
on St Katherine, is based on the *tenor* 'Agmina'.

[86] Oxford, Bod. Lib., E Musaeo 7, pp. x–xi; printed (in reverse order) in Bukofzer, *Studies in Medieval
and Renaissance Music* (New York, 1950; London, 1951), 29–33; *Motets of English Provenance*, nos. 20,
21. The *ars nova* elements in the second piece are probably a later addition.

Ex. 33

Ex. 33, continued

continued

Ex. 33, continued

Triplum. Holy virgin, Katherine, shining jewel of Greece, arisen [from an ancient thorn bush ...], daughter of a king and queen of great excellence ... [she exceeds the role of women] in mastering the literature of the Catholic faith. [She defeats the Persian rhetors, displaying the features] of the art of the French. Conquered in rhetoric, the fifty yield, [who were considered to be] full of the light of wisdom. [They are given to the fire to be burned; it harms them not], but the fire of Urania [yields to them] through the outpouring dew of the grace of the holy spirit.

Motetus. From the thorn grows a rose among the briars of Greece; ... the people breathe the odour of the flower of Alexandria. ... having spurned the damnable [rite of the heathen] she follows her faith. Protected by the shield of purity, ... surpassing the rights of her sex and age, she proclaims the evils of the imperial dignity. Made [strong by faith], the company [of rhetors] perishes, unscorched in the fire. [Finally the empress yields and becomes a martyr ...], and is executed together with Porphyrius. (For full text and translation (not wholly accurate), see PMFC, xv. 178–9.)

   ★ MS 'qui'.
   † MS 'etates'.

to the fore. In the first of the two motets on St Edmund, 'Ave miles celestis curie', not only are the upper parts in *rondellus*, setting a single poem in alternation, but so are the *tenor* and *quartus cantus*, the plainsong 'Ave rex gentis Anglorum' being arbitrarily divided into five sections for the purpose. Much the same techniques are employed in 'Triumphat hodie', a fragmentary motet on St Lawrence from the New College manuscript which can be completed from leaves extant in the British Library,[87] and in a motet on St Nicholas, 'Salve cleri speculum', from the 'Hatton' manuscript, where the *tenor* is based partly on the prose 'Sospitati dedit egros'. Since this prose, a substitute for the melisma on the word 'sospes' in the St Nicholas respond 'Ex eius tumba', is set to a series of repeated musical phrases in the manner of a Sequence, it lends itself well to this technique.[88] Where so much is schematic in construction, a great deal of the interest lies in the concealment of the musical joinery, which is achieved with great skill in 'Ave miles'. The overlapping of phrases is another characteristic technique. In 'Petrum cephas ecclesie', also from the Bury St Edmunds manuscript, each of the parts consists of a series of nine-bar phrases; but the *triplum* with the *quartus cantus*, the *motetus* and the *tenor* each begin their phrases at a different point, as the opening of Ex. 34 shows (overleaf).[89]

The example also illustrates the use of parallel 6–3 chords while the *tenor* is silent, a rather less sophisticated technique than the involvement of the *tenor* itself in the process (as seen in some passages of Ex. 33). This, like the occasional appearance of the *tenor* in the middle of a three-part texture, exemplifies the impact, even at this early stage, of typically English types of descant on more sophisticated polyphonic idioms.[90]

From about the middle of the century there are signs of renewed intellectual vigour in the composition of motets. One of the most adventurous of the New College works, 'Rosa delectabilis', was apparently added to the manuscript at about this time, while one of the motets in the Sloane manuscript (see below) makes particularly striking use of short note-values, a fact that is emphasized if the transcription is on the same scale as the preceding examples (Ex. 35, p. 85).[91]

[87] New College 362, fo. 85ᵛ, and London, Brit. Lib., Add. 24198, fo. 1ᵛ; *Motets of English Provenance*, no. 17. The somewhat indecorous song on which it is based (apparently for no better reason than that its opening 'Trop est fol' corresponds phonetically to 'Triumphat') is shared in *rondellus* fashion between the two lower parts, and makes an attractive addition to the French secular repertory: the text is, unusually, given in full.

[88] Oxford, Bod. Lib., Hatton 81, fos. 45ᵛ and 2ʳ; *Motets of English Provenance*, no. 11. For the plainsong, see *Antiphonale Sarisburiense*, pl. 360. After a free opening, the upper parts carry a textual commentary on the implied text of the lower parts: the work is probably intended as a substitute for the original prose in its liturgical context, i.e. at the repeat of its 'parent' respond.

[89] Oxford, Bod. Lib., E Musaeo 7, pp. vi–vii; *Motets of English Provenance*, no. 18. The fragmentary 'Lux refulget monachorum', on p. viii, shows progressive foreshortening of the *talea* in both *triplum* and *tenor* (*Manuscripts of Fourteenth-Century English Polyphony*, pl. 49).

[90] An example from the New College MS is 'Civitas nusquam conditur' on St Edward the Confessor: the unidentified *tenor* begins 'Cibus esurientem', *Motets of English Provenance*, no. 3. There are Continental examples, such as 'Tribum que non abhorruit' from the *Roman de Fauvel*, attributed by some scholars to Philippe de Vitry (PMFC, i, no. 27).

[91] New College 362, fos. 90ᵛ–91ʳ; London, Brit. Lib., Sloane 1210, fos. 1*ᵛ–1ʳ. *Motets of English Provenance*, nos. 10, 12. In Ex. 35 (*b*) some rhythmic details are uncertain; the text of the second voice is illegible and the *tenor* (lowest voice) is unidentified.

Ex. 34

[Tenor from here has pattern of four bars of rests to five bars of notes]

Triplum. The king of mercy chose Peter, rock of the church, as he was letting down his nets, whereupon he relinquished everything.

Duplum. Peter, most powerful shepherd, was radiant with miracles.

Ex. 35

[R]o - sa de - le - cta - bi - lis spi - na
Tenor [Regali ex progenie]
[R]e - ga - lis ex - o - ri - tur ma - ter de -

ca-rens ex - o - ri - tur;

co - ris a - ni - ma;

[T]ri - um-phus pa - tet ho-di-e le - ti - ci - e ve - xil -

lo vi-cto-ri-o-si prin-ci - pis. Te - la ne-qui-ci-e sunt di - ru-pta,di - ri . . .

(a) *Triplum*. The lovely rose without a thorn arises; *Duplum*. The royal mother arises, the soul of beauty.
(b) Triumph appears today by the joyful banner of the glorious prince. The spears of evil are broken . . . [on the holy Cross].

Works from still later in the century reflect the full impact of the French *ars nova* and call for a reduction to only one-fourth of the original values in transcription. English manuscripts now show the minim (quaver) as a matter of course, mostly in the context of 'major prolation' (6/8 or 9/8 in transcription). The *tenor* may now be laid out in a more generous and regular fashion, lending the whole work a more solid structural support than had been provided by the more haphazardly controlled and faster-moving schemes of the previous epoch. Ex. 36 shows the structural scheme and the opening of 'Omnis terra', on an unidentified *tenor*, from what appears to be a later section of the Bury St Edmunds manuscript (see pp. 88–9).[92]

Here the melodic repetition is twice as fast as the first statement, a common procedure in the works of both Vitry and Machaut. Indeed, a rather similar collection of pieces from Durham actually includes two motets by Vitry,[93] and it cannot therefore be taken as axiomatic that a work in this style in an English manuscript is by an English composer at all. This is no less so if a part other than the *tenor* carries an Anglo-Norman text, as is the case in another of the Bury motets, 'Pura, placens, pulcra', with the *duplum* 'Parfundement plure Absalon' and an unidentified *tenor*.[94] Further evidence of the circulation of French motets in England is provided by the Robertsbridge keyboard manuscript, now thought to belong to the second half of the century, which contains ornamented transcriptions of two motets from the *Roman de Fauvel*.[95]

Another of the Durham motets, 'Musicorum collegio', though exactly comparable in style and structure, is probably by an Englishman; though it is in praise of French court musicians (including one 'J. Anglicus'), the expression 'in curia Gallicorum' suggests the authorship of a non-Frenchman. In any case, it provides further testimony to the interaction between the two countries in musical matters at this time.[96] The same is true of the motet 'Sub Arturo plebs vallata', with *duplum* 'Fons citharizancium' and *tenor* 'In omnem terram', one of three motets in praise of musicians in a late fourteenth-century French manuscript now kept at the Musée

[92] Oxford, Bod. Lib., E Musaeo 7, pp. 530–1; *Motets of English Provenance*, no. 22.

[93] Durham, Cathedral Lib., C I. 20, fos. 336*ᵛ–337ʳ ('Vos quid admiramini') and 337ᵛ ('O canenda', incomplete). These are nos. 7 and 14 respectively of the works of Philippe de Vitry published in *The Roman de Fauvel* (PMFC, i); also in the works of Vitry repr. separately with an introduction by E. H. Roesner, Monaco, 1984.

[94] Oxford, Bod. Lib., E Musaeo 7, pp. 534–5; *Motets of English Provenance*, no. 24.

[95] London, Brit. Lib., Add. 28550, fos. 43ʳ–44ᵛ, containing three *estampies* (the first incomplete), the *Fauvel* motets 'Firmissime fidem teneamus' (no. 30) and 'Tribum que non abhorruit' (no. 27), and the otherwise unknown *cantilena* 'Flos vernalis stirps regalis'. All are printed in CEKM, i, ed. W. Apel; the *estampies* and 'Flos vernalis' also in *English Music for Mass and Offices*, ii, nos. 58–61.

[96] *Motets of English Provenance*, no. 35. In a reprint of the 'musicians' motets from this volume and the companion *Motets of French Provenance* (PMFC, v), Harrison has suggested that the Durham and Robertsbridge MSS may have emanated from the London court of the captive French King, John II. *Musicorum Collegio*, Monaco, 1986.

Condé, Chantilly.[97] The 'people protected by Arthur' are of course the English; welcome things will be bestowed upon them; their militia and clergy flourish; their choir sings joyful songs. Some of the singers named can be identified with members of the chapels of Edward III and the Black Prince, and perhaps of St George's, Windsor. In the *duplum*, which is a brief summary of the main landmarks in the development of musical theory (from Tubal to Franco), the composer identifies himself as 'J. Alani'. It was at one time believed that the motet was composed for the celebration held at Windsor Castle on St George's Day, 1358, to mark the victory of Poitiers two years earlier,[98] but this date is now generally considered to be rather too early. The composer himself has been identified with 'Aleyn', composer of a Gloria in the Old Hall manuscript, and he in turn with a John Aleyn, a canon of Windsor (and elsewhere) and clerk of the Royal Household who died in 1373.[99] There is a good deal of circumstantial probability in all this, though the motet is a work of considerable sophistication, while the Old Hall Gloria is in simple descant style. But there is nothing inherently impossible in these equations, and it may be that the art of motet-writing was further advanced in the fourteenth century than the generality of the sources (which are highly fragmented) might suggest.

There are five motets at the end of the Old Hall manuscript (two incomplete); one is by Byttering, another by the French composer Mayshuet,[100] and three are anonymous. Their function here is evidently as substitutes for the deacon's 'Ite missa est' or its response 'Deo gratias' at the end of Mass, a function made explicit in the texts of 'Are post libamina' and 'Post missarum sollemnia'. In the same way a substantial fragment from Fountains Abbey in Yorkshire[101] contains two motets of which one certainly and the other probably (a fragment based on an unidentified non-plainchant *tenor*) are also 'Deo gratias' substitutes. The former, 'Humane lingue organis' with *duplum* 'Supplicum voces percipe', *contratenor*, and a *tenor* based on a 'Deo gratias' chant, well illustrates the concern for sonority that emerges

[97] MS 564 (*olim* 1047), fos. 70ᵛ–71ʳ; Bologna, Civico Museo Bibliografico Musicale, Q 15, fos. 225ᵛ–226ʳ, 342ᵛ; *Motets of French Provenance*, no. 31. The work also occurs in a privately owned English MS at present in the care of Keble College, Oxford. The *tenor* is cited in the anonymous *Notitia del valore delle note del canto misurato* (*c*.1390), ed. A. Carapetyan (AIM, 1957 = CSM, v), 57.

[98] B. Trowell, 'A Fourteenth-century Ceremonial Motet and its Composer', *AcM*, 29 (1957), 65–75. More recently, the evidence has been reviewed by R. Bowers, 'Fixed Points in the Chronology of English Fourteenth-Century Polyphony', *ML*, 71 (1990), 313–35. He reads the first two words as 'Sub arcturo'—'under the north star'—and suggests a date in the early 1370s.

[99] A. Hughes and M. Bent, 'The Old Hall Manuscript', *MD*, 21 (1967), 109. For the 'Old Hall' MS, see the following chapter.

[100] i.e. Matheus de Sancto Johanne: Hughes and Bent, ibid. 113.

[101] London, Brit. Lib., Add. 40011B: cf. Bukofzer, *Studies*, 86–112.

Ex. 36

Ex. 36, continued

[etc., in strict rhythmic diminution to end. Total length in breves: (4×24)+12+(4×12)+6=162]

Triplum. All the earth strives to worship the true God, ruler of all, of whose bounty it is so remarkably filled; *Duplum.* To them that have shall be given, ...

fully in much of the Old Hall music and was a major factor in what came to be known as the 'contenance Angloise' (Ex. 37, overleaf).[102]

A considerable quantity of music for the Ordinary of the Mass, and for other liturgical purposes, survives from the middle and later fourteenth

[102] The chant is that known as Sanctus VIII of the Vatican edition and was used by Machaut for the Ite of his Mass: it is also found as the 16th in a series of 'Benedicamus Domino' melodies in a 13th-century Exeter Gradual, Manchester, John Rylands Library, lat. 24, fo. 14ʳ (the ultimate source of the melody is a St Nicholas antiphon, 'O Christi pietas', seen in *AS*, pl. 361.) The motet is in *Motets of English Provenance*, no. 36.

Ex. 37

Triplum. Let us with the organ of the human tongue pour out our prayers to the virgin,
to whom the holy parent gave Jesus in a wonderful manner for us wretched ones.
Duplum. Hear the voices of your suppliants, O God, from the seat of the glory that you
have attained. Because you have us always in mind ...

century.[103] This repertory marks the first stage of a typically English concern
for liturgical appropriateness that culminated in the period immediately
before the Reformation. Such a concern could at times be inhibiting, and
it is only when the conventions are transcended that the music becomes
genuinely interesting. But the establishment of the conventions is itself

[103] *English Music for Mass and Offices,* 2 vols. Some of the later 'Worcester' music really belongs
to this period.

of some importance, and they need to be kept in mind if the later medieval English approach to composition is to be properly understood.

The standard number of voice-parts in this kind of music was three, though two-part and four-part settings are also found. It was sung by adult male soloists of whom the highest must often have been a falsettist. Each part tended to move in a broadly similar rhythm (this feature is conveniently known as 'homorhythm') in a succession of consonant chords, though the upper part in particular might carry ornamental figuration. There was a tendency towards a clear separation of the vocal ranges: the theoretical and other sources reveal that the usual terminology was, in the vernacular, 'treble' (or sometimes 'hautain'), 'mean', and 'bourdon' or 'tenor' (and in Latin, *triplex*, *medius*, and *tenor*).[104]

There were two fundamentally different methods of composition: either the music was based on the equivalent plainchant, normally in the middle voice but occasionally in the lowest, rarely in the highest; or else it was freely composed. The latter method was of course inevitable if the text came not from the standard liturgy but was newly composed for 'votive' purposes, that is as an act of devotion that might occur within the context of the liturgical routine without being strictly part of it. 'Liturgical' texts could also be freely composed; if, however, they were based on a chant this could be set in notes of uniform length ('isometric') or in variable durations. The older method, still used in motets, of chopping up the chant into phrases of equal rhythmic structure ('isorhythm') was not normally used in functional liturgical music.[105] The movement of the parts was often parallel, using such chords as 8–5, 10–5, and 6–3 (contemporary English theory admitted the third as a concord and had not yet proscribed the use of parallel consecutive fifths and octaves).[106] When the plainchant was isometric and the intended contrapuntal movement parallel, the music could

---

[104] See B. Trowell, 'Faburden—New Sources, New Evidence', in *Modern Musical Scholarship*, ed. E. Olleson (Boston, Henley, and London, 1978), 28–78.

[105] It was, however, revived in the 'Old Hall' repertory (see Ch. 3), and in a modified form provided the basis of later *tenor*-Mass techniques.

[106] Cf. *Quatuor principalia musice* (1351), IV, ii. 13: 'Consonantie quippe concordantes sunt semiditonus, ditonus, diapenthe, tonus cum diapenthe ac diapason, quibus additur unisonus' ('the concordant consonances are the minor third, major third, fifth, major sixth, and octave, and also the unison': the terminology adopted in this treatise distinguishes between 'concordant consonances' (perfect or imperfect), 'discordant consonances' or 'imperfect discords' (tone, fourth, and semitone), and 'perfect discords' (tritone, minor seventh, and major seventh)). Ibid. IV, ii. 20: 'quia numquam due concordantie perfecte consequenter fieri debent nec ascendendo nec descendendo, nisi pausa intervenerit, aut quando tres cantus simul modulantur. Et [si] non potest fieri aliter bono modo ... tunc unus illorum cantus fiet in concordantiis imperfectis ...' ('two perfect concords should never occur consecutively ascending or descending unless a rest intervenes *or when three voices sing together*. And if it cannot be convincingly done otherwise ... one of the parts should be made in imperfect concords ...'). *CS*, iv. 278, 281.

readily be improvised and doubtless often was;[107] but our written documents naturally show a wider variety of techniques.

There is a growing body of evidence to suggest that such music might equally well be sung in both monastic and secular establishments,[108] though in due course the former fell behind as major centres of composition and performance. It was not always welcomed. According to one Wycliffite writer:

Þan were matynys & masse & euen song . . . ordeyned of synful men, to be songen wiþ *heize criynge . . . deschaunt, countre note & orgon & small brekynge*, þat stiriþ veyn men to daunsinge more þan to mornynge.[109]

Dozens of similarly disparaging comments could be adduced, not only from Lollards but from the most orthodox churchmen. Doubtless the motet was included in their vituperations, but it is the new liturgical music and the paraliturgical *cantilena*[110] that seem to have roused them to opposition. Secular clerks are most frequently named as the culprits, but neither monks nor friars escaped the general condemnation.

The term nowadays most commonly applied to this kind of music is 'English descant'. It is a convenient enough appellation, provided that inappropriate deductions are not drawn from more restricted usages by contemporary writers (who often use *discantus* to refer to improvised counterpoint in two parts), and provided also that too much is not made of its supposed exclusively 'English' character, for it is not without parallels on the Continent. Two further technicalities require comment here. The long-established custom of improvising in parallel concords received a theoretically precise description only in the early fifteenth century, when the movement of successive identical chords was restricted to the 6–3 (interspersed with isolated 8–5s) in order to prevent the occurrence of parallel perfect concords. To this technique, in which the *cantus firmus* was in the

---

[107] *Quatuor principalia musice*, IV, ii. xli: 'Sint quatuor vel quinque homines cantandi habiles, primus incipiet planum cantum in tenore; secundus ponet vocem suam in quinta voce; tertius vero in octava voce; et quartus, si fuerit, ponet vocem suam in duodecima voce. His omnes in concordantiis inceptis, continuabunt cantum planum usque in finem, qui vero in duodecima et in octava, et etiam in quinta continue cantant, frangere debent et florere notas, prout magis decet, mensura servata. Is vero qui discantabit, vocem suam minime ponet in concordantia perfecta, sed tantummodo in concordantiis imperfectis, videlicet in tertia, in sexta, et in decima.' ('Should there be four or five men skilled in singing, the first will begin the plainchant in the *tenor*, the second will place his voice a fifth higher, the third an octave higher, and the fourth (if there is one) at the twelfth above. When everyone has begun at these intervals, they will continue the plainchant to the end; those who sing at the twelfth, the octave, and even the fifth sing continuously, breaking and embellishing their notes as seems best while keeping the measure. But he who sings the highest part should avoid perfect concords on the whole, confining himself to imperfect concords, namely the third, the sixth, and the tenth.') *CS*, iv. 294; cf. Anon. I, ibid. iii. 361. Ex. 41 below offers a written approximation to the technique here described.

[108] See n. 6 above.

[109] Wyclif, *Of Feigned Contemplative Life*, cited Trowell, 'Faburden—New Sources', 40.

[110] For this genre, see below, pp. 95–7.

Ex. 38

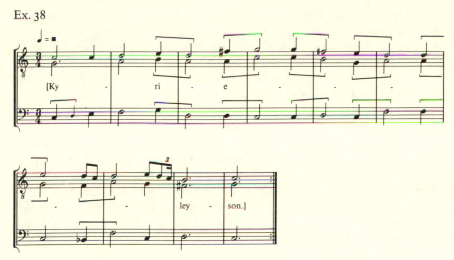

Lord have mercy.

middle voice, the name 'faburden' was given.[111] Secondly, the practice arose of detaching the lowest part of composed or improvised polyphony and treating it as a *cantus firmus* or monophonic piece in its own right; such detached parts came to be known as faburdens (if taken from improvised or improvisable music in the manner of faburden) or as 'squares', a term for which no ready explanation can be found.[112] More will be said on the subject of faburdens and squares in later chapters, but it is important to recognize that their roots lie in the repertory now under discussion.

Only brief samples of this music can be illustrated here. A fragment kept in Durham Cathedral yields, on a single page, practically the whole of a brief three-movement Mass of which the Kyrie may be cited as a typical piece of English descant upon a plainchant, and for comparison with Ex. 8 above on the same plainchant. The absence of a trope will be noted: the reaction against tropes was by now in full swing, and only a few standard ones were retained, poetic energy being diverted to the Sequence and other types of verse not directly linked to the official liturgy (Ex. 38).[113]

[111] The evidence was first correctly interpreted by B. Trowell, 'Faburden and Fauxbourdon', *MD*, 13 (1959), 43 seqq.
[112] See H. Baillie, 'Squares', *AcM*, 32 (1960), 178–93, and J. Bergsagel, 'An Introduction to Ludford', *MD*, 14 (1960), 105–30.
[113] Durham, Cathedral Lib., A III. 11, fo. 1ʳ; *English Music for the Mass and Offices*, i, no. 1. The Durham provenance of this MS is confirmed by the inclusion of the 'Kyrie Cuthberte prece' discussed below.

On the reverse of the same leaf is a complete contrast: an eightfold 'Kyrie Cuthberte prece' in four repeated sections, based on no chant and showing an extraordinary degree of semitonal inflection, rhythmic complexity, and variety of tessitura (Ex. 39).[114]

These are extremes: most of this music proceeds quite straightforwardly in the manner of the Agnus Dei shown as Ex. 40, with a plainchant intonation and isometric mean against moderately independent outer parts in which the normal major prolation of the early *ars nova* is in evidence.[115]

Amongst a number of untroped settings of the Proper of the Mass we find one curious survival: an Alleluya 'Nativitas' for four voices with plainchant in the lowest, for all the world like a survival from the Notre-Dame epoch. It is cited here for comparison with Ex. 10 (Ex. 41, p. 96).[116]

The plainchant in an otherwise normal piece of descant might 'migrate' to another voice for reasons of range, as in Ex. 42, the fragmentary conclusion

Ex. 39

Lord, Cuthbert, by this prayer have mercy on your people, blind with the filth of sin; have mercy on those whom you raised by your holy death from wickedness to glory.

[114] Ibid., no. 8.
[115] London, Public Record Office, E/149/7/23, dorse; *English Music for Mass and Offices*, i, no. 61.
[116] Cambridge, Corpus Christi Coll., 65, fo. 135ʳ; *English Music for Mass and Offices*, i, no. 76.

Ex. 40

Lamb of God, who takes away the sins of the world, ...

of a Te Deum (see pp. 98–9).[117] Other types of liturgical material from the Office may be illustrated from the hymn (Ex. 43, p. 100);[118] and from the Magnificat (Ex. 44, p. 101).[119]

The lowest voice of this example later achieved currency as a detached 'faburden' as previously explained, though in view of its origin in written polyphony the term 'square' might be more appropriate. The plainchant in both these last two examples is in the middle voice, though in Ex. 43 it is transposed and, because of the strictly parallel writing, is scarcely distinguishable from the top part. In such a piece it is the variable rhythm rather than the conduct of the parts that necessitated its being written down; in Ex. 44 the opposite is the case.

In addition to the purely liturgical types of polyphonic music there are others that have been described above as 'paraliturgical'—that is, as adjuncts to the liturgy rather than inherent within it. The motet is the main such form, and there are in addition some curious hybrids that seem to fall between the *conductus* and the motet.[120] But there are others more closely related to the older *conductus* and *versus* in that all parts move in a similar

[117] Cambridge, Gonville and Caius Coll., 727/334, fo. ii[r]; Trowell, 'Faburden—New Sources', 41–2; *English Music for Mass and Offices*, i, no. 93 (in a metrically freer interpretation).

[118] London, Brit. Lib., Sloane 1210, fo. 140[r]; Harrison, *Music in Medieval Britain*, 150–1; Trowell, 'Faburden—New Sources', 42–3; *English Music for Mass and Offices*, i, no. 89.

[119] Cambridge, University Lib., Kk i. 6, fo. 247[r]; quoted Harrison, *Music in Medieval Britain*, 345–6; *English Music for Mass and Offices*, i, no. 90.

[120] Ibid., nos. 94–6, from Oxford, Bod. Lib., Hatton 81; cf. no. 97, and 'Rota versatilis' discussed above, Ex. 16.

Ex. 41

rhythm and carry the same text, which is usually versified in the manner of the Sequence. The term *cantilena*, meaning literally a popular or simple song, has been applied by modern writers to pieces of this kind, and indeed it is generally suitable for a wide range of material from the *conductus* and *versus* in the twelfth and thirteenth centuries to the carol and similar pieces in the fifteenth.[121] A similar style was used for the setting of antiphons of the detached or non-psalmic type, and in the course of time that word was used to denote any text sung, like the four antiphons of the Blessed Virgin Mary, after an Office or at some other stated time in honour of the Virgin herself or of some other (usually a patron) saint. In modern times the term 'votive' has been used to describe such 'antiphons' in order to distinguish them from those sung before and after a psalm or canticle or in procession, and by analogy with votive Masses (and according to

---

[121] Cf. E. Sanders, 'Cantilena and Discant in 14th-century England', *MD*, 19 (1965), 7–52. More recently, the generic term *cantio* has been proposed for strophic religious songs that are not technically *conducti* (i.e. processional) and fall into no well-defined category: J. Stevens, *Words and Music*, 50–51.

some writers 'votive Offices') which lie outside the calendar.[122] In writings on the period now under discussion, the expression 'votive antiphon' has sometimes been applied to works that have more in common with the *conductus* and *versus* than with the true antiphon, even in its enlarged, later medieval, sense. On the whole the term *cantilena*, though in some ways inconveniently large in scope, is the most suitable one for paraliturgical works other than motets.

A typical *cantilena* of the later fourteenth century might embody the parallel movement of much simple descant based on plainchant; but being freely composed it had to be written down no matter how straightforward the movement of its parts. Ex. 45, from a second fragment associated with Fountains Abbey, exhibits a variety of parallel movement in the context of a lively *ars nova* rhythmic idiom (see p. 102).[123]

Many of the surviving fragments of fourteenth-century music yield no clues whatsoever as to their ultimate provenance. Of those that do, including many of those used in this chapter, the majority are from monastic houses— mostly Benedictine (including the cathedral priories) but including the occasional Cistercian or Augustinian foundation.[124] But there are probable survivals from Lincoln Cathedral and from the collegiate foundation of Arundel,[125] while some of the music in one especially interesting fragment appears to hail from the Royal Chapel of Edward III, or possibly from one of his two foundations of Westminster (St Stephen's) or Windsor (St George's).[126] One of the motets in this source, 'Singularis laudis digna', contains a prayer that the war between England and France might cease (Edward having temporarily gained the upper hand), and that the lily 'might agree with the leopard, by which honour would come to King Edward mighty in battle'. The imagery of the poem has been related to the diplomatic good fortune of the English in 1369, a date consistent with the musical setting, which is in the *ars nova* style.[127] But the inference that the other text in this manuscript that refers to an Edward, the hagiographical 'Regem regum collaudemus', must also refer to Edward III and therefore post-date

[122] Cf. *Missale Sarum*, col. 735*: 'Sequuntur Missae votivae communes'. The term 'votive Office' is not medieval. So-called 'votive antiphons' were normally intended for the unofficial ritual that took place after Compline; their introduction as a devotional addition to the canonical Hours may be of monastic origin: see S. E. Roper, 'Medieval English Benedictine Liturgy: Studies in the Formation, Structure –, and Content of the Monastic Votive Office *c*.950–1540' (D.Phil. thesis, Oxford, 1989).

[123] London, Brit. Lib., Add. 63121 (formerly Leeds, Central Lib., Archives Dept. VR 6120), fo. IV'; Trowell, 'Faburden—New Sources', 37–8.

[124] See the lists in EECM, xxvi, p. xvi.

[125] Oxford, Bod. Lib., Barlow 55; London, Brit. Lib., Arundel 14 (cf. EECM, xxvi, loc. cit.).

[126] New York, Pierpont Morgan Lib., 978. Cf. F. Ll. Harrison, 'Polyphonic Music for a Chapel of Edward III', ML, 59 (1978), 420–8; E. Sanders, 'English Polyphony in the Morgan Library Manuscript', 61 (1980), 172–6.

[127] Bowers, 'Fixed Points', 315–17.

Ex. 42

Ex. 42, continued

(b)

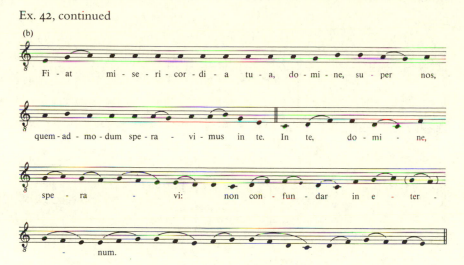

Fi - at   mi - se - ri - cor - di - a   tu - a,   do - mi - ne,   su - per   nos,

quem - ad - mo - dum spe - ra - vi - mus   in   te.   In   te,   do - mi - ne,

spe - ra - vi: non con - fun - dar   in   e - ter -

- num.

O Lord, let your mercy be upon us, just as we have trusted in you. In you, O Lord, have I trusted: let me not be put to confusion for ever.

his death in 1377, is unwarranted. It is almost certainly in honour of Edward the Confessor, and although it is rhythmically advanced there seems to be no obstacle to the view that the fragment reflects the repertoire of a royal establishment in the early 1370s. It would not be surprising that, alongside material known also from the 'Worcester' manuscripts, there should be some very up-to-date pieces in such a collection.

Casual concordances of this kind reveal that a clear distinction between 'monastic' and 'secular' idioms did not exist. There was a good deal of transference of material from place to place up and down the kingdom, and one cannot fail to be struck by the prevailing uniformity of style and convention. But the manuscript just discussed does illustrate the growing importance of polyphonic music in the chapel establishments of royalty and the greater nobility. While the evidence at this period is somewhat patchy,[128] it can hardly be imagined that the Lancastrian revolution of 1399 heralded a sudden change in the pattern of musical cultivation. The strong emphasis in the fifteenth century on the private and collegiate foundations in the surviving sources of polyphonic music must have been preceded by a growing awareness amongst the lay magnates of the value of an advanced musical establishment in promoting a favourable image of themselves to the world.

[128] See, however, the important thesis of A. B. Wathey, *Music in the Royal and Noble Households* (New York, 1989), based on his dissertation, Oxford, 1987, completed too late for detailed use in writing the present chapter. I am grateful to Dr Wathey, however, for much helpful discussion.

Ex. 43

O trinity, blessed light, and princely [unity].

The attention devoted to a private chapel and its music was paralleled in the minstrelsy of a great household. Some idea of the scope of this minstrelsy may be gained from the published lists of musicians employed by the royal households from the later years of Edward I onwards.[129] Dry reading they may make, but they do help one to understand the categories involved. Some musicians were in regular employment; others, freelance entertainers or members of another household, were paid on an *ad hoc* basis; still others, while not on the official rolls ('qui non sunt in rotulo marescalli'), nevertheless received regular payments.

Minstrelsy embraced a variety of activities, not all of them musical. But its most characteristic manifestation took the form of instrumental music in great profusion: the profusion often described in the fourteenth century

[129] See R. Rastall, 'The Minstrels of the English Royal Households', *RMARC*, 4 (1964), 1–41.

Ex. 44

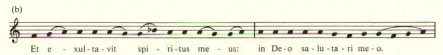

And my spirit has rejoiced in God my saviour.

by some such phrase as 'al maner menstracy'.[130] Not that large numbers necessarily played together: the households employed musicians to fulfil various separate functions in the life of the court. Thus ceremonial occasions called for trumpeters, taborers, and nakerers. The *vigiles* or *vigilatores* were watchmen or 'wayts': the musical instrument played by some of them, probably a kind of shawm, took its name from them. Loud minstrelsy— trumpets, horns, wayts, tabors and the like—was also needed for hunting expeditions. Harpers were needed for the entertainment of the hall; many of them must also have sung, though singers as such are not listed. Their repertory consisted largely of narrative poetry, as did that of the non-musical rymour and gestour (teller of tales, deeds, or *gestes* (Latin *gesta*)). Other musical instruments would be used to accompany dancing or song: fiddles, jigs (played by *gigatores*, their instrument lending its name to the dance),

---

[130] *Sir Orfeo*, l. 565. This early 14th-cent. romance (ed. A. J. Bliss, Oxford, 1954), conveys the flavour of courtly music-making better than any documentation could ever do.

Ex. 45

Hail, rose of the world, the gloss on the Law, mystical chamber.

bagpipes, lutes, organs, crowds, flutes, psalteries, citoles, horns, hornpipes, gitterns, and much else besides.[131]

The evidence of the narrative poetry itself—lays and romances in both English and French—gives a good idea of the circumstances in which the music of a noble household would be heard.[132] The most common context is the feast in which the entire household, including the servants, were gathered together in the great hall of the castle or manor-house. Such feasting was particularly important during the Christmas season, and of course for special occasions such as marriage, or the crown-wearing of the monarch. The reception of a monarch in a nobleman's home, or his return home,

[131] Rastall, 'Minstrels', material relating to the reigns of Edward I–III. For some comments on nomenclature, see C. Page, *Voices and Instruments of the Middle Ages: Instrumental practice and songs in France 1100–1300* (London, 1987), 139–50. For a more general discussion of stringed instruments see M. Remnant, *English Bowed Instruments from Anglo-Saxon to Tudor Times* (Oxford, 1986). For the 'jig' or *giga*, normally considered to be a kind of rebec, cf. German *Geige* etc.: the *gigatores* of Edward I were in fact German. The 'crowd' corresponds to the later Welsh crwth or crwdd, a form of bowed lyre.

[132] Page, *Voices and Instruments*, esp. pp. 151–209.

called for festivities on a lavish scale. It is easy enough to imagine the ceremonial use of music on such occasions. But there was also room for reflection and for pure entertainment, often in the form of narrative or of embryonic drama.[133] English fourteenth-century poems such as *Sir Gawayne* and *Sir Orfeo* are rich in reference to the musical apanage of high society, and the imagery they use, while possibly exaggerated from the point of view of literal description, is an important contribution to the fabric of their writing.

It is harder to assess the place of music in the wider social context, in spite of an abundance of documentation. The 'wandering minstrel' so dear to the romantic imagination must normally have found employment in great houses: indeed he would not otherwise deserve the name. In what other contexts professional musicians might exercise their craft is unclear.[134] There remains the cultivation of music outside the ranks of the specially trained. References to secular song and dance sometimes imply, but rarely state with absolute clarity, the social milieu to which they refer. Between the educated clergy and laity and the rural villeinage lay the great mass of society, Langland's 'faire feeld ful of folke'.[135] There is also the distinction to be drawn between music originating in non-professional circles and that which, while of professional origin, came to be used and imitated more widely.[136]

In spite of such reservations, there is a good deal of evidence for the widespread cultivation and appreciation of music of various kinds during this period. Something has already been said of the actual musical survivals from the later thirteenth and early fourteenth centuries, and for the remainder of the period there is little to add to that.[137] There are numerous references to the singing and dancing of the *carole*, a dance-song with a recurrent choral refrain, usually in terms of strong disapproval. Robert Manning's tale of the cursed dancers,[138] who danced all night in a churchyard and were condemned to doing so for a whole year, illustrates the monotonous, hallucinatory character of such dancing and the dread which it inspired amongst churchmen and moralists. But profane music could be tamed by the Church by substituting pious words for the originals, and there is some

[133] Cf. the English interludes (of which the *Interludium de Clerico et Puella* is the earliest), and the old French secular dramas.

[134] Except of course for the professional use of music in church by trained monks and clergy (including clerks in minor orders).

[135] *The Vision of Piers Plowman* (B-text), ed. A. V. C. Schmidt (London, 1978), *Prologus*, ll. 17 seqq.

[136] Cf. R. L. Greene's broader distinction between poetry 'popular by origin' and that which is 'popular by destination'. *Early English Carols*, pp. cxviii seqq. A fuller discussion of the issue will appear in Vol. II, Ch. 8.

[137] See above, pp. 70–4.

[138] *Handlynge Synne* (begun in 1303), ed. F. J. Furnivall, EETS, Or. Ser., nos. 119, 123 (1901–3), ll. 9015–9232. The earliest version of the story is in the *Life of St Edith* by Goscelin, a monk of Wilton and of St Augustine's, Canterbury: see *Early English Carols*, pp. xlvi–xlvii.

evidence to show that this was frequently done. The so-called Red Book of Ossory, the work of a Franciscan bishop appointed to that see in 1316, contains 60 Latin poems intended to be sung to tunes originally associated with profane words. Some of these are actually named in the document, and by good fortune the text of one of them—'Maid in the moor lay'—has come down in an English manuscript. There is no music, but the English text allows one to get a clearer idea of the musical form, which is that of the *carole*.[139]

Some tunes travelled widely. Chaucer, alluding to a particularly popular melody, wrote in the *Miller's Tale* of Nicholas the poor 'clerke of Oxenforde':

> And al above there lay a gay sautrye,
> On which he made a nightes melodye
> So swetely that all the chambre song;
> And *Angelus ad virginem* he song;
> And after that he song the kinges note;
> Ful often blessed was his merry throte.[140]

Angelus ad virginem may well be of French origin,[141] but it survives in several versions in English manuscripts, in both monophonic and polyphonic forms, and there are two English versions of the words known. Ex. 46 gives the tune with the Latin and one of the English versions of the words.[142]

The intellectual stimulus provided by the coming of the Dominican and Franciscan friars in the early thirteenth century coincided with a rising perception of the moral and practical usefulness of the art. While many writers sanctioned only the study of music as a mathematical discipline, there was a growing appreciation of the link between speculation and practice, provided that the latter was kept within the bounds of decency. Robert Grosseteste, the first regent of the Franciscan school in Oxford, vice-chancellor of the University, and from 1235 Bishop of Lincoln, was, according to Robert Manning, fond of music:

---

[139] 'Peperit virgo' in *The Red Book of Ossory*, fo. 71ʳ; secular text in Oxford, Bod. Lib., Rawl. d. 913, flyleaf. The hypothetical reconstruction in *Medieval English Songs*, no. 16b, is improbable; for a plausible reconstruction of the text see J. Rimmer, 'Carole, Rondeau and Branle in Ireland 1300–1800', *Dance Research*, 7 (1989), 20–46, esp. p. 28. The best account of the *carole* is still the introduction to *Early English Carols* (the spelling *carole* is to be preferred, however, for the secular monophonic dance-song). The later development of the form is discussed below in Ch. 3.

[140] *The Miller's Tale*: A, ll. 3213–18. The identity of 'the kinges note' is unknown.

[141] See n. 64 above.

[142] See n. 61 above. A possible interpretation would allot an equal value to each syllable, but with doubled values on the stressed syllables of 'concláve', 'áve', 'intácta', 'fácta'.

Ex. 46

An - ge - lus ad vir - gi - nem sub - in - trans in con -
Ga - bri - el, fram e - vene king sent to þe mai - de

cla - ve, vir - gi - nis for - mi - di - nem de - mul - cens, in - quit:
swe - te, brou - te hire* blis - ful ti - ding, and faire he gan hire

'A - ve! A - ve re - gi - na vir - gi - num, ce - li
gre - ten: 'Heil be þu ful of grace a - rith, for go -

ter - re - que do - mi - num con - ci - pi - es, et pa - ri -
des sone is e - vene lith; for man - nes loven wile man bi -

es in - tac - ta sa - lu - tem ho - mi - num, tu por - ta
comen and ta - ken fles of þe mai - den brith, ma[n] - ken fre

ce - li fac - ta me - de - la cri - mi - num.
for to ma - ken of senne and dev - les mith.

(From the Latin): The angel, approaching the virgin in her chamber, softening his appearance, said: 'Hail! Hail, queen of virgins, you shall conceive the lord of heaven and earth, and shall bear without sin the saviour of mankind; you are made the gate of heaven and the remission of sins.'

★ MS 'þire'.

> He loued moche to here the harpe,
> For mannys wytte hyt makyþ sharpe;
> Next hys chaumbre, besyde his stody,
> Hys harpers chaumbre was fast þerby.
> Many tymes, by nyȝtys and dayys,
> He had solace of notes and layys.[143]

[143] *Handlynge Synne* (n. 138), ll. 4743–8; a fuller quotation is given in F. S. Stevenson, *Robert Grosseteste* (London, 1899), 334–5.

Both Roger Bacon, much of whose stormy career passed in Oxford and who became a Franciscan friar around 1255, and Robert Kilwardby, regent of the Dominican school then and later Archbishop of Canterbury, found room in their writings for discussions of music; and while their reaction to the practice of the day is not altogether welcoming, it shows a more positive attitude towards the art than had been shown by John of Salisbury in the previous century. The English writer John of Garland (c.1195–1272), though he probably did not write either of the two musical treatises found under his name, and though he lived for most of his life in Paris, was similarly appreciative of its status in his *Morale scolarium* and other works.[144]

The practical side of music was dealt with amongst others by the English writer known as 'Anonymus IV', whose treatise, written around 1280, includes a good deal of important historical information about thirteenth-century music in both England and France.[145] But as a theorist he was surpassed by Walter Odington, whose *Summa de speculatione musice* is one of the most complete summaries of the musical knowledge at that time which we possess. Odington, a monk of Evesham who 'made his deliberations' at Oxford in 1316, deals with the mathematical basis of musical intervals, with plainsong, and with 'harmonia multiplex' or polyphony. With his careful descriptions of musical practice, including remarks on rhythmic style, accounts of musical forms, and an analysis of contrapuntal technique, he fully exemplifies the capacity of contemporary theory for encompassing the full range of speculative and practical music in a coherent system.[146]

English theorists after Odington show less intellectual independence. The curiously named *Metrologus* is a commentary on the *Micrologus* of Guido of Arezzo, while Robert de Handlo's treatise, dated 1326, is a compilation based largely on post-Franconian French sources.[147] The somewhat later

---

[144] Roger Bacon's main discussions of music are in the *Opus maius*, IV. iv, in the long section following ch. 16 (ed. J. H. Bridges, 3 vols., Oxford, 1897–1900, i. 236–8) and *Opus tertium*, chs. 59–64 (ed. J. S. Brewer, London, 1859, 228–68). He divides music, which he regards as important for theological study, into the audible and the visible (*gestus*); the audible into the vocal and the instrumental; and the vocal into *melica*, *metrica*, *rhythmica*, and *prosaica*. Much of what he writes, therefore, has to do with language: cf. T. Adank, 'Roger Bacons Auffassung der Musica', *AMw*, 35 (1978), 33–56. For Kilwardby see the edition of his *De ortu scientiarum* by A. G. Judy (London, 1976). On John of Garland see L. J. Paetow, *The Morale Scolarium of John of Garland* (Berkeley, Calif., 1927); W. G. Waite, 'Johannes de Garlandia, Poet and Musician', *Speculum*, 35 (1960), 179–95 (who, however, equates this philosopher with the author of the treatises referred to). See also Grosseteste's *De artibus liber* and *De generacione sonorum* in *Die philosophische Werke des Robert Grosseteste*, ed. L. Baur (Münster i. W., 1912); and the musical section of Bartholomaeus Anglicus' *De proprietatibus rerum*, ed. H. Müller in *Riemann-Festschrift* (Leipzig, 1909), 245–55.

[145] *Der Musiktraktat des Anonymus IV*, ed. F. Reckow, 2 vols. (Wiesbaden, 1967). Cf. Ch. 1, n. 72.

[146] Ed. F. F. Hammond, CSM, xiv (AIM, 1970).

[147] The *Metrologus* is in *Expositiones in Micrologum Guidonis Aretini*, ed. J. Smits van Waesberghe (Amsterdam, 1957), 59–92; Robert de Handlo in *CS*, i. 383–403.

work of John Hanboys, and the anonymous *Quatuor principalia musice*, dated 1351, are also compilations, the latter marking the full advent of the French *ars nova* in England.[148] Finally, mention should be made of John Trevisa, whose English translations of Ranulph Higden's *Policronicon* and of Bartholomaeus Anglicus's *De proprietatibus rerum*, made towards the end of the fourteenth century, incorporate what appear to be the earliest examples of technical writing on music in the English language.[149]

It would be idle to claim, for English fourteenth-century music, a status comparable with that enjoyed by the great literary masterpieces of Chaucer, Langland, and their contemporaries, or indeed a humanity approaching that of such devotional writers as the Lady Julian of Norwich, Richard Rolle, or Walter Hilton. On the whole it quietly fulfilled its function as an adjunct to the liturgy, as an expression of princely or magnatial dignity, or as pure entertainment (or any combination of these). England produced no individualist comparable to Machaut or Landini; and while we might like to know the names of its composers, the very anonymity of virtually all this music seems appropriate to its humble functionalism. But the first major breaches in the rule of anonymity were shortly to take place, and personal voices to emerge, in the next phase of English musical history.

[148] John Hanboys's *Summa super musicam*, ibid. i. 403–48; *Quatuor principalia musice*, ibid. iv. 200–98 (see above, nn. 106–7, and Plate III). Yet another important treatise from the 14th cent. is the anonymous Cistercian *Musica manualis cum tonale* formerly attributed to John Wylde, ed. C. Sweeney, CSM, xxviii (AIM, 1982).

[149] For the *Policronicon* see *Polychronicon Ranulphi Higden Monachi Cestrensis; together with the English Translations of John Trevisa and of an Unknown writer of the Fifteenth Century*, ed. C. Babington and J. R. Lumby, 9 vols. (London, 1865–86; RBMAS, xli); *On the Properties of Things: John Trevisa's translation of Bartholomaeus Anglicus, De proprietatibus rerum*, ed. M. C. Seymour, 2 vols. (Oxford, 1975).

3

THE AGE OF POWER
AND DUNSTABLE

THE period covered by this chapter coincides broadly with the reigns of the Lancastrian kings, Henry IV, V, and VI, up to the deposition of Henry VI in 1461. While historians naturally see the establishment of the Tudor monarchy in 1485, when the dynastic struggles of the fifteenth century were finally resolved, as a critical turning-point, that moment is of little significance for the history of music. The great movements of the fifteenth century, by and large, were those that were curtailed or transformed only by the upheaval of the Reformation. Two of these, the growth of a sense of national identity and the consolidation of orthodox churchmanship, are of particular importance to us here.

In the fifteenth century the Hundred Years War was being fought between nations that had grown apart in character and ideals. The rejoicing after Agincourt was of a defiantly nationalist kind, and English aggrandizement reached its peak when the young Henry VI was crowned in Paris in 1431.[1] But the tide had turned; the loss of Orléans in 1429 set in train the events that culminated in the final disaster of 1453, and the nation turned to the settlement of its internal problems, becoming culturally more isolated and less influential at the same time.

Henry IV was the first English king since the Conquest whose native language was not French; and it is of some interest that this change of orientation coincides with a renaissance in the setting of English words to music. We should not make too much of this, for the English literature of the fourteenth century was immeasurably superior to that of the fifteenth; but it does betoken a growing acceptance of the English language

[1] For the ceremony see C. Wright, 'The Coronation of Henry VI of England at Notre Dame of Paris', *La Musique et le rite sacré et profane: Actes du XIIIᵉ Congrès . . . Strasbourg . . . 1982* (Strasbourg, 1986), i. 433–8; see further A. Wathey, 'Dunstable in France', *ML*, 67 (1986), 4, and references there given; G. L. Thompson, *Paris and Its People under English Rule: The Anglo-Burgundian Regime 1420–1436* (Oxford, 1991), 199–204.

in courtly and ecclesiastical circles. The polyphonic repertory of secular songs and carols arose in consequence of this acceptance; and this new growth differentiates the new epoch sharply from the previous one, in which secular song might as easily be in French as in English and in which the improvised art of the minstrels and the songs of the people had played a far greater role.

The strengthening of orthodoxy was an important part of Lancastrian policy; the support of the Church was needed to uphold the dynasty, providing it with an appropriate aura of regal pomp and satisfying its devotional predilections. Private chapels, cathedrals, colleges, collegiate churches, and charitable institutions flourished, and liturgical music with them. The music was provided by 'clerks' in minor orders, who might in favourable circumstances sing in polyphony. (The contribution of trained choristers came later.) The religious houses, with a few significant exceptions, declined in musical importance, except for the separate Lady Chapels and their singers that came to be attached to the greater monasteries. A decisive lead was given by the Chapel Royal (the king's own household chapel) in the cultivation of the most elaborate music of the day.[2]

In many ways these developments were a continuation of ideals already well established in the fourteenth century; and they continued unabated until the Reformation, by which time the institutional framework was becoming obsolete and cumbersome. But the achievements of the early fifteenth century were those of a youthful maturity: the conventions laid down somewhat earlier reached their full fruition while retaining the freshness of a new discovery.

English music was more influential on the Continent in the early fifteenth century than it ever had been before or has been since, even in the age of the virginalists. In part this can be linked with the initial success of the English cause in France. An old tradition associates Dunstable with the Duke of Bedford, regent in France during Henry VI's minority;[3] and a poem of the 1430s by Martin le Franc, the Burgundian court poet, assures us that the then novel art of Dufay and Binchois had drawn its inspiration from Dunstable and the 'contenance Angloise', a style characterized, so we are told, by 'sprightly consonance' and a number of specific technical

---

[2] The principal modern works are Harrison, *Music in Medieval Britain*, and Bowers, 'Choral Establishments'.

[3] Cambridge, St John's College, MS 162, a volume of astronomical treatises, bears on fo. 74ᵛ the inscription 'Iste libellus pertinebat Johanni Dunstaple cum duci Bedfordie musico' ('This book belonged to John Dunstable, musician with the Duke of Bedford'; cited M. Bent, *Dunstaple* (London, 1981), 1). But the ascription, even if correct, does not necessarily imply that he was a member of the Duke's chapel staff.

features.[4] In any case Dunstable was, it seems, a trusted servant of Queen Joan, dowager queen of Henry IV, and a recipient of generous gifts and grants of land in France. Still more significantly, he enjoyed the patronage of Humphrey, Duke of Gloucester, whose humanistic interests and contacts with Renaissance Italy may be responsible, at least in part, for the transmission of English music (including that of Dunstable) in Italian manuscripts.[5]

In England, Dunstable evidently had close links with the abbey of St Albans, Duke Humphrey's own favourite foundation; two of his motets, on St Alban and on St Germanus of Auxerre, were composed for the abbey, and John Whethamstede, abbot from 1420 to 1440 and again from 1452 to 1465, composed an epitaph for him, apparently in 1453.[6] Dunstable the composer remains a shadowy figure, and the documents of the 1430s that reveal him to have been a man of substance may well post-date the majority of his surviving compositions. He was, indeed, styled *armiger* by the mid 1420s. It is quite possible that his later life was devoted to the speculative study of the liberal arts; especially perhaps the mathematical disciplines, including music and astronomy, with which later tradition credited him. But his output suggests that in earlier life he must have found employment as a church musician; just what form that took cannot yet be established.

We have more information on the professional career of Lionel (or Leonel) Power, while conversely he seems not to have attained Dunstable's social position or personal eminence. It may be, of course, that the evidence is incomplete, and that the lives and careers of these two outstanding masters were more closely similar than now appears. On the other hand, it is more likely that there was between them a significant distinction in terms of intellectual interests and personal opportunity. Though their mature music can be very similar indeed (and practically indistinguishable from that of their contemporaries), Power's style was rooted in the conventions of a slightly earlier period; and however sophisticated his technical equipment, it did not issue in so noble a monument as Dunstable's eleven isorhythmic motets. But it is difficult to reach conclusions when the ascriptions in Conti-

[4] *Le champion des dames*, cited G. Reese, *Music in the Renaissance* (New York, 1954), 12–13, and others since; see now D. Fallows, 'The Contenance Angloise', *Renaissance Studies*, I (1987), 189–208. For the presence of English musicians at the Council of Constance, 1414–18, and some other foreign contacts, see Harrison, *Music in Medieval Britain*, 243–5; for the Council of (Ferrara)–Florence, below, p. 158.

[5] A. Wathey, 'Dunstable in France', 1–36. The document linking Dunstable with the Duke of Gloucester is printed on pp. 35–6.

[6] Whethamstede's phrase 'melior vir de muliere | Nunquam natus erat' ('better man was never born of woman') echoes the antiphon used as the *tenor* of Dunstable's motet 'Preco prehemencie': 'Inter natos mulierum non surrexit maior Iohanne Baptista'. Another epitaph, originally in St Stephen's, Wallbrook, where the composer was buried, gives the date of his death as 24 Dec. 1453; but the text has to be restored from corrupt 17th-cent. copies, and the final figure of the year is open to doubt. See Bent, *Dunstaple*, 2–3, where both epitaphs are given in full.

nental sources are so unreliable, and Power's standing may yet require a revised critical appraisal.

Power was a member of the household of Thomas, Duke of Clarence, a brother of Henry V, in 1418; he may have been so for some years previously, and he will certainly have been with Clarence in France from late in 1419 until the Duke's death in battle in March 1421. It has been suggested that the Old Hall manuscript, in which Power's music figures prominently, originated in the Duke's chapel before being acquired by the Chapel Royal. He then disappears from view until 1438, when he emerges as an *armiger* at Canterbury, and it has been conjectured that he was the first master of the Lady Chapel choir attached to the Cathedral Priory from about that time until his death on 5 June 1445.[7] Power's service with Clarence will have enabled him to contribute to the renown of English music in France; and it may well be that his activities between 1421 and 1438, like those of Dunstable, put him in touch with those (such as the Duke of Gloucester) whose interests contributed to the above-mentioned dissemination of English music in Italian sources.

Power and Dunstable are merely the most prominent figures in a flourishing musical culture that gave rise to a host of minor masters, many known to us by name, others remaining anonymous. There is a fairly clear-cut distinction between those represented in the Old Hall manuscript (including the Chapel Royal composers of its 'second layer') and those represented mainly in Continental sources, though Power himself appears in both groups. The anonymous repertory includes functional liturgical music, carols, secular songs, and even elaborate Masses and motets. The stylistic range embraced by this music was a wide one, but at the same time represents a synthesis and a distillation of elements that had been thoroughly assimilated.

By the end of the fourteenth century, the technical innovations of the *ars nova* had penetrated everywhere.[8] Even the simplest functional music embodied the fundamental metrical units of the 'four prolations', expressed in the 9/8, 3/4, 6/8, and 2/4 time-signatures of most modern transcriptions. Within this basic framework, three idioms may be discerned, merging into each other at the extremes but quite distinct in principle.

The first of these was 'English descant' (discussed above, pp. 91–3). Arising out of fourteenth-century traditions of simple, sometimes improvised, polyphony, it was characterized by the use of three parts differentiated in range and by similar rhythms in each part. The plainchant, if there was

---

[7] For a detailed discussion of Power's career see R. Bowers, 'Some Observations on the Life and Career of Lionel Power', *PRMA*, 102 (1975–6), 103–27. Clarence incidentally was in possession of one of the manuscripts of the collected literary and musical works of Guillaume de Machaut (*c.*1300–77), now in Paris, Bibl. nat., fr. 9221.

[8] See above, Ch. 2, pp. 86 seqq.

one, was normally placed in the middle part, though considerations of overall range might cause it to 'migrate' from one part to another. At its simplest, moving in parallel 6–3 chords with a plainchant in the middle, such polyphony could be improvised directly from the plainchant books; and the earliest extant description of 'faburden', dating from the early fifteenth century, allows us to conclude that the singer of the top voice (treble) was to sing a fourth higher than the plainchant while the lowest voice moved a third below it, dropping to a fifth below at cadential points. There are some further refinements, but that is the essence of the matter.[9]

Of course, written polyphony was rarely as simple as that; if strictly parallel, the chances are that it would have no plainchant basis; much of what was composed in written form was based on plainchant but far from parallel in style (cf. Ex. 47 below). Contemporary treatises, of which one is by Power himself, describe improvised descant in two parts against a given plainchant, normally in 'counterpoint' or note-against-note writing. Such teaching was an important part of musical training and was given to children as well as adults; but the musical results would not normally have attained the level of sophistication to be expected in written music.

The second style was that of the contemporary French chanson, often adapted by Continental composers themselves for sacred purposes. In this, a prominent and melodious top part was supported by a *tenor* and a *contratenor* moving more slowly beneath, equivalent in range and frequently crossing. The texture was readily adopted by adult singers used to the differentiated but closely similar ranges of English descant. The idiom itself might be quite straightforward, though English composers were not averse to experimenting with the rhythmic complexities of the 'mannered' style that had grown up in France in the late fourteenth century.

The third idiom was that of the motet. Here, the full range of *ars nova* time-values was employed. Two upper parts, in one of the four mensurations listed above, were supported by a *tenor*, or by a *tenor* and *contratenor* together, moving in much slower values, primarily longs and breves, represented by semibreves and minims in modern transcriptions. The *tenor*, and the *contratenor* if there was one, were normally isorhythmic; that is, they were cast in the form of repeated rhythmic units or *taleae* (singular *talea*). Usually the *cantus firmus* in the *tenor* and its supporting *contratenor* embodied a whole number of such *taleae*, after which the entire scheme could be repeated once or more, perhaps in some proportional arrangement of time-values such as 6 : 4 : 3 or 3 : 2 : 1. Such sections of repeated *tenor*-melody are generally known as *colores* (singular *color*). The upper parts might also be wholly or

---

[9] See the articles by Trowell cited in Ch. 2, nn. 104, 111. The vernacular treatises on descant and faburden were edited by S. B. Meech in 'Three Musical Treatises', *Speculum*, 10 (1935), 258–65.

partly isorhythmic from *talea* to *talea*, though not from one *color* to another if proportional diminution were employed.

Such schemes, already practised in England in the fourteenth century, reached their peak of sophistication in the first half of the fifteenth century and were often applied to the movements of the Mass. In a modified form they gave rise to a particularly influential English invention, the *tenor* or *cantus-firmus* Mass in which a single given melody formed the basis of every movement.

A simple categorization of styles such as this cannot convey the wealth and variety of English music at this period, still less account for its appeal and influence. But it provides a useful basis for the study of sources, repertories and individual composers and their works. The most convenient starting-point for such a study, although it is not the earliest document of its kind, is the Old Hall manuscript, the most substantial source to have survived between the St Andrews codex of *c*.1250 and the Eton Choirbook of *c*.1500.

The Old Hall manuscript, which owes its name to its former location in Old Hall College, Ware,[10] may well have been originally compiled (as noted above) for the household chapel of Thomas, Duke of Clarence. There is nothing in its original contents to contradict this assumption, and the prominence of Lionel Power amongst the composers represented lends it a good deal of support. A second group of works is by composers whose connecting link is their membership of the Chapel Royal, and again it may be conjectured with a good deal of plausibility that it came into the possession of the King's Chapel after the death of Clarence in 1421. A final group of additions includes music by Dunstable (here anonymous) and Forest; this is not incompatible with continued Chapel Royal ownership, but the subsequent history of the manuscript is largely unknown until it resurfaced at Ware in the nineteenth century.

The Old Hall manuscript is a collection of music for the Ordinary of the Mass, but without the Kyrie—either because a fascicle or section devoted to Kyries has been lost from the beginning of the manuscript, or because such a fascicle existed separately.[11] Between the Glorias and Credos comes a short series of Marian pieces of the *cantilena* type, sometimes described

[10] Now London, Brit. Lib., Add. 57950. See Bukofzer, *Studies*, 34–85; A. Hughes and M. Bent in *MD*, 21 (1967), 97–147. The standard edition is that of Hughes and Bent in CMM, xlvi (3 vols.); this replaces the older one by A. Ramsbotham, H. B. Collins, and Dom A. Hughes (3 vols., Burnham and London: PMMS, 1933–8), save for some useful plates in the latter. The numbering of items adopted here is that of Hughes and Bent in their article and edition.

[11] Hughes and Bent, in *MD*, 21 (1967), 97–147. The older view, that the verbal expansion of the Kyrie with *prosulae* or verses for particular classes of feast made it inconvenient to set them in polyphony, is untenable for this period; and in 'Lady Masses' (votive Masses of the Blessed Virgin Mary) they were sung untroped ('absque versibus').

as antiphons but probably representing a substitute for the liturgical Alleluia and/ or Sequence. At the end are two or three motets substituting for the 'Ite missa est' (or 'Benedicamus domino') and its response 'Deo gracias'.[12]

The original scribe, who must have been working in the second decade of the century, started each category of piece in a new section of the manuscript; and his successors filled in the gaps and added new gatherings, partly with pieces of the same genre and occasionally with motets. (Hence the term 'layer' to describe each successive contribution to the manuscript.)[13] Much of the simpler music is written in a kind of score-notation (but with little attempt at exact alignment), while the rest is copied in what is known as 'choirbook' format or *cantus collateralis*, the individual parts being noted side by side on the double open page. All the scribes used a 'black' notation, but red and even blue notes are employed to denote various rhythmic complications, and the general level of copying is highly professional. On the whole the manuscript is well preserved, but someone (possibly J. Stafford Smith in the eighteenth century) has removed many of the original illuminated initials, depriving us of the music originally written on their reverse and in some cases perhaps of the evidence of authorship.

The attribution of so many pieces to specific composers is a startlingly novel feature for an English manuscript, and it betokens a new sense of the importance of the individual composer as an artist in his own right rather than as a mere servant or artisan. For many of them, no certain details are available, but some at least must have flourished in the later fourteenth century.[14] They appear to have been drawn from a wide geographical as well as chronological range; some may be associated with Yorkshire and one or other of its major Cistercian foundations, but the firmest identifications are with clerks of the Chapel Royal and of Clarence's chapel, and with singers of Westminster Abbey.[15] Others were foreigners, like Pycard, a northern Frenchman as his name suggests and a clerk in John of Gaunt's chapel from 1391 to 1397.

The most beguiling conundrum surrounds the identity of the composer named as Roy Henry. An early identification of him as Henry VI was based on a mistaken view of the date of the manuscript, while a more recent claim for Henry IV now seems implausible. On the whole Henry V is the most likely candidate, given the probable date of copying, though the music could of course have been composed before he ascended the throne. It would not be incompatible with what we know of his character

[12] On these and comparable motets see Ch. 2, pp. 87 seqq.

[13] The material of the second and subsequent layers is printed consecutively in the third volume ('Vol. ii') of the Hughes–Bent edn.

[14] Apart from those noted below there is Aleyn, discussed above in Ch. 2, p. 87.

[15] See n. 40 below; and for the foreigners Mayshuet and Zacar, Hughes and Bent in *MD*, 21 (1967), 113, 117.

and interests, and the idea that the monarch's musical efforts were part of the repertory of his brother's chapel is inherently attractive and helps to explain the form in which his name appears.[16]

The simple 'descant' style of the manuscript may be illustrated with a Sanctus by W. Typp, possibly the William Typpe who was precentor of the chapel of Fotheringay Castle in 1438. Here the chant migrates between all three voices in various transpositions (Ex. 47, overleaf).[17]

Some examples of English descant are rhythmically more complex, as in a Gloria by Cooke, in which there is no *cantus firmus* (Ex. 48, p. 118).[18] Cooke is one of the most accomplished composers represented in the Old Hall manuscript, which makes it all the more aggravating that he cannot be identified with certainty, but he was probably the John Cooke who was a clerk of the Chapel Royal during the second decade of the century. Another possible candidate is the Richard Cooke who can be found as a clerk of Clarence's chapel in 1420. Other composers of the same name, such as John Cooke, clerk of the Chapel Royal from 1428/9 to 1455 or later, are too young to qualify. Like Power, Cooke is represented in both the main layers of the manuscript; it is most unlikely from the stylistic similarities that more than one composer is involved, and Power's death in 1445 probably represents the limit for the working life of any composer represented in the first layer.[19]

The pure chanson style is comparatively rare in the first layer of the Old Hall manuscript; but it may be found in a Gloria by Excetre amongst other works. J. Excetre, as he is called here, has been confidently identified with a canon of Exeter who was also a member of the Chapel Royal between 1372 and 1397,[20] but this, if correct, would cast considerable doubt on some of the later dates considered possible for other composers, and would in any case make his use of a 'Burgundian' chanson style an implausibly mature example for its date (Ex. 49, p. 119).[21] As with many examples of early fifteenth-century church music in this idiom, there is a contrasting section for the top part and *tenor* alone.

Many of the most characteristically lively and ingenious pieces of the first layer are elaborate canonic and isorhythmic works in a motet-like idiom. A Gloria by Tyes (no. 19), which is isorhythmic in all its voices,

---

[16] Bukofzer, *Studies*, and Harrison, *Music in Medieval Britain*, have favoured the identification with Henry V and Henry IV respectively. The name 'Henrici Quinti' beside an Alleluia in Worcester, Co. Rec. Off., MS b. 705: 4, BA 54 (see *RISM*, B IV⁴, pp. 728–9) is unconnected with the music.

[17] *The Old Hall Manuscript*, no. 95; see Frontispiece for the complete piece.

[18] Ibid. i, no. 7.

[19] For details of Cooke and his various namesakes see A. Wathey, *Music in the Royal and Noble Households*, 35; further information on the Old Hall composers, with reference to sources, may be found on p. 46, n. 1.

[20] Hughes and Bent, *MD*, 21 (1967), 111.

[21] *The Old Hall Manuscript*, no. 80.

Ex. 47

Ex. 47, continued

(b) (chant, transposed up a 4th)

Sanc - - - tus, Sanc - -

- - tus do - mi - nus De - us Sa - ba - oth.

Ple - ni sunt ce - li et ter - ra

Holy, holy, holy, lord God of hosts. The heavens and the earth are full . . .

★ Chant transposed up a 4th.
† Chant transposed up an octave.

is a comparatively straightforward instance without canon. (Tyes was *organista* at Westminster Abbey in 1399/1400.)[22] Byttering, Queldryk, and Power all wrote works using these techniques. But the acme of the style is reached by Pycard, the Frenchman, whose three Gloria settings (nos. 26–8) exhibit respectively the techniques of canon, double canon, and isorhythm. The last two are for five voices, though in each case with an alternative *solus*

[22] Wathey, *Music in the Royal and Noble Households*, 43.

Ex. 48

And on earth peace to men of good will . . . O lord, only-begotten Son Jesu Christ . . .

tenor as a substitute for the *tenor* and *contratenor*. In the first of these five-part works this results in a loss of musical sense, since the two canons are between the first and second treble, and the *tenor* and *contratenor*, respectively. The fifth part is a freely composed third treble. The second five-part work has no strict canon, though it is rich in free imitation. The *tenor* is based on the final versicle, 'Iohannes Iesu care', of the Sequence 'Iohannes Iesu Christo' for the feast of St John the Evangelist; but the Gloria text incorpor-

Ex. 49

(Text in top voice only)

ates the Marian trope 'Spiritus et alme orphanorum'. The first *contratenor* does nothing beyond duplicating the notes of the *tenor* and filling in its rests with repetitions or anticipations of its notes: nothing of substance therefore is lost by the substitution of the *solus tenor* for these two parts. The other parts are two trebles and an *alius contratenor* which moves in rhythms comparable to that of the *solus tenor* (or its constituent parts). The *solus tenor*, which for the sake of simplicity will be regarded as the true *tenor* from now on, and the *alius contratenor* perform a complex dual structure involving a fourfold rhythmic and twofold melodic repetition (Ex. 50, overleaf).[23] This is heard four times in all, in the temporal ratio 12:9:8:12, against which is pitted the lively counterpoint of the two trebles, the whole constructed with a verve worthy of the Dufay of 'Ecclesie militantis'. The result may be sampled in the opening of each major section (Ex. 51, pp. 121–2).[24]

Pycard represents the apogee of technical sophistication in the Old Hall repertory. His employment by John of Gaunt no doubt facilitated the acceptance in an English milieu of the international style current around 1400,

[23] *The Old Hall Manuscript*, no. 28.
[24] Ibid. The editors' interpretation of the relative speeds of the four sections as 12:9:8:6 leads to an improbably fast final section. Dufay's motet would provide a parallel for a return to the original speed. A recently discovered anonymous Credo exhibits the proportions 12:8:6:4:3:2 or, more simply, 4:2:1; see M. Bent, 'The Yoxford Credo', *Essays in Musicology: A Tribute to Alvin Johnson*, ed. L. Lockwood and E. Roesner (American Musicological Society, 1990), 26–51.

Ex. 50

Tenor. John, dear to Jesus.

the idiom of Ciconia, of Arnold and Hugo de Lantins, of Grenon, of Nico-
laus Zacharie, and of others represented in the North Italian Canonici codex
now in Oxford (Bodleian Library, Canonici misc. 213). To the textual clarity
and rhythmic liveliness characteristic of the idiom the English added their
characteristically acute sense of vocal sonority. This could take the form
either of a special concern for euphony (for which they were later to become
especially noted) or, on the contrary, that relish for the harmonic clash
of independently conceived lines which is paradoxically a manifestation
of the same sense and which may be illustrated in an extreme form by
the five-part conclusion of another Gloria by Cooke (Ex. 52, p. 123).[25]

Lionel Power is certainly the most prolific of the composers represented
in the Old Hall manuscript; but one would hardly suspect his subsequent
stylistic development and European reputation from the pieces contained
in it. They are accomplished, it is true, and the range of styles is wider
than that of any of the other composers; but they are not individually
more compelling than the best of those by Pycard, Cooke, Tyes, or Pennard.
Unlike Cooke, Power is represented in the second layer by only one piece,
the Credo no. 73 (it is fragmentary but can be completed from a Continental
source), and that an uncharacteristic one. Apart from an anonymous Agnus,
no. 140, thought to form a pair with a Sanctus (no. 116) attributed to Power
in the manuscript, this is the only Old Hall work by Power with a Continental concordance.[26] Most of his later music is to be found in Continental

[25] *The Old Hall Manuscript*, no. 36.

[26] Both are in Aosta, Biblioteca del Seminario Maggiore, MS A¹D 19 (henceforth Ao.), fos. 238ᵛ–240ʳ
(no. 173, Credo), and fos. 245ᵛ–246ʳ (no. 176, Agnus). The MS was inventoried by G. de Van, 'A
Recently Discovered Source of Early Fifteenth Century Polyphonic Music', *MD*, 2 (1948), 5–74; but
see the revised description in *Census-Catalogue of manuscript sources of polyphonic music 1400–1550*
(Neuhausen–Stuttgart, 1979–88), i. 6–7.

Ex. 51

(a) Et in ter - ra pax ho - mi - ni - bus bo - ne vo - lun - ta - -

(♩ = ♩. of upper voices) Et in ter - ra pax ho - mi - ni - bus bo - ne vo - lun - ta -

tis. Lau - da - mus te.

tis. Lau - da - mus te.

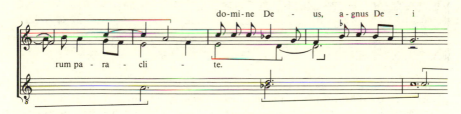

(b) Spi - ri - tus et al - me

(♩ = ♩. of upper voices) Spi - ri - tus et al - me or - pha - no -

do - mi - ne De - us, a - gnus De - i

rum pa - ra - cli - te.

(c) a[d] Ma - ri - e glo - -

(♩ = ♩. of upper voices) ad Ma - ri - e glo - ri -

Ex. 51, continued

(a) And on earth peace to men of good will. We praise you.

(b) Spirit and nourisher of orphans, the comforter; O lord God, lamb of God . . .

(c) to the glory of Mary; you who sit at the right hand of the father, have mercy on us.

(d) with the holy spirit . . . Amen.

Ex. 52

Triplex 1. for you alone are holy, you alone are the lord, you alone are the most high, (*Triplex 2*) Jesu Christ, with the holy spirit in the glory of God the father. (*Both*) Amen.

manuscripts only: one exception is a setting of 'Ave regina celorum, ave domina' (II), in the Selden manuscript (discussed below)—it is anonymous there but is given to 'Leonel' in one of several Continental sources.[27] Others may include an anonymous English setting of the Sequence 'Benedicta ecelorum regina', and the Kyries of the two Masses which are more probably by Dunstable and Benet respectively.[28] The general picture, therefore, is of an early period represented by the Old Hall manuscript, and of a later period represented mainly in Continental sources. It is unlikely, nevertheless, that Power enjoyed any personal connection with European musicians: the transmission of the music overseas (primarily to Italy) was part and parcel of the entire phenomenon of the Continental interest in English music during the first half of the fifteenth century.

Power's later music is discussed below. The first layer of the Old Hall manuscript contains four Glorias, three Credos, seven Sanctus settings, and four Agnus settings attributed to him: in addition the anonymous Gloria, no. 24, is musically a pair with the Credo, no. 84, while the anonymous Credo, no. 77, may well be a pair with the Gloria, no. 21, and the Agnus, no. 140, already mentioned, may be a pair with the Sanctus, no. 116. Musical similarity does not of course absolutely prove identity of authorship, though it renders it highly likely. The Sanctus, no. 118, and the Agnus, no. 141, both attributed to Power, may also have been intended as a pair. There are also several anonymous Mass movements falling adjacent to or within groups of works by Power, and some of these too may be by him. Two of the *cantilenae*, the antiphons 'Ave regina celorum, ave domina' (I) and 'Beata progenies', are by Power (nos. 43, 49), and they are preceded by the anonymously preserved numbers 41–2 and 44–8 respectively. While this may seem an incautious basis on which to assign anonymous works to known composers, it is to be noted that numbers 42, 45–6, and 48 lack the openings of the pieces where the ascription, if any, would have been found.

Power's stylistic range is so wide that style alone would be an unsafe criterion for attribution. Turning to the authenticated works, we find that the Gloria, no. 21 (and its probable pair the anonymous Credo, no. 77)

[27] Oxford, Bod. Lib., Arch. Selden B 26, fos. 5^v–6^r (no. 5, anon.); Trent, Museo provinciale d'arte (henceforth Tr.), MS 92, fos. 132^v–133^r (no. 1491, anon.) and fos. 171^v–172^r (no. 1525, anon.); Ao., fos. 195^v–196^r (no. 146, anon.); Bologna, Civico Museo Bibliografia Musicale, Q 15 (henceforth BL), fos. 277^v–278^r (no. 281 [303], 'Leonel'). Power, *Works*, ed. C. Hamm (AIM, 1969), i, no. 7; *Fifteenth-Century Liturgical Music*, i, no. 4. For BL see G. de Van, 'Inventory of Manuscript Bologna, Liceo Musicale, Q15 (*olim* 37)', *MD*, 2 (1948), 231–57; our references correspond to those given there, ignoring a more recent MS foliation.

[28] The 'Benedicta es' is in the following Continental sources: Tr. 92, fos. 177^v–178^r (no. 1531, 'de Anglia'); BL, fos. 205^v–206^r (no. 185 [218], 'de Anglia'); Bologna, Biblioteca Universitaria, MS 2216 (BU), fos. 41^v–42^r (pp. 82–3, anon.). Printed DTO, lxxvi (Jg. xl), 81; Power, *Works*, i, no. 15. It is also found, with an extra verse, in Oxford, Bod. Lib., Lincoln College Lat. 124, fos. 223^{r-v}, again anonymously: see A. Wathey, 'Newly Discovered Fifteenth-Century Polyphony at Oxford', *ML*, 64 (1983), 58–66, with a plate of fo. 223^r and a transcription of the additional verse (p. 66). The Kyries are in Dunstable, *Works*, ed. M. Bukofzer (2nd edn., London, 1970), nos. 70, 71.

closely resembles the technique of Cooke's Gloria, no. 36 (Ex. 52 above), with its alternation of two-part and four-part sections (the latter scored for two trebles, *contratenor* and *tenor*) and a five-part section to conclude. The rhythmically mannered style of the Gloria, no. 21, and of the Credos, nos. 81 and 83, can be found in the music of Pycard (though not throughout a movement), while the buoyant rhythms and isorhythmic structure of no. 23 are paralleled in works by Pycard, Pennard, Tyes, Typp, and Swynford. This is not to deny originality and resource to Power, but merely to stress his position as one of a group of composers of a high general level. His style also embraced the simpler descant of his contemporaries, an idiom which through its euphony and rhythmic simplicity is more likely to have been the key to Power's later development than were the more complex and mannered techniques. It is illustrated here from the first of the *cantilenae*, 'Ave regina celorum, ave domina' (I) (Ex. 53).[29]

Ex. 53

Hail, queen of the heavens. Hail . . .

* No flat in MS.

The first layer of the Old Hall manuscript is a striking testimony, unique in the breadth of its coverage, to a body of English music about which we should otherwise be much less well informed. It was added to during the succeeding decades by a series of scribes, not all of whom can be very easily distinguished from each other. For our purposes it will be sufficient to distinguish between the addition of works by Power, Cooke, Burell,

[29] *The Old Hall Manuscript*, i, no. 43.

Damett, and Sturgeon, together with a few anonyma, on the one hand, and the still later addition of three works, one by Dunstable and two by Forest, on the other, consideration of the latter being deferred to a later stage.

The 'second-layer' Credo of Power (no. 73) has already been mentioned. All the other second-layer composers have Chapel Royal associations—and it may be mentioned that even the two pieces by 'Roy Henry', though they are in the original hand, are suspected to be a later addition to the manuscript. Burell, who died in 1422/3, held a corrody in the diocese of York,[30] but he was listed as a clerk of the Chapel Royal in 1402, 1413, and 1421. The identity of Cooke has been discussed above. Thomas Damett, certainly the composer, was a clerk of the Chapel Royal from at least 1413 until 1431, and a canon of Windsor from 1431 until his death in 1436 or 1437. Nicholas Sturgeon (the manuscript itself gives the initial 'N') also joined the Chapel Royal in 1413; his many canonries included one at Windsor but he also became precentor of St Paul's Cathedral, a post which he held until his death in 1454. The obvious linking factor between all these men is membership of the Chapel Royal, which strongly suggests that the manuscript became its property during the second or third decade of the century.[31] This is a more probable conjecture than that it migrated to Windsor, on the grounds of the canonries held by Damett and Sturgeon, the latter at least *in absentia*. It has been suggested that the pieces addressed to St George refer to him as patron of England rather than of the chapel.[32]

The second-layer music of the Old Hall manuscript gives the impression of being much more self-contained and insular than either that of the first layer or a great deal of music contemporary with it. Not only does it lack any importation of pieces by Continental composers; only two (discounting the late addition of works by Dunstable and Forest) are found in any Continental source, these being the Credo by Power already mentioned and an anonymous Credo in chanson style immediately following it in the manuscript (no. 74).[33] Though the Continental influence of Power, Dunstable, and their contemporaries must by this time have been well under way, the compilers chose to make their additions largely from what proves to have been a somewhat isolated repertory for its date. This is far from denying it excellence; it is neither the first nor the last insular repertory of merit to have made little or no impact abroad. Nor does it imply that certain aspects of Continental style were not well-known to these composers. The opening of a Gloria by Burell, with its expressive

[30] Hughes and Bent, *MD*, 21 (1967), 109–10; Wathey, *Music in the Royal and Noble Households*.
[31] Above, p. 113. For biographical notes, Hughes and Bent, *MD*, 21 (1967), 122.
[32] Hughes and Bent, *MD*, 21 (1967), 122.
[33] Tr. 90, fos. 207ᵛ–209ʳ (no. 949, copied from Tr. 93 (this MS is kept in the Biblioteca capitolare), fos. 278ᵛ–80ʳ, no. 1780, both anon.).

accented dissonances, comes close to the chanson idiom of Loqueville and his contemporaries (Ex. 54).[34]

Ex. 54

And on earth peace to men of good will.

At the same time, a few pieces in 'English descant' style are scarcely distinguishable from those in the first layer. An example is Cooke's 'Stella celi' (no. 55), though this is marked by the explicit use of the G sharp and even D sharp at the beginning.[35] More characteristic than either of these idioms, however, is a new blend of chanson and descant styles, marked by considerable melodic and rhythmic verve, combined with a freely disso-nant idiom in the management of the parts. This may be illustrated in the opening of an unfortunately incomplete Gloria by Damett, who is perhaps the most impressive of these composers (Ex. 55, overleaf).[36]

The melodic idiom here approaches that of the carol (see below), with its aggressive rhythmic force and compelling line. Damett was also capable of a quieter, more intense style (Gloria, no. 13) and of a more mannered type of rhythmic complexity (the Gloria–Credo pair, nos. 39, 93). In the latter the idiom approaches that of the motet, a manner favoured also by Cooke and Sturgeon. All three composers actually contributed a motet;

[34] *The Old Hall Manuscript*, no. 12.
[35] Compare the two previous pieces, 'Beata Dei' and 'Salve porta', by Damett. 'Stella celi' is addressed to the BVM in time of plague. See M. Bent, 'New and Little-Known Fragments of English Medieval Polyphony', *JAMS*, 21 (1968), 148; Wathey, *ML*, 64 (1983), 64, and the further references there given. Cooke's piece is reprinted in R. Hoppin, *Anthology of Medieval Music* (New York, 1978), no. 71.
[36] *The Old Hall Manuscript*, no. 10 (incomplete).

Ex. 55

And on earth peace to men of good will. We praise you ...

these, together with a Sanctus by Sturgeon, occupy a gap in the series
of first-layer Sanctus settings. These works are more extended in design,
and more euphonious, than the first-layer motets briefly alluded to earlier.
Damett's 'Salvatoris mater' combines a Sequence-text (altered to include
a reference to Henry V) addressed to the Virgin,[37] and a second, Sequence-
like text addressed to St George, beginning 'O Georgi Deo care'. This
too contains allusions to the monarch. The *tenor* is curious. It consists of
a fragment of a troped Benedictus, a variant of Sanctus 3 in the Salisbury
cycle, but embodying an extra musical phrase to accommodate the text,
'Benedictus Marie filius qui venit in nomine domini'. Damett, however,
transposes the melody down a tone and, what is more, truncates it in a
manner which is clarified by the actual text as given in the manuscript:
'Benedictus Marie filius qui ve'. This torso is presented four times in increasing diminution in the ratio 6:3:2:1, each statement of the melody being
divided into two rhythmically equal halves. The idiom, while well managed,
does not achieve the poise and equilibrium of Dunstable—the top part

---

[37] AH, liv. 424.

is rhythmically somewhat nervous, and is more detached from the lower parts—but at the same time it moves to a convincing climax. The poise is more nearly approached in Sturgeon's otherwise less interesting 'Salve mater domini/ Salve templum gracie', the *tenor* of which is simply the continuation, labelled 'It in nomine domini', of Damett's 'Benedictus ... qui ve' (the letter 'n' of 'venit' having been lost *en route*). Sturgeon's *tenor*, nevertheless, is untransposed and is stated three times only in the ratio 3:2:1, each statement once again being divided into two rhythmically equal halves. A further connection was pointed out by Bukofzer: 'the first four measures of the treble in the first four isorhythmic periods have exactly the same rhythm in the two works'. Cooke's 'Alma proles regia/ Christi miles inclite', which falls between the works of Damett and Sturgeon in the manuscript, shares with the former a combination of texts addressed respectively to the Virgin and St George, but differs from either in that its *tenor*, an extract from the litany headed 'Ab inimicis nostris defende nos Christe', has no connection with the Sanctus settings which surround this group of works. Its rhythmic idiom is more old-fashioned and faster-moving than that of its companions, reinforcing the impression that its composer is identical with the 'first-layer' Cooke.

The varied picture conveyed by the Old Hall repertory is confirmed by a large number of smaller and mostly fragmentary sources of the period. One of these, recovered from the binding of a memorandum book belonging to the Cistercian abbey of Fountains in Yorkshire, is written in the newer manner in black-void (i.e. 'white') notation on paper.[38] Six of its seventeen different compositions (one of the Gloria settings is duplicated) do in fact concord with pieces in the oldest layer of the Old Hall manuscript. Like the latter, it provides compositions for the Ordinary of the Mass, probably for the Lady Mass, and it includes a motet which is evidently a substitute for the 'Deo gratias' at the end of Mass.[39] If the music was really intended for use at Fountains Abbey (concerning the musical establishment of which little is known), it is likely to have been performed by a small group of singers maintained in order to provide polyphonic music in the Lady Chapel, rather than for use in choir by members of the monastic community itself. It is not certain, of course, that the binding of the memorandum and hence the origin of the fragment can be located in Yorkshire. But there is at least a suggestion that sophisticated music travelled widely, and it is not

---

[38] London, Brit. Lib., Add. 40011 (B), referred to in Ch. 2: cf. Bukofzer, *Studies*, 86–112. There is a facsimile in *The Fountains Fragments*, ed. M. Bent (Clarabricken, 1987), and an edition by E. Kershaw (Newton Abbot, 1989). The date could be as early as 1410; the text of the final, fragmentary item, refers to a political event of 1385: see P. Lefferts, *The Motet in England in the Fourteenth Century* (Ann Arbor, Mich., 1986), 184; Bowers, 'Fixed Points', 317–20.

[39] 'Humane lingue/ Supplicum voces/ Contratenor/ Tenor [Deo gracias]'; cf. Ch. 2, Ex. 37.

impossible that some of the Old Hall composers, one of whom is actually called Fonteyn, had northern roots.[40] It need not be assumed that far-flung communities in those times of difficult communication would have had to be content with a backward provincialism in music.

The additions to the Old Hall manuscript already described are not altogether typical of the new era which can be discerned from around 1410. This was characterized by two divergent trends: a more consonant and flowing style, coupled with an interest in larger structures, associated above all with the names of Power and Dunstable and destined to prove very fashionable on the Continent; and the first hints of a renewed attention to the smaller forms: songs, carols, ritual antiphons, hymns and the like, which travelled less readily. The former came to an end around 1460 if not before; the latter, however, continued to the end of the century and provided much of the continuity which would otherwise be lacking for the period from 1450 to 1485.

The popularity overseas of the music of Dunstable, Power, and many of their lesser contemporaries is reflected by the existence of a number of Continental manuscripts containing their work, the chief ones being those now at Aosta, Trent, Modena, and Bologna.[41] It is noteworthy that these are all Italian manuscripts, although a widely quoted passage from a poem written by Martin le Franc in 1441–2 testifies to the influence of the *contenance angloise* on Dufay and Binchois.[42] Northern European sources of English music are less common, but the Bruges fragment now in the Archivio di Stato at Lucca, and the important MS 5557 of the Bibliothèque Royale in Brussels, probably intended for practical use at the Burgundian court, are significant instances.[43]

The more insular trends in English music of the period are represented in such collections as the Selden and Egerton manuscripts (discussed below) and a host of smaller fragments, though it must be emphasized that they also contain examples of the exportable commodity in the form in which it was first conceived.

---

[40] It is possible that Gervays ('Gervasius de Anglia' in BL) was connected with the Cistercian abbey of Jervaulx; Queldryk, though he bears the name of an estate owned by Fountains Abbey (see Hughes and Bent, *MD*, 21 (1967), 112–13, 114), was probably employed at Lichfield: see A. Wathey, 'Lost Books of Polyphony in England', *RMARC*, 21 (1988), 1–20.

[41] For Aosta, Trent, and Bologna, see above, nn. 26–8; Modena, Bibl. estense, α X, 1. 11 (formerly Lat. 471, known as Mod. B).

[42] See above, n. 4. Binchois may have been employed by the earl of Suffolk in the 1420s: see Thompson, *Paris and Its People*, 221.

[43] On the Lucca fragment, see R. Strohm, *Music in Late Medieval Bruges* (Oxford, 1985). On Brussels 5557, see the unpublished thesis by G. Curtis, 'The English Masses of Brussels, Bibliothèque Royale, MS 5557', and his edition in *Fifteenth-Century Liturgical Music*, iii (London, 1989).

The earliest stage of English influence abroad is represented by Lionel Power, whose later music, as already stated, is to be found mainly in Continental sources. His importance in this respect should not be exaggerated: of the twenty-six 'motets' assembled by Charles Hamm in his edition, only thirteen can be assigned to Power without dispute.[44] Some of them, such as the beautiful 'Benedicta es celorum regina' already referred to,[45] are indeed described as 'de Anglia' or in some such way; and the eleven attributed and unchallenged works include such beautiful compositions as the four-part 'Ave regina ... ave domina' (no. 7), the first 'Salve regina' (no. 10), two fine settings of 'Anima mea liquefacta est' (nos. 18, 25), and the semi-declamatory 'Quam pulcra es' (no. 26).[46] Almost all the works (including the *dubia*) are votive antiphons of the Virgin Mary destined for the conclusion of the Office in choir or for the short separate services which, in England at least, took place before the image of the Virgin (or other saint) in the appropriate chapel.[47] That such compositions were already capable of reaching a degree of elaboration is shown by the four-part 'Ave regina' (Ex. 56, overleaf).

These works appealed by virtue of their well-balanced melodic lines, their euphony, and their rhythmic straightforwardness. But Power took a step of even greater importance in the composition of his Mass 'Alma redemptoris mater'. In this work, probably for the first time, an entire Mass was composed on the foundation of a single unifying *tenor*, in this case the plainchant antiphon of its title. The work survives only in Continental sources, and is without a Kyrie, although the fragmentary English sources of other 'cyclic' Masses (as such works are usually called nowadays) suggest that a troped Kyrie would originally have been included.[48]

Power's Mass, which is for three voices, treats the *cantus firmus* in a curious but by no means unparalleled way: it is laid out in an irregular series of

---

[44] Power, *Works*, i. If one excludes the three Old Hall motets, one of which is anonymous, from the reckoning, the figure is eleven out of twenty-three works.

[45] See n. 28.

[46] The four-part 'Ave regina' is also in the Selden MS (Oxford, Bod. Lib., Arch. Selden B 26), and is printed in *Fifteenth-Century Liturgical Music*, i, no. 4 (cf. n. 27). Four other works which may be by Dunstable are also in the edition of his *Works*, nos. 40, 60, 62, 63 (= Power, *Works*, nos. 16, 21, 17, 22): of these the last three are more probably by Power, the 'Salve regina' (Dunstable, no. 63 = Power, no. 22) being a particularly fine and extended specimen of his art.

[47] See above, Ch. 2, p. 96.

[48] For the standard English version of the melody (but notated a 5th higher as was usual) see *AS*, pl. 529; the slightly different Continental version is given in modern Roman chant-books, such as the *Liber Usualis* (1934 etc.), 273. The Mass occurs in Ao., fos. 219ᵛ–226ʳ (nos. 162–5, Sanctus and Agnus anon.), in Tr. 87, fos. 3ᵛ–8ᵛ (nos. 3–6, anon.), and in Tr. 90, fos. 112ᵛ–114ʳ (no. 902, Gloria only, anon., copied from Tr. 93, fos. 142ᵛ–144ʳ, no. 1712, anon.); there is a good modern edition by G. Curtis (Newton Abbot, 1982). The fragmentary, anonymous Kyrie 'Deus creator' on the same *tenor* in the Brit. Lib., Add. 54324, does not belong to this Mass: see M. and I. Bent, 'Dufay, Dunstable, Plummer—A New Source', *JAMS*, 22 (1969), 404.

Ex. 56

Hail, queen of the heavens, hail, mistress of the angels;

note-values devised by the composer himself, and moreover it is truncated after the syllable 'po-' of the word 'populo', which happens to fall on the note *g*: thus the tonality of the plainchant, which is in mode 5 (effectively F major) is distorted and the Mass itself is in a form of mode 1 transposed (in effect G minor). What is retained of the chant is presented in each movement as a series of six lengthy phrases, three in triple time and three in duple time, separated from each other by extensive rests. Some of the

TABLE I. *Tenor Layouts in English Masses*

Power, 'Alma redemptoris mater' (GCSA) *a 3*

$$\begin{array}{l} \bigcirc \; \Longmapsto \langle n \rangle + 16 + \langle 4 \rangle + 16 + \langle 8 \rangle + 14 \\ \mathverb{C} \; \Longmapsto \langle n \rangle^{a} + 20 + \langle 8 \rangle + 38 + \langle 8 \rangle + 12 \end{array} \Big\}$$

Dunstable, 'Iesu Christe fili Dei vivi' (GC) *a 3*

$$\begin{array}{l} [\mathrm{C}] \; \Longmapsto^{b} 7 + \langle 12 \rangle + 12 + \langle 2 \rangle + 1; \\ \qquad\quad \mathrm{C}\; 20 + \langle 28 \rangle + 22; \end{array} \Big\}$$

$$\begin{array}{l} [\bigcirc] \; \Longmapsto 7 + \langle 12 \rangle + 12 + \langle 2 \rangle + 1; \\ \qquad\quad \mathrm{C}\; 10 + \langle 14 \rangle + 11 \end{array} \Big\}$$

Dunstable, 'Da gaudiorum premia' (KGCS) *a 3*

$$\begin{array}{l} \mathrm{C}\!\!\!/ \; \Longmapsto^{b} \langle n \rangle + 11 + \langle 2 \rangle + 8 + \langle 1 \rangle + 18 \\ \mathrm{C}\,[2] \; \Longmapsto^{b} \langle n \rangle + 9 + \langle 2 \rangle + 11 + \langle 2 \rangle + 6 \end{array} \Big\}$$

Dunstable, 'Rex seculorum' (KGCSA) *a 3*

$$\bigcirc \; \Longmapsto \langle n \rangle\, n \quad \mathrm{C} \Longmapsto n \quad \bigcirc \Longmapsto n$$

(not isorhythmic; short rests ignored, Credo has $\mathverb{C}$ in middle section and intermediate rest of 14 breves; Sanctus and Agnus have no initial rest.)

Anon., 'Veterem hominem' (KGCSA) *a 4*

$$\begin{array}{l} \bigcirc \; \Longmapsto \langle n \rangle + 24 + \langle n \rangle + 34 \\ \mathverb{C}^{c} \; \Longmapsto \langle n \rangle + 36 + \langle n \rangle + 48 \end{array}$$

Anon., 'Caput' (KGCSA) *a 4*

$$\begin{array}{l} \bigcirc \; \Longmapsto \langle n \rangle + 30 + \langle n \rangle + 12 + \langle n \rangle + 29 \\ \mathrm{C} \; \Longmapsto \langle n \rangle + 46 + \langle n \rangle + 44 \end{array}$$

Note: Layout is as shown in each of the extant movements listed (K = Kyrie, G = Gloria, C = Credo, S = Sanctus, A = Agnus). Angle brackets indicate rests; n = length varies from movement to movement (and may be nil). Sections encompassing between them a single statement of the chant are bracketed together; otherwise each line represents one such statement.

  [a] This section is in $\bigcirc$ in the Agnus Dei.
  [b] The values are doubled with respect to the original to conform to those of the upper parts.
  [c] The signature is C in the Agnus Dei (MS Trent 88), and was probably so originally in every movement.

movements, and some of their duple-time second sections, also begin with lengthy duos, in which the *tenor* is silent (see Table I).

Apart from its artistic merits, which are considerable, this work is of great historical significance. Power may not have invented the device of the unifying *cantus firmus*, but his interest in unity is shown in his paired movements in the Old Hall manuscript. Nor is his Mass necessarily the very first complete example of its kind to have been written. But it is without doubt one of the earliest, and the treatment of the *cantus firmus* as an isorhythmic as well as an 'isomelic' device was to have far-reaching consequences. The exact design could be varied, but the method, especially when combined with other forms of unification such as the 'head-motive' already in use on the Continent,[49] seemed to have an almost limitless application. After about 1450 it took root in France and the Netherlands, where Dufay and others applied it to secular as well as sacred *cantus firmi* in their Masses, and it forms the basis of by far the majority of fifteenth- and early sixteenth-century works in this form.

Power's name is attached to two other cyclic Masses in some sources, but these works are more likely to be by Dunstable and Benet respectively.[50] He wrote no motets in the strict sense of the term as then understood, although the cyclic *tenor* Mass is simply an application of motet technique on a large scale. In Power's case, the whole work resembles a single gigantic motet, with as many melodic statements (*colores*) as there are movements. Later composers, by repeating the *cantus firmus* within each movement, were often able to create, in effect, a cycle of motets of similar construction. This comparison is not purely a technical one, since there is good reason to suppose that the polyphonic Mass came to supersede the motet as the chief ecclesiastical ceremonial form in the fifteenth century.

For the motet proper in its latest medieval manifestation, however, and for much more besides, we have to turn our attention to the commanding figure of John Dunstable. What little can be said of his career has already been mentioned. The conjecture that he may have provided music for the coronation of Henry VI in Paris, while not intrinsically impossible, is purely speculative and relies too heavily on his supposed service in the chapel of the Duke of Bedford.[51] His links with the abbey of St Alban's, for which he wrote two motets, are much stronger. A still more specific piece of information is a report that a work entitled 'Preco prehemencie', combined with the text 'Inter natos mulierum', was performed at Christ Church Cathedral Priory, Canterbury, in 1416. Although the composer is not mentioned, Dunstable's motet of that title, celebrating the feast of St John the Baptist, does indeed use the antiphon 'Inter natos' as its *tenor*, and it is hard to believe that the reference could be to any other work.[52]

---

[49] In this, each movement begins with the same or similar phrase, usually in its harmony as well as its melody. Sometimes not every movement is so treated. A good early example is Arnold de Lantins's Mass 'Verbum incarnatum' (*Polyphonia Sacra*, ed. C. van den Borren (2nd edn., London, 1962), nos. 1–5, after an Italian MS of *c*.1440, Oxford, Bod. Lib., Can. misc. 213). An interesting late use occurs in Byrd's five-part Mass, except in the Sanctus; see also the Gloria and Agnus of the four-part Mass and, less strictly, the first three movements of the three-part Mass. Another means of unification was to adopt the same or similar metrical scheme for each movement: see the Gloria–Credo pair by Dunstable, *Works*, nos. 11–12, and the Gloria–Sanctus–Agnus cycle by Benet, discussed below, p. 143.

[50] See below, pp. 138, 143–5.

[51] See above, n. 3. The works in question are the Mass 'Da gaudiorum premia' and the four-part 'Veni sancte Spiritus': Harrison, *Music in Medieval Britain*, 244–5; but the date of both works is probably earlier (M. Bent, *Dunstaple*, 7–8).

[52] M. Bent, *Dunstaple*, 8. There is in fact a fragmentary manuscript of the work in the Chapter Library at Canterbury, Add. MS 128/3.

Eleven of Dunstable's isorhythmic motets survive complete.[53] They differ markedly from those of his English predecessors, though they do bear points of resemblance to some of the more elaborate isorhythmic structures amongst the Mass movements of the Old Hall manuscript. All his motets are based on the principle of the progressive diminution of a *cantus firmus*, but this structuralism is balanced by his concern for consonance and for melodic grace. The result is a uniquely satisfying art-form.[54] As in some of the French masterpieces of a century earlier, the form seems to grow out of a multiplication of the smallest rhythmic units: the half-beats become beats, two or three beats make a bar, two or three bars a 'super-bar', two or three super-bars a still larger unit, five or six of these a half-section, two half-sections a whole section, and three of these the entire work. But because of the successive diminutions of the *cantus firmus*, and hence of the sections of the work as a whole, a barren symmetry is avoided.

Although all Dunstable's motets are in honour of a saint or religious festival, it is probable that they were composed for specific occasions rather than for general use, and for performance outside the immediate context of the liturgy. 'Preco prehemencie', even if performed on 21 August 1416 'at such short notice ... [that it] must have been in the existing repertory of the choir',[55] is likely to have been composed in the first instance for some more special occasion than the normal twice-yearly celebration of St John the Baptist. This grand four-part work illustrates very well the structural principles just outlined: the first section is in two halves, each of which contains five metrical units which are divided into three 'super-bars', each consisting of three triple-time bars.[56] The three sections are related in the ratio 3:2:1; in section two the triple-time bars become duple, while in section three the 'super-bars' disappear, or rather are assimilated into ordinary triple-time bars. The four-part 'Veni sancte spiritus' (no. 32)

---

[53] Dunstable, *Works*, nos. 23–33. No. 34, a textless puzzle-canon from a late source, is in a different category; but we do also possess a textless *tenor*, attributed to Dunstable in some copies of Johannes de Muris' *Libellus cantus mensurabilis*, which may have belonged to a motet, and a *tenor* 'Ipsum regem', quoted by Morley in his *Plaine and Easie Introduction*, 178 (ed. Harman, 291), as an example of poor word-setting.

[54] It should be noted that in the three-part motets of Dunstable and his English contemporaries, unlike most 14th-cent. works, the second part behaves (as occasionally in Dufay) more like a texted *contratenor* than a true *motetus*, being usually in the same range as the *tenor* and melodically somewhat wayward; in the four-part motets the parts are in function *triplum*, *motetus*, *contratenor* (texted and more mobile than the *tenor*, except in 'Preco prehemencie'), and the *tenor* itself.

[55] M. Bent, loc. cit. The occasion was the celebration of Bedford's victory at Harfleur on 15 August—the very day on which the emperor Sigismund had signed the treaty of Canterbury with Henry. It is possible that Dunstable was named after St John the Baptist and owed a special devotion to him: see n. 6 above.

[56] This is the structure of the *tenor*. But the *contratenor* (though closer to the traditional character of a *contratenor* than usual) is simply divided into 22½ 'super-bars' (13½ + 9), each of which consists of two triple-time bars. In the second and third sections of the motet, the rhythms of the *contratenor* are modified to conform to the layout of the *tenor*.

has exactly the same metrical scheme (and therefore the same number of bars in the modern edition); 'Salve scema sanctitatis' (no. 30), on St Katherine, is even grander, each half-section being divided into six rather than five units.

Such calculations do not of themselves convey the flavour of these impressive compositions, nor do they do more than skate over the surface of their technical ingenuity. They are, however, doubtless the composer's own point of departure, from which he could proceed to make his other decisions: the choice of *cantus firmus* and its rhythmic interpretation; whether to include a fourth part and if so how to relate it to the *tenor*;[57] the choice (and in some cases perhaps the composition) of texts; and finally the filling out of the structure with actual notes in the upper parts. If this sounds schematic, so it is; but the medieval aesthetic is here subjected to the composer's own feeling for consonance and sonority, for tonal completeness, and for melodic grace. The evidence is that the most elaborate works are the earliest, and that in such three-part compositions as 'Albanus roseo rutilat' and 'Ave regina celorum, ave decus' (nos. 23, 24) he was moving towards the less rigid approach of his Masses and antiphons. The opening of the former illustrates his characteristic lyricism at its best (Ex. 57).[58]

Dunstable wrote two cyclic Masses of which we know (although they have not been preserved in their entirety) and of which his authorship is reasonably certain. There is also a number of single and paired movements. One of the latter groupings, the Gloria and Credo on 'Iesu Christe fili Dei vivi'[59] represents the *cantus-firmus* method at its most severe: the scheme of the Gloria, itself an isorhythmic composition of the strictest kind, is exactly repeated in the Credo. This was not a promising model for the future. The Mass 'Da gaudiorum premia' (of which only the Credo and Sanctus survive in full)[60] resembles Power's 'Alma redemptoris mater': each movement contains a single statement of the *cantus firmus*, and this is given the same rhythmic treatment each time, except for a varying number of rests at the beginning of each section. As for the most impressive of these

[57] See nn. 54, 56.
[58] Dunstable, *Works*, no. 23. D. R. Howlett has suggested that this work was composed in 1426, when the Duke of Bedford visited St Alban's abbey: 'A Possible Date for a Dunstable Motet', *MR*, 36 (1975), 81–4. It is possible that Benet's 'Tellus purpurium' (discussed below) was also written for that occasion. Dunstable's other motet for St Alban's was 'Dies dignus decorari' in honour of St Germanus: *Works*, no. 26.
[59] Ibid., nos. 15–16; previously published in DTO, lxi (Jg. xxxi), 114–19, nos. 60–1, and by Feininger in DPL, I/viii. The *cantus firmus* is a respond, without its verse, for Easter (with verse 'Qui surrexisti', AS, pl. 249) or Ascension (with verse 'Qui sedes', AS, pl. 270: the chants in AS, pls. 108, 252, and e are different): see Table I.
[60] *Works*, nos. 17, 18 (Credo and Sanctus), 69 (Kyrie 'Deus Creator', fragmentary), and 72 (incipit only of fragmentary Gloria). The Kyrie and Gloria fragments are printed only in the second edition. The *cantus firmus* (AS, pl. 290) is the verse 'Da gaudiorum premia' of the metrical respond 'Gloria patri geniteque proli' for the second nocturn and for the procession of Trinity Sunday. See Table I.

Ex. 57

Triplex. Alban perpetually reddens the stars with roseate beauty; with his purple blood sea-girt England is stained;

Duplum. And you hasten to yield [the passage to] the mountain whither you were to be led: ... (reading 'montem' for 'mortem', the last word being required to rhyme with 'pontem' in line 2).

works, the Mass 'Rex seculorum' (which may just possibly be by Power), it is not isorhythmic at all, though it does have a unifying *cantus firmus*.[61] Neither Dunstable nor Power, it seems, hit on the so-called double-cursus treatment used in the two great anonymous but enormously influential works shortly to be discussed.

The remainder of Dunstable's works fall into the categories of hymn, Magnificat, votive antiphon, and secular song. All the non-isorhythmic works classified by Bukofzer as motets are perhaps better thought of as antiphons, analogous to the devotional, paraliturgical *cantilena* rather than to the polytextual motet proper. They may or may not be founded upon the chant; of the three works based on what were to become the regular Marian antiphons, 'Ave regina celorum' and 'Regina celi letare' are founded on the chant, while 'Alma redemptoris mater' is not.[62] The first two embellish the chant in the top voice, against which *tenor* and *contratenor* provide a harmonic support in the manner of a Burgundian chanson. In the third, the chant is alluded to here and there, but it is not based consistently upon it and at the main cadential points departs from it altogether in tonality. Otherwise, however, it is indistinguishable from the other two in style.

This style, the 'pan-consonant' idiom already referred to in connection with the isorhythmic motets,[63] has seemed to many to be the essence of Dunstable's art; and yet, confronted as we are by the chaos of conflicting ascriptions in the mainly Continental sources of this music, it is very difficult to say exactly wherein Dunstable's personal voice resides. Not only Power but also Binchois, Bedyngham, Benet, and Forest are contenders for a number of works to which Dunstable's name is also attached, and in those circumstances the unsupported ascription of a single source must be regarded with circumspection. All the scholar can do is to accept the weight of the documentary evidence, such as it is; the evidence of the style is not yet a sharp enough tool for criticism.

A recent study strongly suggests that proportional relationships played a large part in the music of Dunstable—not only in the isorhythmic motets and *cantus-firmus* Masses, where it is only to be expected, but in other works as well.[64] Proportional analysis has helped to resolve difficult or corrupt passages and has sometimes revealed details of the presumed original versions prior to their modification by Continental scribes. It might also prove to be of help in resolving conflicting attributions, but more needs

[61] This is an antiphon of St Benedict, to be found in the Worcester Antiphonal, pl. 301 (see Ch. 2, n. 53). Printed Dunstable, *Works*, nos. 19–22 (Gloria, Credo, Sanctus, Agnus) and 70 (fragmentary Kyrie 'Deus creator'). See Table I.

[62] *Works*, nos. 37, 38, 40. The first two require a plainchant intonation, but this feature is not invariably associated with the use of a *cantus firmus* at this period.

[63] The term was first applied by Bukofzer, 'Fauxbourdon Revisited', *MQ*, 38 (1952), 22–47, to a work by Pyamour (see below).

[64] See B. Trowell, 'Proportion in the Music of Dunstable', *PRMA*, 105 (1978/9), 100–41.

to be discovered about the practice of other composers in this respect. It seems certain that the use of proportion—whether to achieve an abstract mathematical perfection (as for example in the use of 'triangular numbers') or to give a work a symbolic meaning (which might be mystical or quasi-architectural)—was of far greater importance in the fifteenth century than was at one time suspected. Dunstable's mathematical interests may have made him particularly prone to hidden constructionism, but he was far from unique in this respect.

The few works of Dunstable for which dates can be suggested with any plausibility seem to indicate that the majority of his surviving compositions were written by about 1435.[65] However, there are some indications that a particularly consonant form of the Burgundian chanson style was not the final stage in his artistic development. A five-part 'Gaude flore virginali', and also a Magnificat, were once in the Eton College manuscript; and a Marian antiphon, 'Descendi in ortum meum', pieced together from two fragmentary sources, shows some points of resemblance to a four-part 'Anna mater matris Christi' by his younger contemporary John Plummer. A brief quotation will show how skilfully Dunstable adapted his idiom to a four-part texture (Ex. 58).[66] Four-part writing was nothing new, of course, and the strange bitonality of the cadences is a characteristic of some much earlier work;[67] but the manipulative skill whereby the independence of the parts is reconciled with euphony shows the experience of a past master, and we may be grateful for this glimpse of the direction taken by Dunstable's music in his later years (see overleaf).

Dunstable's art did not shine in isolation: he was surrounded by a galaxy of talent in which the names of Forest, Pyamour, Benet, Bedyngham, Standley, Frye, and Plummer are prominent, together with such lesser luminaries as Blome, Richard Markham, Neweland, Soursby, Stone, Tyling, Driffelde, Wyvell, and Richard Cox. Of these, Forest and Benet are closest to Dunstable in manner, and their works (like those of Bedyngham) are often confused with his in the sources.[68] Forest was an imaginative composer. His 'Qualis est dilectus tuus' (ascribed to Forest in the Old Hall manuscript, though to 'Polmier' (i.e. Plummer) in the Modena source) belongs to the then popular genre of antiphons based on texts from the Song of Songs.[69]

---

[65] M. Bent, *Dunstaple*, 7.

[66] *Works*, no. 73. There is in fact a fragmentary Kyrie 'Deus creator omnium' by Plummer in one of the MSS (British Library Add. 54324) from which this edition has been made.

[67] See above, Ex. 52.

[68] For Forest see Bukofzer, 'Forest', in *MGG*; Hughes and Bent, in *MD*, 21 (1967), 97–147; *NGD*, s.v. 'Forest' (Margaret Bent). There was, however, a clerk at Worcester Cathedral who is a more likely candidate (information from Dr A. Wathey).

[69] *The Old Hall Manuscript*, no. 67. For settings of texts from the Song of Songs at this period see S. Burstyn, 'Early 15th-Century Polyphonic Settings of Song of Songs Antiphons', *AcM*, 49 (1977), 200–27.

Ex. 58

And I looked to see if the vines were flourishing ...

Its fluid line oscillates between duple and triple metre, rather in the manner of some contemporary carols (see below); though by no means as homophonic as Dunstable's 'Quam pulcra es', the most celebrated example of the genre,[70] it does contain a declamatory element, again a feature of the carol. Two extracts, the opening section and the setting of the text '[My beloved is] white and ruddy', will illustrate both points; the change of harmony at 'rubicundus' is perhaps to be regarded as a piece of word-painting (Ex. 59).

Somewhat similar is a setting of 'Quam pulcra es', the only recorded work of John Pyamour, Master of the Children of the Chapel in 1420, who died in 1431. Here, too, the third voice enters a few bars after the others, in the middle of a phrase in the text.[71] The work has been highly praised; but even more remarkable is Forest's own 'Tota pulcra es', with its lively treatment of the 'voice of the turtle' and its rhetorical conclusion.[72]

Some of this rhythmic liveliness appears in an isolated Credo copied

[70] *Works*, no. 44. The critical notes to the 2nd edn. cite seven sources and seven earlier modern editions.

[71] The work is printed in *The Oxford Anthology: Medieval Music*, no. 96. See also Burstyn, 'Song of Songs Antiphons' (n. 69), 208–10.

[72] DTO, lxxvi (Jg. xl), 80: the ending is quoted by Harrison, *Music in Medieval Britain*, 303–4. The change to *prolatio maior* (C) towards the end can be paralleled in Dunstable's 'Quam pulcra es' (see n. 70), though it is disguised in the modern edition by a change from halved to quartered note-values at that point.

Ex. 59

How are you to be chosen from the chosen ones, O most beautiful of women? [My friend] is shining and of a good colour.

Ex. 60

... and this is that [most glorious festivity]

twice into MS Trent 92, and in a small number of other compositions.[73]
But Forest's outstanding extant work is the antiphon 'Ascendit Christus',
copied into the Old Hall manuscript next to Dunstable's four-part 'Veni
sancte spiritus' but as different from it as chalk from cheese. Here recur
the fluid rhythms of 'Qualis est dilectus tuus', together with the rhythmic
liveliness and rhetorical pauses of 'Tota pulcra es'. It is historically important
as being one of the earliest examples—perhaps the very earliest—of an
antiphon, its text enunciated in all three voices but based on an 'alien'
cantus firmus, in this case the 'Alma redemptoris mater'. The work is readily
available in modern editions, but the unusual imitative treatment at the
first entry of the *cantus firmus* may be noted (Ex. 60).[74] Such a work is
a remote precursor of the *cantus-firmus* antiphons of the Eton Choirbook.

[73] Credo: Tr. 92, fos. 115ᵛ–116ʳ (no. 1472, anon.) and fos. 188ᵛ–190ʳ (no. 1541, ascribed to 'Forest').
Another Credo, in Tr. 92, fos. 113ᵛ–114ʳ (no. 1471) is anonymous, but is referred to as 'Patrem anglicanus'
in the index and may be by him: it is based on the chant 'Alma redemptoris mater' (see n. 48).
The attribution to Forest of an 'Anima mea liquefacta est' (two versions, one for three and one for
four voices, both published in DTO, lxxvi (Jg. 86–8) rests on Bukofzer's reading ('English Church
Music of the 15th Century', *NOHM,* iii. (1960), 165–213, at 195) of the inscription in Tr. 90, fo.
334 as 'Forest in agone [i.e. in a contest] composuit'. He remarks 'The name is erased but still legible',
but neither the name nor for that matter the word 'agone' are entirely certain. Forest also wrote
two motets, 'Alma redemptoris mater/ Anima mea' *a 3* (DTO, liii (Jg. xxvii/1), 34–5, in a faulty text
a third too low, after Tr. 90, fos. 341ᵛ–342ʳ (no. 1052)), and 'Gaude martir/ Collaudemus/ Habitabat
Deus', on St Oswald, in Mod. B, fo. 129ᵛ–130ʳ (unpublished). See Plates IV, V.

[74] *The Old Hall Manuscript,* no. 68; also in Dunstable, *Works,* no. 61.

John Benet, with about twenty certain or probable ascriptions in the sources, appears a still more considerable figure than Forest. Like many other English musicians of his day, he was a member of the London gild of parish clerks, known as the Confraternity of St Nicholas, membership of which was essential for any practising musician in the metropolis though by no means confined to them.[75] Benet appears on the first extant list of members, in 1448/9; he was also Master of the six choristers at St Anthony's hospital in the city of London in 1443, a post said to have become vacant in 1449.[76] Whether or not that was the date of his death is unknown. But he seems to have been one of Dunstable's older contemporaries, to judge from the style of some of his music. A Gloria–Sanctus–Agnus group combines an almost excessive concern for consonance with a use of major prolation (6/8 or 9/8 in transcription) which recalls some of the Old Hall music.[77] The association of the Gloria with the paired Sanctus and Agnus has been made by scholars on the basis of its similarity to them in metrical structure, texture, and even tonality. Each movement moves from 6/8 or 9/8 to 3/4 and back to 6/8 or 9/8; each is scored for the typical chanson combination of *discantus*, with *contratenor* and *tenor* below in the same range; and each moves from an initial G major towards D minor, though the range of cadential degrees in the Gloria is greater. The openings of the Gloria and Sanctus are similar enough to rank as a 'head-motive' (Ex. 61, overleaf). The Sanctus intonation, which is repeated for the Agnus, appears to have been devised by Benet himself. The frequent hemiolias in the 6/8 or 9/8 sections tend to obscure the underlying metre somewhat, while conversely much of the 3/4 material transgresses into compound-duple territory.

The work which has become known as a *Missa sine nomine* has also been assembled by editors from scattered sources, initially by R. von Ficker from the isolated movements in the Trent codices, in which only the Sanctus and Agnus are grouped together. Most of the movements in Trent are anonymous, except for one copy of the Credo, attributed to 'Leonellus', and one of the Sanctus, attributed to 'Dunstabl'. The subsequent discovery of the Aosta manuscript, which contains the Gloria, Sanctus, and Agnus, has yielded the plausible attribution to Benet, while the still more recent discovery of a fragmentary English source has given us an almost complete

[75] See H. Baillie, 'A London Gild of Musicians, 1460–1530', *PRMA*, 83 (1956–7), 15–28. Other names mentioned in the extant register include those of Plummer, Bedyngham, Burell, and Frye; the death of Nicholas Sturgeon is recorded in 1455.

[76] *NGD*, art. 'Benet' (B. Trowell).

[77] Gloria in Tr. 92, fos. 165ᵛ–167ᵛ, no. 1521, ed. DTO, lxi (Jg. xxxi), 85 (no. 46). Sanctus and Agnus in BL, fos. 24ᵛ–26', nos. 25–6 [26–7]: facsimile in *EEH*, i, pls. 51–4; there is an unsatisfactory transcription in *EEH*, ii, 120 seqq., and a much better one of the Agnus only in *Invitation to Medieval Music*, ed. R. T. Dart (London, 1967), i, no. 17. The view of Bukofzer (*NOHM*, iii. 195) that the Gloria was unrelated to the Sanctus and Agnus is offset by the considerations noted below.

Ex. 61

(a) And on earth peace to men of good will.
(b) Holy, holy, holy.

version of the Kyrie, troped with the text 'Omnipotens pater'.[78] The main interest of this work is in its use of a similar, but not identical, freely composed *cantus firmus* in each movement as a means of unification. It is also strongly unified by structure and above all by key, since not only each movement but each main section within a movement ends on the chord of C or (in the case of the two-part sections) a unison *c'*. For this reason it is not entirely free from monotony, but it is an impressive achievement all the same.

Most of Benet's surviving compositions are for the Ordinary of the Mass;[79] but he also composed an elaborate motet, 'Tellus purpurium/ Splendida flamigero', on a *tenor* as yet unidentified, and two antiphons with *cantus firmus*. The motet is a grand affair, based on the proportional scheme 3:2:1, setting texts in rhymed hexameters on the martyrdom of St Alban. (It is of interest that the distribution of the lines of the texts corresponds exactly to the musical structure: 6 + 4 + 2 in the *triplum* and 3 + 2 + 1 in the motetus.)[80] In the antiphon 'Gaude pia Magdalena', the *tenor*, based on the plainsong 'O certe precipuus', does not declaim the text of the other voices; such works are, perhaps, on the borderline between motet and antiphon. This one even has the 3:2:1 proportions of a motet, and is isorhythmic in all voices in the two halves of each section: it is, however, a less successful work than 'Tellus purpurium', with some rather awkward gaps in the sonority (for example in the bare octaves at bars 46, 88, and 100).[81]

It is characteristic of this period that little of what has survived, though

[78] The work is printed in Dunstable, *Works*, nos. 56–9 (Gloria, Credo, Sanctus, Agnus) and, in the 2nd edn. only, no. 71 (Kyrie); see the Critical Commentary on pp. 203–5, 210–11, for details of sources and ascriptions. The edition by Ficker, without the Kyrie, is in DTO, lxi (Jg. xxxi), 119–26, nos. 62–5.

[79] Amongst them may be cited a Gloria and Credo in Oxford, Bod. Lib., Add. C 87★, fos. 221^r–v, 224^r, imperfect, with concordances in Tr. 90, fos. 116^v–118^r (Gloria, no. 904, copied from Tr. 93, fos. 146^v–148^r, no. 1714) and fos. 188^v–189^v (Credo, no. 941, anon., copied from Tr. 93, fos. 258^v–259^v, no. 1772); Munich, Bayerische Staatsbibliothek, clm. 14274 (*olim* Mus. 3232a), nos. 269 (Gloria), 264 (Credo), both ascribed to Benet; printed in 'original' notation in E. Apfel, *Studien zur Satztechnik der mittelalterlichen englischen Musik*, 2 vols. (Heidelberg, 1959), ii. 123–9. In spite of the scribal pairing of these movements in the Oxford manuscript, and many points of similarity between them, it has been proposed (*NGD*) that the Credo Tr. 90, no. 940 (fos. 186^v–188^r, anon.) is the true 'pair' to the Gloria. There is an ingenious canonic Kyrie 'Deus creator omnium' by Benet in Tr. 87, fos. 130^r–131^r (nos. 107–8), printed CMM, xxxviii. 69–76 (no. 13), and a Gloria and Sanctus on 'Iacet granum' in the Aosta MS, nos. 70, 158.

[80] A modern edition, after Mod. B, is in *Invitation to Medieval Music*, iii, no. 8, ed. B. Trowell; it is also in the *Oxford Anthology*, no. 88. Cf. Dunstable's 'Albanus roseo rutilat', the texts of which are also in rhymed hexameters (though the rhymes are not so regularly distributed), referred to in n. 58.

[81] 'Gaude pia Magdalena' is in *Fifteenth-Century Liturgical Music*, i, no. 18 (the *cantus firmus* is the respond for first vespers of St Mary Magdalen (*AS*, pl. 456), first phrase only). Another motet has been reconstructed from the incomplete copy at the end of Mod. B by B. Trowell and A. Wathey, 'John Benet's "Lux fulget ex Anglia—O pater pietatis—Salve Thoma"', *St Thomas Cantilupe, Bishop of Hereford*, ed. M. Jancey (Hereford, 1982), 159–80.

preserved anonymously or attributed to such figures as Markham, Stone, or Wyvell, about whom nothing is known, falls below a remarkably high level. Stone's two antiphons on texts from the Song of Songs have been favourably noticed.[82] Soursby (or Saursbi, Sorbi) was perhaps John Souresby or Sowresby, instructor of the choristers at St Mary's, Warwick, in 1432/3 and 1448/9.[83] Two settings of the Sanctus, one of which is paired with an anonymous Agnus in the Aosta manuscript, show him to have been a master of euphony and of a wide-ranging melodic line. In the Aosta Sanctus, based on the fifth Sarum chant for the text, the treatment resembles that of a motet, bold in conception and finely wrought.[84]

Bedyngham, Standley, Frye, and Plummer (or Plomer) are more substantial figures, and are of a later generation. Bedyngham has suffered more than most from confusion of ascription: his most famous work, 'O rosa bella', is usually thought of as Dunstable's, while two English songs, 'Myn hertis lust' and 'So ys emprentid' have been given, perhaps correctly, to Frye. Two French songs, 'Durer ne puis' and 'Mon seul plaisir', are also ascribed to Dunstable and Dufay respectively. None of his sacred compositions has been published in full, though the DTO edition of his Mass 'Deuil angouisseux' comes close to being complete.[85]

Bedyngham was a member of the Confraternity of St Nicholas in 1448/9, and his death occurred in 1459 or 1460. The nature of some of his music suggests strong links with the Continent, where it was preserved in quantity; yet nothing is recorded of his life outside London.[86] His Mass 'Deuil angouisseux' is a noteworthy early example of so-called parody technique, in which a composer takes an existing polyphonic composition as a point of departure, quoting not only one or more of the original voice-parts in isolation, but retaining at least some small part of its polyphonic substance. Bedyngham's Mass is based on one of Binchois's finest compositions,[87] a ballade in which

[82] Burstyn, 'Song of Songs Antiphons' (n. 69), 217–19, with quotations. Stone was clerk of the Chapel Royal, 1465–7.

[83] NGD, s.v. 'Soursby' (B. Trowell). An earlier identification with Henry Soulbe, clerk of the Chapel Royal, 1446–52, is rejected.

[84] The first Sanctus setting is in DTO, lxi (Jg. xxxi), 102–3 (no. 53), after Tr. 90, fos. 265ʳ–266ᵛ (no. 977, anon., copied from Tr. 93, fos. 336ʳ–337ᵛ, no. 1808, anon.), Tr. 92, fos. 127ᵛ–128ʳ (no. 1486, anonymous, but described in index as 'Sanctus Anglicanus'), and Tr. 92, fos. 200ᵛ–202ʳ (no. 180, ascribed to 'Sovesby' or, more likely, 'Soresby'), where it is followed by an anonymous Agnus (fos. 253ᵛ–254ʳ, no. 181) based on the third Salisbury chant (GS, pl. 17), said to make a pair with the Sanctus. The Sanctus itself is printed in Invitation to Medieval Music, iv, no. 10, ed. B. Trowell: the plainsong intonation, transcribed from the MS, differs from the opening of the Sanctus in GS, suggesting rather the Continental version of the melody preserved as Vatican XVII, but the continuation of the cantus firmus demonstrates that the Salisbury form of the chant was intended.

[85] DTO, lxi (Jg. xxxi), 127–35, no. 66, without a concluding 'Benedicamus domino' which is said to belong to it.

[86] He became Verger of St Stephen's, Westminster, in 1458 (a post later held by Nicholas Ludford).

[87] Binchois, Die Chansons, ed. Wolfgang Rehm (Mainz, 1957), no. 50. Bedyngham does not seem to have used the four-part version, no. 51.

the 'grief' of the text is sublimated by a treatment that preserves a certain noble detachment. Bedyngham's Mass is by no means limited to this particular quality; it proceeds by a method of subtle allusion to the original far removed from the scissors-and-paste methods of Bartolomeo da Bologna's Gloria and Credo on his own *ballate* 'Vince con lena' and 'Morir desio' respectively.[88] It is perhaps closer in spirit to Dufay's Mass on 'Resveillies vous' (formerly known as 'Sine nomine'), though it has been argued in that case that the Mass came first and the chanson later;[89] and it is not really comparable to Standley's Mass and motet 'Que est ista', probably conceived as a whole from the outset, or to Frye's Mass 'Summe trinitati', of which the corresponding motet 'Salve virgo' may be the contrafactum of a lost Kyrie.[90] The opening of Bedyngham's Sanctus, together with part of the model, will illustrate his technique of allusion (Ex. 62, overleaf).

Bedyngham's other Mass[91] has not been much studied, and of his other sacred music all that remain are three two-part extracts copied, incredibly, by the Windsor musician John Baldwin at the end of the sixteenth century.[92] For the rest, he may have set English as well as French and Italian texts to music. 'Myn hertis lust' and 'So ys emprentid', if they are by him, are a successful transference of the idioms of the French ballade to English texts; to the French songs already mentioned may be added 'Se belle' and the renowned 'Le serviteur', while the Italian settings are 'Gentil madonna' and 'O rosa bella'.[93] The latter, which is really one of the most distinctive compositions of the entire fifteenth century, is also one of the most disputable as to attribution. Bukofzer remarked: 'The authorship of Dunstable appears certain in view of the fact that *Urb* [Rome, Bibl. vat., Urbino lat. 1411, ascribing the work to 'Donstaple'] contains a collection of chansons of an early group of composers active some time before Bedyngham. The scribe of *Porto* [Oporto, Bibl. com., 714, ascribing the piece to 'Johannes Bedyngham'] (a later MS) apparently confused the author of the concordantiae with that of the original composition.' But it has been pointed out that the inscription in the Trent manuscript containing the 'concordantiae'

---

[88] *Polyphonia Sacra*, ed. C. van den Borren (2nd edn., London, 1962), nos. 6, 7: see Bukofzer, 'Changing Aspects of Medieval and Renaissance Music', *MQ*, 45 (1958), 1–18, at 15, for the latter identification.

[89] D. Fallows, *Dufay* (London, 1982), 165–8.

[90] Below, pp. 149, 150.

[91] Tr. 88, fos. 46ᵛ–54ʳ (nos. 225–9, anon.); Tr. 93, fos. 30ᵛ–36ʳ (nos. 1613–15, Gloria, Credo and Sanctus, anon.); Oxford, Bod. Lib., Add. C 87★, fo. 223ʳ (Sanctus, imperfect, ascribed to 'Bedingham': printed in 'original' notation in E. Apfel, *Studien*, ii. 139–42, no. 58). The Kyrie of this Mass is untroped.

[92] London, Brit. Lib., R. M. 24. d. 2, fos. 104ᵛ–107ʳ.

[93] For details, including suggestions as to possible English originals for certain settings of French and Italian texts, see *NGD*, s.v. 'Bedyngham', and D. Fallows, 'English Song Repertories of the Mid-Fifteenth Century', *PRMA*, 103 (1976–7), 61–79. For 'O rosa bella', see MB, viii. 133–4, no. 54, and the Critical Commentary, ibid., 200–2. There is also a photograph of the Oporto source, with the ascription to Bedyngham, pl. 7.

Ex. 62

Ex. 62, continued

(a) Bitter grief, immeasurable rage . . . Woeful heart
(b) Holy, holy . . .

(a set of three additional parts, making six in all) can be taken to imply Bedyngham's authorship of the original, rather than of the concordantiae themselves, which are rather too late in style for Bedyngham.

'O rosa bella' is, in any event, quite unlike any other work of Dunstable. It is a setting of a *ballata* by Giustiniani in which, however, the implied repetition scheme of a *ballata* cannot be carried through since the first part of a composition (with which it ought to end) finishes on a half-close. To the modern ear, at least, this would sound unsatisfying, though two early manuscripts appear to demand it. It is noteworthy for its sensitive declamation of the text, and for its extensive use of imitation in the Burgundian manner. In the later fifteenth century it suffered not only the addition of the three concordantiae already mentioned, but a number of other adaptations including one by Ockeghem.[94]

Of the career of Standley (or Sandley) nothing is known, and of his music little need be said. His canonic Mass in the Trent MS 88 is a *tour de force* in which the *contratenor* is derived from the *tenor* by omitting all its notes below *b*; but it cannot be said to evince a strong character. The antiphon 'Que est ista', though anonymous in the source, is constructed in the same way and is reasonably believed to be by Standley.[95] A further Mass (by 'Standly') has been discovered in the Strahov manuscript in Prague, and there is another short antiphon, 'Virgo prefulgens avia', extant.[96]

[94] A second *contratenor*, making a four-part version, is included in MB, viii. Two duos, consisting of the original top part and one other (Tr. 90, fos. 361–362, belonging to no. 1074), are unpublished. A similar duo by Ockeghem (ibid., fo. 445ʳ, no. 1128), together with a three-part setting of the original top part by one Hert (ibid., fos. 444ᵛ–445ᵛ, no. 1127) are printed in *Invitation to Medieval Music*, iv. 8–15, no. 1.

[95] The Mass and the motet were first published in DPL, I/vi and IV/i respectively by L. Feininger, who discovered the secret of their canonic method and invented the title *Missa ad fugam reservatam*. More recently they have been published in CMM, xxxviii, nos. 9, 8.

[96] Prague, Strahov Monastery, D. G. IV. 47, containing the Mass, is also a source of the 'Veterem hominem' Mass, discussed below. 'Virgo prefulgens' is in Mod. B, ascribed to 'Sandley', and in Tr. 92, ascribed to 'Winchois' (i.e. Binchois), whence its appearance in *Les Musiciens de la cour de Bourgogne au XVᵉ siècle (1420–1467)*, ed. J. Marix (Paris, 1937), pp. 227 seqq.

Walter Frye is a much more considerable figure. He was admitted to the London gild of St Nicholas in 1456/7, and may have died in 1475. Although his music is preserved almost exclusively in Continental sources, there is no evidence that he actually worked or even travelled abroad. Nor is there any good reason to associate him with Ely: the *cantus firmus* of his Mass 'Flos regalis' is so far unidentified from any plainsong source, and the rhythmical antiphon 'Flos regalis Etheldreda', part of an Office in honour of Ely's patron saint, is only one of several texts beginning with those first two words.[97]

This particular Mass is the second of three by Frye to have been copied in the important Brussels manuscript[98] and it is the most elaborate, though not necessarily the last to have been composed. The Kyrie is omitted and does not survive elsewhere. A number of details of texture and tonality—the work is in four parts in G Mixolydian—and even the contour of the *cantus firmus* strikingly parallel those of the anonymous Mass 'Veterem hominem' shortly to be discussed. The third of these Masses, the three-part 'Nobilis et pulcra', for St Katherine, does include a troped Kyrie, 'Deus creator omnium': here the closest parallel is to the anonymous Mass 'Quem malignus spiritus' (see below). The first Mass, 'Summe trinitati', also in three parts, may have been written last: its constant use of duple metre and the simplicity of its rhythms and textures all point to the Continental chanson style of the later fifteenth century. As already mentioned, the antiphon 'Salve virgo mater' may be a contrafactum of the lost Kyrie of this Mass—presumably troped, although the *prosula* cannot be identified. A Mass 'So ys emprentid', ascribed to Frye, has survived in the remnants of a choirbook now in Lucca.[99]

This last piece of evidence strengthens the ascription to Frye of the song 'So ys emprentid' in the Mellon chansonnier, a large and sumptuous collection with a substantial English element. This source also includes two other pieces with an English text, both anonymously: 'Alas, alas', attributed to 'Frey' in the Schedel Songbook,[100] and 'Myn hertis lust', for which, as we have seen, the evidence elsewhere points to Bedyngham as the composer. The question of attribution is not easily resolved; all three songs suggest a composer in touch with the contemporary Continental chanson (as both Bedyngham and Frye clearly were); the emphasis on 5–3 triads perhaps fits Frye better than Bedyngham, even for 'Myn hertis lust', which

[97] For the supposed connection with Ely see S. Kenney, *Walter Frye and the Contenance Angloise*, (New Haven, Conn., and London, 1964), and her article 'Ely Cathedral and the "Contenance Angloise"', in *Musik und Geschichte* (Cologne, 1963), 35–49. See, however, *NGD*, s.v. 'Frye'. Kenney has edited the collected works of Frye in CMM, xix.

[98] Bibliothèque royale, MS 5557, first fascicle, also containing Masses by John Plummer and Richard Cockx (or Cox): cf. n. 43 for the modern edition.

[99] See Strohm, *Music in Late Medieval Bruges* (n. 43): no. 4 of the MS.

[100] Munich, Staatsbibliothek, MS 810 (= Cim 351a, *olim* Mus. 3232).

like the other two is not notably distinct in manner from his popular chanson 'Tout a par moy'.[101]

Frye's other widely copied work, the antiphon 'Ave regina celorum, mater regis angelorum',[102] is similar in style, well deserving the commonly bestowed appellation 'song-motet'. The text of this evergreen composition is not that of the 'Ave regina' in normal present-day use, which has as its second phrase 'ave domina angelorum', though it may be found in modern books with its plainchant melody.[103] Frye does not use the plainchant, and although we have styled the work as an antiphon, he actually employed a Lenten responsorial form of the little versified text, making lines 5 and 6 into a versicle and repeating lines 3 and 4 as 7 and 8.[104] In so doing he virtually created single-handed the form of the 'respond-motet' (ABCB) as it developed in the hands of Continental composers in the late fifteenth and the sixteenth centuries. Not only was his piece widely circulated: it was arranged in various ways and its freely composed *tenor* used as the basis for other composers' works, for example in the Mass and motet 'Ave regina celorum' by Obrecht.

Frye's other sacred works are of less interest, although his prose 'Sospitati dedit egros', for insertion into the ninth responsory of Matins for the feast of St Nicholas, is a rare example of a purely ritual item amongst this group of composers. Its sole source is the 'Pepys' manuscript, to be discussed in the next chapter, and it is perhaps a fairly late work, functional and rather austere. Perhaps Frye wrote his piece for the celebration of the feast by his confraternity.[105]

The last of this group of composers to be considered is John Plummer (Plomer, Polumier, etc.), a member of the Chapel Royal from at least 1437 until 1467 or later, and Master of its Children from 1444 to 1455. He also became verger of St George's, Windsor, presumably sometime between 1455 and 1460, when his name first appears in that connection, and from the records of which he disappears after 1484. Plummer was a man of substance; his importance as a composer has perhaps been exaggerated,[106] but his compositions interestingly reflect the transition to a later

---

[101] CMM, xix, no. 1, attributed to Frye in the Mellon chansonnier. There is a textless piece, probably a ballade, by Frye in the Strahov MS already mentioned (n. 96).

[102] CMM, xix, no. 5.

[103] e.g. *Liber Usualis* (1934 seqq.), 1864.

[104] Reese, *Music in the Renaissance*, 94, citing F. J. Mone, *Lateinische Hymnen des Mittelalters*, 3 vols. (Freiburg im Breisgau, 1854), ii. 202. In view of this, the theory that Frye's work was originally a ballade, ventilated in Fallows, 'English Song Repertories' (n. 93), 68, seems unnecessary. Reese quotes the work in full, pp. 94–5.

[105] CMM, xix, no. 7, and again in CMM, xl (*The Music of the Pepys Manuscript*), no. 91. The 'Deo gratias' and 'Amen' following it in the MS, and included in CMM, xix, do not belong to the work.

[106] e.g. by Bukofzer in *NOHM*, iii. 198–202, a perceptive discussion nevertheless. The authoritative account of Plummer's life is by Trowell in *NGD*.

fifteenth-century style, and his four authentic antiphons[107] make use of such devices as canon and invertible counterpoint as well as employing varied vocal groupings. Two short passages from his 'Descendi in ortum meum' will serve to illustrate the former techniques (Ex. 63).[108] Yet Plummer looked backwards as well as forwards, and the ending of his most elaborate surviving work, 'Anna mater matris Christi', in spite of its picturesque repetition (of which there is a good deal in Plummer), harks back to the archaic cadence of Ex. 52 (Ex. 64, p. 154).[109] The Brussels Mass, on the other hand (if it is really his), is remarkably bold in its melodic floridity and the free use of accidentals.

Amongst the large amount of anonymous English (or apparently English) music surviving mainly in Continental sources, pride of place must be given to the Mass-cycles, several of which are conceived on a large scale and are of considerable intrinsic merit. The criteria for determining the English origin of such works are difficult to formulate precisely, but they would include the following: use of a Salisbury (or other English) version of a chant; inclusion of a troped Kyrie (more particularly with an 'English' *prosula* such as 'Deus creator omnium'); partial survival in an English fragmentary source; and single- or double-cursus layout of the chant in the same arbitrary rhythmicization in each movement, usually in the context of a bipartite (but sometimes tripartite) mensural structure. These are not invariable features, nor do they all necessarily exclude Continental authorship, but taken together they help to reinforce impressions gained from less tangible qualities of style. As for the composers themselves, speculation would be premature, although there are interesting parallels between the anonymous 'Quem malignus spiritus' and 'Veterem hominem', and between Frye's 'Nobilis et pulcra' and 'Flos regalis', respectively.

Of a group of four such works recently published,[110] 'Fuit homo missus' and 'Quem malignus spiritus' are the most straightforward, being in three parts with *cantus firmus* in the lowest voice. Though somewhat similar in general conception, they are not entirely comparable. 'Fuit homo missus', based on the Gradual for the vigil of St John the Baptist,[111] lays out its *cantus firmus* in notes of equal value, and even the length of the duos, in which the *tenor* is silent, are identical in the Kyrie, Gloria, and Credo:

---

[107] *Four Motets*, ed. B. Trowell (PMMS, 1968). 'Qualis est dilectus tuus' is believed to be by Forest (see above).

[108] Ibid., no. 1: cf. Ex. 68.

[109] Ibid., no. 4; also in *Fifteenth-Century Liturgical Music*, i, no. 17. In the source (Oxford, Bod. Lib., MS Add. C 87★, fos. 234ᵛ and 222ʳ), the top part is marked as optional.

[110] *Fifteenth-Century Liturgical Music*, ii (EECM, xxii), containing the Masses 'Fuit homo', 'Quem malignus spiritus', 'Salve sancta parens', and 'Veterem hominem'.

[111] GS, pl. 188. The work was first published by L. Feininger, with an attribution to Power, in DPL, I/ix.

Ex. 63

continued

Ex. 63, continued

(a) [I looked to see] if the vines were flourishing, and the pomegranates ripening.
(b) turn back . . .

Ex. 64

Take us to live with Christ. Amen.

hence those three movements are of equal length. The scheme of the Sanctus and Agnus is varied to allow for duo settings of the 'Pleni', 'Benedictus', and the second 'Agnus dei'. The work is notable for its melodic grace, and for the consonance of its duos, somewhat compromised at the entrance of the *tenor*. One is tempted to suggest that Benet might have composed this work, though some features, such as the speeded-up cadences and the divided chords at the ends of sections, have no exact parallel in his output.

'Quem malignus spiritus', based on a responsory from the rhymed Office of St John of Bridlington, is rather more complex in its layout and in its rhythmic style. The same is true of the Mass 'Salve sancta parens', based on the well-known Marian Introit, and to which a fourth part, probably spurious, has been added in the Continental sources. An English fragment of the work preserves the Kyrie, incomplete, and may reflect its original three-part scoring. The four-part writing of 'Veterem hominem', on the other hand, is intrinsic to the work and is a textural novelty which it shares with Frye's 'Flos regalis' and the anonymous 'Caput'. In each case, the fourth voice is a bass or second *contratenor* below the *tenor*, which shares its range with the (first) *contratenor*. Since none of these works can be dated with any precision, it cannot be proved that any of them preceded Dufay's adoption of the same texture in his later Masses, though it seems likely that 'Caput' in particular (once believed to be by Dufay himself) may have influenced him in this respect. If that is so, this group of works will have been of decisive importance in the development of Renaissance choral texture.

'Veterem hominem' is a work of immense originality, vigour, and finesse.[112] The plainsong melody on which it is based is the first of a series of six antiphons for Lauds on the feast of the Baptism of Christ;[113] unusually, these are all variants of the same seventh-mode melody. This melody is stated in the *tenor*, twice in each movement, in a series of arbitrarily chosen rhythmic values, first in triple time and then in duple time. There are earlier instances of such double statements, but here the duple-time version is not proportionally related to the triple-time one. The chosen values are repeated in each movement; but the movements are not exact replicas of each other because of differences in the lengths of the rests in the passages in which the *tenor* is silent, and because of some further structural variation in the Sanctus and Agnus (see Table 1).

These are the bare bones of the structure. They are clothed in a bold and resourceful web of melody in the three accompanying voices, closely knit without any sacrifice of clarity. The normal four-part texture is relieved by a number of passages for two voices; in the introductory duos to each section these are always the upper two, but elsewhere other combinations are employed, and in the 'Pleni sunt celi' and the second 'Agnus', for example, the combinations I/II, I/III, and II/IV are used in turn (the *tenor* part in the I/III combination retaining its plainchant-bearing role). Some idea of the variety and richness of the four-part writing can be illustrated from the passage which immediately follows these duets in the second 'Agnus' (Ex. 65, overleaf).

[112] It was first edited by L. Feininger, together with the Masses 'Caput' and 'Christus surrexit', with an attribution to Dufay for all these, in his series *Monumenta polyphoniae liturgicae sanctae ecclesiae romanae*, I/ii (Rome: Societas Universalis Sanctae Ceciliae, 1951).
[113] *GS*, pl. 95.

Ex. 65

Ex. 65, continued

... have mercy on us.

The Mass 'Caput', about which so much has been written,[114] is an even grander creation, though it is only slightly longer and if anything rather less vigorous in style than 'Veterem hominem'. It has many points of similarity with it: the general layout, the choice of a seventh-mode *cantus firmus* (though a much longer one), and the use of the 'Deus creator omnium' *prosula* for the Kyrie are three of them. It may well have been written by a different composer in emulation of the other work, but hardly by Dufay, whose authorship is somewhat diffidently attested in the Trent codices and nowhere else. The arguments for an English origin are those relevant to all the anonymous Masses so far discussed: the use of a Kyrie with *prosula* of English Use, the adoption of a chant in its Salisbury version as a basis for the work, and its survival in two fragmentary English sources.

The conceptual link between 'Caput' and 'Veterem hominem' goes deeper than the points so far noted. Just as 'Veterem hominem' was based on an antiphon for the Baptism of Christ, so 'Caput' is based on the final word, set to a lengthy melisma, of the antiphon 'Venit ad Petrum', sung in the Salisbury and some other Uses at the ceremony of the washing of the feet on Maundy Thursday.[115] Christ's own baptism is symbolically complemented by his washing of the feet of the disciples. But Peter requests that not only his feet, but his hands and his head ('caput') be washed. The symbolism reflects not only baptism but Peter's position at the head

---

[114] The fundamental study, though he accepted the then usual attribution to Dufay, is that of Bukofzer in *Studies in Medieval and Renaissance Music*, 217–310: see also his contribution 'Caput Redivivum' to *JAMS*, 4 (1951), 98–102. The authorship and the circumstances have been touched on, amongst others, by T. Walker in *Abstracts of the American Musicological Society*, 1969; by M. and I. Bent in *JAMS*, 22 (1969); by A. Planchart, 'Guillaume Dufay's Masses: Notes and Revisions', *MQ*, 58 (1972), 1–23, and by G. Chew, 'The Early Cyclic Mass as an Expression of Royal and Papal Supremacy', *ML*, 53 (1972), 254–69. There are several editions: DTO, xxxviii (Jg. xix/ I), 17–46; the edition by Feininger (see n. 112); CMM, I/ii, 75–101 (Dufay, *Omnia opera*, ed. H. Besseler); and the edition by Planchart, *Three Caput Masses* (Collegium Musicum, I/ v, no. i; New Haven, Conn., 1964). All carry attributions to Dufay. Among sources not yet used by editors are the Brit. Lib. Add. MS 54324, containing the Kyrie (see M. and I. Bent, *JAMS*, 22 (1969)), and the Lucca fragment described by Strohm, *Music in Late Medieval Bruges* (n. 43), where the *tenor* is headed 'Caput drachonis'.

[115] *GS*, pls. 96–7 (the melisma itself is on pl. 97).

of the Church, and it has been suggested that the Mass may have been composed to commemorate the anticipated reunion of the Eastern and Western Churches, promulgated at the Council of Florence in 1439 though never consummated.[116]

However this may be (and 'Caput' is only one of a number of Masses suggestive of the general notions of anointing and of royal or papal supremacy),[117] the Mass remains one of the finest achievements of the English spirit. As noted above it almost certainly influenced not only Dufay, who adopted its distinctive scoring and some aspects of its *cantus-firmus* treatment in his own later Masses, but also Ockeghem, whose soaring lines are in many ways clearly linked to the English idiom of this and similar works. In his own 'Caput' Mass Ockeghem expressed his indebtedness in the most direct fashion by borrowing not only the *cantus firmus* but also its rhythmic layout, simply transposing it to the bass in order to achieve a wholly distinctive harmonic idiom. He may have believed the work to be by Dufay, but his sincerest form of flattery ensured the preservation of a certain Englishness in the mainstream of European music at a time when direct contact had failed.

These Masses, together with much of the work of Power, Dunstable, Benet, Forest, Bedyngham, Frye, Plummer, and their lesser contemporaries,[118] found such favour on the Continent that they multiplied rapidly there in copies of greater or lesser faithfulness to the originals (some changes were merely scribal; others, such as adaptations of texts—the Kyrie texts were especially subject to tampering and the movement sometimes omitted altogether—or alterations to the mensuration signs, affected the actual music). There was indeed a 'craze' for English musicians and their work that has no parallel in later times; but so short-lived was it that by about 1475 Tinctoris could say that the English were 'popularly said to shout while the French sing', and lament the fact that they had lost their flair for innovation.[119] This is scarcely a fair reflection on the quality of English music in the later fifteenth century, and the isolation was undoubtedly due in part to political factors; but it cannot be denied that native composers

---

[116]   Chew, 'The Early Cyclic Mass', 260.

[117]   Ibid., 256. In addition to the examples which he cites may be mentioned the fragmentary Mass 'Tu es Petrus' in the Coventry source of the 'Caput' Mass (Bukofzer, *JAMS*, 4 (1951), 98–102).

[118]   Estimates naturally differ, but there are at least a dozen further cycles or pairs, preserved anonymously or attributed to such figures as Bloym and Driffelde, in Continental sources; others are found, mostly as fragments, in English sources, and there are numerous single movements in both English and Continental MSS.

[119]   *Proportionale musices* (ed. A. Seay, *CSM*, XXII/iia), Dedication; translated from the text in CS, iv. 153–5, by O. Strunk, *Source Readings in Music History* (London, 1952), 195. In the expression 'anglici vulgariter iubilare Gallici vero cantare dicuntur', the term 'iubilare' is perhaps intended to convey the florid style of English music as opposed to the more syllabic style beginning to be fashionable on the continent (Harrison, *Music in Medieval Britain*, 258); but in its context the remark is certainly intended to be derogatory.

began to turn in on themselves, as it were, and to cultivate more assiduously than before the more homespun elements in the national style.

These elements had never been wholly absent, and the link with the simpler styles represented in the Old Hall manuscript can be traced in the forms of secular song and carol, and in the workaday music for the liturgy that never ceased to be composed.

There seems to have been a revival of non-sacred, or at least non-liturgical, song to English words in the fifteenth century, though this may be due to the accidents of survival rather than to any real change of direction. Monophonic secular music was in any case rarely written down after the end of the trouvère period, though it is something of a mystery why England did not further develop the tradition of the London *pui*[120] and cultivate an art of courtly song in the fourteenth and fifteenth centuries comparable to the German *Minnesang* and *Meistergesang*. England's cultural links were of course with France rather than with Germany, and courtly song in four-teenth-century France was usually a more sophisticated affair, being either polyphonic or, if not polyphonic, at least rhythmically lively and up-to-date. The old trouvère manner, so far as its music was concerned, had disappeared. But there are no remnants of such an art in England either, and most of the lyric poetry of the fourteenth century seems to have been devised to be spoken.[121] The revival of secular polyphonic song in the early fifteenth century does in fact seem to have been the result of renewed contact with French sources. Two of the songs with French texts in the Cambridge Songbook of about 1415 are actually adaptations of late fourteenth-century Continental works, while many others, including most of those with English texts, are in modified virelai form (AbbA, A being in principle a refrain), though the da capo is not normally indicated.[122] The same is true of a similar but now much more fragmentary collection in the Bodleian Library,[123] which is related to the Cambridge MS in so far as one of the songs, 'I rede that thu be joly and glad', is in both. The repertory includes settings of English, French and even Latin and macaronic (Latin and English) texts. Even the Latin ones, however, are very straightforward in character; they include two rounds, a 'Benedicamus domino', and a respond verse, 'Gloria

---

[120] Above, pp. 70–1.

[121] Chaucer's rondeau 'Now welcom somer' at the end of *The Parlement of Foules*, is introduced with the line 'The note, I trowe, maked was in Fraunce'; but it is not certain that Chaucer had a particular tune, or polyphonic composition, in mind. The French title added in one source is in the wrong metre (see the notes to Skeat's edition).

[122] Cambridge, Univ. Lib., Add. 5464; facs. ed. R. Rastall (Leeds: Boethius Press, 1973); for an edition of all the songs see Bibliography II. A, s.v. *Four French Songs*. For details of the adaptations, see Wilkins, *Music in the Age of Chaucer*, 107–9.

[123] MS Douce 381.

in excelsis Deo', in Cambridge and the fragment of an Offertory, 'Felix namque', said to be based on the Bridgettine version of the chant, in Oxford. Since the only Bridgettine house in England was the newly founded Syon monastery on the river Thames, the Oxford manuscript, or at least this particular part of it, may have come from there. Like the 'Gloria in excelsis', and like the macaronic pieces 'Pater noster most of myght', 'Ave Maria I say', and 'Credo in Deum that ys' from the Cambridge manuscript, it is a simple piece of two-part counterpoint in major prolation (modern 6/8).[124]

These features are in fact typical of both collections. The second piece in the Cambridge manuscript, 'Thys ʒol' (i.e. 'yule') has a lower part marked 'Tenor [gap] *quod* Edmund*us*', which may perhaps refer to the authorship of the piece as a whole rather than simply to that of the *tenor*. A short extract will convey something of the flavour of this scrapbook of minstrelsy, in which we may perhaps discern the efforts of a hired musician to cheer up a shivering nobility as they foregathered for the festive season (Ex. 66).

The later history of English song in the fifteenth century illustrates the gradual assimilation of current trends in France, though the sources are pitiful in quantitative terms.[125] A few such songs, including some to French and Italian texts, have already been mentioned. Discussion of this repertory has tended to focus upon settings of English words, but it should be emphasized that some composers, such as Bedyngham and Frye, were equally at home with French and (at least in Bedyngham's case) Italian verse. In any event there was a good deal of adaptation of pieces to different texts—even, on occasion, to Latin sacred texts—and the priority of one or the other cannot always be readily established. When English composers set French texts, these were nearly always in the form of the rondeau (ABaAabAB, in which capital letters represent the refrain and small letters new text to the music of the refrain), such as Dunstable's 'Puisque m'amour', Bedyngham's 'Durer ne puis', 'Mon seul plaisir', and 'Se belle', and the eight or so genuine songs of the expatriate Robert Morton.[126] Songs to English words may be ballades (musical form AAB, the last line of each stanza being the refrain) or freely composed.

Much of this material is part and parcel of the common currency of

---

[124] Printed as organ music by R. T. Dart, 'A New Source of Early English Organ Music', *ML*, 35 (1954), 201–5, and by Apel in CEKM, i. 10. On Syon, see Knowles, *The Religious Orders in England*, ii. 175–81; for the identification of the chant, Harrison, *Music in Medieval Britain*, 193.

[125] Fallows, 'English Song Repertories' (n. 93).

[126] 'Puisque m'amour' and 'Durer ne puis' are in Dunstable, *Works*, nos. 55, 64; 'Mon seul plaisir' is in CMM, I/vi, no. 90, as a doubtful work of Dufay; 'Se belle' is unpublished in its original form, but a keyboard version in the Buxheim Organ Book, Munich, Bayerische Staatsbibliothek, Cim 352b, fo. 91 (no. 171), is edited by B. A. Wallner, *Das Buxheimer Orgelbuch*, 3 vols. (Kassel, 1958–9; Das Erbe deutscher Musick, I/xxxviii–xxxix), i. 224. Morton's songs are available in an edition by Allan Atlas (New York: Broude, 1981).

Ex. 66

At this Christmastide the best advice you can take is to be a merry man, and leave care
and put out strife: thus think I to lead my life.

courtly song at this period and can be deduced to be English only because
an English text is set (and even here an adaptation from a Continental
original is sometimes a possibility) or because of an ascription to an English
composer.[127] Beside these works in an 'international' idiom, however, are
a number of more homely pieces with English (occasionally Latin) texts
in such sources as the Bodleian manuscripts Ashmole 1393 and 191, Selden
B 26, and the slightly later 'Ritson' manuscript (London, British Library,
Add. 5665). Even here, this repertory is not a totally isolated one, as the
unascribed fragment of 'So ys emprentid' in Ashmole 191 indicates. Many
of the songs are in two parts only, but one of the completed Ashmole
pieces, the deservedly well-known 'Go hert hurt with adversite', is a three-
part piece which manages to combine a sophisticated technique with an
attention to the spirit and rhythm of the English words which is not often
found at this date outside the carol. The transference of the beginning

---

[127] Other criteria include those of form (e.g. incompatibility with verbal text as given in the source),
style, and position in the MS. Some of the ramifications are dealt with by Fallows, 'English Song
Repertories' (n. 93), and esp. pp. 69–70.

of line 4 of the poem to the end of its first musical section is (if the words are not more seriously misplaced in the manuscript than appears to be the case) a particularly telling touch (Ex. 67).[128]

Another vein appears in the comic dialogue '"Tappster!" "Drinker?"' from Selden B26,[129] a forerunner of the erotic '"Be pes, ye make me spille my ale"' in the Ritson manuscript, the contents of which will be discussed more fully in the next chapter. But for a firmly established tradition of English text-setting, we must look to the polyphonic carol.

The carol is one of those forms easier to describe in technical terms than to account for. Literary sources make it clear that it was originally a round-dance with a refrain sung by all and stanzas sung by the leader. As such, because of its popularity and its hypnotic character, it was much disliked by the Church. It was apparently a Franciscan idea to adapt the carol (as well as other forms of profane song) to sacred and edifying texts, thereby bringing it within the pale of what was considered tolerable. In this form it must be considered analogous to the Italian *lauda* and the Spanish *cantiga de loor*, but very few examples of the carol at this stage of its evolution have survived with their music. What appears to be a uniquely English phenomenon is the polyphonic carol, at first to English, or a mixture of English and Latin words, and subsequently also to wholly Latin texts, as a predominantly serious and edifying form with a strong link with the Christmas season.[130]

A large number of lyrics in carol form have survived without music, and they embrace all areas of subject-matter, sacred and secular. The carol has been defined by Greene as a poem 'intended, or at least suitable for singing, made up of uniform stanzas and provided with a burden which begins the piece and is to be repeated after each stanza'. The burden, in this sense, is a separate formal unit, the word 'refrain' being reserved for a single line repeated from stanza to stanza. The distinction is a useful one and is retained in the following discussion, though this use of the word 'burden' is an anachronism.

In considering the polyphonic carol, however, it becomes evident that further issues remain—those of language, usage, form, scoring and so on.

---

[128] Edited in full in *Invitation to Medieval Music*, i. 14–15, transposed up a fifth. All the Bodleian sources may be studied in facsimile in *Early Bodleian Music*, 3 vols. (London, 1901–13), i; most of the pieces are edited (not always adequately) in vol. ii.

[129] Also in A. T. Davison and W. Apel, *Historical Anthology of Music* (Cambridge, Mass., 1946), i, no. 85.

[130] Cf. Ch. 2, pp. 103–4. The definitive work, so far as the English texts are concerned, is *The Early English Carols*, ed. R. L. Greene. The music of the 15th-cent. examples, including those to Latin texts, has been edited in full by John Stevens, *Medieval Carols* (London, 1952), MB, iv.

Ex. 67

Go, heart, hurt with adversity, and let my lady see thy wounds; and say this to her as I say it to you: farewell my joy. And welcome, pain, until I see my lady again. ('Hert' is a pun on 'hart', i.e. 'deer', and 'heart'.)

Note: The underlay has been freely adjusted. In the lower staff the *contratenor* has no flat in the key-signature, but the accidental seems to be needed whenever the note occurs. The second line of the *tenor* part also has no key-signature, and its application in bar 7 is editorial; an accidental is added which can be taken to apply to bars 8–11, after which the key-signature is restored. A few incorrect time-values are emended without comment. Neither the *tenor* nor the *contratenor* has text, but the former at least could legitimately be sung.

None of the musical sources bears a generic title, either for collections or for individual pieces; and while there is no dispute that 'carol' is the appropriate term for a substantial body of pieces in both English and Latin, it does not follow that the question of form thereby disappears. Even in purely literary manuscripts, it is not always clear whether a verbal cue for the burden means that it is to be repeated in full between each stanza, particularly if these have a single-line refrain as well. The addition of music simply accentuates the problem, and often adds to it in that verbal directions are, if anything, even less explicit in musical manuscripts. The burden, moreover, may be repeated in fuller scoring, and the question arises as to whether both versions are to be repeated between each stanza. (The term 'chorus' is sometimes used to denote three-part sections.) Sensible solutions are given in the modern edition, but there are in some cases viable alternatives.

The truth is that, well established though the principle of carol form certainly is, it is not the most important thing about the music itself. It should not be surprising that a few pieces in different forms are directly comparable. What is more important is that we have here a body of homely lyric, expressing in English, Latin, or both, the simple truths of revealed religion or natural morality, set to music which in a largely inexplicable way is the perfect accompaniment. It is in a straightforward, mostly cheerful style, well adapted to keeping up the spirits of its hearers during the dark time of the year or to enlivening the liturgy in an unofficial way. The performers are clerics rather than minstrels; clerics typically, one feels, of the large private establishment, available for service in chapel or hall as occasion required. There is literary support for thinking of the carol as another manifestation of the old *conductus*;[131] to serve as a substitute for the 'Benedicamus domino' in the Office is no doubt only one possible function out of many for both forms, but it is one which, if substantiated, can help us to grasp the link between them.[132] Their preoccupation with the Christmas season is another common feature. The polyphonic carol is nearly always a high-minded genre; the musical settings of satirical, amorous, or erotic songs in this form have mostly disappeared. These will have been the province of a lower class of musician, for production at a more advanced stage of an evening's entertainment; and the few surviving specimens with music are perhaps examples of the higher clerical wit rather than of a genuinely popular art.

The earliest collection of carols is the 'Trinity roll', containing the famous Agincourt song;[133] the two other important sources from up to about 1460 are the Selden manuscript (which also has a version of the Agincourt song)

---

[131] e.g. in *Sir Gawain and the Green Knight*, line 1655: 'As coundutes of Krystmasse and carolez newe', cited by R. L. Greene, *Early English Carols*, p. xxviii. Greene is mistaken, however, in believing the *conductus* to be solely a polyphonic form.

[132] Harrison, *Music in Medieval Britain*, pp. 118–19, 127 (as to the *conductus*), 416–18 (as to the carol). The convivial function of the carol is dealt with ibid. 418–19.

[133] Cambridge, Trinity College, MS O. 3. 58.

and the Egerton manuscript, both of which also contain liturgical music.[134] The technical progress of the carol in the fifteenth century—its advance from two to three parts, its tendency to an increase of rhythmic subtlety and formal complexity—can be studied in the pages of the modern edition. All is anonymous, except for the name 'Childe' at the head of '[Y]blessid be that Lorde' in the Selden manuscript (fo. 28^v) and the initials 'quod J.D.' at the end of the words of 'I pray 3ou alle' in the same source. But three of the anonymous antiphons in that manuscript are ascribed elsewhere to Power, Dunstable, and Plummer respectively, and while the identification of J.D. as John Dunstable lacks confirmation, there is no reason in principle why musicians of that calibre, particularly if in the service of a noble house-hold, should not have been involved in that kind of music-making. Various conjectures have been made about Childe,[135] but they cannot be verified, and his carol (if it is his) does not differ in style from the others.

It is difficult to select adequately from this hoard of material, but Ex. 68 overleaf, from the Selden manuscript, will illustrate a number of points: the use of a Latin burden and refrain in an otherwise English text, the scoring for two voices in unison as well as in two and three parts; and the influence of faburden (see p. 112) on the three-part writing. This is a more reflective carol than some, substituting perfect time (3/4) for major prolation (3/8); notice also the cunning use of syncopation (in the medieval sense), the extra beat in bar 32 being lost again in bars 35–6. In some carols, however, such metrical irregularities are not ironed out so neatly.[136]

The liturgical music of the Selden manuscript varies from the highly sophisticated work of Power, Dunstable, and Plummer to some really crude (if imaginative) writing.[137] A few pieces have escaped the net cast by recent scholarship, amongst them the fascinating two-part vernacular sequence 'Glad and blithe mote thou be', based both in text and in music on the Latin Sequence 'Laetabundus exultet fidelis chorus alleluya'.[138]

The origin of the Selden manuscript is not known for certain, though it has been assigned (on no firm evidence) to Worcester Cathedral Priory by Greene.[139] The Egerton source is most convincingly linked with the

---

[134] Oxford, Bod. Lib., Arch. Selden B 26; London, Brit. Lib., Egerton 3307; facsimile of the former in *EBM*, i, pls. 37–97, 109, with transcriptions in ii. 74–180.

[135] Summarized in *MGG*, Supplement, art. 'Childe'.

[136] Selden B 26, fo. 13^v; *Medieval Carols*, no. 23. In my view, there is no need to sing both burdens at the beginning and between each stanza.

[137] The liturgical music of this manuscript is printed in *Fifteenth-Century Liturgical Music*, i. No. 6 of this edition, 'Miles Christi', a hymn in honour of St Thomas of Lancaster, is a good specimen of the bolder use of dissonance.

[138] Oxford, Bod. Lib., Selden B 26, fos. 19^v–20^r. For the music of the Sequence, see *Le Tropaire-prosaire de Dublin*, pls. 21, 46. There was some confusion as to the melodic shape of the fourth double-versicle of this tune: the polyphonic version seems to have been based on the form found at pl. 21 as corrected in the MS. For the Latin text, see *Missale Sarum*, cols. 872, 771★; AH, liv. 5.

[139] *The Early English Carols*, 2nd edn., 314.

Ex. 68

Nourishing mother of the redeemer. As I lay one night I thought I saw a seemly light, called Mary bright. *Nourishing mother of the redeemer.*

Note: Text beneath lowest voice only, though all are to be sung. Three more stanzas follow. It is reasonably certain that BURDEN II (but not BURDEN I) should follow each of them.

★ MS 'say'.

Chapel Royal or St George's, Windsor.[140] Its main interest, apart from the repertory of carols, lies in its provision of a substantial body of music for Holy Week and Easter. This is for the Use of Salisbury, and the alternative suggestion that the manuscript hailed from the remote Cistercian abbey of Meaux is not really compatible with it. The manuscript includes the processional music for Palm Sunday, the St Matthew Passion (incomplete, and not in its liturgical place), a ferial Mass, doubtless for use in Holy Week, the Passion according to St Luke, and a number of other hymns, antiphons, and responds. There is also an impressive four-part antiphon or motet, 'Cantemus domino', with wordless *contratenor* and *tenor*, the latter based on the plainchant 'Gaudent in celo'. This is an accomplished piece, as is the isorhythmic setting of 'O potores exquisiti', a drinking-song which can be traced back to the thirteenth century.[141] This deserves quotation for its matching of a jocular text to music of considerable finesse (Ex. 69, overleaf).[142]

The liturgical music is much more restrained, but it too is highly accomplished in its own way, and the two Passions are two of the three earliest polyphonic settings known (see below). The entire *synagoga* part, that is to say that of the crowd and all the characters other than Christ and the Evangelist, is given polyphonic treatment.[143]

Another liturgical source of about this time or perhaps a little earlier, Shrewsbury School MS VI, also deserves mention. This is the *triplex* partbook of a polyphonic processional, one of an original set of three, from the diocese of Lichfield.[144] Not much of the music can be reconstructed, but what survives exhibits a more old-fashioned idiom than the comparable pieces (such as its setting of 'Salve festa dies') in the Egerton manuscript. It too contains the *synagoga* part of a polyphonic setting of the St Matthew Passion. But the special interest of the Shrewsbury fragment is that it also served as a single actor's part, complete with cues, for three liturgical plays.

[140] Initially by Schofield, 'A Newly Discovered 15th-Century Manuscript', *MQ*, 32 (1946), 509–36; challenged by Bukofzer, *Studies*, 113–75, supported by R. L. Greene, 'Two Medieval Musical Manuscripts', *JAMS*, 7 (1954), 1–34, both of whom put forward a link with the Cistercian abbey of Meaux in Yorkshire. The liturgical difficulties arising from this, and the arguments in favour of Windsor, have been stated by Harrison, *Music in Medieval Britain*, 275, by McPeek in his edition, *The British Museum Manuscript Egerton 3307* (London, 1963), and by Stevens in *Medieval Carols*, 125. Greene does not comment on the presence in the manuscript of a version in honour of St George of the processional hymn 'Salve festa dies'; in summarizing the arguments to date in the 2nd edn., 299–301, he expressed the view that 'if a court connection is to be made, the Chapel Royal is a much more likely choice [than St George's, Windsor]', while continuing to hold a strong preference for Meaux. The MS is edited, except for the carols, by McPeek; all the liturgical music is also in *Fifteenth-Century Liturgical Music*, i, and the carols are in *Medieval Carols*.

[141] The text is in Carmina Burana: Munich, Bayerische Staatsbibliothek, Clm 4660, fos. 89ᵛ–90ʳ (ed. A. Hilka, O. Schumann, and B. Bischoff, 4 vols. (Heidelberg, 1930–70), no. 202), beginning 'Potatores exquisiti' and with numerous other variants.

[142] Egerton 3307, fos. 72ᵛ–73ʳ; facsimile of first opening in Bukofzer, *Studies*, pl. 3.

[143] *Fifteenth-Century Liturgical Music*, i, nos. 24 (St Luke), 38 (St Matthew).

[144] See S. Rankin, 'Shrewsbury School, Manuscript VI', *PRMA*, 102 (1975–6), 129–44. The date *c*.1430 has been proposed.

Ex. 69

Ex. 69, continued

O choice drinkers, although you are without thirst, drink quickly all the same; and do not, unmindful of your cups, let the frequently filled tankards go to sleep. Let unheard of talk resound. Who cannot drink . . .

Note: Tenor and *contratenor* have verbal cues in first section but were perhaps not intended to be sung. *Contratenor* (upward stems) has one flat in key-signature; this is represented by accidentals in this transcription except in bar 18, where the bracketed natural-sign represents an editorial decision to ignore it.

These are for Christmas (*Officium pastorum*) and Easter (*Visitatio sepulchri* and *Officium peregrinorum*), the standard trio of dramas in the English secular Uses. But these plays incorporate both Latin and vernacular texts, the former to be sung, either to plainchant or to polyphony according to what is provided in the manuscript, the latter to be spoken. Clearly, with only a single part extant, the plays are not susceptible of reconstruction; but it is fascinating to reflect both on this evidence for a 'transition' from Latin to vernacular church drama, and on the versatility of the 'clerks' whose task it was to sing polyphonic music and to be actors at the same time.[145]

As for the vernacular drama proper, that too called for music, though not to anything like so great an extent. The great civic ceremony of the Corpus Christi play—that is to say the cycle of so-called mystery plays, each performed on a pageant or wagon at a series of 'stations' in the city by the members of a particular craft-gild—was the principal occasion for medieval drama in English.[146] In some form or other it flourished at a number of centres from the fourteenth to the third quarter of the sixteenth century, when the pressures of the Reformation finally crushed it. The majority of the extant manuscript sources are late in date—even, in the case of the Chester cycle, of a date after the suppression of the performances—but we do possess in the manuscript of the York cycle a witness to the fifteenth-

[145] The plays are edited by N. Davis, *The Non-Cycle Plays and Fragments* (London: OUP for EETS, 1970), 1–7; their music ed. F. Ll. Harrison, ibid., 124–33.

[146] See J. Stevens, 'Music in Medieval Drama', *PRMA*, 84 (1957–8), 81–95, and the articles by N. C. Carpenter listed in the bibliography. The most recent contribution is by R. Rastall, 'Music in the Cycle', in Lumiansky and Mills, *The Chester Mystery Cycle* (Chapel Hill, NC, and London, 1983), 111–64.

century text which even includes some music, six two-part pieces for the Weavers' play of the Assumption of the Virgin.[147]

The many references to music in the mystery plays make it clear both that the music was in the strict sense incidental but at the same time fulfilled a dramatic function. In the words of John Stevens, this was 'to symbolize heaven'. Most of the musical 'cues' could be satisfied by the singing of the appropriate plainchant, and it seems likely that this could be done by the more musical members of the gild itself. But the music for the York play of the Assumption consists of simple two-part pieces to texts from the Song of Songs, and it is probable—given the fact that they are written in high clefs and taking account of some of the external evidence in connection with the Chester cycle—that they were sung by the boys of the Minster choir. It is possible, too, that some of the cues in the York and other cycles may have been intended to refer to simple polyphony in the prevailing style, to be performed by trained singers, boys or men. There is also some evidence for the use of instruments, and it is likely that the day of the performances was marked by a good deal of professional minstrelsy of one sort or another, whether or not in connection with specific plays. In such a context it is possible to catch a glimpse of the more informal functions of music as an accompaniment to a prolonged act of civic celebration.

As in earlier periods, the instrumental repertory of the minstrels remains largely a closed book. Doubtless we should see the first half of the fifteenth century as a period of expansion of opportunities for the non-clerical professional. The names of royal minstrels under the three Henrys have been published,[148] but we should also expect to find the regular employment of minstrels in the larger magnatial households, and increasing evidence of town musicians or 'waits'. Still others would have been freelancers, wandering from place to place in search of work. At a later date the distinctions would become formalized, the musicians institutionalized, and the evidence more plentiful; for the moment, it is possible to say only that the scope of the profession and its social status were advancing.

As for the repertory itself, this would still have included the singing of narrative poetry of various kinds, though the read poem and the prose tale were now serious competitors. Dance music was obviously important, and one can begin to see a new trend here. Increasingly the dance was coming to be a serious polyphonic form, based on a *cantus firmus* which was often a schematic version of a song *tenor*. The technical term for one

---

[147] The manuscript, dating from between 1463 and 1477, is in the Brit. Lib., Add. 35290. See the recent edition by R. Beadle, *The York Plays* (London, 1982), incorporating a transcription of the music by J. Stevens.

[148] Rastall, 'Minstrels', *RMARC*, 4 (1964), 26–31; for the household of Joan, second wife of Henry IV (d. 1437) see also J. Stell and A. Wathey, 'New Light on the Biography of John Dunstable?', *ML*, 62 (1981), 60–3.

Ex. 70

particular variety of such things, *basse danse* or *bassadanza*, did not reach England until later (cf. Chapter 4, p. 259), but the basic musical principle is older and more generally applicable, and it flourished in England as elsewhere in Europe. In one fragment a *cantus firmus* labelled 'Quene note' is provided with a roughly sketched descant.[149] Another melody in the same fragment bears the legend 'Anxcibonyouredelabonestren', meaning apparently 'Ainsi bon jour de la bonne étrenne', 'this is the good day of the New Year's gift'. A setting of the tune, headed simply 'A' by the doubtless puzzled scribe, is found in one of the Trent codices. If it is a genuine specimen of English minstrelsy it is indicative of a high state of the art, since it is an elaborate and sophisticated piece (Ex. 70).[150]

In spite of the unsettled political circumstances of the period, English musical life benefited in a number of ways from the recovered stability of the Church and its association with the ambitions and prosperity of the ruling classes. New collegiate foundations—churches, schools, and colleges—provided new opportunities for education and the cultivation of music. Though many song and grammar schools, attached as they were to the cathedrals and priories, and to the older collegiate churches and

---

[149] Oxford, Bod. Lib., Digby 167, fo. 31ᵛ: printed in *Invitation to Medieval Music*, iii, no. 6.
[150] Tr. 87, fos. 117ᵛ–118ʳ; *Invitation*, iii, no. 7.

colleges, had long been in existence, their number increased considerably in the earlier fifteenth century. The importance in this respect of the newer colleges, whether of fellows or of chaplains (chantry priests), should not be underestimated.[151] The grammar schools did not have specifically musical functions, but they were a preparation for university, at which Music was studied as a liberal art. This was a speculative and mathematical discipline, but the earlier medieval link between theory and practice had not been lost, and it is hard not to believe that the universities were important centres of cultivation.[152]

The period produced nothing to compare in intellectual mastery with Walter Odington's *Summa* in the early fourteenth century; but the substantial compiler John Hanboys probably belongs to this epoch, and there is a plethora of small practical treatises, some in the vernacular.[153] A member of the Augustinian abbey of Waltham Holy Cross, John Wylde, was responsible for the survival of much of this material together with that of a number of fourteenth-century works.[154] The general impression is not one of intellectual supremacy but rather of an intensely practical concern for the day-to-day requirements of musicians.

Behind the great diversity of music in the first half of the fifteenth century it is possible to discern its underlying unity. This can be explained not only in technical terms—the wide stylistic range of the surviving written music can be brought under a remarkably compact set of harmonic and melodic criteria—but also in the context of the cultural background. Although English music of earlier periods possessed certain special characteristics, it was only in the late fourteenth and early fifteenth centuries that it acquired a wholly distinct voice. In this period, and especially during the reign of Henry V, national consciousness took a new turn. It was stimulated by Henry's military victories, of which the Agincourt song is a memorable celebration, but it was underlined by the inevitable historical process towards a wholly English state, a process which had already made it impossible, for example, for diplomatic negotiations with it to be conducted in French.[155] For the first time since the Anglo-Saxon period, English had

---

[151] See in general A. F. Leach, *The Schools of Medieval England* (London, 1915: informative but inadequately referenced). For the role of the gilds see F. A. Westlake, *The Parish Gilds of Mediaeval England* (London, 1919), and on towns in general, S. Reynolds, *An Introduction to the Study of English Medieval Towns* (corr. repr. Oxford, 1982) with its extensive bibliography.

[152] See N. C. Carpenter, *Music in the Medieval and Renaissance Universities*; F. Ll. Harrison in *The History of the University of Oxford*, ii (forthcoming).

[153] See above, p. 112, n. 9.

[154] Wylde's collection is preserved as London, Brit. Lib., Lansdowne 763; for an earlier work contained in it see above, Ch. 2, n. 148.

[155] E. F. Jacob, *The Fifteenth Century* (Oxford, 1961), 179; see however Thompson, *Paris and Its People*, 214. The transition from French to English as the medium of instruction in grammar schools took place in the 14th cent.: see A. F. Leach, *Schools of Medieval England*, 196–7, citing John Trevisa's translation of Higden's *Policronicon*.

become the mother tongue of all classes. But the country continued to play an important political role abroad, and the war with France, though increasingly unsuccessful and eventually disastrous, neither weakened England's ties with the Continent nor diluted her sense of national identity. Only the power-struggle between the houses of York and Lancaster threatened the unity of the nation. But even this had a less disturbing effect on life and art than might be imagined; and in the period with which we have been concerned, English music was able to build on to a largely insular substructure an edifice that excited European admiration.

4

THE LATER FIFTEENTH AND EARLY SIXTEENTH CENTURIES

THE period covered by this chapter witnessed the composition of a great quantity of music of unquestionable stature, much of it hardly performed in modern times and still waiting to take its place in the heritage of national classics. It does not matter that contemporary Continental opinion ignored or misunderstood it; and it should not matter that it has often been neglected since. Judged on its own terms, it cannot fail to impress and uplift.

The principal novelty in the period was the growth of a quality that can only be called architectural. This may seem a strange proposition in view of the mathematical and proportional basis of much of the music of the preceding era. But the quality which now emerges is based not on numerical proportions as such (though they may indeed be exploited in some cases) but on the realization of the possibilities provided by larger choirs: the distribution of masses of sound in order to provide effective contrasts, the development of harmonic thinking, and the cultivation of a highly decorative superstructure. This is closely parallel to the late Gothic and Perpendicular styles of architecture, in which the resources of space were more imaginatively planned than hitherto, and in which a balanced use of ornament was an essential feature. The parallel must not be pushed too far, if only because architecture was ubiquitous and polyphonic music, even the grandest sort, merely the decorative surface of a musical culture of which the staple commodity was still the age-old plainsong of the Church; but it is perhaps the most helpful way in which to approach the essence of this splendid music.

The durability of plainsong is a remarkable phenomenon: during the Tudor epoch it entered on the eighth century of its written existence. Though much expanded by later additions, it was in substance the same

repertory as it always had been. In spite of what has been written about
the 'decadence' of plainchant in the fifteenth and sixteenth centuries, the
music remained virtually unchanged, such differences as exist being in matters of pure detail. This is in great contrast to the ravages which it suffered
on the Continent in the later sixteenth century, but the rewriting of plainsong to suit Renaissance ideals was an irrelevance to post-Reformation England. Until the Edwardian Reformation, and even during the Marian
reaction, the medieval plainchant tradition, like the liturgy which it clothed,
remained intact. Performance practice may have changed insensibly during
the passage of many centuries—plainsong may have been sung more slowly
and subjected to rhythmic modification during this latest phase—but essentially it remained unaltered. This is a point of great importance, since it
underlines that respect for tradition which lies at the heart of the polyphonic
repertory, and which in some ways survived the Reformation itself.

As for the liturgy, it too developed along conservative lines until the
Reformation. It could be said to have achieved its final form in the printed
breviaries, hymnals, missals, processionals, and other ritual books of the
late fifteenth and earlier sixteenth centuries, and above all in the great
antiphonal and four graduals of the Salisbury Use, the first printed in two
volumes in Paris, 1519–20, the graduals in 1508, 1527, 1528, and 1532 respectively.[1] In southern England, the Salisbury or 'Sarum' Use, and local customs
closely related to it, predominated: only that of Hereford was sufficiently
independent to warrant its own printed liturgies. In much of the north,
that of York, which differed in many respects, held sway. But all over
England the monastic rites also made their contribution. The Benedictine
was the chief of these, for it determined the form of service in the cathedral
priories, of which those of Canterbury, Worcester, Winchester, and Durham
were perhaps the most important.[2] But the other major abbeys—St Albans,
Gloucester, and Chester, for example—and the Cistercian foundations such
as the great northern abbeys of Fountains and Meaux, all contributed their
particular pattern of worship. The Augustinian or black canons, however,[3]
employed the Use of Salisbury, and the Friars usually adopted local custom.
In spite of their diversity, all these Uses were essentially that of Rome,
with purely local modifications. They did not differ organically from it
as did that of Milan, or, at earlier times, that of Spain. In many ways the
English pre-Reformation rites were closer to the universal customs of those

[1] The full details may be found in *STC*, ii, s.v. 'Liturgies'.
[2] The others were Bath (under the Bishop of Wells), Coventry (under the Bishop of Lichfield),
Ely, Norwich, and Rochester. Wells and Lichfield themselves, like London, Lincoln, Hereford,
Chichester, Salisbury, Exeter, and York, were served by secular chapters.
[3] These included Waltham Holy Cross, Oxford (St Frideswide), Osney (just outside Oxford), and
Leicester (St Mary). The cathedrals at Carlisle, and at St Andrews in Scotland, were served by Augustinian
chapters. (The remaining Scottish sees, like the Welsh, were secular except for Whithorn, which
was Premonstratensian.)

days than they were to the post-Tridentine rite, which was a severer disruption of established practice than is sometimes realized.

This musical culture—that of the liturgical plainchant and its polyphonic decoration—was sustained by an institutional framework of some complexity and considerable variety. The Church was never, perhaps, so richly endowed or so ready to devote its income to the maintenance of worship as at this time. The major institutions were of course the secular cathedrals, amongst whose large staff professional musicians played a small but important role. The canons, whether resident or not, had long ceased to fulfil their obligation of singing the daily Office. Their place was taken by 'vicars choral', in priest's, deacon's, or subdeacon's orders, and by 'clerks of the choir' in lower orders, whose primary duty was to sing plainchant.[4] But the real contribution of the epoch was the growth of boys' choirs under the direction of a *magister choristarum*; they were trained to a pitch of musicianship almost inconceivable today and with the vicars choral and clerks provided the fundamental conditions for the cultivation of elaborate polyphony.[5]

In the greater monasteries and cathedral priories,[6] the monks themselves carried on the daily Office and the daily Conventual and High Mass which were *de rigueur*. But the greatest of them established separate Lady Chapel choirs in order to perform the service of the Blessed Virgin Mary in the Lady Chapel, which like the nave of the monastic church was open to the general public. No doubt such choirs would also assist at High Mass when occasion demanded: the existence of some compositions is scarcely conceivable otherwise. But their main function was to provide a focus for public devotion, and to that end they attained a peak of sophistication in the early sixteenth century.

Beside the cathedrals and monasteries had grown up a mass of lesser institutions: colleges, household chapels, and collegiate and parish churches. The Fellows of the Oxford and Cambridge Colleges, like those of Eton, Winchester, and some others,[7] had never been expected to maintain the

---

[4] For the vicars, see Harrison, *Music in Medieval Britain*, 4–9. The rise of the singing clerks in the 15th cent. (often referred to nowadays as 'lay clerks', although they would normally be in minor orders; they were sometimes called 'clerici generosi', i.e. 'gentlemen clerks', implying a quasi-lay status) is dealt with by Bowers, 'Choral Establishments within the English Church', 4040–50. They were 'career musicians' rather than 'apprentice priests' (ibid. 4041).

[5] Harrison, *Music in Medieval Britain*, 9–12, 177–85, 194–7. Boy choristers under a *magister* were an ancient institution, but their functions were ceremonial as well as musical, the latter being confined at first to the singing of plainchant. Only in the second half of the 15th cent. did the teaching of the skills necessary for them to sing polyphonic music become usual, though this surely need not exclude their occasional use for this purpose earlier in the century. See Bowers, 'Choral Establishments', 6001 seqq., and 4051–3, where it is argued that the role of the choristers in the early 15th cent., despite the rise in their numbers, was still 'more decorative than musical'.

[6] Harrison, *Music in Medieval Britain*, 38–44, 185–94.

[7] Ibid. 30–8, 157–69.

daily Office by their own efforts. But all of them made provision for it in their statutes, whether for said or for sung performance. A common feature was the provision for the daily singing of the antiphon of the Blessed Virgin Mary, not necessarily in polyphony. But the largest colleges—Eton, and King's, Cambridge, for example, or Magdalen, New College, St John's (known then as Canterbury College), and Cardinal College (later Christ Church) at Oxford—cultivated polyphonic music on a regular basis. The largest household chapels—those of the King himself, the comparable institutions at St Stephen's, Westminster, or St George's, Windsor, or the chapels of the Dukes of Richmond and Northumberland[8]—maintained the daily Mass and Office, and the service of the Blessed Virgin Mary, the latter at least often in polyphony. Colleges of chantry priests (the 'collegiate churches' of the later Middle Ages) also made provision for the maintenance of services and in some cases at least cultivated polyphonic music.[9] Hospitals and schools also made their contribution. Parish churches, finally (in addition to collegiate churches fulfilling that role), were a significant repository of musical culture.[10] It would be hard to say in what proportion of them music was to be heard in the later Middle Ages—in some, at least, it would have been impracticable to sing even plainchant—but a significant number will have performed the rite with appropriate ceremony, and a small but growing number catered for polyphony. The music, with much else, was in the charge of the parish clerk; in a parish which aspired to polyphony, additional clerks, known as conducts, were employed. The musical establishment of St Mary-at-Hill in the city of London was one such.[11]

Even where elaborate vocal polyphony was precluded, the organ might be used. The role of the organ was rarely, if ever, accompanimental at this period. Its function was to act as a substitute for one side of the plainsong choir in those forms in which alternation from side to side was employed (predominantly the hymn) or for the whole choir in other circumstances, such as at the Offertory at Mass or the antiphon at the conclusion of a psalm or canticle.[12] In an extreme case, a single clerk and the organist could provide the entire music for a service between them.[13] Cathedrals and other large churches might have two or more organs to fulfil different ritual functions, while even quite small churches could often boast one

---

[8] Ibid. 19–26, 170–4.

[9] On these institutions generally, see Bowers, *passim*. Amongst the more notable collegiate foundations were St Mary's, Warwick (refounded 1392), Fotheringay (1398, 1411), Manchester (1421), and Higham Ferrers (1422). These and several others employed clerks and choristers in addition to the Master and chaplains (or, following the older nomenclature, dean and canons), whose principal duties were to say Masses for the soul of the founder.

[10] Harrison, *Music in Medieval Britain*, 197–201.

[11] See H. Baillie, 'A London Church in Early Tudor Times', *ML*, 36 (1955), 55–64.

[12] On the later medieval organ and its ritual use, see Harrison, *Music in Medieval Britain*, 209–18.

[13] Ibid. 215.

in the early sixteenth century. The surviving written repertory, it is fair to say, represents but a fraction of what must have been needed. In all probability, performance was for the most part improvised from plainchant books.

The period of the final flowering of the medieval liturgy and its music was also touched by elements of humanism and the Renaissance. We may discount monastic humanism, such as might be attributed to John Whethamstede, abbot of St Albans, as having little or no influence on music, though it is a curious coincidence that amongst the few fifteenth-century settings of Latin hexameters are two motets on St Alban.[14] But neither the composition of hexameters (particularly of rhyming hexameters) nor the setting of them to music are necessarily evidence of humanism. There are no equivalents in English music of Ockeghem's 'Intemerata Dei mater' or of Josquin's 'Huc me sydereo descendere iussit Olympo'. Humanism came to English music through the medium of English verse, when composers began to show a new attention to the rhythms and the sense of the poetry. These first manifestations were trivial enough in themselves, but they achieved a certain fulfilment in such works as the Passion carols of Cornysh and Browne. The more overtly Renaissance ambience of the court of Henry VIII enabled the new spirit to flourish, though in a curiously half-hearted way. In England at this time the Renaissance was not, as it later became and as it already was in Italy, the guiding theme of an entire culture; rather was it a medium for experiment, an occasion of courtly irresponsibility, almost, and always to be tested against the solid achievements of the medieval tradition. It was not yet capable of sustaining the highest flights of the imagination, and for the time being at least it was the medieval tradition that prevailed.

Artistically, the period is one of stability and steady growth. This was not much affected by the dynastic struggles of its earlier years, and while it is true that no great masterpieces can be assigned with any confidence to the years 1460–85, it is quite likely that some of the earlier music in the Eton Choirbook (see below) goes back to that time. Nor can we ascribe the apparent loss of music to the depredations of civil war. Changes of fashion were a far more serious threat, as the numerous fragments recovered from the bindings of later manuscripts show. Though Eton itself, a foundation of Henry VI, was suppressed from 1463 to 1476,[15] the Wars of the Roses were not fought as a conflict of ideals: the ecclesiastical establishment was not a point at issue. Quite different was the effect of the Reformation,

---

[14] For Whethamstede see Knowles, *Religious Orders*, ii. 193–7, 267–8. For the motets referred to see above, Ch. 3, pp. 136, 145. It is just possible that Whethamstede himself wrote these texts, though the actual rhymed Office of St Alban is much older.

[15] Harrison, *Music in Medieval Britain*, 34–5; King's College, Cambridge, was also temporarily under a cloud.

the first phase of which began, at around 1530, within the period covered by this chapter. Though Henry VIII's policy was to retain Catholic doctrine and liturgy, the break with Rome provided a suitable climate for liturgical experiment: the limited use of the vernacular, the simplification of church music, and the growing cult of the person of Jesus as an antidote to that of Mary. Though the old view that Taverner ceased to compose after 1530 is now discredited, he did not subsequently aspire to the grandeur of his three great six-part Masses, though his music may have gained in subtlety thereafter. From 1530 to the death of Henry the Church was beset by doubts as to its legitimacy and its ultimate direction; and this could not but be reflected to some extent in its music.

The humbler forms of music continued on paths already established earlier in the century. Two collections, the 'Pepys' manuscript at Magdalene College, Cambridge, and the 'Ritson' manuscript at the British Library, will serve to illustrate contemporary trends. The former is an anthology of liturgical music, apparently from the diocese of Canterbury.[16] All seasons of the Church's year are represented, particularly that of Easter, together with some of the more important feasts of the sanctorale. There is also a series of Alleluias for the daily Mass of the Virgin, and one or two other votive items. The ritual forms are very diverse: in addition to the Alleluia they include processional items (hymns, litanies, antiphons with psalm), hymns, antiphons, responds, lessons, Benedicamus settings, and blessings. Some of these, such as the dramatic *propheta* trope for 'En rex venit' on Palm Sunday, are rarely if ever met with outside plainchant sources. A unique feature is the provision of measured monophonic music, either based on the plainchant or its faburden or else freely composed. Although some of this may have been intended as a basis for improvised polyphony, like the 'squares' of which more will be said in this chapter, there are others which seem too elaborate for that,[17] though it must be admitted that the interest is not always maintained. The music of the *propheta* trope just mentioned, also monophonic, is based on the antiphons from which the texts of its three sections were derived rather than on the melodies associated with it in the few printed processionals which contain it.[18]

[16] *The Music of the Pepys Ms 1236*, ed. S. R. Charles (CMM, xl); see F. Ll. Harrison, 'Music for the Sarum Rite', *AnnM*, 6 (1958–63), 99–144. The evidence for the provenance of the manuscript is discussed by Bowers in I. Fenlon (ed.), *Cambridge Music Manuscripts, 900–1700* (Cambridge, 1982), 111–14, with the further suggestion that it was compiled by (or for) one of the priests of the chapel of the Almonry of Christ Church priory. The almonry was in effect a boarding school for the cathedral boys, but its chapel observed the Salisbury, not the monastic, Use, and could have performed the kind of music collected here. Though more of a private collection than a properly liturgical manuscript (it also contains treatises), there can be little doubt that it represents the musical repertory of just such an establishment.

[17] e.g. nos. 99, 100, though not no. 67.

[18] Harrison, *AnnM*, 6 (1958–63), 126–8.

The polyphonic music in the manuscript covers a wide range of styles, some of it dating from several years at least before its compilation around 1465 (Walter Frye's 'Sospitati dedit egros', discussed in the previous chapter, is an example), and much of the anonymous music is clearly contemporary. The other named composers, however—Gilbert Banaster, William Corbronde, John Tuder, [John] Fowler, Garnesey, Sir W. Haute (or Haut), and J[ohn] Nesbet—seem to belong to a slightly later generation. Banaster (whose surname is spelt Banastre here) became Master of the Choristers of the Chapel Royal in 1478 and died in 1487. Like Nesbet, he reappears in the Eton Choirbook (see below). Nesbet and Corbronde were successive Masters of the Lady Chapel Choir at Christ Church Canterbury (the cathedral priory), in 1470 and 1474–80 respectively. Haute was a local landowner whose knighthood in 1465 gives a *terminus post quem* for the completion of the manuscript. He reappears as Sir W. Hawte, *miles*, in the Ritson manuscript (below), which has Devonian associations; this suggests a surprisingly wide currency for the music of one who must have been an amateur composer.

Most of the music in the manuscript is for three voices. Apart from settings of plainchant (whether strictly presented or in an ornamented form) and freely composed works, we find here, perhaps for the first time, settings of the faburden of the chant in which the faburden is treated as an entity in itself. Faburden as a technique of improvisation has been described in the previous chapter. It involved the embellishment of the plainchant by duplicating it a fourth above in the 'treble' and providing a 'faburden' a third below, falling to the fifth at cadences and in certain other circumstances.[19] During the second half of the fifteenth century, however, there was a tendency to regard the plainchant, even though transposed, as lying in the top rather than the middle voice. This was not perhaps so much because of the greater audibility of the part on top as because the effect was to create tonal unity between the chant and its faburden. Whatever the reason, from this time onwards the faburden usually came to be thought of as lying a sixth below the chant, falling to the octave at cadences. At the same time, we may suppose, an increase in the skill of singers practising the improvised form led to a greater freedom in the manipulation of the material. This is reflected in the humbler forms of written polyphony, in which it is sometimes hard to tell whether the ultimate basis is the plainsong in the top (or even, still, the middle) voice or the faburden below. At times, only the principal tonal points of reference may remain.

In the Pepys manuscript, for example, in the setting of the Processional Psalm 'Laudate pueri' (no. 66) the antiphon 'Alleluya' is freely composed but is for the most part in the appropriate tonality; in the psalm itself,

---

[19]   e.g. at the ends of words, though this rule was not always observed.

however, the chant[20] appears essentially in the middle voice in a faburden-like setting. In Banaster's 'Vos secli iusti iudices', however (a setting of the even-numbered verses of the hymn 'Exultet celum laudibus', no. 11), the middle part is so free that the chant must be regarded as being, though highly ornamented, in the top voice; the lowest voice is often faburden-like, but departs from this function more readily than the top voice does from the plainchant. The style of this beautifully euphonious piece would not seem out of place as the product of the period of Dunstable, and indeed it could well have been composed before or shortly after 1450. The very next piece in the manuscript, however, a Kyrie for the processional Litany, is definitely based on the faburden, the chant itself being less consistently in evidence. The procession seems to have been a favoured context for this technique, and five settings of the 'Salve festa dies' in the Pepys manuscript conform to it to a greater or lesser degree. It may be illustrated from the hymn-verse 'Eterne rex altissime' (no. 78), where the lowest part, representing the faburden, is noticeably closer to its expected form than the top part is to the chant (here transposed for the sake of comparison). As for the middle part, it is quite free (Ex. 71, overleaf).[21]

The interest of the collection, however, is not dependent on its technical aspects. Its chief significance is in providing examples of a wide variety of liturgical forms at a time when the evidence is very thin on the ground. If for the most part the technical achievement is modest, the music has a quiet beauty which is in large part a reflection of its liturgical appropriateness.

This is a convenient point at which to raise the subject of 'squares', which are analogous to monophonic faburdens. Many examples of the latter have come to light, often scribbled roughly into hymnals or processionals. Since improvised faburden did not, by definition, require notation, these were presumably intended, as we have suggested in the case of some of the Pepys examples, as a basis for improvised descant. In some cases the melodic line departs quite radically from the strict faburden. Usually this can be explained as a convention, perhaps originating in the improvised form, intended to obviate tonal awkwardness;[22] but in one instance at least, the faburden of the first Magnificat tone, it can be traced back to an existing written composition (see Ex. 44, p. 101 above).

---

[20] *AS*, pl. 239.

[21] Ed. Charles (n. 16), 108.

[22] e.g. the 'Salve festa dies' in Rome, Bibl. vat., Ottob. lat. 308: see F. Ll. Harrison, 'Faburden in Practice', *MD*, 16 (1962), 11–34, Ex. 6(c). The faburden of the Te Deum incorporated a variant designed to bring the two melodies that form its second half within the same tonal orbit: see Harrison, *Music in Medieval Britain*, 388–9, and the slightly different explanation in my article, 'The "Te Deum" in Late Medieval England', *Early Music*, 6 (1978), 188–94.

Ex. 71

(a) chant (up a 4th)

(b) Pepys 1236, no. 78

(c) Faburden: from Oxford, Bod. Lib., Digby 167 (down a 5th)

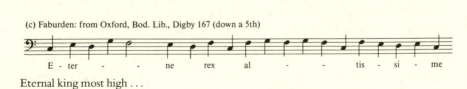

Eternal king most high . . .

As has already been said,[23] there is little distinction between a 'faburden'
of this kind and a 'square'. From the existence of a small number of mid-
sixteenth-century Masses said to be 'upon the square', it has been established
that the 'square' in these cases at least is a monophonic, measured melody
of a type found in a number of sources of the later fifteenth century. The
term is also found in documentary sources from the mid-fifteenth century

---

[23] See above, pp. 93–5, and the references there given.

onwards, and scholars have generally applied the term to the whole body of this material—settings, for the most part, of the Kyrie, Sanctus, and Agnus. The origin of some of these melodies was subsequently discovered in existing polyphonic compositions, and it has since been assumed that all, or at any rate the great majority, must have been so derived. One at least has been traced to a secular chanson,[24] and there appears to be an analogy here with the derivation of some *basse-danse* melodies from polyphonic chansons; these too were used as a basis for improvised polyphony, instrumental in this case.

The phenomenon of faburdens and squares is really part and parcel of a whole ethos of composition in which the re-use of existing material played a far larger part than it does today. Elaboration, simplification, and subsequent re-elaboration were processes that were almost second nature to many musicians. Different liturgical observances acquired their conventions, so that faburdens, for instance, became characteristic of the Office and of processions, 'squares' of the Lady Mass (the daily votive Mass of the Blessed Virgin Mary). They were used not only in improvised polyphony, but, with ever increasing sophistication, in many varieties of written composition. The Tudor Magnificat, usually based on a faburden, and Lady Masses (such as those of Nicholas Ludford), based on squares, are two of the most important; organ hymns 'on the faburden' are another large category.

Returning to our survey of the extant material, the next important source is the so-called Ritson manuscript, an anthology like the Pepys source but much more heterogeneous in content.[25] It was compiled over a period of time, perhaps from 1470 to 1510 or even later. Miscellaneous deeds and receipts added to the manuscript around 1510 connect it with the county of Devon; and Richard Smert, one of the composers named, was rector of Plymtree, near Exeter, from 1435 to 1477.[26] The other composers represented are John Trouluffe, Richard Mower, Sir Thomas Packe (or Pakke), Sir William Hawte, Edmund Sturges, John Cornysch, 'W.P.' (possibly William Pasche or William Parker), T.B. (or B.T.),[27] and J. Norman. There are also two copies (one incomplete) of a piece by Henry VIII, 'Passetyme with goode cumpanye'.

The principal contents of the manuscript are carols; sacred works by

---

[24] This is 'Or me veult bien esperance mentir' from the Mellon Chansonnier, fos. 70^{r-v}, ed. L. L. Perkins and H. Garey (New Haven, Conn., and London, 1979), 172–5, no. 49. See below, p. 224, and nn. 91, 93. The principal source of squares is Brit. Lib., Lansdowne 462.

[25] London, Brit. Lib., Add. 5665. See *Early English Carols* (2nd edn.), 307–8; *Medieval Carols*, ed. J. Stevens.

[26] Stevens, *Music and Poetry in the Early Tudor Court* (London, 1961; Cambridge, 1979), 338. Smert may have been only the author of the texts, however.

[27] The initials are superimposed in the form of a monogram. The piece in question is also subscribed 'quod r.c.', but this may refer only to a brief musical puzzle added at the end.

Packe and others, interrupted by a collection of English songs in chanson style; and a final group of English songs. Apart from this last group, which in view of the ascription 'The kyngys balade' attached to the second copy of 'Passetyme' must have been copied, if not necessarily entirely composed, after 1509, the music may be discussed here without distorting the general chronological picture. The carols continue and develop the manner of those in the Selden and Egerton collections. They are longer and more elaborate than the majority of these, and invariably include a second, three-part burden and often intermediate three-part sections as well, though none is entirely in three parts like 'Ave rex anglorum' from the Egerton Codex.[28] Each carol is given a quasi-liturgical heading, except for a few marked 'ad placitum', though some of the others are purely convivial or moralistic. Major prolation (3/8) is entirely eliminated.

It is instructive, for instance, to compare 'Alleluya ... Now may we myrthis make' (no. 105), marked 'de nativitate', with the earlier version in the Selden manuscript, 'Alleluya: Now wel may we merthis make' (no. 20). The texts, which incidentally are based on the Christmas Sequence 'Letabundus exultet fidelis chorus',[29] are virtually identical, but the music, while similar in some respects, is here greatly extended and of greater contrapuntal refinement. However, it is no more advanced than some of the Egerton pieces. What seems to be new in the Ritson collection is a feeling for the declamation of the English language, as in the affecting 'Meruelle noȝt Iosep' (no. 81) or the lively 'Nowell ... Dieu vous garde' (no. 80), subscribed with the name of Smert. Here the burden (like the first stanza) is laid out as a little dialogue, dramatizing and extending the usual alternation between two- and three-part sections (Ex. 72).[30]

The little block of secular works in chanson style later on in the manuscript[31] also refines on the genres established earlier in the century. The first of them, 'My wofull hert' (no. 2) is perhaps the most accomplished, and is the most extended and best preserved of ballades to English texts, with two stanzas intact. The setting would pass muster in any Continental collection of the later fifteenth century, and indeed is not unlike Binchois or Busnois in manner. The syllabic versification and the respect shown in the music for the lyric caesura reflect this, as does the care taken over textural clarity. The effective use of musical rhyme in the melismatic postlude to the two sections reinforces the view that this is the work of a sophisticated composer fully immersed in the Continental tradition.

[28] *Medieval Carols*, no. 52. The numbering of this edition is employed in the following discussion, but the original orthography of the verbal texts is followed.

[29] See above, p. 165; a text-only version belonging to Bridgwater Corporation actually gives the first stanza of 'Letabundus' as burden (*Early English Carols*, no. 14a).

[30] London, Brit. Lib., Add. 5665, fos. 8ᵛ–9ᵛ.

[31] *Early Tudor Songs and Carols*, ed. J. Stevens (London, 1975), nos. 2–9. Numbered references in the text are to this edition.

Ex. 72

[No - welle,   no - welle,   no - welle,   no - welle.]

No - welle,   no - welle,   no - welle,   no - welle.

Who ys there,   that syng-eth so,   No -

Who us there   that syng-eth so,   No -

w[elle],   no - welle,   no - welle?

welle,   no - welle,   no - welle?

[I am here,   sire Cri - stes - masse.]

I am here,   sire Cri - stes - masse.

Welle - come,   [my lord,] sire   Cri - stes - masse.

well - come,   my lord,   sire   Cri - stes - masse.

The other pieces in the group give a more insular impression, in some cases because of their more declamatory treatment of the text, in others because of a less sophisticated technique. 'Thow man, envired with temptacion' (no. 7) is a moralizing piece, musically a ballade, not entirely successful in its combination of declamation and melisma. 'Absens of you' (no. 4) is a more successful, purely secular, ballade, like the former in duple time but with a more complete form of stanza and a better-balanced approach to word-setting. 'Be pes, ye make me spille my ale' (no. 3), a lively comic dialogue culminating in the capitulation of the girl, is an effective setting of the first stanza, but fails to cope with the metrical variations of the second and third, and hence to reflect the little drama as a whole. It deserves mention, however, as an early instance of musical humour.

Of the many sacred Latin works in the manuscript, one group belongs to the period of the carols already discussed, and is not of outstanding interest, except for an anonymous four-part 'Ave regina celorum, mater regis angelorum' which is curiously close to the manner of Busnois and Ockeghem. Though it can hardly be other than the work of an Englishman, there were perhaps cross-currents at this time which the documentary sources have not as yet revealed. The opening serves to reveal its long-breathed lines and closely knit texture (Ex. 73).[32]

A second group of pieces (fos. 62^v–65^r, 73^v–131^r) is largely devoted to music by Sir Thomas Packe (or Pakke), though it also includes works by Sir William Hawte (see above, p. 180), Edmund Sturges (i.e. Turges), Henry Petyr(e), John Cornysch (so spelt here), and a number of anonymous compositions. Several of these, like the Mass by which Henry Petyr is represented, are in 'plainsong' notation, a modified form of which was sometimes adopted in polyphonic music of this period when only a restricted range of note-values was required. One such piece, ascribed 'W.P.' (possibly for William Pasche), 'Anima mea liquefacta est', is a simplified reworking of a piece by Power or Dunstable.[33]

Petyr's Mass is not a particularly inspired composition, though it deserves mention as the precursor of the more imaginative 'plainsong' Masses of Taverner and Sheppard. There are three other Masses, or parts of Masses, in the manuscript, all similarly for three voices: the Kyrie and Gloria by 'Sturges' is fully worthy of the composer better known for his elaborate compositions in the Eton and Caius College choirbooks, while the two by Packe himself have many picturesque moments. However, Packe's individuality is most strikingly evident in two refrain-compositions, a five-part setting of the antiphon 'Lumen ad revelacionem gencium', for Candlemas, with the second half of each alternating verse also in polyphony, and a

---

[32] Brit. Lib., Add. 5665, fos. 58^v–59^r.
[33] See Benham, '"Salve Regina"', *ML*, 59 (1978), 28–32.

Ex. 73

Hail, queen of the heavens, mother of the king of the angels . . .

macaronic (Latin/ English) paraphrase of the Te Deum, again with a five-part refrain. The latter is one of the curiosities of the period, both from the musical and the verbal point of view. The refrain and the opening of the first stanza of the paraphrase will serve to indicate the flavour (the refrain carries the faburden of the chant in the *tenor*) (Ex. 74, overleaf).[34]

[34] Brit. Lib., Add. 5665, fos. 95ᵛ–96ʳ.

Ex. 74

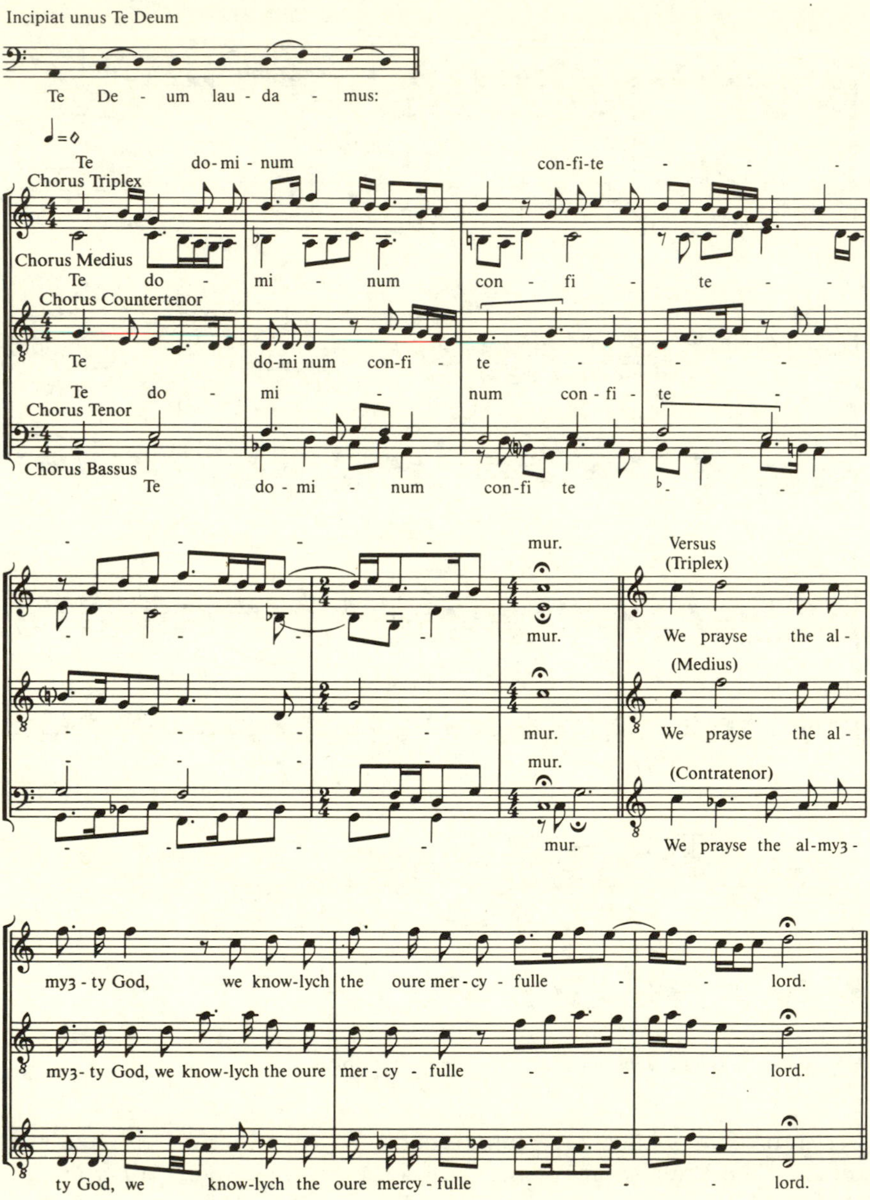

(Latin): We praise thee, O God, we confess you to be lord.

The paraphrase is divided into nine stanzas, of which the first three are in three-part polyphony of the kind shown, the next three in metrical monophony (the fourth stanza is also given an alternative polyphonic setting), and the last three have no music at all. The text of the first stanza continues thus:

> All erth worshyppeth the[e] fader everlastynge lorde of hevyn and
>   kinge.
> All angelys hevyn and alle potestates yn on acorde
> Cherubin et seraphyn incessabile voce proclamant and synge
> [*Refrain*] Te Deum laudamus [*etc.*]

Evidently this is some kind of unofficial popular church music, tinged with a provincial accent, designed to bring the message of the hymn closer to simple people. But the five-part refrain presupposes a well-trained choir, and the composition, so naïve in some respects, is not lacking in sophistication. Nothing certain is known of Packe, but he may have had Devon connections like Smert and Trouluffe; at all events, his music serves to illustrate the early Tudor style in a somewhat unexpected context.

That style bursts forth in all its glory in the contents of the Eton College manuscript (MS 178 of the College Library).[35] The Eton Choirbook, as it is generally called, is a very different kind of book from the two which we have just considered, though it resembles them in that the parts are written out separately on the facing pages of an opening (a procedure known technically as *cantus collateralis*). The Eton book, however, is in a far larger format—23″ × 17″—being designed to be read from a lectern by a choir of perhaps ten choristers and seven clerks.[36] Even so, the music was probably learnt in substance beforehand—the highest parts are inscribed at the top of the huge volume, where the choristers would least be able to see them, and it shows little or no sign of markings or corrections for performances. The immense complexity of much of the music would certainly require its preparation beforehand, and it has been possible to identify fragmentary sources intended for that very purpose.[37] The volume therefore served a ceremonial and mnemonic function, but it is from such sources that our knowledge of musical history so often derives.

[35] *The Eton Choirbook*, ed. F. Ll. Harrison, 3 vols. (London, 1956–61). Certain fragmentary and missing works are supplied from other sources. The numbering of the edition has been used in the following discussion, and the musical examples drawn from it. See also Harrison, 'The Eton College Choirbook', *Kongressbericht Utrecht 1952* (Amsterdam, 1953), 224–32.

[36] These are the numbers given in the statutes of 1476: they were subject to some variation subsequently. Harrison, *Music in Medieval Britain*, 34–5.

[37] e.g. Cambridge, Univ. Lib., MS Buxton 96, part of a roll containing the bass voice of John Browne's 'Stabat mater dolorosa'. See the description by Bowers in I. Fenlon (ed.), *Cambridge Music Manuscripts, 900–1700*, 114–17.

Because of its size and the number of composers represented, the Eton manuscript provides a convenient basis for summarizing the nature of the musical style current in the reign of Henry VII. The index at the beginning lists 66 antiphons of the Virgin, followed by 24 Magnificats, and the Passion according to St Matthew by Davy; the nine-part 'Salve Regina' by Wylkynson (no. 9), and his thirteen-part canonic setting of the Apostles' Creed (no. 50), are later additions. Twenty-nine pieces are now lost completely, and several others are incomplete or fragmentary. But even as it stands it is a monumental collection. There are no Masses, which were perhaps not sung polyphonically at Eton, although no fewer than seven were said or sung daily under the statutes of 1444. The manuscript helped to fulfil the requirement that an antiphon be sung every evening before the image of the Blessed Virgin: in Lent the 'Salve regina' with its 'verses' (metrical tropes inserted before each of the three final invocations of the text), of which the manuscript provides fifteen settings; otherwise, and also on feast days in Lent, some other antiphon.[38] It is not clear whether, in the late fifteenth and early sixteenth centuries, the daily performance was invariably polyphonic—practical considerations would suggest perhaps not.

Of the twenty-five composers listed in the index to the manuscript, Dunstable, whose five-part 'Gaude flore virginali' is unfortunately one of the lost works, was the oldest; otherwise the earliest generation represented is that of Horwood and Banaster (d. 1487), Nesbet (see above, p. 180), and perhaps Hugo Kellyk, about whom nothing is known, but whose style is relatively unformed. Horwood was made Master of the London Gild of Parish Clerks (see above, p. 143) in 1474; he became a vicar choral at Lincoln Cathedral in 1476, and was Master of the Choristers there from 1477 until his death around 1484. His 'Salve regina' (no. 10) shows how quickly the style evolved: here already are the full five-part texture which was to become standard, the greatly increased length (here 82 bars of triple time followed by 130 in quadruple time and a final short triple-time section of 14 bars),[39] and the characteristic alternation between sections for reduced voices and those for full choir. More archaic features are a certain tonal instability (in this case as between transposed Dorian—G minor, in effect, with one flat—and Mixolydian—G major with no signature), and the scoring for *tenor* and *bassus* in the same range. In spite of this, there is already a strong feeling of triadic harmony supported by the metrical divisions,

[38] The next most frequently set text is 'Gaude flore virginali': the only other one set more than once is 'Stabat mater dolorosa'. The performances would have taken place after Compline.

[39] The actual proportions, taking the breve as the unit and including the full value of final notes, are 83, 261, 17. It is not certain, however, that the breve was performed at the same speed in duple as in triple time: probably it was performed rather more quickly. If a 4 : 3 increase in speed is assumed for the middle section, the relative lengths of each section can be expressed very roughly in the form 10 : 25 : 2. It is very doubtful if there is any symbolic significance in these or similar approximate relations in other works of the period.

Ex. 75

O sweet Mary, hail.

as may be illustrated by the conclusion of the work, showing the fluid yet vigorous melodic line that is so typical of this music (Ex. 75).[40]

Horwood's Magnificat, on the eighth tone in G with some hints of faburden here and there, is rather more advanced still, and may be studied for the sake of the conventions which it embodies. The texture is more

[40] *The Eton Choirbook*, i. 107, transposed down a fourth.

Ex. 76

(a) verse 3

Qui - a re - spexit humilitatem an - cil - le su - e: ecce enim ex hoc be - a -

tam me dicent omnes gene - ra - ti - o - nes.

(b) verse 4

Ex. 76, continued

For he has looked on the humility of his maid-servant; behold from now on all generations shall call me blessed. For he who is mighty has made me great.

standardized, the *tenor* and *contratenor* being in the same range and the *bassus* decidedly lower. As always, only the even-numbered verses of the canticle are set, the others being chanted in plainsong. Each polyphonic half-verse ends with a strong cadence, in this case on to C. The arrangement is even more symmetrical than that of the antiphon, for verses 2 and 4 are in triple time, 6 and 8 in quadruple (or duple), and 10 and 12 again in triple. Verses 4 and 8 (but not 12, since it is the last), moreover, are for reduced forces.[41] In verse 4, still further variety is obtained by dividing the *tenor* (a device known in England as 'gymel' or *cantus gemellus*, meaning 'twin song'), and combining them with the *contratenor* to form a rich three-part sonority (Ex. 76).[42] The short passage of *rondellus* (see p. 47) will be noticed, but this is merely an incident in a passage in which imitation and sequence (cf. the second-*tenor* entries in bars 40 and 43) play an important part throughout.

We shall have occasion to mention other settings of the Magnificat, but apart from the choice of different tones and the greater use of faburden or chant in some settings the conventions hardly changed at all prior to the Reformation.

Nesbet and Kellyk, whose Magnificats (nos. 43, 45) surround that of Horwood in the Manuscript, are perhaps less interesting composers, though Kellyk's seven-part 'Gaude flore virginali' (no. 2) exploits the potential richness of the medium with perfect confidence. Banaster's 'O Maria et Elizabeth' (no. 28), on the Visitation of the Blessed Virgin, has been connected with the pregnancy of Elizabeth of York, wife of Henry VII.[43] She gave birth on 19 September 1486; but although the text of the antiphon

[41] In later settings, verse 12 sometimes begins with reduced forces in order to maintain a symmetry of textural contrast.
[42] *The Eton Choirbook*, iii. 70–1 (chant, verse 3, and bass 36–46; faburden for comparison quoted from London, Brit. Lib., MS Royal Appendix 56, fo. 23ᵛ).
[43] *The Eton Choirbook*, ii, Preface.

includes a prayer for the king, he is referred to only as 'N', and the work may originally have been composed with an earlier monarch in mind. The setting of the lengthy text is more declamatory than usual—even so it extends to 274 bars in the modern transcription. Banaster's death in 1487 is a reminder that the declamatory idiom developed well before the end of the century.

A second group of composers consists of those whose working lives drew to a close around the turn of the century or slightly later; Walter Lambe, and probably John Browne and Richard Davy, belong to this group, together with such minor figures as Hygons, Mychelson, and Sutton (the last a Fellow of Eton until 1499). Harrison's estimate of Browne as 'the outstanding figure of the collection and perhaps the greatest English composer between Dunstable and Taverner' is possibly exaggerated: Lambe, whose music is marked by a rare freshness and facility, is a close rival, and we shall have occasion to mention others whose music is scarcely if at all inferior. Browne and Lambe are nevertheless the two best represented composers in the collection, and in their different ways exhibit the style in its full maturity.

We now know that Browne was an Oxonian, though in what precise sense remains obscure.[44] It hardly matters. In spite of his subsequent obscurity, he must have been one of the most highly regarded composers of his day. The Eton manuscript originally contained fifteen of his works, and the three carols in the Fayrfax Book (see below, p. 254) are almost certainly by him. His great 'O Maria Salvatoris Mater', in eight parts, opens the collection. Its ringing self-confidence is characteristic (Ex. 77).[45] The standard five-part texture is expanded by the duplication of the *bassus* to provide overlapping parts of equivalent range, the duplication of the *contratenor*, making with the *tenor* a block of three parts in the same range, and the addition of the *quatriplex* above the *triplex*. The *tenor* part in this piece is a *cantus firmus*, unfortunately not identified as yet: its irregular rhythmic progress is a typical device of this period and the early sixteenth century, and with the supporting bass-line it provides the solid harmonic foundation on which much of the composition rests. The strong textural contrasts of this work are not a novelty, but the effect of such passages as the duet for *quatriplex* and *triplex* which immediately follows the passage just quoted is all the more striking in view of the richness of texture just encountered.

Browne was equally at home in a more sombre idiom, and the related settings of 'Stabat mater dolorosa' (no. 4), 'Stabat virgo mater Christi' (no. 5, an otherwise unknown text), and 'Stabat iuxta Christi crucem' (no. 6)

---

[44] Bowers in Fenlon, *Cambridge Music Manuscripts*, 114–17: the composer's name is given in the MS referred to as 'Johannes Browne Oxoniensis' (the final 'e' of the surname seems to be clearly present, though it is omitted in Bowers's transcript).

[45] *The Eton Choirbook*, i. 1–2. The text of this antiphon is otherwise unknown.

Ex. 77

continued

Ex. 77, continued

O, Mary, mother of the saviour . . .

are perhaps his best title to fame.[46] The first and third of these (the third for low voices) are often quoted: the second, which is unfortunately imperfect in its opening section, is understandably less well known. The opening of the second section, however, for reduced voices with divided *medius*, is so characteristic of his art at its reflective best that it deserves quotation. The gradual intensification of the rhythmic movement and of the counterpoint, as the setting of the words resolves into an extended melisma of wonderful intricacy, is accomplished with great skill (Ex. 78).[47]

Walter Lambe, a clerk of St George's, Windsor, from 1479 to 1484 (and Master of the Choristers from 1482), and again from 1492 to 1499 or later, was originally represented in the manuscript by twelve compositions, of which only seven remain in whole or in part. Fortunately one of the incomplete works, his masterly 'O Maria plena gracia' for six voices (no. 3), can be transcribed from the slightly later Lambeth Choirbook (see below, p. 209), while the otherwise lost five-part 'Gaude flore virginali' has been partially recovered from a fragmentary source.[48] Lambe's art is mostly more predictable than Browne's, but a second, four-part, setting of 'Gaude flore virginali' (no. 39) is an unexpectedly complex essay in florid writing against a slow-moving *cantus firmus* (Ex. 79, p. 199).[49]

The third important member of this group, Richard Davy, a scholar of Magdalen College, Oxford, who acted as *informator choristarum* and organist jointly with one William Bernard in 1490–1 and alone until 1492 at least, and who is perhaps also to be identified with a vicar choral of Exeter Cathedral (1497–1506), was a more facile composer than Browne or Lambe—he is said according to a note in the Eton manuscript itself to have written 'O domine celi terreque' in a single day while at Magdalen— but is certainly not to be ignored. Of the ten works originally entered

---

[46] A four-part 'Stabat virgo' (no. 36) is a less expansive work.
[47] *The Eton Choirbook*, i. 59.
[48] See M. and I. Bent in *JAMS*, 22 (1969), 394–424, where it is convincingly argued that the extensive fragment of a 'Gaude flore virginali' in Brit. Lib., Add. 54324, is from Lambe's missing work rather than from that of Dunstable, which is also missing and had the same vocal range.
[49] *The Eton Choirbook*, iii. 47. Wedge-shaped brackets indicate red-void notes.

Ex. 78

continued

Ex. 78, continued

You stand, mother, joyless, discerning those terrifying crimes of the Jews.

Ex. 79

. . . a seat in the heavenly kingdoms, Rejoice, virgin mother of Christ . . .

into the manuscript, one Magnificat is completely lost and another survives only as a fragment. The celebrated *Passio domini in ramis palmarum*, or Passion according to St Matthew (no. 49), is also incomplete in the manuscript, the first eleven choruses having been supplied by the editor from the music of later sections, and the two surviving voices of numbers 12–23 having

Ex. 80

Truly this was the son of God.

also been supplemented editorially. The work is a setting of the *synagoga* part[50] for four voices, and originally totalled 42 sections. Its somewhat bland style is best suited to the more reflective moments, of which the final chorus is a representative example (Ex. 80).[51]

Of the seven votive anthems, all but the six-part 'Gaude flore virginali' (no. 51) are complete. 'O domine celi terreque' (no. 23) is long and highly florid, for all its speed of composition, and its second section opens with a delicately scored passage for divided *triplex* and *medius*, the *bassus* entering later on, a device that prefigures its even more effective use (with divided mean) in Taverner's Mass 'Corona spinea' (see below, p. 227). Apart from the five-part 'Salve regina' (no. 11), Davy's remaining antiphons follow

---

[50] See above, p. 167.
[51] *The Eton Choirbook*, iii. 134.

in a block (nos. 24–7): all are distinguished from those of Browne and Lambe by their greater, almost excessive, floridity, though there is pathos too in his own 'Stabat mater'.

A final group of composers would include Robert Fayrfax, William Cornysh junior, Edmund Turges, and Robert Wylkynson, as well as such minor figures as William Brygeman, John Hampton, Robert Hacomplaynt, and John Sygar and, in all probability, Fawkyner, William monk of Stratford, and Edmund Sturton. Of these, Fayrfax is a major figure demanding separate treatment: of the six works copied into the manuscript, four are lost (though the Magnificat 'Regali' has been recovered from the Lambeth Palace manuscript), the antiphon 'Ave lumen gracie' is incomplete, and only a five-part 'Salve regina', unique to this manuscript, survives in full. Cornysh, however, though his contribution has also suffered depredations, is more fairly represented by such of it as remains intact. Three complete compositions, one completable work, and one fragment, remain out of the original eight. There can be no doubt that Cornysh, a Gentleman of the Chapel Royal from 1501 or earlier, and Master of the Children from 1509 until the year of his death (1523), was a composer of the first rank—perhaps, with Browne, Fayrfax, and Ludford, as fine a musician as the Henrician period produced before Taverner. Compared even with these, let alone with Lambe or Davy, his music is outstanding for its delicacy of scoring and sensitivity to the text. His short 'Ave Maria mater Dei' (no. 41), in four parts for men's voices, and written in duple metre throughout, is a marvel of understatement, enlivened though it is by the picturesque reduction to the two lowest voices for the setting of the words 'mundi imperatrix inferni'. His 'Salve regina' (no. 12) is perhaps the finest of all the many settings by English composers of this period. Selective quotation is a poor method of indicating its merits, but one passage, setting the text 'gementes et flentes in hac lacrimarum valle', will serve to illustrate Cornysh's remarkable capacity for working up to, and then resolving, an emotional climax (Ex. 81, overleaf).[52] Technically, the passage is remarkable for the extreme dissonance in bar 68, and its gradual 'mollification' in bars 70 and 71. The diminished fourth (or augmented fifth) is something of a leitmotiv in this work, as it occurs earlier, at bar 20, and, almost at the end, at bar 355. Cornysh's lengthy duple-time 'Stabat mater' (no. 30, unfortunately imperfect at the beginning) is another masterpiece, varied in scoring and confident in its manipulation of tonal change for expressive purposes.

Cornysh's Magnificat from the Eton manuscript has not survived, but there is a splendid setting in the Caius College manuscript[53] which exhibits his style, and indeed that of the early Tudor period itself, at its apogee.

[52] *The Eton Choirbook*, i. 117–18, transposed down a fourth.
[53] *Early Tudor Magnificats*, ed. P. Doe (London, 1964), no. 4 (pp. 49–64). See below, p. 209.

Ex. 81

Ex. 81, continued

. . . mourning and weeping in this vale of tears.

Its five voices cover the enormous range of 26 notes (C–g'' as written, probably sounding a tone or so higher in performance by today's standard). It is remarkable for the variety of its scoring, with much division of the *tenor* and *contratenor* parts, and for the floridity of its final verse, 'Sicut erat'. But in other respects it is quite traditional, not departing at all in outline from the pattern previously described (p. 193), and indeed opening with the same phrase as Horwood's work. Cornysh has merely transposed the tone (the eighth) down a fifth, and based his setting rather more consistently on the faburden.

We shall have occasion to return to Cornysh. Amongst the remaining 'Eton' composers, Edmund Turges, about whom nothing certain is known, is in some ways a comparable figure. He is no doubt the same man as the 'Edmundus Sturges' who is recorded as the composer of a modest three-part Kyrie and Gloria in the Ritson manuscript. Three Magnificats are lost from Eton, one of them for men's voices in four parts, but again there is a splendid setting from the Caius manuscript by way of compensation.[54]

Turges's two antiphons, both settings of 'Gaude flore virginali' (no. 33, for five voices, and no. 40, for four) are less consistently interesting than those of Cornysh, but the first of them is distinguished by its lightness of texture (the scoring is for two trebles, mean, *tenor* and bass) and its use of duple time from the outset, reverting to triple metre only for a short concluding passage. One passage will serve to illustrate his capacity for harmonic adventurousness—so short an excursion into the 'flat side' forbids us to think of 'modulation', but the technique is one which has interesting parallels, both English and Continental (Ex. 82).[55]

Turges's Magnificat has been described as 'perhaps the most florid work of this period in any form'.[56] Based on the faburden of the seventh tone, transposed down a fifth, it is certainly of great rhythmic complexity. At one point (bars 172–5 of the edition) a form of syncopation is used in which an extension of the four-beat unit by half a beat (bars 172–3) is compensated for by an equivalent subtraction later (bar 175). This is a revival of an old concept, taught by Philippe de Vitry and familiar in Continental music of the late fourteenth century.[57] It is found in the Tudor organ repertory, too,[58] but it remains something of a rarity at this period. Perhaps

---

[54] *Early Tudor Magnificats*, no. 5 (pp. 65–89).

[55] *The Eton Choirbook*, iii. 4–5. Cf. the passage from Sturton's 'Gaude virgo mater christi' quoted below (Ex. 83), and, for a Continental parallel, the 'Christe' of Obrecht's Mass 'Maria zart'.

[56] Harrison, *Music in Medieval Britain*, 350. See n. 54 above.

[57] W. Apel (ed.), *French Secular Music of the Late Fourteenth Century* (Cambridge, Mass., 1950).

[58] See the setting of the Introit 'Resurrexi' by Thomas Preston: *Early Tudor Organ Music*, ii. *Music for the Mass*, ed. D. Stevens (London, 1969), 22, where the editor's time-signatures conceal a regular duple metre, displaced by one beat between his bars 52 and 58 (the second beat of bar 52, and the fourth of 58, are metrically strong beats).

Ex. 82

... That you obtain [our] desire, [as you do] Whatever, O virgin, you demand From Jesus most sweet.

the most impressive part of Turges's setting is again the 'Sicut erat', in which various solo groupings are deployed to usher in the final majestic tutti.

Robert Wylkynson was 'parish clerk' (an office deriving from the old parish church of St Nicholas before it became the chapel of Eton College) at Eton from 1496, and Master of the Choristers from 1500 until 1515. Originally the manuscript contained seven of his pieces, but he himself added his nine-part 'Salve regina' and his thirteen-part round, 'Iesus autem/ Credo in Deum', after the compilation of the second index. With most of his original contribution lost or incomplete, generalization is impossible, but there can be little doubt that the nine-part 'Salve' (no. 9) is his master-piece. It is also an admirable summation of the spirit of the Eton music, rich and complex but without pretensions to any great depth of feeling. Based on the antiphon 'Assumpta est Maria in celum', heard three times in ever-increasing speeds, the piece hardly seems suited to the Lenten season and was perhaps intended for some joyful occasion such as the feast of the Assumption itself, the College's patronal festival. 'Iesus autem transiens' (no. 50) is a curiosity, a thirteen-part round in which each singer begins with a nine-note *cantus firmus* (the beginning of a Magnificat antiphon mean-ing 'Jesus however passing in their midst . . .') and continues with the text of the Apostles' Creed. The twelve parts allotted to the latter correspond nominally with the assignment of each clause of the Creed to one of the twelve apostles, but the actual disposition of the text leads to changes of assignment within the individual phrases. The piece was copied by that collector of curiosities, John Baldwin of Windsor, into his own common-place book at the end of the sixteenth century, probably from the Eton manuscript itself.[59]

It is a characteristic sign of the music of this period that the works of the lesser composers are so high in quality. Indeed, it is in many cases only because of the smaller number of their surviving compositions that the word 'lesser' is applicable at all. A work like Sturton's six-part 'Gaude virgo mater Christi' (no. 8) is not in any objective sense inferior to the greatest masterpieces of the epoch. The occurrence of the flat seventh in the plainsong on which it is based, a transposed version of 'Alma redemptoris mater', leads to the purple passage in Ex. 83.[60] But much the same could be said of Sutton, composer of a magnificent seven-part 'Salve regina' (no. 15—the final 'O dulcis' is a particularly impressive example of suave euphony, for all its bold dissonance), Hacomplaynt, Hampton, Huchyn, or Hygons,

---

[59] For Baldwin, who also completed the 'Forrest–Heyther' part-books of English Masses, see below, p. 390.
[60] *The Eton Choirbook*, i.87; plainsong from *AS*, pl. 529. Sturton, whose identity remains uncertain, is also represented in the Lambeth Choirbook.

Ex. 83

(a) section of chant (transposed down a 5th)

tu - um   san - ctum   ge - ni - to - rem

(b) antiphon

(a) ... your holy parent ...
(b) Where the fruit of your womb ...

or for that matter Fawkyner, who was probably one of the youngest contributors.

   Although so much has been lost, the Eton manuscript offers a very fair
picture of the antiphon and Magnificat as they were cultivated around
the turn of the century. But for the third major form, the Mass, we must
turn to other sources, chief among them the magnificent, and closely related,
Caius College and Lambeth Palace choirbooks. This will also offer the
opportunity to introduce the music of Fayrfax and Ludford, the two

outstanding composers represented in these manuscripts. A few prefatory remarks about the earlier development of the polyphonic Mass, however, are necessary.

The polyphonic Mass, which had attained considerable heights in such works as 'Caput' and 'Veterem hominem' (see Chapter 3, pp. 155–8), seems to have been less assiduously cultivated during the second half of the fifteenth century. There were, however, some significant developments: in particular, the polyphonic troped Kyrie (i.e. with *prosula* or inserted text) was abandoned, and the complete *alternatim* Mass made its appearance. The Kyrie without *prosula* continued to be set, both independently and as part of a cycle, but this was for use in 'Lady Masses' (votive Masses of the Blessed Virgin Mary), for which untroped melodies were prescribed in the Salisbury ritual.[61] There was an increasing tendency, too, to base such settings on a 'square' (see above, p. 181), rather than on the plainsongs actually specified. Henceforth, when English composers wrote an elaborate 'festal' Mass, it was without Kyrie, this being sung, with its *prosula*, in plainchant. Cyclic compositions for the Lady Mass, however, did include the Kyrie, and the whole Mass might well be based on the appropriate 'square'. The *alternatim* structure, too (in which sections of polyphony and plainchant were sung in alternation), seems to have been devised especially for the Lady Mass, though it was by no means an invariable feature of it.

These developments must be charted in a small number of sources, amongst them the Ritson manuscript and a fragmentary choirbook now in York. As we have seen (p. 186), the Ritson manuscript includes three Masses, each for three voices, in addition to the Kyrie and Gloria by 'Sturges'. Two of these, entitled 'Rex summe', and 'Gaudete in domino', are by Sir Thomas Packe. Both are partly *alternatim*—the former in its Kyrie, Gloria, and Credo, the latter in its Kyrie only—and neither is based on plainchant. The titles are thus hard to explain, since even 'Rex summe' is not amongst the Kyrie melodies prescribed in the Sarum Missal for the Lady Mass. These two works are of some elaboration and are not without interest; the third, Henry Petyr's 'plainsong' Mass, is without Kyrie and is set in full (like, for example, Taverner's later such work). It may therefore not have been intended for the Lady Mass at all, though its simplicity would have made it appropriate enough.

The York manuscript,[62] a series of fragments dating from perhaps as

---

[61] *Missale Sarum*, ed. F. Dickinson (Oxford and London, 1861–83), col. 761*. They were usually identified, however, by the *prosula* text originally associated with them, as they are in modern books.

[62] York, Borthwick Institute, MS 1. See H. Baillie and P. Oboussier, 'The York Masses', *ML*, 35 (1954), 19–30. The authors' assumption of a Lincoln origin for the manuscript, based on William Horwood's presence there from 1476, was revised by Baillie, 'A London Gild of Musicians', *PRMA*, 83 (1956–7) in favour of London, where Horwood became Master of the Gild of St Nicholas in 1474 and John Cook (also named in the manuscript) in 1501.

late as 1515, is too incomplete to allow firm conclusions; but it contains parts of four Kyries, one of which at least, ascribed to 'Horwod' and based on the melody 'O rex clemens', was *alternatim*; two Gloria–Credo pairs, again *alternatim*, three Masses consisting (as far as can be ascertained) of Gloria, Credo, Sanctus, and Agnus; and finally a three-part Gloria and Credo, nearly complete, for men's voices. The four Kyries were presumably all intended for the daily Lady Mass (the melody 'O rex clemens' was prescribed in the Sarum Missal for Mondays); the remaining works, except perhaps for the third Mass, though not musically related to them, may well have also been so intended. The first of the Gloria–Credo pairs is actually based on the melody—a 'square'—later used by Nicholas Ludford in his Tuesday Lady Mass (see below, p. 224). The second is based on a Compline versicle, 'Custodi nos', while the fifth, more elaborate than the others and ascribed to 'Johannes Cuk', is based on a Marian antiphon, 'Venit dilectus meus'.

We know from inventories that festal Masses in five and six parts were written by composers of the 'Eton' period, but we have to wait until the sumptuous Lambeth and Caius choirbooks for surviving complete examples. These manuscripts share to a certain extent the same repertory; the statement in the Caius manuscript that it was the gift of Edward Higgons, 'canon of this church', can be taken as meaning that it was destined either for St Stephen's, Westminster, or for Salisbury Cathedral, of which the former is much the more probable.[63] The Lambeth manuscript is similar in script but differs, at times quite radically, in its musical text. It has a more old-fashioned repertory, including Lambe's 'O Maria plena gracia' (from which the fragmentary Eton version, no. 3, can be completed), and a six-part antiphon, 'Ave Maria ancilla trinitatis', by the excellent Sturton, another 'Eton' composer. It also contains Fayrfax's 'Regali' Magnificat, which was once in the Eton Choirbook but is now lost from it. The two manuscripts together are major sources of the music of Fayrfax and Ludford, the latter of whom worked at St Stephen's. Although the Lambeth and Caius manuscripts may well have issued from the same workshop, the former would seem to be slightly the earlier of the two (the latter being perhaps of 1525 or so) and was perhaps intended for a different church.[64]

---

[63] The Caius College Choirbook (MS 667) is described by Bowers in Fenlon, *Cambridge Music Manuscripts*, 126–8, where the probability of the connection with St Stephen's is stressed. Higgons was a London lawyer of some eminence: the phrase 'ex dono et opere' implies that it was commissioned by him for presentation to the church, not that he himself was the copyist.

[64] The contents of the Lambeth Choirbook (MS 1 of the Lambeth Palace Library) are listed by Harrison in *The Eton Choirbook*. The theory that it was intended for St Stephen's is based solely on its inclusion of several works of Ludford: there is no reason to connect it with Higgons, even if both MSS came from the same workshop. Geoffrey Chew, 'The Provenance and Date of the Caius and Lambeth Choir-books', *ML*, 51 (1970), 107–17, concludes that the Lambeth MS was intended for St Stephen's and the Caius MS for Salisbury; but it is altogether more probable that the Caius MS was intended for St Stephen's and the Lambeth MS for some other comparable institution—possibly St George's, Windsor.

Robert Fayrfax was the leading figure in the musical establishment of his day, a member of the Chapel Royal from 1497 or earlier, on the musical establishment of St Albans Abbey in 1502 (a post which will have been compatible with membership of the Chapel Royal, which he never relinquished), Doctor of Music at Cambridge (1504) and Oxford (by 'incorporation', 1511). He died in 1521.[65] We possess the 'exercise' for his doctorate, presumably composed for the Cambridge degree (the Mass 'O quam glorifica'), and four other complete Masses as well as the fragmentary 'Sponsus amat sponsam'. The Mass 'Regali ex progenie' was copied at King's College, Cambridge, in 1503–4,[66] and its companion Magnificat, as we have seen, was included in the Eton Choirbook, presumably by 1502. The other Masses cannot be dated, though we may suspect 'Tecum principium' from its mastery to be the latest.

Two of Fayrfax's Masses, 'Regali' and 'O bone Iesu', are musically linked both to a Magnificat and an antiphon, while the Mass 'Albanus' is connected to an antiphon, 'O Maria Deo grata'. Unfortunately the antiphon in every case survives incomplete, but it seems that 'O bone Iesu' preceded its eponymous Mass and Magnificat since they took their titles from it. The Mass is therefore a 'derived' Mass, though not the earliest by an English composer;[67] nevertheless, perhaps under Continental influence, it marks a fresh start in the direction of what has usually been called the 'parody' Mass, the prototype of examples by Taverner and Tallis and perhaps others too. The academic requirement for a Mass and an antiphon by supplicants for musical degrees at Oxford no doubt stimulated the composition of related pairs of works, though the question as to which would have been written first, in such a context, is scarcely relevant.

The 'O bone Iesu' trilogy, or rather the Mass and Magnificat from it, is not especially striking, though we should beware of thinking it early on that account; rather, the simplicity of some of the writing, for example at the 'et incarnatus' of the Mass, suggests a late date. We can assume that the 'Regali' trio was in existence by 1502, and it may very well be earlier still, as the Mass and Magnificat at least are very conventional, the former being based on two statements of the antiphon 'Regali ex progenie' in each movement.[68] The chant can also be made to fit what survives (the bass) of the related antiphon, 'Gaude flore virginali'.[69] The Magnificat

[65] On Fayrfax see E. B. Warren, 'The Life and Works of Robert Fayrfax', MD, 2 (1957), 134–52.
[66] Harrison, Music in Medieval Britain, 164.
[67] See above, p. 146.
[68] Fayrfax, Collected Works, ed. E. B. Warren, 3 vols. (AIM, 1959–66), i. 104–36. Subsequent references are to this edition.
[69] H. Benham, Latin Church Music in England c. 1460–1575 (London, 1977), 123. But there seem to be no grounds for believing it to be later than the Mass on that account. The surviving part is in the Collected Works, iii. 28–9.

is more tenuously linked, but the connection is there all the same.[70] Its freedom from a *cantus firmus*, however, imparts a spontaneity lacking in the Mass.

The rhythmic complexities of the Mass 'O quam glorifica',[71] which are at times excessive, are obviously to do with its function as a degree exercise, the earliest identifiable one to have survived. The *cantus firmus*, a hymn for the Assumption, is laid out once, in freely devised rhythms, in each movement. The 'Albanus' Mass[72] is rather more interesting, both for its own sake as a repository of appealing melody and as a structure. Fayrfax based it on a nine-note motive, part of an antiphon of St Alban previously used by Dunstable in his motet 'Albanus roseo rutilat'.[73] He took only the phrase used to set the word 'Albanus' itself, however, and for the purposes of his structure reduced it to six notes by omitting repetitions (or rather by divesting them of any significance, since his layout incorporates many note-repetitions). This motive, consisting of the notes c d' e' c' d' c', appears altogether 40 times, either in its basic form, or in retrograde, inversion, or retrograde inversion (Ex. 84).[74] The last ten appearances occur

Ex. 84

in the 'Dona nobis pacem', where the nine-note shape is restored as a string of semibreves (original notation): five times in each of the voices in turn, like a fugal exposition, and then, finally, five times in the *tenor* alone in a series of descending steps (Ex. 85, overleaf).[75]

'Tecum principium',[76] based on a Vespers antiphon for Christmas and Epiphany, is rather finer still, though it still suffers from a certain rhythmic and formal stiffness. In part this is due to a continued concern for motivic working, which is prominent in this Mass, and can be seen for example in the section of the Gloria given in Ex. 86 (pp. 214–15).[77]

In assessing Fayrfax, however, it should be remembered that he was

---

[70] *Collected Works*, ii. 1–11; *The Eton Choirbook*, iii. 96–103 (no. 47).

[71] *Collected Works*, i. 64–103.

[72] Ibid. 33–63.

[73] See above, p. 136.

[74] The first appearance of each, from which the examples are derived, is as follows: (a) Gloria, bars 14–22; (b) Gloria, bars 30–7; (c) Credo, bars 23–31, followed by two successive statements in sequence, each one degree lower than the preceding (bars 31–46); (d) Credo, bars 121–7, followed by two statements each a tone higher, bars 128–37; thus the fourth, fifth, and sixth statements in this movement are the exact retrogrades, so far as pitch is concerned, of the third, second, and first respectively.

[75] *Collected Works*, i. 62–3.

[76] Ibid. 137–71, with revised version of part of Gloria, 172–3.

[77] *Collected Works*, i. 143; plainsong from *AS*, pl. 54.

Ex. 85

Ex. 85, continued

Grant us peace.

Ex. 86

(a) plainsong

Te - cum prin - ci - pi - um in di - e   vir - tu - tis

(b)

Ex. 86, continued

(a) With you [greatest] of princes in the day of virtue . . .
(b) You who sit at the right hand of the father, have mercy on us. For you only are holy. You only are the lord.

clearly a pioneer in the development of the large-scale Mass. He was not lacking in self-criticism, as may be seen from the greatly improved version (assuming that it is his) of the 'Qui tollis' that immediately precedes the above quotation in the Forrest–Heyther and Peterhouse part-books. In any case, Fayrfax was clearly more readily stimulated by a special text, and two or three of the antiphons are finer than anything in the Masses. Even the two surviving 'Eton' antiphons, a 'Salve regina' (no. 19) and 'Ave lumen gracie' (no. 53, incomplete) have greater rhythmic fluidity than they. He was not a formal innovator in this sphere, and all his antiphons except the 'Salve regina' (which concludes with a third, triple-time, section) are divided into the usual two sections, triple and duple. But in such works as 'Ave Dei patris filia', 'Eterne laudis lilium', and 'Maria plena virtute', all settings of the lengthy texts in 'poetic prose',[78] there is a successful amalgam of a more declamatory style and a broad structural layout. This is most apparent in 'Maria plena virtute', a kind of meditation on the seven last words from the cross, placed in the context of a prayer to Mary. The choice of G minor as the tonality, with a key-signature of two flats in two of the five parts and the frequent use of A flats, while not unprecedented in England, is carried through more consistently than (for example) in certain works of Cornysh. Possibly, as with the schematic use of an ostinato in the Mass 'Albanus', and as in a certain predilection for proportional complex-ities of notation, there is an element of Continental influence here. At all events, the music is deeply felt, as a short passage from the opening

---

[78] *Collected Works*, ii. 36–46, 47–56, 59–71. 'Ave Dei patris filia' is a text later used by Tallis; there is also an anonymous setting in the Lambeth Choirbook.

of the second section will make clear (Ex. 87).[79] After such restraint, which is characteristic of the whole work, the final lengthy tutti (bars 138–202) is all the more striking. Something of its onward momentum can be sensed from the concluding bars (Ex. 88, p. 218).[80]

This is perhaps the point at which to mention the curious Mass 'O quam suavis' for long considered a work of John Lloyd, a clerk of the Chapel Royal from 1511 to 1520. This attribution rested on a misreading of its enigmatic ascription as 'Hoc fecit Io[hann]es maris', 'John of the Sea' being interpreted as John Floyd or Lloyd. The true reading of the name, however, in defiance of grammar, appears to be 'm[atr]es maris', and the real identity of the composer remains unknown. Mystification is not confined to the ascription. The *tenor* part is written out as a series of riddles which must be solved before the work can be performed, though the style of the music itself is quite straightforward. The sumptuously designed choirbook in which it is preserved—perhaps a presentation copy for a wealthy patron—also contains a three-voiced votive antiphon, 'Ave regina celorum', again cryptically written.[81]

Nicholas Ludford was clearly a younger composer than Fayrfax: he joined the Fraternity of St Nicholas in 1521, the year of Fayrfax's death, and died around 1557. He was a member of St Stephen's, Westminster, at its dissolution in 1548; there he had held the office of verger, an important post like that of St George's, Windsor.[82] He may all the same have been older than Taverner (d. 1545), since his music is included in the Lambeth and Caius College choirbooks. In the former are preserved his five-part Mass 'Lapidaverunt Stephanum' and the six-part Mass 'Benedicta'; the Caius College manuscript has these and the five-part 'Christi virgo', the six-part 'Videte miraculum', and the Magnificat 'Benedicta'. His music is not included in the Forrest–Heyther part-books (see below, pp. 226 seqq.), but 'Christi virgo' and two more Masses, 'Inclina cor meum' and 'Regnum mundi', with four votive antiphons, were copied into the late Henrician

[79] Ibid. 65–6.

[80] Ibid. 71.

[81] The manuscript (Cambridge, Univ. Lib., Nn. vi. 46) is described, and the inscription clarified, by Bowers in Fenlon, *Cambridge Music Manuscripts*, 118–19, with a plate of one opening on pp. 120–1. The Mass was first published without any attribution by H. B. Collins as *Missa O Quam Suavis* (Burnham, 1927). See also Harrison, *Music in Medieval Britain*, p. 268. The *cantus firmus* is a Corpus Christi antiphon, derived from one for the feast of St Nicholas, 'O Christi pietas', and also used for a well-known Sanctus melody, no. VIII of the Vatican editions. I remain attracted by an informal suggestion of Dr Ronald Woodley that the name should be read antithetically as Wylkynson, i.e. son of the welkin or sky. If the Mass were originally based on the identical melody of the antiphon 'O Christi pietas', that would not be inappropriate for the parish clerk of Eton College, the chapel of which was previously dedicated to St Nicholas. For the melody see Ch. 2, n. 102.

[82] Cf. the career of John Plummer, above, p. 151.

Ex. 87

Jesus said to his disciples: 'I thirst for the salvation of the peoples.' Hear our prayers in your mercy, O Jesu.

Ex. 88

★ Edn. marks ♭ here.

part-books belonging to Peterhouse, Cambridge.[83] Ludford's posthumous reputation quickly faded, unlike that of Fayrfax, and it may well have been more localized during his lifetime; yet he was a musician of the very highest calibre, less versatile and more experimental than Taverner, but fully his equal in contrapuntal skill and in the resourceful use of the human voice.

If the order in which Ludford's Masses were composed corresponds to their distribution in the extant manuscripts, we need not be surprised that 'Lapidaverunt Stephanum', for all its technical maturity, is somewhat lacking in variety.[84] The six voices for which the Mass and Magnificat 'Benedicta' are scored offered greater scope,[85] and it is perhaps more a matter of astonishment that such mastery should be displayed by a composer of whom virtually nothing was known until modern times. It was not yet a cliché to score the 'Et incarnatus' for high voices and the 'Crucifixus' for low; here the plaintive phrase to which the words 'ex Maria virgine' are set, the rich sonority of the 'Crucifixus', and the wonderful manipulation of harmony in the following 'Et resurrexit' (note the suspended dissonance in bar 136, imparting a curiously questioning note to an otherwise confident passage), seem to speak to us with a directness that transcends the intervening centuries (Ex. 89, pp. 220–2).[86]

The Magnificat is based, most unusually, on a *cantus firmus*, the same as that of the Mass, making it effectively a fifth movement. The two works are also related in other ways. The chant is heard once in each movement, including the Magnificat itself: it would be hard to think of a more splendid way of celebrating a Marian feast than by performing the whole ensemble at Mass and Vespers.

All Ludford's Masses have a 'head-motive', a similar passage at the start of each movement, but those of 'Christi virgo' and 'Videte miraculum' are more sharply marked off. That of 'Christi virgo' makes an especially impressive start to the Gloria (Ex. 90, p. 223).[87] These Masses are more subtle in some ways than 'Benedicta', but they do not exceed it in self-assurance and command of the medium.

Quite different, at least superficially, are the seven three-part Masses written for the daily celebration of the Lady Mass, perhaps initially at least for the use of St Stephen's. They are preserved in a set of part-books

---

[83] MS 471–4, kept in the University Library. See N. Sandon, 'The Henrician Partbooks, at Peterhouse, Cambridge', *PRMA*, 103 (1976–7), 106–40, and his thesis 'The Henrician Partbooks' (Exeter, 1983); see below, p. 243.

[84] Nicholas Ludford, *Collected Works*, ed. J. D. Bergsagel, 2 vols. (AIM, 1963–77), ii. 1–38. The *cantus firmus* is an antiphon for Lauds on St Stephen's day (*AS*, pl. 60).

[85] Ibid. 130–79, 180–93; Magnificat also in *Early Tudor Magnificats*, i, no. 7. The *cantus firmus* is the verse of the respond 'Beata es virgo', for the feast of the Assumption (*AS*, pl. 497).

[86] *Collected Works*, ii. 151–5.

[87] Ibid. 39.

Ex. 89

Ex. 89, continued

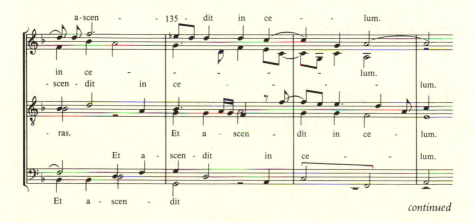

continued

Ex. 89, continued

And he was made flesh by the holy spirit of the virgin Mary. And was made man. He was crucified also ... And he rose on the third day as foretold by the scriptures. And ascended into heaven.

Ex. 90

And on earth peace to men of good will.

which may conceivably be in the composer's own hand;[88] of the four
books, three contain the polyphonic parts, and the fourth, uniquely, the
plainchants and other monophonic music intended to alternate with the
polyphony. Each Mass contains a Kyrie, Gloria, Alleluia, Sequence, Credo,
Sanctus, and Agnus, the Offertories and Communions being given in plainchant. The Sanctus and Agnus settings, and the Credo on ferias iv and
vi (i.e. Wednesday and Friday) are set in full; otherwise the music is *alternatim*.
   Perhaps the most interesting feature of these by no means insubstantial
works is that the movements of the Ordinary are based on 'squares'. In
the Kyrie and Gloria, and in all but the two Credos just mentioned, the
phrases of these melodies are first heard monophonically, followed by a
polyphonic setting of the same phrase or its continuation. The general
character and origin of these melodies have been discussed above (pp. 181
seqq.). Ludford's choice of melodies, one for each day, is comparable but
not identical to the rather larger selection in the Lansdowne source. For
example, his 'Sunday' melody, entitled 'Leroy' in yet another manuscript,

[88] Brit. Lib., Roy. App. 45–8, using printed music-paper datable to *c.*1530 (see J. Milsom, 'The
Date of Ludford's Lady Masses', *ML*, 66 (1985), 367). The Masses are published in the *Collected Works*, i.

is one of the three assigned to Sundays in Lansdowne.[89] (To anticipate slightly, we shall find that Taverner used this melody in his Kyrie 'Leroy', and that this was therefore probably intended for the Sunday Lady Mass.) On the other hand, his melodies for ferias ii and v (Monday and Thursday) are the other two 'Sunday' melodies of Lansdowne (where one of them is ascribed to 'Dunstapel'), while the others are not found elsewhere at all in monophonic form. Ludford's 'Tuesday' melody is particularly interesting, as it is derived from an anonymous chanson, 'Or me veult bien esperance mentir', now to be found only in a manuscript of Neapolitan provenance, the so-called Mellon Chansonnier.[90] It is possible that this chanson is by an English composer, but the piece enjoyed Continental popularity, as it was arranged as a motet, 'Ave tota casta virgo', and as an organ piece with the curious title 'Portigaler' (following the name of the *tenor* tune, 'Portugaler', in the motet version).[91] We have already noted the occurrence of the melody in one of the 'York' Masses.[92] It can also be found in an organ 'Kyrie' in a manuscript of Ludford's time,[93] and, slightly later, as the basis of a short keyboard piece with the title 'Orma vulte', obviously a corruption of 'Or me veult'.[94]

The opening of Ludford's Kyrie for Tuesday will serve to illustrate both his style in these works and the melody itself (Ex. 91).[95]

The Alleluias and Sequences are based not on squares but on the appropriate plainchants, with which they alternate. The seven Alleluias are those assigned to each day of the week in Lady Masses from the Purification (2 February) to Advent in the Salisbury Missal.[96] The choice of Sequences, which was free according to the rubrics, does not exactly follow the selection

[89] Brit. Lib., MS Lansdowne 462, fo. 151ᵛ, no. 7; entitled 'Leroy' in Rome, Bibl. Vat., Reg. lat. 1146, fo. 73ʳ. The ultimate derivation is from a Kyrie based on a plainsong found in Oxford, Bod. Lib., Rawl. liturg. d. 3, fo. 72ᵛ; see R. Bowers and A. Wathey, 'New Sources of English Fifteenth- and Sixteenth-Century Polyphony', *EMH*, 4 (1984), 330–46, describing Oxford, New College, MS 7, fos. 299–300. There are fragments of a four-part 'Leroy' Mass by Ludford in Brit. Lib., Add. 30520, fos. 2ʳ⁻ᵛ.

[90] Cf. n. 24. The identification was made by Margaret Bent: see her article 'The Transmission of English Music 1300–1500', *Studien zur Tradition in der Musik* (Munich, 1973), 68.

[91] The motet version occurs anonymously in Munich, Staatsbibl., clm 14274 (the St Emmeram Codex); printed in Dufay, *Opera Omnia* (Rome, 1964 (CMM, i)), vi, no. 88 (a two-part version in the destroyed Strasbourg MS 222 C. 22 was ascribed to Dufay). The organ piece is in the *Buxheimer Orgelbuch*, ed. B. A. Wallner (Kassel, 1958–9), i, no. 43.

[92] Above, p. 209.

[93] Brit. Lib., Roy. App. 56, fo. 15ʳ (*Early Tudor Organ Music*, ii. 16–17). The second section is wrongly called 'Christe'; it is in fact a second treatment of the first phrase, presumably for use in a ninefold *alternatim* performance with the monophonic melody.

[94] Oxford, Christ Church, Mus. 361, fo. 19ᵛ (*Early Tudor Organ Music*, ii. 18). There is also a monophonic version entitled 'Ormavoyt' scribbled in a copy of the 'Matthew' Bible once belonging to Evesham Abbey: see R. T. Dart, 'Notes on a Bible of Evesham Abbey (ii): A note on the music', *English Historical Review*, 79 (1964), p. 777.

[95] Ludford, *Collected Works*, i. 44.

[96] *Missale ad usum . . . Sarum*, ed. Dickinson, col. 781*.

Ex. 91

Lord have mercy.

given there.[97] The Offertory and Communion, sung in plainsong throughout, are those of the same season (that is, of the *Missa Salve*); but alternatives
for other seasons are given in an appendix.[98] The Introits and Graduals
are not included.

If John Taverner (*c.*1495–1545) outshone even his most talented contemporaries, it was at least partly because he combined many of their best qualities:
Cornysh's clarity of texture, Fayrfax's sensitivity to the text, Ludford's

[97] Ibid., cols. 769*–755*, referred to at col. 781*. Ludford's Sunday Sequence is 'Ave preclara'
(col. 879, for the Octave of the Assumption); those for Monday to Saturday are the first three and
nos. 5–7 of the selection in cols. 769*–775*.
[98] MS 48, fos. 25ʳ–27ᵛ; *Collected Works*, 153–4.

grandeur of design. In addition, he was a substantial innovator, above all in his development of the shorter forms of Mass and antiphon, and in the importance given to ritual forms, in particular the respond. In these ways he set the pattern for much of what was to follow. But these considerations do not adequately explain the very special attraction of his finest music. It is perhaps in sheer melodiousness that he transcends the common currency of his day; and this, allied to his superlative command of contrapuntal resource, entitles him to be regarded as the outstanding figure between Dunstable and Byrd.

The old legend that Taverner stopped composing after 1530 because of his 'Protestant' sympathies is now discredited. Indeed, much of his innovatory work would be inexplicable on that hypothesis. A native (it would seem) of Lincolnshire, he is found as a clerk-fellow of Tattershall collegiate church in 1525, and in the following year he became the first *informator choristarum* at Cardinal College, newly founded by Wolsey (subsequently known as 'Christ Church' and, from 1546, the seat of Oxford's bishopric).[99] He left Cardinal College in 1530 and emerges later as a substantial citizen of Boston, where he was buried. His involvement with Lutheran activities at Oxford in 1528 led to his arrest and subsequent release; this was perhaps no more than a temporary escapade, though Taverner was certainly a supporter of the Royal Supremacy as his actions at Boston as Cromwell's agent show.[100]

We are fortunate in possessing a set of part-books which in all probability originated at Cardinal College while Taverner was there. Known as the 'Forrest–Heyther' part-books, they contain eighteen Masses of which the first eleven relate to that period.[101] (It should be explained that by this time the old 'choirbook' format had been largely abandoned in favour of separate part-books, from which the music could be learnt and subsequently performed in choir. The change is perhaps to be associated with a tendency for the polyphonic choir to occupy choir-stalls in preference to singing from the middle of the choir, but the exact chronology of this

---

[99] Harrison, *Music in Medieval Britain*, 27, 36–7. Cardinal College was built around the Augustinian abbey of St Frideswide, suppressed by Wolsey in 1525. A planned new chapel never rose above the foundations. On Wolsey's fall the new foundation was dissolved and became in 1532 'King Henry VIII's College in Oxford'. For the later history see below.

[100] For the biography see the works of C. Hand and D. S. Josephson listed in the Bibliography, and the article in *NGD*.

[101] Oxford, Bod. Lib., Mus. Sch. e. 376–81: fac. edn., New York and London, 1988. Dom A. Hughes, *Medieval Polyphony in the Bodleian Library* (Oxford, 1951), 43–6; J. Bergsagel, 'The Date and Provenance of the Forrest–Heyther Collection of Tudor Masses', *ML*, 44 (1963), 240–8; editions (other than of Masses by Fayrfax, Sheppard, Tye and Taverner) in *Early Tudor Masses*, ed. Bergsagel, 2 vols. (London, 1963–76) (EECM, i, xvi). The books are named after William Forrest, a petty canon of Osney Cathedral, who once owned them, and William Heather, a Chapel Royal singer who founded Oxford's Chair of Music and gave the books to the university.

development cannot be ascertained at present.) The first Mass is Taverner's own 'Gloria tibi trinitas',[102] adorned with initial letters bearing what has been plausibly taken to be a likeness of the composer himself; the other composers represented in the first layer are Fayrfax, with four Masses, and Avery Burton, John Marbeck, William Rasar, Hugh Aston, Thomas Ashewelle, and John Norman, with one each. Taverner, with two more Masses, Ashewelle, and Aston reappear in the second layer, along with the later Sheppard, Tye, and Alwood.

The two Masses of Taverner in the second layer are 'Corona spinea' and 'O Michael', both for six voices,[103] and it seems certain that they too pre-date his departure from Cardinal College. Indeed, 'O Michael' appears, from a certain stiffness and a preoccupation with technique, to be rather earlier than either of the other two.[104] 'Gloria tibi trinitas' and 'Corona spinea', on the other hand, are masterpieces of the highest order. The former is best known for the 'in nomine' section of the Sanctus, which gave rise to a whole genre of pieces like it, all based on the plainsong 'Gloria tibi trinitas' and called either that or 'In nomine'. It is a passage of wonderful beauty, but its fame should not be allowed to obscure the merits of the Mass as a whole, which reside chiefly in the grandeur of its design and the vigour of its counterpoint. The latter may be illustrated by a passage from the Credo (Ex. 92, pp. 228–30).[105]

'Corona spinea' is characterized by the clarity and variety of its scoring, the flexibility of its melodic lines, and its structural strength. The *cantus firmus*, easily recognizable as such in the score, has not been identified. The vocal orchestration, as it may justly be called, is subtle and sophisticated throughout; almost every conceivable disposition of the six parts is employed, together with the subdivision of trebles and means, to bring about a constantly shifting range of tone-colour in the context of a continuously flowing stream of melody. This sense of colour may best be illustrated by some extracts from the second Agnus, where it may be seen how Taverner was able to transcend his predecessors in the exploitation of contrast and luminosity of texture. The unexpected entry of the second

---

[102] TCM, i. 126–56; Taverner, *Six-part Masses*, ed. Benham (London, 1978), 1–74.

[103] TCM, i. 157–93, 194–225; *Six-part Masses*, 75–169, 170–245.

[104] The *cantus firmus* is the respond 'Archangeli Michaelis interventione' for Matins on two feasts of St Michael (St Michael in Monte Tumba, 16 Oct., and the Apparition of St Michael, 8 May). The melody is printed, from the Salisbury Processional of 1519, ibid. 260. The Mass is noteworthy for several extended passages in canon, five in all.

[105] *Six-part Masses*, 32–3; plainsong ibid. 256–7, after the Antiphonal of 1520, fo. ii of the *Temporale* (*AS*, pl. 286 has the identical form of the melody). The original *cantus firmus* is in long notes with many textual omissions; the long notes have been split up by the editor to accommodate the full text on the basis of variant readings in another source and parallel treatment in other works. Our quotation from the original written form is from his Appendix, p. 258.

Ex. 92

Ex. 92, continued

(b) plainsong, with the above section of *cantus firmus* as originally notated

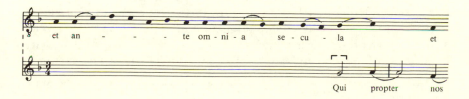

Glo - ri - a ti - bi tri - ni - tas e - qua - lis u - na de - i - tas

et an - - - te om - ni - a se - cu - la et

Qui propter nos

continued

Ex. 92, continued

(*a*) Who for us men and for our salvation descended from the heavens.
(*b*) Glory to you, trinity of equals, single deity from before all ages, now and for ever.
   * Liquescent neume, usually interpreted in polyphony as a prolongation (in isochronous settings as a note of double length, or as two notes of the same pitch).

bass in bar 92 is a telling stroke, lending solidity to the ethereal superstructure (Ex. 93, pp. 231–3).[106]

   These two Masses mark a turning-point not only in Taverner's own work but in that of Tudor music as a whole. In one sense they belong to the florid tradition represented by Ludford, Fayrfax, Cornysh, and the Eton composers generally. In other ways, however, they opened up new possibilities in the realms of vocal scoring, structure, and harmonic manipulation, possibilities that were exploited both by Taverner himself and by Tallis, Byrd, and their contemporaries. As the anthologies of the later sixteenth century clearly show, Fayrfax and Taverner in particular were the fountain-head from which later composers drew their inspiration, a new beginning which the upheavals of the Reformation could not obliterate.

   Where the chronology of his works is so uncertain, and his development so personal, it would be wrong to infer that all Taverner's more 'advanced' compositions are later than the works just discussed. The 'Western Wind' Mass[107] is a case in point. It falls into no clearly defined category—it is, for example, neither 'festal' nor 'short' in the senses generally understood by these terms—and while highly original, it does not by any means fulfil all the expectations which a late date might raise. Its principal novelty lies in its use of a profane melody, treated as the theme for a set of variations,

   [106] *Six-part Masses*, 156–62. For parallels cf. Ludford (Ex. 89 above) and Cornysh's 'Stabat Mater' (*The Eton Choirbook*, no. 30).
   [107] TCM, i. 3–29; *Four- and Five-part Masses*, 37–90; also ed. P. Brett (London, 1962). For the melody on which this and the later Masses by Sheppard and Tye were based, see Vol. II, Ch. 8.

Ex. 93

continued

Ex. 93, continued

Ex. 93, continued

Lamb of God, you who take away the sins of the world . . . have mercy on us.

nine in each of the four movements. Since the melody is virtually unchanged throughout, variety is achieved by the different contrapuntal contexts in which it is placed; and it is a great tribute to the composer's skill that no hint of monotony is present. The work was evidently highly regarded, since both Sheppard and Tye later wrote Masses in imitation of it, and Taverner's own composition was copied out later in the sixteenth century.

Taverner's other Masses are of less consequence, though none is without interesting features. The Mass 'Playn Song'[108] is based, like Henry Petyr's, on a restricted range of note-values, such as could have been represented by plainsong symbols and perhaps originally was, although the extant source uses ordinary notation. The full text of the Gloria, Credo, Sanctus, and Agnus is set, except for the conventional omission in the Credo from 'Et in spiritum sanctum' to 'in remissionem peccatorum'.[109] For all its restraint, it is a work of considerable charm and inventiveness. 'Mater Christi' and 'Small Devotion'[110] are based on polyphonic antiphons by Taverner himself. The rather curious name of the second of these is believed to be a corruption of 'S Will Devotio', an abbreviation of 'Sancti Willelmis Devotio'. The antiphon from which it is derived, 'O Christe Iesu pastor bone', is thought originally to have been addressed to St William of York, to whom the statutes of Cardinal College prescribed the singing of an antiphon every evening. The very similar text 'O Christe Iesu', incorporating a prayer for Henry as 'founder' of the College, was substituted for 'O Willelme'

---

[108] TCM, i. 30–49; *Four- and Five-part Masses*, 1–36.

[109] R. Hannas, 'Concerning Deletions in the Polyphonic Mass Credo', *JAMS*, 5 (1952), 155–86 (esp. 169–70, 172–4). At this period, however, the omissions probably indicate no more than a desire to keep the length of the setting within reasonable bounds. The chart on pp. 184–5 is insufficiently representative to give a plausible picture of the general pattern of omissions in English Masses of the early Tudor period.

[110] TCM, i. 99–125, 70–98; *Five-part Masses*, 1–67, 68–123.

after Wolsey's fall and the re-foundation in 1532. Later still, the antiphon was further adapted to include a prayer for Queen Elizabeth.[111]

'O Christe Iesu' (or 'O Willelme') is a short and quietly impressive work, and the very simple Mass based on it shares much of its quality. Unfortunately the *tenor* part is missing both from the Mass and the antiphon, the latter in both its sources, and also from an English adaptation of 'Small Devotion' made at some later date.[112] We are more fortunate in the case of the Mass 'Mater Christi', though it too lacks a *tenor* part, since the antiphon on which it is based survives complete. As the adaptation is fairly close, a good part of the Mass can be reconstructed with confidence. The antiphon[113] has always been held to be one of Taverner's most advanced works, with its sensitive declamation of the text and effective use of antiphonal contrast; but it shares many of its features with 'O Christe Iesu', which was evidently composed before 1530; the observation serves to reinforce the difficulties of arriving at a satisfactory chronology.

The 'Meane' Mass, also known as 'Sine nomine', has been described as 'the most obviously novel of Taverner's shorter pieces'[114] on account of its consistent use of concise points of imitation, harmony, and antiphonal contrasts. Like the other two short Masses it is for five voices, here extant in full. Its brevity is such that exaggerated claims for its significance are out of place, but the version of the head-motive used in the Sanctus (in which, as in the openings of the other movements, the middle voice is silent) offers some relief from the predominantly syllabic style (Ex. 94). Like 'Small Devotion', this Mass was later adapted to English words, at times rather freely.[115]

Taverner's 'Leroy' Kyrie, a short but beautiful piece based on a 'square', was intended as we have seen for the Lady Mass.[116] His other ritual works include three Magnificats, a Te Deum, and several responds. The Magnificats, which are not amongst his most inspired works, are all *alternatim* settings based on the first tone, in four, five, and six parts respectively.[117] The

---

[111]   Harrison, *Music in Medieval Britain*, 341. The Elizabethan text beginning 'Christe Iesu', found in Oxford, Christ Church, Mus. 979–83, fits better the rhythm of the putative 'O Willelme' and may therefore have been made directly from it. Edited (as 'O Christe Iesu') in TCM, iii. 73–7, and in *Votive Antiphons*, ed. Benham (London, 1981), 124–30, with discussion of sources and texts on pp. 181–2.

[112]   From the 'Wanley' part-books (see below, pp. 278–9); printed TCM, iii. 169–98.

[113]   TCM, iii. 92–8; Taverner, *Votive Antiphons*, pp. 110–23.

[114]   Benham, *Latin Church Music*, p. 138. Printed TCM, i. 50–69; *Four- and Five-part Masses*, 91–138. The original title indicates the lack of trebles (i.e. the higher boys' voices).

[115]   TCM, iii. 143–68.

[116]   Above, p. 224. Printed TCM, iii. 54–5; Taverner, *Ritual Music*, ed. Benham (London, 1984), 136–9 (with alternating 'square'). The three short settings of 'Christeleison' (TCM, iii. 56–7; *Ritual Music*, 140–1) are based on the middle section of Ludford's 'Tuesday' melody (above, p. 224).

[117]   TCM, iii. 3–8, 9–16, 17–25; *Ritual Music*, 40–52, 22–39, and 1–21 respectively (with plainchant insertions). Much of the top part of the six-part work is missing, as is the whole of the *tenor* of the five-part.

Ex. 94

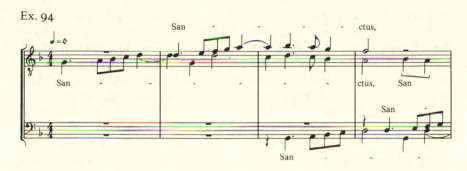

Holy, holy, holy:

first and third are based on the chant itself, the second on the faburden.
The Te Deum is a rather similar work in five parts for men's voices only:
the *tenor* is missing from the only source, but can be reconstructed as it
carried the plainchant.[118] The responds, which are of two kinds, have several
points of interest. The first type, which is the older, sets the music allotted
in the rubrics to the cantors. Taverner's 'In pace'[119] is a typical specimen,
setting the opening intonation to the respond itself, the verse, and the
Gloria Patri, leaving the main part of the respond and its abbreviated repetitions to be sung in plainchant, thus:

R.	Pol.	In pace
	Pl.	in idipsum dormiam et requiescam.
V.	Pol.	Si dedero somnum oculis meis, et palebris meis dormitationem:
R.	Pl.	dormiam et requiescam.
V.	Pol.	Gloria patri e filio et spiritui sancto:
R.	Pl.	dormiam et requiescam.

---

[118] TCM, iii. 26–34; *Ritual Music*, 53–74 (with plainchant insertions and a superior reconstruction
of the *tenor*).

[119] TCM, iii. 48–51; *Ritual Music*, 100–8 (with plainchant insertions).

Taverner's music in this case is a very straightforward setting of the text and melody of the cantors' sections, laying out the chant as a row of longs (semibreves in quartered note-values) in the top part. His other two solo responds, for liturgical reasons, are more picturesquely scored for high voices. At Matins on All Saints' Day (1 November) the eighth lesson ('of virgins') was directed to be read by a boy; following it the respond 'Audivi vocem de celo' was to be sung by five boys from the altar steps, their heads covered with white amices and carrying lighted candles.[120] Taverner's setting[121] is in four parts, the second being divided for just one chord: it is of great complexity, particularly in view of the conditions under which it was intended to be performed. 'Gloria in excelsis' is the verse of the respond 'Hodie nobis celorum rex', sung after the first lesson at Matins of Christmas (which preceded Midnight Mass). Here the respond proper was sung by two clerks, and was not set in polyphony; the verse again, however, was to be sung by five boys, arrayed as before, from a high place beyond the high altar, facing the choir.[122] An extract from Taverner's setting[123] will give an idea of what was expected of them (Ex. 95, pp. 237–8).

These texts and some others continued to be set in this way by later composers such as Sheppard. But at the same time a new method of setting responsorial texts had come into being, whereby the choral sections of the chant, not those for cantors, were given polyphonic treatment. Taverner's two settings of 'Dum transisset sabbatum',[124] the third and last respond of Easter Matins, appear to be the earliest extant examples; in them the text is laid out as follows:

R.	Pl.	Dum transisset
	Pol.	sabbatum, Maria Magdalena et Maria Iacobi et Salome emerunt aromata, ut venientes unguerunt Iesum, Alleluya, Alleluya.
V.	Pl.	Et valde mane una sabbatorum veniunt ad monumentum, orto iam sole.
R.	Pol.	Ut venientes unguerunt Iesum, Alleluya, Alleluya.
V.	Pl.	Gloria patri et filio et spiritui sancto.
R.	Pol.	Alleluya, Alleluya.

In both settings, the chant is placed in the *tenor*. This became the normal

---

[120] *Breviarium Sarum*, ed. F. Procter and C. Wordsworth, 3 vols. (Cambridge, 1879–86), iii, cols. 974–5.

[121] TCM, iii. 35–6; *Ritual Music*, 91–4 (with plainchant insertions).

[122] *Brev. Sar.*, i, col. clxxxiv; Antiphonal (1519), *Temporale*, p. lii.

[123] TCM, iii. 46–7; *Ritual Music*, 95–9 (including the plainchant respond 'Hodie nobis').

[124] TCM, iii. 37–40 (*a* 5, with a four-part variant, 40–2), 43–5 (*a* 5); *Ritual Music*, 109–18 (arranged *a* 4, 119–26), 127–35. The sources of no. 1 in its five-part version, followed in TCM, include an adaptation of the opening words, properly left in plainchant. The second setting does not incorporate clean breaks at the points from which partial repetitions would be made in a liturgical performance.

Ex. 95

(a) Iste versus cantetur a quinque pueris

continued

Ex. 95, continued

Glory to God in the highest:

method for later composers; it has been pointed out that it reflected the fact that the polyphonic music of a secular establishment such as Cardinal College was provided by a true choir, and that 'the effect was to restore the kind of contrast between choir and soloists which was originally contemplated by the liturgy'.[125] The same method was usually employed in the sixteenth century for the responsorial chants of the Mass, for example in the Alleluias of Ludford's Lady Masses, and in Taverner's similar setting of the 'Thursday' Alleluia, 'Veni electa'.[126]

Taverner's ritual works also include a fine setting of the prose 'Sospitati dedit egros', for Matins of St Nicholas, and a few other odds and ends.[127] The votive antiphon is another important category; of the three large-scale settings 'Ave Dei patris filia', based for some reason on the Te Deum chant, is a rather dull piece; 'Gaude plurimum' is considerably more accomplished, while 'O splendor glorie' is a fine, closely knit work, part of which is elsewhere attributed to Tye. Two of the shorter antiphons have already been mentioned; of the others, four are unfortunately lacking both *triplex* and *tenor* parts; there are also two three-part fragments of a larger work

[125]   Harrison, *Music in Medieval Britain*, 369.

[126]   TCM, iii. 53; *Ritual Music*, 146–9, showing the plainchant verse and the repetition of the polyphony to the words 'speciem tuam', which in the original plainchant is set to the same neuma as the word 'Alleluya'; the music is then performed a third time to accommodate the responsorial repetition of 'Alleluya' (unless a Sequence is to follow). Taverner's other Alleluia (TCM, iii. 52; *Ritual Music*, 150–1) has not been identified; its *cantus firmus* resembles the chant of the Marian Alleluias 'Salve virgo' and 'Virga Iesse', but is identical to neither.

[127]   The prose is in TCM, iii. 110–16, and, with the appropriate plainchant sections (including the respond 'Ex eius tumba', on to the repeat of which the prose is to be grafted), in *Ritual Music*, 75–90. This volume includes one or two pieces not in TCM; in all, the minor ritual items include four isolated Sequence verses, a Tract verse (the metrical 'Tam peccatum'), and two processional items. Most of these owe their survival solely to John Baldwin's penchant for collecting passages of three-part counterpoint in the late 16th cent. (Brit. Lib., R. M. 24. d. 2).

and, finally, a textless piece entitled 'Quemadmodum' of which the original function remains obscure.[128]

Taverner also wrote some secular pieces, but all but one are again incomplete.[129] In spite of the imperfect preservation of his music, however, the range and grandeur of his genius are very evident. We might, perhaps, feel differently if his three or four great Masses had not survived in full. They are the setting in which his more innovatory, or more purely functional works, can be judged. In that context, his whole output can be seen as a remarkably complete statement of the early Tudor style at its zenith.

The number of composers known to have reached maturity during the reign of Henry VIII, and more particularly between 1520 and 1545, is considerably greater even than the comparable figure for the reign of Henry VII, even if this epoch is extended by a decade or so to 1520. If the total for the earlier period is about 40 names (with perhaps a few more very minor figures), that for the later period must be close to 70. In part this reflects a greater proportion of ascribed, rather than anonymous, compositions in the sources, particularly in the case of secular works; but it also reflects the continuing vitality of the musical tradition, now beginning to be susceptible to Continental influence once more.

Of Taverner's contemporaries, in addition to Ludford, the Forrest–Heyther books contribute the names of another six: Burton, Marbeck, Rasar, Aston, Ashewelle, and Norman. Ludford, Aston, Marbeck, Norman, and Rasar (as well as Fayrfax, Pasche, and Taverner himself), together with about twenty others, appear in the late Henrician part-books now in the collection belonging to Peterhouse, Cambridge.[130] Although this set is imperfect, lacking the *tenor* and part of the *triplex* books, it is an enormously valuable source. From Scotland the Scone Abbey, or 'Carver', Choirbook[131] preserves a mainly earlier repertory but adds the name of Robert Carver, alias Arnat, himself. Many more names can be added from the lesser sources of church music in this period, together with the palpably earlier material of later sets such as the 'Gyffard' part-books,[132] which belong to the reign of Mary.

Of the composers just named, Burton, Rasar, and Norman are fairly minor figures. Avery Burton's Mass 'Ut re mi fa sol la' from the Forrest–Heyther Books was copied out as a five-part work, but an essential bass voice is lacking, which rather suggests that a set of part-books such as this

---

[128] The votive antiphons and the 'Quemadmodum' are printed in TCM, iii, and, with improved texts, in Taverner, *Votive Antiphons*.

[129] Printed in Josephson, *John Taverner*, and in Taverner, *Ritual Music*, 158–75.

[130] See above, n. 83.

[131] Edinburgh, National Library of Scotland, Adv. 5. 1. 15.

[132] London, Brit. Lib., Add. 17802–5, a set of four part-books once the property of a Dr Philip Gyffard. Their ultimate origin is unknown.

was not actually used. In any event, the work is not one of great distinction.[133] Norman's Mass 'Resurrexit Dominus' is a straightforward *cantus-firmus* setting, while Rasar's 'Christe Iesu', in duple time throughout, might conceivably be based on a polyphonic model, perhaps on the same text as Taverner's antiphon '(O) Christe Iesu pastor bone' ('O Willelme pastor bone').[134]

Rather more interest attaches to John Marbeck's Mass 'Per arma iusticie', though more for the sake of its composer than any intrinsic qualities in the music. In fact it is a *cantus-firmus* Mass like many others of the period, illustrating Marbeck's thorough if conventional musicianship. The sources preserve two of his votive antiphons, one a Jesus antiphon, 'Domine Iesu Christe', the other a Mary antiphon, 'Ave Dei patris filia', of a kind which he presumably would not have wished to see preserved. At first sight the charming little Christmas piece, 'A virgin and mother', looks more characteristic of the reformer, but it too must pre-date his public disavowal in 1550 of his former study and practice of music, and for all we know it may be an adaptation from a setting of a Latin text.[135]

The two most important contemporaries of Taverner, apart from Ludford, are Ashewelle and Aston. Both may have been slightly older than he, perhaps more nearly contemporary with Fayrfax. Ashewelle was a chorister at St George's, Windsor, from 1491 to 1493, and is listed amongst the singing clerks (*clerici conducticii*) in 1502/3. He subsequently became *informator choristarum* at Lincoln Cathedral (by 1508) and master of the Lady Chapel choir at Durham Cathedral Priory (1513).[136] Apart from his two Masses in the Forrest–Heyther books there are some fragmentary works including the Masses 'Sancte Cuthberte'[137] and 'God Save King Harry', based on a five-note motive (*f g a bb a*, used also in works by Alen, Pasche, and Alwood, amongst others) which may very well be based on the sol-fa names implied by its title (Ex. 96).[138]

Ashewelle's surviving complete Masses are splendid affairs. 'Ave Maria'

---

[133] Burton, whose first name sometimes appears as 'Davey' or 'David', and his second as 'Burnett', was a member of the Chapel Royal from 1509 to 1542. His life is summarized by L. D. Brothers, 'Avery Burton and his Hexachord Mass', *MD*, 28 (1974), 153–76, at 154–8; the earlier assumption that he composed a vocal Te Deum appears not to be borne out (for his organ Te Deum see below, pp. 252–3). Brothers's belief that the numerous 6–4 chords in the hexachordal Mass were the product of deliberate experiment cannot be sustained. The Mass is in duple time throughout, suggesting that it can have been written no earlier than the 1520s.

[134] Above, p. 233. The Masses of Norman and Rasar are in *Early Tudor Masses*, ii.

[135] The polyphonic works of Marbeck are printed in TCM, x. In the Preface to his biblical *Concordance*, published in 1550, Marbeck refers to his having 'consumed vainly the greatest part of my life' in 'the study of Musike and playing the organs'.

[136] *Early Tudor Masses*, ii, p. x.

[137] London, Brit. Lib., Add. 30520, fos. 3ʳ⁻ᵛ, possibly based on the Salisbury respond 'Sancte *N*. Christi confessor' (*AS*, pl. 693).

[138] N. Sandon, 'F G A B Flat A: Thoughts on a Tudor Motif', *Early Music*, 12 (1984), 56–63, at 62 (reconstructed from the two part-books of an otherwise lost set; Cambridge, Univ. Lib., Dd xiii. 27, with ibid., St John's College MS K31).

Ex. 96

(*b*) And on earth peace to men . . .

is noteworthy for its rhythmic qualities and the brilliance of its scoring.[139] 'Iesu Christe', for six voices, is if anything even more sophisticated: its *cantus firmus* is laid out as a study in proportions, and the whole thing is a superbly confident assertion of the 'post-Etonian' aesthetic.[140]

Hugh Aston (or Assheton, etc.) was a composer of a similar stamp—indeed the scribes occasionally confused the two men. He was given permission to supplicate for the degree of Bachelor of Music at Oxford in 1510, and is next heard of as Master of the Choristers at Newarke College, Leicester, in 1525, when the choir there, probably for reasons beyond his control, was in a bad way. Although proposed as a possible *informator* for Cardinal College in 1526, he remained at Leicester until the dissolution of the College in 1548.[141] He died there in 1558.

Aston's music is rather more massively scored, and more motivically conceived, than that of Ashewelle. These qualities are fully evident in what is perhaps his most impressive work, the six-part Mass 'Videte manus tuas',

[139] *Early Tudor Masses*, i. 61–124. Note for example the Gloria, bars 69–87, for divided trebles and means.

[140] *Early Tudor Masses*, ii. 1–72. For the layout of the *cantus firmus* see ibid., Appendix II. The chant is that employed by Dunstable in his Gloria/Credo 'Iesu Christe fili Dei vivi'.

[141] Harrison, *Music in Medieval Britain*, 28–30. A fuller summary of Aston's career is offered by N. Sandon, 'Another Mass by Hugh Aston?', *Early Music*, 9 (1981), 184–91.

and may be illustrated by a short passage from its Gloria, where the building up of the texture at 'Gracias agimus' is particularly striking (Ex. 97).[142]

Ex. 97

We give thanks to you . . .

Aston's Mass 'Te Deum' needs to be considered in conjunction with his antiphon 'Te matrem Dei laudamus', a setting of a Marian adaptation of the Te Deum text, using some of its plainsong material and opening similarly to the Gloria, Credo, and Sanctus of the Mass. The antiphon was later provided with a non-Marian text, 'Te Deum laudamus' (used in the *Tudor Church Music* edition),[143] though this is not by any means identical to the liturgical Te Deum. It has been suggested that the Mass and antiphon were written in fulfilment of the requirements for proceeding to the degree of Bachelor of Music,[144] but the Mass seems considerably more assured in technique than the antiphon, and its title 'Te Deum' in all but one of the sources may indicate that it was composed after the antiphon had been adapted to the Trinitarian text.

The Mass is based entirely on phrases from the first half of the Te Deum chant, giving it something of the character of an ostinato Mass. The material is, however, presented with some freedom, in different voices and transposi-

---

[142] TCM, x. 40–1.

[143] Ibid. 99–113. The adaptation is found only in a late source, the Sadler part-books (Oxford, Bod. Lib., Mus. Sch. e. 1–5); and while this itself was naturally copied from an earlier source now lost, it is quite certain that the Marian text is the original.

[144] There is no record that Aston actually took this degree. In those days, permission to 'supplicate' was granted on the strength of previous lengthy study, and subject to the composition of a Mass and antiphon. Only when this had been done would the degree actually be granted. The 'exercises' were supposed to remain in the hands of the proctors, but no original copies have come down to us from those times.

tions, while the openings of the Gloria, Credo, and Agnus make use of the initial motive of the chant, which differs from that of the remaining verses. The opening of the Sanctus is based, naturally, on the 'Sanctus' melody of the Te Deum; this movement is also tonally contrasted with the others, cadencing on to G while they are in C. The effect is of a well-planned and convincing structure. The Mass is quite independent of the antiphon except in its head-motive (in the Gloria, Credo, and Agnus), which is a refinement of the opening of the latter. The Sanctus does not utilize the threefold 'Sancta' of the antiphon.

Of Aston's remaining sacred works, only the antiphon 'Gaude virgo mater Christi' is complete, though three others survive with three or four voices out of their original five. 'Gaude virgo mater Christi', setting part of a text previously used by an anonymous composer in the Ritson manuscript (see above, pp. 183 seqq.) is a fine work culminating in a splendid 'Amen'.[145] Aston also composed a 'Hornepype', and possibly other works, for keyboard solo, and a famous 'Ground' for three–part consort (see below, p. 342). It has been suggested that the fragments of an anonymous Mass of the period, to which this ground can be fitted, are the remains of a Mass by Aston himself.[146]

The study of the very considerable quantity of music by the lesser composers of this period is beyond the scope of this book. Much of it is contained, though sadly incomplete, in the set of part-books belonging to Peterhouse and now kept at the University Library, Cambridge.[147] Copied around 1540, it is a very diverse collection embracing music by composers as early as Fayrfax and Pasche (to whose generation such figures as Arthur Chamberlayne and Edward Martyn can be assigned); by the major masters whom we have been discussing, Ludford, Taverner, and Aston, with whom Richard Pygott, William Rasar, John Mason, Richard Bramston, Thomas Knyght, and Robert Jones are contemporary; and the earlier works of such figures as Thomas Tallis, Christopher Tye, William Whytbroke, Thomas Appleby, and indeed Marbeck, whose activity as a composer must have ceased by about 1540. The more eminent of these will be dealt with in the following chapter, to which their most characteristic contribution belongs. It should be remembered, however, that for many of them any attempt to force their careers into the pattern imposed by even so strong an external factor as the Reformation and its consequences results in a highly artificial picture

---

[145] TCM, x. 85–98. It too survives in the Sadler part-books with an alternative text, 'Gaude mater matris Christi' (on St Anne); it has been edited in this form by Sandon.

[146] By Sandon in *Early Music*, 9 (1981), 184–91. See also comments ibid. 519–20 (by J. Blezzard) and in vol. 10 (1982), 215–16 (by O. Neighbour).

[147] See above, n. 83.

of their development. This applies not only to Tallis, Tye, and Sheppard, who were mature masters by 1545, but also to such lesser men (in addition to Appleby and Whytbroke) as Philip Alcoke, John Blytheman, William Mundy, Robert Okeland, and Thomas Wryght, all of whom are represented in the Gyffard part-books, of Marian date, mentioned above. Whether their compositions in individual instances are Marian or Henrician is in some cases difficult to determine; but it is quite clear that a large part of that collection looks back to the earlier reign. Some of its composers are palpably of a still earlier generation: Bramston and Knyght have been mentioned, and another is John Redford, the almoner (and organist) of St Paul's who died in 1547.

During the 1530s and 1540s the rich and highly decorated style that is so characteristic of Ludford, Taverner, and Aston began to give way to a leaner, sparer, idiom characterized by bolder melodic lines, a freer use of dissonance, a predominance of duple time over triple, and a tendency to write in a smaller number of parts. There was also a renewed attention given to the setting of the minor ritual forms at the expense (to some extent) of the large-scale votive antiphon and the festal Mass. On the whole, these developments are more characteristic of the younger composers; but we have seen how Taverner cultivated the ritual forms and a more syllabic style, and in the case of John Redford, a composer whose contribution to vocal church music shows him to have been a bold and resourceful musician, another factor is brought into play, the experience of writing liturgical organ music (see below).

One of the principal exponents of a 'bold' style[148] was Sheppard; but for the purposes of this chapter it may be illustrated by an anonymous Te Deum from the Gyffard part-books. In this fine work, an *alternatim* setting based on the faburden of the chant, the freer use of dissonance will be immediately apparent (Ex. 98).[149]

Although Scotland was politically and ecclesiastically independent of England at this period, something may be said here of Scottish church music, since much of it shows a strong affinity to English idioms. We do not possess any document that can be linked with the Chapel Royal of James IV, refounded in 1501 on a basis that clearly made provision for elaborate polyphony; but we do have, in the so-called 'Scone Antiphonary' or 'Carver

---

[148] The term is not entirely fanciful: Morley in 1597 introduces the name of 'one maister *Boulde*' as the supposed protagonist of a then archaic style characterized by 'harsh allowances'. *A Plaine and Easie Introduction*, 117–19.

[149] Brit. Lib., Add. 17802–5, fo. 1ʳ. Plainchant version from a contemporary miscellany, ibid., Roy. App. 56, fo. 30ᵛ (even numbered verses only, possibly for *alternatim* performance with an organ setting).

Ex. 98

(a) Plainchant, verse 4, transposed down a tone

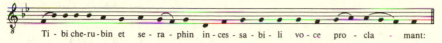

Ti - bi che-ru-bin et se - ra-phin in-ces-sa-bi-li vo - ce pro - cla - mant:

To you cherubs and seraphs with ceaseless voice proclaim:

Choirbook',[150] an impressive testimony to the musical repertory of a well-endowed establishment of the early sixteenth century. Robert Carver (alias Arnat), born in 1487 or 1488, was a member of Scone Abbey (Augustinian) from 1503 or 1504, and was still active as a composer in 1546, 'in his fifty-ninth year'. It seems likely that the book belonged to the abbey and represents the core of its repertory.

The choirbook includes music by Fayrfax, Nesbet, Lambe, and Cornysh, here anonymous, and a copy of Dufay's Mass 'L'homme armé', indicating Scotland's closer links with Continental music at this time. There is also a certain amount of music of which the composers cannot be identified, including a fine Mass beginning with a troped Kyrie, 'Rex virginum'. But the outstanding figure is Carver himself, with five Masses and two antiphons. It is quite possible that his ten-part Mass 'Dum sacrum misterium', composed in his twenty-second year 'in honour of God and St Michael', was intended for the coronation of James V in the Royal Chapel of Stirling castle on St Michael's day (29 September), 1513.[151] The *cantus firmus* of his own 'L'homme armé' Mass[152] may have been suggested to him by his knowledge of Dufay's work though it owes nothing to Dufay in point of style and indeed presents the theme in the major mode, as had Ockeghem and some others but not Dufay himself. The work dated 1546 and ascribed to his fifty-ninth year is a four-part Mass, 'Pater creator omnium'. His most impressive published composition is the nineteen-part antiphon 'O bone Iesu', a *tour de force* exceeded in later years only by Tallis amongst English Renaissance composers.[153] In spite of some understandable weaknesses of counterpoint it is a wholly convincing essay in textural richness, an expansion of the traditional insular texture to undreamt-of proportions unaided by any division into separate choirs. 'Gaude flore virginali', for five voices, is a less obviously successful experiment in tonal manipulation: as the extract in Ex. 99 shows, the range of chords is quite wide, but the melodic idiom is not especially compelling and the 'joy' of the text is scarcely hinted at.[154] Perhaps here too the influence of the Franco-Flemish school can be detected; if there is an English parallel, it is in some of the more experimental work of Fayrfax.

The rather later 'Dunkeld' part-books are a collection of mainly foreign

[150] See above, n. 131. Described by D. Stevens, 'The Manuscript Edinburgh, National Library of Scotland, Adv. MS. 5. 1. 15', MD, 13 (1959), 155–67, and by K. Elliott, 'The Carver Choir-Book', ML, 41 (1960), 349–57; some compositions printed in *Music of Scotland 1500–1700*, ed. K. Elliott (London, 1957; 2nd edn., 1964).

[151] The date 1513 is given in the manuscript, but it has been altered first from 1506 and then from 1508 (or possibly 1511). Clearly if Carver was in his 22nd year in 1513 he cannot have been in his 59th year in 1546. Scone Abbey itself was dedicated to the Trinity and St Michael, so the work may have originally been written somewhat earlier for that establishment.

[152] *Music of Scotland*, 30–57.

[153] Ibid. 87–102; Carver, *Collected Works*, ed. D. Stevens (AIM, 1959), i. 1–20.

[154] *Collected Works*, i. 24–6.

Ex. 99

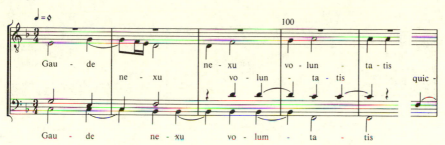

continued

Ex. 99, continued

Rejoice in the entanglement of the will ... Whatever, O virgin, you demand from Jesus most sweet. Rejoice, mother of the wretched, because the father of the ages will give to those who worship you here a fitting and a rich reward.

music; but at the end are two six-part Masses of insular provenance, one of which, on the Offertory 'Felix namque', has been published.[155] This is not a *cantus-firmus* Mass, but is based rather freely on the intonation of the chant; there is an untroped Kyrie.

This discussion of sacred music in the early sixteenth century cannot be concluded without a brief discussion of the surviving repertory of liturgical organ music. Reference has been made above to the function of the organ

[155] *Music of Scotland*, 58–86. The part-books are in the Edinburgh University Library, MS 64 (lowest part missing).

in the liturgy; the written sources tend to bear out the view that its principal use was on occasions on which a polyphonic choir would not have been present, and for establishments which did not rise to vocal polyphony at all. Monastic churches, including the cathedral priories, frequently had one or more organs, both in the monastic and the public parts of their churches.[156]

As has been said, organ music must normally have been improvised. This will invariably have been true in the fifteenth century, from which no written organ music survives. There is evidence from the later fifteenth century that choirboys were taught to play the organ,[157] and a strong implication that it was still essentially an improvisatory art at that period. Nevertheless, there are a few written sources preserving a Henrician and Marian repertory, and an art of some sophistication quickly arose. In the reign of Henry VIII the most considerable master was John Redford; to his name must be added those of several lesser men, such as Avery Burton, Robert Coxsun, Philip ap Rhys, John Thorne, Richard Wynslate, and Thomas Preston. A slightly earlier repertory of purely anonymous music has left some traces.[158]

Liturgical organ music is almost invariably based on the appropriate plainchant or its faburden; there are, however, one or two fragments based on a 'square', namely that used by Ludford for his 'Tuesday' Lady Mass.[159] In the case of the most important pre-Marian source,[160] the compilation appears to have been put together by a provincial organist from materials gathered in London. There is a strong possibility that the compiler may have been Richard Wynslate, who was a singer at St Mary-at-Hill, that well-known cradle of composers, in 1538; in 1541 he became Master of the Choristers at Winchester Cathedral, a post which he held through all the subsequent upheavals. His name is one of only two to appear in a form that does not rule out his possible status as the copyist of the music; and of the two, his is the career that fits in better with the supposition.[161] Since the manuscript refers to Philip ap Rhys as organist of St Paul's Cathedral

[156] See esp. Harrison, *Music in Medieval Britain*, 209–18, on the late medieval organ and its ritual use. Further information is in Bowers, *Choral Institutions*, in Knowles, *Religious Orders*, iii. 19–20, and in the introductions to the two volumes of *Early Tudor Organ Music*.

[157] In the deed appointing William Horwood instructor of the Choristers in 1477 (Harrison, *Music in Medieval Britain*, 177, citing Lincoln Chapter Acts 1536–47, 31) and in later similar appointments there; similarly Hygons at Wells in 1479 (Harrison, 179), Foderley (1496), Tildesley (1502), and Thomas Ashewelle (1513) at Durham (Harrison, 187; Ashewelle's indenture is translated by Knowles, *Religious Orders*, iii. 17–18); and James Renynger at Glastonbury, 1534 (Harrison, 191).

[158] The complete repertory is published in *Early Tudor Organ Music*, 2 vols. (London, 1966 and 1969), supplemented by *The Mulliner Book*, ed. D. Stevens (London, 1951; 2nd edn., 1954).

[159] See nn. 93, 94.

[160] London, Brit. Lib., Add. 29996, first section (fos. 6–48, of which fos. 6ʳ–45ʳ contain the repertory in question).

[161] The other is Robert Coxsun, who was a member of the choir of St Nicholas, Wallingford, in 1548, when he was aged 58 (information kindly supplied by Dr Bowers). On St Mary-at-Hill, see Baillie in *ML*, 36 (1955), 55–64.

'in London', it is certain that it was copied (outside London, no doubt) in 1547 or later; if substantially complete by 1549, as the nature of the repertory strongly suggests, its initial usefulness would have been short-lived, though its owner may have brought it out of mothballs for the period of the Marian reaction. Together with two similar manuscripts, probably of Marian date,[162] it came, much later, into the hands of Thomas Tomkins, who had them bound together with other material; the whole was indexed and the folios numbered by his son Nathaniel, presumably after Thomas's death in 1656. Tomkins's manuscript comments on some of the liturgical pieces afford a fascinating glimpse into the mind of a conservative musician of the early Stuart period.[163]

Philip ap Rhys had himself been organist at St Mary's before going to St Paul's; he may have been a pupil of Redford and a means of the wider dissemination of his music.[164] His organ Mass, a setting of the Kyrie 'Deus creator omnium', Gloria, Sanctus, Agnus, together with the Offertory 'Benedicta sit' for Trinity Sunday,[165] is a unique survival so far as England is concerned, though the form had long been current in Continental Europe. John Thorne, who was organist of York Minster from 1543 until his death in 1573, was himself at St Mary-at-Hill in 1539/40.[166] Tallis, Preston, Blytheman, and William Shelbye (organist of Canterbury Cathedral for six years from 1547) are others whose extant organ music, though surviving largely or wholly in later sources, may date in part at least before 1549.[167]

All these were overshadowed at that time by John Redford, who laid the foundations of the style and was its most distinguished exponent. His music is characterized by the freedom and energy of the counterpoint, as may be seen in this passage from his lengthy Offertory, 'Precatus est Moyses' (Ex. 100).[168]

The Offertory (and particularly the 'Felix namque' for the Lady Mass

---

[162] Add. 29996, fos. 49–71, of which fos. 49ʳ–67ᵛ, together with fos. 45ʳ–47ᵛ of the first section contain liturgical organ music; and fos. 158–183, with liturgical organ music on fos. 158ʳ–178ᵛ. All this music was apparently copied by the same person; it is considered in the following chapter.

[163] The manuscript is fully described in my thesis (1965), and its liturgical music critically examined. A briefer discussion may be found in my *English Keyboard Music Before the Nineteenth Century* (Oxford, 1973), 21–37.

[164] On Ap Rhys, see Baillie in *ML*, 36 (1955), 55–64.

[165] *Early Tudor Organ Music*, ii. 1–16.

[166] See Baillie, 'Some Biographical Notes on English Church Musicians', *RMARC*, 2 (1962), 18–57 at 55.

[167] Up-to-date information on these, and on Redford, may be found in *NGD*.

[168] *Early Tudor Organ Music*, ii. 103–4; plainsong (from the Gradual of 1532), ibid. 137. The chant is in the lowest part, ornamented, but on the basis that each note of the plainsong corresponds to one semibreve (minim in transcription), in the setting. This 'monorhythmic' or 'isochronous' treatment was usual in the organ repertory; the method of ornamentation, or 'breaking the plainsong', is described by Morley, *A Plaine and Easie Introduction*, 96, citing Redford, Tallis, Preston, 'Hodgis', Thorne, and 'Selbie' (i.e. Shelbye) as its main exponents. Hodges, none of whose music has survived, was an organist of Hereford Cathedral.

Ex. 100

(b) plainchant

(memento) A - bra - ham   I - sa - ac et   Ia -

continued

Ex. 100, continued

cob: qui - bus iu - ra - sti da - re ter - ram   flu - (entem lac et mel)

(b) [Remember] Abraham and Isaac and Jacob: to whom you swore that you would give them a land flowing [with milk and honey].

from Septuagesima to Advent) was one of the two most frequently set forms; the other was the hymn, for which composers usually provided enough music for the odd-numbered stanzas. The original custom with all these forms was to allow for the vocal performance of the intonation: by the celebrant in the case of the Magnificat and Te Deum; by the ruler (or rulers) of the choir in the case of the hymn, Kyrie, Sanctus, Agnus, Offertory, and other items of the Proper of the Mass; and by the celebrant followed by the ruler in the Gloria of the Mass. It became usual in the hymn, however, to assign the whole of the first verse, including the intonation, to the organ. The procedure with the hymn, Magnificat, and Te Deum was the opposite of that adopted in vocal settings, which was to provide polyphony for the even-numbered verses. In Preston's Gradual 'Hec dies' and Alleluia 'Pascha nostrum' for Easter Day,[169] the organ takes the part of the cantors, a procedure followed in one or two later examples of the Alleluia.[170]

While some of the liturgical organ music that has come down to us is contrived and mechanical, the best of it has a charm and playfulness, bordering sometimes on eccentricity, that is absent from other forms. Some of these qualities may be seen in a verse from a very fine anonymous Magnificat, based on the faburden of the eighth tone transposed down a fifth (Ex. 101).[171]

Of our four extant complete Te Deum settings, one by Avery Burton and two by Redford certainly belong to this early period; Burton's is a remarkably sophisticated treatment on the faburden transposed down a tone. It is instructive to compare his technique with that of the vocal setting quoted earlier (Ex. 98); the stylistic 'match' is so good that the vocal and

[169] Early Tudor Organ Music, ii. 26–30. The complete composition, though possibly one of Preston's earlier works, is discussed in the following chapter.

[170] e.g. Tallis's Marian Alleluia, 'Per te Dei genitrix', printed as a 'Fantasy' in Tallis, Complete Keyboard Works, ed. D. Stevens (London, 1953), 8–9.

[171] Early Tudor Organ Music, i. 24–5. For a version of the faburden, untransposed and for a different verse, see Ex. 76.

Ex. 101

(timentibus)

organ settings could almost be used in alternation, though there is no evidence that this was actually done (Ex. 102, overleaf).[172] Altogether, the

[172] Ibid. 1; plainchant, ibid. 151. For a discussion of the conventions as to the written pitch of both vocal and organ settings of the Te Deum, and of their possible relation to a single performing pitch (in the case of Exx. 98 and 102 perhaps up to a minor third higher in terms of the present-day standard) see my article in *Early Music*, 6 (1978), 188–94, and, more generally, in 'The Pitch of Early Tudor Organ Music', *ML*, 51 (1970), 156–63.

Ex. 102

(a) Tibi omnes

(b)

Ti - bi o - mnes an - ge - li, ti - bi ce - li et u - ni - ver - se po - te - sta - tes:

(b) To you all angels, to you the heavens and the universal powers . . . [proclaim]

organ music of this period provides a fascinating mirror image of its vocal counterpart in its imaginative response to the ritual needs of the Church.

After the Ritson manuscript,[173] the next major source of music to profane and vernacular texts is the Fayrfax Book of c.1502.[174] It has been so named from the fact that it contains music by Fayrfax, from the presence of his arms on the title-page and a somewhat inaccurate indication there as to which songs are his, and from its subsequent ownership by members (though

---

[173] See above, pp. 183–9. For some remarks on the changed context of courtly music under Henry VIII see the following chapter, pp. 322–3.

[174] London, Brit. Lib., Add. 5465, edited in full in *Early Tudor Songs and Carols*. A critical edition of the texts appears in J. Stevens, *Music and Poetry in the Early Tudor Court*.

not apparently the direct descendants) of the composer's family. But there is no evidence that Fayrfax himself planned, wrote, or commissioned the manuscript, and it must remain a somewhat mysterious source so far as its intended destination and function are concerned. It originally contained fifty-one songs, of which two are now missing entirely and another seven are incomplete as a result of leaves having fallen out. Even so, it is a splendid document of early Tudor song, second only to the 'Henry VIII' manuscript (below) in extent and variety, and second to none in the quality of its music.

Apart from those of Fayrfax, the manuscript contains songs by William Newark(e) (d. 1509), Sheryngham, Hamshere, Richard Davy, Edmund Turges, Tutor, Sir Thomas Philipps (MS 'Phelyppis'), Browne, William Cornys(s)h Junior (so named and spelt), and Gilbert Banaster (here 'Banastir'). Newark, Sheryngham, and Philipps are unique to this manuscript, and little is known about them; Tutor may perhaps be the John Tuder of the Pepys manuscript (Banaster and probably Turges appear in both sources); Hamshere and Browne are presumably the Hampshire and John Browne of the Eton manuscript; Banaster, Cornysh, Davy, and Turges provide an unquestionable link with it. Fifteen of the songs are anonymous, in some cases perhaps because of missing leaves.

The high quality of the music is not immediately apparent, for the manuscript begins with a dozen two-part songs (not now fully extant), to courtly amorous texts, of no very great interest. Nor can it be said that Fayrfax's own contribution is of great distinction, though his songs pay careful attention to the declamation of the text, particularly (as with Newark, Hamshere, and Sheryngham) in those that are for three voices. Many of the songs are short monostrophic compositions (though the settings are often extended by means of elaborate melismas at the ends of lines of the verse); others are through-composed settings of poems in two or more stanzas, which tended to encourage composers to greater concision and variety: Fayrfax's 'Sumwhat musyng'[175] is a good example, with a sense of progress through the stanzas and a mournful little melisma to illustrate the poet's summary of his mistress's character at the end. Most interesting of all are those in carol form, generally with a varied burden and through-composed stanzas.[176] Philipps's 'I love, I love, and whom love ye?'[177] is a lively secular carol, with only minimal variation in the burden and an essentially strophic setting of the six stanzas. The burden itself will convey its musical character (Ex. 103, overleaf).

There are a number of rather similar pieces, but with through-composed stanzas and more varied burdens, by Browne, Davy, Cornysh, and others.

[175] *Early Tudor Songs and Carols*, 62–4.
[176] For the carol form, and the term 'burden', see above, pp. 162–5.
[177] *Early Tudor Songs and Carols*, 70–3.

Ex. 103

But the finest works in the collection are the religious carols, mostly on the Passion, and particularly those in four parts, of which the supreme examples are Browne's 'Jhesu, mercy' and Cornysh's 'Woffuly araid'.[178] The latter has often been quoted; it does indeed transcend the normal limits of musical expression current at the time. As in other works, the burden is reduced to a simple refrain-line on its repetitions; here these

[178] Ibid. 80–5, 92–7.

Ex. 104

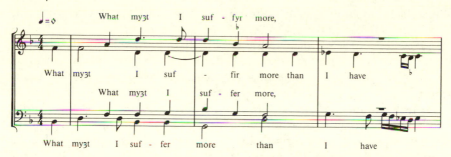

are not literal returns but are recomposed each time in phrases of ever-increasing intensity, culminating in a final cadence of overwhelming poignancy (Ex. 104, p. 257).[179]

Expressive though such music is, it is hardly touched by Renaissance idioms; rather is it a counterpart to the intense realism of the last phase of Gothic art. The first hints of a truly Renaissance culture are to be found in the second group of secular songs from the Ritson manuscript.[180] Here are to be found for the first time short homophonic pieces, strophically set, profane or moralizing in tone, side by side with longer works in the older idiom and even a two-part piece based on the *tenor* of a chanson by Binchois.[181] One of the strophic pieces is King Henry's own 'Passetyme with good cumpanye', copied twice, to a feebly moralistic text. There is much more of this sort of thing, including thirty-three pieces by the king himself, in the manuscript that has come to be known by his name.[182] Its original ownership cannot be determined with certainty. It has been plausibly suggested, however, that it was prepared on behalf of Sir Henry Guildford, Controller of the Royal Household.[183] Its contents suggest that it was compiled by or for someone familiar with the repertory of court entertainment; its general character suggests a library or presentation copy rather than one destined for performing use at the court itself. The date is probably around 1520, after which the copying of an anthology reflecting the young king's enthusiasms and preoccupations would have seemed less appropriate.

The collection is in fact very varied. Apart from pieces of the kind already described, there are chansons and other works by Continental (French and Flemish) composers, instrumental pieces, puzzle-canons, and rounds, as well as longer and more deeply felt works. The general tone, indeed, is professional and serious, and even the probable association of some of the music with courtly 'revels' must be interpreted in the context of a strictly regulated court etiquette. Though Henry himself was a performer as well as a composer, this music will most often have been played and sung, whether before the king or in the houses of the nobility and administrative classes, by professional musicians. To show off one's talents in company was a risk which only a privileged few could take with impunity.

Apart from the king, the composer most frequently represented is again

---

[179] Ibid. 97. For Cornysh's use of the diminished fourth, here very probable though not expressly notated, see above, Ex. 81.

[180] Above, p. 184. Published ibid. 11–22 (nos. 10–19).

[181] 'Votre trey dowce regaunt' (*sic*), ibid. 18 (no. 17), and the informative note on p. 157.

[182] London, Brit. Lib., Add. 31922, edited as *Music at the Court of Henry VIII*, ed. J. Stevens (London, 1962). 'Passetyme' reappears here, fos. 14ᵛ–15ʳ: ibid. 10–11, with the first Ritson version, and a valuable note on pp. 101–2. The two Ritson versions, which are virtually identical, are conflated in *Early Tudor Songs and Carols*, 14 (no. 12).

[183] Originally by Chappell; reported and refined on in *Music at the Court of Henry VIII*, p. xxiii.

Cornysh, whose talents are displayed in a more varied guise than in earlier collections. As Master of the Choristers in the king's Royal Chapel he was responsible for organizing much of the entertainment of the court, and the repertory no doubt reflects something of his predilections as well as the needs of his client. A new generation of composers was emerging: Cowper, Pygott, Farthing, Lloyd, and some others of lesser consequence.[184] A piece like Cowper's 'Farewell my joy' (no. 63), while clearly bound to the idiom of his predecessors, has the greater freedom of expression that one would associate with a contemporary of Taverner. We see also the beginnings of a new kind of harmonically conceived writing, based perhaps on the contemporary Continental chanson but in the case of Ex. 105 (overleaf) certainly the work of an English (though anonymous) composer.[185] This is highly expressive, and looks forward to the next phase of English part-song; but it is not altogether typical of a collection which for the most part remains tied to a somewhat superficial, because not deeply rooted, courtly culture.

The pieces for instrumental consort in the 'Henry VIII' manuscript, lively though some of them are, do not convey the impression of being associated with courtly dance. Cornysh's three-part 'Fa la sol' (no. 6) is a lengthy contrapuntal study which was printed incomplete, together with two four-part textless pieces respectively by Fayrfax and Cowper, in XX Songes.[186] Apart from a few textless pieces by Continental composers, the other such works (called 'consorts' in the edition) are short, but generally contrapuntal and irregularly structured pieces. The various 'puzzle-canons' by Lloyd, Dunstable, and Fayrfax are still less dance-like. It is possible, of course, that the 'consorts' were intended for mimed dancing in semi-dramatic entertainments, rather than for what we now call ballroom dancing.

England was, however, heir to two traditions of formal courtly dancing, the French and the Italian, themselves inextricably intertwined at an earlier stage of their history. From France came the basse danse (also current in Italy in the fifteenth century as the bassadanza); this took the musical form of a lengthy cantus firmus, played in long notes on a slide trumpet or sackbut, accompanied usually by one or two shawms improvising around it. (It is a little uncertain just how such collective improvisation would have worked,

---

[184] Pygott, whose music also occurs in the Peterhouse part-books, was a member of Cardinal Wolsey's household chapel, c.1516–29, and was probably a Gentleman of the Chapel Royal thereafter: he was still alive in 1552 (Sandon in PRMA, 103 (1976–7), 139). Cowper (Oxford D.Mus., 1507) and Pygott, with John Gwynneth, Taverner, Fayrfax, Cornysh, Ashewelle, Taverner, and Robert Jones (Chapel Royal c.1520 to 1533 or later: Sandon, ibid.) are represented in XX Songes (1530), the only secular collection to be printed in England before 1571 (only the bassus part-book survives complete).

[185] Music at the Court of Henry VIII, 53 (no. 67).

[186] See n. 184.

Ex. 105

★ gy = 'guide'.

but pictorial sources from fifteenth-century France frequently show such
a three-part ensemble and it is reasonably clear that the players are playing
extempore, in however circumscribed or routine a manner.) It is tolerably
certain that the same musical conventions obtained in England, while for
the choreography we do possess, in a treatise by Robert Coplande entitled
*Here followeth the manner of dancing of bace dances after the use of France and
other places translated out of French into English* (1521), and in a manuscript
leaf of slightly earlier date, the evidence that the French methods were
adopted.

A detailed history and description of the *basse danse* is beyond the scope
of this book.[187] Originally, each long note of the *cantus firmus* was allotted
a single 'step' (containing two or four movements); the *cantus firmi* were
compiled from various sources—frequently they are adaptations of fifteenth-
century chanson tenors—in such a way as to provide the right number
of notes for the predetermined choreography. This is still the presumption

---

[187] The main authority is D. Heartz, 'The Basse Dance: Its Evolution circa 1450 to 1550',
AnnM, 6 (1958–63), 287–340. See also Bukofzer, *Studies in Medieval and Renaissance Music*, 190–216.

behind the choreographies of Coplande and the Salisbury fragment.[188] In France in the early sixteenth century, however, the various special choreographies came gradually to be superseded by a single one, the *basse danse commune*, for which any *cantus firmus* of the appropriate length might serve. This in turn facilitated a musical change that was taking place simultaneously, the adaptation of existing polyphonic chansons, instead of the old *cantus firmi*, for the purposes of the *basse danse*.

Another sign of change was the emergence of new dances. The *basse danse* had never stood alone, for even in the fifteenth century there had been courtly dances characterized by leaps ('sauts')—the very antithesis of the *basse danse*—and others for which rhythmical monophonic tunes were required. In the sixteenth century there arose the *branle* (originally the name of a *basse-danse* step), the *gaillarde*, the *tourdion*, and, from the Italian, the *pavane*. In Italy itself, the leaping dance was called *saltarello*; with the *quaternaria* and *piva* it formed one of a group of derivatives of the *bassadanza*, being based on increasingly shorter units of time in comparison with it. The music came more and more to be based on the popular songs of the day, and on their implied harmonic structure. New dances were created: the *passamezzo* and the *pavana* (or *paduana*, sometimes a triple-time dance at first), again often linked to a series of pre-ordained harmonies. In addition there were the *balli* or mimed dances.

This discussion provides us with the background to English practices extending well beyond the reign of Henry into those of all his Tudor successors. The musical evidence from Henry's own reign is very limited, but something of the flavour of the courtly dances of his day can be gleaned from a small number of three-part pieces notated in keyboard score on two staves.[189] Here we have 'The emperorse pavyn' (in triple time, apparently recalling the visit of Charles V in 1520), 'A galyard', 'The kingys pavyn', 'The crocke', 'The kyngs maske', and another 'Galyard'. The rather primitive counterpoint and simple structures are persuasive as evidence that here we have specimens of the 'real thing', though the music itself may be at least partly French. Also in the same manuscript and a closely related one are some freer ensemble pieces—'La belle fyne' and 'Myne cuckes co'—and a series of transcriptions of Parisian chansons of the 1520s; here

---

[188] This fragment, printed by Heartz, is the flyleaf in a copy of a *Catholicon* published in Venice in 1497, and now in the Chapter Library at Salisbury. The main sources of *basse-danse* tunes are a sumptuous MS in the Royal Library in Brussels (MS 9085; fac. edn. by E. Closson, Brussels, 1912), and an incunabulum, *L'Art et instruction de bien dancer*, published in Paris before 1496 by Michel Toulouze (fac. edn. by V. Scholderes, London, 1936). There are modern editions of all the tunes by J. L. Jackman, *Fifteenth Century Basse Dances* (Wellesley College, Mass., 1964), and T. W. Marrocco, *Inventory of 15th-century Bassedanze, Balli and Balletti* (New York, 1981).

[189] London, Brit. Lib., Roy. App. 58, fos. 47ʳ–49ᵛ; ed. for ensemble in P. Holman, *Seven Dances from the Court of Henry VIII* (Corby, 1983).

too are the earliest true 'secular' keyboard pieces, and some lute music, which, however, belongs to the following reign. The keyboard pieces[190] are especially interesting. Hugh Aston's 'Hornepype' is a kind of *piva*, though it employs two different triple-time measures; 'My lady Careys dompe' and 'The short mesure off my lady Wynkfylds rownde' are named after the wives of two prominent members of Henry's court. The first two are based on a simple alternation of tonic and dominant harmony; all three bear some resemblance to extant dances for keyboard from northern Italy in the early years of the sixteenth century, and it seems probable that they reflect to some extent the style of performance brought to Henry's court by the Venetian player Dionysius Memo, who accompanied the Venetian Ambassador in 1516. His performances were emulated by Sagudino, the ambassador's secretary, and by Henry himself.

As these considerations show, contacts with European musical culture, which appear to have been somewhat limited during the later fifteenth century, were gradually being restored in the early sixteenth, and especially during the reign of Henry VIII. Earlier, there had certainly been a continuous trickle of English musicians making a career abroad. Two of the most important were Robert Morton, who served at the Burgundian court under Charles the Bold and Philip the Good (1457–75), and John Hothby, a Carmelite friar who was chaplain and choirmaster at Lucca Cathedral from 1467 to 1486; he then returned to England, where he died in the following year. A Robertus de Anglia (not Morton) was at Ferrara from 1460 to 1461 at least, and *magister cantus* at San Petronio, Bologna, from 1467 until 1474, when he returned to England. The same name crops up, together with those of Bedyngham and a mysterious Galfridus de Anglia, in an important song manuscript now in Oporto.[191] References to performing musicians abroad, singers and minstrels, are rather more frequent, but there is little to suggest a regular traffic in the opposite direction. In Henry's reign, however, apart from Dionysius Memo we can instance Benedictus de Opitiis, organist of Our Lady's church in Antwerp, who came to England in 1516 to become a court organist to the king; and Philip van Wilder, a Dutch composer who lived in London from 1525 and served as a court lutenist. Wilder became one of the most important composers of secular music

---

[190] Edited (with the two-stave dances just mentioned and a keyboard version of 'La belle fyne'), by F. Dawes: *Schotts Anthology of Early Keyboard Music* (5 vols., London, 1951), i. There is a keyboard transcription of 'Myne cuckes co' in the companion MS, Roy. App. 56: a forthcoming volume of MB will include this and much other hitherto unpublished keyboard music of the period.

[191] For a full discussion of the Oporto manuscript and the identity of Robertus see D. Fallows in *PRMA*, 103 (1976–7), 61–79, and his 'Robertus de Anglia and the Oporto Song Collection', *Source Materials and the Interpretation of Music*, ed. I. Bent (London, 1981), 99–128. The songs of Galfridus and Robertus have been edited by Fallows (Newton Abbot, 1977).

in the later part of Henry's reign, and he was responsible for making the inventory, still extant, of the king's musical possessions on his death in 1547.[192]

In the other direction, English musicians had an opportunity of demonstrating their skills at the Field of the Cloth of Gold, a purely ceremonial meeting between the kings of England and France in 1520. The highly placed Richard Sampson, who later became bishop of Lichfield and Coventry, had previously held diplomatic appointments at Antwerp and Tournai. His compositions, with some by Benedictus de Opitiis, were inscribed in a small but beautiful manuscript which may have been intended as a gift to Henry VIII.[193] They reflect the limits to which an English musician might go in the direction of Continental style at that time, at least in the realm of church music. The manuscript also includes two psalm-motets, a genre already common in Europe but hitherto unknown in England.

Hothby was more of a theorist than a composer, and he is the most distinguished English writer on music in this period. He wrote on plainchant, counterpoint, and proportions, and engaged in a vigorous controversy with Bartolomé Ramos de Pareja, a Spaniard of dangerously modern (though to the present-day reader refreshingly unprejudiced) views.[194] But Hothby's work is totally detached from the main current of English music at that time, and had no discernible influence upon it. Indeed, the era of theoretical influence on composers had passed; but compilers such as John Tucke and John Dygon at least reflect the concerns of the English musicians of their day. Tucke, a scholar and later Fellow of New College, made little contribution of his own; but he was widely read and devised a complex scheme of coloration (blue, red, yellow, etc.), to indicate complex proportions.[195] Dygon, who was prior of St Augustine's, Canterbury, also wrote on proportions, and gave some attention to the needs of keyboard players.[196] One must not forget, of course, that many of our manuscripts of earlier writings, both English and foreign, date from this period. The English church musician of the later Middle Ages drew his inspiration from many sources, and must often have been an exceedingly broadly educated man.

Little was produced in English for the lay reader, but this period marks

---

[192] On Wilder, see the following chapter. The inventory has often been printed, e.g. in F. W. Galpin, *Old English Instruments of Music* (4th edn., New York, 1965), 215–22, after Brit. Lib., Harl. 1419.

[193] London, Brit. Lib., Roy. 11. E. xi; Harrison, *Music in Medieval Britain*, 338–40.

[194] For modern editions of Hothby's works, see the Bibliography.

[195] London, Brit. Lib., Add. 10336; Lambeth Palace Library, MS 466. See Harrison, *Music in Medieval Britain*, 44.

[196] Cambridge, Trinity College, MS 1210; cited by H. J. Steele, 'English Organs and Organ Music from 1500 to 1650', Ph.D. thesis (Cambridge, 1958), 40 seqq.

the beginnings of printed music theory—in the vernacular as it happens. Caxton's *Mirrour of the World*, written and first published by himself in 1481, includes a very brief section on music in its description of the liberal arts. Rather more important is his edition of Ranulph Higden's *Policronicon*, in the English version by John Trevisa, in 1482.[197] The *Policronicon* is basically a narrative of Higden's own day, the thirteenth and early fourteenth centuries, but it begins with a fanciful history of the world incorporating a fairly lengthy discussion of Pythagorean musical theory. John of Trevisa lived in the second half of the fourteenth century, and his translation (with that of Bartolomaeus de Anglia's *De proprietatibus rerum*) therefore embodies what must be the earliest extended piece of writing on music in English; but Caxton's edition gave it a far wider circulation and effectively marks the beginning of literature on music for the general reader.

In this period, finally, we can dimly discern the beginnings of a genuinely popular musical culture in the modern sense—the music, that is, of literate or semi-literate urban folk and of such of their country cousins as lay within its reach, supplied by clerks and educated entrepreneurs for the edification and amusement of the lower orders. We do not often have the tunes; but we have, from the fifteenth century, manuscripts of ballads and other kinds of popular verse, and, from the early sixteenth century at least, printed ballads, 'Christmas carols', and the like. The precise cultural orbit of the manuscript materials is sometimes difficult to assess, but the printed sources were produced as broadsheets and pamphlets for popular consumption. More will be said on this topic in Volume II; here we may note the particular popularity of the narrative ballad (not the only kind, in spite of modern writers' definitions), whether on traditional themes, as often in the manuscript sources (ballads of Robin Hood, 'Seynt Steuene was a clerk', etc.), or whether topical and satirical, as so often in the printed examples. The popular carol was just beginning to shed the form of a dance-song and to acquire its later invariable association with the Christmas season.

The nature of popular melody can be sampled in an occasional manuscript fragment, or in the use made of it in art-music, most notably in this period by Taverner in his 'Western Wynde' Mass. But music sung, hummed, whistled, or merely retained in the head is as likely as not to have been harmonized in its original form; one of the few broadsheets to survive with music (and the only one from the early sixteenth century) is a fragment in which the musical part can only be from a polyphonic setting.[198] It has been suggested that this ballad and its music may have been written

---

[197] For the modern edition of Higden (in both Latin and English), see the Bibliography.

[198] This is from a broadsheet published *c.*1520 by John Rastell. See A. H. King, 'An English Broadside of the 1520s', in *Essays on Opera and English Music* (1975), 19–24, where the dating is discussed.

Ex. 106

* The inner part has crotchets (quavers in transcription). These may perhaps be intended as 'coloured' minims, consistently with the value of the outer parts when interpreted according to the rules of major prolation.

for 'one of the street pageants which were a feature of state visits and for which Rastell [the printer] was regularly in demand as an organizer'.[199]

Rastell also wrote and published a play, *A New Interlude and a mery of the Nature of the iiij Elements*, which includes a three-part song, 'Tyme to pas with goodly sport'.[200] This is the only surviving piece of music to be included with the text of a secular drama in the sixteenth century, though we know of others, such as Redford's *Wyt and Science*,[201] which called for music. But we should also instance the songs associated with the Taylors and Shearmens Pageant of the Nativity at Coventry.[202] The miracle plays, which were still being played at this period, were one of the most widespread forms of popular entertainment, and a highly effective platform for the music associated with them. One of the two three-part songs in this particular play was sung by the shepherds (the two stanzas are separated by dialogue), the other by the women of Bethlehem (doubtless played by men) as they await the slaughter of their children. The manuscript of this cycle of plays was copied in 1534 by one Robert Croo, though the music was added only in an appendix dated 1591.[203] There is no reason, however, to doubt that it belongs to the early sixteenth century. The first song was made generally known only quite recently;[204] the other, which has long been deservedly popular, is given here, partly in order to offer an alternative to the usual rhythmic interpretation (Ex. 106, p. 265).[205] It may also serve to symbolize the impending destruction of a culture in a climate of ever-increasing hostility between religious opponents.

---

[199] King, ibid. 24. It will be remembered that the emperor Charles V visited London in 1520 (above, p. 261).

[200] King, 'The Significance of John Rastell in Early Music Printing', *The Library*, 26 (1971, with fac.); G. Reese, *Music in the Renaissance*, 878; *Music at the Court of Henry VIII*, 14 (no. 9a).

[201] London, Brit. Lib., Add. 15233; ed. J. O. H. Phillips (London; Shakespeare Society Publications, 1848). See also A. Brown, 'An Edition of the *Play of Wyt and Science* by John Redford', MA diss. (London, 1949). There is an excellent discussion of music in early Tudor drama in J. Stevens, *Music and Poetry in the Early Tudor Court*, 252–9.

[202] *Coventry Mysteries*, ed. J. O. H. Phillips (London: Shakespeare Society, 1841), also ed. Hardin Craig, *Two Coventry Corpus Christi Plays* (London: EETS, extra series, 1902; 2nd edn., 1957).

[203] The manuscript was destroyed in a fire at the City of Birmingham Reference Library in 1879. The music has survived only because it had been transcribed by Thomas Sharp in his *Dissertation on the Pageants or Dramatic Mysteries Anciently performed at Coventry* (Coventry, 1825), 113–18; all subsequent versions depend on his.

[204] J. P. Cutts, 'The Second Coventry Carol', *Renaissance News*, 10 (1957), 3–8; now also in R. Rastall (ed.), *Two Coventry Carols* (Totnes, 1973).

[205] The original version was printed, after Sharp, in *The Oxford Book of Carols* (London, 1928), 44–5 (no. 22); see also Rastall, *Two Coventry Carols*. Sharp's transcription may have been unduly literalistic and even mistaken in certain respects. I have assumed a regular triple (compound duple) metre, and *alteratio* in bars 1, 4, 6, 8, 11, 14.

5

THE PERIOD OF THE REFORMATION

A CHURCH musician of the later years of Henry's reign would have had little adjustment to make in the practice of his art, provided that he could accept the royal supremacy and, if employed by a monastic foundation, was in a position to find an alternative sphere of activity. So far as the first was concerned, the virtually complete capitulation of the ecclesiastical hierarchy would have made protest by ordinary individuals a pointless exercise. There is no record of any professional musician making an issue of the matter at this period; indeed, the few instances of trouble with the authorities, as in the cases of Taverner and Marbeck, were on the grounds of their Lutheran opinions. These were equally repugnant to the monarch, whose policy was to preserve the outward forms and doctrinal essence (as he saw it) of Catholicism.

The suppression of the monasteries had nevertheless a catastrophic effect on the musical life of the country, since they were devoted to the maintenance of the liturgy and its music, for the most part in a form that differed from English secular usage and was closely bound up with European tradition. But the professional element in the monasteries was primarily associated with the Lady Chapel choirs, and its skills were readily applicable to non-monastic foundations: cathedrals, collegiate churches, colleges, household chapels, and parish churches. Thomas Tallis, for example, who had been in turn a clerk at Dover Priory, a 'conduct' (or singing clerk) at St Mary-at-Hill, and Master of the Choristers at the large Augustinian abbey of Waltham Holy Cross, subsequently became a Gentleman of the Chapel Royal. He was a musician of exceptional gifts, but his career illustrates the ease with which such transferences could be made, and with which subsequent changes of religious practice could be assimilated, at least to outward appearance.

The suppression of the smaller monasteries took place in 1536, and of the larger ones between 1538 and 1540, Waltham itself being the last to surrender. Still more serious from the musical point of view was the suppression early in the next reign (1548) of the collegiate churches as a consequence of the bringing into effect of the Chantries Act.[1] Men such as Aston and Ludford were pensioned off; others no doubt found re-employment, but by then a drastic liturgical reform was in the offing. In the meantime, Henry's expansion of the diocesan structure had found a role for some former abbeys. The cathedral priories—Canterbury, Rochester, Norwich, Ely, Winchester, Worcester, Durham, and Carlisle—were refounded with secular chapters; Bath and Coventry were dissolved but subsequently became parish churches. At Oxford, St Frideswide's had been suppressed by Wolsey and its church used as the chapel of his new College (1526); in 1542 the new diocese of Oxford was given Osney Abbey just outside the city as its cathedral church; but this was transferred in 1546 to Christ Church, as Henry VIII's refoundation of Cardinal College was now known. So from then on the college chapel served as the cathedral of the diocese, a not entirely happy arrangement that still persists. The former abbeys of Peterborough, Gloucester, Chester, and Bristol also became cathedral churches, as did Westminster for a brief period (until 1550, when it was joined to the see of London; it was refounded as a Benedictine monastery under Mary Tudor, after which it joined St George's, Windsor, the only collegiate church of importance to have escaped suppression, as a 'Royal Peculiar').[2]

Although few liturgical changes were carried out during Henry's lifetime, the royal supremacy enabled some minor adjustments to be made and facilitated the wholesale revisions of the following reign. Of a purely political nature were the excision of the Mass and Office of St Thomas of Canterbury, and of all references to the Pope, from all missals, breviaries, and other service books. These changes were enshrined in the breviaries produced by Edward Whitchurch, and by Whitchurch and Richard Grafton, from 1541 to 1544.[3] More significantly, the Royal Injunctions of 1536 required inter alia that a Bible in Latin and English be set up in every parish church by 1 August 1537. The English Bible in question would have been the so-called 'Matthew' Bible, an amalgam of the translations by Coverdale and Tyndale with notes by 'Matthew'. The injunctions of 1538 repeated the order for an English Bible, and in 1539 the 'Great Bible', a reissue of 'Matthew' without his notes, was printed by Grafton and Whitchurch and set up in every parish church.[4] From 1543, lessons at Matins and 'Evensong' (i.e. Vespers) had to be read in English.

---

[1] The Act of 1545 was confirmed in 1547.

[2] Knowles, The Religious Orders in England, iii. 389–92. For the constitutions of the new foundations see Harrison, Music in Medieval Britain, 195–7.

[3] See the list in Breviarium Sarum, iii, p. xlvi; STC, s.v. 'Liturgies'.

[4] The prose psalter from this version was often separately printed (initially in both Latin and English, 1540) and became the standard liturgical version in the Anglican Church from 1549 onwards.

It is quite clear that Archbishop Cranmer, who with Thomas Cromwell as Vicar-General was responsible for the content of Royal Injunctions, would have liked reform to proceed faster than circumstances permitted. In the convocation of 1542, which established the Use of Salisbury throughout the realm, he advocated a reduction of ceremonies.[5] His English Litany with simplified music, for use in processions in time of need, was prepared by royal command and published in 1544. Two editions of that year are extant. In October Cranmer wrote his famous letter to Henry, reporting on his progress in translating the 'festal' processions (i.e. those used on Sundays and holy days) and giving his views as to the appropriate kind of music: 'as nere as may be, for every sillable, a note'.[6] In the last years of Henry's reign, he was working on liturgical reforms (albeit in the context of the Latin breviary), such as the compression of the eight Offices into two (Matins and Evensong), a revised lectionary, and a monthly recitation of the psalms, that were to be fulfilled rather more radically in the *Book of Common Prayer*.[7]

With the accession of the nine-year-old Edward VI on 29 January 1547, the reforming party came into power. A Protectorate was established under Edward Seymour, Earl of Hertford, soon to be created Duke of Somerset. In July a Royal Visitation to every diocesan cathedral was inaugurated. Injunctions of general application included the reading of the Epistle and Gospel in English, and the use of Cranmer's Litany at all processions (in spite of its obvious unsuitability for festal occasions). In January 1548 the Protector and Council abolished the special ceremonies for Candlemas, Ash Wednesday, Palm Sunday, and Good Friday; in February the removal of images was ordered; in March an English *Order of Communion* (that is, for the actual reception, not for the whole service) was published. Of the particular injunctions, those issued to Lincoln Cathedral in April 1548 have been especially noted: antiphons of Our Lady or other saints were forbidden, with her Office and that of the dead, to be replaced by English antiphons (or 'anthems') of Our Lord only, 'setting thereunto a plain and distinct note for every syllable one'.[8] There is here a marked echo of Cranmer's earlier phrase.

In the meantime, Compline had already been sung in English in the

[5] *Oxford History of England*, vii. 431. The Royal Injunctions of 1538 had spoken against the abuse of images and the ceremonies connected with them.

[6] *State Papers of Henry VIII*, i (1830), 760–1, *s.a.* 1543 (repr. in J. Marbeck, *The booke of Common praier noted*, fac. ed. R. A. Leaver, 1980, pp. 77–8). In the letter itself the year is not given, but only 1544 fits the circumstances.

[7] P. Le Huray, *Music and the Reformation in England, 1549–1660* (London, 1967; 2nd edn., Cambridge, 1978), 7. The standard work on the Anglican liturgy is F. Procter and W. H. Frere, *A New History of the Book of Common Prayer* (London, 1908). The Edwardian books were reprinted in the Everyman Library (London, 1910), and the Elizabethan in the Ancient and Modern Library of Theological Literature (Edinburgh, 1909).

[8] Injunctions 25, 28, cited Le Huray, *Music and the Reformation*, 9.

Royal Chapel, initially on Easter Day (11 April), 1547, while at the Mass celebrated as usual at Westminster Abbey to mark the opening of the new Parliament in November, the Gloria, Credo, Sanctus with Benedictus, and Agnus Dei were all sung in English. By May 1548 Latin had been excluded altogether from St Paul's Cathedral and the Royal Chapel. Undoubtedly this was a period of much liturgical experiment, both as to vernacular text and as to music; but many of the details will always remain obscure. All this, however, was merely a preliminary to the Act of Uniformity, passed on 21 January 1549, which imposed the *Book of Common Prayer* from the following Whitsunday, 9 June. Here in one book was contained all that was necessary (apart from the Holy Scriptures) for the performance of the services as laid down by authority. But it was issued without a psalter, of which several editions were separately published. One of these also included 'all that appertein to the clerkes to say or syng . . .'. This so-called *Clerks' Book* appears to have been consulted by Marbeck in compiling his *Booke of Common praier noted*, published by Richard Grafton in 1550.

It might have been thought that matters could be left at that point. But the more radical reformers, who were in close contact with Continental divines, wished to make more sweeping changes. 'Catholic' practices, including elaborate vocal music and organ playing, continued in many places; the old chants were being adapted to the new words,[9] and in some quarters the Prayer Book was being ignored altogether. In the West Country the reforms provoked a rising. Control was by royal and archiepiscopal injunctions, and by orders in Council. These adopted an increasingly 'Protestant' tone, and eventually the second Prayer Book, authorized by an Act of April 1552, was brought into compulsory use by All Saints' Day, 1 November, in that year. It marks the extreme limit of liturgical change in England; on 6 July 1553, Edward VI died; Mary Tudor acceded to the throne with little opposition, and in due course brought England back not only to the Latin rite but to union with the Roman Church. Her increasing vindictiveness lost her the goodwill with which her reign began; she and her stern minister and relation Cardinal Pole died on the same day, 17 November 1558. Elizabeth moved swiftly to restore the position under Edward VI; the Prayer Book of 1552 was reissued with minor modifications; the bench of bishops was almost totally replaced; and the Church of England, steering an unsteady course between puritanism and 'popery', moved forward to the next phase of its troubled existence.

The chief effects of the Reformation on English church music were, first and foremost, a drastic curtailment of what was required; and, second, the adoption of the English language and with it the search for a simple and intelligible style. At no point was there a serious threat to abolish poly-

[9] Hooper to Bullinger at Zurich, 27 Dec. 1549 (cited Le Huray, ibid. 23).

phonic music altogether (although some divines may have wished for it), still less to limit music to the singing of metrical psalms. From the point of view of the musical heritage, the closest analogy is with Lutheran practice, though the Anglican tradition was subsequently enriched by the adoption of a Calvinist style of psalmody.

The curtailment has two aspects, institutional and liturgical. The principal outcome of the dissolution of the monasteries and collegiate churches was to channel the stream of musical excellence into the cathedrals and a very few other favoured institutions. Of the latter, the Royal Chapel was by far the most important. As has been very wisely said, the royal supremacy enhanced its already considerable significance,[10] for its practices became a model for imitation and a guide to what might be considered permissible elsewhere. Elizabeth's moderation and tolerance in its ordering were of decisive importance for the future of the Anglican tradition.

The liturgical curtailment went hand in hand with the change from Latin to English and may be assessed at a glance by comparing the requirements of the first Prayer Book with those of the Salisbury missal and breviary. Gone are antiphons, responds, Graduals, Alleluias, Tracts, and Sequences; the Introit becomes a complete psalm without antiphon, the Offertory and Communion a small selection of 'sentences'. Subsequently even the Introit and Communion (called 'post Communion' in the first Prayer Book) disappeared. All processions except the Litany, many feasts, and all the special ceremonies connected with Holy Week and Easter, Candlemas, and Ash Wednesday were abolished. The eightfold Office was reduced to Matins and Evensong, retaining the Venite, Te Deum (or Benedicite), Benedictus, Magnificat, and Nunc Dimittis. The 1552 book replaced the Kyrie by the Ten Commandments, and placed the Gloria at the end of the 'Lords supper, or Holye Communion', as it was now called; the Lord's Prayer was transferred to a position after the Communion, and even the rudimentary 'Pax' of the 1549 book disappeared.[11] At Matins and Evensong, various psalms were specified as alternatives to the Gospel canticles.

The translations of the first Prayer Book had been preceded by others, dictated by devotional and experimental motives. The earliest were those of the various Primers, renderings of the eightfold Office for the benefit of the laity: the first extant example dates from 1534.[12] Their original purpose

---

[10] Le Huray, ibid. 11. The larger colleges at Oxford and Cambridge, Eton and Winchester, St George's, Windsor, and Westminster Abbey (Royal Peculiars), and a very few Anglican private chapels and parish churches, were the other institutions in which a greater or lesser degree of professional music was maintained.

[11] 'The Supper of the Lorde and the Holy Communion, commonly called the Masse' (1549) included, after the giving of the peace, a devotional sentence, 'Christ our Pascall lambe', of which a setting by Sheppard exists.

[12] A prymer in Englyshe, ed. W. Marshall (STC, 15986), based on G. Joye, Ortulus anime (Antwerp, 1530; STC, 13828.4), an unofficial 'Protestant' version.

was Catholic and devotional, but their texts, and particularly those of King Henry's own Primer of 1545, would have provided material for a vernacular liturgy, such as was tried out in the Royal Chapel from Easter 1547. Translations of the Ordinary of the Mass were made for the state opening of Parliament and Convocation in November 1547, and their wording appears to have been adopted in some of the earliest polyphonic settings to have come down to us, since their texts differ from those of the 1549 book.[13]

The most interesting of the early translations, since it also contains the music, is Cranmer's Litany of 1544. The publication consisted of 'An exhortation vnto prayer, ... to be read to the people in euery church afore processyons', and 'a Letanie with suffrages to be said or song in the tyme of the said processyons'.[14] This is merely the last part of the elaborate Salisbury processional rite 'causa necessitatis vel tribulacionis factis', including the Mass 'pro fratribus et sororibus',[15] and there is no reason to suppose that it was intended at this stage to be detached from it. The general tone of the publication, however, with its lengthy exhortation and additional short explanatory preface, is remarkably 'Protestant' for the period. The invocations to the saints are reduced to three (to Mary, to the angels, and to all other saints), and amongst the prayers for deliverance is one 'from the tyranny of the bisshop of Rome and all his detestable enormyties', a phrase that seems to go beyond what the maintenance of the royal supremacy might require. As for the music, the simplicity of the Latin Litany itself precludes any judgement of Cranmer's skill in adaptation. In any case, his exact source for the chant has not been determined. It is clear, however, that he strove for an entirely natural setting of the English text; he did not hesitate to rearrange the notes to fit the changed accentuation, and he adopted the available range of note-shapes (the *plica* ⌐, and the square and diamond *punctum*) to ensure a natural delivery. These shapes are familiar from their later use by Marbeck, who explained their meaning (⌐ ˸ ⊟ ; ▪ ˸ ◇ ; ▪˸♩) and added the dotted punctum (▪·˸◇·) to the repertoire. That they were intended by Cranmer to be given precise durations is debatable, as it is in the case of plainchant; but the issue tends to be clouded by modern views as to what constitutes a natural delivery. Polyphonic settings were certainly metrical in the strict sense, though with some revision of the actual note-values.

The phrases of Cranmer's Litany, readily adaptable to subsequent revisions, have remained familiar, largely through polyphonic settings of

[13] Le Huray, *Music and the Reformation*, 177, referring to nos. 1, 4, 5, and 7 of the 'Wanley' MS (see below). In these, the Apostles' Creed is used in a translation drawn from the Primer of 1545; this may have been dictated by the lack of a ready translation of the Nicene Creed, as suggested by Le Huray, or possibly by a desire for concision, since the Latin text of the latter was normally abbreviated in polyphonic settings.

[14] Fac. ed. J. E. Hunt (London, 1939).

[15] See, for example, the printed Sarum Processional of 1502, fos. 162ʳ seqq. (fac., 1980).

which that of Tallis has been the most influential.[16] It is a pity that Cranmer did not fulfil his intention to set 'some devoute and solempne note' to the text of the festival processions that he had prepared. But the plan to pursue this was overtaken by the decision to order the use of the Litany for all processions, festal or otherwise, and in the event the only other publication to provide monophonic music for the English liturgy was to be that of Marbeck in 1550.[17]

The booke of Common praier noted,[18] as it was called, has acquired its present familiarity from its revival for congregational use in the nineteenth and twentieth centuries. But it was originally intended to supply simple plainchant for the priest's and clerks' parts of the 1549 Prayer Book; the simplicity was designed to make the words intelligible to the hearer, not to enable the music to be sung by the congregation. It was soon rendered obsolete by the appearance of the 1552 book, and may never have been widely used; its significance should not be underestimated, however, for the book is representative of several years of liturgical and musical experiment, and in some respects—notably in the chanting of the psalms—it provided patterns that were of use to those who were endeavouring to preserve continuity in the early Elizabethan period. As with Cranmer's Litany, its ethos was inherited by simple polyphonic practice as much as by monophonic chant. This sense of tradition and continuity is one of the most attractive and interesting aspects of early Anglican polyphonic music, and it is that to which our attention will primarily be drawn.

The two major sources of early Anglican polyphony are the so-called 'Wanley' and 'Lumley' part-books, both sets dating from the Edwardian period.[19] In each, unfortunately, one book is lacking, though restoration of the missing part is often possible, particularly in the Wanley set, in which the lost tenor book frequently carried the plainchant or faburden. The repertory consists of anthems and canticles, with a good deal of music for the 'Communion' in the Wanley books, and some settings of metrical psalms in both collections. A third important source is John Day's printed *Certaine notes*, which may have been planned as early as the Edwardian period, though it was not actually published until 1565.[20] In addition there are

---

[16] There is an anonymous setting, with the chant in the tenor, in Day's publication of 1560/5. In Tallis (EECM, xiii. 150–9), the chant is mostly in the treble, but is ignored in some responses altogether.

[17] For Cranmer's letter see n. 6. A copy of the 1549 prayerbook in the Christ Church Library (e. 6. 3) contains MS adaptations of the Salisbury chants for the priest's parts of the Mass: these follow the Latin originals very closely. An article by Dr Milsom, who discovered the new material, is in course of preparation.

[18] Facsimiles (*inter alia*) ed. J. E. Hunt (London, 1939) and R. A. Leaver (Oxford, 1980).

[19] London, Brit. Lib., Roy. App. 74–6; Oxford, Bod. Lib., Mus. Sch. e. 420–2. There is an edition of the former by Dr J. Blezzard (*The Tudor Church Music of the Lumley Books*, Madison, Wis., 1985). For the Wanley books see n. 33 below.

[20] See below, p. 283, and n. 39.

a number of significant fragments, and a good deal of patently early material survives in later Elizabethan, Jacobean, and even Caroline part-books.

Except for the Litany, of which there are settings in both the Wanley and Lumley books, the earliest sources do not include settings of the simplest parts of the Anglican service, the responses and psalms. Probably, if not merely said, they were normally intoned in the manner indicated by Marbeck's publication, that is to say, to simple phrases suggested by the outlines of the Latin tones. Marbeck did not include a psalter, but he included tones for the Venite (tone 8 first ending), Benedictus (5^I, 8^I), Magnificat (1^I, 8^I), and Nunc Dimittis (5^I, 7^4). The few other specimens of psalms in the book are all set to tone 8 with the first ending. Marbeck may have expected the whole psalter to be sung to this simple formula, and for all we know to the contrary this was the normal Edwardian and early Elizabethan practice in those cathedrals and other establishments in which singing had not fallen prey to extreme puritan sentiment.

The harmonized singing of responses and psalms was associated originally with important feasts, and may have been an innovation of Elizabeth's Royal Chapel. Tallis's settings may be studied in this connection, although the sources are late, since they conveniently illustrate the aims and methods of the early Elizabethan composer of liturgical music. Barnard in 1641 printed two sets of 'preces';[21] one for four and one for five voices, and three portions of Psalm 119 for five voices. His selection of psalms is incomplete, and their relation to the preces doubtful, since the psalms are tonally closer to the four-part preces than to the five-part set to which Barnard links them. From part-books in the Bodleian Library and St John's College, Oxford, however, comes a more complete collection of Tallis's psalms, from which it emerges that those printed by Barnard were part of a series originally intended for Christmas Eve, Christmas Day, and St Stephen's Day (26 December).[22] Those for Christmas Eve and St Stephen's Day are simply the portions of Psalm 119 appointed for Evensong on the 24th and 26th respectively of each month, i.e. Ps. 119, vv. 1–32, 145–76. In between, however, come two of the three proper psalms for Evensong on Christmas Day, as appointed in the second Edwardian and Elizabethan prayer books (Pss. 110, 132). It is thus quite clear that Tallis intended a

---

[21] 'Preces' is the term conventionally given to the opening versicles and responses in the Anglican Offices, 'Responses' that given to those sung after the Apostles' Creed. The text of the 1549 preces is closer to the Latin model than that of 1552 and later books, but it was only in 1662 that the Gloria Patri was divided into a versicle and response, and 'Praise ye the Lord' treated as a versicle with the further response 'The Lord's name be praised'. Tallis's text is that of the 1552 and Elizabethan books.

[22] Oxford, Bod. Lib., Mus. e. 40, and St John's College, MS 180 (bass decani only), in which they are preceded by the tonally appropriate four-part preces, possibly in a five-part version. I am grateful to Dr Milsom for drawing the Bodleian source to my attention: it contains a set of psalms by Robert Parsons which appear to be otherwise unknown.

coherent set for these particular days, though the lack of the first psalm for Evensong on Christmas Day (89) is difficult to explain.[23]

Each of these psalms is a quite straightforward setting of one of the Gregorian psalm-tones in the tenor. In the case of those that survive in full (119: 9–16, 17–24, 25–32), the first two use tone 1, fourth ending (but in different harmonizations), the third one tone 7, first ending, transposed down a fifth. The tones used in the other settings, of which only the bass part survives, can be deduced with reasonable certainty, and on that basis a reconstruction made. What is harder to understand is the reason for the choice of tones in the first place, since the antiphons which would originally have determined this were no longer sung. A verse from the third of the complete settings will serve to illustrate the style (Ex. 107).[24]

Ex. 107

My soul cleav-eth to the dust; O quicken thou me, ac-cord-ing to thy word.

My soul cleav-eth to the dust; O quicken thou me, ac-cord-ing to thy word.

Psalm-settings such as these must be looked at in a larger context. Their simple sequences of 5–3 chords reflect a harmonic style that had long displaced the fifteenth-century usage, based largely on 6–3 triads, in written music, though the latter was still familiar to musicians of Tallis's generation in the form of improvised faburden, for example in the singing of the Magnificat and processional psalms. In Italy, the new style came to be known as *falsobordone*, and was used for the chanting of psalms in Latin. In England, settings of festal psalms must have provided a precedent for the eventual custom of having the daily course of psalms sung in harmony, though this may not have become common until after the Restoration. Even then they were still based, if loosely, on the Sarum tones, and such 'chants' became the nucleus of the repertory that developed from then on.[25]

The canticles (Benedictus, Magnificat, and Nunc Dimittis, with the

---

[23] Barnard's intonation for Ps. 119: 9 is clearly spurious. His versions are printed in Tallis, *English Sacred Music*, ed. L. Ellinwood, 2 vols. (London, 1971; 2nd edn., 1974), ii. 125–43, while single verses from those for which only a bass part exists are given on p. 189.

[24] Tallis, ibid. 138.

[25] Le Huray, *Music and the Reformation*, 158–60.

Venite, Te Deum, and Benedicite, later also the Jubilate, Cantate domino, and Deus misereatur) from the outset provided composers with greater scope. The Wanley books contain examples of each of the first six of these, with a preponderance of settings of the Magnificat, Nunc Dimittis, and Te Deum. Several are based on modified plainchant, and others, more surprisingly, on the faburden.[26] Others occur in *Certaine notes* and minor sources. Several settings of the Te Deum, four of them in the Wanley books, make use of adapted plainchant, or in one case of both faburden and plainchant.[27] This last is the fourth of the Wanley versions, and it has the added interest of being adapted for antiphonal singing in the Lumley part-books; for the alternating verses, it preserves the complete texture. It is noteworthy that in this work the division between faburden and plain-chant follows pre-Reformation precedent. In none of these works does polyphony alternate with monophonic chant, a custom virtually unknown to the Anglican rite. An interesting feature of some Magnificats, however, is the spreading of one statement of the chant or faburden over two verses, resulting in as many statements as would have been heard in the polyphonic sections of an *alternatim* setting.[28]

Little of Tallis's service music has survived from early sources, though a Benedictus for men's voices, using the text of Henry VIII's Primer of 1545, has been preserved in the Lumley part-books.[29] But a five-part Te Deum 'for meanes', though extant only in sources of 1625 and later, shows unquestionably archaic features.[30] For one thing, it sets the 1549, not the 1552 or later texts (e.g. 'Heav'n and earth are *replenished* with the majesty of thy glory'). The first half-verse is left to be intoned, and the tonal scheme of the work is closely modelled on that of Latin settings based on the chant or faburden transposed down a tone. This is the explanation for the startling change to cadences on the chord of A major at 'Thou art the King of Glory, O Christ' and many of the following verses including the last (Ex. 108).[31]

The work alternates between the decani and cantoris sides of the choir in all voices for much of its length, and exploits divided upper voices in an interesting setting of 'Thou didst not abhor the Virgin's womb', marked

---

[26] See J. Aplin, 'A Group of English Magnificats', in *Soundings*, 7 (1978), 85–100.

[27] J. Aplin, 'The Survival of Plainsong in Anglican Music', *JAMS*, 32 (1979), 247–75.

[28] In later Anglican usage, the first two verses are compressed into one in any event; this is not made explicit in the 1549 or 1552 Prayer Books, but it is the practice adopted by Marbeck and may have been usual from the outset.

[29] Tallis, *English Sacred Music*, ii. 102–19. All four parts are extant.

[30] Ibid. 78–101.

[31] Ibid. 100–1. The medius (or mean), contratenor 2, and bass decani parts are missing but can mostly be reconstructed from an organ score. Small notes indicate purely conjectural restorations; square brackets enclose missing text from a surviving part; a few syllables of text (most of it editorial in any event) are omitted in the antiphonal passages to accommodate the compression of the score on to three staves.

Ex. 108

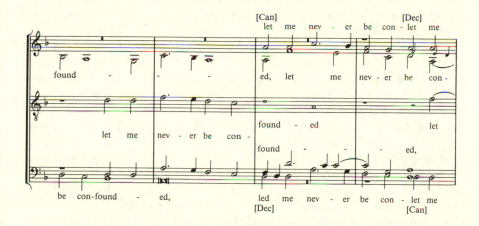

continued

Ex. 108, continued

in the organ part 'gimmell 4 meanes': this indicates that the decani and cantoris mean parts are each themselves divided. This may be compared with the scoring of Mundy's service 'in medio chori' (discussed below), in which the top two parts are similarly divided. In Mundy's case, however, the top part is a genuine treble, while that of Tallis is simply the decani mean. It is not clear whether Tallis's work is for men only; if the mean parts are intended for boys, an upward transposition (by modern standards) would be appropriate, but in view of the early date this is somewhat unlikely. In later Anglican practice, the 'mean' became the standard boys' part, but this did not immediately oust the older usage: Day's *Certaine notes* (see below) provides evidence of both. The reason for the terminological change is not known, but it may have been the result of a decline in the standard of boys' singing during an age of confusion and turmoil. Boys had been entrusted with the mean part in some early Tudor choirs; this may now have seemed the appropriate designation for a relatively undemanding top part for boys. When standards improved, the terminology stuck, and the word 'treble' came to be reserved for an exceptionally high boy's part.[32]

The relatively large provision in the Wanley books[33] of music for the 'Communion' reflects the needs of a period in which this service was still 'commonly called the Masse' and might be celebrated frequently.[34] Four of the complete settings of the Ordinary use a pre-1549 version of the text in which the Apostles' Creed is substituted for the Nicene (see above, and n. 13). The remaining six settings use the 1549 text with Nicene Creed;

[32] For further remarks on Anglican scoring and the high 'treble', see Ch. 6, pp. 352–3; on the constitution of earlier Tudor choirs, above, p. 189.

[33] Oxford, Bod. Lib., MSS Mus. Sch. e. 420–2, so named after their 18th cent. owner Humfrey Wanley. The tenor book is missing: the others are countertenor, countertenor, and bass, suggesting perhaps that most of the music was intended (at least by the compiler) for men's voices. There is a summary list of contents in Le Huray, *Music and the Reformation*, 173–5. An edition by J. Wrightson is in preparation.

[34] See n. 11 above. Frequent, if not daily, celebration is implied by several rubrics in the 1549 order.

the last two, however, are adaptations of Masses by Taverner in which the Kyrie was consequently omitted.[35]

Though the Wanley books were probably compiled between 1549 and 1552 for a parish church or private chapel, the repertory itself reflects a wider chronological span and may well embrace works written for a larger institution such as the Chapel Royal itself. The extracts in Ex. 109 illustrate, first, the simplest kind of plainchant setting; secondly, a freely composed Magnificat in a style that is typical of much of the music in the manuscript; and finally the richer textures of a Communion service subtitled '5. parts for men' (pp. 280–3).[36] There are also simpler settings of Offertory and 'post-Communion' sentences, while the two settings of 'Christ our paschal lamb' would also have been intended for the Communion.[37] There are a number of minor ritual items, for example for weddings and funerals, or for Ash Wednesday, and several 'antems', the humble descendants of the Latin votive antiphon. There was still a strong sense of attachment to the Latin rite: two of the three settings of 'Christ rising again', with its verse, 'Christ is risen', are entitled 'Christus resurgens'. In the 1549 book, these texts were prescribed to be sung or said on Easter Day 'in the mornyng, afore Mattyns'. They are a pale reflection of the solemn visit to the sepulchre in the Use of Salisbury, the 'elevatio crucis' with procession and restoration of the Blessed Sacrament to the tabernacle. Even the texts to be sung are considerably modified. Yet the ceremony retained its outward form of antiphon with verse, followed by versicle with response and collect, and the connection was not lost on the contemporary composer.[38]

As for the composers, most of this very early music has survived anonymously. A few works in the Wanley books can be ascribed on the basis of later sources to Sheppard, Tye, and Tallis (whose contribution is discussed more fully below), and a few more to such lesser figures as Okeland, Johnson,

---

[35] TCM, iii. 143–68, 169–98. The adaptations are from the 'Meane' Mass and 'Small Devotion' (i.e. Sancti Willelmi Devotio: see above, p. 233) respectively. Details of the adaptation are given in the preface to the same volume. The second of the ten Communion settings in the Wanley Books (fos. 11ʳ, 10ʳ, 10ᵛ) is also evidently an adaptation in view of its florid style and the lack of a Kyrie; but the original is not known.

[36] (a) from a Litany (fos. 58ʳ, 59ᵛ, 57ᵛ): tenor supplied from chant. The 6–4 chord at the cadence seems extraordinary, but it also appears very clearly at the end of each of the three following, musically similar responses, and may have been intended to make an 'acoustic' bass sounding B flat. (b) precedes a Nunc Dimittis known to be by Tye but is musically unconnected with it: tenor supplied (fos. 7ʳ, 6ᵛ, 6ᵛ); (c) carries the additional rubric 'ii bassys'; the missing part for harmonic reasons is evidently one of them (fos. 95ᵛ, 98ʳ, 93ᵛ: MS 422 carries the other bass and the top part, 'contertenor', on opposite pages). Original spelling has been retained in order to convey the atmosphere of the period, and, to a smaller extent, the pronunciation.

[37] Both are preceded by Communion settings in the manuscript. The second is by Sheppard, who may therefore have written the preceding Communion.

[38] In 1552 the antiphon and its verse alone were retained, and sung in place of the Venite at Matins. In this form, without the word 'Alleluya' at the end of each part, they were frequently set by Elizabethan composers from Tallis onwards (though Tallis—if the work is really his—has 'Alleluya' at the end of the second part only).

Ex. 109

(a)

O   god the fa - ther of heven   have

mer - cy up - on us my - se - ra - ble syn -   ners

(b) And   my sprete   re - yoy - sethe in   god   my

And   my sprete   re - yoy - sethe in god my sav -

sa - vy - our   for he   hathe re - gard - ede the low - ly -

- y - our for he hathe   re - gard - ede the   low - ly - nes
              . [for   he   hathe re - gard - ede the
              for he   hathe re - gard - ede the low - ly -

nes   of hys hand may - den

of   hys   hand may - den   of   hys hand mayd - en
low - ly - nes of   hys hand]
nes   of   hys   hand   mayd - en

Ex. 109, continued

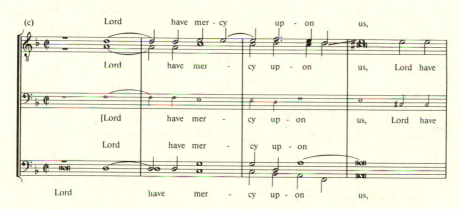

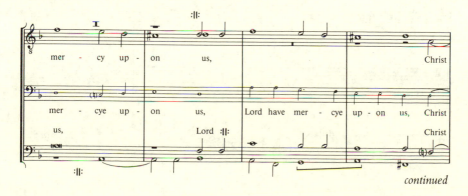

continued

Ex. 109, continued

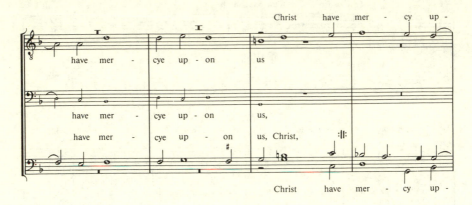

Ex. 109, continued

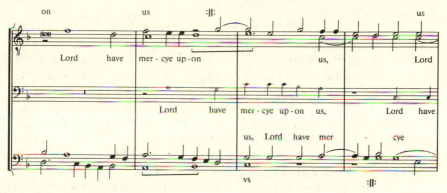

Stone, Whytbroke, Causton, and Heath. Except for Tye, all these reappear in John Day's *Certaine notes* (1565), together with Robert Hasylton and Knyght. It has been plausibly suggested that *Certaine notes* was originally planned prior to the appearance of the 1552 Prayer Book, and that it was revised for publication in 1560 before eventually being issued in 1565.[39] Certainly all the composers about whom anything is known were active in Edwardian times, and in one case at least, that of a Communion Ordinary by Heath, the version of the Wanley books is updated and included in Day's collection. Thomas Causton, the principal contributor, was a member

---

[39] See J. Aplin, 'The Origins of John Day's "Certaine Notes" ', *ML*, 62 (1981), 295–9. Although there are copies in the British Library of the medius and bassus books bearing the title *Certaine notes* and the date 1560, they have a colophon dated 1565. The Bodleian bassus, with the same title, lacks the last two leaves (and hence the colophon), reflecting an earlier stage in the planning of the collection. In all probability it was issued thus by mistake, since there is no evidence that the other part-books ever existed in this form. Finally, Day reissued the collection with a new title-page, *Mornyng and Evenyng prayer and Communion*, with the date 1565.

of the Chapel Royal, apparently from Edwardian times, until his death in 1569.

One of the main constituents of English musical life during this period and for a long time after was the metrical psalter. The idea of providing versified translations of the psalms for private devotional use was widespread amongst the Continental reformers. Their versions varied considerably in tone, but the most interesting from our point of view are those which were of sufficiently general appeal to be sung in domestic gatherings or even in vernacular liturgies. Many of Luther's hymns were paraphrases of this type, and it was under Lutheran influence that Miles Coverdale, the reformer and biblical translator, published his *Goostly psalms and spirituall songes* around 1545. This was ordered to be burnt in 1546; it was not, therefore, a particularly influential publication, though it may have helped to pave the way towards the more general use of metrical versions.[40]

Another early psalter was that of Robert Crowley, with its 'note of four partes' (1549). This was the earliest complete metrical psalter, and the first to contain harmonized music. But it seems to have been little used, possibly because of the austere and restricted nature of the music. Although the translation could have been used with metrical tunes, the composer merely provided a single harmonization of tone 7, which is placed in the tenor: it even imitates the reciting notes of prose psalmody.[41]

A very different future awaited the paraphrases of Thomas Sternhold, 'groom of the King's Majesty's robes' under Henry VIII and Edward VI. A small collection of nineteen psalms was published (without music) in 1548 or 1549. An enlarged edition of thirty-seven psalms, together with an appendix of seven by John Hopkins, was published, after Sternhold's death, in December 1549. This went through a number of reprints, in one of which, that of 1553, a further seven psalms by William Whittingham (later Dean of Durham) were added. With the accession of Mary, the most influential of the exiles from her regime congregated in Geneva, where in 1556 the first edition with music appeared: *One and fiftie psalmes of David in Englishe metre, whereof 37. were made by Thomas Sterneholde: ād the rest by others. Cōferred with the hebrewe, and in certeyn places corrected as the text and sens of the Prophete required.* The title conceals a substantial revision of Sternhold's versions, not all of it necessitated by a concern for verbal accuracy. The contributions of Hopkins and Whittingham were now

---

[40] Frost (*ESPHT*, 293) gives the date of burning from Bishop Bonner's Register (certificate dated 26 Sept. 1546), a more trustworthy source than the 1st edition of Foxe's *Book of Martyrs*, which gave the date as 1539. As for the date of publication, Frost says: 'words and music suggest not earlier than 1543'. Many of the tunes occur in the Erfurt *Enchiridion* and in Johann Walter's polyphonic *Geystliche gesankbuchleyn*, both of 1524; but others are known, if at all, only from later sources. The 41 tunes are printed, with sources where known, in *ESPHT*, 294–339.

[41] Printed Le Huray, *Music and the Reformation*, 372; not in *ESPHT*.

mingled with those of Sternhold according to their numerical place in the psalter; and it was in this form that 'Sternhold and Hopkins' became the basis of future editions.[42]

All but two of Sternhold's paraphrases, and all of those of Hopkins, were in the simple metre (8 6 8 6) later known as 'ballad metre'. But this was little used by the Continental reformers, and the tunes for the English psalter had to be newly composed, not, however, without retaining some echoes of the existing Calvinist repertory. In subsequent expansions the Continental metres, and hence the Continental tunes, were freely drawn upon. The Anglo-Genevan psalter was expanded to 62 psalms in 1558, and to 87 in 1561. This latter was the basis of John Day's 16mo edition of the same year; and in 1562 Day finally achieved his 'Whole Booke of psalms', the forerunner of an immense line of English and Scottish metrical psalters, both with and without music. This version, for all its many subsequent modifications in both text and music, held the field until 1687, when it was supplanted by the 'New Version' of Nahum Tate and Nicholas Brady; and even after that it continued to be printed.[43]

Another psalter printed during the period was that of Archbishop Matthew Parker, with nine harmonized tunes by Tallis. Parker may well have been working on this for many years before its publication around 1567, perhaps even before his elevation to the see of Canterbury in 1559. It seems not, however, to have been intended for public use. Tallis's tunes also, though by a distinguished musician, were too few in number to provide the needful variety if the psalter were to be in constant use; and the very fact that they were harmonized (even though the tunes might be extracted) may have made them less generally serviceable. In them the Gregorian tones were abandoned, but there was a quaint attempt by means of an introductory rhyme to express the character of the eight modes in which they were written: 'The first is meeke: deuout to see, | the second sad: in maiesty' (etc.). The ninth tune is the familiar 'Ordinal', set to Parker's version of the 'Veni creator spiritus', 'Come holy ghost eternall God'.[44]

The Dutch Calvinist population in London was catered for by the versions of Utenhove (John Day, 1561, 1566), while incomplete psalters of the period would include Francis Seager's *Certayne Psalmes* (1553, with two four-part tunes), and William Hunnis's *Seven Sobs of a Sorrowful Soule for Sinne*, i.e. the seven penitential psalms, to which he annexed two collections entitled

---

[42] On the early history of this psalter, with particular reference to Sternhold's own contribution and the revisions to which it was subjected, see R. Zim, *Metrical Psalm Poetry: Praise and Prayer, 1535–1601* (Cambridge, 1987).

[43] The 'Old Version' was also the basis of the Scottish psalters published under various titles from 1564 onwards. For bibliographical details of the most important editions, see *ESPHT*, 3–50; the tunes of the complete psalter, with subsequent harmonizations and adaptations down to 1677, ibid., 55–290.

[44] Ed. *ESPHT*, 374–93; Tallis, *English Sacred Music*, ii. 160–77.

A Handful of Honisuckles and *Comfortable Dialogs between Christ and a Sinner*.
The first extant edition is dated 1583, but as it is described as 'newlie printed
and augmented' it is clear that there was at least one earlier edition; and
there is other evidence that Hunnis's verse and simple tunes had been
current for some time.[45] Tye's *Actes of the Apostles* (three editions in or
around 1553, with harmonized music for fourteen chapters) are an analogous
essay in paraphrase,[46] while John Hall's *The Courte of Vertu* (1565) is another
collection of pietistic song with thirty melodies and one four-part tune
(it was originally published without music in 1550).

John Day himself published a collection of harmonized settings of the
tunes of the Sternhold and Hopkins psalter in 1563. Entitled *The Whole
Psalms in Foure Parts, whiche may be song to al Musical Instrumentes*, it includes
settings by R. Brimle[y], W. Pearson (i.e. Parsons) T[homas] Causton, N.
Southerton, J. Hake, R[ichard] Edwards, Tallis (two prayers, one of them
being a version of 'Remember not'), and a composer identified as 'W.P.S.'.
Only the first stanzas were printed, and the words of some psalms do not
appear at all; but the entire psalter could now be sung in harmony by
means of cross-reference to the monophonic editions. Like these it included
paraphrases of the canticles and other liturgical items, as well as a few non-
liturgical prayers. It is most unlikely that it was used much if at all in churches;
it was intended, rather, to promote devotion in the home and as a substitute
for 'vayne and trifling ballades'. Day's collection was never reprinted, though
it was superseded, later in the sixteenth and in the early seventeenth centuries, by a number of similar harmonized psalters.[47]

The religious upheavals of the Reformation period might seem to indicate
that it would have been an unpropitious one for the cultivation of the
more complex styles of Anglican church music; yet the evidence suggests
that there was a demand for music of some elaboration during the Edwardian
and early Elizabethan periods. Although many of the manuscript sources
are much later, there is often evidence both from the texts and from biographical details of the composers themselves of an early date. It is practically
certain, for example, that John Sheppard died in 1559 or 1560; his Anglican
music, therefore, must belong very largely, if not entirely, to the Edwardian
period. Some of it is simple enough, and often remarkably arresting on

---

[45] Seager's tunes printed *ESPHT*, 339–42; one of them (based on tone 6 in the tenor) in Le Huray,
Music and the Reformation, 384. Hunnis, *ESPHT*, 458–67. Hunnis was Master of the Children of the
Chapel Royal from 1566 to 1597.

[46] Ibid. 343–73; Tye, *English Sacred Music*, ed. J. Morehen (London, 1977), 274–315.

[47] For these, including the Scottish harmonized psalters, see Ch. 7, pp. 395–6.

that very account, as in a sensitive setting of 'Christ our paschal lamb' for men's voices from the Wanley part-books. He also composed settings of a large number of the Sternhold and Hopkins psalms and metrical prayers.[48] But the so-called Second Service for double choir (decani and cantoris *a 4*, full sections *a 5*) is of quite remarkable sophistication. Sheppard was a gentleman of the Chapel Royal from 1552 or earlier (possibly from 1548, when he left Magdalen College, Oxford, where he had been *Informator choristarum* since 1543) until the coronation of Queen Elizabeth on 17 July 1559, after which his name disappears from the records. Whether this and other settings of 1552/1559 texts are Edwardian or very early Elizabethan it is impossible to determine; given the increasingly Protestant sentiment of Edward's reign, the latter is perhaps more probable, but in any event there was evidently scope for a style in no sense inferior to that of contemporary Latin settings (Ex. 110, overleaf).[49] Although such music is not easy to sing well, the predominant impression is of contrapuntal refinement, a natural response to the verbal rhythms, and a strong sense of continuity, rather than of technical brilliance for its own sake.

These qualities are less evident in the Anglican music of Christopher Tye (*c*.1505–?1572), who (apparently unlike Sheppard) came under strong Protestant influence. Unfortunately the documentary evidence does not permit a precise account of his career, but it is consistent with the view that his opinions moved in line with those of the more ardent reformers during Edward's reign, and that he did not resume the composition of Latin ritual music during that of Mary—though that would not necessarily apply to Latin psalms and similar pieces. He was *Magister choristarum* at Ely Cathedral from 1543 until perhaps 1548 or even later; he is described on the title-page of his *Actes of the Apostles* (1553) as 'Gentylman of his grace's [i.e. Edward VI's] most honourable chappell', and may have been associated with it from the beginning of the reign, possibly without relinquishing his post at Ely, at least in the first instance. His name does not appear on any of the extant lists of the Chapel Royal between 1545 and 1560, however; he seems to have resumed his post at Ely in 1558 or 1559 (perhaps only after Elizabeth's reformist position had become clear), but subsequently took orders and resigned in 1561 to take up the living at

---

[48] 'Christ our paschal lamb' is in *An Anthology of English Church Music*, ed. D. Wulstan (London, 1971), no. 8: cf. n. 37 above. Two of the metrical settings are in *The Mulliner Book* (nos. 44, 82); the rest, of which only a single voice survives, are in London, Brit. Lib., Add. 15166.

[49] *Anthology of English Church Music*, no. 9 (from Nunc Dimittis, bars 1–18). The two countertenor parts belong to decani and cantoris respectively, but are divided to permit five-part writing in the 'full' sections; otherwise the writing is for two antiphonal four-part choirs. The bass decani voice is missing and has been supplied by the editor. For the transposition adopted in this example and in many modern editions, see n. 73.

Ex. 110

(transposed up a minor 3rd)

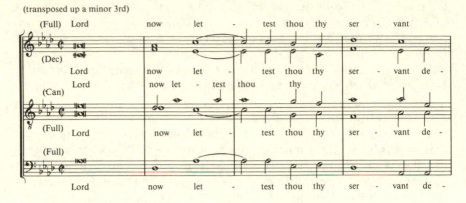

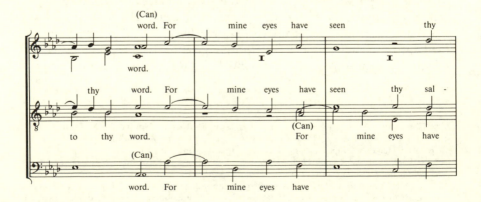

Ex. 110, continued

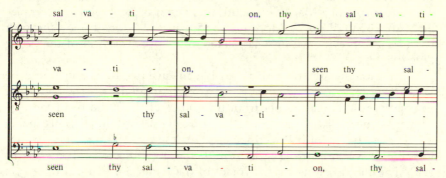

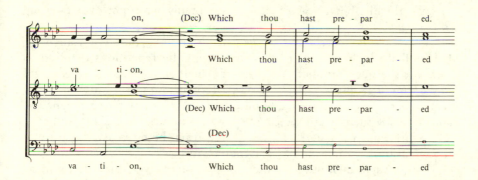

Doddington. He died sometime between 27 August 1571 and 15 March 1573.[50]

One of Tye's earliest Anglican works is the Nunc Dimittis, 'Lord, let thy servant now depart in peace', from the Wanley part-books and one later source.[51] Its text pre-dates the 1549 translation and probably even that of 1545; while the exact date of the piece itself cannot be determined, it may well have been written for private use at some time before the accession of Edward VI. Musically it is somewhat disappointing, in spite of its flowing lines, for each verse is set as a musically separate section

---

[50] Tye's date of birth has been given as c.1505 on the basis that he was awarded the B.Mus. at Cambridge in 1536 after ten years' study and practice of the art; but he may of course have been slightly younger. He obtained the D.Mus. in 1545 (and at Oxford by 'incorporation' in 1548). On Latin works that may be of Edwardian date, see below, p. 303, and n. 77. Tye was succeeded at Ely by his son-in-law, Robert White, in 1562.

[51] Tye, *English Sacred Music*, 238–48.

with a full close in the tonic (so to speak) in all but one instance. Much
the same is true of a Magnificat and Nunc Dimittis composed as a complement to Osbert Parsley's Morning Service in G minor, though the fault
is much less in evidence in what seems to be a later version of the Nunc
Dimittis.[52]

Tye's anthems are somewhat variable in quality, though it would be
hard to relate this to a gradually increasing confidence in the setting of
English words. Three settings from the Office of the Dead from the 1545
Primer are perfectly controlled, 'Deliver us, good Lord' in particular being
a little masterpiece of balanced feeling.[53] At the other end of the chronological scale is 'Christ rising again from the dead' (with a second part 'Christ
is risen again'), a setting for six voices of the Easter Anthems in their 1552
(or later) form.[54] It is a fortunate chance that has preserved five of the
six parts in a late sixteenth-century source; whether it is a late Edwardian
or an early Elizabethan work, it is undoubtedly his finest extant setting
of English words.

The much-discussed *Actes of the Apostles* is in a different category.[55]
It is difficult to imagine a performance with the repetitions required to
cater for the huge number of stanzas of which each 'chapter' consists: 76
in the case of chapter 13, implying 38 performances of its music. The verse
is quite peculiarly unappealing, but the settings are not ineffective vignettes,
and some of them were later reused to make attractive short anthems.
The work enjoyed a *succès d'estime* at the time, being issued three times
(in two distinct editions) in 1553 and thereabouts.

Tallis's Anglican music is rather more austere even than Tye's in its
general character. Some of his more functional service-music has already
been mentioned, but something should be said of the so-called 'Dorian'
service, an early example if not indeed the very first of a 'complete' Anglican
service consisting of Venite, Te Deum, Benedictus, Responses to the Commandments, Creed, Sanctus, Gloria, Magnificat, and Nunc Dimittis. The
order and text of the 'Communion' items reveal their connection with
the 1552 (or 1559) rite: the Responses to the Commandments replaces the
Kyrie, and the Gloria is transferred to the end.[56] Later on, it became unusual
to set either the Sanctus or the Gloria, since even when the service was

---

[52] Ibid. 249–73; the fragments of a variant Nunc Dimittis (more sectional in structure and retaining
as its *Gloria Patri* that of Parsley's Benedictus), ibid. 351–2; Parsley's Service is in TCM, x. 271–89.

[53] Tye, *English Sacred Music*, 24–34.

[54] Ibid. 10–23.

[55] Cf. p. 286 and n. 46.

[56] Tallis, *English Sacred Music*, ii. 1–62. The text of the 10th Response to the Commandments there
printed is not that of 1552; but Barnard (1641) gives a setting of the 1552 text at this point, and there
is no reason to believe that this is not what Tallis composed.

not curtailed after the Offertory, as was not infrequently the case, the latter part came increasingly to be said and not sung.[57]

'Dorian' is a nineteenth-century title for a work which conforms to the normal criteria for polyphonic writing in mode 1 (in effect D minor, though without key-signature). It is neither specially archaic nor indeed particularly noteworthy in any other respect: yet it enjoyed a considerable vogue and continued to be copied even in the seventeenth century. Its quiet austerity guaranteed its continued use, and much the same may be said of Tallis's other Anglican music. His own 'Christ rising'[58] is considerably more restrained than Tye's, but it has survived in two seventeenth-century sources. The other anthems are mostly very simple indeed, though sometimes, as in the declamatory 'Remember not, O Lord God, our old iniquities', very impressively so;[59] the more elaborate ones are transcriptions, probably not by Tallis himself, of some of the *cantiones sacrae* published in 1575.

This picture of Anglican church music before about that date may be rounded out by reference to a younger generation of composers: William Mundy, Richard Farrant, Robert White, Robert Parsons, and of course William Byrd, though his contribution will be discussed more fully in a later chapter. Mundy, who was born around 1530 (he became head boy at Westminster Abbey in 1543) was both a prolific and an imaginative composer of Anglican music. His most spectacular work is the Evening Service 'in medio chori'. Like Sheppard's Second Service, this is more plausibly to be considered an early Elizabethan than a late Edwardian service, and perhaps as a test of the skill of the Chapel Royal singers, whom Mundy joined in 1563. The subtitle is best explained by its scoring, which harks back to the pre-Reformation days in which polyphonic service-music really was sung 'from the middle of the choir'. Conceivably Mundy intended that the choir in this instance, or a group of soloists from it, should actually stand in the middle; but this is far from certain.

Mundy's service (in spite of its traditional designation 'in nine parts') is in the standard six-part texture of treble, mean, two countertenors, and bass, familiar from the larger Latin works of Taverner, Sheppard, Tye, and Tallis. In the seventeenth-century source (from which the second

---

[57] The bass parts only of two further complete services by Tallis are known. One, 'of five parts, two in one', is printed ibid., 179–88; the other is in Shrewsbury, Shropshire County Record Office, MS 356/2 (information kindly supplied by Dr Milsom). The texts of both the former and the 'Dorian' service have echoes of the 1549 versions; it is possible that they have been adapted from settings of the 1549 rite, but more likely perhaps that Tallis relied on his memory and tended to slip into the older wording at times.

[58] Ibid. 63–77. See p. 279 and n. 38 above. Cf. the setting by Sheppard (*Anthems for Men's Voices*, ed. Le Huray and others, 2 vols. (London, 1965), ii. 5–11), with 'Alleluia' at the end of *both* parts.

[59] Tallis, *Sacred Music*, i. 43–50, after Day's *Certaine notes*; an earlier version, from the Lumley part-books, ibid. 111–16. Yet another in *The Mulliner Book*, 36–7.

countertenor cantoris and both tenor books are missing), the treble part is accommodated in the mean decani book; both this and the actual mean (written in the mean cantoris book) are frequently divided, again in the manner established in Latin compositions, such passages being marked 'gymel'. In these sections, as far as can be determined, only the decani or cantoris sides of the lower parts are used, thus effecting a reduction of forces comparable to that apparently intended in similar passages in Latin works. Mundy's composition stands as a bridge between earlier practice and that of the standard Anglican repertoire, in which the treble was regarded as an exceptionally high part.[60]

Mundy also wrote the still popular anthem, 'O Lord, the maker of all thing', and has been credited with the fine 'Rejoice in the Lord always', which survives, anonymously and without words, as a keyboard score in the 'Mulliner Book'.[61] The other composers mentioned above are of less consequence for the Anglican rite (except of course for Byrd), but between them they carry the Anglican tradition forward to the middle years of Elizabeth's reign. Mundy, Richard Farrant (d. 1581), and Byrd were apparently the earliest to cultivate the accompanied 'verse anthem', usually a setting of a metrical psalm or comparable poem in which sections (or 'verses') for a solo voice were accompanied by the organ and followed by brief choral refrains. The contrapuntal style of the accompaniment was adapted from that of the contemporary 'consort-song' (for which see below). The principle was later adopted in Services as well as anthems; it was also applicable to compositions in which (as in the Mundy Service just discussed) the solo parts themselves provided full harmony, and in which therefore the organ was inessential if used at all. Later on, however, when the organ almost invariably supported the voices in any case, verse sections were normally for single voices or small groups, the organ contributing essential contrapuntal material.

Farrant's 'When as we sat in Babylon' is a good example of the earliest type of verse anthem, a metrical version of Psalm 137 with a choral refrain after each stanza.[62] He also wrote the still familiar short full anthems 'Call to remembrance' and 'Hide not thou thy face',[63] and a Morning, Communion, and Evening Service (Te Deum, Benedictus, Commandments, Creed,

---

[60] The unique source is Cambridge, Peterhouse, MSS 475–81. The work is unpublished: I am grateful to Mr Peter Phillips for an opportunity to consult a transcription.

[61] 'O Lord, the maker of all thing' is in *The Treasury of English Church Music*, ii, 22–7, and the *Oxford Book of Tudor Anthems* (London 1978), 240–7, both ed. P. Le Huray; 'Rejoice in the Lord always' is in *The Mulliner Book*, 53–4.

[62] Le Huray, *Music and the Reformation*, 221. A rather more sophisticated verse anthem by Mundy, 'Ah helpless wretch', to words by William Hunnis, may be seen in *The Treasury of English Church Music*, ii. 28–32.

[63] These, with 'Lord, for thy tender mercy's sake', also ascribed to John Hilton the Elder, are in *The Oxford Book of Tudor Anthems*, 50–6, 94–8, 152–6, ed. Anthony Greening; see also *The Treasury*, ii. 46–9.

Magnificat, and Nunc Dimittis) known variously as the 'Third', 'High', or 'Short' Service.[64]

From its tentative beginnings in the later 1540s, Anglican church music had developed from an experimental idiom, in which composers were not always certain of their direction, to a medium of expression which was to serve as the starting-point for the masterpieces of Byrd, Gibbons, and Tomkins. It was a remarkable achievement, and it reflects the confidence inspired, in this respect as in so many others, by the leadership of a queen in whose character a love of music and ceremony played an important part.

The composition of Latin sacred music occupied musicians throughout the period covered by this chapter. The earlier stages of the careers of such composers as Tallis, Tye, and Sheppard, to say nothing of innumerable lesser figures, took place within the later years of Henry's reign. If there was ever a general cessation it will have been between 1549 and 1553, since the Chapel Royal under Edward seems not to have encouraged Latin poly-phony and indeed to have pioneered the use of English even before the publication of the first Prayer Book.[65] But with Mary's accession the stage was set for a renewed cultivation of the old genres both by the generation of Tallis and by those who now came to the fore for the first time; and the substitution of the votive antiphon by the psalm-motet and by settings of texts (such as Latin collects) addressed solely to the deity may also have gathered strength in this reign. With the accession of Elizabeth, there were several good reasons for the continued cultivation of these newer types (which for practical purposes may be referred to as motets, though English composers rarely used the word). To begin with, the queen herself seems to have encouraged the use of Latin in her chapel. The publication of Walter Haddon's *Liber precum publicarum*, a Latin version of the *Book of Common Prayer*, in 1563 suggests as much; and while there is no evidence of its use in sung services either in her chapel or in the universities at this period, it indicates a climate favourable to the composition of Latin 'anthems'. Secondly, English musicians of this period will have wanted to maintain their growing links with the current Franco-Flemish school, and it was in the composition of Latin motets that the style could be most closely followed and their credentials as serious composers maintained abroad. Finally, there must have been a genuine expectation that the position

---

[64] The morning and evening canticles were edited by E. H. Fellowes in 1928 in the *Tudor Church Music octavo series*, nos. 62, 33. Details of these and many other single editions of Anglican church compositions are given in R. T. Daniel and P. Le Huray, *The Sources of English Church Music 1549–1660*, 2 vols. (London, 1972). Amongst the too little-known masterpieces of the period must be counted Robert Parsons's so-called First Service, first printed by Barnard in 1641, of which the fine Nunc Dimittis is in *The Treasury*, ii. 33–4. For the sacred music of Thomas Whythorne, see below, p. 332.

[65] See, however, p. 303 and n. 77 below.

might once more be reversed and the Latin rite with the papacy restored a second time. The opinion gains ground that the Gyffard part-books, a body of music for the Latin rite,[66] may have been compiled at the behest of a romantic reactionary during the decade following Elizabeth's accession. They were apparently never used, but they may have been copied for the private chapel of a recusant nobleman.

At the end of that decade, however, such expectations will have receded sharply. The failure of the northern rising in 1569 was followed by the papal bull of 1570, excommunicating Elizabeth and releasing her subjects from their oath of obedience. That had the effect of polarizing the situation, and it was reinforced by two important events in liturgical history, the issue by Pius V of the new Roman Breviary in 1568, and of the Missal in 1570, in conformity with the decrees of the Council of Trent. These effectively rendered the Salisbury liturgy obsolete for practising Roman Catholics, despite a provision that long-standing local customs might be retained; since every new priest was trained abroad in the Tridentine rite and as there was not immediately available any corresponding edition of the chant, they will have had to resort to crude patchwork if musical services were to be attempted at all. As it happened, the political circumstances made any overt cultivation of the Roman liturgy impossible.

It is greatly to Elizabeth's credit that she was willing to retain the recusant Byrd as a Gentleman of the Chapel Royal, to patronize him and Tallis by granting them a monopoly of music printing, and to look favourably on the publication of their joint *Cantiones* in 1575. Her ability to distinguish between genuine religious sentiment and political intrigue was rarely put to such good use as here.

The archetypal response to the changing conditions is that of Tallis, whose career has been briefly outlined above. His Latin compositions are rarely datable with precision, but a broad outline is discernible. To the earliest period of his career, the 1530s and 1540s, belongs a series of Marian antiphons of the type still cultivated by Taverner, but infrequently thereafter: 'Ave rosa sine spinis', 'Salve intemerata virgo', 'Ave Dei patris filia', and the massive 'Gaude gloriosa Dei mater'. This last is a work of such monumental proportions, and of such technical mastery, that it may perhaps, as has been suggested,[67] belong to Mary's reign, when William Mundy for example was still writing in this manner; but it would be dangerous to assume that Tallis was incapable of producing such a piece by (say) 1545, and it bears strong signs of youthful vigour. In this kind of work it was usual to begin with a lengthy section in triple metre, and to conclude in duple

---

[66] London, Brit. Lib., Add. MSS 17802–5; discussed in detail by R. Bray in *RMARC*, 7 (1969), 31–50.
[67] P. Doe, *Tallis* (London, 1968; 2nd edn., 1976), 16.

Ex. III

continued

Ex. III, continued

Rejoice, O virgin Mary, whom deservedly the church celebrates with praise, . . .

time.[68] That is what is done here, but the bold sweep of the lines, and the assurance with which the masses of sound are juxtaposed, are sufficient to dismiss any impression that the composer is working to a formula. His procedures are not without their precedents, however, and the passage in Ex. III (pp. 295–6) for divided trebles and means, with a delayed entry of a bass far below, provides a strong reminder of Taverner's Mass 'Corona spinea' (see above, Ex. 93), as well as a foretaste of Mundy's Evening Service 'in medio chori' (see p. 291).[69] Two further sections for reduced voices, separated by one for the full choir, precede the last glorious tutti, 87 bars in length. The final 'Amen' deserves close study for its treatment of two separate (though related) points of imitation (Ex. 112, pp. 297–8).[70]

Of Tallis's three Masses, 'Salve intemerata' is closely based on its eponymous antiphon and is probably also an early work. The unnamed four-part Mass, presumably for men's voices, is a short functional work of either late Henrician or Marian date. It has been suggested that the massive seven-part Mass 'Puer natus est nobis' may have been written for performance at Christmas 1554, when Philip II and his chapel were still in England following his marriage to Mary.[71] Certainly the music has pronouncedly Flemish characteristics, and in some ways might almost pass as one of Nicolas

---

[68] In fact 'Ave Dei patris filia' is in duple time throughout, though in view of the lateness of the source this may be a scribal modification, and 'Salve intemerata' in triple; since neither formula was previously unknown, no conclusion regarding their date can be drawn from these facts.

[69] TCM, vi. 131–2. The barring and note-values in this and the following example have been made to conform to the practice normally adopted for music of the Henrician period.

[70] Ibid. 142–3. Notice the sequential transposition of bars 251³–252³ and 252⁴–254⁴ respectively (a five-beat unit).

[71] See Doe, *Tallis*, 21.

Ex. 112

continued

Ex. 112, continued

Gombert's more grandiose conceptions. The reason behind the choice of note-values for a *cantus firmus* is often an impenetrable mystery to the modern scholar, but on this occasion the formula has proved to be deceptively simple: every note is given a numerical value (calculated in semibreves) according to the vowel of the syllable originally associated with it (initially a = 1, e = 2, i = 3, o = 4, u = 5) (Ex. 113).[72] Thanks to recent discoveries, every movement except the Credo can be satisfactorily reconstructed. The grandeur does not preclude moments of quiet reflection: the opening of

---

[72] Doe, *Tallis*, 22, where the numbers are given but their significance is not remarked upon. I am grateful to Professor Doe for subsequently pointing out to me the vocalic relationships, which vary from movement to movement.

Ex. 113

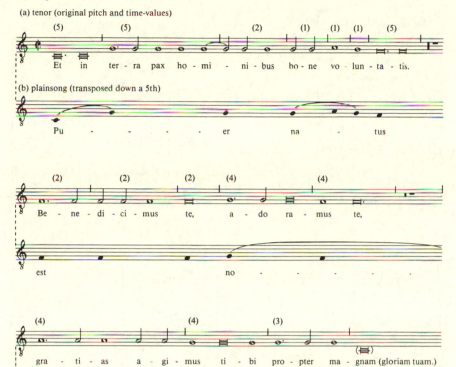

(a) tenor (original pitch and time-values)

Et in ter - ra pax ho - mi - ni - bus bo - ne vo - lun - ta - tis.

(b) plainsong (transposed down a 5th)

Pu - - - er na - tus

Be - ne - di - ci - mus te, a - do - ra - mus te,

est no - - - - -

gra - ti - as a - gi - mus ti - bi pro - pter ma - gnam (gloriam tuam.)

- - - - - - bis

(*a*) And on earth peace to men of good will. We bless you, we adore you, we give you thanks for your great glory.
(*b*) A child has been born to us . . .

the 'Benedictus' is perhaps as solemn an inspiration as the century produced (Ex. 114, pp. 300–1).[73]

Tallis's shorter ritual pieces no doubt also belong for the most part to the Marian period. Many of the *alternatim* hymn settings and short responds are quietly impressive. At one time it was thought that the two sets of Lamentations must also date from this period, as they are settings of Salisbury texts—but quite apart from the fact that they do not provide for the full

[73] Ed. S. Dunkley and D. Wulstan (Oxford, 1977; 2nd edn., 1980), 25–6. The transposition up a minor third, though it can scarcely be applicable to all the Latin liturgical music in 'normal' clefs at this period, as is sometimes argued, does in this instance give a more satisfactory performing pitch and conforms to what would appear to be the normal pitch-standard for Anglican church music of the Elizabethan and Jacobean period.

Ex. 114

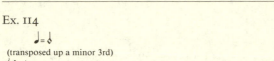

(transposed up a minor 3rd)

Ex. 114, continued

Blessed is he who comes in the name of the lord.

ritual of the service of *Tenebrae* to which they belong, their style is far removed from the merely functional. On the other hand, the several large responds, most of which were printed in the *Cantiones Sacrae* of 1575, were certainly composed with the ritual in mind: they observe the layout established by Taverner for this form (see p. 236 above), making them textually incomplete at the beginning unless the plainsong is supplied.[74]

Other works in the *Cantiones*, however, are non-ritual and probably belong to the 1560s or, in some cases, the early 1570s: prayers such as 'Absterge domine' and the seven-part 'Suscipe quaeso', biblical or Roman liturgical settings like 'Derelinquit impius' and 'In ieunio et fletu', and short devotional pieces such as 'O sacrum convivium' or the two settings of 'Salvator mundi'. 'Miserere nostri' is a display of canonic skill. To the same period belong, in all probability, the major psalm-motets, 'Domine quis habitabit' and 'Laudate dominum', and, as has already been implied, the two sets of Lamentations.

These last must surely be accounted their composer's masterpiece (or masterpieces, since they are two independent compositions). The great skill which has gone into their making has been put to the service of a deep and immediate emotional impact. Perhaps for the first time, a composer

[74] Tallis's contribution to this famous publication, which is discussed more fully in the following chapter, is printed in TCM, vi. 180–241, though unfortunately in alphabetical order, not that of the original. Tallis's contribution of seventeen items is made up by counting the long bipartite 'Suscipe quaeso' as two items; the setting of '[Dum transisset] sabbatum' on p. 257 is also part of the *Cantiones*. The titles of the responds in TCM do not include the chanted *initia*.

Ex. 115

Weeping, he wept in the night, and his tears ran down his cheeks: ...

has used the major mode to illustrate the grief that goes beyond its conventional expression (Ex. 115).[75]

At the opposite pole lies his triumphant forty-part motet 'Spem in alium numquam habui'. This *tour de force* for eight five-part choirs was, according to an early seventeenth-century account, written in response to a polychoral work by Striggio (doubtless his forty-part 'Ecce beatam lucem') and performed in the long gallery at Arundel House, the London home of the Dukes of Norfolk. A work of the early 1570s, it is a remarkable demonstration of virtuosity with which to set the seal on his life's work.[76]

It was Tallis's achievement to enter into the Elizabethan age with a formidable array of skill and experience, and to come to terms with its new aesthetic. This was denied, for various reasons, to his near contemporaries Tye and Sheppard. Tye was hardly behind Tallis in technical skill, and his seven-part 'Peccavimus cum patribus' is a worthy companion to 'Gaude gloriosa'. Its prayerful text, addressed to Christ, and penitential tone, however, put it in a rather different category, for all the technical similarities, and it is conceivable that it echoes the feelings of a reformer at Mary's accession. The two fine psalm-motets, 'Miserere mei, Deus' and 'Omnes gentes', may date from the same period or even later.[77]

Tye's Masses and smaller ritual works, on the other hand, are probably Henrician. Little need be said about the latter, of which only small fragments survive; but the Masses are a significant achievement. The six-part 'Euge bone' is musically related to a motet, 'Quaesumus, omnipotens', the text of which is in the form of a prayer for the reigning monarch; as the name of Henry in one of the standard versions of this prayer is here replaced by the phrase 'famulos tuos', it has been conjectured that the motet was intended to refer to Edward VI and the Protectorate collectively, and that both Mass and motet were composed to celebrate Edward's accession.[78] The Mass itself is somewhat stiff in conception, though concisely written and clear-cut in its tonality, which is essentially a modern C major. If the divided trebles and means in the second 'Agnus' look back to Taverner, the passage of choral homophony that immediately follows, like the chordal

[75] TCM, vi. 106; see also the new edition by Philip Brett (London, 1969).

[76] For the arguments in favour of the Arundel House performance and much supporting information, see D. Stevens, 'A Songe of Fortie Partes', *Early Music*, 10 (1982), 171–81; see also, however, the comments of P. Brett, 'Facing the Music', ibid. 347–50. The motet is discussed by P. Doe, 'Tallis's "Spem in alium" ', *ML*, 51 (1970); it has been published in TCM, vi. 299–318, and in a new edition by P. Brett (London, 1966).

[77] See Tye, *Ritual Music and Motets*, ed. N. Davison (London, 1987). H. Benham, 'Latin Church Music under Edward VI', *MT*, 116 (1975), 477–9, has attributed Tye's 'In quo corrigit' and 'Domine Deus celestis' to the reign of Edward VI.

[78] Tye, *Masses*, ed. P. Doe (London, 1980), p. xv; the Mass printed ibid. 105–56, and the motet, which lacks the tenor, in Tye, *Ritual Music*, 78–92.

opening of the Sanctus, is extremely up-to-date. The metre is duple through-out.

The 'Mean' Mass, as it has been called, is a short five-part work dating from no later than c.1540.[79] As for 'The Western Wynde', for four voices,[80] it is clearly inspired by Taverner's work, and complements it in so far as the tune is placed throughout in the alto (or medius) part, the one voice in which it never appears in Taverner's work. That was no doubt in order to avoid transposing the melody, and in fact Tye's work is in a different key from Taverner's (D minor as opposed to G minor). In other ways it could hardly be said to emulate its model, though it is an attractive enough piece.

Sheppard's artistic personality is in sharp contrast to that of Tye. A younger man, he devoted much of his energies to the provision of polyphonic music for the Latin rite, and a great deal of it must have been intended for the use of the Chapel Royal under Mary. His Latin works comprise five Masses, two Magnificats, a Te Deum, seventeen Office hymns, twenty Office responds, six votive antiphons, several psalm-motets (including a non-liturgical canticle), and a quantity of miscellaneous ritual material for the Mass and Office.[81] No other sixteenth-century English composer was so productive in this area, and if occasionally the procedures seem a little stereotyped, the consistent inventiveness and richness of his polyphony are a perpetual source of amazement.

Of the Masses, the six-part 'Cantate', on an unidentified plainsong, is the most retrospective in technique, though it can hardly be determined whether it is a Henrician or Marian work. The others, all for four voices, are generally plainer in style: that on 'The Western Wynde' is more closely modelled on Taverner's Mass than is that of Tye, but there are fewer statements of the theme, and Taverner's structural logic is abandoned. The 'Frences Mass' (the title of which, formerly read as the 'French' Mass, has occasioned a good deal of speculation) is a very brief and highly sectionalized affair on the lines of Taverner's 'Mean' Mass. 'Be not afraid' is another puzzling title: its recurrent motives have not been identifiable as belonging to a known chant, and the title has been held to refer to the exceptionally high level of dissonance in the work. The 'Plainsong Mass for a Mean' is an attractive short *alternatim* work including the Kyrie, presumably for the Lady Mass.

Sheppard's hymns and responds are amongst his most characteristic creations. In the hymns, it is invariably the even-numbered verses that

---

[79] Tye, *Masses*, 47–104, from the Peterhouse part-books (above, p. 239), tenor supplied by the editor.

[80] Ibid. 1–46, from the Gyffard part-books (above, p. 294).

[81] For the Masses, see the edition by Sandon (EECM, xvii), while there are transposed editions of the responds and hymns in the collected edition inaugurated by D. Wulstan (see Bibliography).

Ex. 116

The wise men went, following the star that they had seen going ahead of them, . . .

are set, usually with the plainsong stated in long notes of equal value, either in the top voice, the tenor, or (rarely) in some other part. Usually, but not always, the top voice is a treble; the subdivision of the standard vocal ranges often yields textures of seven or eight parts. The second verse of his 'Hostis Herodes impie', beginning 'Ibant magi', will illustrate a standard texture and procedure (Ex. 116).[82]

Sheppard's larger responds, of which there are fourteen, follow the pattern previously noted. One of them, 'Gaude, gaude, gaude, Maria', is of special interest as it incorporates the prose 'Inviolata', assigned to the second Vespers

[82] *Collected Works*, ii. 52. The performing pitch would perhaps be a little higher than the original notation would suggest in modern terms, but not (in my view) as high as that suggested by the transposition adopted in the edition cited. Cf. n. 73.

TABLE 2. *John Sheppard's 'Gaude, gaude, gaude, Maria'*

Function	Text	Type	Forces
R intonation	Gaude, gaude, gaude Maria	Plainsong	3 cantors
R continuation	virgo cunctas hereses sola interemisti que Gabrielis archangeli dictis credidisti. ★Dum virgo Deum et hominem genuisti. †Et post partum virgo inviolata permansisti.	Polyphony	a 6 (treble, mean, 2 countertenors, tenor, bass)
V1	Gabrielem archangelum . . .	Plainsong	3 cantors
R from ★, interrupted	Dum virgo Deum et hominem genuisti. Et post partum virgo	Polyphony	a 6
(Prosa versa 1)[a]	Inviolata integra et casta es Maria.		
	A.[b]	Plainsong	chorus
Prosa verse 2	Que es effecta fulgida celi porta	Polyphony	a 6
	A.	Plainsong	chorus
Prosa verse 3	O mater alma Christi charissima	Polyphony	a 5 (divided trebles and means, bass)
	A.	Plainsong	chorus
Prosa verse 4	Suscipe laudum pia preconia	Polyphony	a 5 (as above)
	A.	Plainsong	chorus
Prosa verse 5	Nostra ut pura pectora sint et corpora	Polyphony	a 5 (as above)
	A.	Plainsong	chorus
Prosa verse 6	Que nunc flagitant devota voxque et corda	Polyphony	a 5 (as above)
	A.	Plainsong	chorus
Prosa verse 7	Tu da per precata dulcisona	Polyphony	a 5 (divided trebles and means, 1st countertenor)
	A.	Plainsong	chorus
Prosa verse 8	Nobis perpetua frui vita	Polyphony	a 5 (divided trebles and means, bass)
	A.	Plainsong	chorus
Prosa verse 9 (R from ★, concluded)[c]	O benigna que sola inviolata permansisti	Polyphony	a 6
V2	Gloria patri et filio et spiritui sancto	Plainsong	3 cantors
R from †	Et post partum virgo inviolata permansisti.	Polyphony	a 6

[a] Sung to a variant of the music of 'inviolata permansisti'.
[b] The plainsong of each verse in turn is sung as a melisma to the vowel 'a'.
[c] To the original music, which is introduced without a break from the preceding section.

of the Purification (2 February) in the Salisbury ritual.[83] The scheme is outlined in Table 2. The whole thing is a fascinating example of musico-liturgical joinery, enhanced by the ethereal quality of the five-part sections and the majestic conclusion of the respond itself. A similarly interesting structure is found in the antiphon 'Media vita' to the canticle 'Nunc dimittis', the latter being followed not by the antiphon itself but by a series of verses ('Ne proiicias', etc.) which 'hitch on' to partial repetitions of the antiphon as though it were a respond. This liturgical curiosity was sung at Compline on the third and fourth Sundays of Lent.[84]

Sheppard also provided music for the Kyrie on the melody 'Lux et origo' and for the Gradual 'Hec dies', both for the second Vespers of the Resurrection.[85] His Te Deum is a work of great grandeur, while the short responds, especially those for Compline ('In manus tuas' I–II, 'In pace'), are quietly reflective. The psalm-motets and votive antiphons, like the Te Deum, are as yet unpublished.[86]

Amongst the contemporaries of Tallis, Tye, and Sheppard, Osbert Parsley, a singing clerk of Norwich Cathedral for fifty years until his death in 1585, deserves brief mention for his psalm-motet 'Conserva me, domine' and for his own Lamentations, both copied out by John Sadler in the late sixteenth century.[87] The Lamentations, unlike those of Tallis or White (to which they are musically much inferior) make use of the proper plainchant melody; they are a setting of the Sarum *Lectio prima* for Matins on Holy Saturday, but with the correct Hebrew letters and verse-division. It is possible that they were composed for English liturgical use, but it is likely in any case that the use of plainchant and the correctness of the verse-division stem from a Continental setting used by Parsley as a model.

The psalm-motet became the major form for the next generation, amongst whom Mundy and White are the chief. Mundy's Latin works include two Masses 'apon the square' (Lady Masses), two Magnificats, and a few other liturgical works, as well as three votive antiphons (one fragmentary), ten psalm-motets (one fragmentary), and three motets on

[83] *Brev. ad usum Sar.*, iii, col. 145. Sheppard, *Collected Works*, i. 22–31 (transposed); *Responsorial Music*, ed. D. Chadd (London, 1977), 99–117 (untransposed); a version of the plainsong (giving only the single 'Gaude' used at first vespers), *AS*, pls. 402–3.

[84] *Brev. Sar.* i, cols. dcliii–dcliv. The full scheme was also sung on the immediately preceding Saturdays, and on feasts of nine lessons within the third and fourth weeks of Lent. For the plainsong, see *AS*, pls. 170–1. Sheppard, *Collected Works*, i. 89–100. Compare the *versus ad repetendum* of early Introit psalmody. The 15th-cent. German song 'Mitten wir in Leben sind' (expanded by Luther) is based textually on the antiphon itself, but some of its melodic content is derived from the verse 'Ne proiicias'.

[85] *Collected Works*, i. 77–9, 80–2.

[86] The psalm-motets are discussed in Benham, *Latin Church Music*, 202–3; the occasional practice of repeating the first verse at the end of a psalm may be compared with that of Josquin in a few works.

[87] Oxford, Bod. Lib., Mus. Sch. e. 1–5; TCM, x. 237–47, 247–55.

non-psalmodic texts.[88] The antiphons are lengthy works in an old-fashioned style, presumably dating from Queen Mary's reign; the psalm-motets are consistently more advanced in idiom (lacking for example triple-time sections in all but one case), and may well be Elizabethan. They are technically confident, and imbued with a certain Flemish gravity; there are few points of repose, but there is here and there a sense of harmonic tonality as an expressive device (Ex. 117).[89]

Robert White (or Whyte) was a still more accomplished musician. Born perhaps about 1540, he was a chorister at Trinity College, Cambridge, in and around 1555; he obtained the degree of Bachelor of Music at Cambridge in 1560, and in 1562 succeeded his father-in-law Christopher Tye as Master of the Choristers at Ely Cathedral. He was himself succeeded there in 1566 by John Farrant; he became organist of Chester Cathedral and was involved in the performances of the mystery cycle there in 1567 and 1568. He was appointed *Magister choristarum* at Westminster Abbey in 1569; he, his wife, and his youngest child all died of the plague within a month or so in November 1574.

White left few liturgical works. His Latin Magnificat is a splendid, if rather conventional piece, while the four settings of the hymn 'Christe qui lux es et dies' (i.e. of the even-numbered verses beginning 'Precamur sancte domine') look as though they might have been undertaken as an exercise in contrapuntal techniques.[90] His glory resides in the twelve psalm-motets and the Lamentations. Compared with Mundy's psalms, those of White preserve rather more of the old English vigour of contrapuntal line; he also uses divided voices and triple time more freely. But his mastery may be seen in a work that shows neither of these devices, the rather sombre 'Deus misereatur' (Ps. lxvi) for six voices in a lowish tessitura. The restrained gravity of the setting of the words 'Letentur et exultent gentes', at the beginning of the second part, leads inexorably to the final 'et metuant eum omnes fines terre' (Ex. 118, pp. 311–13).[91]

As for the two sets of Lamentations, they are unquestionably one of the high points of the epoch. For five and for six voices respectively, they each set part of the *Lectio tertia* on Maundy Thursday, and the *Lectio prima* with part of the *Lectio secunda* on Good Friday in the Sarum rite, so continuing the scheme initiated by Tallis; but these works are wholly non-liturgical in conception. It is difficult to account for two settings of the same words, but a comparison enables one to point to the five-part set as perhaps the

---

[88] See William Mundy, *Latin Antiphons and Psalms*, ed. Harrison (London, 1963); the other Latin works are unpublished. For 'squares' see above, p. 181.

[89] Ibid. 74–7, from Ps. cxviii: 141–4, 'Adolescentulus sum ego', bars 30–51 (transposed up a minor third).

[90] Cf. the similar settings by Byrd (see Ch. 6). White's sacred music is published in TCM, v; the Latin church music is also now available in a better edition by D. Mateer in 3 volumes (see Bibliography).

[91] White, *Six-Part Latin Psalms*, 57–8, 65–7 (TCM, v. 69, 74–5).

Ex. 117

continued

Ex. 117, continued

Your justice is for ever, and your law the truth.

Ex. 118

★ MS ♯ before *b*

continued

Ex. 118, continued

Ex. 118, continued

(a) Let the people rejoice and be glad . . .
(b) and let all the ends of the earth fear him. Amen.

maturer and more deeply considered of the two. But it would be difficult to choose between them for originality, as the two versions of 'O vos omnes' clearly demonstrate (Ex. 119).[92] What could not have been expected of such a composer, had he been allotted the life-span of his contemporary, William Byrd?

A considerable amount of minor liturgical music—including liturgical organ music—has survived from the reign of Mary or a little later. Much of the extant vocal music is in the Gyffard part-books, to which reference has already been made.[93] The evidence for their date is conflicting, but for reasons already explained, there will have been little reason to collect music for the Salisbury ritual after 1570. The works ascribed to 'mr. birde' and 'John mundye' were composed for that ritual, and while it is possible that these are references to their well-known eponyms (William Byrd, 1543–1623; John Mundy, son of William Mundy, ?c.1545–1630), it is rather more likely that they concern earlier composers of the same name.

The other minor figures represented in the source include Philip Alcoke, Thomas Appleby, Robert Barber, Blytheman, Robert Johnson, Thomas Knyght, Robert Okeland, William Whytbroke, and Thomas Wryght. Some of these (with others not mentioned) may have been more nearly contemporaneous with Taverner (born c.1495) than with Sheppard, Tallis, Tye, or White (all of whom are represented); but the majority were probably still active in Mary's reign. The liturgical forms include Kyries, Alleluias, and complete Ordinaries for the Lady Mass, a Proper of the Mass for the Name of Jesus, short responds, and minor ritual forms such as the 'Asperges' and 'Vidi aquam' before Mass, the 'Gloria laus' for Palm Sunday and the 'Christus resurgens';[94] there are also Magnificats and settings of the votive antiphon 'Sancte Deus', a Te Deum and the three 'Western Wynde' Masses of Taverner, Sheppard, and Tye. Some passages from an anonymous 'Asperges me', the second item in the collection, will illustrate the plain but liturgically appropriate idiom of the more modest pieces. This one is based on the faburden of the chant, stated monorhythmically in the lowest voice (Ex. 120, pp. 319–20).[95]

---

[92] TCM, v. 28–9, 42–4. Ex. 100 (b) is preceded by a setting of the same text for sexta vox, discantus, and tenor; the tenor part is editorial.

[93] Above, p. 294 and n. 66.

[94] For the 'Christus resurgens' and its associated ceremonial, see above, p. 279.

[95] Add. 17802–5, fos. 5ᵛ, 4ʳ, 4ʳ, 4ʳ (MS 17803 is top part). Plainchant, following the intonation in all part-books except MS 17803 (note the phonetic spelling), from the printed Processional of 1502 (fac. edn.), fo. A2ᵛ. Since the intonation and following psalm-verse are untransposed in the source, the faburden may be thought of as 'thirds' faburden against the untransposed plainsong rather than as 'sixths' faburden against the plainsong transposed up a fourth. See p. 180 for the origin of the distinction, and Ex. 98 above, from the first piece in the same source, where the weight of the evidence is in favour of 'sixths' faburden.

Ex. 119

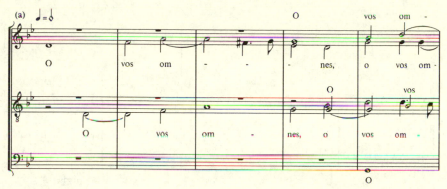

continued

Ex. 119, continued

Ex. 119, continued

continued

Ex. 119, continued

(a) and (b) O all you who pass by the way, wait, and see if there is any grief like mine:

These vocal forms are paralleled by a substantial written repertory of liturgical organ music, most of it from a collection now in the British Library and once the property of Thomas Tomkins.[96] The second layer of this contains the entire liturgical output of Thomas Preston, whose career took him from Trinity College, Cambridge, and Magdalen College, Oxford, to St George's, Windsor. He seems to have remained a Roman Catholic; and while some of his surviving music may date from Henry's reign, the majority of it is probably Marian.[97] The range of his style may be illustrated, first, by an extract from the Introit of his Easter Day Mass, and, second, by the opening of his fifth setting of the Offertory 'Felix namque' (Ex. 121, pp. 321–2).[98]

Whereas the rhythmic nervousness of the former passage is a development of an idiom favoured by John Redford, the suave euphony of the latter is a creation of Preston himself, at least so far as organ music is concerned. A third aspect of his character is displayed in the virtuoso demands of his first 'Felix namque' and his Offertory 'Diffusa est gratia'. This kind of writing foreshadows the idiom of John Bull (Ex. 122, p. 322).[99]

Contemporaries of Preston who also wrote liturgical organ music include Richard Wynslate, Philip ap Rhys, John Thorne, Shelbye, Alwood, Blytheman, Richard Farrant, and Tallis himself; there is also a large anonymous repertory, in particular a collection of *alternatim* hymns 'upon the faburden'. Blytheman and Tallis both emulated the virtuosity of Preston, though Tallis's two elaborate settings of 'Felix namque', dated 1562 and 1564 respectively in the Fitzwilliam Virginal Book, are perhaps demonstrations of virtuosity

[96] London, Brit. Lib., Add. 29996: see above, pp. 249–50.
[97] See D. Mateer, 'Further Light on Preston and Whyte', *MT*, 115 (1974), 1074–7.
[98] Add. 29996, fos. 62ᵛ, 57ʳ (cf. *Early Tudor Organ Music*, ii, nos. 5, 16); plainchants from the printed Salisbury Gradual of 1532.
[99] Add. 29996, fo. 50ʳ (cf. *Early Tudor Organ Music*, ii, no. 8).

Ex. 120

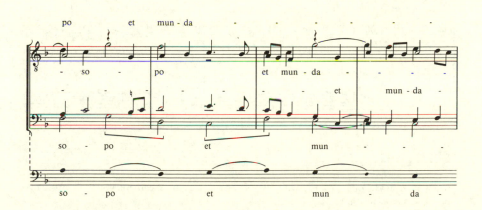

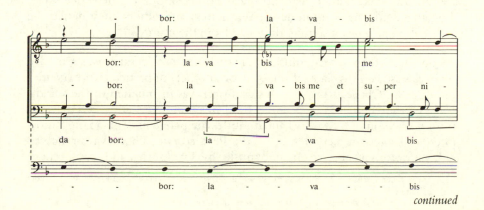

continued

Ex. 120, continued

You will sprinkle me, O lord, with hyssop and I shall be cleansed: you will wash me and I shall be made whiter than snow.

for its own sake rather than liturgical compositions in the strict sense. Together with the In nomines of Blytheman and others, they herald the later cult of plainchant settings divorced from the liturgy.[100]

A good deal of the 'secular' music of the early sixteenth century was provided by ecclesiastical musicians of one sort or another, in particular the 'gentlemen' of the Chapel Royal.[101] This tradition was maintained in the middle years of the century, for example by Tallis and Tye. The latter became tutor to the young Edward VI and doubtless helped to encourage the atmosphere of Protestant piety desired by the Protectorate. There was a renewed cultivation of serious instrumental music, by Tye himself and many others,

[100] For a fuller discussion of this repertory, see my *English Keyboard Music*, 19–38, and the older literature cited there.

[101] For an account of the repertory in the early years of Henry VIII's reign see Ch. 4, pp. 258–9.

Ex. 121

(a)

Re - sur - re - xi,

et   ad - huc

te - cum sum,   al -   (leluya:)

(b)

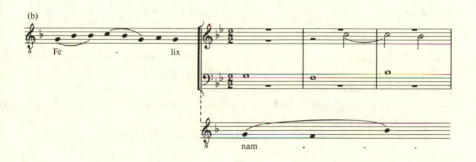

Fe -   lix

nam - - - -

continued

Ex. 121, continued

que   es,   sa -   cra
                                                            (virgo Maria)

(*a*) I have arisen, and I am with you, alleluia.
(*b*) For you are indeed happy, holy virgin Mary . . .

Ex. 122

while in the part-song a high moral tone was generally observed. This persisted into the early years of Elizabeth's reign and is typified by the popularity of metrical psalm-singing in courtly circles and elsewhere.[102]

At the same time there had been a gradual change of emphasis in the organization of court music under Henry VIII. Though the replacement of 'minstrels' by 'musicians' is in some respects a change of nomenclature only, it symbolizes the growing status of art-music outside the Church. The minstrels—in the widest sense the whole of the entertainment industry with its hierarchy, its privileges, and its restrictive practices—were in decline. In their heyday they had embraced the best in secular art-music as then conceived, but they had been overtaken by events: the increasing complexity of art-music outside the Church and above all the increasing need for musical literacy. Minstrelsy, indeed, had been essentially an orally communicated skill: when this no longer sufficed, the summit of the profession lost its *raison d'être*.

Minstrels (of whatever kind) had always been distinguished in royal lists

[102] Above, pp. 284–6.

from the more specialized musical (or semi-musical) functionaries such as trumpeters and *vigilatores* or 'waits'.[103] Now, under Henry VIII, the minstrels gradually decreased in number and 'musicians' and specialized singers and instrumentalists increased. At his burial, those provided with liveries included 'Gentilmen of the Chapell' (20), 'Trumpettors' (18), 'Singing men and children under Philips' (9), 'Mynstrells' (7, including Hughe Wodhouse their marshal), 'Musytyans' (5, all of the Bassani family), 'Shackebuttes' (4), 'Vyolls' and 'Vialls' (6 of the former, all Italian, and 2 of the latter, apparently both Flemish), 'Fluttes' (5), and a 'Fyfer', 'Drume player', 'Harper', and 'Bage piper'. In 1555 there were still five Bassani musicians and one other, eight sackbuts, six flutes, six violins, two viols, three 'dromslades', two fifers, two harpers, and a 'lewter'.[104] The minstrels did not die out completely for some time, but the tradition of a large and specialized household establishment of professional musicians was maintained and enhanced in the reign of Elizabeth.[105]

The 'Philips' (often called 'Mr Philips' or 'Phillips') in charge of the household singing men and children was almost certainly Philip van Wilder (or Welder), a Flemish musician who with his relative Peter was in the royal service under Henry VIII. Philip is described as a minstrel in 1526, but later had charge of the music of the Privy Chamber.[106] He took care of the King's instruments and inventoried them at his death,[107] and continued in the service of Edward VI until his own death in 1553. His extant works include a small amount of Latin church music, a wedding psalm (128) to the metrical paraphrase of Thomas Sternhold,[108] and several chansons and a madrigal. The chansons became very popular, and were often copied in keyboard or polyphonic instrumental versions.[109]

---

[103] See Rastall in *RMARC*, 4 (1964), 1–41. On the waits at a later date see below, Ch. 8, p. 496.

[104] *The King's Musick*, ed. H. de Lafontaine (London, 1909), 7–9.

[105] Ibid., *passim*. The term 'King's Musick' was not in use before the 17th cent., and then only informally, but it has been used by scholars as a generic label for royal household music as far back as the records go. Lafontaine in the edition cited used the Lord Chamberlain's records in the Public Record Office, which go back to 1460–1. W. Woodfill (*Musicians in English Society* (Princeton, NJ, 1953), 177) argued the case for a decisive change of pattern in the reign of Henry VIII, basing it on the decay of the travelling minstrelsy, and the growing substitution of a permanent body of musicians. But there is no need to regard late medieval minstrels as being necessarily wanderers, and their 'decline' is more probably due to the causes given above. Many of Henry's 'musicians', including most of the large number of foreigners, were employed on a temporary basis: see, e.g., J. Stevens, *Music and Poetry*, 308.

[106] J. Stevens, ibid. 307.

[107] Printed in R. Russell, *The Harpsichord and Clavichord: An Introductory Study* (2nd edn., rev. H. Schott, London, 1973), 155–60; Galpin, *Old English Instruments* (4th edn.), 215–22.

[108] *An Anthology of English Church Music*, 141–8. The text is Sternhold's original version, not the later Genevan revision (information from Dr R. Zim).

[109] On van Wilder see Milsom, 'English Polyphonic Style in Transition: A Study of the Sacred Music of Thomas Tallis', 2 vols. (Oxford, 1983), i. 61 seqq.; ii, Appendix 3.3 (list of works in English sources).

The royal example helped to foster amateur musicianship in the nobility and gentry, and an appreciation of those kinds of music that only the profession could provide. The higher echelons of that profession were still largely supplied through the traditional medium of the song-school, but the Reformation broke the existing pattern whereby the career thus inaugurated led automatically to a cathedral or collegiate clerkship, or beyond to the major orders of subdeacon, deacon, and priest. A cathedral post now often meant poverty and a 'part-time' approach to the duties; but by the same token, the trained musician became more readily available as a tutor, an instrumentalist, or a composer of 'secular' music, seeking the patronage of the local gentry and nobility.[110] The 'Gentlemen of the Chapel Royal' became a musical élite, exhibiting the standards by which the accomplishments of the provinces could be measured, and offering London the rich and varied tapestry of musical life for which the reign of Elizabeth has become famous.

The final outcome of these developments lay in the future; but the Reformation, and the consequent secularization of much that had formerly been within the ecclesiastical sphere, hastened what was in any case a natural result of the Tudor love of music and ceremonial. There is little evidence from the middle decades of the century of a preoccupation amongst noble and wealthy householders with a professional 'private music'; the Seymours, the family of the Protector, were perhaps somewhat unusual in this respect.[111] The rewarding of tutors and the purchase of instruments and music books for amateur use is more frequently met with.[112] Quite exceptional is the very substantial acquisition of music books, largely from abroad, by Henry Fitzalan, 16th Earl of Arundel (1512–80); but it is uncertain to what extent it was used for actual performance, amateur or professional.[113] As with the collection of Edward Paston at a later date, its character was largely determined by his continued adherence to the Roman·Catholic faith.

The written 'secular' repertory of the period was principally governed by adherence to a set of more or less elevated ideals, which may be considered under the headings of chivalrous accomplishment, learning, and piety. The

---

[110] David Price, *Patrons and Musicians of the English Renaissance* (Cambridge, 1981), 60–2.

[111] Ibid. 15–17, 118–24.

[112] Ibid. 3, 13–14.

[113] The dissemination of foreign music in England at this time is discussed by Milsom, 'English Polyphonic Style', 71–82, with particular reference to the Fitzalan (later Lumley) library. (Fitzalan was the son-in-law of Henry Howard, 4th Duke of Norfolk, for whom Tallis's forty-part motet 'Spem in alium' was apparently written: see above, p. 303.) Milsom has found that the musical items listed in the Lumley catalogue of 1609 (and printed by S. Jayne and F. R. Johnson, *The Lumley Library: the Catalogue of 1609*, London, 1956) in most cases identify only the first item of several bound together in each of the part-books concerned; so that the amount of music attributable to Fitzalan's purchases is greatly increased.

first of these was related to the perennial medieval theme of 'courtly love', though with a typically Renaissance emphasis on the accomplishments themselves. Music, as such an accomplishment, was recommended to the nobility and gentry in the 'courtly' literature of the period: Sir Thomas Elyot's *The Boke named the Governor* (1531), Baldassare Castiglione's *Il cortegiano* (1528, translated by Sir Thomas Hoby as *The Book of the Courtyer*, 1561), and Roger Ascham's *Toxophilus* (1545).[114] But it is the attitudes of the Renaissance gentleman as a whole, derived from such sources as *Il cortegiano*, that pervade the poetry of Surrey and Wyatt, and through it a large amount of lesser verse. Their poetry made increasing use of Italian forms (sonnet, strambotto, etc.) over French and older English models and showed, at least in the versions of Thomas Tottel's *Songes and Sonnettes* (1557), a new conception of metrical regularity.[115]

The learning was deep-rooted. The Tudor monarchs were scholars and Latinists, patrons of the educational system propounded by Colet, More, and Erasmus. The study of classical languages and literature influenced thought to such an extent that even the leisured products of schoolmasters and academics were founded upon it, and those of educated men shot through with allusions that escape all but specialists today. In this connection the part played by educational institutions in public entertainment is especially significant: the song-schools, universities, and Inns of Court in particular.

As for piety, it is a current never far from the surface, and often visible upon it.[116] The spirit of the Reformation merely encouraged a trend that was already clearly noticeable, for example, in the devotional literature of the 1530s and 1540s. But it was not confined to specifically Christian verse, 'Protestant' or 'Catholic'; it adds a colouring to many treatments of classical themes, and to a great deal of love-poetry of whatever inspiration.

The written forms of secular song were principally the part-song, the consort-song, and the lute-song, though the last was but in its infancy. The part-song had developed along lines comparable to the standard types of Italian madrigal and French chanson of the 1530s (the former being at first no more than a monostrophic *canzone* or a through-composed setting of some originally repetitive form such as the madrigal or sonnet); that is, it had acquired a generally homophonic four-part texture, frequently

[114] Price, *Patrons and Musicians*, 5–6. Their recommendation was qualified by warnings against 'over moche studie' of the art (Ascham, *Scholemaster*, 1570).

[115] Modern edition by H. E. Rollins (2 vols., Cambridge, Mass., 1928–9). Wyatt's poems, which in their original form are based on syllable-count but show little regularity of stress, were revised by Tottel or an assistant to bring them into line with the greater regularity practised by Surrey, the poet chiefly represented in the collection.

[116] In so far as this was fostered by metrical psalmody and similar exercises, see above, pp. 284–6.

with imitative entries, and a melodious top part.[117] The chanson style was familiar to English musicians from imported manuscripts and printed copies, from copies made by English scribes (generally working in England from one of the first two categories), and from the dissemination of music by foreign musicians resident in England (such as Philip van Wilder). It is clear that the madrigal style was also known and appreciated, mainly through the medium of imported copies of printed music by such composers as Festa, Arcadelt, and Verdelot, but its influence at this date does not appear to have been anything like so widespread.[118]

The part-songs of Tallis, Sheppard, Robert Johnson, and others, as represented in the Mulliner Book in particular,[119] show the change wrought by the Parisian chanson style in comparison with the earlier Tudor manner. Many of them exhibit the pervading imitation, equality of voices, and even the dactylic opening rhythm (♩ ♪♪) of the stylistic model. This last feature occurs for example in Sheppard's 'O happy dames' (no. 111), and in a setting, surviving only in late sources as a solo song with lute accompaniment, of Richard Edwards's poem 'In youthfull [or 'youthlye'] yeares'.[120] A more chordal manner is found in 'In going to my naked bed' (no. 81); again the words are by Edwards, and again he may well be the composer.[121] The Mulliner Book presents the music in reduced score for keyboard and is without texts, but in most cases a restoration is possible, either because the text is known from a literary source, or because the piece itself has survived in a later musical manuscript (or both). For example, Robert Johnson's 'Defiled is my name', a setting of a poem once thought to refer to Anne Boleyn, survives in the 'Hamond' part-books of c.1560–90.[122]

---

[117] The Italian madrigal was always monostrophic: it often had musical repetitions, occasionally to new text. To the extent that English part-songs are monostrophic, they might well be termed 'madrigals'; but the word is anachronistic at this date. For further remarks on this topic, see Ch. 7, pp. 397–8.

[118] The whole subject has been treated exhaustively by J. Milsom in his dissertation (see n. 109), with documentary information in the appendices in vol. ii.

[119] Ed. D. Stevens. For other sources, mostly fragmentary, see Milsom, 'English Polyphonic Style', ch. 4, with reconstructions in vol. ii. Milsom has convincingly reconstructed a large part of the important bass part-book in the Public Record Office (MS 1/246, earlier described by D. Stevens in The Music Survey, 2 (1950), 161–70); he has also identified contemporary settings of several of the poems by John Heywood, John Redford, John Thorne, Richard Edwards, and others in the 'literary' section of Brit. Lib., Add. 15233. Tallis's secular songs are in Tallis, English Sacred Music, i. 95–110, based on all sources.

[120] 'O happy dames' is also in the Public Record Office Book; the poem is by Surrey. 'In youthfull yeares' is in Brit. Lib., Add. 15117, fo. 14ᵛ, and in the Dallis lute-book (Dublin, Trinity College, MS D. 3. 30, pp. 204–7), where it is ascribed to Parsons. It shows every sign of having been written as a part-song; it has been edited by Greer in Songs from Manuscript Sources, ed. D. Greer, 2 vols. (London, 1979), i, no. 1; see also Joiner in RMARC, 7 (1969), 84–5 (fac.), 103–4. The words are in Add. 15233 and were later published by Edwards in his anthology The Paradyse of daintie Deuises (London, 1576; ed. H. E. Rollins, Cambridge, Mass., 1927). Edwards was Master of the Children of the Chapel Royal, 1565–6, and he may be the true composer as Milsom suggests.

[121] The words were printed in The Paradyse of daintie Deuises.

[122] London, Brit. Lib., Add. 30480–4.

This fine piece may stand as one of the best extant representatives of this particular style, an intense and impassioned plea couched in a satisfying bipartite form (Ex. 123, overleaf).[123]

Robert Johnson was a Scottish priest who had fled to England 'lang before reformation'—before the Scottish Reformation, that is, and presumably to take advantage of the English one under Edward VI. Thomas Whythorne (1528–96) was a musician whose views happily developed in line with those current in his day, though he may have had to conceal them during Mary's reign. Brought up by an uncle priest, he was sent to Magdalen College School in 1538 as a chorister; after six years there, and a further one as a demy of the College itself, he served an apprenticeship with John Heywood. Heywood was a Roman Catholic, unheroic enough to admit the royal supremacy under pressure and content to lie low during Edward's reign, but who rose to sufficient prominence under Mary to have to flee in 1558. He was a poet and dramatist, master of a company of choirboy actors and a performing musician of considerable repute. Under him Whythorne learnt the craft of versification and the approved postures of a poet of the day. He applied himself to the study of musical instruments, and after three years felt himself able to pursue the profession of a music tutor in the houses of the wealthy. His unique autobiography[124] provides an amusing insight into the trials and temptations of a young man in such circumstances; he does not name his patrons, although in some cases they can be identified or guessed at. In 1571 he published his *Songes for three, fower and five voyces*, and immediately afterwards was asked to direct the music in Archbishop Parker's private chapel in Lambeth Palace. After Parker's death in 1575 he was again left to his own devices, and here the autobiography ends, shortly before his marriage in 1577. His only other publication was a collection of *Duos*, which appeared in 1590.

Whythorne was a typical product of his time, though anything but a typical composer. The clue to his distinctiveness lies in his literary approach. Although music was his first and lifelong love, his early training was as a singer, a player of instruments, and as a maker of verses. He developed a curious fondness for putting his feelings into verse, and almost all his music sets his own poetry. Although, as the autobiography makes clear, Whythorne himself often sang his verses to the accompaniment of the virginals or the lute, the conventions of the day dictated a contrapuntal format for publication. But although some of the published works may indeed

---

[123] *Music of Scotland*, 165–6 (no. 44); *The Mulliner Book*, 59–60 (no. 80). In the latter, the music of the first section is marked to be repeated at the end, but this is less convincing, both verbally and musically, than the repeat indicated in the Hamond part-books, which is of the latter part of the second section. In other respects, too, Mulliner's text is less satisfactory.

[124] Ed. J. M. Osborn (Oxford, 1961).

Ex. 123

Ex. 123, continued

* The Mulliner Book has *a'* here, and may be right; the point necessarily occurs in both forms.

have originated as solo songs, even the simplest of them are elaborated with care, while many are lengthy compositions of considerable complexity.

At the beginning of Mary's reign, Whythorne travelled to the Netherlands, Germany, France, and Italy. He became acquainted with the vogue for madrigalian composition and publication, and the *Songes* are in part the product of an ambition to emulate that kind of endeavour. Stylistically, they are remote from true madrigals, but to Whythorne belongs the credit of actually getting a set of 'secular' part-books into print. His publisher, John Day, was more experienced in promoting psalters and church music, and although the standard of production was high the slim volumes did not sell well; nevertheless, their historical importance is considerable, for Whythorne set a pattern that lasted almost into the second quarter of the seventeenth century.[125]

Whythorne's limitations as a composer stem not from any lack of skill as such, but rather from a certain pedestrianism that hampered him as a poet and is evident in the somewhat earthbound quality of his melodies. He was not at all an amateur musician, but he displays an amateurish enthusiasm as a composer: he promises at the end of his autobiography to compose large numbers of further songs in two, three, four, five, even six parts, though only the duos, fifty-six of them, saw the light of day. The *Songes* of 1571 are sufficiently numerous; there are seventy-six, far more than in most later publications, though many are very short. Two brief pieces, one in four, the other in five parts, will illustrate his essential conventionality: the melody of the second harks back to idioms current in Henry's time, though the contrapuntal dressing is more elaborate (Ex. 124, overleaf).

Some of Whythorne's music is much more elaborate than this, however: the four-part 'Since I embrace the heav'nly grace', for example,[126] though beginning quietly enough, works up to a positive torrent of counterpoint in setting the final word 'rejoice'. It is just here, however, that his weakness is apparent, for the conclusion merely disturbs the balance of what is basically

[125] See Ch. 7, p. 422. The precedent of *XX Songes* (1530) was, of course, long forgotten.
[126] Ed. Peter Warlock (OUP, 1927: *Oxford Choral Songs*, no. 357).

Ex. 124

(a) Though cho-ler cleapt the heart a-bout And set it all on fire, Which caused the tongue in ha-sty wise To blast out for my hire, A dread-ful change for me to have if it had ta-ken place: Yet now the storm is gone and past, And I in qui-et case. Yet

(b) As thy sha-dow it-self ap-ply'th To fol-low thee where-

Ex. 124, continued

so thou go, And when thou bends, it - self it wry'th, Turn -

ing as thou both to and fro: The flat - ter - er doth

e - ven so, And shopes him - self the same to gloze, With

man - y a fawn - ing and gay show, Whom he would frame for his pur - pose. With

rather ordinary music. Whythorne's most elaborate compositions are the five psalms (95, 100, 123, 134, and 130) that conclude his four-part section: these are through-composed settings of the ordinary prayer-book texts,[127] and it is tempting to think that they may have been responsible for Parker's decision to appoint him to his chapel.

Whythorne was, however, a somewhat isolated figure in English music. One of his songs has the text in one part only—a consort-song, that is, for solo voice and instrumental accompaniment, though it may be that this method of performance was often used even for music with words in all parts. However that may be, there is a substantial repertory of music expressly for solo voice extant, the accompaniment being in most cases presumably for viols, to which the range and character of the accompanying parts are well suited. The voice-part is invariably in the treble or 'mean' range, being the top or second part of the standard five-part texture. Such pieces were especially suited to choirboy plays and for the musical training and moral education of choristers, and it is quite possible that the genre originated in that context. At the same time, it has to be admitted that, while there is plenty of evidence for the public performance of choirboy plays from the time of Henry VIII onwards, and while many of the examples of consort-song before 1575 are clearly dramatic in form, in not one case has it proved possible to link such a song with a specific play.[128] We should remember, however, that all kinds of ceremonies and pageants called for music in which choristers might play a part.

Apart from Byrd, whose contribution will be considered in the following chapter, the early consort-songs are by such men as Richard Farrant, Robert Parsons, and Nicholas Strogers, the last a shadowy figure of the early Elizabethan period. They can be of considerable eloquence, as in the anonymous 'Come tread the paths', which with Parsons's 'Pour down you pow'rs divine' and Farrant's 'Ah, alas, you salt sea gods' belongs to a tradition of 'death-songs' in triple time; or Farrant's 'O Jove, from stately throne', the text of which clearly suggests a dramatic situation (Ex. 125).[129]

The origins of lute-song in England are obscure. It seems certain that the genre originated within the period covered by this chapter, although virtually nothing for voice and lute (as opposed to arrangements of popular

---

[127] The publication also includes a couple of settings of metrical psalms.

[128] See G. E. P. Arkwright, 'Elizabethan Choirboy Plays and their Music', *PMA*, 40 (1913–14), 117–38, and the discussion in Ch. 7 below. The song 'Awake ye woeful wights' in Edwards's play *Damon and Pithias* (?1564) survives in a version for voice and lute: see below, p. 335.

[129] *Consort Songs*, ed. P. Brett (London, 1967), 17–18. The term 'death-song' is that of Peter Warlock, whose *Elizabethan Songs* (3 vols., London, 1926) is an earlier anthology of consort-songs.

tunes for lute alone) was written down within it. Some later sources contain songs of an incontestably early period, but many of them are evidently arrangements of consort-songs or part-songs. 'Pour down you pow'rs divine', for instance, occurs in a later manuscript, the Turpyn lute-book, in a version for voice and bass lute; it is followed by a second part, 'No grief is like to mine', which is almost certainly also an arrangement although no other version has survived.[130] The 'Dallis' and 'Ballet' lute-books of the 1580s and 1590s also include songs, but some of these at least are also arrangements;[131] the 'Brogyntyn' manuscript (c.1595)[132] includes arrangements of consort accompaniments for the lute, while still others simply arrange the three or four lower voices for lute irrespective of whether the original vocal part was at the top or not.[133] Song arrangements for solo lute are not uncommon, and these may often have been performed as solo songs, the player himself (or herself) singing along with the arrangement: the pieces in the British Library MS Royal Appendix 58 (after 1547) and Le Roy's *A briefe and plaine Instruction* (translated by 'F. Ke.', 1574) provide possible examples within the period. It seems likely, in any event, that songs were often improvised over simple harmonic grounds strummed on a plucked instrument, a practice well attested in Italy though less so in England.[134]

Another late source, British Library Add. MS 15117,[135] preserves genuine early lute-songs amongst its arrangements and a number of seventeenth-century songs. Amongst the former, 'In youthlye yeares' has been mentioned above, and there is also an arrangement of part of Johnson's 'Defiled is my name' under the title 'Unto my fame'.[136] (The latter, incidentally, is accompanied by a lute-part in the 'treble' tuning $c\ f\ bb\ d'\ g'\ c''$, while others have the 'bass' tuning $D\ G\ c\ e\ a\ d'$, as compared with the normal or 'mean' tuning $G\ c\ f\ a\ d'\ g'$. It is not clear to what extent these tunings correspond to genuinely differentiated sizes of lute, although Dowland and Danyel later score specifically for the 'bass' and 'mean' lutes simultaneously, while literary sources refer to all three, though often in a way that suggests that 'mean' and 'treble' were virtually synonymous.)[137] But one genuine example of early lute-song from this source is The Willow Song, 'The

[130] Cambridge, King's College, Rowe Library MS 2, fos. 5ᵛ seqq. (fac., Boethius Press). See *Consort Songs*, nos. 6a ('Pour down') and 6b ('No grief'). The second of these is of course for voice and lute, the only extant version, but the first is given only as a consort-song: the lute-song arrangement appears to be unpublished. I find it difficult to accept the editor's suggestion that the consort version is itself adapted from a lute-accompanied song: the part-writing is not awkward, and the accompaniment in genuine lute-songs rarely embodies an independent top part such as is here an essential part of the conception. The actual surviving lute version is clearly a later arrangement.

[131] Dublin, Trinity College, D. 3. 30 (Dallis) and D. 1. 21 (Ballet). See John Ward and others in *LSJ*, 9 (1967), 17–40, 10 (1968), 15–32, and 12 (1970), 43–4.

[132] Aberystwyth, National Library of Wales, Brogyntyn 27. *Consort Songs*, passim.

[133] e.g. Brit. Lib., Add. 29246–7 and 31992, compiled for Edward Paston (see Ch. 7).

[134] See the extensive discussion in Poulton, *John Dowland* (London, 1972; 2nd edn., 1982), 182–8. Some of the material in Royal Appendix 58 and others such as Stowe 389 evidently has a bearing on this: see Ward in *JAMS*, 13 (1960), 117–25, and his edition of the *Dublin Virginal Manuscript* (3rd edn., London, 1983).

[135] See Joiner in *RMARC*, 7 (1969), 51–109.

[136] Ibid. (with fac. of both).

[137] There are also examples of tunings on *A* and on *E*, which further confuses the issue. Later, the need for lower notes was satisfied on the normal lute by additional bass courses. Accompaniments at strange pitches are often a sign of arrangements: see further below, Ch. 8.

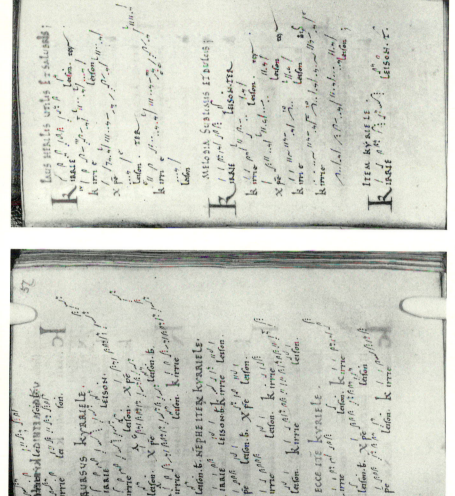

P L A T E I. Cambridge, Corpus Christi College, MS 473, fos. 57ʳ, 137ᵀ
(11th century: see Ex. 1)

PLATE II. Oxford, Bodleian Library, MS Rawlinson g. 22, fos. 1ʳ, 1ᵛ
(13th century: see Ex. 7)

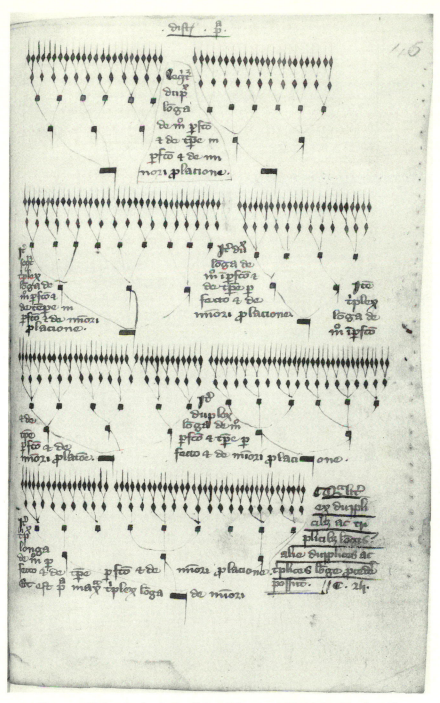

PLATE III. Oxford, Bodleian Library, MS Digby 90, fo. 45ʳ
(*Quatuor principalia musice*, 1351, copied between then and 1388). Part
of a series of diagrams showing duple and triple subdivisions of every
value from *maxima* to *semibrevis*.

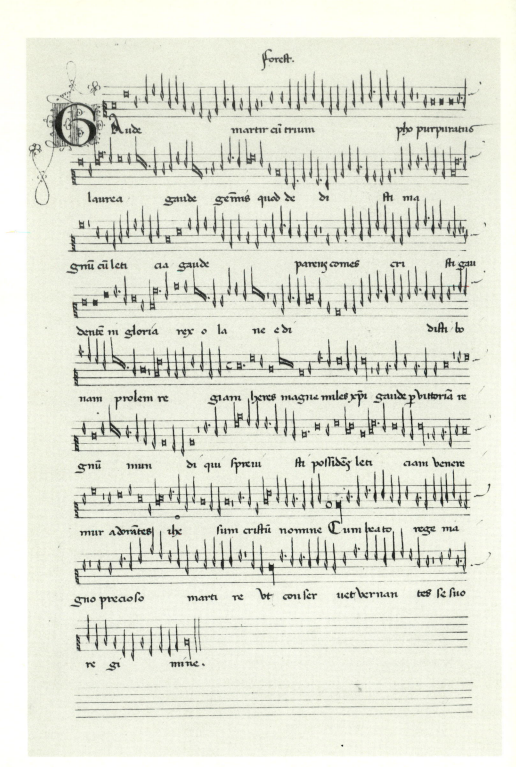

PLATE IV. Modena, Biblioteca estense, MS *a* X 1. 11, fo. 129[v]
(15th century: Forest, 'Gaude martir/Collaudemus/Habitat Deus')

PLATE V. Modena, Biblioteca estense, MS *a* X 1. 11, fo. 130ʳ
(15th century: Forest, 'Gaude martir/Collaudemus/Habitat Deus')

PLATE VI. Durham, Dean and Chapter Library, MS B II 30, fo. 81ᵛ
(round lyre from a MS of Cassiodorus, 8th century)

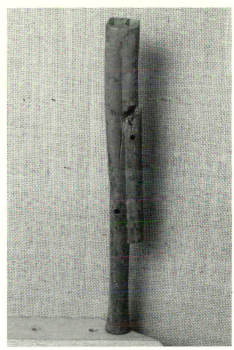

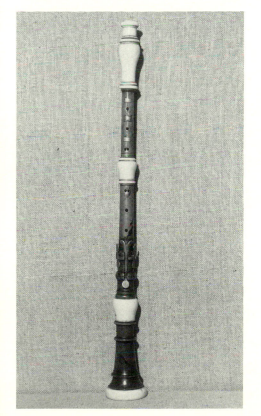

PLATE VII. (*a*) Medieval double pipe, front and back, probably of the 2nd half of the 15th century (Oxford, All Souls College, on loan to the Bate Collection of Historical Instruments)

(*b*) The 'Galpin' oboe, probably English (but possibly French), *c.*1685 (Oxford, Bate Collection, no. 200)

PLATE VIII. Virginals by Thomas White, probably of 1654 (St Fagans, Cardiff, Welsh Folk Museum). The original date has been altered to 1684 by a restorer. The compass is B_1–f''', but the lowest notes were probably tuned as a short octave descending to G_1.

PLATE IX. Portrait of Sir Henry Unton: detail showing mixed consort
of treble violin, transverse flute, lute, cittern, bass viol, and bandora
(partly hidden) (London, National Portrait Gallery)

PLATE X. (*a*) Nicholas Lanier, self-portrait (Oxford, Faculty of Music) (*b*) William Lawes (Oxford, Faculty of Music)

Plate XI. (a) Christopher Simpson (Oxford, Faculty of Music) (b) Matthew Locke (Oxford, Faculty of Music)

PLATE XII. Oxford, Bodleian Library, MS Mus. Sch. c. 93, fo. 81ᵛ
(hand of Thomas Tomkins)

PLATE XIII. Oxford, Bodleian Library, MS Mus. b. 1, fo. 19ᵛ
(hand of Edward Lowe)

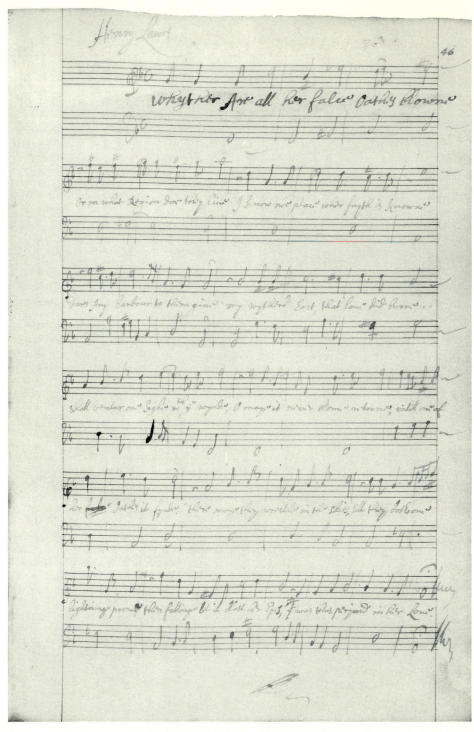

PLATE XIV. British Library, MS Add. 53723, fo. 46^r
(hand of Henry Lawes: see Ex. 193)

PLATE XV. British Library, MS Add. 31432, fo. 24ᵛ
(hand of William Lawes: see Ex. 196)

PLATE XVI. Oxford, Bodleian Library, MS Mus. c. 23, fo. 11ʳ
(hand of Matthew Locke: the introductory symphony to his
motet 'Audi, domine')

poor soul sat sighing', made famous by Shakespeare's use of it in the last act of *Othello*. Its exact date is uncertain, though Desdemona refers to it as 'an old thing'. Its style, with its lilting triple rhythm and haunting refrain, is not inappropriate to the early 1570s.[138]

The Willow Song is too well known to be quoted; but another early song, 'Awake ye woeful wights', may serve to illustrate the flavour of the style. This was composed, presumably by Richard Edwards himself, for his play *Damon and Pithias*, probably performed at court by the Children of the Chapel Royal at Christmas 1564–5.[139] In the play-text the accompaniment is said to be for regals. The lute version is thus again an arrangement, but the principle of a single accompanying instrument is maintained, and the simplicity of the writing is in keeping with what we should expect of truly artistic lute-song in its earliest phase (Ex. 126, overleaf).

The written repertories of instrumental music parallel the predominantly learned and serious tone of the vocal genres to a surprising degree. Of course the noisier ceremonial music, and the repertories of the lower classes of minstrel, designed solely for entertainment of a not very demanding kind, have mostly disappeared, if indeed they were written down at all. But a certain amount of dance music for 'whole' and 'mixed' consort, and in arrangements for solo keyboard and lute, has survived.[140] It enables us to point to the pavan and galliard, the *passamezzo* (*antico*), and other simple harmonic patterns, as the basic dance-types at this period. The mixed consort was characterized by the simultaneous ornamentation of simple lines by a variety of plucked instruments, such as the lute, cittern, and bandora. It reached its apogee in the later Elizabethan period, but the sound must already have been a familiar one in the middle decades of the century.[141]

---

[138] The earliest source is the 'Osborn' MS of *c.*1575–80 (see n. 146). For a different musical setting of this song see Ch. 7, n. 70, and the references given there. Another haunting triple-time piece from the Brit. Lib. MS, 'O death rock me a sleepe', I believe to be a mangled version of a consort-song, the original of which must be reconstructed from a keyboard version in Christ Church Mus. 371 (dating from the 1560s); see also J. M. Ward, '*Joan qd John* and other Fragments at Western Reserve University', *Aspects of Medieval and Renaissance Music* (New York, 1966), 837–44. This is a different setting from the duple-time one in *Consort Songs*, no. 1.

[139] See J. M. Long, 'Music for a Song in "Damon and Pithias"', *ML*, 48 (1967), 247–50. It was Hazlitt who suggested that the unnamed tragedy of 1564–5 was probably *Damon and Pithias*. Long gives a facsimile and a transcription.

[140] London, Brit. Lib., Royal Appendix 74–6 (the Lumley part-books: additional matter printed in *Elizabethan Consort Music*, ed. P. Doe, 2 vols. (London, 1979–88), i. 153–77, 199–208); ibid., Royal Appendix 58 (two-stave arrangements of three-part consorts, printed in *Schott's Anthology of Early Keyboard Music*, i; Dublin, Trinity College, D. 3. 30 (*The Dublin Virginal Manuscript*, ed. J. Ward, who prints many of the originals on which these keyboard versions are based). The two latter MSS, with others, also include dance music for lute.

[141] So much is implied by the isolated, heavily ornamented lines from the Lumley part-books, printed in *Elizabethan Consort Music*, i. 199–206. For the later repertory see Ch. 8 below, pp. 469–70.

Ex. 126

A - wake ye woe - ful wights* that long hath wept in woe; re - sign to me your plaints and tears, my hap - less hap to show.

* MS 'weights'.   † MS *f′* for *c′*.

More serious and reflective types of instrumental consort music continued the tradition begun in the reign of Henry VIII. In the middle of the century the genre included arrangements of vocal works, imitations of vocal forms such as *cantus-firmus* settings (e.g. of 'Dum transisset', 'Miserere', or 'Gloria tibi trinitas'), and learned exercises employing complex rhythmic proportions or canonic techniques. The principal early source is a manuscript laid out as a 'table book' (i.e. with the separate parts on each double page arranged in such a way that the performers could read them while sitting at a table on which the book was placed), entitled 'A book of In Nomines & other solfainge songs of v: vi: vii: & viii: pts for voyces or instruments'. It appears to have been copied or completed in 1578.[142] While textless vocal performance, using the sol-fa or hexachordal syllables, is thus given as much prominence as instrumental, it is hardly conceivable that much if any of this music was originally intended to serve so highly pedagogic a function. It is true that the hexachordal system, being the method by which the ability to sing at sight was attained, was deeply ingrained in the musical consciousness of the time; but some of the pieces at least are highly instrumental in conception, and there is no shortage of evidence for the existence of consorts (such as chests of viols) on which they could be played.[143]

The composers include Tye, Tallis, White, Parsons, Preston, Thorne, Robert Johnson, and other still lesser men; there is also the early work of William Byrd. The chief form, and a novelty for the period, was the In nomine. Such pieces took as their point of departure the section of the Sanctus of Taverner's Mass 'Gloria tibi trinitas' which sets the words 'in nomine domini'; this is in four parts with the *cantus firmus* laid out in breves in the mean. Taverner's own music exists in arrangements for four and for five instrumental parts (as well as for keyboard and for voices), and other men's works often imitate its opening motif and tonal structure (ending on a chord of G) as well as invariably using the 'Gloria tibi trinitas' chant. The most impressive corpus of such works is the set of twenty-one by Christopher Tye; many of these have titles, which might be an exhortation to the performers (e.g. 'Howld fast'), descriptive ('Rachells weepinge'), or more remotely allusive. One such is 'Crye', with its more than usually 'instrumental' idiom (Ex. 127, overleaf).[144] The In nomines of

---

[142] London, Brit. Lib., Add. 31390. See J. Noble, 'Le Répertoire instrumental anglais (1550–1585)', in *La musique instrumentale de la Renaissance* (Paris, 1955), 91–114, for a full discussion and inventory. The format of this huge book enables it to be looked at either way up, and it appears in fact to have been copied in the reverse order to that suggested by either the modern or the 'original' foliation.

[143] See for example the references given by D. C. Price, *Patrons and Musicians of the English Renaissance*, 2–3; Henry VIII's instruments at his death included 'A chest collered red with vi Vialles hauing the Kinges Armes' (Galpin, 220).

[144] Add. 31390, fos. 27ᵛ–28ʳ (formerly 46ᵛ–47ʳ: cf. n. 142). Tye, *The Instrumental Music*, ed. R. Weidner (New Haven, 1967), 34–8; *Elizabethan Consort Music*, ii, 116–18.

White are richly expressive, while one by Robert Parsons clearly influenced the young William Byrd and is found adjacent to one of his in several sources.

Ex. 127

    * The ♯ is placed *below* the note in the MS: it is possible that this (and others similarly placed) are scribal afterthoughts, not the work of the composer.

    Other *cantus-firmus* pieces include such things as the four settings of 'Dum transisset' by Tye; they have the subdivisions associated with the liturgical form but can hardly have been intended as settings of the text. Arrangements and imitations of vocal music without *cantus firmus*, which frequently occur, are forerunners of the fantasia (fantasi, fancy); the distinction is sometimes difficult to make, and titles can be confusing, as when for example Tye's 'Amavit' turns out to be a version of his anthem 'I lift my heart'. Other mysterious titles (like Taverner's earlier 'Quemadmodum') may conceal similar arrangements, while a work such as Tye's 'Rubum quem' gives the impression of being wholly original. Compositional exercises are represented by Tye's 'Sit fast', a hair-raising essay in proportions; and a small genre of wholly picturesque (and otherwise unclassifiable) pieces would include such works as Parsons's 'The songe called trumpetts' and 'De la court'.[145]

        [145] *Elizabethan Consort Music*, i, nos. 70, 34.

Little solo lute music was written down at this period. Amongst the few remains are 'The Duke of Somersetts dompe', based on an Italian harmonic ground, together with half a dozen fragments, mostly song arrangements.[146] The former implies a date between 1547 and 1552 (the Protector was created Duke in the former year and died in the latter: his heir did not inherit that title). It has been proposed that 'dompes' are memorial pieces, like the later French 'tombeaux'; but there is little evidence (least of all philological) to support the assertion, and the dompe (or dump, thumpe, etc.), appears to have been in the first instance a lively stamping or 'thumping' dance, and subsequently, through a very natural linguistic confusion, a sad piece, illustrating but also alleviating the sorrows of a named personage. What is indisputable, however, is that nearly all dompes are based on some simple harmonic ground, whose incessant repetition provides a suitably haunting quality.

A few sources of rather later date (such as the Dallis and Ballet lute-books)[147] preserve what is apparently earlier material, such as simple settings of the *romanesca* and *folia* harmonies. One of these, for two lutes, is a version of 'Greensleeves' rather different from that generally known (Ex. 128, overleaf).[148]

Keyboard music is much more fully represented in sources before 1575. The Mulliner Book, the Dublin Virginal Manuscript, and several smaller manuscripts are still extant, while even the liturgical manuscript, Add. 29996, contains two or three non-liturgical pieces from the epoch. The Mulliner Book is the anthology of a London organist, compiled during the quarter-century 1550–75.[149] Though it includes several liturgical items, they were probably copied for private diversion on a domestic instrument, whether organ, clavichord, or harpsichord ('virginals'). Apart from these, it includes original keyboard works (non-liturgical *cantus-firmus* settings, freely composed works in contrapuntal style, and dances), and many transcriptions

[146] Brit. Lib., MS Royal Appendix 58, referred to above (n. 134). The lute music has been edited by Ward in *JAMS*, 13 (1960), 117–25. Other early MSS include British Library Stowe 389 ('Raphe Bowle's MS', 1558), discussed by Ward in *The Dublin Virginal Manuscript*, 40–1, 43; the 'Giles Lodge' Book of c.1559–71, 1572–6 (Washington, Folger Shakespeare Library, MS v. a. 159: see *NGD*, 'Sources of Lute Music', sect. 7); and the Osborn MS of c.1575–80 (New Haven, Conn., Yale University Library, J. M. Osborn MSS, Mus. 13: see *RISM*, B VII, 234–5).

[147] See above, n. 131. The Dallis book was inscribed by a pupil of Thomas Dallis, Fellow of Trinity College, Cambridge, in 1583; some of the pieces are ascribed to Dallis himself. On 'Dr Dallis', or 'Dally', see F. W. Sternfeld, *Music in Shakespearean Tragedy* (London, 1963; 2nd edn., 1967) 47. The Ballet book is one of two quite distinct MSS within the same covers; it dates from c.1590, while the second one is somewhat later.

[148] Washington, D.C., Folger Shakespeare Library, MS v. b. 280 (formerly 1610.1, known as the 'Dowland Book'), fo. 5ʳ, after J. Ward, 'Music for *A Handfull of pleasant delites*', *JAMS*, 10 (1957), 157, where the whole piece is given; see also Ward, '"And Who But Ladie Greensleeues"', *The Well Enchanting Skill* (Oxford, 1990), 181–211.

[149] London, Brit. Lib., Add. 30513; ed. D. Stevens, *The Mulliner Book*. Mulliner was also for a time organist of Corpus Christi College, Oxford.

Ex. 128

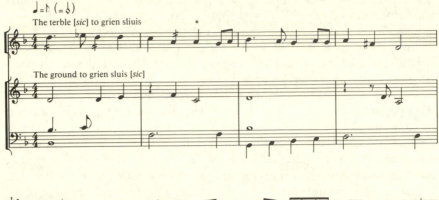

The terble [sic] to grien sliuis

The ground to grien sluis [sic]

4 more variations, over the same ground, follow.

★ Ward prints *b′* [flat].

from vocal and instrumental compositions. It is a major source of the keyboard music of Blytheman, who is represented by several liturgical items and by six settings of 'Gloria tibi trinitas'. These are the complement of the consort In nomine (of which the Mulliner Book contains three transcriptions for keyboard), but the name of the plainchant itself is given by way of title, presumably by analogy with the liturgical repertoire. Subsequently either name might be used, or even both; but it seems certain that not even the earliest of them were liturgical in function. The liturgical context of this antiphon was not amenable to organ substitution, as far as is known, and a set of six like Blytheman's (or the still larger sets of Bull and Tomkins) far exceeds functional requirements. Blytheman's set is in fact an essay in different kinds of figuration against the chant, ending with a beautiful quiet piece in which it is slightly ornamented in the bass (Ex. 129).[150]

This style could be readily adapted to freely composed works, of which Alwood's 'Voluntary' (no. 17) is an early example, and perhaps the very

[150] Ibid., no. 96. For the chant, see Ex. 92 (*b*).

Ex. 129

earliest to which that title is given. Another novelty is the earliest extant English psalm- or hymn-melody in a keyboard version; this is the 'Psalmus: O Lord turn not away' (no. 109), a setting of a tune in 'double common metre' (8686 × 2).[151]

The transcriptions include Latin and English sacred works, and part-songs of which this manuscript is sometimes the only source. Some of the pieces are incomplete in texture, lacking one or two inner parts or (in two cases) the melodic line, suggesting the combination of keyboard with other instruments. 'A fansye' by Newman is perhaps from the sparseness of its

---

[151] The text is not a psalm but 'The Lamentation of a Sinner', first printed in the psalter of 1561: see *ESPHT*, 61.

texture arranged from a work for lute. Original 'secular' keyboard music is less well represented, but there are two or three dance-like pieces at the beginning, and Newman's expressive 'Pavan', in four sections, at the end.

The secular forms of keyboard music in the 1560s are rather better represented in the Dublin Virginal Manuscript, so called only from its present location.[152] It looks again like a Londoner's anthology; the one named composer, Tailer, might perhaps be John Taylor, Master of the Choristers at Westminster Abbey during the 1560s. Amongst several pavans and galliards is a fine pair on the *passamezzo antico* harmonic ground (Ex. 130).[153]

Even more remarkable is a set of variations on the *romanesca* harmonies.[154] A simple version of this ground, from a much later manuscript, is entitled 'Q.M. Dump' (or 'Queen Mary's Dump'), from which it may perhaps be inferred that the variations of the Dublin source are by Mary Tudor's virginalist John Heywood.[155] It is also possible that English musicians obtained their knowledge of this harmonic pattern from some member of King Philip's chapel, perhaps Antonio Cabezón, who used it in his keyboard variations 'O guardame las vacas'.[156]

Several other sources help to round out this picture without significantly modifying it. A manuscript now in York contains a number of transcriptions of French, Italian, and English vocal works.[157] The recently discovered 'Winchester Anthology' of medieval English verse contains a certain amount of roughly written keyboard music, including a version of Hugh Aston's Ground.[158] Perhaps the most attractive of this group of manuscripts is a small oblong folio at Christ Church, Oxford, written on printed music-paper and still in its original parchment wrapper.[159] Herein are liturgical pieces by Redford and others; song-arrangements including one of 'O Death rock me asleep' and of part-songs by Philip van Wilder; a 'Gloria tibi trinitas' subtitled 'ij partes on a rownde time' and a liturgical piece by Tallis; and

[152] Dublin, Trinity College, MS D. 3. 30 (see n. 140). This keyboard manuscript is bound with the Dallis lute-book (see n. 131) but was originally separate and is partly foliated in an early hand.

[153] *The Dublin Virginal Manuscript*, ed. Ward, nos. 1, 2 (pp. 2–7).

[154] Ibid., no. 9 (pp. 14–17). This harmonic pattern is similar to that of the *passamezzo antico* (Ex. 130 (*c*)), but the notes are half the length and the first note is *b* flat.

[155] Cf. ibid. 44.

[156] At least three sets by Cabezón, and one anonymous setting, are known (W. Apel, *The History of Keyboard Music to 1700* (Bloomington, Ind., 1972), 263–4). All are in triple time, as are all Continental pieces entitled 'Aria della romanesca', whereas the untitled English examples are in duple time. Nevertheless, the use of the generic term *romanesca* for this harmonic pattern seems well justified.

[157] York, Minster Library, MS M. 91 (S), from perhaps 1575 or 1580, discussed by Milsom, 'English Polyphonic Style', i, 121, with inventory in vol. ii, App. 3.5. The manuscript is unique in giving in most cases the originals in open score with the transcriptions beneath.

[158] London, Brit. Lib., Add. 60577. See J. Blezzard, 'A New Source of Tudor Secular Music', *MT*, 122 (1981), 532–5. I am grateful to Dr Blezzard for making available to me her unpublished transcriptions. In the consort version in Christ Church, Mus. 984–8, there is an additional part by William Whytbroke.

[159] Mus. 371.

Ex. 130

(b)

(c)   Ground (normal pitch and time-values)

* The Dublin MS has *c* (i.e. *g* when untransposed) at this point. The usual version implies minor harmonies over each *g*, but the chords of C major in the Dublin version are quite consistent throughout the Pavan and Galliard and do not require editorial modification.

three In nomines (the third incomplete) and a hexachord setting by N[icholas] Strowger (or Strogers). This last is probably a keyboard duet. It is not a unique example, but it is testimony to an inventive and perhaps underestimated mind.[160]

It is tempting to think of the period of the Reformation as an age of transition. That is all very well, provided that we do not allow ourselves to be unduly obsessed by the peaks of achievement on either side. All periods are transitory; this one is so in the sense that almost all musicians, of whatever standing, suddenly found themselves obliged to come to terms with the undermining of what they had hitherto taken for granted. That the seeds of the Reformation had been sown long before, and had already put forth the first shoots, is of little consequence; most of those involved must have been taken aback with the speed of change. Religion and human-ism, in whatever guise, spoke the same message: simplify, be understood, appeal to the reason. Even the Marian reaction could not stem this tide, which flowed irrespective of 'Catholic' or 'Protestant' currents of thought. It was of European dimensions, and a nation newly alive to what its neigh-bours had to offer could not remain unaffected. In the field of musical endeavour, it was a challenge which some side-stepped, many met only half-heartedly, and a few rose to with resourcefulness. It was after all the age of Tallis, Tye, and Sheppard, of Mundy, White, and Parsons, to mention only the most significant of those in the last category. In Tallis the country produced a master of European stature; one whose immense technical skill was always at the service of the matter in hand; and one whose music, because he cultivated so many different genres, is astonishingly varied in style. It is his principal distinction over the others that he truly symbolizes the age in which he lived, reflecting all its moods and spanning its length and breadth with assurance, the tone-poet of an intellectual revolution.

---

[160] Several pieces from this and other manuscripts were given in Denis Stevens's anthology *Altenglische Orgelmusik* (Kassel and Basle, 1953). A collection of all non-liturgical keyboard music before about 1580 (with the exception of the Mulliner and Dublin MSS) is in preparation.

6

THE ELIZABETHAN AND JACOBEAN PERIOD: MUSIC FOR THE CHURCH

THE reign of Elizabeth was one of gradually increasing national self-confidence, mirrored with curious exactness in its artistic (and especially its literary and musical) productions. Once it became clear that there could be no accommodation, at least in the short term, between the English Church and the papacy, the consequences had to be faced with determination. Adherence to Roman Catholicism implied at best disloyalty and at worst treason. It ceased to be mere conservatism, a longing for a vanished past, and became instead an association with a Continental movement of immense vigour. It could not be ignored; the wonder, rather, is that recusancy—so called from the refusal of Roman Catholics to attend their parish church—played so large a part in English intellectual life, despite the risk of severe penalties for those involved. Elizabeth, whose personal position as daughter of Anne Boleyn was a large part of the problem, acted with courage, resolution, and scrupulous fairness. These qualities were put to a severe test when Mary Queen of Scots was brought to trial; but Elizabeth emerged unscathed, and when in the following year the Armada was defeated by a combination of circumstances, the tide of national fortunes seemed truly to have turned, subsequent reverses notwithstanding.

The artistic and cultural movement unleashed by the prosperity and well-being of the country under Elizabeth could not be halted by the many inadequacies of James I, a monarch of a very different stamp. For all the change of dynasty, the different style of government, and the lack of set purpose, the forces of continuity prevailed. Again this is reflected in literary and musical history. It is not simply that the active working lives of several of the greatest figures spanned both reigns; the formal and other conventions pioneered by poets and musicians of the Elizabethan period retained their vitality in the Jacobean. But one particular innovation of the early seventeenth century must be singled out. The dramatic masque, though not wholly without Elizabethan precedent, was essentially a novelty in its marriage of fine literature, music, and the dance; it led to a new conception of the dramatic and the declamatory in music, and eventually provided the conditions under which the idioms of Italian monody could take root. These developments first arose in the Jacobean age.

The period just defined has been called the 'madrigalian'; yet its three greatest figures—Byrd, Dowland, and Gibbons—produced scarcely a 'true' madrigal between them. It would be more apt to describe it as one in which the ideals of the high Renaissance reached their finest flowering, achieving in some respects a greater depth and brilliance than had been possible in Italy itself, let alone France or Germany. One of these ideals was the expression of the text, by which the music might be, in Byrd's arresting phrase, 'framed to the life of the words'.[1] It is surely not chauvinism to see in some of the best native products of the age a more profound application of that spirit than can be discovered elsewhere. The gradually increasing mastery of even minor composers over their musical 'language' is comparable to the forging of blank verse as a medium for dramatic speech by the Elizabethan and Jacobean playwrights. But the development went further than this; by virtue of its capacity to reflect the text in its fullness, musical language acquired a self-sufficiency that allowed it to stand on its own in the form of instrumental music, and to become a fully expressive medium in its own right. It cannot really be said that this had been attained hitherto, or that it became true of European music generally before the later seventeenth century. In this respect England was in the vanguard.

The literary culture that formed the backdrop to these achievements was marked by an ever-increasing refinement and ingenuity. The manner tended towards the rhetorical, the matter towards the metaphysical. Rhetoric, in origin, is simply the art of putting one's thoughts across in the most effective way. But the Elizabethans, like all children of the Renaissance, sought to emulate the precepts of Antiquity, and above all those of late Antiquity as purveyed by Cicero and Quintilian. It would be hard for any poetry, let alone drama, to avoid rhetoric, and Shakespeare is the most naturally rhetorical of all poets. But in the minor writers of the time we may sometimes see the results of an undue reliance on rhetorical tricks: reinforcements of meaning by technical devices such as alliteration, rhyme, metrical variation, antithesis, progressions of thought, and the like. These are often reflected or emphasized in musical settings; and music itself acquired a repertory of devices analogous to those of literature. Form and tonality on a broad scale, rhythmic displacements and harmonic subtleties on the small, are examples of musical 'rhetoric'; they had always existed,

---

[1] In the title of his *Psalmes, Songs, and Sonnets*, 1611, ed. E. H. Fellowes (London, 1964).

but the sense of conscious manipulation is a good deal stronger in this period than previously.

The term 'metaphysical' was applied by Dryden to poets conspicuous for their use of extravagant imagery and remote analogies. It may be traced back to Italian poetry through Wyatt, Surrey, and their imitators, but it became the *raison d'être* of much Elizabethan and Jacobean verse. In a sense, metaphor and allegory being themselves a form of rhetoric, there is often no real distinction between style and content. Music is a language in which the distinction is inherently pointless, which is perhaps why it was so important to a culture nurtured on style.

That it was important is beyond question. From the point of view of the higher musical culture, the Tudor and Stuart epochs exhibit a transition between the all-embracing patronage of the Church in the Middle Ages and the inherently professional, self-supporting attitude of the eighteenth century onwards. Already in the early Tudor period there are signs that the cultivation of secular music was beginning to acquire a higher status than that of 'minstrelsy' in however splendid a guise. At first the providers of this more exalted music were ecclesiastics of some kind; but the Reformation as we have seen dealt the *coup de grâce* to what was often a purely nominal link. Even in households that still maintained a private chapel, the ecclesiastical connection became very tenuous. Apart from the very special case of the Chapel Royal, the provision of a musical establishment became a great rarity. Partly this was for economic reasons, partly because, for many highly placed Anglicans, music had ceased to be an essential or even a desirable concomitant of worship. The obligation to attend the parish church made a private chapel something of a luxury; conversely, the parish church itself might take on the functions of a chapel for the local squire and patron of the living. Even for recusants, for whom a private chapel was a necessity, there is little evidence for formalized musical establishments. If any existed, they will have lacked the institutional cohesion of earlier times, though it is true that in any case we should not expect them to have been documented. But it is much more likely that chapel services were normally celebrated without music (for practical and liturgical reasons), and that much of the Latin sacred music collected by recusants, if performed at all, is to be considered as a form of domestic music.

It is in the sphere of domestic music that Tudor and Stuart patronage was paramount. The great families of the time employed skilled musicians to teach both their young and their own more humble minstrels, and to provide music for private entertainment and social occasions. They also bought music, and musical instruments, for their own and for professional use. These activities scarcely warrant the term 'patronage', except in a sense so wide as to rob it of significance. But the term is justified when the employment, or other assistance, was such as to afford a musician the leisure to compose works of permanent value. Just as the medieval Church may reasonably be said to have been the 'patron' of those composers in its employment whose labours far exceeded the call of duty, so the great families of the Elizabethan and later periods patronized a vast body of household music: sacred, secular, and instrumental. This support is acknowledged in the dedications of printed music, particularly of the period 1575–1650; but it is also the background to much if not most of what was written but remained in manuscript. On the other hand, dedicatory letters may sometimes conceal a minimal relationship between composer and 'patron'; they cannot always be taken at face value, but may afford valuable supporting evidence for conclusions gained from the study of family archives.[2]

What has been said implies a contemporary appreciation of music going beyond that associated with its original function. There are medieval parallels to this more sophisticated approach, for it is inherent in the collecting of music in written form after the initial occasion of its composition had passed. This is true both of collections of manuscripts or printed editions by wealthy amateurs, and of collections of works into a single volume by enthusiasts or by the composers themselves. The reverence thus given to the written form is analogous to that shown for poetry. A collection of verse such as Shakespeare's *Sonnets* cannot have been published for readers familiar with the original circumstances of composition; then as now, these will have been a matter of speculation, the true value of each poem resting in its intrinsic qualities. So it is with a published collection of madrigals, or with manuscript anthologies made by such men as Robert Dow, John Sadler, or Francis Tregian; so also with the myriad of works embodied in the collections of a Paston or a Lumley, in spite of the ideology which may lie behind their formation. This aspect of written collections has sometimes been neglected by comparison with their supposed primary function as a source for actual performance.

One might expect such evidence of musical 'appreciation' to be confirmed by a literary genre of aesthetics and criticism; but on the whole this is not so. The study of music as a liberal art, to which lip-service was still paid in the universities, had bequeathed an apparatus of ethical, acoustical, and cosmological speculation. An imaginative writer like John Case might build upon the former, one like Robert Fludd on the two latter. There was also a growing body of practical instruction. But of criticism in the modern sense, let alone analysis, there was virtually nothing. In spite of some hints in the writings of Thomas Morley, Charles Butler, and Christopher Simpson, the beginnings of a modern attitude are to be found only

---

[2] The outstanding works on this topic are Woodfill, *Musicians in English Society*, and D. C. Price, *Patrons and Musicians of the English Renaissance*. See also L. Hulse, 'The Musical Patronage of Robert Cecil, First Earl of Salisbury (1563–1612)', *JRMA*, 116 (1991), 24–40.

in the writings of the late seventeenth-century amateur Roger North.[3] But it would be very rash to conclude from this that Elizabethan lovers of music were not alive to its many subtleties of construction and expressive device, and did not relish them for their own sake. Modern criticism, when allied to a knowledge of external factors affecting the composition of both individual works and whole classes of music at this period, has demonstrated some of its profundities for the first time; but it is a quest inherent in the nature of the music itself.

It is fitting to begin this quest with a look at Anglican church music, the form in which so many composers served their apprenticeship and the ground in which their deepest roots were laid. This was hardly less true of the recusant Byrd than of his Anglican contemporaries. William Byrd (c.1543–1623) became organist and choirmaster of Lincoln Cathedral in 1563, when he was about 20 years old. His appointment was typical of the post-Reformation arrangement whereby the organistship was linked to the duties of instructor of the choristers—not only in music but in general education and with responsibility for their welfare. Byrd was sworn in as a Gentleman of the Chapel Royal on 22 February 1570, following the drowning of Robert Parsons at Newark-on-Trent on 25 January;[4] but he was not replaced at Lincoln until 7 December 1572 and may have continued to carry out the duties until then. In 1573, at the instance of 'certain noblemen and counsellors of the queen's highness', he was granted by the Cathedral Chapter an annuity for life of five marks (£3. 6s. 8d.), to which his continued provision of 'songs and divine services well set to music' was subsequently added as an attempted condition. Even so, he suffered a financial loss by the move; evidently this was dictated by a longer-term view of his career prospects and a desire to be at the centre of developments at this exciting period.[5]

There can be little doubt that Byrd had been trained as a composer by Tallis, and he may well have been a chorister in the Chapel Royal.[6] If so, he will have experienced the trauma of changing attitudes under Edward VI, Mary, and Elizabeth, and may have been quite uncertain of his personal position on Elizabeth's accession. The Lincoln authorities, for their part, seem to have spared no pains to secure his services: the full

---

[3] The title of M. C. Boyd's *Elizabethan Music and Musical Criticism* (Philadelphia, Pa., 1940; repr. 1967) might suggest the reverse, but the writings discussed in it hardly amount to criticism in the present-day sense. The origins of a genuinely critical attitude—the endeavour, that is, to describe, evaluate, and place in their historical context individual works of musical art—in Europe is worthy of closer investigation than it has received.

[4] *The Old Cheque-Book*, ed. E. F. Rimbault (London, 1872), 2 (the year 1569 is 'old style').

[5] For Byrd's Lincoln years see W. Shaw, 'William Byrd of Lincoln', *ML*, 48 (1967), 52–9.

[6] Thomas Byrd, 'clarke of the checke', who may have been his father, died in Feb. 1562 (1561 old style): *The Old Cheque-Book*, 1.

force of the Puritan reaction was evidently still to come. If a Chapter Act of Michaelmas 1570 reads like an attempt to curtail Byrd's enthusiasm for playing the organ, they still hoped for compositions from his pen even long after he had left.[7] Although we are rightly warned against too rosy a picture of cathedral music in Elizabeth's reign,[8] we must allow for the likelihood that a certain respect for tradition and dignity of worship was still a powerful factor.

It seems fairly certain, in any case, that some of Byrd's Anglican music was written while he was at Lincoln, even if he had the resources of the Chapel Royal in mind at the time. There is little difficulty in attributing the two sets of preces and 'festal' psalms, the first two and possibly the third service, and several of the anthems, to the decade 1563–72. Most of this music is for five and even six voice-parts, utilizing the characteristically Anglican antiphony between 'decani' and 'cantoris'; in some of these works, too, a solo voice with independent organ accompaniment is used. There is no reason to suppose that such music could not have been performed at Lincoln, though polyphonic settings of the psalms and canticles were probably reserved for Sundays and holy days.

While Byrd's debt to Tallis is everywhere apparent, he shows his independence in a number of ways. The preference for a larger number of voices (particularly in his anthems) is one. When we look at the 'festal' psalms we discover that, while structurally they are a form of harmonized chanting, there is scarcely any reference to the plainchant tones in them.[9] 'Teach me O Lord' (Ps. 119: 33–8) from the second set, and the fragmentary Psalm 100 found in some sources of the first set, are accompanied solos alternating with chorus. Several do not call for psalmodic intonation, while 'Save me O God' (Ps. 54) from the first set calls for alternation not between the two sides of the choir, but between 'verse' sections scored for a group of high voices (medius dec., medius cant., contratenor cant., tenor dec.) and 'full' sections for the divided contratenors, tenors, and basses, to which the medius is added for the Gloria Patri. The surviving sets of psalms do not fulfil the requirements of the Book of Common Prayer for special feasts, and it is possible that they were selected by seventeenth-century compilers from a larger body of such material.

It is tempting to dwell on these psalms and their many arresting features, but the early canticles and anthems are still more rewarding. The Short Service, while akin in tonality and expression to Tallis's Dorian, is

---

[7] Shaw, 'William Byrd', 55–7.

[8] A. Smith, 'The Cultivation of Music in English Cathedrals in the Reign of Elizabeth I', PRMA, 94 (1967–8), 37–49.

[9] The 'Glory be' of no. 2b ('O clap your hands', Ps. 47) does in fact quote the eighth psalm tone: The Byrd Edition, ed. P. Brett, 17 vols. (London, 1970–), xa, pp. 18–19. This volume contains all Byrd's Anglican service music except for the 'Great Service'.

noteworthy for its gradually increasing textural complexity. The Venite, Te Deum, Benedictus, Kyrie (Responses to the Commandments), Creed, Magnificat, and Nunc Dimittis are set. The second service, a Magnificat and Nunc Dimittis only, employs the accompanied solo idiom, while the third, also a Magnificat and Nunc Dimittis, is in triple time throughout (hence the titles in some manuscripts 'Mr Birds 3 minoms' and 'Mr Byrds pricke Semibriefe'). Byrd's manipulation of the rhythmic possibilities of this metre, the gentle undulation of the antiphonal structure, and the exquisite balance between homophonic and contrapuntal writing, make this work a fascinating precursor of his later masterpieces (Ex. 131).[10]

Ex. 131

Byrd's early anthems are not without their roughness, as might be expected in a young composer striving to emulate and in some respects

[10] Ibid., no. 7: from the Nunc Dimittis, p. 145. In the 'Full' sections the second part of the score corresponds to the 1st countertenor decani with the 2nd countertenor cantoris, and the third part to the 2nd countertenor decani with the 1st countertenor cantoris, while in the passages for decani or cantoris alone the distribution is as marked.

to outdo his elders. There is much to be said for the view that sees a model for them in the early Elizabethan Latin motet and its contemporary English adaptations.[11] However, the future of the anthem depended on the sensitive handling of the English text, in which considerations of comprehensibility and a feeling for its natural rhythms were paramount. Byrd steered the difficult course between the pious part-song and the motet with consummate skill, and in a work like 'Arise O Lord' and its (originally separate) second part 'Help us O God'[12] achieved something very like a classical shape for the shorter full anthem. Byrd was also a pioneer in the composition of 'verse' anthems, a name usually given to those which employ solo voices with an independent accompaniment in alternation with passages for the full choir. The earliest, 'Alack when I look back', seems to have started life as a consort-song to which choral sections were subsequently added.[13] But this in turn is based on a tune first published in 1583 in William Hunnis's *Seven Sobs of a Sorrowful soule*, which it is unlikely to antedate; in the circumstances the application of the principle to the festal psalms and other service-music may well be of greater historical importance.

To turn from the early service music to the Great Service[14] is like emerging from the foothills for an assault on the highest peaks. Apart from the grandeur and cohesion of its design, its aptness of word-setting, and its many incidental beauties, this work can also serve as a textbook for the choral layout of the period. Byrd here employs the full resources of the standard five-part division on both the decani and cantoris side of the choir, with the added distinction between 'verse' and 'full' on both sides. Only the rare high trebles (never used by Byrd) are missing. While in many anthems and services of the sixteenth century the complexities of part-division must often have been solely due to their having been copied into the standard seventeenth-century format of ten (sometimes eight) part-books, one can be sure in this case that they are part and parcel of the original conception. The work has all the appearance of having been written as a show-piece for the Chapel Royal, perhaps during the 1580s or 1590s.

Composers of this period rarely, if ever, wrote in as many as ten real parts for the full choir, however, except at brief moments when the two choirs overlap; their choral medium must therefore be seen in a different light from that of their English predecessors, and from that of many of their Continental contemporaries when writing for double choir. In fact the number of separate voice-parts is almost infinitely variable, and the dynamic contrasts between verse, decani, cantoris, and full sections are as

---

[11] *The Byrd Edition*, vol. xi, p. v.
[12] Ibid., no. I.
[13] Ibid., no. II; cf. p. ix.
[14] This work occupies the whole of vol. xb in *The Byrd Edition*.

important as the actual interplay of parts. If there is a Continental parallel, it is with the use of contrasting forces in Venetian choral music and with the concertante style generally.

Although the seventeenth-century sources in which this work alone exists include organ parts, the organ is nowhere essential and may not originally have been used. (It is important to remember that the use of 'verse' sections, as here, does not necessarily entail an independent organ part. Although the designation 'verse' is not consistently applied in the extant part-books, it is done so with sufficient frequency to imply the distinction throughout, a distinction confirmed by the nature of the scoring and, paradoxically, by the use of the term in the organ books themselves.) Indeed any kind of instrumental participation would be superfluous in this most carefully conceived specimen of vocal scoring.

Any of the regular ten parts could qualify for 'verse' (i.e. solo) duty, and in this work they all frequently do. They are normally deployed in contrasting groups of endless variety, their antiphony cutting across the regular choral activities of decani and cantoris. These verse sections are of considerable extent: in the second half of the Benedictus, for example, from 'That we being delivered', there are 70 bars of such music, divided into two unequal sections, for six voices (42 bars) and four voices respectively. The flow of counterpoint seems quite inexhaustible (Ex. 132, pp. 354–5).

As will be seen, there is a very strong feeling for the major mode, and in the original notation the work is in fact in C major, with frequent cadences on to G and D, and using the keys of F major, D minor, and A minor for tonal variety. The Te Deum, however, although not based on the plainchant, is influenced by it to the extent that the final cadence of each half, and of several verses in the second half, leads to a chord of E major. This is neither the tonic of E major (or E minor), nor strictly speaking the dominant of A minor, but the *finalis* of the fourth mode, although it is true that until the final chord we might be tempted to think of it as a dominant (Ex. 133, pp. 356–7).

Byrd's anthems[15] make a long list, but many of them are pious part-songs or consort-songs rather than anthems in the true sense, and only a relatively small number survive in 'liturgical' sources. The mature verse anthems include the attractive 'Christ rising again', with two soprano (i.e. medius) soloists; this was published in 1589 with an accompaniment for instrumental consort, which may be the form in which it was originally conceived. 'Hear my prayer' and 'O Lord rebuke me not' are still later verse anthems, with a freer structure and a richly expressive treatment of their texts. 'Sing joyfully', a version of Ps. 81: 1–4, is his maturest and most 'madrigalian' full anthem. It is curious that Byrd should have published a setting of the

---

[15] Published in *The Byrd Edition*, xi, to which reference is here made.

Ex. 132

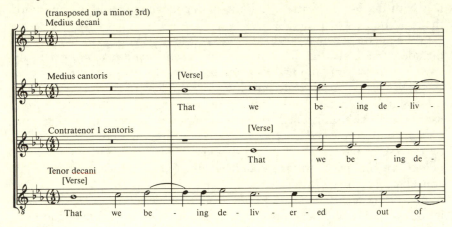

Ex. 132, continued

same psalm-verses, in a different translation, in his *Psalmes, Songs, and Sonnets* of 1611, but the differences are instructive. The madrigalianism of 'Sing joyfully' is contained within the conventions of the full anthem: its six voice-parts are conventionally disposed amongst the ten books of the seventeenth-century liturgical sources as well as being found in various sets of 'secular' part-books. The alla breve notation, while broad enough to allow for incidental detail, clearly implies an allegro tempo. 'Sing we merrily', on the other hand, like some other late sacred works, owes nothing in its vocal layout to the conventions of the choral establishments of the time, being for three high voices and two lower ones. Its speed is also fast, but the notation is in crotchets and minims rather than minims and semibreves. Thus of the two settings of 'Blow the trumpet' the second, while notationally similar, must be sung more slowly (Ex. 134, pp. 358–9).[16]

It would be difficult to match 'Sing joyfully' as a vigorous and picturesque piece of word-setting, and few of Byrd's contemporaries did so. William Mundy (d. 1591), Richard Farrant (d. 1591), Osbert Parsley (d. 1585), and presumably Tallis (d. 1585) remained content with an older idiom, while Robert White, who was more nearly his own age, died too early (1574) to make a profound impact. Of those younger than he, Edmund Hooper (c.1553–1621), Thomas Morley (c.1557–1603), and Nathaniel Giles

[16] Ibid., no. 10; *Psalms, Songs, and Sonnets* (EM, xvi), no. 21.

Ex. 133

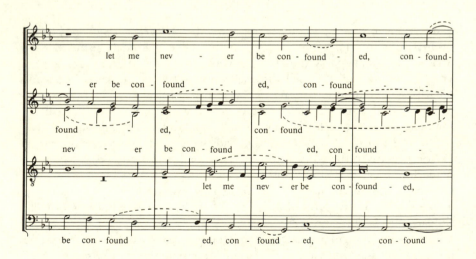

Ex. 133, continued

(c.1558–1633) are the most important. About another thirty names can be adduced,[17] of whom John Bull at least achieved high stature in other fields. John Holmes, organist of Winchester Cathedral, and John Mundy, organist of St George's, Windsor, are of some interest, the former as an early practitioner of the verse anthem.[18] Hooper and Giles were both associated with the Chapel Royal, Hooper as a Gentleman after a period as Master of the Choristers at Westminster Abbey (1588–1604), and Nathaniel Giles as Master of the Choristers from 1597, a post which he held concurrently with the similar one at St George's, Windsor.[19] Much of Hooper's music is ambitious and elaborately scored, and a modern writer has described his verse anthems as 'splendid'; so in many ways they are, but the elaboration is not matched by that unity of textual declamation and musical expression that we find in Byrd and which was to be recreated in the best work of Gibbons and Tomkins. Giles is rather less interesting still, though he experimented with chromaticism and (for some obscure reason) in the use of a very low-pitched notation.[20]

Morley is a more significant figure than either of these, though his surviving Anglican church music is small in quantity.[21] Like Byrd he was (almost certainly) a recusant; yet he was employed as organist of Norwich Cathedral

[17] Le Huray, *Music and the Reformation in England*, 228.
[18] Ibid. 268.
[19] Giles became Master of the Choristers at Windsor in 1585 after having been similarly employed at Worcester Cathedral for five years previously. His anthems, ed. J. Bunker Clark, have appeared as EECM, xxiii.
[20] Ibid., no. 1, 'He that hath my commandments', necessitating transcription one octave higher: even so, the pitch is suitable for men's voices. Two surviving organ parts are notated respectively a fourth higher and an octave higher than the vocal parts.
[21] Le Huray, *Music and the Reformation*, 246–55.

Ex. 134

Ex. 134, continued

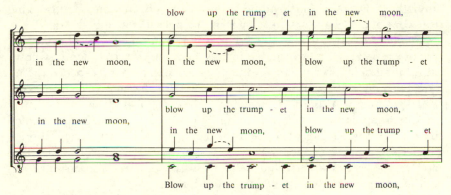

(sharing the duties with William Inglott) and later became organist of St Paul's Cathedral and a Gentleman of the Chapel Royal. He was far from being a typical church musician, however, and in his *Plaine and Easie Introduction* has a harsh word or two for the organists of his day. He was a pupil of Byrd, whom he greatly revered, and emulated him in his own 'Three minnoms' service, and perhaps also to a certain extent in his seven-movement 'verse' service, although this employs an independent organ part. His verse anthem 'Out of the deep' and his Burial Service (the earliest of its kind) are also noteworthy.

Though the tenor of London's musical life, centred as it was around the Chapel Royal, was notable for its continuity, we can mark a new generation with Thomas Tomkins (1572–1656), Thomas Weelkes (*c.*1575–1623), and Orlando Gibbons (1583–1625). Well over forty contemporaries can be listed, of whom John Amner (*c.*1585–1641), Adrian Batten, and John Ward (1571–1638) may be singled out.[22] Thomas Tomkins made a substantial contribution to Caroline musical life, and his church music was published by his son Nathaniel in an impressive set of part-books, *Musica Deo Sacra*, in 1668. Much if not most of it, however, was probably composed during the period covered by this chapter. Tomkins, who was another pupil of Byrd, became organist of Worcester Cathedral in 1596, a post which he held until the surrender of the city in 1646; he was also a 'Gentleman Extraordinary' of the Chapel Royal, possibly from as early as 1603, and served as organist from 1621 until 1625 at least. After 1628 he seems to have lived permanently at Worcester, where he continued to compose, writing for example some very elaborate and difficult keyboard music and perhaps such things as the three-part anthems which were included in *Musica Deo Sacra* but are not found elsewhere. The more complex church music, however, must have been conceived for the Chapel Royal; a Chapel Royal

[22] Ibid. 274. Tomkins's music is discussed on pp. 274–96.

book of anthem texts, dating from *c*.1630, contains more of his than of any other composer. Although he has not always been seen as epitomizing the work of the Jacobean Chapel, it is in that light that he is best judged.

Musica Deo Sacra includes five services (with varying choice of canticles), the preces and responses with two psalms, forty-one verse anthems, twenty-nine full anthems, six anthems for men's voices, nineteen three-part anthems, and five metrical psalm-tunes. Of the services, the first two are 'short', and the third is a 'great' service for two antiphonal choirs and a small 'verse' group consisting of two means (sopranos), countertenor (alto), and tenor. As in Byrd's Great Service the organ part is not independent, though Tomkins employs a much smaller group of solo voices. The other two are 'verse' services with an independent organ part; two more similar sets of canticles survive incomplete in manuscript.

The full anthems include the remarkable 'O Praise the Lord', in twelve parts, and much other estimable music. But fine though they and many of the canticles undoubtedly are, it is for his verse anthems that Tomkins must particularly be remembered.[23] It is here that his penchant for vocal scoring, textual declamation, and coherence of structure comes to the fore. The last must be seen within the conventional framework of solo (or concertante) passages followed by choral refrains, but there is consummate artistry in the balance between the sections, whether this is seen in terms of tonality, of relative length, or of the relationship between the forces employed. One kind of juxtaposition may be seen in 'Behold, I bring you glad tidings',[24] in which a (spectacularly accompanied) soprano solo is succeeded by a ten-part chorus, one of Tomkins's most elaborate conceptions and one of the few of its kind in Anglican church music. The tonality is F major throughout. More often, however, there are several alternations between verse and chorus; there may well be tonal contrast in the sectional cadences, musical continuity between verse and chorus, and varied scoring from verse to verse. Although a diagrammatic representation cannot convey the essence of such music, Table 3 will serve to illustrate the tonal and structural variety that is possible.[25]

Tomkins's response to the text is most vividly illustrated by his declamatory solo verses. These abound in his verse anthems: it is almost impossible to be representative, but some passages from 'O Lord let me know mine end' will serve to indicate the extent and indeed the limitations of his expressive range. As far as the latter are concerned, it should be noted that there is little of the Baroque in Tomkins's thought: his technique is bounded by a Renaissance conception of vocal enunciation, however

[23] All the verse anthems, with the three- and four-part full anthems, have been edited by Bernard Rose in four volumes of EECM: v, ix, xiv, xxvii.

[24] EECM, ix, no. 12.

[25] The work is published in EECM, v, no. 6.

TABLE 3. *Thomas Tomkins's 'Christ rising again from the dead'*

Section	Bars	Scoring	Opening tonality	Cadence	Key	Chord
1.	1–14	Verse (Bass)	A major	imperfect	A minor	E major
	15–19	Chorus *a 4*	G major	perfect	A minor	A major
	20–31	Verse (ATB)	A minor	perfect	A minor	A major
	31–2	Chorus	E minor	perfect	E minor	E major
2.	33–42	Verse (ATB)	A minor	imperfect	D minor	A major
	43–52	Chorus	G minor (♯6) (or G major ♭7)	plagal	G major	G major
3.	53–61	Verse (SATB)	indeterminate	perfect	G major	G major
	62–71	Chorus	indeterminate	imperfect	A minor	E major
4.[a]	72–80	Verse (ATB)	(A minor)	perfect	A minor	A major
	81–8	Chorus	A minor	perfect	A minor	A major
5.	89–109	Verse (ATB)	(C major)	perfect	G major	G major
	110–14	Chorus	(A minor)	perfect	C major	C major
	115–30	Verse (ATB)	F major	perfect	A minor	A major
	130–44	Chorus	(G major)	perfect	A minor	A major
	145–7	Chorus ('Amen')	(A minor)	plagal	A minor	A major

Note: Bracketed tonalities are confirmed by cadences some little way in. The two marked 'indeterminate' do not cadence sufficiently soon to enable an 'opening tonality' to be identified.

[a] Triple time.

elaborately expressed, and the accompaniment is entirely contrapuntal in method (Ex. 135, pp. 362–4).[26]

Thomas Weelkes was probably very slightly junior to Tomkins. After an initial period as organist of Winchester College, he became organist and choirmaster of Chichester Cathedral in 1601 or 1602, and was still on its staff at his death in 1623. His personal life was a tragedy. After a brilliant start, with the publication of three books of madrigals between 1597 and 1600, the award of the degree of Bachelor of Music from Oxford in 1602, a satisfactory marriage, and an apparently blameless initial period at the Cathedral, the record is punctuated by ever more frequent mentions of his failure to perform his duties, his drunkenness, his brawling, and his propensity to utter blasphemies. It is not difficult to imagine the vicious circle of disillusionment and the remedies he sought. For Chichester Cathedral in the early seventeenth century was a sorry place, poorly endowed and understaffed, its officials careless of their obligations. Its choir was a 'half-choir', unable to maintain the traditional antiphony of decani and cantoris, and presumably quite unable to perform Weelkes's finest music.[27]

[26] EECM, ix, no. 16. The form is simply that of three solo verses each followed by a choral reworking of their last few words. Our extracts are from the second and third verses.

[27] D. Brown, *Thomas Weelkes* (London, 1969), 40–1.

Ex. 135

(a)   (transposed up a minor 3rd)

Be - hold,   be - hold,

thou   hast   made   my days   as   it   were   a

span long,   as   it   were   a   span   long,

Ex. 135, continued

For man, for man walk-eth in a vain shad - ow, and dis-qui-et-eth him-

self in vain.

continued

Ex. 135, continued

them.   And   now,   Lord, and   now,   Lord,   what   is   my

hope, what   is   my   hope?   tru - ly   my

hope,   tru - ly my   hope is ev'n in   thee.

There are many indications that he sought, and failed to obtain, the position of Gentleman of the Chapel Royal.[28] It may be that he enjoyed some standing there, and that he spent a good deal of his time in London. Of one common failing he remains unconvicted; and he survived his wife's early death by only a year, dying at the London house of a friendly creditor and leaving the will of an exemplary, though impoverished, family man.

Yet this earthly vessel was that of a near genius. Most of his madrigalian works are early, but we must grant him at least a decade of productive life after the Chichester appointment. Nearly fifty anthems and no fewer than nine services are known; unfortunately only twenty-five anthems and parts of three services survive complete, or sufficiently so to enable plausible reconstructions to be made. Much of the service music is known only from the organ book formerly attributed to Adrian Batten, a monumental source dating from about 1630.[29] Two of the partial survivals, however, serve to show Weelkes's range. The Magnificat and Nunc Dimittis 'for trebles' provide a rare instance of the use of this high-pitched boy's voice. The part itself does not survive (perhaps understandably since a treble book was not part of the standard equipment) but has been plausibly reconstructed from the top line of the organ part in the 'full' sections.[30] The work also contains substantial 'verse' sections for two means (i.e. for boys, but the title does not refer to them), to which two basses are added in one section; there is also a short tenor solo. The scoring is characterized by a soft brilliance throughout.

The ninth service, a Magnificat and Nunc Dimittis only, is a much grander affair in the 'great service' manner, for antiphonal choirs with verse sections. No organ part has survived, nor is one necessary; both tenor parts and one of the countertenors are missing, but the tenor would have been mostly undivided, and much of the missing countertenor would have coincided with surviving material. In the masterly reconstruction now available,[31] the distinction between 'verse' and 'full' sections is editorial but entirely plausible: the soloists, drawn from each of the ten voice-parts, are arranged in various combinations exactly as in Byrd's Great Service. Much of the writing is in six and seven parts, but the ending of the Magnificat implies a further subdivision into the maximum of ten. The predominant impression is of massivity, but there are also moments of quiet reflection, as in the lovely setting of 'He rememb'ring his mercy' or the opening of the Nunc Dimittis (Ex. 136, pp. 366–7).

---

[28] He is indeed so described on the title-page of his *Ayeres or Phantasticke Spirites* (1608), but there is no independent confirmation of this. He may have been a 'Gentleman Extraordinary': Brown, *Thomas Weelkes*, 33.

[29] Oxford, Bod. Lib., MS Tenbury 791.

[30] See the edition by P. Le Huray (London, 1962).

[31] Ed. D. Wulstan (Oxford, 1979).

Ex. 136

Ex. 136, continued

Music on this scale must have been quite beyond the Chichester choir, and the same is true of several of the full anthems,[32] particularly those in six or seven parts. Some of these are amongst the composer's finest conceptions: 'Gloria in excelsis Deo/Sing my soul', 'Hosanna to the Son of David', 'O Lord, arise' (*a 7*), 'O Lord, grant the King a long life' (*a 7*), and 'When David heard' with its second part 'O my son Absalom'. Some of the anthems survive mainly or wholly in 'secular' sources, and it is probable that such a one as 'When David heard' (from Thomas Myriell's manuscript *Tristitiae remedium* of 1616, and elsewhere) was never intended for church use at all. The broken phrases at the end of this work are amongst the most affecting from the entire period (Ex. 137, overleaf).[33]

But the true anthems are marked by a very personal blend of dignity and brilliance. 'Alleluia: I heard a voice' is an interesting case, for it seems to have been composed as a full anthem and later reworked as a verse anthem. This involved some rhythmic expansion and the provision of an independent organ part in two passages originally assigned to the first bass alone. Unfortunately the sources of the 'verse' arrangement are late and incomplete, but their authenticity seems confirmed by Weelkes's use of a substantial section of the work (bars 8–23, repeated in 47 seqq.) in the Gloria of the Nunc Dimittis of the fourth service 'for trebles' (discussed above), which is of course a 'verse' service.[34] This is one of several instances in which Weelkes recapitulates the music of an anthem in a service: presumably such works were intended to be performed on the same occasion. In some manuscripts anthems and services are 'paired' for liturgical convenience, even when there is no obvious musical connection.

[32] The *Collected Anthems*, ed. D. Brown, W. Collins, and P. Le Huray, are published as MB, xxiii.
[33] Ibid., no. 16 (original pitch).
[34] See above, n. 30: the anthem confirms the correctness of Le Huray's reconstruction.

Ex. 137

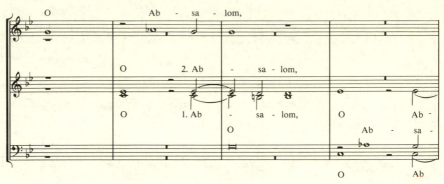

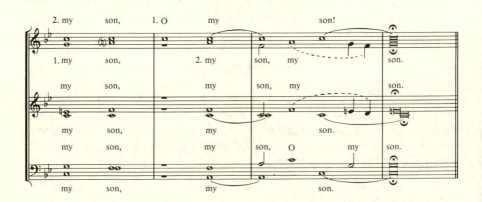

The publication of Weelkes's verse anthems has necessitated a reassessment, for they had until the late 1960s suffered almost total neglect. On the whole we are conscious of dignity rather than extravagance in the word-setting. The bass solos of 'In thee, O Lord, have I put my trust' are nobly conceived, but the effect of the whole is somewhat static. There is more variety in some others, for example 'Give the king thy judgments', where thematic unity between the verses (for two means and countertenor) and the six-part chorus, and the repetition of the first chorus as the third and last, give a sense of cohesion. The result is still powerful and massive. Two factors are responsible for the solid brilliance of much of Weelkes's output, at least when writing for six or more voices: a very strong and steady harmonic tread, often reinforced by long notes in the bass, and a tendency to write rather high mean parts in pairs so that a continuously high top-sounding part occurs. In 'verse music', a similar effect may be created by the organ accompaniment.

But it is perhaps Orlando Gibbons who best epitomizes the special flavour of Jacobean church music. His professional career is symbolized by his membership of the Chapel Royal—he was Gentleman from 1605 and shared the organist's duties from 1615. In 1623 he also became organist of Westminster Abbey. Two years later he died at Canterbury while the Chapel Royal was awaiting the arrival of Charles I's bride, Henrietta Maria. It was as a keyboard player that he was chiefly noted in his lifetime, but he practised virtually all forms of composition then in use, and his Anglican church music in particular[35] is distinguished by that suave gravity which is a hallmark of his style.

Gibbons's preces and responses, his festal psalms and canticles, convey the essence of the contemporary Anglican ethos. Mostly they are grave and unassuming; but the second service in particular has many picturesque moments. The setting of 'He hath scattered the proud: in the imagination of their hearts', for instance, shows how vivid musical symbolism could arise out of an extension of normal contrapuntal technique (Ex. 138, pp. 370–2).[36]

Only a handful of full anthems has survived, but they cover a wide range. The setting of the collect 'Almighty and everlasting God' (for the third Sunday after the Epiphany) exhibits his quieter style, while 'Hosanna to the Son of David', 'Lift up your heads' and 'O clap your hands together' are exuberant show-pieces. 'Hosanna to the Son of David' allows an interesting comparison with Weelkes's setting of the same text: where Weelkes is massive and powerful, Gibbons is nimble and fleet-footed. 'O clap your hands' is a lucky survival, for it exists complete in only one set of part-books dating from after the Restoration.[37] It is there described as 'Dr Hethers commencement song', meaning that it was composed to celebrate William

[35] Published in TCM, iv; the anthems, ed. D. Wulstan, in EECM, iii, xxi.
[36] TCM, ix. 108–10, transposed up a minor third.
[37] York, Minster Lib., I/1–8 (c.1675, signed 'William Gostling').

Ex. 138

Ex. 138, continued

continued

Ex. 138, continued

Heather's Honorary Doctorate of Music at Oxford in 1622. The academic occasion presumably explains its eight-part layout, and the work is not without a certain formality and stiffness of declamation. (Both of these works, incidentally, like Byrd's 'Sing joyfully', are often lamed in performance by an over-cautious choice of tempo.)

It is, however, for his verse anthems that Gibbons is chiefly to be admired. Sixteen survive complete, or nearly so, and a further nine have been expertly reconstructed from organ scores. Nearly half are preserved in a score-book once thought to be in Gibbons's own hand but now recognized as a later seventeenth-century copy. In this, the instrumental parts of the 'verse' sections are written on to the staves which in the choral sections are occupied by the voices. It is not quite clear what this implies in terms of Gibbons's intentions or of contemporary performing practice. It is quite possible, however, that he conceived at least some of his anthems in a stylized contrapuntal medium, leaving copyists either to adapt the accompaniment to the organ or to retain the separate parts for performance by an instrumental consort. The latter would be appropriate for private and domestic music-making, the former for church use in most instances.

In 'This is the record of John', for example, the contrapuntal writing has the ring of authenticity, and the organ part the appearance of an adaptation. According to a note in the score, this anthem was written at the request of William Laud, then President of St John's College, Oxford. One can well imagine that the rather special and perhaps intimate circumstances of its first performance called for special care in its composition, and that an adaptation for more general church use might quickly follow.

The superb declamation of this anthem is matched in a number of others including the most elaborate of them all, 'See, see, the word is incarnate',

Ex. 139

written to a text by Godfrey Goodman, Dean of Rochester. Here there is no contemporary organ part, or indeed any 'liturgical' source, and there is a strong feeling of chamber music, of the consort song with choruses, in fact. The same is true of 'Behold thou hast made my days', an affecting setting of Psalm 39 dating from 1618, although this does survive in several 'liturgical' sources. 'Blessed are all they' (Ps. 128) is another occasional piece, composed for the Duke of Somerset's wedding in 1613.

For other anthems, however, only an organ accompaniment survives, and the predominant impression is of liturgical propriety. This is true for example of 'Almighty god, who by thy son' (for St Peter's Day), and the rather more elaborate 'Behold I bring you glad tidings' (for Christmas). The range of expression is not wide, but within its limits it is perfectly conceived. The opening verse of 'If ye be risen again with Christ', for instance, not only illustrates the text but is a fine example of Gibbons's sense of melodic development (Ex. 139, p. 373).[38]

A number of lesser composers emulated the styles established by Byrd and Gibbons and helped to preserve the traditional Anglican idioms in London and the provinces during the reign of Charles I. Adrian Batten and Martin Peerson of St Paul's, John Amner of Ely, Michael East of Lichfield, and John Ward (who held no ecclesiastical post) are the most important, while in a slightly lower category might be placed William Smith, the minor canon of Durham whose Preces and Responses have endured to the present day; Thomas Ravenscroft, music-master at Christ's Hospital; Ben Cosyn, music-master at Dulwich and Charterhouse; John Lugge of Exeter; and Richard Nicholson, organist of Magdalen College, Oxford, and the first Professor of Music at the University. Batten was by far the most prolific, with more than fifty anthems and a good deal of service music to his credit. His work is too little known, and too extensive, for a just appraisal, but it was not widely circulated even in his lifetime, and the charge of harmonic and tonal monotony is probably justified. Batten is no longer believed to have compiled the enormous organ-book that has traditionally borne his name; but he was an enthusiast for his functional art, a true child of the early Stuart epoch in his concern for the liturgy and its embellishment.

Nicholson, Lugge, Smith, East, and Ravenscroft were less prolific but in some ways more individual; Martin Peerson was something of an eccentric, Amner a notable and competent practitioner (his curiously named 'Cesar's Service' is still performed), and John Ward a striking master in the madrigalian field whose anthems would deserve revival. Much of their sacred music, however, was intended for private devotional use. One final figure deserves mention: John Barnard, whose own enthusiasm bore fruit in the splendid *First book of Selected Church Musick* (1641), a wonderfully catholic anthology ranging from Tallis to Barnard's own day.[39] In these ten part-books are preserved numerous compositions which would otherwise have perished, and many more known only fragmentarily from other sources. By that date, however, new stylistic currents had begun to infiltrate

---

[38] EECM, iii, no. 8; transposed, as there, up a minor third (but a major third down from the extant organ part which because of differences in pitch-standard was often notated, as in the present case, a fifth above the voices).

[39] Barnard also copied, or had copied on his behalf, the part-books in the Royal College of Music, MSS 1045–51.

the quiet waters of English church music, and all was to be swept away before the end of the decade in the Civil War and its aftermath.

The Latin motet is not so far removed from the Anglican anthem as may at first appear. Many of the motets of Tallis and his contemporaries are found in English versions, apparently for church use, and the same was to be true of Byrd. The Chapel Royal may initially have sung Latin motets regularly, though perhaps less so as the Anglican repertory grew. On the other hand the motet, even if capable of fulfilling a public function, frequently became a repository of private emotion—in Byrd's case especially so.

The word 'motet' was hardly used by English composers of their Latin works: 'Cantiones sacrae' was the usual collective term, while 'Gradualia' had a more technical meaning. 'Motet' is retained here, however, as a convenient label for all sacred Latin forms other than the Mass, except indeed when a more specific term such as hymn or respond is appropriate. Few English composers apart from Byrd wrote motets: Morley is the most important, apart from the exiles Philips and Dering. Byrd's contribution is altogether outstanding and represents the peak of his own personal achievement.

Byrd's earliest work in this sphere shows clear signs of his apprenticeship in a tradition of enlightened conservatism. His raw materials were the texts of the Salisbury Use or the Vulgate Bible, and the liturgical chants associated with the former. His very earliest efforts may even have been intended for that rite before its abolition when he was aged 15 or so. For the next few years, the contrapuntal setting of liturgical chants (both with and without texts) and the employment of Salisbury texts without chant, will have fulfilled the needs both of the fledgling composer and of the religious conservative for whom the Elizabethan settlement might prove to be but a temporary set-back. After that, however, and certainly from 1570 onwards, the use of Latin texts will have been more and more the result of a conscious decision to retain the language of Roman Catholicism. Queen Elizabeth's learning and her willingness to allow Latin in her chapel may have made such decisions easier to take, but there is good reason to suppose that behind the public cultivation (within certain well-defined limits) of Latin motet-composition lay the private language of the composer and his intimates.

A broad chronological picture of Byrd's motet output can be discerned from dates of publication and other evidence; but many details remain uncertain.[40] Byrd continued to include earlier work in his published collections, even as late as 1605, while the manuscript motets cover a wide range.

---

[40] Byrd's *Gradualia* were published in TCM, vii; his Masses, manuscript motets, and contributions to the 1575 *Cantiones*, in TCM, ix. The old *Collected Works*, ed. E. H. Fellowes, is in the course of complete replacement as *The Byrd Edition*, under the general editorship of Philip Brett.

Apart from juvenilia and doubtful works, which need not be considered here, there are experimental and derivative pieces of the 1560s or early 1570s, and mature works that could have been written at any time up to about 1590. Amongst the former, 'O salutaris hostia', for six voices, is notable for the harshness occasioned by its three canonic parts, and may have been intended to emulate Tallis's setting of 'Salvator mundi' (no. 2), published in the 1575 *Cantiones*. In such company the crudities of 'Reges Tharsis' seem less surprising, though this, if genuine, must be one of Byrd's earliest works, a *cantus-firmus* setting of a respond (without verse) in which the intonation is left to the cantor. Far more assured are the Lamentations, a fine work in which the debt to Tallis is chiefly evident in an expanded sense of tonality. A still further advance is to be discerned in a group of which 'Audivi vocem de caelo' is typical, a free setting of a respond for All Saints' Day, again without the verse; the break at 'Beati mortui', though perhaps originating in a liturgical convention, has been turned to rhetorical use (Ex. 140).[41]

We are here at the level of the most mature of the 1575 *Cantiones*. The majority of the remaining manuscript motets are psalm-settings, and some at least may reflect (like the Lamentations) Byrd's increasing sense of alienation from the religious establishment of his country. This at any rate is likely to be the case with 'Quomodo cantabimus', a huge eight-part canonic setting of part of Psalm cxxxvi, written in 1584 in response to Philippe de Monte's 'Super flumina Babylonis'; this latter, which had been sent to Byrd in the previous year, was based on the opening verses of the same psalm. The precise circumstances of this musical correspondence are unknown, but it is hard not to see in Byrd's reply something of his feelings: 'How shall we sing the Lord's song in a strange land?' (*in terra aliena*); 'if I forget thee, O Jerusalem, may my right hand forget her cunning'. The symbolism of the canonic writing is clear. But another side of Byrd's character is to be seen in the six-part 'Circumspice Ierusalem': 'Look around thee, O Jerusalem, towards the East, and behold the joy that cometh to thee from God.' This splendidly optimistic work (to a specially composed text) is marked by the rhythmic vigour and the appropriateness of word-setting characteristic of the greatest of the 1589 and 1591 motets, and must surely belong to the late 1580s: it may indeed be a response to the defeat of the Armada.

The motets published in 1575[42] are an epitome of Byrd's achievement up to that point and include several designed to demonstrate his technical

[41]   TCM, ix. 182 seqq., transposed up a tone.
[42]   *The Byrd Edition*, i, ed. C. Monson. In the following discussion the bracketed numbers are those of the original volume as a whole (i.e. including the works by Tallis), while the unbracketed numbers are those of Byrd's own contribution as numbered by modern editors.

Ex. 140

(transposed up a tone)

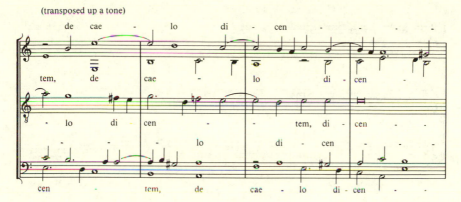

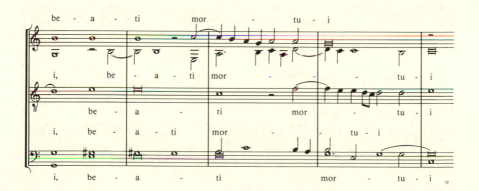

[I heard a voice] from heaven saying: Blessed are the dead ...

Ex. 141

Ex. 141, continued

... and because of the glory of your name release us.

skill. Such are the eight-part 'Diliges dominum' with its canon 'recte et retro', the hymn 'O lux beata Trinitas' with its canonic third verse, and the elaborately devised *cantus-firmus* setting of the antiphon 'Miserere mihi Domine'. Neither the hymn nor the antiphon has any stylistic or formal resemblance to its liturgical equivalent, and the same is true of 'Siderum rector', a quaintly stilted setting of the last two verses of the hymn 'Virginis proles'. Many of the texts are responds in the (Continental) Roman rite, though as most of them are also Salisbury it is difficult to deduce on the basis of their texts exactly to which stage of Byrd's religious and technical development they belong. The music can help here; the respond for the dead 'Libera me de morte aeterna' (no. 17 (33)), with its *cantus firmus*, looks like a Salisbury-inspired piece and indeed is closely related to a similar one by Robert Parsons. On the other hand, 'Emendemus in melius' (no. 1 (4)), a non-Salisbury respond, is clearly one of the most 'advanced' compositions in the entire volume. It is a beautifully contrived piece in which a fundamentally homophonic and declamatory conception is enlivened by contrapuntal detail of a particularly finely wrought and sensitive nature. The closing bars will make the point (Ex. 141). The rising phrase in the tenor in bars 55–6 not only recalls the setting of the words 'Adiuva nos' at the beginning of the second section (the 'verse' of the respond), but anticipates the treatment at the opening of the very next piece, 'Libera me domine et pone me iuxta te'. But this is a more thoroughly contrapuntal work, and the same is true of the majority of the remaining motets in this volume. The variety obtainable from within a single stylistic standpoint may be conveniently illustrated by two consecutive works: 'Aspice, Domine, quia facta est desolata' (no. 4 (10)) and 'Attollite portas' (no. 5 (11)), the one an intensely reflective but never harsh meditation on the desolated city (Jerusalem, perhaps taken figuratively for England), the other a brilliant evocation, with bold themes and picturesque antiphony, of the entry of the 'King of Glory'.

It is curious that the boldest musical conception in this publication, the tripartite 'Tribue Domine' (nos. 14–16 (30–2)), should be allied to an improvisatory text redolent of the old votive antiphon. A veritable symphony in the unusual written key of B flat, the words are a freely invented devotion to the Trinity. The prayer to be 'steadfast in faith, effectual in work' might be taken as a swipe at the Thirty-Nine Articles. But in general Tallis and Byrd published little if anything to cause offence to the Establishment. Their venture failed, but for predictable commercial reasons: the music was difficult and sophisticated, the time for its more general appreciation not yet ripe.

So far we have set Byrd's achievement mainly in the context of the work of his English contemporaries and elders. However, mention must be made of one very important external influence, that of Alfonso Ferrabosco. Ferrabosco, born into a Bolognese family of musicians, was an exact contemporary of Byrd. He entered the service of Queen Elizabeth in 1562, and finally left in 1578 on being suspected of grave crimes. The question of his guilt remained unresolved, but he was a popular and influential musician in England and remained so after his departure. He has been said to have been a secret agent for Elizabeth, and may indeed have been reporting to her on the movements of expatriates and on what he could glean of Italian policy. But though clearly an Anglophile he seems to have remained a Roman Catholic, and it is hard to imagine him wanting to jeopardize the advance of his faith. While in England he fathered two children, one of whom, Alfonso Ferrabosco the younger (born between 1575 and 1578), became a leading composer of the next generation in this country. Alfonso the elder's large output of Latin motets survives almost exclusively in English sources.

Resemblances alone do not prove the influence of Ferrabosco upon Byrd, but when close similarities coincide with stylistic novelty, it may be reasonably inferred.[43] This is particularly the case with Byrd's hymn 'Siderum rector', which follows exactly the structure of Ferrabosco's 'Ecce iam noctis', and his 'O lux beata Trinitas', which is similarly related to Ferrabosco's 'Aurora diem nuntiat'. In both cases the moderate crotchet rhythms of the Italian 'note nere' style are adopted; in the first, the settings are based on simple tunes of the composer's own devising, an apparently unique device for this period. Ferrabosco also set a fashion for the composition of responds from the (Roman) Mass and Office for the Dead, and probably introduced English composers to other texts from the Roman rite as well.

---

[43] In what follows, as in other matters, I am indebted to J. Kerman, *The Masses and Motets of William Byrd* (London and Boston, 1981), esp. pp. 35 seqq.

In the period prior to the publication of the Tridentine Missal and Breviary such influence would have been of considerable significance. Parsons's 'Credo quod redemptor' is based directly on Ferrabosco's eponymous motet, and even his Salisbury-based responds 'Libera me domine de morte aeterna' (a model for Byrd's setting) and 'Peccantem me quotidie' break with English liturgical tradition in setting the entire chant. Byrd's 'Domine secundum actum meum' is closely related to Ferrabosco's 'Domine non secundum peccatis nostris', while his 'Emendemus in melius' is based in part on Ferrabosco's psalm-motet 'Qui fundasti terram'.

After the failure of the *Cantiones Sacrae*, Byrd did not venture into print again for another thirteen years; when he did so it was with a series of retrospective publications of which two (1588 and 1589) were devoted to works with vernacular texts and two (1589 and 1591) to Latin motets. These latter have a strong claim to be the most striking of all Elizabethan publications in their concentration of mastery. During the 1580s Byrd attained complete assurance in his response to the texts which he chose, combining a sensitivity to their verbal resonances with a perfection of technical resource that no other composer could match. From the depths of 'Tristitia et anxietas' (1589/4) to the exuberance of 'Laudibus in sanctis' (1591/1),[44] there is no grade of emotion that he cannot illuminate. What Englishmen were still to achieve in madrigal and ayre had already been realized to perfection in his Latin compositions.

Although the livelier works are in some ways the most arresting, the predominant mood in these publications is elegiac and penitential. In this context the three *cantus-firmus* motets and a piece like 'Infelix ego' (which with its B flat major tonality and monumental proportions recalls the 'Tribue Domine' of 1575) do not seem out of place. In the more recent compositions, however, the expressive range is greatly increased, and the technical resource refined. In a work such as 'Recordare Domine', for example (1591/11), we may note how sequence is used, in a strictly contrapuntal context, to give point to the hopefulness of the words 'Ut non desoletur terra' and to enlarge the expressive scope of the music by suggesting new harmonic vistas (Ex. 142, overleaf).

If anything, the musical language is more deeply expressive in the first book, which apart from 'Tristitia et anxietas' contains the sombre 'Deus venerunt gentes' and 'Ne irascaris Domine' amongst a series of settings which can be readily construed as an indication of penitence and sorrow at the religious condition of England at the time, and of hopefulness for change in the future. No single text could be regarded as subversive; but in combination their tendency is unmistakable, and it is a wonder that

---

[44] These numbers are those of *The Byrd Edition*, vols. ii and iii respectively (i.e. treating multi-partite works as one and so differing from the original enumeration).

Ex. 142

Ex. 142, continued

... that the earth may not be laid waste.

they did not cause their composer more trouble than was actually the case. But their overt meaning was always a defence, and only the Marian antiphon 'Salve regina' could be regarded as inherently non-Anglican by the lights of that time.

The joyful motets should not be ignored, however, and in 'Laudibus in sanctis' (1591/1) we have a unique masterpiece, a thoroughly madrigalian setting of a version of Psalm cl in elegiac couplets. The madrigalian effect is partly a consequence of the notation which, moving swiftly in crotchets and minims rather than more soberly in minims and semibreves, permits a musical style responsive to every nuance of the text. To take just one example, the delicious setting of the line 'Hunc arguta canant tenui psalteria corda' ('Let sharp-toned psalteries praise him with delicate string') conveys just that hint of sharpness implicit in the word 'arguta' (Ex. 143, overleaf). The same example shows, however, that Byrd was not unduly sensitive to the niceties of Latin scansion; he seems to have wanted to convey something of the flavour of a metrical text, but largely ignores and in some places totally contradicts the quantities. From the humanistic point of view the work is a failure; we do not know if this worried the anonymous author of the rather ingenious paraphrase (which may have been written specially for Byrd), but it has worried few people since.

Byrd's Masses[45] were first published and probably written during the 1590s: first the four-part Mass, then the three-part one, and finally that for five voices. The three works were published surreptitiously without title-pages: the bibliographical evidence for the order in which they were published coincides with such musical evidence as exists for the order of composition. There were no post-Reformation English precedents for these

[45] *The Byrd Edition*, iv. Their history of publication was clarified in an important article by P. Clulow, 'Publication Dates for Byrd's Latin Masses', *ML*, 47 (1966), 1–9.

Ex. 143

works; their inspiration would seem to be primarily Continental, and yet it has been rather surprisingly established beyond reasonable doubt that for the four-part work Byrd had recourse to a pre-Reformation English model, Taverner's 'Mean' Mass.[46]

In spite of the similarity, however, Byrd's Masses are Tridentine, not pre-Reformation English: they set the Kyrie (confined in earlier English sixteenth-century composers to the Lady Mass, which was often set *alternatim*) and the remainder of the Ordinary in full. Taverner's Mass, for example, has no Kyrie and omits a large section of the Credo text in the then customary English fashion. This is not to deny Byrd's use of such a work as a point of departure, but to emphasize his very different standpoint as a Tridentine Catholic. On the other hand, he is indifferent to some current Roman conventions, such as the varying treatment of long and short texts in order to arrive at a series of comparably weighted movements. The Kyrie of the three-part Mass, for instance, is minute (none is strictly ninefold, but the three-part Kyrie has room for only one enunciation of each of the three petitions), and none of the Credos explores the possibilities of con-

[46] See P. Brett, 'Homage to Taverner in Byrd's Masses', *Early Music*, 9 (1981), 169–76.

cision. The composer has arrived at an interpretation of the liturgy in which the text as such is paramount; it owes very little to the purely musical conventions established elsewhere, but conveys (as Bach's and Beethoven's Masses were later to do) his own intensely personal reaction to the meaning of the words—words which, far from being a familiar formula, were intensely charged with significance for him, as seems to be the case with the deeply felt prayer for peace at the end of the five-part work (Ex. 144, overleaf).

The surviving copies of Byrd's Masses are bound with copies of the *Gradualia*, with which they are conceptually linked.[47] The Masses provided the Ordinary (or permanent) texts of the Mass, the *Gradualia* the Proper (or special) texts for the Marian and other greater feasts of the Church year, and for the Saturday votive Masses of Our Lady at different seasons. They were published in two sets of part-books, in 1605 and 1607, but it is likely that Byrd had been at work on the collection for several years. Some other genres are also represented, and the 1605 set even has an old-fashioned working of a Salisbury chant, 'Christus resurgens'. The two sets by no means amount to a complete liturgical cycle, but they do provide appropriate music for all the most important occasions, and were probably more than adequate for the needs of the English Roman Catholic community at the time. Indeed, it is hard to imagine them being performed in all their glory in those unpropitious times; circumstances have scarcely ever given them the airing they deserve in the liturgical context for which they are so superbly fitted.

As with the Masses, the *Gradualia* ignore the established conventions, one of which was to vary the style of the setting according to the liturgical genre (Introit, Gradual, Alleluia, Offertory, and Communion). Byrd is aware of no such stylistic distinctions, and when the liturgy repeats the text (or part of the text) of one item in another, he is prepared to repeat the music also. It is only latterly that his full scheme has been revealed, for it depends on the identification of such repetitions in the light of the liturgical requirements.

In his moving preface to the 1605 publication, Byrd explained how the close study of the texts led inevitably to his finding the right notes with which to explore them. It is the experience of every true composer, but it is often taken for granted, and Byrd thought it worth while to set out for his readers just what was involved. His achievement can be illustrated on every page of the *Gradualia*, whether from the calm contemplation of the Christmas motet 'O magnum mysterium' or from the vivid dialogue in the Easter Sequence 'Victimae paschali laudes'. In the group of pieces outside his main scheme he has left a garland of minor liturgical and

---

[47] TCM, vii; *The Byrd Edition*, v–vii (in progress). There is a penetrating discussion of the *Gradualia* in Kerman, *Masses and Motets*, 216–340.

Ex. 144

Ex. 144, continued

... grant us peace.

semi-liturgical works, including the finely wrought 'Ave verum corpus', the exquisite three-part Marian hymn 'Ave maris stella', and the 'Voces turbarum', his simple but effective setting of the choruses of the St John Passion. His collection is a remarkable achievement, and all the more so for being composed to fulfil a private ideal rather than a public function.

Few other composers of Byrd's generation, apart from those living abroad, cultivated the Latin motet, and none did so with anything like his distinction or versatility. Amongst his younger contemporaries Morley produced no more than a dozen works at the very outside; of these, one is apparently a consort song from which the vocal line is missing, a second survives in one voice-part only, and a third is an English part-song with a Latin refrain and is almost certainly by an older composer. Two are very early works, dating from 1576 when the composer was 19; 'Gaude Maria virgo' is based on a motet by Peter Philips, while the rest are mature compositions, four from the *Plaine and Easie Introduction* and the others from seventeenth-century anthologies.[48] The short 'Agnus Dei' and 'Eheu sustulerunt me' from the former are marvels of concise expressiveness.

But Morley's masterpiece is the six-part 'De profundis clamavi', included with 'Laboravi in gemitu meo', a reworking of the setting by Philippe Rogier, in Thomas Myriell's manuscript *Tristitiae remedium* of 1616. We are far removed in this work from Byrd's instinctive approach. It is imbued with a delicate gravity that both matches the text and yet foreshadows the idiom of consort writing as it developed in the hands of the Jacobean and Caroline masters.

John Baldwin, to whose activities as a copyist we owe so much of our knowledge of this repertory,[49] himself occasionally set Latin texts, as did

[48] The complete collection, ed. H. K. Andrews and R. T. Dart, was published in 1959.
[49] For Baldwin as a copyist see Ch. 7, n. 3.

Nathaniel Giles, Wilbye, Weelkes, and Ravenscroft. Alfonso Ferrabosco the younger, and Thomas Lupo, both of Italian descent and members of James I's household, also cultivated the motet, the former with some distinction. Their conservative style remained paramount until the end of the reign.

The expatriates Peter Philips and Richard Dering are often mentioned together, but their careers and personalities differed. Philips was about twenty years older than Dering. Trained as a chorister at St Paul's under Sebastian Westcote, he fled to the Continent in 1582, at the age of about 22, on account of his faith. In Antwerp he published several collections of motets. Two of them, for five and for eight voices respectively, were later republished with *basso continuo*. The other three contain between them motets for one, two, and three voices with *basso continuo* and anticipate baroque methods; but neither the motets for large forces nor those for small seem to have been influential in England. Philips's music for harpsichord and for consort was collected by Francis Tregian, but this does not imply a widespread recognition.

The case of Dering is somewhat different. Born out of wedlock around 1580, he probably received his musical training in England; this led in due course to his taking the degree of Bachelor of Music at Oxford in 1610. It is not known exactly when he became converted to Roman Catholicism and emigrated, but he is found as organist to the English convent in Brussels in 1617. In the same year he published in Antwerp his *Cantica sacra*, in five parts with *basso continuo*; and in the following year a similar six-part collection appeared.[50] In 1625 he became organist in the chapel of Charles I's queen, Henrietta Maria, a congenial post that he was able to enjoy until his death in 1630. It was perhaps at this period that he composed the two- and three-part motets with *basso continuo* that were eventually published after the Restoration. He may also have written the large collection of organ music for the Tridentine rite that survives in the Christ Church library, though this theory has not gone unchallenged.[51]

After Byrd, few English composers in this field were able (or wished) to recapture the exalted style of the high Renaissance. The a cappella motet with *basso continuo* and, later on, the orchestrally accompanied motet, became an occasional medium for Anglican and Roman Catholic composers alike. More characteristic, however, was the 'few-voiced' type, occasionally monodic, that took its place alongside other forward-looking genres in the seventeenth century and so contributed to the slow growth of the baroque style in England.

---

[50] Published as EECM, xv.

[51] The manuscript, Christ Church 89, was attributed to Dering by R. T. Dart, 'An Early 17th-Century Book of English Organ Music for the Roman Rite', *ML*, 52 (1971), 27–38. Richard Vendome has suggested William Browne, another expatriate: see his edition of Browne (Oxford, 1983), 5.

7

SECULAR VOCAL MUSIC,
1575–1625

THE secular music of Elizabethan and Jacobean England does not fall into such neatly defined categories as was once supposed. Even the word 'secular' is not very helpful for the purpose of definition, since much that was written for domestic use was unambiguously sacred in content.[1] Consort-song, lute-song, and part-song (embracing the madrigal), are all interrelated. In addition, there are the various genres of domestic psalmody and sacred songs, including those for voice or voices with the accompaniment of 'whole' or mixed consort.

Apart from medium and content, there are the questions of social function and the circumstances of performance and publication to consider. It is now known that the somewhat uniform-looking series of polyphonic vocal publications issued by East and others between 1588 and 1624 conceals a considerable variety of genres, and that works written for special occasions might be reissued and even rescored for general use. A certain amount was conceived for the stage—choirboy plays, masques, and so on; or special events might be commemorated in song. The deaths of notable personages, such as Sir Philip Sidney in 1586 or Prince Henry in 1612, provoked an outburst of funereal verse and music.[2] The manuscript anthologists—Dow, Hamond, Merro, Myriell, Tregian, Wigthorpe, Nicholson, and others, to

---

[1] See above, Ch. 5, pp. 324–32.

[2] Byrd wrote three consort-songs on the death of Sidney: 'In Angel's Weed' (*The Byrd Edition*, xv, no. 31: the text, modified to apply to Mary Queen of Scots, originally began 'Is Sidney dead'), 'Come to me, grief', (ibid. xvi, no. 27), and 'O that most rare breast' (ibid. xvi, no. 28: these two were subsequently published as works for five voices in *Psalmes, Sonets, & Songs of sadnes and pietie* (1588), nos. 34, 35). For Prince Henry we have Byrd's 'Fair Britain Isle' (see n. 15), Ward's 'Weep forth your tears' (1613), Coprario's *Songs of Mourning* (1613), and (probably) Gibbons's 'Nay let me weep' (1612). Henry Noel, a favourite courtier of Queen Elizabeth who died in 1597, was commemorated by Dowland (seven 'funerall psalmes', printed and discussed in Poulton, *John Dowland*, 330–6), Weelkes ('Noel, adieu', 1600), and Morley ('Hark, Alleluia' in his *Canzonets*, 1597). If Noel is to be identified with the 'Bonny-boots' so often referred to, the list can be increased. Byrd wrote an elegy on the death of Tallis in 1585 (see below), and Weelkes one on Morley, published in 1608; and doubtless there are many more.

say nothing of the copyists who worked for Edward Paston[3]—might be motivated by their personal circumstances and predilections, by their religious orientation, or by the desire to evoke a single idea (as with Thomas Myriell's *Tristitiae remedium* of 1616). In any case, their part-books preserve material of very various origin.

Another element to bear in mind is the influence of popular song in the art-music of this period. Popular song as such is to be considered in a later chapter;[4] but it is necessary at this stage to be aware of its significance as a unifying agent in a musical culture that embraced wide extremes. The use made of popular material in instrumental music serves as a reminder that the vocal and instrumental genres are also interlinked at several levels.

With these reservations, we may consider in turn the forms of consort-song, part-song, and lute-song, together with such kinds of domestic sacred music as do not fall clearly into any of these categories, and concluding with a discussion of music for the stage.

That the consort-song survived beyond the 1560s as a major musical form is largely due to Byrd. He probably cultivated it from his earliest years, though the elegy on the death of Mary I, 'Crowned with flow'rs and lilies', does not look like a work of that period, whether or not it is really by Byrd himself (about which there is some uncertainty).[5] The year 1588 makes a suitable dividing-line between his earlier and later contributions to the genre, since it was then that he included thirty-five of them, with text in all parts, in his *Psalmes, Sonets, & Songs of sadnes and pietie*.[6] Many of these survive in pre-publication form in manuscripts of the period;[7] and for the others the consort versions are easily reconstructible, Byrd having

---

[3] Robert Dow, Fellow of All Souls (d. 1588): owner and probable copyist, Oxford, Christ Church Mus. 984–8. Thomas Hamond: Oxford, Bod. Lib., Mus. Sch. f. 20–24; owner of London, Brit. Lib., Add. 30480–4. John Merro of Gloucester: Oxford, Bod. Lib., Mus. Sch. d. 245–7; New York, Public Lib., Drexel 4180–5; London, Brit. Lib., Add. 17792–7. The Revd Thomas Myriell (*c*.1580–1625): Brit. Lib., Add. 29372–7, an anthology prepared for publication and entitled *Tristitiae remedium*; also Add. 40657–61 (discovered by Dr K. S. Teo), and several other MSS in part (see P. J. Willetts, 'Musical Connections of Thomas Myriell', *ML*, 49 (1968), 36–42). Francis Tregian the younger (1574–1619): Brit. Lib., Egerton 3665; New York, Public Lib., Drexel 4302 (the 'Sambroke' MS); Cambridge, Fitzwilliam Museum, 32. g. 29 (the Fitzwilliam Virginal Book). For the scribes associated with Edward Paston, a Norfolk Catholic gentleman, see P. Brett, 'Edward Paston (1550–1630)', *Transactions of the Cambridge Bibliographical Society*, 4 (1964–8), 51 seqq. John Baldwin of Windsor wrote a famous Common-place Book (Brit. Mus., R. M. 24. d. 2); Christ Church, Mus. 979–83; *My Ladye Nevells Booke*; and made additions to Bod. Lib., Mus. Sch. e. 376–81. John Sadler of Cambridge wrote Bod. Lib., Mus. e. 1–5; and ibid., Tenbury MS 1486 together with the privately owned Willmott MS. This list includes but a fraction of MSS within this period written by identifiable scribes.

[4] See Vol. II, Ch. 8.

[5] *The Byrd Edition*, xv, no. 29, and p. 175.

[6] EM, xiv (= Byrd, *Collected Works*, xii). The original versions are printed in *The Byrd Edition*, xvi. The most important MS is that of Robert Dow (see n. 3), though two of his versions were, like many later ones, copied from the print.

[7] See the dedicatory Preface of the 1588 publication with its reference to 'many vntrue incorrected coppies of diuers my songes'.

marked 'the first singing part' in most cases. According to his own testimony, they were 'originally made for Instruments to express the harmonie and one voyce to pronounce the dittie'. Many more were included in Byrd's later collections,[8] and over fifty, from all periods of Byrd's life, survive only in manuscript.[9]

Amongst Byrd's earliest consort-songs will have been his free settings of metrical psalm-texts, many of them in the 'Old Version' going under the names of Sternhold and Hopkins, others in translations not otherwise known. In several of these, the character of the writing suggests that the conventional repetition of the last line of each stanza should be sung chorally, thus providing a link with the then embryonic verse anthem.[10] Similar in their general conception are some of Byrd's settings of other religious poems, designated in the 1588 publication as 'songs of sadnes and pietie'. Amongst these are a number of elegies: three on the death of Sir Philip Sidney (see above, n. 2), and 'Ye sacred muses' (for Tallis, who died in 1585). The best of these is undoubtedly the lengthy setting of 'O that most rare breast', a poem in memory of Sidney attributed to Sir Edward Dyer. The second section shows Byrd's command of melodic line to good effect (Ex. 145, overleaf).[11]

But perhaps the finest song of this period is his 'Lulla, lullaby, my sweet little baby', an affecting setting of a carol on the massacre of the innocents and the flight into Egypt. In its manuscript version, like several others, it stands in the 'elegiac' key of C minor, and the stanza itself recalls the triple-time idiom of the earlier Tudor 'death-song'.[12]

In the category of 'sonets' stand a number of moral songs and those of a lighter character, such as 'Though Amaryllis dance in green'[13] and 'La verginella', the latter later expanded and rewritten as a madrigal. Byrd was not altogether happy in setting Ariosto's Italian words on this occasion, though he matches the mood of the text well enough. Byrd adapted it twice: for publication in his 1588 set, with Italian words in all parts; and

[8] *Songs of Sundrie Natures* (1589: ed. EM, xv, = *Collected Works*, xiii); *Psalmes, Songs and Sonnets* (1611: ed. EM, xvi, = *Collected Works*, xiv). J. Kerman (*The Elizabethan Madrigal* (New York), 106), lists nine works in this style from the 1589 publication (counting 17–18, 29 with 34, and 42–3 as one each), printed with texts in all voices and without designation of the 'first singing part'; of these, three survive in 'prior' MS versions (1589, nos. 29, 31, and 32: = *The Byrd Edition*, xvi, nos. 29–31). In addition (cf. Kerman, op. cit. 107) there are eight works from 1589 and 1611, printed with untexted accompaniments in their relevant sections: a pastoral dialogue (1589, no. 41, *a* 6), two serious solo songs (1611, nos. 31 and 32, both *a* 6), three verse anthems (1589, nos. 46–7, *a* 6 with vocal duet and choral sections; 1611, no. 25, *a* 5 with vocal solo and choral conclusion *a* 6, and no. 28, *a* 6 with vocal solo and choral conclusion), and two carols (1589, no. 35, *a* 5 with vocal solo and four-part choral refrain no. 24, and no. 40, *a* 6 with vocal duet and four-part choral refrain no. 25).

[9] *The Byrd Edition*, xv (41 authentic consort-songs), xvi (13 fragmentary works, nos. 34–43, 45–7).

[10] See above, Ch. 5, p. 292.

[11] *The Byrd Edition*, xvi, no. 28 (= EM, xiv, no. 35).

[12] *The Byrd Edition*, xvi, no. 25 (= EM, xiv, no. 32).

[13] *The Byrd Edition*, xvi, no. 12 (= EM, xiv, no. 12).

Ex. 145

Ex. 145, continued

will   my life   it - self   would   yield   If

heath - en   blame   ne   might   my   faith   dis - tain:

for Nicholas Yonge's *Musica Transalpina*, also first published in 1588, with
English text ('The fair young virgin') and with a second part ('But not
so soon') to a translation of the next stanza in Ariosto's poem.[14]

The 'sonets' are generally marked by a greater rhythmic liveliness than
the other songs, and this is often maintained in his later works, even those
that are elegiac, such as 'Fair Britain Isle' on the death of Prince Henry
in 1612.[15] One of Byrd's most entrancing songs is 'My mistress had a little
dog', a mock-heroic piece on the death of a dog (possibly belonging to
Penelope, Lady Rich) at Appleton Hall, the Norfolk home of his friend
and admirer Edward Paston.[16] Here we see in fully developed form the
sense of drama and occasion that had animated so many of his earlier pieces:
the sacred dialogue 'Triumph with pleasant melody';[17] 'Quis me statim',

[14] *The Byrd Edition*, xvi, no. 19 (= EM, xiv, no. 24); the 'madrigalian' version is newly edited
in *The Byrd Edition*, xvi, no. 1.
[15] *The Byrd Edition*, xv, no. 34.
[16] Ibid., no. 36.
[17] Ibid., no. 12.

for a production of Seneca's *Hippolytus* at Christ Church, Oxford, in 1592,[18] and the sadly fragmentary 'Look and bow down', a through-composed setting of a poem by Queen Elizabeth herself on the defeat of the Armada, and sung before her (presumably in Byrd's setting) outside St Paul's on 24 November 1588.[19]

No other composer could match Byrd in the field of the consort-song. The named composers, after the generation of Parsons, Strogers, and Farrant, include such figures as Nathaniel Pattrick and William Cobbold, and, still later, Nathaniel Giles, John Tomkins, John Bennet, and the Oxonians Richard Nicholson and William Wigthorpe. The psalm-settings of John Cosyn are also in consort-song format, as are various works by Whythorne, Greaves, John Mundy, Gibbons, Peerson, Ravenscroft, and others.[20] Some of these will be referred to later in another context. Nicholson and Wigthorpe were enthusiasts who preserved much of the earlier repertory as well as making their own contribution, which was predominantly of a light and witty nature.[21]

One further subspecies of the consort-song demands a special word, and that is the 'Cries', those curious evocations of city and country life within a strictly contrapuntal framework. 'The Cries of London' by Orlando Gibbons is based on two statements of the 'In nomine' theme (see p. 337).[22] Each part is both instrumental and vocal; possibly the players themselves were expected to sing the various calls as they occur. In Weelkes's fine setting,[23] which is freely composed, the top part, and the top part only, is vocal throughout. The cries in these and other settings are traditional; many of them recur with small differences (sometimes due to bowdlerization) in each one, although the musical evocation appears to be entirely the composer's. To 'The City Cries' Richard Dering adds 'The Country Cries'; once more the cries are shared between all the voices.[24] These settings are lively, even somewhat crude in workmanship, and immensely long. William Cobbold's 'New Fashions',[25] which lacks one part in the source, is a set of variations on the 'Browning' melody, into which other popular tunes are introduced from time to time.

The purely secular consort-song in the seventeenth century undoubtedly displays a tendency to triviality. It had been overtaken by the part-song

---

[18] Ibid., no. 37. The words are thought to be by William Gager, who wrote additional scenes for this production of the play.

[19] *The Byrd Edition*, xvi, no. 41 (incipits of each of the three sections in lute tablature) and pp. 197–8 (discussion with transcript of text).

[20] For Whythorne see Ch. 5, pp. 327–32.

[21] For the repertory as a whole, excluding Byrd and works printed in EM, see *Consort Songs*, ed. P. Brett (MB, xxii).

[22] Ibid., no. 67.

[23] Ibid., no. 66.

[24] Ibid., nos. 69, 70. The 'Country Cries' are intended to be Welsh.

[25] Ibid., no. 71. For the Browning song see Ch. 8, n. 14.

and lute-song as the most characteristic expressions of the spirit of the age. It is to these that we now turn, prefacing the former with a discussion of harmonized metrical psalms.

Accounts of Elizabethan music are inclined to neglect domestic psalmody on account of its musical simplicity, but this is to ignore its social importance and its comprehensive influence. The development of the Old Version psalter, with its harmonized edition and the analogous collections of the early Elizabethan period, has been touched on in Chapter 5. Day's harmonized edition of 1563 was followed by a number of others, of which those published by Thomas Est[e] (1592, 1594, 1598 [?], 1604, 1611) and Ravenscroft (1621 (twice), 1633, 1728 (twice), 1746) were in direct succession to that of Day. Ravenscroft's composers included himself, Edward Blanks, Richard Alison, John Bennet, John Milton, Thomas Tomkins, John Dowland, and John Ward. Meanwhile William Damon, a naturalized Fleming, had published his own harmonized version of the same tunes in 1579; and he followed this with yet another collection, published in two parts (*The former Booke* and *The second Booke*) in 1591.[26]

Other harmonizations of the church tunes included those of John Cosyn (*Musike of six, and five partes*, 1585), which are in consort-song format, and Richard Alison, whose *Psalmes of Dauid in meter* (1599) were designed to be accompanied by a mixed consort of lute, orpharion, cittern, and bass viol. William Leighton's *Teares or Lamentacions of a Sorrowful Soule* (1614) included a number of simple tunes to the accompaniment of a larger mixed consort, and these too were stated by Leighton to be suited to psalmodic texts in the Long Metre of Psalm 51.[27]

Psalmody was not of course confined to settings of the church tunes or to the Old Version itself. Many free compositions to texts from the latter are extant: we have noted consort-songs by Byrd, but a complete census from the manuscript and printed sources would fill many pages. As for other metrical versions, these too are numerous, and are found in settings ranging from simple tunes to complex polyphony.[28] Henry Ainsworth's psalter, with forty-seven tunes of which some are new, ran to four editions from 1612 to 1644; William Barton's official Commonwealth version appeared in five editions from 1644 to 1654. Edmund Prys's *Llyfr y Psalmau* was published in London in 1621, while the Scot, George Buchanan,

---

[26] For a comprehensive review of all this material, see *ESPHT*, 55–290; for the full repertory of harmonized tunes in Scotland, see *The Scottish Metrical Psalter of A.D. 1635*, ed. N. Livingstone (Glasgow, 1864).

[27] A few of Cosyn's psalm-settings are reconstructed in *Consort Songs* (nos. 41–4). Two examples from Alison's 1599 publication are given in Alison and others, *Twenty Songs from Printed Sources* (ELS, II xxi). Leighton's collection has been republished as EECM, xi.

[28] Many literary versions exist, of course, without music, for example by Sir Philip Sidney and the Countess of Pembroke—though it is possible that at least some may have been written with the standard tunes in mind.

had a Latin version first published in Frankfurt in 1585, and William Slatyer issued a version in four languages in 1643. Buchanan's verses received simple four-part settings, one or more for each metre and adhering to the quantities of the Latin text, by one Statius Olthoff: they were enormously popular on the Continent, running to innumerable editions in Herborn and elsewhere; but they first appeared in Britain only in 1640. Far more interesting musically are Robert Tailor's *Sacred Hymns. Consisting of Fifty Select Psalms ... and by Robert Tailour, set to be sung in Five parts, as also to the Viole, and Lute or Orpharion* (1615). Finally, mention must be made of two collections by George Wither: *The Songs of the Old Testament* (1621) and *The Hymnes and Songs of the Church* (1623). Both have treble tunes with bass accompaniment, those for the latter being by Orlando Gibbons.[29]

The influence of metrical psalmody was all-pervading. Its peculiar diction, the result of forcing biblical translations into the mould of regular rhyming verse, permeated all kinds of literature in which no such restrictions were necessary, while the official body of tunes, largely taken from the Calvinist repertoire and often borrowed for use outside the context of the Old Version, exercised a comparable influence on melodic writing in both sacred and secular music. This influence lasted well beyond the end of the period covered by this chapter, but it is of particular relevance to the Elizabethan and Jacobean era, and most of all in the sphere of domestic part-song.

If simple harmonized psalmody, performed in various ways, formed the foundation of domestic music-making in the homes of the educated, the pious or discreetly amorous part-song represents the next level of sophistication. The sententious note was struck by Thomas Whythorne in his publication of 1571 (discussed in Chapter 5). It never disappeared, in spite of the growing taste for light verse corresponding to the *poesia per musica* of the Italians. It could have a deadening effect even on Byrd, the supreme master of the age; but it would be wrong to dismiss the part-songs of Byrd as merely parochial achievements, or indeed to draw too sharp a distinction between the part-song and the 'true' madrigal. Byrd cultivated both, and also a large area falling clearly into neither category.

Many of Byrd's part-songs, as we have seen, were simply adaptations of consort-songs with text added to all voices. In most cases the 'first singing part' is so labelled and would in any case stand out by virtue of its relative plainness and lack of textual repetition. Occasionally a part-song with no known consort original betrays such characteristics. More often, however, the 'pervading imitation' inherited from the previous generation and deriving in part from the Parisian chanson of the 1530s and 1540s was the primary structural element.

Since virtually all of the songs published in 1588 are adaptations of consort-

[29] For Ainsworth see *ESPHT*, 394–405; Barton, ibid. 453–9; Prys, ibid. 405–8; Buchanan, ibid. 507–31; Tailour, ibid. 468–506; Wither, ibid. 408–33.

songs, the 1589 volume is Byrd's first major collection of purely vocal part-songs. It cannot be a coincidence that here and in 1611 Byrd adopted Whythorne's plan in 1571 of starting with three-part works and ascending to four, five and in Byrd's case six voices.[30] Similarly, both of Byrd's books embody a wide stylistic range, from severe settings of psalm paraphrases to examples of overt madrigalism. There is also far less emphasis than in 1588 on strophic settings: three of the strophic poems in 1589, and two in 1611, are through-composed. Many poems have but one stanza, as in the case of the three-part penitential psalms of 1589. These paraphrases are unattributed, and it is not known if they ever existed as complete versions of the psalms in question. Although the very fact of metrical paraphrase tends to place them within the 'Protestant' sphere, it is conceivable that Byrd was endeavouring to emulate, though on a much smaller scale, the Continental tradition exemplified by Lasso's five-part *Psalmi Davidis poenitentiales* (1584). Though undemonstrative, they are marked throughout by a concentrated intensity of expression.

Many of the remaining vocal part-songs of Byrd's 1589 and 1611 collections come much closer to the madrigalian spirit. Modern comment is apt to be inhibited by a somewhat restrictive view of what actually constitutes a madrigal. Essentially, a madrigal is a monostrophic poem, set to music in a way that underlines the verbal and semantic content of the text. This latter requirement rules out altogether the strophic treatment of a strophic poem, and normally (though not quite always) the reuse of old music to new text within a single stanza. This usage first arose in Italy in the early sixteenth century, when poets took to imitating the old madrigalian form of the fourteenth century (which *was* stanzaic, verbally and musically), and treating it for the purposes of musical setting as monostrophic. The same was done with *sonetti*, *ballate*, *strambotti*, and other forms; and it is really only chance that has given us 'madrigal' (Italian *madrigale*) rather than these others as a generic name.

It was only in England that a repertory of vernacular 'madrigals' so called came into existence. Flemish and German composers, for example, gave the name only to settings of Italian texts. In England, it became current through the translated Italian madrigals collected in Nicholas Yonge's *Musica Transalpina* (1588) and Thomas Watson's *Italian Madrigalls Englished* (1590). Several other such sets followed including a second set of *Musica Transalpina* in 1597. The first book of music by an English composer to bear the title was Morley's of 1594; but Byrd himself had contributed to both Yonge's and Watson's publications, and the concept was familiar enough even before that from manuscript copies of Italian madrigals and from imported prints,

---

[30] The scheme was also adopted in *Musica Transalpina* (1588) and in several later collections, but is very rarely found on the Continent.

of which latter those of the older Ferrabosco (two five-part sets published in Venice in 1587) appear to have been the best known.

In the circumstances, a monostrophic or otherwise through-composed part-song by an English composer of this period is by definition a madrigal, although present-day usage tends to restrict the term to pieces exhibiting certain specific 'madrigalisms', even to the extent of contradicting a publisher's or composer's own title. This has yielded the concept of 'transitional' songs[31]—transitional, that is, between the strophic part-song or consort-song and the fully fledged madrigal; but this is to impose an unduly limiting pattern on a complex and by no means rectilinear development. The terminological question has perhaps been given undue prominence by a generation of scholars anxious to counter earlier misconceptions.

Byrd's part-songs, as has been said, are widely varied in style. The question as to whether or not he was writing a 'madrigal' probably never entered his head. 'The fair young virgin', adapted from his consort-song 'La verginella' and published in *Musica Transalpina*, is an excellent madrigal, neither its madrigalism nor its excellence diminished by the slight predominance and verbal simplicity (without text-repetition) of the top part. Byrd complemented this adaptation with an entirely new setting of a translation of the next stanza of Ariosto's poem.[32] For Thomas Watson's publication he wrote two settings, one in four and one in six parts, of 'This sweet and merry month of May'. The six-part version (the two settings have much in common) is rightly considered to be a high point of Byrd's achievement, but it is a stylistic apex in the cultivation of a genre that covers a wide range rather than the practically unique phenomenon that is sometimes made of it.

Byrd was capable of being defeated by a feebly pietistic or allegorical text, and several of the 1589/1611 part-songs suffer more from this than from any 'transitional' status they may have. 'Is Love a boy', with the second part 'Boy pity me' based on an inversion of the original idea, is typical of sound but uninspired workmanship. On the other hand, a number of far more animated pieces are ruled out as madrigals by virtue of their strophic construction or internal repetitions to new text. But a piece like 'Penelope that longed for the sight' (1589, no. 27) is both through-composed and an affective response to a text that, if not poetically distinguished, at least utilizes a classical simile to the purpose; it is interesting to compare it to the very next piece, 'Compel the hawk to sit', a miserable offering by Thomas Churchyard (a poet whose calibre is adequately suggested by his name) that evoked little response from the great composer. The close of 'Penelope' illustrates his affective power when roused (Ex. 146, pp. 399–400).

[31] Kerman, *The Elizabethan Madrigal*, 111–17.
[32] See above, n. 14.

Ex. 146

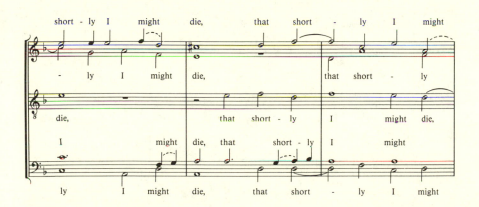

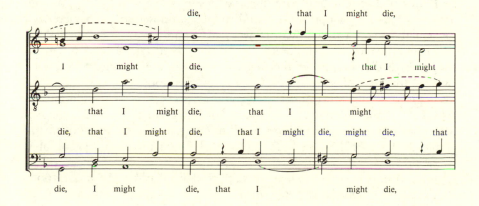

continued

Ex. 146, continued

Byrd's 1611 set contains a mixture not dissimilar to that of 1589, though there is a rather higher proportion of through-composed songs characterized by tangible madrigalisms. 'Come woeful Orpheus' (no. 19) imitates the chromaticisms of contemporary Italian and Netherlands composers in response to the imagery of the text; 'Awake mine eyes' and 'Come jolly swains' (nos. 12, 13, *a* 4) are even more conventionally madrigalian. The example of 'This sweet and merry month' (no. 9, *a* 4, first published in 1590) is a reminder not to accept uncritically a late date for anything in this book, though the concision, rhythmic tautness, and sheer novelty of a piece like 'What is life' (no. 14) may be tantamount to proof of it (Ex. 147).

John Mundy (*Songs and Psalmes*, 1594), Richard Carlton (*Madrigals*, 1601), Richard Alison (*An Howres Recreation in Musicke*, 1606), and Orlando Gibbons (*Madrigals and Mottets*, 1612) are amongst the composers nowadays associated with the older part-song rather than the newer madrigalian

Ex. 147

tradition.[33] As with Byrd (though except for Gibbons on a vastly inferior level), their publications are a mixture that includes consort-songs (Mundy, Alison, Gibbons), strophic vocal part-songs (Carlton), and even anthems (Alison). Carlton's achievement is so very far from matching his evident ambition that it is hardly worth while deciding whether his title can be justified. Gibbons is in a different category, but he has added to the difficulty by not revealing which are the madrigals and which the motets. Probably the remarkable elegy 'Nay let me weep', almost certainly a consort-song in memory of Prince Henry (d. 1612), is to be counted as a motet; the three-stanza poem is through-composed, and the final couplet is apparently a choral conclusion, the mood of which is a curious anticipation of that of the end of Purcell's *Dido* and Blow's *Venus and Adonis* (Ex. 148, pp. 402–4).

There is a later example of a consort-song by Gibbons in his Welcome Song composed for James I's visit to Scotland in 1617, 'Do not repine, fair sun';[34] but attempts to identify this medium in other works published in 1612 are less well founded. The conventional expression on the title-page, 'apt for Viols and Voyces', would no doubt permit performance as consort-songs as well as allowing for instrumental doubling and the use of instruments alone; but it can be counter-productive to seek evidence of adaptation at all costs. The deadening effect of inferior verse is unfortunately apparent even in this distinguished publication and particularly in the more ambitious pieces; but at its best the composer's incomparable melodic gift emerges, and in 'The silver swan' and 'Ah dear heart' we can judge what Gibbons

[33] Kerman, *The Elizabethan Madrigal*, 118–27.
[34] See the edition by P. Brett (London, 1961).

Ex. 148

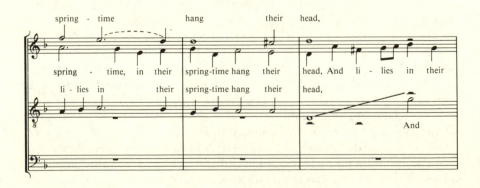

Ex. 148, continued

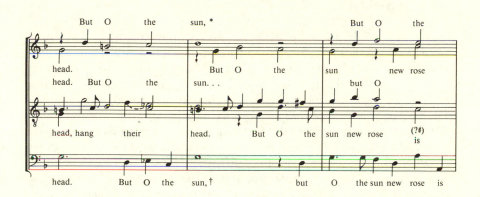

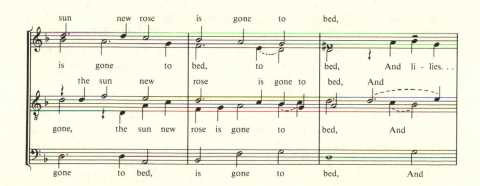

continued

Ex. 148, continued

* In the original print these notes are set to the words 'is gone to bed'.
† Original words 'the sun new rose'.

might have produced by way of a volume of lute-songs.[35] The latter, a setting of a poem once attributed to Donne, shows Gibbons's 'nucleic' approach to melodic construction; but the underpinning of the melody by the inexorable rise of the bass in bars 6–11, its subsequent extension by sequence, and the subtle transition to the second section, show a master in control of all aspects of composition (Ex. 149, pp. 405–6).

With Morley we come to the first English composer to have assimilated thoroughly the Italian idioms of his day. This is evident in his editing of Italian compositions for the English market, in his imitations of them, in his wholly original compositions, and in the markedly Italianate orientation of *A Plaine and Easie Introduction*. The distinction between transcription, imitation, and free composition is not always an easy one to draw: *The First Booke of Balletts to Five Voyces* (1595) and *The First Booke of Canzonets to Two Voyces* (1595) contain both imitations (of varying degrees of fidelity) and free (or almost free) compositions. Each, incidentally, was published in both an Italian and an English edition, though the Italian edition of the *Canzonets* is no longer extant. For the balletts, which are dance-like pieces with 'fa la' refrain, Morley relied partly on Gastoldi's *Balletti* of 1591, partly on other composers such as Vecchi and Marenzio; his book also contains a miscellaneous group of canzonets and madrigals, and a dialogue, 'Phyllis I fain would die now'. In most cases, apparently, Morley set his English texts first and then adapted the music to the Italian texts, even when he was imitating an Italian composition in the first place.[36]

Both the *balletto* and the *canzonetta* were light strophic poems; but English

[35] *First Set of Madrigals and Motets*, nos. 1, 15. Both are in ABB′ form (B′ having different words from B). The text of 'Ah dear heart' was also set by Dowland; but there is no evidence that he was the poet.
[36] Kerman, *The Elizabethan Madrigal*.

Ex. 149

continued

Ex. 149, continued

editions of Italian canzonets, and hence their imitations, lack all but the first stanza. Thus the distinction between a canzonet and a light English madrigal is all but lost. Many of the two-part canzonets are modelled on four-part examples by Felice Anerio and others, an ingenious example of compressed imitation. The three-part canzonets (1593) and the five- and six-part canzonets (1597), on the other hand, are entirely original compositions. The three-part canzonets are still closer to the madrigal than are the largely homophonic five- and six-part works; the set embraces the splendid 'Arise get up my dear' (no. 20), 'the first full-fledged example of Morley's narrative madrigal',[37] and a number of more serious compositions including the attractively sentimental 'Cease mine eyes'. It was left to Weelkes and Wilbye, however, to exploit more fully the potential of the three-part madrigal.

Morley actually used the term 'madrigal' in his four-part collection of 1594. Its status is unique in that it defined once for all the characteristic flavour of the English madrigal. This flavour (though 'texture', in the gastronomic sense, would make a better metaphor) is best described as 'light', a term that is not easily defined but can nevertheless be justified. The distinction in the Italian madrigal between the light and the serious does not depend entirely on the subject-matter of the poem, but in part on its treatment as verse and as music. A light poem of the type known as *poesia per musica* demands a comparable lightness of touch in the setting, even if the subject-matter is 'serious'. The setting itself may be 'serious' in so far as it responds to the subject-matter, but 'light' in its reflection of the underlying character of the verse. It is in this sense that English madrigals are almost invariably light, even when dealing with a serious theme.

This understanding of an important distinction is almost the exact opposite of the one hitherto generally current, according to which it has been main-

[37] Ibid. 181.

tained that 'Marenzio ... even when he sets a very trivial poem ... still keeps an aesthetically serious approach to the music, a sophisticated consciousness of his task as an artist'.[38] This is true, but not in the sense that the style is appropriate to a more literary type of poem. It is precisely Marenzio's seriousness as an artist that enables him at once to reflect the level of the verse he is setting and to transcend it as a medium for the conveying of the intended emotion. This is of some importance in view of Marenzio's position in the shaping of the English madrigal.[39] Morley's immediate models may have been composers of much lesser stature; but he was himself an artist of comparable sensitivity to the level of a text, and must have been inspired by a deep knowledge of his Italian heritage.

The English went far further than the Italians in their rejection of the best poetry of the day as a source of texts. In avoiding the deadly sententiousness that could hamper even Byrd and Gibbons, the madrigalists resorted very largely to triviality. The marriage of this kind of verse to true music is the very special achievement of Morley, Weelkes, Wilbye, and several others. Only John Ward demonstrated a more serious taste in poetry, but by that time it was too late to reform the polyphonic madrigal: the recognized medium for the setting of verse of that calibre had come to be the solo song.

In Morley's collection of 1594 (enlarged by two pieces in the edition of 1600) we can recognize the English madrigal in its classic shape. The generally short rhyming lines, variable design, and conventionally amorous sentiments of the texts (could they be, in many cases, the original work or translations of the composer himself?) are matched by the volubility, textural clarity, and sudden contrasts of the settings. The apparently effortless flow of ideas conceals an art based on variety and balance. In no. 2, 'Clorinda false', for example, we can see how a conventionalized response to conventional sentiments is enlivened by tonal and textural variety. After the repeated contrapuntal opening, for example, we have the beautifully judged passage quoted as Ex. 150 (overleaf). The pace of contrast quickens, there is a modulation to the dominant (D minor), and the little work ends with a more extended, and in large part repeated, coda to the final couplet:

> Thus spake Philistus on his hook relying,
> And sweetly fell a-dying.

We should miss neither the *double entendre* nor the ambiguity with which the composer keeps us at arm's length, as it were, from a too literal interpretation

---

[38] Ibid. 172.

[39] His contribution to Thomas Watson's *Italian Madrigalls Englished* (1590) is extensive; it is less so, however, in other anthologies. Watson's texts were adaptations rather than translations. For full documentation of the entire field see A. Obertello, *Madrigali italiani in Inghilterra* (Milan, 1949).

Ex. 150

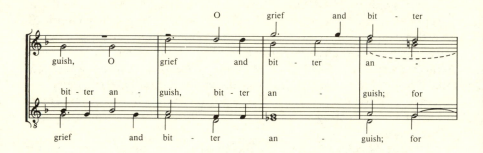

Ex. 150, continued

of 'death': his dominant pedal and falling phrases suggest both the sadness of real death and the ecstasy of sexual fulfilment (Ex. 151, overleaf).

In 'In dew of roses steeping | Her lovely cheeks, Lycoris thus sat weeping' (no. 7), the complaint of the bereft maiden is set to a music that reflects the pastoral liquidities of the text by its scoring for high voices and its repetitive, echo-like quality. Here there is no relaxation: the music presses onwards to the vengeful insistence of 'Yet my ghost still shall haunt thee' (Ex. 152, overleaf).

But the collection, like so many others, spares a thought for requited love and faithfulness, and culminates in the brilliantly descriptive 'Hark jolly shepherds' and 'Ho! who comes here', the latter a splendid evocation of the morris dance. In retrospect Morley's technical equipment may look conventional enough, but the apparent straightforwardness conceals an art of incomparable delicacy and sophistication.[40]

We can gain an idea of the strengths and weaknesses of the English madrigal at the dawn of the new century from *The Triumphes of Oriana*, published by Morley in 1601. The idea behind such a collection came from *Il trionfo di Dori*, a Venetian anthology first published in 1592, and from one specific madrigal therein, Croce's 'Ove tra l'herb' e i fiori'. This madrigal became known in England from its inclusion, to the translation

---

[40] Kerman's commentary (*The Elizabethan Madrigal*, 184–9), is indispensable.

Ex. 151

Ex. 152

'Hard by a crystal fountain', in the second *Musica Transalpina* (1597). It was in this translation that Dori became Oriana, and in which the final couplet

> Then sang the shepherds and nymphs of Diana:
> Long live fair Oriana

first appeared.[41] Morley himself set the text in his *Triumphes*, and his setting is actually a free version of Croce's composition. The refrain had also attracted Michael Cavendish, whose 'Come gentle swains', first published in 1598, was extensively revised for the *Triumphes*.

Whereas 'Dori' had been the mythological name of the bride of a wealthy Venetian nobleman,[42] however, 'Oriana' was now applied to the praise of a sixty-seven-year-old virgin queen. We do not know what Morley thought of such a transformation, but it is certain that he was at a disadvantage compared with Leonardo Sanudo, the Venetian patron. Sanudo was able to commission twenty-nine poets and musicians to honour his bride; Morley scraped the barrel to find twenty-two composers besides himself, and was content to identify the author of two of his twenty-five poems by the initials I. L. (perhaps John Lyly). Several of his composers are minor masters, to put it no lower than that; yet the collection is an impressive achievement. It has been suggested that the madrigals were originally gathered for the elaborate 'Maying' of 1601, a 'triumph' in the Renaissance tradition devised to solace the queen and divert the populace after the execution of Essex.[43] To accompany such a festivity with music would have been no novelty; but to do so with a newly commissioned set of madrigals was a bold gesture in view of the youthfulness of the form in England.

Some of the composers represented—Daniel Norcome, Ellis Gibbons, Richard Carlton, George Marson, and the mysterious John Lisley—scarcely call for any comment, their contributions being either picturesque but technically unsound, or simply dull. Even some of the better composers, such as Michael East and Robert Jones, were less than sparkling on this occasion. But some other minor figures, amongst them Bennet, Holmes, Hilton, Hunt, and Milton, rose to their best level; and Morley was able to draw on Tomkins, Weelkes, and Wilbye, as well as on himself, to add real lustre to the collection. Weelkes's 'As Vesta was from Latmos hill descending' is one of the finest madrigals of the period, the huge augmentations of the bass in the refrain underpinning the structure to an unprecedented

---

[41] The Italian words are: 'Poi concordi seguir ninfe e pastori: | Viva la bella Dori'.

[42] See Kerman, 'Morley and the "Triumphs of Oriana"', *ML*, 34 (1953), 185–91; and *The Elizabethan Madrigal*, 194–209.

[43] See the introduction to the modern edition (EM, xxxii). The collection may have been prepared in advance of publication.

degree.[44] It was Weelkes and Wilbye in particular who were able to take the madrigal forward to its next phase by giving it a structural solidity that is absent from Morley's approach.

These qualities are not so much in evidence in Weelkes's first collection,[45] in which the three- and four-part madrigals carry Morley's penchant for picturesqueness even further than the master himself, while those for five and six voices are mostly short and often predominantly homophonic. It is true that in 'Cease sorrows now' he considerably enlarged the expressive range of the three-part madrigal, while in 'My flocks feed not' we have a tripartite madrigal-sequence of considerable ingenuity.[46] The picturesqueness of 'Three virgin nymphs' (for three high voices, with a bass to help characterize 'rude Sylvanus') and 'Lo country sports' (four voices, written in the treble, treble, mezzo-soprano and alto clefs) hardly needs stressing. In the *Balletts and Madrigals to fiue voyces* (1598, second edition 1608), the conventionally designed balletts are interspersed with madrigals, some of which also carry the 'fa la' refrain. Conventional design, of course, need not mean dull music, and this volume has rightly been praised for its 'impression of bubbling spontaneity'.[47] One of Weelkes's technical usages here fully exploited is the use of a quick triple metre (three crotchets in the time of two): 'Sing we at pleasure' uses no other, and it is heard at the beginning of the elegy for Lord Borough, 'Cease now delight', that concludes the volume. This, and the importation of the 'fa la' into a 'serious' madrigal (such as no. 21, 'Farewell my joy') heightens the sense of ironic contrast of which Weelkes was a master.

Weelkes's qualities are exhibited to perfection in the *Madrigals of 5, and 6. parts*, published in 1600. There is no lack of sparkling wit, but in several cases there is an increased spaciousness made possible by the composer's mastery of tonal design. In three of the four bipartite madrigals, the first part ends on what we should nowadays call an imperfect cadence or half close.[48] The exception, 'O care, thou wilt despatch me', is for other reasons one of Weelkes's finest compositions. The 'fa la' is here deeply ironic, and the second part opens with a veritable paroxysm of chromatically expressed grief, resolved by a modulation to the relative major to introduce the balm of 'Music, sick man's Jewel' (Ex. 153, pp. 413–14).

---

[44] The technique is not exactly 'antiquated' (Kerman, 231): rather, it anticipates later structured principles based on broad harmonic schemes. A similar technique is used, as Kerman points out, in 'When Thoralis delights to walk'.

[45] *Madrigals to 3. 4. 5. & 6. voyces*, 1597 (EM, ix).

[46] Ibid., nos. 2–4. The words are from *The Passionate Pilgrim*, a compilation first published in 1599 with an ascription to Shakespeare.

[47] Dart in the introduction to EM, x.

[48] This technique was pioneered in the late 15th cent., for example by Obrecht in his motet 'Laudemus nunc dominum'. It is frequent in Continental motets and madrigals of the 16th cent., though the vestiges of modal independence sometimes make the procedure tonally ambiguous. Weelkes's usage is tonally very clear-cut.

Ex. 153

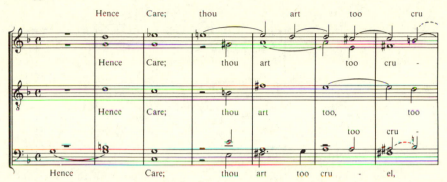

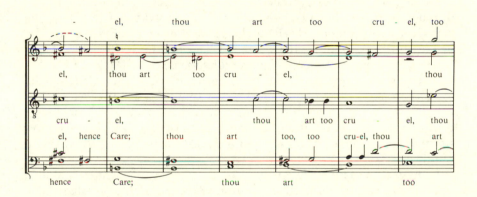

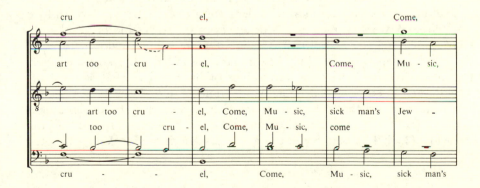

Ex. 153, continued

'What have the gods', another bipartite madrigal calling on the power of music to solace, has a certain anthem-like massivity, while 'Thule the period of cosmography' revels in the strange imagery of the text. The volume concludes with the fine extended elegy for Henry Noel.

The *Ayeres or Phantasticke Spirites for three voices* show Weelkes in lighter mood: this is a book of balletts and canzonets, two of the latter being to Italian texts.[49] The volume concludes with a third six-part elegy, composed in memory of Morley, though the words, by John Davies, were originally written on the death of Henry Earl of Pembroke. It is the most affective of the three, its broken phrases recalling those of 'When David heard'.

John Wilbye (1574–1638) appears in his madrigals as a more polished and certainly a more balanced and consistent composer than Weelkes. Wilbye provides a rare instance of a musician of his stature remaining over many years in the service of one family, in this case the Kytsons of Hengrave Hall near Bury St Edmunds. The dedication to Sir Charles Cavendish of Wilbye's first set of madrigals is dated 'from th' Augustine Fryers the xii. of Aprill. 1598': that is from the Kytson's town house in London. However, it is with Hengrave that Wilbye is primarily associated: the extensive papers still extant reveal even the furnishings of his room as well as the large and very interesting collection of instruments and music books 'in the chamber where the musicyons playe'.[50] It is clear that the establishment was a model of enlightened patronage. It was broken up in 1628 on the death of Lady Elizabeth Kytson, and it seems that thereafter Wilbye devoted

[49] These have but one stanza, though several of the English ones have two or more. At this date the nomenclature is beginning to be used very carelessly.

[50] EM, vi, p. x. Fellowes's extensive introduction to this volume is a most illuminating commentary on domestic music of the period.

himself to the service of her youngest daughter Lady Rivers in Colchester.[51]
Wilbye was unmarried, and the conditions of a lifetime's service in the
provinces might otherwise have proved irksome; but they must have suited
what was evidently an equable temperament. Apart from his two sets of
madrigals only a few sacred works and instrumental pieces have survived.
Whether he actually cultivated these and other forms more extensively
is unknown; as things stand, his reputation is unique in a composer of
his gifts in resting almost exclusively on a modest collection of works in
a single medium.

Wilbye was closer than Weelkes to Morley in spirit. But his five- and
six-part madrigals in particular exhibit a power of emotional expression
and a sense of musical organization that are his alone. Fine as the first
set is, it is on the second (published in 1609)[52] that Wilbye's reputation
hangs. The emotional power of 'Weep, weep mine eyes' (no. 23, for five
voices) and 'Draw on sweet night' (no. 31, for six) is virtually unparalleled
in English madrigalian music. The former makes its bow to Dowland's
Lachrimae[53] in its opening bars; thereafter the music shifts uneasily between
the (D) major and minor modes, its every tonal movement corresponding
to an emotional shift in the text. This is still more evident in 'Draw on
sweet night', in which nature's balm is represented by a very definite D
major, leaving the singer's private griefs to other keys (Ex. 154, overleaf).

But even where the emotions are less bared, there can be an exquisite
bitter-sweetness, as when in the second part of 'Sweet honey-sucking bees'
(nos. 17–18) the protagonists, having been encouraged to gather their nectar
from 'Melisuavia's lips' are warned of the consequences of stinging her
(Ex. 155, p. 418).

The passage is twice repeated, first in the lower three voices, then in
still another grouping, and finally the musical pun illustrative of 'sharp'
is carried through into the elaborately worked G major coda. In the very
next number, 'All pleasure is of this condition', the imagery is continued:

> The honey being shed away doth flee,
> But leaves a sting that wounds the inward heart.[54]

The second of these lines is set to a passage that is not only emotionally
compelling but illustrates Wilbye's structural powers: the downward transposition by a fourth of a contrapuntal nucleus to propel the music forward

[51] Sir Thomas Kytson had died in 1602; Lady Rivers, who had become separated from her husband
Lord Davy (later Viscount of Colchester and Earl Rivers) in 1594, died in 1644, six years after Wilbye.
Wilbye left her the sum of £20; and his 'best vyall' to the future Charles II. Fellowes, EM, vi, *passim*.
[52] EM, vii.
[53] See below, p. 429, and Ch. 8, pp. 470–4.
[54] It is, however, a quite separate work, with different scoring, from the pair just discussed.

Ex. 154

Ex. 154, continued

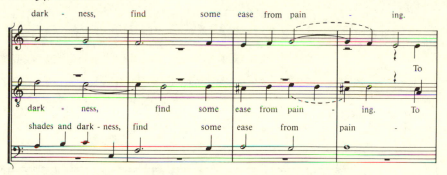

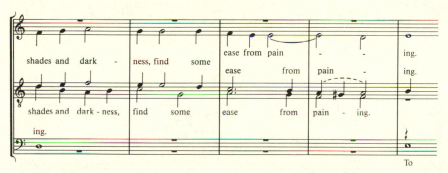

is an old device,[55] but the mastery with which it is concealed in the web of counterpoint (but revealed in our example) is of the highest order (Ex. 156, pp. 419–20). The concluding passage, if transcribed in units of equal length, reveals an ingenious rhythmic augmentation in the bass (Ex. 157, p. 421).[56]

Passages like these raise again the question of 'level'. To what extent were Weelkes and Wilbye aware of contemporary Italian achievement in the madrigal, and to what extent would it have provided a model for a 'serious' approach? The Italian madrigalists of the 1590s and early 1600s, even those who were not yet ready for monody, were seeking new means of expression that threatened to destroy the balance, the instinctive response to the text, with which we have credited Marenzio. Marenzio himself enlarged his musical language in this direction; to varying degrees and in

[55] It can be traced back to Josquin at least; for an earlier English example see Tallis's 'Gaude gloriosa': above, Ch. 5, Ex. 112 and n. 70. Kerman (*The Elizabethan Madrigal*, 241–2) has a valuable passage on Wilbye's sequential writing.

[56] The values are 2, 4, 5, 6, and 6 semibreves respectively, if one counts from the accented syllables and disregards repetitions on unaccented ones. Fellowes's transcription quite disguises this process, as well as the cross-rhythms in the upper parts.

Ex. 155

1. For if one flam - ing dart come from her
For if one flam - ing dart

eye,   come from her eye,   come from her eye,   was
come from her eye,   come from her eye, was   nev - er dart so

die,   then you Ah,
nev - er dart so sharp, Ah   then you die, you   die, 2. die,
sharp,   Ah,   ah,   then you

then you die   then you die, you   die.
then you die, then you   die, Ah,   then you   die.
die, Ah,   then you die,   you   die.

Ex. 156

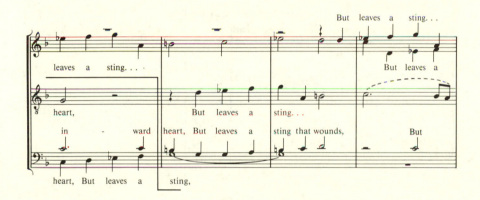

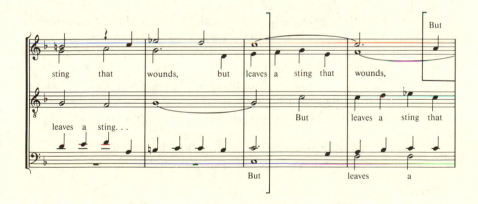

continued

Ex. 156, continued

different ways this was also attempted by such composers as Giaches de Wert, Pallavicino, the young Monteverdi, and above all Gesualdo. On the whole, English composers did not pursue this path: their Italian models (five of the texts in Wilbye's first set are versions of Italian poems)[57] when identifiable are of a more conventional cast. We can see from his three-part 'Ah cruel Amaryllis', no. 3 of his second set, how far Wilbye was from the spirit of Pallavicino, let alone Monteverdi.[58] His music, for all its boldness and imagination, remained an appropriate vehicle for a type of verse which, while in this case it is by no means of poor quality, generally lacks poetic depth.

Of the two other major English madrigalists, John Ward (1571–1638)[59] was a fine composer whose 'seriousness' is reflected in his choice of texts

---

[57] Kerman, 234–5; Obertello, 128–33.

[58] The text 'Crud' Amarilli' is from Guarini's *Il pastor fido*: Pallavicino's setting is in his sixth book (1600), Monteverdi's in his fifth (1605). D. Arnold, *Monteverdi* (London, 1963), 62–3.

[59] For the dates, see *NGD*, ad loc. The will was proved on 31 Aug. 1638.

Ex. 157

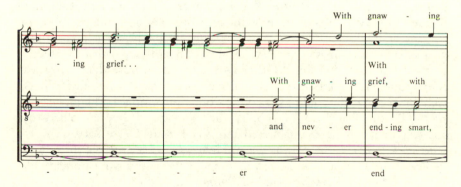

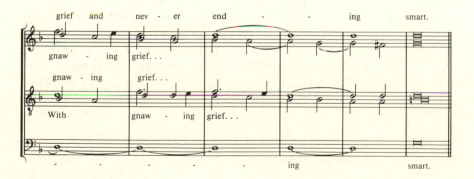

by poets such as Sir Philip Sidney and Michael Drayton. Ward was a household musician to Sir Henry Fanshawe, Remembrancer of the Exchequer,
where Ward also held a post. He was a musician of similar cast to Wilbye;
but his one set of madrigals was published only in 1613,[60] while a far higher
proportion of his surviving output consists of sacred and consort music.
His best work (like that of Weelkes and Wilbye) was in five- and six-part
writing; in some of his music there is a massivity that goes even beyond
that of Weelkes. It is characterized by bold suspensions, sharp contrasts,
and an approach to vocal scoring that is dictated less by the demands of
part-writing than by a desire for sonorous effect. There is also a tendency
to monotony, and a sacrifice of continuity for the sake of detailed characterization. Both strengths and weaknesses may be seen in his most ambitious
composition, the madrigal-pair 'If the deep sighs' (nos. 23–4) to a text
by Michael Drayton.[61] The syntax of the opening lines is all but destroyed
by a disjunction of ideas. The pastoral imagery of the second part is imaginatively handled, but the immense work suffers from repetitiveness and tonal
monotony. In his elegiac mood, however, he can be most impressive: 'Come
sable night' and the elegy for Prince Henry, 'Weep forth your tears' (nos.
27, 28), are in his best manner.

A final composer of distinction is Tomkins, whose *Songs of 3. 4. 5. and
6 parts* were published in 1622.[62] Overt madrigalisms are here subsumed
in the composer's passionate individuality of style, and indeed there are
settings of biblical texts that cannot by any means be termed madrigals.
One of these is his masterpiece 'When David heard', a worthy counterpart
to the setting by Weelkes.[63] Other works are little more than canzonets.
Many have 'fa la' refrains (though being non-strophic they are not balletts);
sometimes these are used in the context of an uncomplicated light-hearted
style ('To the shady woods', no. 13); at other times they are allied to a
sad text in the manner established by Weelkes in 'Cease sorrows now'.
The *locus classicus* is the pair 'O let me live' and 'O let me die' (nos. 7–8),
dedicated to Dowland and Danyel respectively, and paying homage like
so many other works to Dowland's *Lachrimae* (Ex. 158).

In any more extended discussion the following at least would merit close
attention: Kirbye (1597), Bennet (1599), Bateson (1604, 1618), Michael East
(1604, 1606, 1610, 1618, 1618, 1624, 1638, though the last two books contain
no madrigals, while that of 1610 and the second of 1618 are miscellanies),
Jones (1607, unfortunately incomplete), and Pilkington (1613, 1624). Pilk-

---

[60] Modern edition: EM, xix.
[61] The text is adapted from the ninth eclogue of Drayton's *The Shepherds Garland* (1593). *EMV*,
714.
[62] EM, xviii. There were two editions, one undated but almost certainly of the same year: ibid.,
p. v.
[63] See Ch. 6, p. 367. Both settings are superior to that of Michael East (1618a, no. 20).

Ex. 158

ington, whose second set ranks as the swan-song of the whole tradition, may stand as representative:[64] a competent provincial practitioner (he was a singer in Chester Cathedral), a lutenist, and composer of airs, whose dancing rhythms preserve the spirit of Morley. His unpretentious griefs are less demanding than those of Ward, Weelkes, or Wilbye. True to the spirit of the age, his second volume includes a couple of dialogues with instrumental accompaniment, one of them an elegy on the death of one Thomas Purcell, and 'A Pauin made for the Orpharion by the Right

[64] His two sets reprinted as EM, xxv, xxvi. The composer referred to the contents of both as 'madrigals and pastorals'.

Honourable William, Earl of Derby'. But it is as a true English madrigalist
that he deserves to be remembered.

The miscellaneous collections of Ravenscroft (*Pammelia* and *Deuteromelia*,
1609, and *Melismata*, 1611) offer a far more heterogeneous collection of
rounds, light polyphonic songs, and sacred pieces, as interesting to the student
of literature and life as to the musical historian.[65] East's fourth, fifth, and
sixth 'sets of books', as he was content to call them, contain a similar variety,
as does the *Priuate Musicke* of Martin Peerson (1620).[66] Leighton's *Teares*
(1614), after the rather uninteresting songs to the accompaniment of a mixed
consort, contain a surprisingly valuable anthology of domestic sacred music
by Byrd, Bull, Gibbons, Ward, Weelkes, Wilbye, and many others. Hilton's
Ayres or Fa Las (1627) form a bridge between the tradition of light-hearted
Renaissance polyphony and the vocal chamber music of the baroque period.
The collections of Cavendish (1598) and Greaves (1604) include lute-airs
as well as madrigals and (in Greaves's case) consort-songs. Modern publications have not succeeded as yet in making available the whole of this rich
variety; and where they have penetrated, it is often in a piecemeal fashion
that conceals its full extent.[67]

The phenomenon of the English madrigal has been the source both
of admiration and of ill-founded comment. Its fountain-head was an enthusiasm for things Italian that found partial expression in the printing of Italian
madrigals to English texts. When adaptation and imitation followed, English
composers found themselves working a rich vein. But their approach was
pragmatic; what was congenial, they used, adapting it to native traditions
and substituting these when they felt like it. It is as pointless to quarrel
with their terminology as it is to try to isolate their madrigalism in a pure
form. The English polyphonic song[68] is *sui generis*, an inimitable and unre-
peatable *mélange*. Comparison with its Italian counterpart is a necessary stage
in its criticism, but in the end it must be judged for what it is.

We have seen that lute-songs were often issued simultaneously as part-songs,
and it has been claimed that in some instances the part-song versions came
first. The use of solo (or duetting) voice connects the lute-song with the

---

[65] See the texts printed in *EMV*, 201–46, with those from his *Brief Discourse*, 246–55.

[66] East's texts in *EMV*, 95–100. The fifth book has only text incipits (cf. Whythorne's *Duos*, 1590,
and East's own seventh book, 1638). The sixth book consists entirely of church music except for
the air of a canzo in honour of Princess Elizabeth. Peerson's texts, with those of his later *Mottects
or Grave Chamber Musique* (1630) are in *EMV*, 174–89. The title of the *Priuate Musicke* specially mentions
the possibility of a keyboard realization of the harmonies: 'and for want of viols, they may be performed
to either the virginall or lute, where the proficient can play upon the ground, or for a shift to the
base viol alone'.

[67] Leighton's *Teares* (see above, p. 395) in EECM, xi; Hilton: texts only, *EMV*, 114–18; Cavendish
and Greaves, EM, xxxvi; the lute-songs of Cavendish in ELS, II/vii, and of Greaves in ELS, II/xviii.

[68] Here I think of the consort-song and the purely vocal part-song as different manifestations of
the same impulse, though the former also looks towards the aesthetic of the true solo song.

consort-song, as does the occasional use of a 'choral' refrain in both. But in reality the lute-song has a distinctive aesthetic, characterized by a sharply defined and self-sufficient type of melody, and with an accompaniment which need be no more than a purely chordal foundation. A tendency towards polyphonic elaboration in the accompaniment was replaced by idiomatic developments that led to the emergence of continuo song, in which the melody was all important and the necessary harmony inherent in the bass-line.

Enough has been said in Chapter 5 to make it clear that Dowland's first songbook of 1597 by no means marks the emergence of a new art form. Even within the sphere of printed music, it was beaten to the post by the songs in William Barley's *A new Booke of Tabliture* (1596), though there are only two of these and the accompaniments are for the bandora.[69] Much more important, however, are the manuscript sources, several of which pre-date 1597, and of which others, though copied later, contain earlier songs. Some of these were mentioned above (p. 334). As the songs which they contain cannot be dated with precision, it is often a pointless exercise to assign them to the period before or after 1575: the Willow Song is a good example of such uncertainty. Its triple rhythm and elegiac tone are characteristic of the earlier period, in both consort- and lute-song; but the care taken with the accompaniment and the artistry with which it complements the melody are features that look to the future. Curiously enough a second setting of the same or similar words has survived, and it may be this, rather than the more familiar one, that Shakespeare had in mind when writing *Othello*.[70] Though the two are quite different in detail there is a generic resemblance that suggests a similar date.

Dowland did, however, in 1597 initiate a tradition of publishing that in itself promoted a fashion for lute-song and swelled the tide of such compositions. His book was the first printed collection to be laid out in 'table-book' fashion, the top part with the lute accompaniment being placed on the left-hand page and the right-hand one being occupied by the three lower vocal parts arranged so as to be read around three sides of a table. Not all songbooks included four vocal parts: one, two, and three are all found, while others include a textless bass. Still other variants were possible,

[69] Barley's work was published in full by W. W. Newcomb under the title *Lute Music of Shakespeare's Time* (Pennsylvania and London, 1966); the songs, which are anonymous, also in ELS, II/xx, nos. 11–14, with informative notes. An even earlier precedent was that of the third part of *A briefe and plaine instruction* (1574), mostly taken from Adrian Le Roy's *Airs* of 1571; the other two parts, which also contain music, were based on lute tutors published by Le Roy in and around 1567. See I. Harwood, 'On the Publication of Adrian Le Roy's Lute Instructions', *LSJ*, 18 (1976), 30–6.

[70] It is found in a version for lute solo in the 'Lodge' book: Washington DC, Folger Shakespeare Library, MS v. a. 159, fo. 19ʳ, and in a similar arrangement with a variant of the melody, by Dallis (Dublin, Trinity College, MS D. 3. 30, p. 26): see F. W. Sternfeld, *Music in Shakespearean Tragedy*, 44–9, with facsimiles and transcriptions; J. M. Ward, 'Joan qd John', 845–53.

and the variety of performance-practice implied by these is a matter for separate discussion. But it is as well to remember from the outset that the concept of solo lute-song has to be modified by the admission of additional or alternative parts, both vocal and instrumental. While there is something romantically satisfying about the solitary singer accompanying himself (and while such solo performance was, perhaps, the contemporary ideal), the rich textural variety illustrated by the songbooks is not to be forgotten. From time to time the additional parts are found to be essential, and the inclusion of such pieces in volumes otherwise devoted to purely lute-accompanied songs is in no way contrary to the spirit and aesthetic of the age.

Dowland himself was a new kind of musician, the first of his class to achieve anything like such eminence. He was never a Gentleman of the Chapel Royal (in spite of Anthony Wood's statement to the contrary),[71] and became a royal lutenist only in 1612. His origins are obscure, and his immediate family is likely to have lived in humble circumstances. He is not known to have been a singer in adult life, and it may be that he was never even a chorister. He must, however, have had a good general education and had studied music from his childhood;[72] in 1580, at the age of 17, he travelled to Paris in the service of the Ambassador, Sir Henry Cobham, perhaps with the intention of gaining musical experience in what would then have been the only practicable way. He returned a couple of years later,[73] but in 1594–7 he travelled abroad again, this time to the courts of Wolfenbüttel and Hesse, and then to Italy, where he fell in with a group of disaffected exiles. Realizing his mistake, he wrote an abject letter to Sir Robert Cecil, disclaiming any continued adherence to Roman Catholicism, and came home early in 1597 after a further visit to Hesse.[74]

Finally, in 1598, Dowland obtained a post as lutenist to King Christian IV of Denmark; this he held, with increasingly lengthy absences, until 1606, when he was paid off and came home for good. Outwardly Dowland's life is that of a successful career musician and family man; he was famous, widely travelled, a virtuoso performer, and an acclaimed song-writer; a Bachelor of Music of 'both the Universities' (i.e. of Oxford and, presumably by incorporation, of Cambridge), and finally a Doctor of Music, probably

---

[71] D. Poulton, *John Dowland*, 20. I have drawn extensively on this standard biography.

[72] Address 'To the courteous Reader', *First Booke of Songes* (1597) (transcribed Poulton, 219–20). His command of Latin is evidenced by his translation of Ornithoparcus' *Micrologus*. Nothing is known, however, of any period of residence at a university (see n. 75 below).

[73] The exact year is uncertain (Poulton, 26–7).

[74] Dowland admitted to conversion to Roman Catholicism during his visit to France, and his letter implies that he had held the faith continuously until his disillusionment in Italy. The text of the letter is in Poulton, 37–40; discussed ibid. 40–5.

of Oxford.[75] He had married and fathered a gifted son, Robert, and the family lived in decent circumstances in Fetter Lane from 1603 or 1604 until his death early in 1626. But he had a somewhat unstable temperament, with a disposition to melancholy exacerbated (it may be) by his failure to gain a place at the English court before middle age. Yet he had not been neglected, either by his fellow musicians or by royalty and the nobility.[76] His irascibility and feeling of isolation in his later years were part and parcel of his emotional sensitivity as a man and artist.

Dowland is revealed in his songs as a composer of extraordinary range. The number (88) and the medium may seem limited, but he had the capacity to express every mood with unfailing aptness. His response is always a purely musical one: he is untrammelled by literary theory and, while he could turn his hand to commendatory verse in the somewhat unappealing style of the day and may have written some of his own song texts, he is not to be compared with his friend Campion as a littérateur. The second and subsequent stanzas of his songs will not always fit the music composed with the first in mind, though this happens less frequently than is sometimes asserted. Though he may have been widely read and seems to have been well acquainted with the Elizabethan literature of rhetoric,[77] this can never have been more than a starting-point for what for him was generally an apparently spontaneous reaction to the text.

Dowland had had the opportunity of assimilating all the main musical currents of his day, but he was drawn above all by those of Italy. He was an admirer of Marenzio, whom, however, he never met, and must have come across Caccini at court in Florence. Caccini had acquired a European reputation by the early seventeenth century. Two of his best-known songs, 'Dovró dunque morire?' and 'Amarilli mia bella', were actually included in Robert Dowland's *A musicall banquet* (1610) with the thorough-bass accompaniment realized for lute, probably by John Dowland himself.[78] Dowland was closer to the spirit of Italian monody than any other English

[75] The taking of the B.Mus., though it necessitated matriculation and membership of a College, in this case Christ Church, did not require residence or previous admission to the BA. The degree was probably not affected by the religious tests applicable to the BA and MA (see Wood, cited Poulton, 42), and consequently is not good evidence against his continued Roman Catholicism; though, again, his faith could have been disguised or laid aside in England, and university residence between 1582 and 1588 cannot be altogether ruled out.

[76] He became lutenist to Lord Howard de Walden after his return from Denmark, and was admired by, among others, Thomas Campion and Henry Peacham (see Poulton, 46, 71); he was also given tributes by Richard Barnfield and Francis Meres (ibid. 50–1).

[77] For an illuminating discussion, see R. H. Wells, 'The Ladder of Love', *Early Music*, 12 (1984), 173–89.

[78] The originals were printed in Caccini's *Le nuove musiche* (1602). This publication was imitated in the *Prime musiche nuove* (London, 1613), by Angelo Notari, a much inferior musician who was in the service of Prince Henry and Prince Charles, continuing with the latter after he became King in 1625. See I. Spink, 'Angelo Notari and his "Prime Musiche Nuove"', in *Monthly Musical Record*, 87 (1957), 168–77; P. J. Willetts, 'Autographs of Angelo Notari', *ML*, 50 (1969), 124–6.

composer at that date, as two of his three songs in the same collection
('Far from triumphing Court' and 'In darkness let me dwell') abundantly
testify. He deepened his understanding still further in *A pilgrimes solace* (1612);
but equally Italianate in many ways are his simple ayres and songs in dance-
rhythms. Some of these originated as instrumental pieces;[79] others were
subsequently arranged for lute or consort, or both. As an example of the
latter kind, from his first book (1597), we may cite 'My thoughts are winged
with hopes' (no. 3) for its immaculate adaptation of galliard rhythm to
a pretty poem by Sir Walter Ralegh (Ex. 159).[80]

Ex. 159

My thoughts are wing'd with hopes, my hopes with love.

Mount, Love, un - to the moon in clear - est night

Note: The vocal bass, given here in square brackets when it differs from the lute bass, may have
been used independently of the other voices (not shown here); and it may have been played or sung.

★ *f'* om 1597.

[79] e.g. 'If my complaints could passions move' from the first book (no. 4), arranged from a piece
for lute solo called 'Captain Digorie Piper's Galliard' (Poulton, 134–5, where the priority of the various
versions is discussed).

[80] Poulton, 223–4, confirming the priority of the vocal version and the authorship of the text. The
lute arrangement was called 'Sir John Souch his Galliard'. (Here and elsewhere in our examples, small
notes represent the separate bass part; if this was texted, as it was here, the words are given only
when ambiguity would otherwise result.)

The more serious songs of the first book—such as 'Go crystal tears' (no. 9), or 'All ye whom love or fortune hath betrayed' (no. 14)—do not stray outside the limits of the regularly constructed ayre, even if in solo performance they seem to call for a declamatory manner. In the second book (1600), in which a sombre mood predominates, there is a definite attempt, in such a song as 'Sorrow stay' (no. 3), to break the shackles of the ayre and to write what is in effect a deeply felt solo madrigal.[81] The most declamatory portion is in the first part, though paradoxically the very next phrase recalls the idiom of the mid-sixteenth-century part-song (Ex. 160, overleaf). The juxtaposition here is not altogether convincing, and the final section, with its extended repeat, is perhaps still unduly contrapuntal in conception (Ex. 161, p. 431).

This is the point at which to consider the scoring and performance of Dowland's songs. The title-page of his first book, in the flowery fashion of the time, reads: *The first booke of Songes or Ayres of foure partes with Tableture for the Lute: So made that all the partes together, or either of them seuerally may be song to the Lute, Orpherian, or Viol de gambo*. This cannot be taken literally: one would hardly want to sing (say) the altus, or even the cantus, with the bass viol alone. The obvious alternatives are to sing the ayres as part-songs, or as solo songs with lute accompaniment, with or without a bass viol playing from the vocal bass part.[82] The latter can hardly be regarded as compulsory, since earlier lute-songs seem to have done without it; but later examples of solo lute-song always have a textless bass part as well, and in the more elaborate songs it can play a quasi-essential role. In any case it adds a welcome firmness to the evanescent bass notes of the lute.

In the second book (1600) the songs are described as being 'of 2. 4. and 5. parts: With Tableture for the Lute or Orpherian, with the Violl de Gamba'. In fact the first eight songs (those 'of 2 parts') have a texted bass, which might indeed be sung as well as (or instead of) being played;

---

[81] This book also contains (no. 2) one of Dowland's most famous pieces, the song 'Flow my tears'. This originated as a lute pavan, 'Lachrimae', and was subsequently arranged for instrumental ensemble as the first of a set of seven pavans (see Ch. 8). The specially composed text, possibly by Dowland himself, calls for the repetition of the first two strains of the three-strain pavan, but is otherwise monostrophic (see Poulton, 255–8). Nos. 4–8 are completely monostrophic (nos. 6–8 are a tripartite cycle), without any musical repetition except to the same text. 'Sorrow stay' was arranged as a consort-song by William Wigthorpe.

[82] The orpherion (or more correctly the orpharion) was a wire-strung instrument of the bandora family, tuned like the lute (see *NGD*, ad loc.). It is not always clear whether the solo or part-song versions came first, though in most cases some awkwardness in the word-setting in the inner parts suggests that it was the former. The harmonies of the lute and vocal parts do not always coincide. Performance with lute and *vocal* bass accompaniment may have been common, as this is what is provided in several other publications. Most modern editions fail to cater for all the possibilities, though MB, vi, includes all the vocal parts of those songs by Dowland which are not merely solos. The solo versions of all his songs are in ELS, 1st ser.

Ex. 160

Note: The original vocal bass, given in square brackets where it differs from the lute bass, may have been played or sung.

numbers 9–20 have four texted parts in the manner of the first book,[83] while numbers 21–2 have five texted (or in the case of the dialogue with chorus, number 22, partially texted) parts of which the quinto, in the tenor clef, is marked 'For a treble Violl'.[84]

In the 'third and last' book (1603), 'newly composed to sing to the Lute, Orpharion or viols', the first four songs have a textless bass, while numbers 5–20 are again presented as four-part songs.[85] Number 21 is described as 'a dialogue for a base and meane Lute with five voices to sing thereto';[86] here the dialogue is between the 'Cantus prima' (*sic*) and 'Secunda pars', which are accompanied by the ordinary ('meane') and bass lutes in turn. The 'secunda pars' is also accompanied by the three lower parts without text, while for the final section all five voices sing together with text.

[83] MB, vi, nos. 22–33.   [84] Ibid., nos. 34–5.
[85] Ibid., nos. 36–51.   [86] Ibid., no. 52.

Ex. 161

but down,   down,   down,   down I fall,   down,

fall,   but down,   down,   down,   down, down,   down I fall,

and a - rise,   down, and a - rise

down, and a - rise,   down, and a - rise, a -

I   nev - er shall.

rise, a - rise, a - rise, a - rise, a - rise. I nev-er shall.

★ *F* in (vocal) bass.

In *A Pilgrimes Solace. Wherein is contained Musicall Harmonie of 3. 4. and 5. parts, to be sung and plaid with the Lute and Viols*, numbers 9–11 have instrumental cantus and bassus in addition to the vocal part and lute accompaniment. Numbers 1–8 and 12–18 are again presented as four-part vocal works in addition to the tablature, though in number 8 the four parts are simply a chorus to what is basically a solo song, the bass being textless until that point.[87] In *A Musicall Banquet*, finally, Dowland's three songs each have a bass, which is textless in the case of 'Far from triumphing Court' and 'In darkness let me dwell', the former being marked 'For one Voice onely to sing'.

The main impression is of a variety of possibilities, not all of which are discoverable from the modern editions. Viols might clearly be used in appropriate cases to double with or replace texted voice-parts; textless parts are purely instrumental. There is no particular reason why the lute should not be played with the fuller versions, provided that the occasional harmonic discrepancy is resolved. Above all, the retention of the vocal and/or instrumental bass is acoustically desirable and sometimes musically essential.

In his third book, Dowland reverted to a predominantly lighter tone; all but the final dialogue are strophically set, and there is little evidence of a declamatory style, even in the more serious numbers. But the *Pilgrimes Solace*, together with his contribution to *A Musicall Banquet*, exhibits his profoundest manner. 'In darkness let me dwell', from the latter, has a good claim to be considered his finest song, and as such one of the finest ever written. The final phrase, a repetition of the first, ending on an unresolved dominant chord, symbolizes the very depths of despair. But several of the *Pilgrimes Solace* songs approach it in expression. Of the three songs with instrumental cantus and bassus, 'Lasso vita mia' is a particularly noteworthy essay in the Italian monodic style, though the cantus part in particular is a hindrance to complete metrical freedom in performance. For Dowland a certain purely musical discipline was still a necessity. He amused himself by representing the syllables of his Italian text wherever possible by the equivalent in solmization (Ex. 162, pp. 433–4).

The very next song, 'In this trembling shadow', the first of a group of religious songs, deserves quotation for the sake of its fine contrapuntal argument, which makes it possible that, like some others, it was originally conceived as a part-song (Ex. 163, p. 435).[88]

Quite different are the dialogue and chorus 'Up merry mates', with its touch of comedy and its hint of a musico-dramatic expression new to England. The last two songs in the book are a pair: 'Welcome black

[87] Ibid., nos. 53–62, 63a–c, 64–5.
[88] Printed as such in MB, vi, no. 61.

Ex. 162

continued

Ex. 162, continued

mi fa so - frir

mil - le, mil - le mar - ti - re, mar - ti - re.

(viol)

Weary, my life makes me die . . . [love] makes me endure a thousand deaths.

   ★ No key-signature; *b″* flats are marked, *b′* flats are inferential.
   † Altus: no key-signature; remaining *b′* flats, after the first, are inferred.
   ‡ No key-signature; flats, where required, are marked or can be inferred. Divergencies from the lute bass are placed in square brackets and marked 'viol'.

night', technically a strophic song invoking the aid of Hymen to sanctify the delights of Love, is followed by 'Cease these false sports', in which her arrival is foreseen. The argument of the verse depends on the singing of the second stanza of the first song, though it is difficult to match with Dowland's setting, which gains considerably from its omission.[89] He has in any case treated the rather feeble text with the utmost seriousness, as though the approach of night were an invitation to melancholy rather than to love. The final section of the second song, however, expresses beautifully the sense of anticipation and marks his final farewell to song in print (Ex. 164, p. 436).

   [89] It has been suggested that these songs were written to celebrate the marriage of Lord Howard de Walden with the Lady Elizabeth Home in 1612. For the details, and the difficulties, see Poulton, 313–14.

Ex. 163

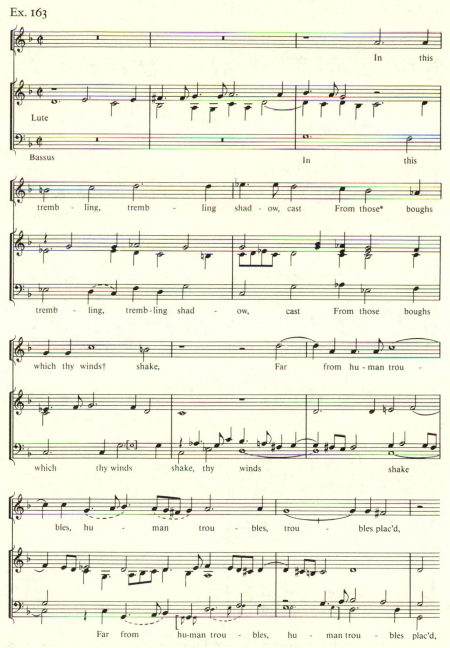

Note: Variants in the original (texted) bass are given (small) in square brackets; this may have been used independently of the altus and tenor parts (not shown here), and may have been sung or played.

★ ELS prints 'these'.   † In the voice part (followed by ELS) 'wings'.

Ex. 164

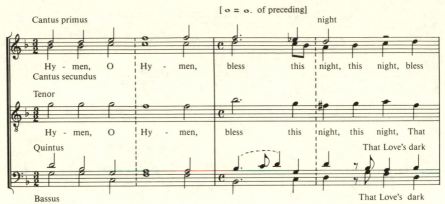

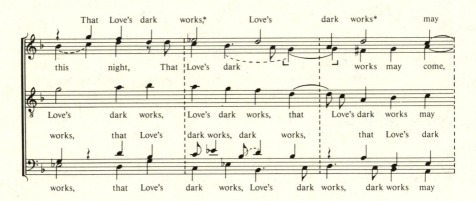

Note: The original lute accompaniment is omitted. The barring (other than editorial dotted barring) is from the original score for voice (i.e. cantus secundus, which takes the solo part in the verse) and lute. ⌐ ⌐ or ⌐ ⌐ = black semibreve in the original.

★ 'work' in orig. edn.   † *f* in orig. edn.

After the publication of Dowland's first book, English solo song polarized in two main directions: the polyphonically elaborate, usually serious song, and the short and simple 'ayre'. Of Dowland's contemporaries, Morley and Danyel cultivated chiefly the former, while Rosseter, Campion, Jones, Ford, Pilkington, and others concentrated on the latter. Of course there was much common ground between the two types, and some, like Dowland himself, were equally at ease in both. To these should be added a third tendency, towards a declamatory type of song, much influenced by the new Italian monody, from which contrapuntal elements in the accompaniment were gradually eliminated. The short ayre and the declamatory song (together with the associated genre of dialogue with or without chorus) became the basis of the baroque continuo-accompanied song in England. Songs came to be written out in score with only a bass-line for accompaniment from about 1610 onwards; and while this is at first likely to have been filled out by a lute or theorbo rather than by a keyboard instrument, the precise details of such an accompaniment ceased to be a concern of the more 'advanced' composers of that period. The major early figure in this development was Robert Johnson.

Morley's songbook of 1600, his last collection of secular music, well illustrates his meticulous approach to the craft of composition. It contains several fine and serious songs, such as 'I saw my lady weeping',[90] 'Who is it that this dark night', and 'Come, sorrow, come', this last being one of the most expressive examples of the entire epoch. There are also some attractive short songs, of which 'With my love my life was nestled', a setting of an allegorical poem by Robert Southwell on the outlawing of the Roman Catholic faith, has a particularly enchanting melody. The volume is famous, of course, for its setting of 'It was a lover and his lass', so often heard in a corrupt form. It used to be assumed without question that Morley had composed the music specially for the production of *As You Like It* around 1600; a more recent opinion is that Shakespeare borrowed a song already made popular by Morley's publication.[91] It seems impossible to decide the question with finality; the latter hypothesis seems the more probable, though it implies perhaps that fewer of 'Shakespeare's' songs are actually his than was once thought, even amongst those that are not obviously from the context quotations of older material.

In any event, Morley's song deserves close attention for its exquisite harmonies and its rhythmic subtlety. The only surviving copy of his book is incomplete (though two songs have been recovered from a manuscript giving only the treble and the bass), and we are left with but a glimpse of his genius in this area.

[90] This poem is a slightly corrupt version of the first song in Dowland's second book, where three stanzas are given.

[91] The song may of course have been current prior to publication.

John Danyel's *Songs for the Lute Viol and Voice* (1606)[92] represent the first tendency noted above in an extreme form. He too could write relatively straightforward songs ('Why canst thou not', 'I die whenas I do not see'), though even in these a contrapuntal element can be detected. But the most typical expression of his manner is to be found in two 'madrigalian' cycles, *Mrs M.E. her Funerall teares for the death of her husband* (nos. 9–11) and 'Can doleful notes', the latter to a poem of vivid musical imagery:

I   Can doleful notes to measur'd accents set
    Express unmeasured griefs which time forget?
II No, let chromatic tunes, harsh without ground,
    Be sullen music for a tuneless heart;
    Chromatic tunes most like my passions sound,
    As if combin'd to bear their falling part.
III Uncertain certain turns, of thoughts forecast,
    Bring back the same, then die, and dying last.

The poem is commonplace and its musical illustration largely predictable; yet the overall effect is greatly enhanced by Danyel's sense of form and technical discipline. The final bars are a good illustration of his ability to build up tension over a prolonged dominant pedal, giving the final tonic a deeply consolatory effect (Ex. 165).

The *Funerall teares* are if anything still more richly expressive, and the whole volume is a remarkable testimony to a master whose output was small and whose music has never been widely known.[93]

The declared opposition to this kind of song was spearheaded by Philip Rosseter and Thomas Campion in their joint publication of 1601,[94] the preface to which (almost certainly written by Campion himself) is a sort of manifesto against contrapuntal elaboration and preludes for the lute alone. Rosseter and Campion did not provide four-part versions of their songs in this instance. But already in 1600 Robert Jones had published a first collection of mainly simple and homophonic ayres, with a title-page and disposition closely modelled on Dowland's first book; that is, every ayre was furnished with a four-part version, and the various possibilities were described in the ambiguous terms already noted. Future practice was inconsistent, but on the whole it was the homophonic ayre that lent itself best to part-song treatment.

[92] ELS, II/viii.

[93] John Danyel was a brother of the poet Samuel Daniel (as his name is usually spelt), and took over his court appointment on his death in 1618. John himself died in 1625 or later.

[94] ELS, I/iv, xiii (Campion) and viii, ix (Rosseter). Campion's own first and second books, formerly ELS, II/i–ii, have been newly edited (see Bibliography); the third is in ELS, II/x, while the fourth remains unpublished except in facsimile. See also *Collected English Lutenist Partsongs*, ed. D. Greer, i. 90–216. There are editions of his literary work by P. Vivian (Oxford, 1909) and W. R. Davis (London, 1969, with some musical transcriptions).

Ex. 165

Campion's own qualities have sometimes been underrated,[95] especially by comparing his music unfavourably with his verse, where his mastery is obvious. But whereas the perfection, on a small scale, of the best of Rosseter, Jones, Ford, and Pilkington, may be readily conceded, there was in Campion a searching quality which, if it sometimes resulted in an ungainly phrase, more often gave rise to unexpected subtleties of expression. In Campion's songs, the second and subsequent stanzas invariably fit the music like a glove—for the very good reason that they were written precisely with that in mind.

Campion's intellectual standing was unique amongst English composers of this period. He published two volumes of Latin verse (in 1595 and 1619),

[95] e.g. in P. Warlock, *The English Ayre* (London, 1926), 105.

Observations in the Art of English Poesie (1602), and a large quantity of lyric verse, mostly in his own five songbooks but also in other collections such as the various descriptions of masques to which he contributed and in the songbooks of Coprario (*Songs of Mourning*, 1613), and, conceivably, Rosseter. He also published a musical treatise, *A New Way of Making Fowre Parts in Counter-point* (*c.*1613), which in turn is closely related to John Coprario's manuscript *Rules How to Compose*[96] of about the same date. Both are noteworthy for their harmonic conception of music in parts; and Campion's treatise secured a new lease of life when incorporated into the second and subsequent editions of John Playford's *A Breefe Introduction to the Skill of Musick*.[97] It was indeed the chief instructional manual of its kind in England until it was replaced in the twelfth edition of the *Brief Introduction* by one by Purcell himself.

Campion's *Observations* were devoted to the application of classical metrics in English prosody, though he differed in his approach from earlier occasional 'classicists' such as Sidney, Spenser, and Spenser's tutor Gabriel Harvey. His attack on rhyme drew a protest from Samuel Daniel, brother of the composer. But curiously enough Campion hardly ever forsook rhyme in his own lyrics, whether in favour of classical metres or for any other reason. One exception is the last song of his first book, 'Come let us sound with melody', written in Sapphic metre to a musical setting in which the quantities are strictly observed. This kind of thing is very similar to the *musique mesurée* cultivated by Claude Lejeune and others, setting the *vers mesurés à l'antique* of Jean Antoine de Baïf and his followers of the *Académie de poésie et de musique* (founded in 1570). Campion must have heard of these experiments and may have admired them, but he was too much of a realist to make them the basis of his own lyric art.

Campion's true achievement was to forge a new relationship between the 'words' and the 'notes':[98] 'to couple my Words and Notes lovingly together', as he puts it in the preface to his *Two Books of Ayres* (*c.*1613). It is not simply that the musical settings are appropriate to the verbal texts; it is that neither is complete without the other; that although the poems may indeed be read with pleasure, their versification has as its final justifica-

---

[96] ed. in facsimile by M. F. Bukofzer (Los Angeles, 1952).

[97] This is the title of the 1st edn. (1654). The next edn. (1655) included Campion's treatise 'with large annotations' for the first time; but (lacking the word 'brief' in the title) it seems not to have been taken account of in the subsequent enumeration of editions. The next edn., the 'true' 2nd, lacked Campion's treatise; but it was included in the 3rd (1660, repr. 1662), 4th (1664, repr. 1666, 1667, 1670), 6th (1672), 7th (1674), and 8th (1679); in the 10th (1683) and 11th (1687) a compilation by Playford himself was substituted. The 5th and 9th editions are unrecorded.

[98] On Campion see the publications of Warlock (1926), Kastendieck (1962), and Pattison (1948); Greer in *LSJ*, 9 (1967), 7–16; and C. Wilson, *Words and Notes Coupled Lovingly Together: Thomas Campion, A Critical Study* (New York, 1989).

tion a premeditated melodic and indeed harmonic content by means of which alone full aesthetic satisfaction is given. Only a composer who was also a poet could achieve such a union, as he himself says; and it is on these terms that his work should be judged.

Campion's first songbook was included in a double volume published jointly with his friend Philip Rosseter; thereafter he cultivated the double volume on his own account with the *Two Bookes of Ayres*, *c.*1613, and *The Third and Fourth Booke of Ayres*, *c.*1617. In effect, therefore, Campion published the equivalent of five 'normal' books: 116 songs in all, together with three more from published collections of masque-music (though one of the three has music identical to that of an earlier song). It is a larger total than for any other writer of lute-songs, and while that is no guarantee of quality it is a symbol of commitment. A number of them survive in ornamented versions in manuscripts of continuo-song.

It is assumed that Campion wrote the unsigned preface to Rosseter's collection, in which he inveighs against contrapuntal accompaniment and undue length: 'What Epigrams are in Poetrie, the same are Ayres in musicke, then in their chiefe perfection when they are short and well seasoned.' Although Rosseter's name appears first on the title-page, Campion's songs come first in the volume, which he probably instigated. In this first book there are no four-part versions; all, however, have a textless bass to be played on the viol (which there is no reason to regard as optional). Though Rosseter's aesthetic is close to Campion's, his more natural musicianship is everywhere apparent, while Campion seems to strive for variety and for melodic and metrical ingenuity. There is nothing forced, however, about Campion's beautiful song 'Blame not my cheeks', where the melodic originality of the second part in no way interrupts the flow (Ex. 166, overleaf).

In his *Two Bookes of Ayres* (*c.*1613), Campion supplied part-song versions of all the songs except for the last one in each book. However, four of those in the first book, and all of those (except the last) in the second book are in three rather than in four parts, an arrangement unique in the lute-song books. It has been suggested that in many instances the part-song versions may have been composed first, though this cannot be proved. The first book contains 'Diuine and Morall Songs', including the still popular 'Never weather-beaten sail'; the second, 'Light Conceits of Louers'. In *The Third and Fourth Booke of Ayres* (*c.*1617), the part-song arrangement is abandoned once more, and the viol part stated to be an alternative to the lute or orpharion (though it is surely permissible to play both). Some of these later songs are concise in the extreme, as little as eight bars of four crotchets each (plus repetitions) in some instances. But many of them compress a great deal into their tiny space. One of the most beautiful, 'Shall I come sweet Love to thee' from the third book, will bear quotation together with part of the ornamented version from a later songbook

Ex. 166

Blame not my cheeks, though pale with love they be,
To cher - ish it that is dis - mayed by thee,

The kind - ly heat un - to my heart is flown,
Who art so cru - el and un - stead - fast grown:

For na - ture, called for by dis - tres - sed hearts,

Neg - lects and quite for - sakes the out - ward parts.

Note: Small notes in square brackets represent the original untexted bass (i.e. 'viol') part where it differs from that of the lute. In bars 4 and 8 it takes the upper note including the rest (the rests being bracketed because only inferential as regards the lute part).

(Ex. 167, pp. 444–5).[99] Here the musically unexpected fourth line provides an element of tension that is released by the more animated setting of the final couplet (the shorter note-values being compensated for by verbal repetition). The ornamentation confirms a slow tempo for this deeply felt little song.

Of the other composers of lute-songs, Robert Jones comes closest to Campion in spirit. His five published books[100] contain 105 songs, some of them perhaps as with Dowland originally conceived as four-part ayres. The title-page of Jones's first book, indeed, is worded in exactly the same ambiguous way as that of Dowland's first book, and likewise gives all the songs in four-part versions. His later publications, however, are more explicit in their directions for performance. His particular contribution lay in the field of the vocal duet for high voices, though not the dramatic dialogue that was already being cultivated in the first decade of the new century. For a man of the theatre—he was, with Philip Rosseter and two others, a director of the Children of the Queen's Revels[101]—that is perhaps surprising, but Jones's talent was intrinsically a musical, not a dramatic or literary one. His interest was in sonority and in musical balance, as one might expect of a Bachelor of Music: the second book includes an alternative tablature for the lyra viol, a unique feature in the songbooks. At his best, he was capable of an exquisitely turned melody perfectly matched to its text (Ex. 168, pp. 446–7).[102]

Jones has occasionally been over-praised, or admired for the wrong reasons—the false relations so relished by Warlock are mostly misprints—but his output bears the marks of a sharply defined personality with a particular talent for lively musical characterization.

Jones must stand for many a minor figure, such as Cavendish (1598), Rosseter (1601, jointly with Campion), Pilkington (1605), and Ford (1607); all cultivated the short and simple, occasionally serious ayre, often with distinction. At a rather lower level stand Greaves (1604), Hume (1605, 1607), Bartlet (1606), Handford (1609), and Corkine (1610, 1612). Robert Dowland's *A Musicall Banquet* (1610) includes, in addition to the three fine songs by John Dowland already mentioned, excellent examples by Richard Martin, Robert Hales, Anthony Holborne, and Daniel Bacheler, as well

---

[99] London, Brit. Lib., Add. 29481, fo. 20ʳ. The version in ELS, II/x is disfigured by the halving of the note-values, and by an unacknowledged (and unnecessary) emendation in the 4th line of the tune.

[100] 1600, 1601, 1608 (*Ultimum Vale*), 1609 (*A Musicall Dreame*), and 1610 (*The Muses Gardin for Delights*): ELS, II/iv–vi, xiv–xv; cf. *Collected English Lutenist Partsongs*, i. 23–77, 145–73; ii. 46–89. He also published a set of madrigals (1607) and contributed to Leighton's *Teares* (1614).

[101] From 1610 until 1616, when the project for a new theatre fell foul of bourgeois sentiment. Warlock, *The English Ayre*, 81; *NGD*, ad loc.

[102] Book III, no. 2; the text is by Anthony Munday. Small notes show the untexted bassus, where this differs from the lute bass: in the former the repeat is written out in full.

Ex. 167

(a)

Shall I come, sweet love, to thee, When the even - ing beams are set? Shall I not ex - clud - ed be? Will you find no feign - ed let? Let me not for pi - ty more Tell the long, long hours, tell the long hours at your door.

Lute

Viol

(viol)

Ex. 167, continued

(b)

Shall I come, sweet love, to thee, When the

    ★ In the original edition the bars are placed after every two minims.

as Italian, French, and Spanish songs.[103] John Maynard's *The XII Wonders of the World* (1611) is a mere curiosity devoted to a series of character-sketches, and is of little musical interest. The collection by Mason and Earsden (1618) is a rare example of the music provided for a specific entertainment, in this case that of the King at Brougham Castle in 'Westmerland', though this particular one was devoid of dramatic action and possessed little musical substance. Finally, to round off the period, come the *Ayres* of John Attey (1622), the last genuine lutenist publication, and a traditional one cast in the mould of Dowland's first book.

Several of these publications were in fact of a composite nature, containing madrigals and/or instrumental music along with lute-songs in various scorings—such are those of Cavendish, Greaves, Hume, and Ford.[104]

Two composers stand out amid the general level, Alfonso Ferrabosco the younger and John Coprario. In Ferrabosco's *Ayres* (1609) a new note is sounded—that of the incipient continuo-song. It is sounded only tentatively, for the accompaniments are still laid out in the traditional way for lute and bass viol.[105] Moreover, although seven of the songs (counting the tripartite 'If all these cupids' as one) are actually from masques or (in one case) a play by Ben Jonson, the dramatic context neither calls for nor receives a declamatory style of vocal writing. More truly dramatic are the three dialogues with which the volume concludes, though even here the idiom is controlled by Renaissance polyphonic convention. The real novelty in these songs lies in those turns of phrase that defy analysis but bespeak the spirit of the baroque. It is curious that they should feature in the work of so accomplished a contrapuntist as Ferrabosco; yet in his first song, 'Fly

[103] Their composers include Caccini and 'Tesseir'; i.e. Guillaume Tessier (fl. *c.*1582), not the Charles Tessier whose *Premier livre de chansons* was published in London in 1597, though the two may well have been related. *NGD*, ad loc.

[104] Some of Hume's songs are accompanied by the lyra viol, an instrument of which he was particularly fond, and in one case by two lyra viols; all but one of these are given in ELS, II/xxi. But Hume's was a very slender talent.

[105] Some MS versions give a bass-line only. This is also the case with his three songs to Italian texts in Oxford, Bod. Lib., Tenbury MS 1018, ed. I. Spink in ELS, II/xix with other songs by Ferrabosco from MS sources. The Italian settings, though hardly comparable with those of the Italian monodists, deserve to be better known.

Ex. 168

Beau-ty sate bath-ing by a spring, Where fair-est shades did hide her, The winds blew calm, the birds did sing, The cool streams ran be-side her. My wan-ton thoughts en-tic'd my eye To see what was for-bid-den; But bit-ter me-mo-

Lute

Viol

Ex. 168, continued

ry cried 'fie', So vain de - lights were chid - den.

from the world', it is precisely the combination of technical control and expressive freedom that is so striking (Ex. 169, overleaf).

John Coprario, whose surname according to Anthony Wood was an Italianization of 'Cooper', was another rare spirit whose songs diverge sharply from popular notions of the lutenists' ayres. Like the younger Ferrabosco an admirable contrapuntist, his two published sets of 1606 and 1612, in memory of the Earl of Devonshire and Prince Henry respectively, contain duets and solos of a passionate gravity that finds no exact parallel in the songs of the period. 'When pale famine', from the latter, shows him profiting from a familiarity with the Italian monodic style, though Anthony Wood's account of an Italian sojourn is unconfirmed by documentary evidence (Ex. 170, p. 449).

This is a convenient point at which to discuss the music of the Elizabethan and Jacobean theatre, in which solo song played such a significant role. Mention has already been made of the Elizabethan choirboy plays and their music. Originally these were devised, by their choirmasters and others, for the edification of the boys themselves; but in the capital at least the performances of the most important choirs—those of St Paul's, Westminster Abbey, and the Chapel Royal—became popular as public entertainments. Eventually the 'Children of the Queen's Chapel' came to be organized as a quasi-professional company under a somewhat unscrupulous manager, one Henry Evans; they performed at the Blackfriars' theatre from 1596, and on the accession of James I in 1603 became known as the 'Children of the Queen's Revels' (i.e. of James's wife Anne of Denmark). After a succession of scandalous performances the company was suppressed in 1608, though the children continued to act elsewhere for a while.[106]

The importance of music in the choristers' plays is obvious, though the most striking thing about them is the length and sophistication of the plays

[106] The standard account of the choristers' plays is still that given by G. E. P. Arkwright in *PMA*, 40 (1913–14), 117–38. The Blackfriars' theatre was the refectory of the former Dominican house on the north bank of the Thames, furnished for theatrical use by Burbage in 1596.

Ex. 169

Fly from the world, O fly thou poor dis-tress'd,
Lute
Viol

Where thy dis-eas - ed soul in-fects thy soul; And where thy thoughts do mul - ti-ply un-rest.

themselves. The culmination of the tradition is to be seen in the three masterpieces written for them by Ben Jonson—*Cynthia's Revels* (1600), *The Poetaster* (1601), and *Epicoene*, this last performed in 1609 or 1610 at Whitefriars. The surviving songs[107] are simple enough, but they are to be seen as dramatic highlights in an evening characterized by an aura of music, from the three preliminary 'soundings' or introductory toccatas onwards. Much of this music will never be recovered; what remains is

[107] Ed. M. Chan, *Music in the Theatre of Ben Jonson* (Oxford, 1980), 59–60, 65–6. Henry Youll's setting of 'Slow, slow, fresh fount' in his *Canzonets to Three Voices* (1608: printed ibid. 50–3, the text from *Cynthia's Revels*) is less certainly connected with its play.

Ex. 170

When pale fam-ine fed on thee With her in-sa-tiate

Lute

Viol

jaws, When ci-vil broils set mur-ther free Con-temn-ing all thy laws,

When heav'n en-rag'd con-sum'd thee so With plagues that

none thy face could know,

enough to convey something of the rarefied atmosphere of these demanding entertainments.

With the choristers' plays may be classed other amateur or student productions: those of the schools, the universities, and the Inns of Court. They are all characterized by a dependence on classical history or mythology, or some comparably learned subject-matter; their music, if any, was often of minimal importance and is rarely recoverable. One final class of amateur production was the cycle of miracle plays, still occasionally to be seen in the Elizabethan period in a modified form, but soon to be suppressed for good. Their use of open-air stages provides a link with the habits of the professional adult companies.

These latter originated in the minstrel troupes of the royalty and greater nobility. Even in the Middle Ages, their entertainment could take a dramatic form. In the Tudor period, this consisted of 'interludes', 'merry' or 'moral', set pieces within the evening's festivities.[108] The players, their masters' 'servants', might take their performances to the public by playing on improvised stages in inns and elsewhere; but members of independent companies were regarded as vagabonds and were subject to the penalties appropriate to that class.[109] From the notion of the troupe as a nobleman's servants arose that of a theatre company under patronage; and this was the general rule throughout the Tudor and early Stuart periods. Burbage's great experiment of 1576—the formation of a completely independent company—was in advance of its time and succeeded only because it established itself outside the City's jurisdiction. It too sought and achieved the patronage of the Lord Chamberlain (Lord Hunsdon) around 1594, and in 1603 it became 'The King's Men', a fitting recognition of the finest company of its time, the one for which Shakespeare wrote, in which he acted, and which he partly owned.

Burbage himself built London's first purpose-built theatre—actually called the Theatre—in 1576 on land in the parish of St Leonard's, Shoreditch. Like its improvised predecessors it consisted of an open-air stage, but now surrounded by a roofed gallery, with quarters for the actors and their impedimenta and an open arena surrounding the stage on three sides. Others followed: the Curtain, the Rose, the Swan, and finally the Globe on the South Bank after the lease on the Theatre had expired. (It was destroyed by fire in 1613 but immediately replaced.) For the Globe Shakespeare's finest plays were written; but in 1608, on the suppression of the choristers' company, the King's Men took over Blackfriars, which Burbage had bought speculatively in 1596. This was an indoor theatre, and its use encouraged a greater intimacy in the drama, with obvious implications for its musical

---

[108] See above, Ch. 4, p. 266 and n. 201.
[109] See Woodfill, *Musicians in English Society*, 56–8. I have drawn extensively on this authoritative work in this chapter and the next.

potential. But the company continued to use the Globe as well, and their plays (both before and after the move to Blackfriars) were often put on at court too.

If the choirboys' and adult companies represent two distinct traditions of Elizabethan and Jacobean drama, masques and dramatic entertainments provide a third. These were associated primarily but not exclusively with the royal court; any great nobleman and even the lesser gentry might command similar entertainment, and the masque as a genre actually survived the closure of the public theatres and the collapse of the monarchy. The masque may be defined as a dramatic 'excuse' for the social dancing which invariably concluded it; but it was not the only semi-dramatic genre cultivated amongst royalty and the nobility. The subject comes most clearly into focus from a wide angle: the Jacobean masque at its most elaborate is the heir to a history of 'disguisings' and acts of homage from the early Tudor period onwards, and it is the near cousin of the many less highly formalized enactments of its own day.

The music provided for Elizabethan and Jacobean drama seems to have been governed by one overriding principle: that it should be consonant with the dramatic mode employed. This may seem an obvious point, but it would appear to rule out some musical usages that have become familiar since, for example in opera and above all ballad opera and its relatives. If for example the mode is realistic, the music (a song, let us suppose) will be believable in the context. It may be the spontaneous utterance of a principal character (as with Desdemona and the fragments of the Willow Song that she sings), or more or less extraneous to the action, as with 'It was a lover' (performed by two pages) in *As You Like It*, 'Orpheus with his lute' in *Henry VIII*, or the unnamed song with which Lucius attempts to keep Brutus awake in his tent.[110] In each case the accompaniment, or lack of it, is dictated by the dramatic context.[111] A further illustration may be afforded from the second act of *Cymbeline* (c.1609), for which a contemporary setting, almost certainly composed by Robert Johnson for the play itself, survives:

CLOTEN. I would this music would come: I am advised to give her music o' mornings; they say it will penetrate.

[Enter musicians]

---

[110] *Julius Caesar*, IV. iii. 264. Scholars generally refer to songs of which the text is not given as 'blank' songs; but sometimes, though not here, a title is given, and this may occasionally lead to the recovery of the music.

[111] The use of two pages in *As You Like It* probably implies that one will accompany the other; the boys who took parts like that of the woman in *Henry VIII*, or of Lucius in *Julius Caesar*, would have accompanied themselves, though mention of the use of the regal in the plays of Marston (as earlier in *Damon and Pithias*) suggests the possibility of a non-naturalistic accompaniment off-stage in such cases.

Come on; tune: if you can penetrate her with your fingering, so; we'll try with tongue, too: if none will do, let her remain; but I'll never give o'er. First, a very excellent good-conceited thing; after a wonderful sweet air, with admirable rich words to it,—and then let her consider.

It would seem that a purely instrumental piece should first be played, and only after that the 'song' for which the 1623 folio provides the text (Ex. 171),[112] after which:

CLOTEN. So, get you gone. If this penetrate, I will consider your music the better: if it do not, it is a vice in her ears; which horsehair and calves' guts, nor the voice of unpaved eunuch to boot, can never amend.

[*Exeunt Musicians*

A purely instrumental parallel occurs in Marlowe's *Tamburlaine*, part 2 (?1588):

ZENOCRATE. Some musicke, and my fit will cease my Lord.

[*They call musicke.*

TAM. Proud furie and intollerable fit,
   That dares torment the body of my Love [*etc.*]

[*The musicke sounds, and she dies.*

Here the music acts magically to release the soul from the body, but the mode of action remains realistic. Rather different is the position at the end of *The Winter's Tale*, where the 'statue' of Hermione is brought to life:

PAULINA.   It is requir'd
   You do awake your faith. Then all stand still
   Or those that think it is unlawful business
   I am about, let them depart.
LEONTES.   Proceed:
   No foot shall stir.
PAULINA. Music, awake her: strike!—   [*Music.*

Here the illusion is created of a supernatural event, and the music is part of the illusion.[113] The supernatural use of instrumental music is most readily associated with the tradition of dumb-shows and masques in plays from

[112] Ed. I. Spink in ELS, II/xvii (Johnson), no. 20, from Oxford, Bod. Lib., MS Don c.57, p. 78. The musical source does not set the complete stanza; the suggested repetition will serve to accommodate the missing portion. In the example, I have preserved several variants of the song MS as compared with that printed in the 1623 folio.
[113] As Chan points out, the music is 'played by Paulina's household musicians' (*Ben Jonson*, 317). Her deception, however, requires their identity to be concealed; the bystanders are taken in, at least to the end of the play, and the audience is at liberty to suspend its disbelief in sympathy. Chan has much valuable comment on the role of music in this play and in *The Tempest*, 308–31.

Ex. 171

Hark!   hark!   hark! hark! the   lark   at heav'n gate   sings,
[His steeds to   wa - ter   at those   springs,

at   heav'n   gate   sings,   And   Phoe - bus   'gins   to   rise.
at   those   springs,   on   chal - ic'd   flow'rs   that   lies;

The   wink - ing   Ma - ry - buds be - gin   To   ope   their   gold - en
And]

eyes;   With   ev' - ry - thing that   pret - ty is, My   la - dy sweet, a-

rise,   a - rise,   a - rise,   my   la - dy   sweet, a - rise.

★ Orig. not.

Har - - ke

Gorboduc (1561) onwards, culminating in the memorable instances in *Macbeth* and *The Tempest*.[114]

The use of music in supernatural scenes approaches the conventions of opera, and has often been seen in that light, although it is not necessarily 'unrealistic' for spirits, let us say, to sing. But realism is itself a relative concept in the theatre, and, the supernatural aside, we may think of a graded series of departures from pure realism, from ordinary prose discourse, through blank verse and soliloquy, to the use of song as a medium of dramatic expression. This last, indeed, is the mode of opera, which in its early history is nothing but the continuous use of this medium. It was in the masque that the early operatic ideal of continuous song was most nearly approached: completely so in the case of Jonson's *Lovers made men* (1617), if we are to believe the note in the 1640 edition that the text was set throughout in recitative by Nicholas Lanier. But with this doubtful exception, dramatic song was restricted to moments of heightened emotion or dramatic stasis, or both, like the arias of *opera seria* at a later date. Seen in this light, it was an effective resource; as in the 'straight' theatre, however, there was always a temptation to introduce song without due regard for its dramatic appropriateness, and in the course of the seventeenth century this was often violated.

The Stuart masque was, like its Tudor predecessor, an ambivalent form, shifting uneasily between high-minded dramatic allegory and the requirements of courtly entertainment.[115] As far as the music is concerned, the principle of 'dramatic consonance' still applies, but with the reservation that much of the entertainment might be only tenuously dramatic if at all. On the whole we might distinguish between three levels: the truly dramatic, in which professional actors played specific parts, and in which the use of music corresponded to that in the normal theatre; the emblematic, characterized by dances performed by noble masquers, and songs interspersed with and pertaining to them;[116] and the social, the 'revels' danced by the masquers and the ladies of the audience, and by members of the audience

---

[114] See Chan, 11–12. She points out that the use of 'hautboys' in *Macbeth* to welcome Duncan's arrival and the preparations for the banquet in Act I carries malevolent overtones; but there is a distinction between this and their *supernatural* use in the 'Show of eight Kings' in Act IV. The use of the same instruments in both contexts helps to relate the natural and the supernatural levels in the same dramatic action. Hautboys (i.e. oboes, but in a more primitive state of development and graded in size to form a consort) are also used supernaturally in *Hamlet* (III. ii. 145), in Middleton's *Hengist*, and in *Antony and Cleopatra* (IV. iii); in this last, supernatural music accompanies natural action. This does not violate the principle of 'consonance' mentioned above: the music provides a dramatically legitimate and effective illustration of the psychological state of the characters. A supernatural event may be witnessed by 'natural' characters (*The Tempest*, *Macbeth*, etc.); or their state of mind may be illustrated by aural means alone. See Sternfeld, *Music in Shakespearean Tragedy*, 214–26.

[115] For a résumé see Chan, *Ben Jonson*, 139–46.

[116] The degree of integration within the dramatic whole (as represented by our first two levels) naturally varied considerably.

with each other. In the Stuart period, the 'antimasque' was introduced: this was a grotesque scene performed as an introduction or interlude in marked contrast to the main allegorical action. Both might be described as dramatic; but the latter was followed by a series of emblematic dances and songs, symbolizing the overall 'conceit' of the masque and apostrophizing the monarch and his courtiers, and by the revels themselves. Finally, the audience would be recalled in a speech, and the entertainment would be concluded with a grand dance and song. Many variants of this scheme were possible, but its essentials were always preserved.

These three levels of presentation corresponded to the three areas of action: the stage with its scenery, the dancing place below and in front, and the main part of the hall in which the monarch and spectators were seated, and in which the revels were danced.[117] The musical element was far more elaborate than in the normal theatre, and the semi-dramatic character of much of it permitted a non-realistic disposition of the instrumentalists in full view of the audience. Surviving descriptions make it clear that our musical sources preserve only the skeleton of the richly scored originals, and also that large quantities of music have completely disappeared.

Masque-music survives in the musical appendices to two of Campion's printed 'descriptions' of masques, in printed collections such as the *Ayres* of Ferrabosco (1609) and Adson's *Courtly Masquing Ayres* (in five parts for instruments, published in 1621), and in manuscript part-books and song-collections, as well as in arrangements for keyboard and lute. Campion's masque for the marriage of Lord Hayes, solemnized at court on 6 January 1607, was printed in the same year with a musical appendix; of the seven songs in the masque, only two are given in their musical settings, together with three dances (with words added for domestic performance).[118] The instrumental resources were originally specified as follows: a 'consort of ten' consisting of 'Basse and Meane lutes, a Bandora, double Sackbutt, and an Harpsichord, with two treble Violins'; a contrasting group consisting of '9 Violins and three Lutes'; 'and to answere both the Consorts (as it were in a triangle) sixe Cornets, and sixe Chappell voyces ... in a place raised higher in respect of the pearcing sound of those Instruments'. The *Songe of transformation*, 'Night and *Diana* change', was performed by a total of forty-two musicians. It is difficult to recover, even in the imagination, the richness of such performances.

Other evidence suggests that the dances were normally performed as a five-part ensemble of 'violins' (members of the violin family), usually

---

[117] See the printed descriptions of Campion's masques, and the diagram in Davis's edn., p. 206.

[118] Ed. Davis, 203–30; songs in ELS, II/xxi, nos. 1–2, and in J. Sabol (ed.), *Songs and Dances for the Stuart Masque* (Providence, RI, 1959), nos. 2, 3. Of the four 'new dances' specified in the text, the first is identical to the song 'Move now with measured sound'; the other three were composed by Lupo and Giles.

with an accompaniment of assorted plucked instruments.[119] The most interesting collection of dances of the period consists of a treble and a bass
book, now bound together; they are either the sole survivors of a set of
five or, more probably, an enthusiast's record of the musical essentials,
to which an improvised 'filling' could be supplied.[120] The collection consists
mainly of pantomimic dances associated with the regular theatre and with
antimasques, and the lighter social dances used for the revels. The titles
usually reveal a dramatic origin, but they are not free from ambiguity,
and they have sometimes been interpreted incautiously.

Theatre songs of the Jacobean period were composed by such men as
Campion, Coprario, Ferrabosco, and Robert Johnson. Nicholas Lanier, John
Wilson, and Robert Ramsey, like Henry and William Lawes, were younger
men whose contribution fell mainly in the following reign. The surviving
theatre songs of Campion, Coprario, and Ferrabosco were printed with
the accompaniment written out in lute tablature, usually with a bass viol
part in addition; but several of Ferrabosco's survive also with only the bass-
line for accompaniment, as is the case also with many non-theatre songs
by Morley, Campion, and others. It is possible to exaggerate the distinction
between lute-song and continuo-song. Not all lute accompaniments were
contrapuntal in conception, and the essence of a chordal accompaniment
could often be perfectly well expressed by a bass-line and be realized from
it on a plucked stringed instrument. After about 1610, the continuo-song
became the more usual written form, though it was confined at first to
manuscript sources, while accompaniments in tablature continued to be
printed until 1622 at least.

The most distinguished exponent of the early continuo song was Robert
Johnson (c.1582–1633), a lutenist of the royal household. In the chaotic state
of manuscript preservation, texts and ascriptions are often doubtful, but
there is enough to demonstrate his progress from an early 'lutenist' idiom
to the most advanced declamatory techniques. Well over half of his fully
authenticated songs are from plays, and were in all likelihood written for
their first productions; if the conjectural ascriptions are added, the proportion
rises to over two-thirds. They include settings from Shakespeare's *Cymbeline*
(see Ex. 171 above), *The Winter's Tale*, and *The Tempest*, as well as from
plays by Beaumont and Fletcher, Webster, Jonson, and Middleton. Middleton's play was *The Witch*, produced by the King's Men around 1616, material
from which was also incorporated in revivals of Shakespeare's *Macbeth*.
Several dances from this play are extant, together with a song by John
Wilson, and Johnson's 'Come away, Hecate', a good example of dramatic

---

[119] See P. Holman, 'The English Royal Violin Consort in the 16th Century', *PRMA*, 109 (1982–3),
39–59.
[120] London, Brit. Lib., Add. 10444. The treble book is in the hand of Nicholas Lestrange.

Ex. 172

alternative forms of melodic line (transposed):

(a)

(variant bass extracted from lute part)

(b)

dialogue in the context of the adult theatre.[121] The genre is justified by the supernatural character of the text, though in *Macbeth* the piece is no more than an entertaining interlude.[122] Johnson's most impressive song is probably 'O let us howl some heavy note' from Webster's *The Duchess of Malfi* (*c*.1613), where the 'howling' is suggested by the remote key of F minor and the use of a striking false relation (Ex. 172, p. 457).[123] His most ambitious work, on the other hand, is the dramatic dialogue 'Charon, O Charon, come away', the text of which is not from any known play. This is a miniature cantata, the prototype of a whole genre of such things

Ex. 173

Cha - ron, oh Cha - ron, come a - way! Why dost thou let me call so long?
When time, thou know'st, for none will stay; In which thou dost me
dou - ble wrong. Ho!   ho!   What hast-y wight doth call?
[Charon]

---

[121] Ed. Spink from New York, Pub. Lib., MS Drexel 4175, in ELS, II/xvii, no. 22; fac. of the song from Cambridge, Fitzwilliam Mus., MS 52. d. 25 (the 'Bull' MS) in the Oxford Shakespeare *Macbeth*, ed. N. Brooke (Oxford, 1990), 230–1; J. Cutts (ed.), *Musique de Scène de la troupe de Shakespeare* (Paris, 1959), no. 6. Brooke (pp. 65–6) argues that the 'Hecate' material was introduced into *Macbeth* before being reused in *The Witch*.

[122] On the other hand the three-part dialogue 'Get you hence' (Spink, no. 23; Cutts, no. 9) from *The Winter's Tale* is 'realistic', at least as sung in the play: Autolycus chooses a 'merry ballad' to sing with Dorcas and Mopsa. But the surviving setting looks a bit too complex for the dramatic context, which suggests a popular tune simply harmonized.

[123] Spink, no. 14, based on New York, Pub. Lib., Drexel 4041/II, no. 26; Cutts, no. 22 (separate transcriptions from this MS, from Drexel 4175, no. 42, and from London, Brit. Lib., Add. 29481, ff. 5ᵛ–6ʳ, both anon., from which our extracts are respectively drawn). The alternative versions are written a tone higher (with a key-signature of one flat): the first is given a lute accompaniment (substantial divergences from the bass-line only are noted here); the second is a melodic line only, considerably ornamented. It is not impossible that the first alternative is closest to the song as originally written, though its very corrupt tablature cannot be relied on for the bass and inner harmony.

outside the theatre, and the nearest approach to the operatic mode at that
time (Ex. 173).[124]

In Johnson, the transition from Renaissance to baroque song is
accomplished, and the form poised to embark on its career as a fully dramatic
medium.

[124] Oxford, Bod. Lib., Tenbury 1018, fo. 7ᵛ; Cambridge, Fitzwilliam Museum, 52. d. 25, fo. 105ᵛ;
ed. Spink, no. 19.

8

INSTRUMENTAL MUSIC, 1575–1625: MUSICAL LIFE AND THOUGHT

INSTRUMENTAL music existed in great variety and profusion during this period, far exceeding in quantity the written survivals from the preceding thirty years when it had first emerged as a fully independent repertory. Solo lute and keyboard music were assiduously cultivated, the former for the first time as a sophisticated and self-sufficient art-form, the latter newly weaned from its liturgical dependence. In the field of chamber music, while the 'whole consort', especially of viols, retained its pre-eminence, there was much experiment with the artistic use of new media, particularly of various kinds of 'mixed' consorts and, in the reign of James I, the combination of a keyboard instrument (usually the organ) with others.

The consort of viols, with or without organ, was certainly the major ensemble medium of the period. The treble, tenor, and bass instruments were used singly, in pairs, or in groups of three to provide music in from two to seven parts, as they had done previously and were to do until the time of Purcell. But the supremacy was being challenged by other combinations such as the consort of violins. These instruments, made in treble, tenor, and bass sizes like the viols, seem to have reached England from Italy during the 1550s or perhaps even earlier:[1] they had four (at first three) strings, unfretted, and the two smaller members were held under the chin, not, like the treble viol, on the lap. In the Elizabethan drama *Gorboduc* (1562), the first act is preceded by a pantomime accompanied

---

[1] *The King's Musick*, 9 (1555). But the Italian musicians described there as 'violons' had appeared earlier, at the burial of Henry VIII, as 'vyolls'; and the nomenclature alternates in succeeding entries. The early history of the family is bedevilled by terminological confusions, and many uncertainties remain. D. D. Boyden, *The History of Violin Playing from its Origins to 1761* (London, 1965; repr. Oxford, 1990), 15–17; Holman in *PRMA*, 109 (1982–3), 39–59. A comprehensive study by Mr Holman is in preparation.

by a consort of violins;[2] and there are references to such consorts on the title-pages of publications by Holborne and Dowland. When the highest member of the family was intended, it was always specified as the 'treble violin', though of course the frequently found word 'treble' is ambiguous, perhaps designedly so. After the Restoration of Charles II we find the 'band of violins' used orchestrally in emulation of that of Louis XIV and conforming to its traditional tunings,[3] in which the strings of the bass instrument were B_1 flat, F, c, g. It is not altogether certain that these tunings were current in England during the Renaissance, and the practice of combining instruments from the violin and viol families may in any case have been widespread.

There were also consorts of wind instruments: 'flutes' (presumably recorders), hautboys, sackbuts with shawms or cornets, and so on. Their written repertories are small and their precise make-up not always certain, but as to their ubiquity, alone or in combination with instruments from other families, or in support of vocal ensembles, there can be no doubt.[4]

The standard mixed consort of the sixteenth and early seventeenth centuries consisted of a transverse flute (the Renaissance flute descending to g), the treble viol, cittern, lute, bandora, and bass viol.[5] The three plucked instruments provided a simultaneous ornamentation of the basic harmonies. Not only was this consort provided with music to play on its own (such as the 'lessons' of Morley and Rosseter); it could also be used to accompany voices, as in Alison's *Psalmes* of 1599 and Sir William Leighton's *Teares or Lamentations of a Sorrowful Soule* (1614).

A popular variant of the bass viol from the early seventeenth century onwards was the 'lyra viol', with a flatter bridge to facilitate the playing of chords. Its music was usually written in tablature, like that of the lute; it could be used on its own, or in twos or threes, or in combination with other instruments. The ordinary bass viol was also used on its own, either in ensembles for two or more (there is even a mid-sixteenth-century pavan for five 'basses'),[6] or alone for the purpose of playing 'divisions'.

In the sixteenth century it became usual to accompany consorts of viols

---

[2] Spelt 'violenze'; see E. H. Meyer, *Early English Chamber Music from the Middle Ages to Purcell* (London, 2nd edn., 1982), 139 (conjecturing 'viols' for 'violins', though unnecessarily); Chan, *Ben Jonson*, p. 11.

[3] These were first detailed by Philibert Jambe de Fer in his *Épitome musical*, 1556.

[4] Lists of royal musicians from the early 16th cent. on give a good idea of the recognized categories (*The King's Musick, passim*). Municipal records are another source (Woodfill, *Musicians in English Society, passim*), stage directions and theatrical records yet another. The second, third, and fourth acts of *Gorboduc* were introduced by consorts of cornets, flutes, and hautboys respectively, the fifth by drums and (transverse) flutes (Meyer, Chan, locc. citt.). Andrew Ashbee's *Records of English Court Music*, in course of publication, will eventually supersede Lafontaine, at least from 1603 on.

[5] See Plate IX. Sometimes the recorder and violin were substituted for the flute and treble viol respectively.

[6] London, Brit. Lib., Roy. App. 75, fo. 35^v; *Elizabethan Consort Music*, i. 173.

on the chamber organ; and a repertory of ensemble music for one or two viols, obbligato organ, and bass viol also sprang up. The novelties of the Caroline period will be considered in the following chapter, but the consort suite for violin, organ, and bass viol was already being cultivated in the reign of James I, by Coprario in particular.

The most versatile domestic keyboard instrument was the virginals: the term was used generically, as we do harpsichord, to mean any keyboard instrument in which the strings are plucked by quills attached to jacks. The larger instruments resembled the later harpsichord in shape, though the finest music of Byrd and Bull was written for a single-manual instrument with a range no wider than C–a''.[7] In the seventeenth century the compass was extended downwards to A_1. The smaller virginals was oblong in shape, the strings at right angles to the keys: the downward range usually extended no lower than c.[8] The chamber organ was a descendant of the older 'porta-tive' or regal (in England these names were given to instruments of the 'positive' type): a typical specification would have been stopped diapason, principal, fifteenth, two-rank mixture, and a reed stop.

Keyboard instruments were rivalled in popularity by the lute, which could be played from an easily learnt tablature and lent itself to song accom-paniment. The six-course Renaissance lute was enlarged by the addition of one or more bass courses which on certain instruments ran alongside the fingerboard and sounded only the one specific bass note to which they were tuned.[9] Apart from the bass lute (tuned a fourth lower than the standard 'treble' or 'mean' lute), there were also the orpharion (tuned as the lute and played with a plectrum), the cittern, the gittern, and the bandora, the last a lower-pitched instrument with wire strings.[10] All these instruments

---

[7] English instruments seem not to have employed the 'short octave', in which the apparent lowest note was E and the lowest six pitches (with the apparent note following in brackets) were distributed as follows: C (E) F (F) D (F♯) G (G) E (G♯) A (A) (etc.). The only English composers whose music necessitates this system were resident abroad.

[8] In other words a 'four-foot' virginal, on which music of extended lower range could be heard an octave higher. Distinctions of octave were not always considered important in Renaissance music—just as in solo song the male or female range might be equally valid—and on the organ a stop of 'four-foot pitch' could be used either as such or as an 'eight-foot stop' in music of limited lower range.

[9] These were known as 'theorbo-lutes'; the true theorbo was a larger, long-necked instrument constructed in the same way.

[10] For the orpharion, see Ch. 7, n. 82. The cittern, wire-strung and played with a plectrum, had a flat, or nearly flat, back, shallow sides and (usually) a longish neck in relation to its small body. 17th cent. instruments, like the one illustrated in Thomas Robinson's *New Citharen Lessons* (1609), might have as many as fourteen courses, seven fretted and seven free. Its name, originally 'citole' in England, may have been corrupted by analogy with 'gittern', the English name for the medieval and Renaissance guitar. The bandora was first explicitly written for in Barley's *A new booke of tabliture* (1596); the tuning was (G_1)–C–D–G–c–e–a. (It is not to be confused with the mandore, a kind of small lute. The nomenclature of the medieval ancestors of all these instruments has been satisfactorily elucidated once and for all by L. Wright, 'The Medieval gittern and citole: A case of mistaken identity', *GSJ*, 30 (1977), 8–42.)

could be used alone or in combination with other instruments or with voices; John Dowland even wrote a duet for two players on one lute.

The written repertories convey something, but not all, of the instrumental variety of the Elizabethan and Jacobean epochs. The oldest forms, those for 'whole' consort, were also the longest lasting and the most productive of purely musical invention. The discussion in Chapter 5 revealed a marked preference amongst mid-century composers for plainchant settings, the In nomine (or 'Gloria tibi trinitas') in particular. Dance music was still largely functional; abstract instrumental music was dominated by transcriptions of vocal music and exercises in mensuration or contrapuntal manipulation. This was the tradition inherited by Byrd.

Byrd's numerous consort hymns and Misereres[11] do not quite belong to this tradition, however; some of them may simply be the best of the juvenile exercises through which he learnt his craft, while others (such as the two rather similar three-verse sets for 'Christe qui lux') may be youthful liturgical works shorn of their texts. While they are scarcely ever less than competent, they have little further claim on our attention.

The In nomines are very different, for while they are all in their various ways derivative they show the budding composer gradually gaining confidence in his own individuality. In his fifth five-part In nomine, for example, while it is closely related to a similar work by Parsons, there is a fine sense of developing animation over a strongly controlled harmonic tread.[12] Indeed it was Byrd's appreciation of the role of harmony in overall design that enabled him to break free of the technical constraints that bound lesser men. This is still more evident in the freely composed fantasias, a form in which Byrd was the first to make substantial headway. His three- and four-part fantasias are mostly short and are not uniformly interesting;[13] but in one case at least, that of the delightful four-part work in G minor (later published by Byrd in his *Psalmes, Songs and Sonnets*, 1611, though probably composed around 1590), there are signs of the wider vocabulary of the five- and six-part works. In this case the tripartite structure, with a middle section devoted to the antiphonal treatment of homophonic phrases, was a fruitful development.

None of Byrd's five- and six-part consorts necessarily post-dates this four-part work, but the greater potential of the larger forces excited him to bolder and more resourceful experiment. Two of them, indeed, were based on existing themes: the five-part Prelude [and Ground] in F on a

---

[11] These, with Byrd's other, more idiomatic, consort music, are in *The Byrd Edition*, xvii.

[12] O. Neighbour, *The Consort and Keyboard Music of William Byrd* (London, 1978), 48. This masterly treatise is an essential companion to the repertories described in its title.

[13] Neighbour suspects the authenticity of nos. 4 and 5 *a* 4, and points out that no. 3 *a* 4 (single part only extant) is identical with 'In manus tuas' from *Gradualia I: Consort and Keyboard Music*, 88, 92.

tune known as 'Good night', and the fine Browning, also in five parts, to the widely popular melody 'The leaves be green'.[14] The five-part Fantasia in C incorporates a canon in its two upper voices throughout, and most effectively quotes another popular tune—'Sick, sick, and very sick'—as part of the canonic structure.[15] This is a more extended example of a tripartite structure, the middle section being written predominantly in triplets. The choice of canonic pitch-interval, the fourth above, means that sequential repetitions one note away in the canonic parts will tend to create cycles of fifths (real or implied); the time-interval of six minims tends to dictate the harmonic rhythm. The splendid transition into the third section illustrates these points (Ex. 174, pp. 465–6).

Of Byrd's six-part fantasias, the first is an immature piece in F, later reworked as a motet, 'Laudate pueri', and included in the *Cantiones Sacrae* of 1575, while the two others, both in G minor, are resourceful and imaginative works, probably of the 1580s. The second of these is the more serene and balanced, and may therefore be the later of the two as has been suggested;[16] the first is bold and confident in spite of a somewhat experimental note. It consists of a lengthy duple-time section, a galliard in three repeated strains, and a short but massive coda. There are signs that the coda and even the galliard were an afterthought,[17] the coda being needed, perhaps, to draw together the disparity created by the juxtaposition of the first and second sections. As for the first section itself, it is a complex structure in which an imitative opening is succeeded by a succession of more homophonic ideas treated antiphonally. This subsection is itself susceptible of a threefold division (marked by clear cadences), and moves at its climax to a statement of a familiar theme, 'Greensleeves', over its *romanesca* bass.[18] The bass is repeated with varied upper parts before the music plunges into the galliard (Ex. 175, p. 467).

There is a strong anticipation here of the later 'consort suite', a form consisting usually of a large (sometimes tripartite) fantasia, two dances, and a unifying coda. In the second G minor work, however, the tendency towards a differentiation between movements is sacrificed in favour of a more unified and, in Renaissance terms, more satisfying structure. Byrd also wrote a five-part pavan in C minor, later arranged for keyboard,[19]

[14] The words were nothing but a simple refrain to some longer poem that has not survived: 'The leaves be green, the nuts be brown, They hang so high, they will not come down.' Meyer (*Early English Chamber Music*, 112) notes consort settings by John Baldwin, Elway Bevin, Byrd, Parsons, Henry Stoninge, and Clement Woodcocke.

[15] Neighbour, *Consort and Keyboard Music*, 78.

[16] Neighbour, 86.

[17] Neighbour, 85.

[18] For the *romanesca* see Ch. 5, n. 154; and on Greensleeves in particular J. Ward, '"And Who But Ladie Greensleeues?"'

[19] *The Byrd Edition*, xvii, no. 14; keyboard version, from several sources, in MB, xxvii, no. 29a.

Ex. 174

continued

Ex. 174, continued

and a six-part pavan and galliard pair in which yet another popular tune, 'The woods so wild', seems to be paraphrased in the second section of the galliard.[20]

Byrd's immediate contemporaries did not remotely achieve his distinction as a composer of consort music. Two who might have done so—Robert Parsons and Robert White—died young and belong effectively to the preceding epoch, along with Tallis, Tye, and a host of lesser men whose art was nevertheless still cultivated by connoisseurs in the later sixteenth and even in the seventeenth century. A large collection carrying the date 1578[21] contains arrangements of Continental Latin motets, madrigals, and chansons alongside native fancies and plainsong settings. A much later set of part-books in the Bodleian Library[22] is devoted to In nomines by such figures as Tallis, Preston, Thorne, and others of the mid-century, alongside similar works by Gibbons, Ward, Bull, and Weelkes. Other, less eccentric, compilers formed mixed collections of fancies, In nomines, and other types of *cantus-*

[20] *The Byrd Edition*, xvii, no. 15.
[21] London, Brit. Lib., Add. 31390. See Ch. 5, n. 142.
[22] Mus. Sch. d. 212–16.

Ex. 175

firmus pieces or grounds (such as the Browning), but they often had to be content with a mediocre level of attainment.[23]

In marked contrast to this earnest cultivation of serious forms stand Anthony Holborne's *Pavans, Galliards, Almains* of 1599.[24] These are described on the title-page as being for 'viols, violins, or other Musicall Wind Instruments', a phrase presumably designed (with quite remarkable illogicality) to encourage players of any type of consort instrument to buy the collection. Most of the pieces (about two-thirds, in fact) survive in versions for lute, bandora, or cittern, or indeed for two or even all three of these instruments; and in some cases at least these may represent the original versions. But simple dance music of this kind could obviously be transferred readily from one medium to another, and a variety of whole consorts or indeed mixed consorts could have adapted the published version to their special needs. The possible social range of such music clearly extended from the politest circles (plucked solo instruments, consort of viols) to professional music-making including that of town and city waits (mixed consort, violins, and wind instruments). What is fascinating is the cultural unity of a society in which the same music could have such a wide appeal.

In Holborne's publication, pavans and galliards follow each other in alternation for the first 54 numbers, though in many cases a specific title ('Mens innovata', 'The funerals', 'Muy linda', 'My selfe', etc.) supersedes the generic indication. (The significance of such titles cannot normally be determined, though a few have been traced to poems by Spenser and to contemporary events.) While the detailed construction of these dances is in fact quite varied, the majority of them have three repeated strains in the standard fashion, and in a few at least they are of uniform length in the regular style favoured by Morley ('a straine they make to containe 8. 12. or 16. semibreues as they list ... and looke howe manie foures of semibreues, you put in the straine of your pavan, so many times six minimes must you put in the straine of your galliard').[25] In Holborne, this equation is not often maintained (the pavan–galliard pair, numbers 13–14, being a rare exception); nor is the galliard normally 'a kind of musicke we make out of the other' (as Morley puts it), a few brief melodic references, as in numbers 37–8, excepted; but the pairs are invariably unified as to key, and the collection as a whole is an invaluable paradigm of the late sixteenth-century genre, the principal English prototype of the baroque suite.

The publication is rounded off by six almains and five dances apparently intended as corantos. The former are perhaps recognizable as Morley's 'more

---

[23] Michael East and Richard Mico were two who, perhaps, stand out above the general level. Meyer, *Early English Chamber Music*, 195–6; much of the work discussed there, however, belongs to the following epoch.

[24] See the edition by B. Thomas (London, 1980).

[25] *A Plaine and Easie Introduction*, 181.

heauie dance than this' (the galliard) if one thinks of a minim beat, though lively enough if counted in crotchets, while the latter[26] are in quick 6/4 time with a good deal of hemiola (3/2); neither is as regular as Morley's description again implies, both having two or three strains of variable length.

Also published in 1599 was Morley's *First Booke of Consort Lessons* (reissued in 1611 with two extra pieces),[27] to which Philip Rosseter's *Lessons for Consort* (1609) is a pendant. These are for the standard mixed consort described above. There are also two slightly earlier manuscript collections: those known as the 'Walsingham consort books', compiled in 1588 for use in the household of Sir Francis Walsingham; and a set in the hand of Matthew Holmes of Oxford around 1595.[28] None of these sources is complete, and much of the music, to be playable at all, requires extensive supplementation, either from parallel sources if these are available, or else by the editor himself. Yet these are in some ways the most characteristic of all the specimens of Elizabethan consort music in existence. Their instrumentation is redolent of occasional music-making, whether in the theatre or in the hall. A well-known portrait of Sir Henry Unton (painted shortly after his death in 1596) shows such a consort playing at a sumptuous feast (see Plate IX). The manuscript sources include pavans, galliards, almains, and settings of well-known tunes; the Walsingham books include music by Alison, Daniel Bacheler,[29] and others; the Holmes books settings by Richard Reade, Richard Nicholson, and unnamed composers. A good deal of the music is arranged: a named composer might be either the original creator of the piece or its arranger, the latter even without the conventional formula 'set by . . .'.

The highly decorative writing, especially that for the lute, suggests a slowish tempo, and may perhaps serve as a warning against the over-hasty performance of nominally undecorated dance music of the period. That said, the delicate timbre of this kind of music makes it unsuitable for actual dancing and may be indicative of a more reflective approach to interpretation than would be otherwise called for. A short section of a famous pavan, 'Johnson's Delight' (variously ascribed to John, Richard, and Edward Johnson, and known also in versions for lute and solo keyboard), in which

---

[26] These are the 'short aeirs' of the title-page. Thomas considers them a type of galliard, but they are surely too sprightly for that. The volta is another possibility (ibid.).

[27] See the reconstruction by S. Beck (New York, 1959). For notice of two missing lute parts see *LSJ*, 4 (1962), 31.

[28] *Music for Mixed Consort*, ed. W. Edwards (MB, xl).

[29] This composer is considered to be the father, or other elder relative, of the well-known lutenist composer of the same name. One of the consort pieces is dated 1588, one year after the publication of a pictorial record of the funeral of Sir Philip Sidney, in which 'Daniell Batchiler' is shown as a small page on horseback; and this is presumed to represent the lutenist. See MB, xl, and *NGD*, s.v. 'Bacheler'.

all the parts are extant, will illustrate the characteristic scoring of this fascinating repertory (Ex. 176, pp. 471–3).[30]

The rather 'drab' quality (to borrow a term of literary criticism) of some sixteenth-century music for whole consort makes the vigorous survival of traditional forms in the Jacobean era a pleasant surprise. Beside Gibbons, Bull, Weelkes, Ward, Tomkins, Dowland, and some lesser practitioners in the established manner, stand the more adventurous Ferrabosco and Coprario, together with immigrants like Thomas Lupo, expatriates like Philips and Dering (their music preserved by the indefatigable Francis Tregian), and collectors of consort dances such as Adson, Brade, and Simpson.

Gibbons is at once the most traditional and the most refined and deeply considered of all these composers. His range is wide: fantasias for two, three, and four viols (some with the 'double bass' viol), In nomines for five viols, fantasias and other pieces for six.[31] Two of the four-part works have frequent tempo-changes, indicated by such words as 'Long' and 'Away'; at times their bold harmonic and melodic gestures seem to foreshadow the style of William Lawes. The same feeling crops up in the six-part fantasias, especially the first with its vivid contrasts and angular themes. The variations on 'Go from my window' are a masterpiece of classical counterpoint in the service of perpetual surprise. If there were no keyboard variations on it to raise our expectations we should be astonished at the composer's resourcefulness in dealing with this simple, square-cut theme.

Composers whose main strengths lay elsewhere must be passed over here, but a word should be spared for Tomkins, whose thirty-five extant works in this medium count as a major contribution. Particularly noteworthy are the seventeen pieces for various combinations of three viols, of which those for two trebles and bass provide an interesting hint of the coming baroque.[32] Lupo was another composer whose three-part writing was lively and adventurous.[33]

Dowland's *Lachrimae* pavans are in a class of their own, their intensity of expression unparalleled in the chamber music of the period. Published in 1604, they are described on the title-page as *Lachrimae, or Seaven Teares*

[30] *Music for Mixed Consort*, no. 13, from the Walsingham books; for other versions see the notes thereto.

[31] O. Gibbons, *Consort Music*, ed. J. Harper (MB, xlviii).

[32] I am grateful to Dr J. A. Irving for making his transcriptions available to me.

[33] E. Meyer, *Early English Chamber Music*, 143–9. For the Lupo family see *NGD*, ad loc. Coprario, Ravenscroft, and Ferrabosco are three further composers rightly singled out by Meyer: ibid. 149–53. See further *Jacobean Consort Music*, ed. R. T. Dart and W. Coates (MB, ix), and below, pp. 474–9.

Ex. 176

continued

Ex. 176, continued

Ex. 176, continued

figured in Seaven Passionate Pauans, with diuers other Pauans, Galiards, and Almands, set forth for the Lute, Viols, or Violons, in fiue parts.[34] This description of the forces involved as usual demands interpretation. These pieces could not be performed on the lute alone, and in most of them the lute part contains material which, if omitted from a performance on five-stringed instruments, would result in a serious impoverishment.[35]

Diana Poulton's eloquent characterization of the seven pavans deserves quotation:

The first part of the book, made up of the 'seaven teares', constitutes a prolonged expression of deeply-felt tragic emotion, only equalled in intensity among the secular compositions of the period by the very greatest examples of madrigalian art.

The first pavan, here called 'Lachrimae Antiquae', was arranged from a lute piece and had also appeared in the form of a song, 'Flow my tears'.[36] From this starting-point arose the remainder of the sequence, to which the quaint titles 'Lachrimae Antiquae Nouae', 'Lachrimae Gementes', 'Lachrimae Tristes', 'Lachrimae Coactae', 'Lachrimae Amantis', and 'Lachrimae Verae' were given. It is difficult to find adequate expression for the range and finesse of the emotions hinted at in this superficially monotonous but in fact well-varied collection. Though lacking even as much surface variety as Haydn's *Seven Last Words* (to which it offers a curious parallel), the collection must undoubtedly be thought of as a coherent whole, its thematic material being constantly transformed in a myriad subtle ways. What is perhaps missing is a sense of progression; the pieces might be played in any order, or a selection made, without a noticeable loss. But a complete performance in the published order is a richly rewarding experience all the same.

The seven *Lachrimae* do not exhaust Dowland's introspective vein, for the very next three pieces are all sombre pavans, the first the famous 'Semper Dowland semper dolens', originally for lute. Then follow nine galliards, many of them also arrangements, and two 'almands'. The composer's charm and versatility is nowhere more strikingly displayed than in this splendid anthology.

Amongst composers of lesser rank, Alfonso Ferrabosco the younger deserves mention as a master of the traditional polyphonic style. This mastery

---

[34] See the fac. edn. (Boethius Press), and the transcriptions by Warlock (1927) and Giesbert (seven pavans only, 1954). Full commentary in D. Poulton, *John Dowland*, 342–75.

[35] Poulton, ibid. 345–6.

[36] Cf. Poulton, 124–6.

is displayed not only in the skilful deployment of vigorously conceived melodic lines, but in the bold sweep of his harmonic and tonal conceptions. In the following passages, taken from the twelfth of a set of twenty four-part fantasias, we can see how the apparently innocent opening idea gives rise to a sequence of modulations that take us from F major as far afield as E major (Ex. 177, overleaf).[37]

This penchant for chromatic modulation is taken a stage further in two hexachordal works in which the six-note scale is presented on successive degrees of the chromatic scale, ascending from c' to g' in the first piece and descending in downward scales in the second.[38] Coprario, too, lent distinction to the traditional form, for example in a fantasia for five viols (accompanied as was now becoming usual on the organ) exploiting contrasted instrumental groupings (Ex. 178, pp. 477–8).[39] A few works of Peter Philips that crossed the Channel and are preserved in one of Francis Tregian's monumental anthologies show that he too kept in touch with English methods. The Pavan and Galliard 'Paggett' (which also exist for keyboard) and a six-part *passamezzo* pavan are especially memorable.[40]

Dance music forms a larger proportion of the Jacobean whole consort repertory than of the Elizabethan. Not all of it was intended for social dancing, the masque, or for public entertainment. Ferrabosco's 'Four-note Pavan', to which Ben Jonson wrote the poem 'Hear me O God', is as profound a work as any in a purely contrapuntal form (Ex. 179, p. 480).[41] But the printed collections preserve a more functional repertory. John Adson's *Courtly Masking Ayres for violins, consorts and cornets* (1611) put five-part flesh on the skeletal forms of dance music preserved (in one manuscript) only in treble and bass.[42] On the Continent, William Brade and Thomas Simpson issued anthologies of English dance music of the kind made

[37] London, Brit. Lib., Add. 29996, fos. 94ʳ–96ʳ (and other sources not here collated). There is a complete list of Ferrabosco's four-part fantasias in Meyer, *Die mehrstimmige Spielmusik des 17. Jahrhunderts in Nord- und Mitteleuropa* (Kassel, 1934); Add. 29996 contains twenty of them in score in the hand of Thomas Tomkins.

[38] *Jacobean Consort Music*, nos. 23 (*a 4*, descending) and 39 (*a 5*, descending). Both works (i.e. with ascending and descending hexachords respectively) exist in both four- and five-part versions and should obviously be performed as a pair in one or other version.

[39] *Jacobean Consort Music*, no. 36, bars 1–12, 40–end (organ part omitted).

[40] *Jacobean Consort Music*, nos. 71, 90. On the *passamezzo antico*, see *The Dublin Virginal Manuscript*, ed. J. Ward, 40, and pp. 342–3 above.

[41] *Jacobean Consort Music*, no. 63; it is preceded by a similar work by Daniel Farrant.

[42] Woodfill, *Musicians in English Society*, 51; there was a 2nd edn. in 1621 or 1622. One piece given in *Jacobean Consort Music*, no. 54. Of the 31 pieces, 21 are five-part, 10 six-part; three of the five-part works are designated 'for sackbuts and cornets'. London, Brit. Lib., Add. 10444, consists of the treble and bass part-books of an extensive series of dances for stage works: there may originally have been three further books for the inner parts.

Ex. 177

(a)

(b)

Ex. 178

(a)

continued

Ex. 178, continued

fashionable through diplomatic contacts between England and Germany.[43] And hidden amongst the extensive manuscript compilations of the period lie innumerable dances of a lighter character, their titles, as with Tregian's own 'Balla d'amore', in ten contrasting sections, hinting at some social context that can often be only guessed at.[44]

The most important new development of the period was the emergence of the consort suite, or 'fantasia-suite', as it has been called. The terms are modern: the word 'suite' was not used in England at this period, though 'set' came to be used both for single unified works as well as for groups of works (such as a pair of suites in the same key). The consort suite seems to have been the invention of John Coprario, who scored them for one or two violins, organ, and bass viol. There are sixteen works for one violin (the last surviving only as an organ part), and eight for two. While consort music of this kind was in great repute at the court of Charles I, and while it is known that Coprario was involved with Charles's music from 1622 at least (when Charles was still Prince of Wales), this music is essentially of Jacobean inspiration. Coprario died in 1626, one year after being appointed composer-in-ordinary to Charles, and was in his prime during the second decade of the century. The peculiar form and instrumental texture of these works is more likely to have been a response to the composer's own searching intellect than to the specific needs of a royal patron, and their conception and composition must have occupied him over a lengthy period. Their introspection and formal discipline may well have appealed to the most artistically minded of all our monarchs, but it does not follow from that that he had any hand in their devising.

Each of these splendid works[45] consists of a lengthy fantasia (which may itself be tripartite in structure), an almain, and a galliard, usually concluding with a short coda in duple time. The form, which owes nothing to the early baroque suite, such as it was, or to such units as the interrelated pavan and galliard, proved durable in England, and was extended to other media; but for Coprario it was confined to the ensemble just described.

[43] Brade, *Newe ausserlesene Paduanen, Galliarden*, [a 5] (Hamburg, 1609); *Newe ausserlesene Paduanen und Galliarden . . .* [a 6] (Hamburg, 1614); *Newe ausserlesene liebliche Branden . . .* [a 5] (Hamburg and Lübeck, 1617); *Newe lustige Volten . . .* [a 5] (Berlin, 1621). Simpson (ed. and comp.), *Opusculum newer Pavanen . . .* [a 5] (Frankfurt, 1610); *Opus newer Paduanen . . .* [a 5] (Frankfurt, 1611 [lost]; 2nd edn., Hamburg, 1617); *Taffel-Consort* [a 4] (Hamburg, 1621). Brade also published a volume in Antwerp, and there are miscellaneous minor sources for both composers. Modern publication has been sporadic, but there are editions of Simpson by H. Mönkemeyer (Wilhelmshaven, 1962) and of both composers in *Jacobean Consort Music*; see also B. Engelke, *Musik und Musiker* (Breslau, 1930); A. Moser, *Geschichte des Violinspiels* (2nd edn., Berlin, 1966) (for Brade); G. Oberst, *Englische Orchestersuiten* (Wolfenbüttel, 1929) (11 pieces by Simpson); and above all for the whole sphere of musical links between England and Germany at this period, W. Braun, *Britannia abundans* (Tutzing, 1977).

[44] *Jacobean Consort Music*, no. 74. The city and municipal waits may often have been called upon to provide consort music of all kinds: see Woodfill, *Musicians in English Society*, 85–7.

[45] Ed. R. Charteris (MB, xlvi). See also Charteris, *John Coprario: A Thematic Catalogue of his Music* (New York, 1977).

Ex. 179

The organ plays a partly independent, partly harmonic, role; in the latter case with a good deal of doubling of the violin parts. Later composers, and in particular Coprario's pupil William Lawes, were to make more of this medium, both in the virtuosity of their string-writing and in the independence of their organ parts; but to Coprario belongs the honour of the invention, to which he applied his special brand of courtly gravity.

Alfonso Ferrabosco published his lessons for one, two, and three lyra viols in 1609, and there are comparable works in the publications of William

Corkine and Tobias Hume.[46] The combination of two or more lyra viols, alone or with other instruments (such as the violin and bass viol), results in a sound of incomparable richness such as can only be guessed at from printed transcriptions (the original notation being in tablature). Their wide range permits a constant interweaving of melodic lines and exchange of harmonic function. Nevertheless, splendid though some of this music is, the repertory reached its apogee in the following epoch.

The lute and other plucked instruments were frequently heard in combination with voices and with other instruments; they also, and the lute in particular, commanded a large solo repertory. The virtuoso composers of the day, chief among them John Dowland, inhabited a different world from the amateur strummers whose resources they adopted and transformed. True, virtuosity on the lute was no new thing, but the emergence of a sophisticated written repertory was indeed a novelty of the period in England, an era of lute music to which the name 'golden age' has been aptly applied. The lutenist who had thoroughly mastered his instrument had at his command an expressive range second to none, in spite of its low dynamic level. The latter, indeed, added to the effect of the performance by guaranteeing an intimacy that lent it a unique charm.

The lute sources of the sixteenth century, even towards the end, give little hint of the new exploitation of the medium that was certainly under way by the 1580s. The Ballet and Dallis lute-books[47] contain simple dances and song arrangements. As in the case of solo song, the genius of Dowland gives the impression of a sudden flowering. Most of his predecessors retain their merited anonymity; yet it was out of such unpromising materials that his art came to fruition.[48] It was nourished abroad, particularly in Italy and in Germany, where his later fame was considerable; yet in spite even of his long sojourn in Denmark it remains wholly English in character. The elder Ferrabosco was one source of a new sophistication.[49] The large output of Anthony Holborne well illustrates the functional level of much of this repertory, as also the cultivation of the cittern and bandora in addition to the lute.[50] There are also numerous examples of music for plucked

---

[46] Examples in *Jacobean Consort Music*, nos. 110–32.

[47] See Ch. 5, n. 131.

[48] One composer whose merits deserve to be investigated more thoroughly is John Johnson (d. 1594), father of Robert Johnson; his 'Delight Pavan' was cited above in an arrangement for mixed consort (Ex. 176).

[49] His lute music ed. N. North, 2 vols. (Oxford, 1979) (Music for the Lute, viii/1–2).

[50] Ed. M. Kanazawa as the first two volumes of a projected *Complete Works* (Harvard Publications in Music, i, v; Cambridge, Mass., 1967–). There are now numerous facsimile editions of manuscript sources of solo lute music in the Boethius Press series Musical Sources. These are, in order of publication, *The Burwell Lute Tutor* (1974), *The Sampson Lute Book* (1974), *The Mynshall Lute Book* (1975), *The Board Lute Book* (1976), *The Robarts Lute Book* (1978), *The Brogyntyn Lute Book* (1978), *The Willoughby Lute Book* (1978), *The Trumbell Lute Book* (1980), *The Marsh Lute Book* (1981), *The Hirsch Lute Book* (1982), *Jane Pickeringe's Lute Book* (1985), and *The M. L. Lute Book* (1986).

instruments in combination, either with each other or with melodic instruments, or both. Music for such combinations stands at the threshold of the 'official' mixed-consort repertory already discussed.[51]

As a composer of music for the lute, John Dowland towers above his contemporaries. Both in quantity and in quality he far excels even his nearest rivals, Daniel Bacheler and Francis Cutting. In stature he can be compared only with Byrd; yet his nature is more akin to that of the next generation of virginalists—Bull in particular, with whom he shares a Continental reputation, a penchant for virtuosity, and some technical features; and Gibbons and Tomkins, whose profoundest introspection he more than matches.

His lute music was first printed, without authority, in William Barley's *New Booke of Tabliture* (1596), and subsequently in his own song books and in his brother Robert Dowland's *Varietie of Lute-Lessons* (1610). Abroad it was published, though often in mangled versions, in Heidelberg, Utrecht, Cologne, Augsburg, Nuremberg, Strasbourg, Amsterdam, and (after his death) in Haarlem; it is preserved in over thirty manuscripts, English and foreign. Yet within a short time after his death it was virtually forgotten, the legend of his reputation alone remaining. Only in the present century has his true worth gradually been recognized, culminating in the splendid edition of his lute music now available.[52]

Dowland's most characteristic compositions are his fantasias (or fancies), pavans, and galliards. There are also some almains, corantos, variation-sets, and a few other pieces less readily classifiable. The fantasias and pavans enshrine his deepest thoughts; the galliards, with one or two exceptions unrelated to the pavans, are of an exquisite lightness of touch.

The first fantasia presents an unproblematical picture; but with the very next piece, 'Forlorn Hope Fancy', we are plunged into the composer's most 'melancholic' mood. The subject is the downward chromatic fourth (used also by Bull and Sweelinck, and by John Danyel in the *Chromatic Tunes* cycle discussed above, pp. 438–9, treated with the utmost gravity and freedom of harmonic resource (Ex. 180).[53] The next piece, entitled 'Farewell', uses the same theme ascending; but the true companion to this appears to be the anonymously preserved fantasia, no. 71, where the descending fourth appears in the same rhythm. No. 72, again anonymous, has yet another variety of chromatic fourth. No. 4, entitled 'Farewell' like no. 3, is an In nomine, gravely beautiful but without harmonic complexity.

Of the pavans, no. 8, 'Piper's Pavan', forms a pair with 'Captain Digorie Piper's Galliard' (no. 19), later used as a song, 'Can she excuse my wrongs?' Number 9 is the famous 'Semper Dowland semper dolens', but the most celebrated of these deeply moving works is of course 'Lachrimae' (no.

[51] See *Music for Mixed Consort*, p. xiii. There are examples by Holborne in the edition just cited.
[52] Ed. D. Poulton and B. Lam (London, 3rd edn., 1981).
[53] *Collected Lute Music*, no. 2.

Ex. 180

15), which again has its own slightly less distinguished galliard (no. 46). But it is difficult to award the palm in such a field, and the most affecting music is not necessarily that in a minor key. 'Sir John Langton's Pavan' (no. 14a), a revised version of an earlier work (no. 14), is highly ornate and in the major mode; yet it incorporates some of the composer's profoundest utterances, as in its second strain (Ex. 181, overleaf). The eight bars (breves) of such a passage are as far removed from the conventional dance as one could hope to get; yet their attraction lies precisely in the discipline exerted by the 'ideal' form that lies in the background—a discipline that permits so striking a harmonic route to the dominant key while insisting on the modulation itself. Incidentally, it is perhaps from such music as this that the French lutenists' idiom of the *grand siècle* took wing.

Dowland's galliards are relatively uncomplicated, with little use of

Ex. 181

hemiola. One of the best known, the 'Frog Galliard' (no. 23, used for the song 'Now, O now I needs must part'), may not even be by him; its rounded binary form is certainly not typical of the galliard form, and its nickname may be the result of some misconception that will never be penetrated. 'The Most High and Mighty Christianus the Fourth, King of Denmark, His Galliard' (no. 40) is a three-strain melody with three variations; the idiom is of an appropriately (and not unhumorously) high-and-mighty character.

Dowland's shorter works and sets of variations are scarcely ever without some charming turn of phrase that renders them memorable. The variations are not great structures of the kind that the virginalists sometimes attained; yet the best of them—'Walsingham', 'Loth to depart', and 'Robin', for instance—are imbued with such delicacy and refinement that their melodic material, fascinating to begin with, is invariably enhanced and transmuted into something precious. He was in truth a composer for all seasons, a solace to the melancholy and a companion to the cheerful.

It has been conjectured that most of Dowland's lute music was written by 1600 or shortly after; and much the same may be said of Francis Cutting, an obscure contemporary who as far as is known wrote only for the lute.

About forty works survive, mostly pavans and galliards (occasionally in paired sets). His work is solidly structured, with strong counterpoint and rigorously controlled ornamentation.[54] Daniel Bacheler, on the other hand, was a more adventurous composer, active in the reign of James I (it is probable that he is not to be identified with the 'Daniell Bachiler' of the Walsingham mixed-consort books, but rather with a younger man, who may have been the son or other younger relative of the former).[55] His music lacks the sheer textural richness that is so characteristic of Dowland; it is less cogent harmonically, but in some ways more allusive and subtle. One of his most attractive pieces is a set of variations on a song here called 'La (usually 'Une') jeune fillette', known in Germany as 'Ich ging einmal spazieren' and familiar in a later form as the choral 'Von Gott will ich nicht lassen'. A few bars of the theme and its first variation will illustrate its loose-limbed textures and contrapuntal freedom (Ex. 182, overleaf).

The lute music of Francis Pilkington—a priest and singing-man of Chester whose vocal music there is good cause to admire—is somewhat eccentric and amateurish, the persuasive advocacy of its editor notwithstanding.[56] Robert Johnson, on the other hand, was an innovative master of the first order. It is true that his principal claim to fame is in his vocal music and other music for plays and masques, and the man of the theatre may be discerned in his lively almains for solo lute; but he also cultivated the traditional forms, on which he impressed his strong personality. The tally of his surviving lute music is small, but it is of uniformly high quality.[57] The pavan in F minor, for example, is a quite remarkable piece of work, the subtlety of its structure enhanced by the idiomatic quality of the decorative repeats. The wonderfully plangent C minor pavan is if anything still freer: the old dance-pattern is cast in an irregular mould and on repetition is dissolved into a freely running embellishment that defies all constraint (Ex. 183, pp. 487–8).[58]

His almain 'To the Stump' is an unusual and vigorous piece of writing for a 'stump', a kind of theorbo-lute invented by Daniel Farrant; it had nine free running basses extending in modern notation down to E_1 flat.

The lute and its music are in many ways the epitome of Elizabethan and Jacobean culture. Its capacity for emotional expression over a wide range and at all levels of technical refinement made the lute uniquely popular

---

[54] *Selected Works for Lute*, ed. M. Long (Music for the Lute, ii; London, 1968).

[55] *Selected Works for Lute*, ed. M. Long (Music for the Lute, v; London, 1972). See n. 29.

[56] *Complete Works for Solo Lute*, ed. B. Jeffery (Music for the Lute, iii; London, 1970).

[57] *Complete Works for Solo Lute*, ed. A. Sundermann (Music for the Lute, iv; London, 1972). The edition is by no means complete, however; there are other pieces, for example, in *The Board Lute Book* (c.1620–30: see the Boethius Press facsimile).

[58] The text is, however, woefully corrupt, and some of the freedoms in the edition cited are more apparent than real. We have attempted a comparison of sources and some emendations.

Ex. 182

and a symbol of cultural unity in a diverse society. The repertory for keyboard instruments is much smaller: possibly as little as one-third of that for plucked instruments as was once claimed,[59] certainly no more than half. The church organ was in decline, its liturgical function severely reduced, so much so that in many places it was looked on as an unnecessary luxury at best, an unjustifiable frivolity at worst. The Jacobean liturgical revival had little impact on the written repertory for organ solo. At the level of domestic amusement, the virginals were harder than the lute to master, probably more expensive to buy, and certainly more troublesome to maintain, tune, and transport. Only at the level of professional courtly

---

[59] R. T. Dart in the introduction to Lumsden's *Anthology of English Lute Music* (London, 1954).

Ex. 183

continued

Ex. 183, continued

entertainment, and in providing personal satisfaction to the skilled practitioner, could keyboard instruments rival the lute.

That is not to say that there is not a great quantity of low-level keyboard music to hand—merely that there is less of it than for lute, and that on the whole it lacks the artistry both of the comparable lute repertory and of the larger keyboard works. Only in Bull, perhaps, and his disciple Giles Farnaby, does the keyboard trifle have the intrinsic value of their more ambitious pieces. Byrd wrote no trifles to speak of; those of Gibbons and Tomkins are rather sharply distinguished from their best work. Otherwise the survivals are by much lesser men.

Keyboard instruments, in spite of their greater power, could not rival the expressive qualities of the lute. But they were on the whole much better equipped to develop solid musical structures. Keyboard fantasias usually lack the subtlety and the improvisatory character of the best of those for lute, but they are often longer and more thoroughly contrapuntal. Plainchant settings are rare in the lute repertory, but they are a mainstay of the keyboard music of Bull and Tomkins at any rate, and of several lesser figures. Variations and grounds may be worked out at far greater length than would have been considered appropriate for the lute, and in the best examples their contrapuntal and formal planning is at an altogether more sophisticated level. Only in the stylized dance do the two repertories meet on potentially equal terms; and here it is the lute repertory that has the advantages of intimacy and flexibility.

English keyboard music of the 'golden age' may usefully be considered in the light of the genres just outlined. Plainsong settings and fugal forms make up one large group, variations and dances another. Lighter genres and miscellaneous pieces fall into the latter category.

Plainsong settings are a curious, and very English, offshoot of earlier liturgical practice. We have seen how Blytheman applied existing techniques to create a set of six non-liturgical settings of the antiphon 'Gloria tibi trinitas'.[60] To that tradition was added an element of contrapuntal severity derived from the consort In nomine, a genre, as we have seen, based on the same chant. Sometimes the figurative, sometimes the contrapuntal factor prevailed; in the best works they are intermingled.

The keyboard In nomine was developed to its highest point in the twelve surviving examples by John Bull.[61] In them rhythmic and figurative complexity reaches its peak, their decorative quality enhanced by a strong sense of musical continuity and development. It is not warm music; it is, rather, intellectually and emotionally somewhat forbidding, but supreme of its kind. In the Caroline epoch, the severity of the form was mitigated by Thomas Tomkins,[62] whose eight examples are more thoughtfully fashioned to combine melodic interest with brilliant virtuosity.

The In nomine was ideal in length for the demonstration of contrapuntal and decorative skill. Tallis might have inaugurated a tradition with his two huge settings of 'Felix namque';[63] but the plainchant was too long for practical purposes and his tour de force was not emulated. Shorter melodies, on the other hand, were much used, sometimes strung together to make miniature sets of two or three variations. The hymn 'Salvator mundi domine' was used like this by Bull; much commoner was the antiphon 'Miserere', of which several brilliant settings by Bull and Tomkins are extant. Some composers used this melody for pedagogic purposes, and in particular for the writing of canons. Little in the way of idiomatic keyboard writing, however, is to be expected from such treatment.

[60] Ch. 5, p. 340.
[61] Bull, *Keyboard Music*, i, ed. J. Steele and F. Cameron (MB, xiv), nos. 20–31.
[62] *Keyboard Music*, ed. S. Tuttle (MB, v).
[63] Mentioned above, pp. 318–20.

Another, more schematic type of *cantus firmus* was the hexachord, the first six notes of the major scale ('ut, re, mi, fa, sol, la') starting on C, F or G. Both kinds were cultivated by Bull, whose 'chromatic' setting (no. 17)[64] is an interesting counterpart to those for consort by Alfonso Ferrabosco the younger. The problem of reconciling fully chromatic keyboard music with what is known of contemporary systems of temperament is a difficult one, but whatever the actual sounds created by such music it is evident that seventeenth-century composers were not afraid of them. Bull's second hexachord piece (no. 18), a hair-raising essay with 23 statements, is rivalled only by that of Tomkins, 32 statements long, with a further 6 in an appendix and various sketches attached. Tomkins composed his work in stages, a habit to which he became increasingly prone in later life, and formal coherence is all but abandoned.

Such works are a half-way house to the freely composed fantasia (or fancy, fantasie, etc.). The name was given to a variety of types: arrangements or reworkings of vocal works (such as Bull's two pieces on Palestrina's madrigal 'Vestiva i colli'), programme music (such as John Mundy's naïve programmatic work beginning with 'Faire Wether'),[65] pedagogic pieces (often called Praeludium or the like), and independently conceived contrapuntal works. These last are obviously of superior interest, though the keyboard form took some time to come into its own. A comparatively early effort by Byrd (no. 13)[66] imitates the metrical structure of Tallis's second (and longer) 'Felix namque', though it is not based on any chant.[67] Some of Byrd's fantasias are based on earlier consort pieces, but there are also two or three wholly original works of high quality (e.g. nos. 46 in D minor, 62 and 63 in G). In general, Byrd likes to divide his work into definite sections, as in his consort fantasias, with a second section that may imitate antiphonal part-writing (Ex. 184).[68]

Quite different is Gibbons's rigorous approach. In his Fantasia for Double Organ (no. 7, the earliest surviving example for that medium), the Fantasia 'in gamut flatt' (no. 9), and in the great work revised for and contributed to *Parthenia* (no. 12), the emphasis is on contrapuntal continuity.[69] New themes are introduced, but the *modus operandi* remains unchanged as in

[64] Numbers in the text are those of the editions cited: in the case of Bull, nos. 1-61 are in *Keyboard Music*, i, while nos. 62-143 are in *Keyboard Music*, ii, ed. R. T. Dart (MB, xix).

[65] The *Fitzwilliam Virginal Book*, ed. J. A. Fuller-Maitland and W. B. Squire (Leipzig, 1899), no. 3.

[66] *Keyboard Music*, i (nos. 1-45), and ii (nos. 46-95), ed. A. Brown (MB, xxvii, xxviii).

[67] Another work related to Tallis's second 'Felix namque' is Tomkins's huge 'Offetary' (no. 21), based on the plainchant intonation throughout in the same transposition (to A *finalis*) as Tallis. Both Byrd's Fantasia and Tomkins's 'Offetary' imitate Tallis's use of cross-rhythms in the proportions 9:2 and 3:1 (or 3:2); and both are in A minor.

[68] *Keyboard Music*, ii, no. 46. This work begins with what looks like an allusion to the 'Salve regina' chant; his setting of the text was published in *Cantiones II* (1591), though there the chant is not used.

[69] References are to Gibbons, *Keyboard Music*, ed. G. Hendrie (MB, xx). Byrd did, of course, also write purely contrapuntal fantasias and similar works.

Ex. 184

a motet. In the work for double organ, left-hand solos to be played on the Great Organ (while the right hand continues on the Chaire Organ or *positif*) provide tonal contrast but do not disrupt the flow. The small number of truly independent fantasias by Bull includes a fine one on the 'chromatic fourth' idea noted above.[70]

Further development on these lines was not possible in the sphere of the keyboard fantasia, though in the Caroline period the voluntary for double organ continued where Gibbons had left off, gradually becoming more dependent on colour than counterpoint. The quieter type of verse and voluntary cultivated by Tomkins also continued to enhance the Anglican liturgy in the context of a greatly reduced role for the organ. It may be that Byrd, Bull, and Gibbons contributed their liveliest inventions to the service of the Chapel Royal: the playing of Gibbons in particular was much admired.[71] But deaths and departures put an end to that brilliant tradition around the year 1625.

Plainsong settings and fantasias were not confined to the organ, of course; nor was the organ exclusively a church instrument. But with keyboard variations and dances we come to the true domain of secular music for the virginals. Here Byrd is the unqualified master. His grounds and variation-sets occupied him for most of his composing career, ranging from comparatively

[70] *Keyboard Music*, i, no. 4, 'on a theme by Sweelinck', dated 15 Dec. 1621. No. 5, on a very similar theme, is less rewarding.

[71] He was described, in a posthumous account of a visit of French ambassadors to Westminster Abbey in 1624, as 'the best finger of that age'. Le Huray, *Music and the Reformation in England*, 166, citing J. Hacket, *Scrinia Reserata* (1692). Le Huray gives a good account of the Chapel Royal organists, ibid. 65–7.

crude efforts like the Hornpipe (no. 39, imitated from Hugh Aston's much earlier work) to sophisticated settings such as 'John come kiss me now' (no. 81), Gypsies' Round (no. 80), and 'O Mistress Mine', which apparently post-date *My Ladye Nevells Booke* (1591) since they are not in that comprehensive collection of his work. That of course is not a conclusive argument as to date (though in these cases the argument is backed up by stylistic indications), and in any case Byrd had achieved full maturity by 1591 as is shown by his superb confidence in handling variation form in such pieces as 'Walsingham', 'Sellenger's Round', 'The Maiden's Song', 'The Woods so Wild', and others. What is so striking is his concern for overall form: the care with which different figurations are introduced and replaced (often in the middle of a variation); the sense of progression from one variation to another, of needful contrast and repose; the handling of the melody itself and its transfer to different parts of the texture; the sense of climax and the addition of a short coda when the circumstances suggest it. In all these respects the 'Walsingham' variations are at the summit of his achievement. In later works an increased formalism and brilliance may sometimes be discerned, but he never exceeded the subtlety of these rather earlier sets.

Bull's 'Walsingham' variations, when placed beside those of Byrd, conveniently illustrate his strengths and his limitations. They are longer and more brilliant than Byrd's, and are not badly arranged; but they are lacking in genuine formal cohesion. Bull is more successful in less pretentious works, as in the three settings of 'Why ask you' (nos. 62–4) or 'Bonny Peg of Ramsey' (no. 75). Gibbons's few variation-sets are somewhat disfigured by their excessive elaboration; much the same applies to Tomkins's earlier sets, while 'Fortune my foe' is a ripe affair of his extreme old age (it is dated 4 July 1654), still unfinalized at his death.

Byrd's mastery of the dance forms was equally complete, but his peers approached him more closely here than elsewhere. If Byrd's 'Passamezzo' Pavan and Galliard (no. 2) are the supreme example of the *passamezzo antico* in England, then Bull's 'Quadran' Pavan and Galliard represent the *passamezzo moderno* at its highest point. Byrd's dozen or so mature pavan–galliard sets are remarkable for their lyrical warmth; those of Bull for their brilliance and posturing (even in such a work as the 'Melancholy' Pavan and Galliard). To Bull also belong a number of exquisite almains and corantos, where he exercised a lighter hand than Byrd himself. The pavans of Gibbons are of a wonderful austere gravity; but there is only one pavan–galliard set, the beautiful 'Lord Salisbury' (there are several separate galliards). Of Tomkins there are four or five sets and several separate dances, some of them late works as introspective as anything written in the golden age proper.

Amongst the close contemporaries of Bull and Gibbons, Morley and

Weelkes wrote small amounts of fine keyboard music.[72] Giles Farnaby, though a lesser musician, left a quantity of pieces that deserve a closer inspection.[73] It has been conjectured that he may have been a pupil of Bull, though he was only a few years younger. He was a joiner by trade and may have been involved with the making of keyboard instruments. In that sense he was an amateur, though his reputation was sufficient for his harmonized psalms to be incorporated into Este's psalter (1592), and later into that of Ravenscroft. In 1592 he also obtained the degree of Bachelor of Music from Oxford. His *Canzonets* were published in 1598, and sometime between 1625 and 1639 he compiled a complete harmonized psalter, dedicated to Dr Henry King, a prebendary of St Paul's. He died, if the identification is correct, in 1640.

Farnaby's more ambitious keyboard works often recall those of Bull in the brilliance of their writing. The eleven fantasias (one of which certainly and others possibly are ornamented transcriptions of vocal works) together with an immense Ground are ambitious and resourceful. Many of his dances are settings of lute and consort works by John and Robert Johnson, Dowland, Byrd, and others; and the apparently independent works exhibit a similar, occasionally rather mechanistic, ornamentation. The 'masks' are also probably all settings of masque-tunes by others—one at least is by Coprario. But Farnaby comes into his own in his lighter dances or genre pieces and sets of variations on popular tunes. He does not attempt the structural cohesion achieved by Byrd; but the variety of his embellishments, as with the best of the lutenists, is always pleasing and creates an effect analogous to that of viewing some object from several angles. In such pieces as 'Bonny sweet Robin' (which may be expanded from an earlier set by Bull), 'Daphne', 'Mal Sims', and 'Why ask you', the themes are enhanced rather than concealed by the delicate tracery with which they are overlaid. 'Giles Farnaby's Dream', 'His Rest', and 'His Humour' are a charming sequence of vignettes. Four pieces by his son Richard continue in the same vein.

Ben Cosyn is another composer who seems to have been associated with Bull and to have been influenced by his style, which he carries to extremes. He was organist first of Dulwich College (1622–4) and later of Charterhouse (from 1626); but his own virginal book, containing music by Bull, Gibbons, and himself, was completed by 1620;[74] and his index to a manuscript believed to be in Bull's hand, with many additions by Cosyn himself, is dated 1652. He died in 1653.[75] A few quiet contrapuntal

---

[72] Morley, ed. R. T. Dart (SBK, xii–xiii); Weelkes: *Keyboard Music in facsimile . . . with introduction and transcriptions*, ed. D. Hunter (Clifden, 1985).

[73] Giles and Richard Farnaby, *Keyboard Music*, ed. R. Marlow (MB, xxiv). See also *Elizabethan Keyboard Music*, ed. A. Brown (MB, lv).

[74] London, Brit. Lib., R. M. 24. l. 4

[75] The 'Bull' MS is in Paris, Bibl. nat., Fonds du Conservatoire, Réserve 1185. For the biography, including the date of burial, see D. Dawe, *Organists of the City of London*, 90.

works subscribed 'B.C.' may reflect the manner of Cosyn the organist.[76] But most of his music is of an ebullient virtuosity, peppered with ornament-signs which he freely added to the works of others as well. The 'Bull' manuscript may have been left in Cosyn's hands when Bull left England for the Low Countries in 1613: Cosyn filled the pages with works by himself and by the younger generation of Caroline composers.

Little need be said here of Bull's own personal life. By the time he came to leave England he had achieved the summit of the profession, and had become a Doctor of Music of both universities and Gresham Professor of Music at the Guildhall in the City of London. But his Roman Catholicism had apparently made life impossible in England; he fled first to Brussels, where he will have encountered Pieter Cornet and Peter Philips; and after a few years as organist of the royal chapel there he settled in Antwerp as cathedral organist from 1617 until his death in 1628. The keyboard music that he wrote on the Continent illustrates his adaptability: it includes fantasias on material of Continental origin, *alternatim* settings of the 'Salve regina', and settings of Dutch folk-tunes and carols.[77] But he must also have continued to play his 'English' works: they exerted a strong influence on Sweelinck at Amsterdam, and some of them are to be found in a collection of his and others' music made shortly after his death by one Guilelmus Messaus.[78]

Curiously enough Peter Philips himself, though exiled abroad from 1582 at the age of 21 or 22 and a noteworthy exponent of up-to-date styles of vocal music, retains a decidedly English character in his keyboard music. His pavans and galliards have an expressive richness that guarantees their central place in the repertory; and even the intabulations of works by Caccini, Lasso, and Marenzio have the organically controlled quality of the best kind of English decorative writing. After living in Italy and Antwerp, Philips eventually (in 1597) became organist of the archducal chapel in Brussels, a post which he held until his death in 1628, the same year as that of Bull.

The music of Farnaby and Philips, together with a great quantity of that of Byrd and Bull, was copied out by the younger Francis Tregian (c.1574–1619), apparently while a prisoner in the Fleet.[79] The Tregians were

---

[76] Oxford, Christ Church, Mus. 1113: a selection in Cosyn, *Three Voluntaries*, ed. J. Steele (London, 1959). A few more pieces by Cosyn are in *Twenty-five pieces for keyed instruments*, ed. J. A. Fuller-Maitland and W. B. Squire (London, 1923); but the bulk of his output remains unpublished. An edition by Mr O. Memed is in preparation.

[77] His fantasia on a theme by Sweelinck has been referred to above, n. 70.

[78] London, Brit. Lib., Add. 23623.

[79] His manuscript, the famous Fitzwilliam Virginal Book, is kept in the Fitzwilliam Museum, Cambridge, MS 32. g. 29; ed. J. A. Fuller-Maitland and W. B. Squire (Leipzig, 1899, and reprints). For other MSS copied by Tregian, see Ch. 7, n. 3. Mrs. R. R. Thompson, who is preparing a comprehensive study of all the 'Tregian' MSS, feels that they were in fact the product of a well organized scriptorium.

a noted Cornish recusant family, constantly in difficulties for the sake of their faith; and Tregian the copyist's tastes were inclined towards the music of his co-religionists, though by no means exclusively so. His famous virginal book is a fascinating 'retrospective' of most of the best of the Elizabethan and Jacobean repertory, together with much of a distinctly minor character that nevertheless illustrates the breadth of contemporary musical culture as no other source does.

A few other important sources may be mentioned here, apart from the Bull and Cosyn manuscripts already referred to. *My Ladye Nevells Booke*, copied in 1591 by John Baldwin, is devoted entirely to music by Byrd. One of the most important manuscripts is now thought to have been copied by Thomas Weelkes around the year 1610, while Will Forster's magnificent collection is dated 1625.[80] Mention must also be made of *Parthenia* (1612 or 1613), a printed collection of music for the virginals, and the first to appear in England. The volume was finely engraved by William Hole— another novelty—and contained music by Byrd, Bull, and Gibbons. Though it is by no means representative of their best work, it is a landmark in the history of music-publishing in this country, and was popular enough to be several times reprinted from the original plates.[81]

One curious survival now in the library of Christ Church, Oxford,[82] is an anonymous collection of Roman Catholic liturgical organ music, apparently of Netherlandish provenance but written down by an Englishman. Various theories have been advanced as to who the scribe (and hence the probable composer) may have been; the most plausible and attractive is that Richard Dering compiled it for use in Brussels where from 1617 he was organist of the English nuns' convent, and that he brought it to England when he became organist of Queen Henrietta Maria's chapel in 1625.[83] It could indeed have been put together specifically for the latter establishment, but the old-fashioned style and the inclusion of pieces by Philips and Cornet argue for a Brussels origin, and in any case there is no proof that the manuscript reached England so early.

The English keyboard repertory, like that of the lute, reflects the whole breadth of the musical culture of the day. There is no corner of experience that is not somehow represented, even if only in work of little intrinsic value. Programme music, stage music, popular song in all its shapes and forms, jostle side by side with the learned genres. And rich though it is,

---

[80] *My Ladye Nevells Booke* is privately owned (ed. H. Andrews (London, 1926; and reprints)). The Weelkes MS is London, Brit. Lib., Add. 30485; Will Forster's Book ibid., R. M. 24. d. 3. For the two latter see *Elizabethan Keyboard Music*, ed. A. Brown (MB, lv). The date of Forster's MS, given as 31 January 1624, is presumably 'old style'.

[81] The dates are uncertain; but according to Dart's modern edition they are 1613(?), 1646, 1651, and 1655. Hole also engraved Angelo Notari's *Prime musiche nuove* (1613).

[82] Mus. 89.

[83] See Ch. 6, n. 50.

the solo keyboard repertory is but a part of that infinitely more varied tapestry represented by instrumental music as a whole, in which a seemingly endless range of possibilities is exploited in the endeavour to create an authentic and self-sufficient medium of musical expression.[84]

The practice of instrumental music is closely bound up with the history of the musical profession at this period. The profession of a singer was still associated primarily with the Church, and in the provinces at least was in decline for that reason. Only in London and its environs, with the Chapel Royal, Westminster Abbey, St Paul's Cathedral, and St George's, Windsor, providing the main opportunities, were pre-Reformation standards of attainment kept up.[85] It was of course these bodies, and especially the Chapel Royal, that provided the vocal complement, not only for state occasions such as royal weddings and funerals, but also for masques and diversions at other times. A purely 'secular' singer would at first have been an entertainer with many other strings to his bow—recitation, acting, or instrumental playing for example. In the seventeenth century we begin to hear of individuals—Nicholas Lanier for example—referred to as singers *par excellence*. But the royal household music (as opposed to its chapels) was dominated throughout the seventeenth century by its instrumentalists, the inheritors of the medieval tradition of minstrelsy and amassed by the monarch in response to the requirement for lavish display as much as to satisfy specifically musical needs.

In London and the provinces, the main outlet for professional musicianship was the institution of the town or city waits, those descendants of medieval watchmen who now played a variety of instruments and gave concerts as well as exercising their traditional function.[86] There is some reason to believe that their music could be quite sophisticated. Otherwise professional musicians were either free and self-employed or were retained by a royal or noble patron. The free musicians of London were controlled, at least in theory, by the Company of Musicians; outside London only those of York maintained a company, though others attempted to do so.[87] In London the focus for retained musicians was of course the royal house-

---

[84] I have written more fully on the keyboard repertory of this period in my *English Keyboard Music Before the Nineteenth Century*, 52–140.

[85] The main centre for the Chapel Royal was in the palace of Whitehall. Its activities between 1561 and 1744 are monitored in *The Old Cheque-Book*, ed. E. F. Rimbault (1872). No such document exists for the other institutions referred to. The relevant modern works include J. S. Bumpus, *The Organists and Composers of St Paul's Cathedral* (London, 1891); E. H. Fellowes, *Organists and Masters of the Choristers of St George's Chapel in Windsor Castle* (London, 1939); and E. Pine, *The Westminster Abbey Singers* (London, 1953). Some material relating to special occasions (coronations, royal funerals, etc.) may be found in *The King's Musick*, ed. H. C. de Lafontaine (1909).

[86] Woodfill, *Musicians in English Society*, 51, 247–51 (on the London waits); 74–108, 293–5 (on the provincial waits).

[87] Woodfill, 3–32; 110 seqq.

hold, to which might be added in the reign of James I the households of his consort, Anne of Denmark, and of the two successive Princes of Wales, Henry and Charles.

There was in fact a noticeable change of emphasis in the constitution of James I's royal music as compared with that of Elizabeth. A list of offices and of fees pertaining to them, dating from 1593, includes sixteen trumpeters and their 'sergeant', six 'sagbuttes', eight 'vyalls', three 'drumslads', two flute-players, three virginalists, four foreign musicians (Venetians, presumably members of the Bassano family), eight 'players of enterludes', and two 'makers of instruments'.[88] Accounts of payments to individual members of the household music rarely reveal the names of significant composers. Amongst the seven violins, seven recorders, seven flutes, six 'hoboies and sagbuttes', six 'lutes and others', twenty-two trumpeters, and four 'drums and fiffes' allowed mourning livery for Queen Elizabeth's funeral,[89] only Thomas Lupo, senior (violin), James Harding (flute), and 'Alphonso Forobosco' stand out as composers of any prominence, though there are several members each of the important musical families of Lupo, Bassano, and Lanier. At the funeral of James,[90] by contrast, 'the chamber of our late Sovereign Lord King James' included, apart from trumpeters and drummers, no fewer than thirteen 'musitions for Violins' (including Thomas Lupo 'composer'),[91] twenty-one 'musicians for windy Instruments', and above all 'the Consorte', eleven musicians including Charles Coleman, Robert Johnson, John Dowland, Daniel Farrant, and Nicholas Lanier 'singer'. The Chapel Royal and Westminster Abbey fielded especially distinguished teams. In the same year the twenty-four musicians of Charles I included John Danyel, Angelo 'Notarie' (Notari was an Italian composer whose monodies had been published in England),[92] Ferrabosco, Coprario, Robert Tailor, and Robert Marsh. This new emphasis on composers of distinction in the royal household heralded the further substantial enhancement of the 'King's Musick' in relation to the Chapel Royal in the Caroline period.

Not all those musicians resident in the houses of wealthy families were its servants. Some, like John Attey with the Earl of Bridgewater, were 'gentlemen and practitioners in music',[93] who may have had their own sources of income and could be treated as companions as well as being tutors to the young of the family. Comparatively few noblemen will have felt the need for the resources required to mount elaborate ceremonial events with music on a regular basis; they could always hire independent

---

[88] *King's Musick*, 38–9.

[89] Ibid. 45–6. See Woodfill, 300–1, for a fuller list based on additional sources.

[90] *King's Musick*, 57–8; Woodfill, 303–4.

[91] Lupo was 'composer to the violins' from 16 Feb. 1621 until his death in 1628, and for a time 'composer to the lute and voices', in which he was succeeded by Robert Johnson. *NGD*, ad loc.

[92] Notari (cf. n. 81) was still in the royal service in 1663, when he died aged 97.

[93] Woodfill, 59.

musicians for a special occasion as did the monarchy itself from time to time.

Rich though the records are in details of music in its ceremonial aspects—as adjuncts to ambassadorial receptions and foreign missions, as table-music, dance music, and dramatic music, all designed to enhance the status and dignity of the royal personage[94]—it is the growth of the amateur appreciation of music that is the most striking feature of the period. With the example of the monarchy to hand, music became a desirable social accomplishment, most frequently exemplified in the study of an instrument such as the lute, virginals, or viol. In the seventeenth century this led to a widespread connoisseurship, to the growth of amateur instrumental ensemble music, and to amateur participation in masques and other forms of private entertainment. Many composers were themselves 'amateurs' in the sense that they did not occupy salaried positions (or that they were employed in a non-musical capacity). The best of them can hardly be distinguished from the true 'professionals' in the calibre of their work. They had received a rigorous training, possibly in connection with a university degree, and contributed in no small way to the more general cultivation of music amongst the gentry.[95]

With the important exception of the song-schools, music did not normally figure in the formal education of children. The song-schools themselves provided an excellent general and musical education until the age of fifteen or sixteen, but in many cases that was evidently the end of the matter.[96] Further musical training could take the form of apprenticeship, which was more suited to a trade than to a profession and which because of its length was heavily dependent on the calibre of the master;[97] or it could be through private tuition (in the case of wealthier families), or as an optional element in the curriculum of certain schools or colleges. It is difficult to generalize because there was no single pattern of schooling as there is today. The curriculum of a grammar school was intended as a preparation for study at a university; but it was possible to go to university without having been to a grammar school, and it was possible to be well educated by the standards of the time without going to a university at all.[98]

The function of a grammar school did not necessitate the teaching of music, even in the purely formal sense applicable to the arts course of a university. Any musical experience gained in such an environment will

[94] The toing and froing of English and German royalty, and the musical accompaniments of their embassies and feastings, are well described in W. Braun, *Britannia Abundans*, 11–36.

[95] On the amateur cultivation of music see Woodfill, 201–39.

[96] The general picture may be plausibly extracted from the fascinating history of the Salisbury Cathedral Grammar and Song Schools in D. H. Robertson, *Sarum Close* (London, 1938; 2nd edn., Bath, 1969).

[97] Woodfill, 16–25.

[98] Many aspects of this non-university learning are discussed in C. Hill, *Intellectual Origins of the English Revolution* (Oxford, 1965, repr. 1980), 14–84.

have been incidental: one may assume for example that the pupils of a grammar school within the cathedral close (as at Salisbury) would frequently have attended choral services and may have benefited from the availability of trained musicians. But at some boarding-schools music was taken more seriously. Winchester and Eton colleges still had their own choir schools and singing-men, and the proximity of these cannot have been without effect. Richard Mulcaster, headmaster of the Merchant Taylors' School, positively encouraged the use of music in education.[99] Christ's Hospital actually had a full-time music-master, who in 1609 was the composer John Farrant; and other charity schools may have been similarly endowed.[100] As we have seen, Benjamin Cosyn, a gifted composer, was organist of Dulwich College from 1622 to 1624, and of Charterhouse from 1626 until 1643, when the 'organs' were 'prohibited'.[101] In such cases the pupils received the equivalent of private tuition at school. As for the girls of that epoch and for long after, private tuition at home was the almost invariable pattern.

At the English universities, Music was formally a part of the arts course leading to the degrees of Bachelor of Arts and Master of Arts; but it was based exclusively on the study of ancient musical theory as transmitted in Latin by Boethius in the sixth century, and there is reason to believe that it was largely a dead letter by the sixteenth. Nevertheless, educated men had Boethius' *De Musica* at their disposal as a basis for philosophical arguments about the nature of music and its place in society, and, since the Latin language gave them no difficulties, it is not surprising that its contents were widely known.[102] More significant, however, was the introduction of degrees in Music, the Bachelor of Music and Doctor of Music, at both Cambridge and Oxford. Some of the earlier recipients of these have faded into obscurity, but in the later sixteenth and early seventeenth centuries there is a surprisingly good correlation between excellence as a composer and the award of a degree. These degrees could be awarded immediately upon matriculation to men who had not studied at the university—the qualification was the study of music over a period of years and the composition of an 'exercise'—and were evidently prized by the composers themselves as contemporary title-pages make clear.

At this period, before the establishment of the Oxford chair in 1627 provided further encouragement, both Oxford and Cambridge were the

---

[99] Price, *Patrons and Musicians of the English Renaissance*, 37.

[100] Ibid. 37–8; F. G. Edwards, 'Music at Christ's Hospital', *MT*, 46 (1905), 573–83. After Farrant came Ravenscroft (1618–22). The Robert Dow who increased the stipend after 1609 cannot have been the Fellow of All Souls known as a musician, for he died in 1588 (see ch. 7, n. 3, and below).

[101] See the article on 'The Charterhouse' by 'Dotted Crotchet' in *MT*, 44 (1903), 777.

[102] See my brief contribution to the *History of Oxford University*, vol. iii.

scene of pageants and other events, in which music played a part, for the
entertainment of visiting royalty. The surviving inventories of deceased
members of Oxford University, too, show a regular pattern of private music-
making. A somewhat exceptional instance of musical cultivation is provided
by the magnificent set of part-books compiled by Robert Dow, Fellow
of All Souls College and BCL, who died in 1588. It is not known for
certain whether there actually existed in Oxford a circle of musicians capable
of performing such music effectively, but the will to preserve it in a practical
format existed. Several of the colleges at both universities, of course, still
kept the establishment needed for the regular performance of choral services;
and while the exact patterns are now difficult to recover, there is enough
circumstantial evidence to suggest a vigorous musical life.

On the subject of 'academic' music, lastly, we should note the foundation
of the chair of music at Gresham's College in the City of London in 1596,
the first holder being John Bull. His twice-weekly lectures were to be
divided equally between theoretical and practical music—a surprisingly
modern and certainly an enlightened arrangement.[103]

The musical writings of the epoch mirrored the academic distinction
between the speculative and the practical. The Oxford don John Case
published in 1588 his *Apologia musices*, a defence of music based on classical
authorities. Two years earlier an anonymous author had published, again
at Oxford, a *Praise of Musick* relying on Biblical and Patristic writings. Some
people thought that this too had been written by Case.[104] There is a certain
amount of speculative material—the science of proportions in its musical
applications—in Morley's *Plaine and Easie Introduction to Practicall Musick*
(1597) and Dowland's translation of Ornithoparcus' *Micrologus* (1609). But
the climax of speculation occurred in Robert Fludd's *Utriusque cosmi . . .
historia* (Oppenheim, 1617–24), in which he likened the universe to a musical
instrument played by the soul.[105] His views were attacked by Kepler and
Mersenne, whom he had criticized; but it may be doubted whether his
ideas had much impact on musical thought in this country.

Writings on practical music took the form of instruction in singing (which
included the reading of music and little else), in the playing of instruments,

[103] Price, *Patrons and Musicians*, 39. Bull was rather quaintly described as 'Doctor of Musicke to
the Kinge': *King's Musick*, 49. The division into theoretical and practical music was of course an ancient
one; what was modern was the adoption of the latter—that is, actual performances—as part of an
academic course. The same principle was to be maintained in Heather's foundation at Oxford; and
there, surprisingly enough, it was the practical, not the theoretical, part of the instruction (again in
the form of concerts) which survived.

[104] On Case, see J. W. Binns, 'John Case and *The Praise of Musick*', *ML*, 55 (1974), 444–53, where
the anonymity of *The Praise of Musick* is proved.

[105] *NGD*, s.v. Fludd. It is the *Tractatus secundus*, published in 1618, that contains the treatise 'De
templo musicae'.

and in descant (i.e. counterpoint) and composition.[106] Two rather different but very brief treatises on notation had been attached to the monophonic psalters of 1561 and 1569 and their successors respectively. Morley's publication of 1597 was by far the most comprehensive of all such guides.[107] Printed manuals on instrumental playing were confined at this period to the plucked stringed instruments, especially the lute, the cittern, and the gittern. The earliest of these were based on books published in Paris by Adrian Le Roy from 1551 onwards. The later publications of Anthony Holborne (1597) and Thomas Robinson (1603, 1609) were more independent.[108]

Descant and composition were treated at length by Morley with numerous examples illustrative both of faulty and of good counterpoint. Much of his material was drawn from Italian sources, but everywhere his robust English good sense is apparent. No one could learn composition solely by reading a treatise, but Morley provided a foundation that could hardly be bettered. Yet techniques were constantly being refined; and the treatises of Coprario (*Rules How to Compose*, *c.*1610, in manuscript) and Campion (*A New Way of Making Fowre Parts in Counter-Point*, *c.*1613) broke new ground by effectively regarding the bass as the foundation.[109] The two treatises are clearly related, and of the two men Coprario was undoubtedly the better equipped to write such a method; yet it was Campion's that was printed, and reprinted again and again with Playford's *Brief Introduction* up to 1687.

A final genre is exemplified by the chapter on music in Henry Peacham's *Compleat Gentleman* (1622, with new editions in 1634 and 1661).[110] Peacham is the heir to the tradition of Castiglione's *Il cortegiano* and its English translation by Sir Thomas Hoby (1561), and to the writings of Elyot and Ascham. The general burden is that music is desirable and even necessary for health and equanimity—provided that it is not overdone. Fortunately Peacham's wise moderation was no match for the enthusiasm of some seventeenth-

---

[106] The notion that writings on music might themselves be either 'theoretical' (speculative) or 'practical' is a medieval one, going back at any rate to Jehan des Murs. It led to a narrowing of the range of topics considered appropriate to 'speculation'.

[107] Facsimile edn., Farnborough, 1971. Ravenscroft's *Briefe Discourse* (1614): fac. edns. London and Amsterdam, 1971; Clarabricken, 1984, with its parallel MS version (Brit. Lib., Add. 19758), has been studied by D. Mateer, 'A Critical Study and Transcription of *A Briefe Discourse* by Thomas Ravenscroft' (M. Mus. diss., London, King's College, 1970).

[108] The earliest such tutor was *A Briefe and Easye Instru[c]tion* (1568), translated from a manual published by Le Roy in 1567; a translation of Le Roy's gittern tutor of 1551 is now lost. See also Ch. 7, n. 69. Holborne, *The Cittharn Schoole* (1597); Robinson, *Schoole of Musicke* (1603: modern edn. by D. Lumsden, Paris, 1971), and *Newe Citharen Lessons* (1609).

[109] Facsimile of the Coprario treatise, ed. M. F. Bukofzer (Los Angeles, 1952); Campion's is included in the editions of his works by P. Vivian (Oxford, 1909), and W. R. Davis (London, 1969).

[110] There are useful articles on Peacham by A. R. Young, 'Henry Peacham, Ben Jonson, and the Cult of Elizabeth-Oriana', *ML*, 60 (1979), 305–11, and S. Hankey, 'The Compleat Gentleman's Music', ibid. 62 (1981), 146–54.

century amateurs, and the culture of the whole epoch was of a vitality that could hardly have been achieved on such a milksop diet.

This culture had derived its main nourishment from Italy. The love-affair with that country had not ceased with the absorption of the madrigalian idiom; it was a key factor in the development of declamatory song and dialogue in the early seventeenth century. England exported what it had learnt to Germany and the Netherlands in the context of the political and matrimonial alliances of those days.[III] England considered itself a Protestant country, and its policies were designed to neutralize the power of Catholic Spain and France. This extended to the marriage of James I himself, and was further enhanced by the marriage of his daughter Elizabeth to Prince Frederick, Elector Palatine of the Rhine, an event which *Parthenia* was published to celebrate. England's cultural standing in Europe was founded on its self-confidence in an international role. When its sense of direction began to falter, as was shortly to be the case, the consequences for music in England were supremely interesting; but it lost its European pre-eminence. In the England of Elizabeth I and James I, music was at once the intimate concern of the nation as a whole and a means by which it displayed its character to the world outside. It is a proud boast for the music of any nation; that it can be made for this country at this period, and perhaps only at this period, tells us something about the nature of Elizabethan and Jacobean England which the most comprehensive account of its political, social, or economic history could never do.

[III] Braun, *Britannia abundans*. For the Netherlands, see A. Curtis, *Sweelinck's Keyboard Music* (Leiden and London, 1969).

9

CHARLES I, THE COMMONWEALTH, AND THE RESTORATION

THE seventeenth century in England was a period of transition: politically and constitutionally, from the medieval to the modern state; in philosophy and science, from a deference to authority to the rational interpretation of observed facts. Twice the monarchy veered towards absolutism; twice it was repelled, first by an extremism which became self-defeating, on the second occasion by an accommodation that satisfied the majority. The Church rose and fell with the monarchy; but when the monarchy itself became overtly Roman Catholic, a conflict arose which only the Revolution could put down.

The scientific revolution was swifter, and effectively complete (in terms of attitudes) by 1662, the year in which the Royal Society received its charter. Science was closely linked to architecture, and Sir Christopher Wren, a genius in both, laid the foundations of an architectural mode that was largely new. In literature and in art, the whole epoch was so dominated by classicism of one kind or another that to speak of a broad movement is difficult; but the general tendency was in the direction of the greater formalism that characterizes the eighteenth century. So in music, the pragmatic Italianism of the Elizabethan and Jacobean composers was supplanted, after many vicissitudes (in which French influence played a large part), by a more formal and respectful dependence. France and Germany made the same pilgrimage from different starting-points, so that wherever English composers looked, they found an Italianized model.

These developments, as in politics, literature, and the fine arts, occupied the whole century and more; but the essentials of the change occurred during the fifty years covered by this chapter. Up to about 1625, English composers were equals in a European community in which much was given and taken; what they had learnt from Italy, they exported to Germany and the Low Countries in particular.[1] But thereafter a more insular attitude predominated; some composers turned in upon themselves, while others were a prey to every passing fashion. In such circumstances a national integrity is hard to foster; the miracle is that this country nevertheless produced a procession of masters culminating in Henry Purcell himself. The traditional reaction to the phenomenon of Purcell is to place him on a lonely pedestal; but it is in many ways more interesting to examine his position in relation to the trends of his time, trends fostered by the minor masters of his epoch and engendered by the heroes[2] of this chapter: John Jenkins, Henry and William Lawes, and Matthew Locke.

In a period of marked political extremism it is perhaps surprising that in music the forces of continuity were so strong. The tendency, already apparent in the reign of James I, for the royal court to become the focal point of patronage became even more accentuated under Charles I. The Chapel Royal as such began to lose its pre-eminence in musical life, notwithstanding the individual excellence of many of its servants, and in spite of its importance to a monarchy devoted to the theory of divine right; the great provincial families gradually withdrew from their culturally dominant position. Yet when the monarchy fell, the most characteristic forms of the epoch, chamber music and song, continued to flourish in the lesser establishments, and provided a solid background to more brilliant manifestations under the later Stuarts. The curious pragmatism of the epoch allowed musicians to satisfy the social needs for their art in abundance and variety whatever the political conditions.

The amateur cultivation of music was greatly advanced by the rapid development of music publishing from the middle of the century. In 1651 John Playford, who had been apprenticed to John Brown (whose name appears on some editions as co-publisher with Playford), began publishing music on a scale hitherto unknown. Not only was he a vigorous and enterprising businessman; he had also the musicianship to act as collector and editor of numerous anthologies. He was even a composer in a small way, but his greatest importance was as a catalyst for a more widespread appreciation of good music than had been possible in the past.

It was of course in the sphere of church music that the effects of political change were most apparent. James I had declared himself unequivocally for episcopal government, and under Charles I the growing trend towards ritual elaboration was reflected in a renewed enthusiasm for the liturgy and its appropriate musical expression. Yet the undercurrent of simple puritan piety persisted, finding expression in renewed editions of the metrical psalter and in other ways. The psalter was also cultivated in Royalist circles,

---

[1] See previous chapter, n. III.
[2] Roger North called Locke 'ultimus herooum' (*Roger North on Music*, ed. J. Wilson (London, 1959), 349. See below, pp. 549 seqq.

where the writing of new paraphrases, together with simple new tunes or more elaborate settings with *basso continuo* provided a foil to more conventional publications. Here, in the sphere of private devotion, Puritans and High Churchmen could find common ground, though the extremism of the ecclesiastical reform under the Commonwealth, expressed liturgically in the *Directory* and in a new metrical psalter, destroyed the continuity of public worship.

At the Restoration, every effort was made to put things on the same footing as before; understandably there were practical difficulties, but in the event the tradition was revived in its essentials and refined in its details. In a conservative revision of the *Book of Common Prayer (1662)* the changes that were made were in a 'Catholic' direction. Edward Lowe (Oxford's Professor, and organist of Christ Church) in his *A Short Direction of the Performance of Cathedral Service* (1661), and James Clifford in *The Divine Services and Anthems* (1663, second edition 1664) endeavoured to provide the appropriate guidance for the recovery of the old traditions.

The sacred music of this turbulent period may be considered in terms of three successive waves of activity. In the first place there was the continuing practice of the old Renaissance contrapuntal style, with its decani and cantoris division of the choir, its 'full' and 'verse' sections, and its organ accompaniment playing a partly essential, partly inessential role. Secondly, there was the adoption of the new accompanied solo or duet style of the early baroque, hailing from Italy and somewhat modified in England to suit the more cautious native taste. Finally, after the Restoration, came the orchestrally accompanied anthem, a courtly entertainment fashioned largely in imitation of the *grand motet* of Lully and his French contemporaries.

The first two genres, however, did not die out; rather, they developed in such a way that in the Restoration period all three co-existed and interacted upon each other to produce a distinctively English 'middle-baroque' accent, running parallel to, influencing, and being influenced by the numerous secular and instrumental idioms of the day. This phase of development was virtually complete by the deaths of Pelham Humfrey in 1674 and of Matthew Locke in 1677: what followed was a consolidation, though we are constantly reminded until long after Purcell's own death of the unstable and parochial character of the English musical heritage.

Of all the composers who preserved the Renaissance idiom into the reign of Charles I, Thomas Tomkins was by far the most resourceful and inventive.[3] A rather later generation of broadly conservative composers is represented by Robert Ramsey (fl. 1610–44), Henry Loosemore (d. 1670), William Child (1606–97), and Benjamin Rogers (1614–98). Child and Rogers

---

[3] His contribution, and that of several minor figures such as Amner, Batten, and East, has been discussed in Ch. 6.

were prolific and long-lived figures who were by no means immune to more radical trends—Child indeed published a set of baroque psalms in 1639—but they nevertheless belong essentially to the older tradition.

The polyphonic style of these and many like them has been described as 'weak'—and so in a sense it is. The firm harmonic progressions, the subtle balance between the claims of linearity and verticality, so characteristic of Gibbons, Weelkes, and Tomkins, are replaced by a curious uncertainty of direction. There can be strangely uncouth declamation of the text, unorganic vacillation in the scoring of adjacent passages, and a sentimental style of melody at odds with the function of the music. Much of it is quite simply rather dull. Yet it is not wholly devoid of charm—the awkward charm of metamorphosis.

Ramsey and Loosemore were Cambridge men—Ramsey organist of Trinity College from 1628 until 1644 (and Master of the Children from 1637), Loosemore organist of King's College from 1627 until his death in 1670. Much of their music is preserved in the 'Caroline' part-books at Peterhouse, Cambridge, unfortunately without the organ parts that are sometimes essential. Some of their works are agreeable specimens of pure Renaissance counterpoint. Ramsey's verse anthem for bass solo and chorus, 'My song shall be alway of the lovingkindness of the Lord',[4] approaches the declamatory fervour of Tomkins. But his service music, including a Latin Te Deum, Jubilate, and Litany, is of a kind that seeks to relieve the monotony by the occasional quaintly picturesque moment or a sudden change of texture.[5] His competence is not in doubt, but his control of idiom is suspect. The remarkable dialogue 'In guilty night' demands consideration in another connection below.

Child and Rogers were both associated with St George's, Windsor: Child as lay clerk from 1630 and organist and Master of the Choristers from 1633; Rogers as lay clerk in 1641–4 and again from 1662 until 1664, when he became organist and choirmaster at Magdalen College, Oxford. Child also became organist of the Chapel Royal at the Restoration. He was one of the most distinguished musicians of his day, associated with the 'High Church' movement in the Caroline period and an innovator in his choice of keys and scoring. Like Ramsey he has a Latin Te Deum and Jubilate in the Caroline part-books; his English services (of which at least seventeen are known)[6] might be in keys as far afield as E major or B flat major; or scored with four 'meanes' (i.e. boys' voice-parts). He is both conscious of tradition and anxious to expand it. His neglect is understandable, given the extent of his output (which includes over fifty anthems) and its

---

[4] Ramsey, *English Sacred Music* (EECM, vii), no. 9.

[5] Ramsey, *Latin Sacred Music* (EECM, xxxi). The inclusion of Latin services in the Peterhouse books is due to the influence of John Cosin, Bishop of Durham, who became Master of Peterhouse.

[6] Le Huray, *Music and the Reformation*, 358.

undoubted unevenness; yet at its best, as in the fine motet 'O bone Jesu', his music has an austere gravity that is genuinely compelling.

'O bone Jesu' affords a useful illustration of the stylistic terrain that had to be traversed by English composers on their journey from a Renaissance to a Baroque idiom. It is one of a quite large number of works by Child, Jeffreys, Locke, and others, to English or Latin texts, in which a basically complete vocal polyphonic texture is supplemented by a *basso continuo* part which nevertheless from time to time plays an essential supporting role. The ultimate models for this idiom were to be found in the motets of Giovanni Gabrieli and his Italian contemporaries; but it had quickly become the lingua franca of Continental composers of sacred music everywhere, both Catholic and Protestant. It was slower to take root in England, where the Anglican tradition of a fully written-out organ part, conceived poly-phonically *pari passu* with the voices (and hence comparable with them in function even when independent) survived until the Commonwealth and even beyond.

The newer idiom was also characterized by a more intense reaction to the meaning of the text, always within the bounds of a metric scheme that visually at least made obeisance to Renaissance convention even though in performance some relaxation of strict tempo was usually inevitable. The use of Latin reinforces the impression of an Italianate and Catholic ethos fully in accord with the spirit of the Royalist, High Church circle in which these composers mostly moved. Such works might be used for private devotion, or in the chapels of the monarch and his family. During the Commonwealth they helped to keep that spirit alive, and at the Restoration they became a natural concomitant of the 'official' Anglican repertory of services and anthems. Though Charles II had learnt to prefer the livelier rhythm of contemporary French music, many of his servants never lost their liking for the deeper resonances and more subtle flavours of an Italianate idiom.

It is not known when 'O bone Jesu' and Child's other motets were composed. While some of them may indeed post-date the Restoration, the strongest influence is that of the early Italian baroque. In 'O bone Jesu', the rhythmic flexibility and the harmonic richness do recall the idiom of Gabrieli quite strongly (Ex. 185, overleaf).[7]

This four-part texture with *basso continuo* stands in the centre of a technical range that extends from the solo motet on the one hand to the elaborate and extended composition, be it anthem, motet, or ode, in several sections and perhaps with both solo and choral and independent instrumental parts on the other. In England the development was to a certain extent

---

[7] Oxford, Bod. Lib., Mus. Sch. c. 204 (fo. 31ʳ). There are also copies in Mus. 156. d. 93, and in the British Library.

Ex. 185

Ex. 185, continued

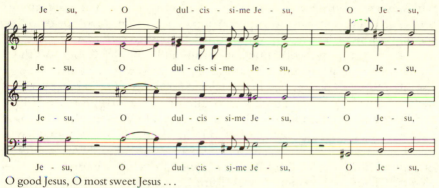

O good Jesus, O most sweet Jesus . . .

chronological. A few composers, such as Johnson and Lanier, had written solo motets quite early on, perhaps even in the reign of James I. For them, such works were an extension of their cultivation of the continuo-song. Outside the country, Peter Philips and Richard Dering had explored the baroque manner, the latter in a series of sacred solos and duets that must have gained a certain currency in England. Although they were not published here until 1662 and 1674, Dering himself had returned to England in 1625 as the organist in Queen Henrietta Maria's chapel.[8] He died in 1630, but he had helped to found a tradition of great importance; and the very fact that his compositions in this vein were published posthumously is sufficient to demonstrate both their continued circulation in the intervening years and their usefulness in the post-Restoration context.

Dering's motets (or 'cantica sacra') are musically comparable only to those of his lesser Italian contemporaries; but what they may lack in rhetorical force they make up for in musical balance. They are a good deal more successful than those of Walter Porter, a pupil of Monteverdi's who became Master of the Choristers at Westminster Abbey from 1639 until 1644, when the choral music was abolished.[9] His baroque sacred music was not published until 1657, apart from one or two anthems with instrumental interludes in his earlier volume of Ayres in 1632. There are motets for two voices with basso continuo, and settings of George Sandys's psalm-versions for the same forces, but in no case is a strong musical personality established.

Sandys had published his Paraphrase upon the Psalmes in 1636. In 1638

[8] Cf. Ch. 6, p. 388. Dering's English publications were the Cantica sacra (1662), and eight motets for two voices and continuo, whose authenticity is doubtful, in a similarly entitled collective publication of 1674 (RISM, 1674², containing music by J. Blackwell, Dering, C. Gibbons, J. Jackson, Jeffreys, H. Lawes, Locke, J. Playford, Rogers, Wise, and anonymous composers).

[9] Pine, The Westminster Abbey Singers, 115 seqq. The other details of Porter's career are retailed in NGD. He died in poverty in 1659.

it reappeared (together with other Biblical paraphrases) in an edition to which twenty-four settings by Henry Lawes were added. These are simple tunes for treble and bass, to be filled in on the organ, theorbo, or other accompanying instrument, in the manner established by Orlando Gibbons and others in the two collections of hymns and songs by George Wither. (Some of them are retained in hymn books of the present day.) Lawes also used Sandys's paraphrases in the *Choice Psalmes* of 1648. This collection includes short psalm-settings (usually of the first verse only) for two trebles and bass, with *basso continuo*, by Henry Lawes and by his brother William, together with a set of eight elegies on the death of William, who was killed at the siege of Chester in 1645. (There is also an elegy on the death of John Tomkins in 1638 by William Lawes himself.) One or two of the elegies, which are by Henry Lawes, John Wilson, John Taylor, John Cob, Edmund Foster, Simon Ive[s], John Jenkins, and John Hilton, will be referred to below. The whole collection is dedicated in the most effusive terms to Charles I, an interesting but ineffectual exercise in pious propaganda.[10]

Henry Lawes's contribution is serviceable but no more, while that of his brother, a few striking passages notwithstanding, is a sad disappointment to anyone familiar with his instrumental music or even his secular songs.[11] Abounding in ineffective and ungrammatical part-writing, it cannot even be excused by inexperience, since little if any of it can have pre-dated Sandys's publication of 1636. Nor is the stylistic novelty so great as to engender a conflict between invention and technique. A sample from Henry's contribution is sufficient to illustrate the character of this music at its limited best (Ex. 186).[12]

William Lawes appears to better advantage in his curious collection of verse anthems 'to the Common Tunes'.[13] These are settings, twelve in all, of 'Old Version' paraphrases, in which plain harmonizations of the standard melodies are interspersed with verses scored for countertenor, tenor, and bass soloists (both separately and in various combinations) with *basso continuo*. This scoring is itself of some interest in that it anticipates the standard 'verse' texture of much Restoration service-music: it was by no means the norm in the pre-Commonwealth period. But interest has understandably centred around the use of the traditional melodies in this relatively sophisticated environment. The original function and context of these anthems are unknown. The Sunday services at the Minster during the siege

---

[10] Milton's famous sonnet in praise of Henry Lawes was first printed amongst the commendatory poems in this collection, though he could hardly have been sympathetic to its cause.

[11] M. Lefkowitz, *William Lawes* (London, 1960), 237–44. The four Latin works of the collection, with four of the English settings and all of the canons, are to texts not by Sandys.

[12] *Choice Psalmes*, no. 2.

[13] Oxford, Christ Church, Mus. 768–70, copied by Edward Lowe.

Ex. 186

* The original has Ⲥ in cantus 1, cantus 2, and basso continuo parts.

of York in 1644, at which Lawes was present, have been suggested;[14] but the evidence is not particularly compelling, and the set may simply have been a private experiment.

William Child, whose *Psalmes* of 1639 (reprinted in 1650 and 1656) are settings of English prose versions for two *cantus*, *bassus*, and *basso continuo*, was a more generally successful exponent of the baroque declamatory idiom. His technical control enabled him to combine it with strict binary form, to which the apparently wayward tonal shifts are ultimately subservient (Ex. 187, pp. 513–14).[15]

Child was clever enough not to link his publication with a political cause, and the editions and manuscript copies[16] are a testimony to their popularity and usefulness throughout the period of Rebellion and Restoration. John Wilson's *Psalterium Carolinum* (1652) combined political inexpediency with musical blandness; the publication quickly disappeared from view, however, probably through pressure from the authorities. On the whole the musical predilections of Royalist composers were not in conflict with the prevailing taste in other circles, and the use of the psalter provided a convenient point of contact with Presbyterian sentiment. Their most personal utterances were never intended for public worship, and together with the repertories of secular song and instrumental music they helped to guarantee the historical continuity on which the future of English music was to depend.

The revival of Anglican liturgy and music at the Restoration embraced every level of activity from the unharmonized chanting of psalms[17] to the presentation of elaborate anthems in the Chapel Royal. There were practical difficulties everywhere, too, from the lack of trained choristers in the greater establishments to the discontinuities and disruptions at parochial level. But in due course matters settled down to their previous state as a three-tiered system embracing the Chapel Royal and the major establishments of London and Windsor; the provincial cathedrals and colleges with their sometimes humdrum routine; and the parish churches, which ranged in their musical potential from that of a lesser cathedral to the wholly negligible. While these levels merged into each other at their extremes, it can be said that the Chapel Royal was the sphere of elaborate, instrumentally accompanied anthems, the cathedrals that of honest functional music in a cappella style (that is, accompanied by the organ only), and parish churches

---

[14] See D. Pinto, 'William Lawes at the Siege of York', *MT*, 127 (1986), 579–83. Thomas Mace (*Musick's Monument* (London, 1676), 18–20) refers to accompanied congregational psalmody during the siege, but gives no further particulars.

[15] *The First Set of Psalmes* (1639), no. 1 (1st section).

[16] e.g. Oxford, Bod. Lib., Mus. Sch. c. 32–7.

[17] Or for that matter the monotoned singing of prayers, versicles, and responses. Hawkins refers to the continued use of Marbeck's *Booke of Common Praier Noted* even in the 18th cent. (p. 539 of the 1853 edn.).

Ex. 187

continued

Ex. 187, continued

that of the metrical psalm, led by the clerk and perhaps accompanied by the organ. Here and there an endowed or voluntary choir might produce more sophisticated music, but the 'cathedral' form of service was rarely encountered.[18]

In many places, including some parish churches, there was a great building, or rebuilding of organs removed, damaged, or destroyed during the Civil War and Commonwealth. Some of these became famous: John Loosemore's new instrument at Exeter Cathedral (1665), those of Robert Dallam at Magdalen College, Oxford, Eton, and York, of Bernard Smith at Christ Church, Oxford, and of Renatus Harris at St Paul's, London.[19] Nearly all have now been destroyed, or changed out of recognition, in response to the musical demands of the German classical and French romantic repertories, the liturgical requirements of the Oxford movement and its Evangelical counterparts, and the desire for ever more mechanization, in the nineteenth and twentieth centuries.

The parochial repertory as such need not detain us here: something will be said in the next chapter of its state at the end of the Stuart period. Of the revival of the cathedral routine, too, only a brief account is necessary, though it is equally relevant to the Chapel Royal and its fellow-establishments. The simpler pre-Commonwealth services and anthems, particularly if they could be sung by men only, were often restored unchanged. Post-Restoration manuscripts often retained the repertory and copying conventions (for example, with an organ part fully written out) of those written before the Civil War. The pre-Commonwealth custom of supporting the voices with wind instruments proved especially useful in the period when choirs were being brought back to their former strength, though before

---

[18] There were a few exceptions to this generalization amongst former abbeys and collegiate churches converted to solely parochial use. The musical tradition of Ludlow Parish Church (see A. Smith in *ML*, 49 (1968), 108–21) continued until the Commonwealth at least.

[19] For a good summary of English organ-building in the 17th cent. see P. Williams, *A New History of the Organ* (London, 1980), 133–6; cf. W. L. Sumner, *The Organ* (3rd edn., London, 1962), 122–63; C. Clutton and A. Niland, *The British Organ* (London, 1963).

long they were dropped altogether;[20] and (with the decline of the string-accompanied anthem) the organ remained as the sole supporting instrument in a repertory more and more governed by considerations of seemliness and propriety. The harmonized chanting of the psalms and canticles was gradually emancipated from its hitherto invariable basis in a plainchant psalm-tone in the tenor; and this chanting eventually came to be the normal way of singing the daily psalms rather than a purely 'festal' technique as before.[21]

The functional post-Restoration repertory of services and anthems was supplied by the revived or newly composed music (the distinction is not always easy to draw) of such figures as Child, Rogers, Henry Lawes (and even of William Lawes in the case of his isolated masterpiece 'The Lord is my light'),[22] Christopher Gibbons, Matthew Locke, and the young Humfrey, Wise, and Blow. The plain a cappella style with *basso continuo* for organ (or indeed with a fully-written organ part) might be enlivened with verses for one or more soloists, for example for the now popular combination of countertenor, tenor, and bass. (The solo countertenor enjoyed a great vogue, in secular as well as sacred music, in the later seventeenth century, and its role as the uppermost voice of a male trio or chorus survived until the nineteenth century in innumerable anthems and glees. It may have been influenced by the similar function of the *haut-contre* in French baroque music.) But the chief interest of the period centres on the instrumentally accompanied verse anthems and motets of Matthew Locke, Pelham Humfrey, and their respective contemporaries. While the bulk of this repertory can be associated directly with the Chapel Royal of Charles II, a number of Latin works (in particular those of Locke) can be more plausibly attributed to the Roman Catholic chapels of Queen Catherine and the Queen Mother, and in some cases to private use in London and Oxford.[23]

Amongst the older composers who figured prominently in the post-Restoration scene, apart from Locke himself, were William Child,

---

[20] Woodfill, *Musicians in English Society*, 150; cf. *Roger North on Music*, 40, 286; Evelyn, *Diary*, 21 Dec. 1662 (see n. 23 below).

[21] For harmonized chanting see Le Huray, *Music and the Reformation in England*, 158–60. There is a collection of 21 chants in score in Brit. Lib., Add. 17784 (c.1670). But monophonic chanting clearly remained an alternative possibility for many decades. Normally the whole of the psalms in any service were sung to the same chant; the older tradition of a different, 'festal' setting for each psalm fell into abeyance after the Restoration. Harmonized preces and responses continued in use. Cf. C. Dearnley, *English Church Music 1650–1750* (London, 1970), 102–6, 285–7.

[22] Lefkowitz, *William Lawes*, 257; E. Walker, *A History of Music in England* (Oxford, 1907; 3rd edn., 1952), 156. The work is a verse anthem with chorus, setting Ps. 27.

[23] See Matthew Locke, *Anthems and Motets* (MB, xxxviii), p. xv; Dearnley, *English Church Music 1650–1750*, 278–80. Evelyn records (21 Dec. 1662) the introduction of the string-accompanied anthem in the Chapel Royal: 'instead of the ancient, grave and solemn wind musiq accompanying the organ, was introduced a concert of 24 violins betweene every pause, after the French fantastical light way, better suiting a tavern or playhouse than a church'.

Christopher Gibbons (1615–76), and Henry Cooke (c.1616–72). Henry Lawes, though he provided an anthem for the coronation, died in 1662. George Jeffreys (c.1625–85), who wrote a considerable quantity of English and Latin church music[24] and who had been a member of the pre-Commonwealth Chapel Royal, entered the service of Lord Hatton at Kirby Hall (Northamptonshire) in 1646 and and remained there at the Restoration.[25] Child's contribution has been sufficiently characterized above: he remained an influential figure for many years longer but was understandably not at the forefront as an innovator at this period. Christopher Gibbons, whose output included a few anthems, was organist both at the Chapel Royal and at Westminster Abbey; but he too played only a small part in the forming of the new idiom. Far more important was 'Captain' Henry Cooke, who became Master of the Children of the Chapel Royal and played the major role in re-forming the choir and re-establishing its tradition. His seven verse-anthems with strings, including the coronation anthem 'Behold O God our defender' (1661), are apparently the earliest of their type, in which a three- or four-part 'band of violins' (perhaps in conjunction with viols and theorbos) provided introductory and intermediate 'symphonies' or ritornelli and (perhaps) accompanied the choruses.[26]

It is, however, in the later works of Matthew Locke, composed between 1660 and his death in 1677, that the distinctive features of the post-Restoration style are most clearly demonstrated in all their boldness and variety. His output of church music was not large, but it covers a wide range, and his idiom is uniquely compelling in the period before Blow and Purcell lent the added distinction of their mature style to the forms which he cultivated. Apart from a number of works for one, two, and three voices with *basso continuo*, including several for men's voices only, there is a respectable body of pieces for larger forces, many with independent instrumental parts. 'How doth the city sit solitary' (no. 8), a verse anthem with a variety of solo groupings and a choral refrain, shows Locke at his best in writing for voices and organ only.[27] The organ part was written out by Locke himself and, although it was later reduced to the status of

[24] On Jeffreys, see P. Aston, 'Tradition and Experiment in the Music of George Jeffreys', *PRMA*, 99 (1972–3), 105–15, and in *NGD*, ad loc. In a recent reassessment it has been pointed out that the materials in Jeffreys's own manuscript compilation (dated 1648) are earlier than previously thought, and that his importance as a pioneer of the Italianate style in England is correspondingly greater: see R. Thompson, 'George Jeffreys and the "Stile Nuovo" in English Sacred Music: A New Date for his Autograph Score, British Library, Add. MS 10338', *ML*, 70 (1989), 317–41.

[25] Other minor composers include Benjamin Rogers, whose eventful career terminated at Magdalen College, Oxford (1665–86: he lived on until 1698, however, when he was aged 84), and Albert Bryne (c.1621–71), organist of St Paul's before and after the Protectorate, and then of Westminster Abbey (1666–8).

[26] On Cooke's anthems see Dearnley, *English Church Music 1650–1750*, 185–90, and I. Cheverton, 'Captain Henry Cooke', *Soundings*, 9 (1982), 74–86.

[27] The numbering of items is that of Locke, *Anthems and Motets* (MB, xxxviii).

a mere *basso continuo* in a score written by John Blow, it contains imitative and other details in the 'verse' sections (for example at the opening) that reveal it to have been an essential part of the conception from the outset. Two or three other anthems by Locke belong to this type, in which the ancestry of the pre-Commonwealth verse anthem is most clearly apparent. But in others, such as the long and justly popular 'Lord let me know mine end' (no. 10), though a fully written-out organ part exists, it is inessential except as regards the bass-line and may not have been originally written in that form. This impressively meditative piece ends remarkably enough for the solo group rather than the full choir; its final bars, to the words 'and be no more seen', carry the successive directions 'soft' and 'softest of all'. In this sober and reflective idiom lies the origin of a great quantity of humble but worthy church music up to the middle of the nineteenth century.

Several of Locke's anthems have independent instrumental parts. 'O be joyful in the Lord, all ye lands' (no. 12) shows his willingness to adopt an idiom pioneered by his younger contemporaries, with its jaunty triple-time symphony at the beginning. Here, as is usual in this kind of work, the accompaniment is for strings in four parts. But Locke's most ambitious achievement, and the most spectacularly scored piece of church music before the coronation of James II provoked an orgy of musical magnificence, was the *Song of Thanksgiving*, 'Be thou exalted, Lord' (no. 7), composed to celebrate Charles II's victory over the Dutch in 1666 and performed in the Chapel Royal on 14 August in that year. Pepys, who heard it on that occasion, described it as 'a special good anthem', as indeed it is: the scoring for three choirs may perhaps indicate the participation of Westminster Abbey and St George's, Windsor, as well as that of the Chapel Royal itself. The exact details of the instrumentation are obscure (the work survives only in the composer's autograph score, which is understandably imprecise on matters over which he would have had control in performance), but one section is assigned to 'violins, theorbos, and viols, to the organ'; and the 'band of violins', at the opening and elsewhere, is scored in five parts using the treble, soprano, mezzo-soprano, alto, and bass clefs. With this is contrasted a 'consort' in four parts, possibly for wind instruments.[28] The construction and musical invention are not less noteworthy. The 'song' proper ('The King shall rejoice', Ps. 21) is framed by a 'grand chorus' setting the last verse of the same psalm, 'Be thou exalted'. There is much picturesque detail in the body of the work, particularly in the antiphonal setting of 'And why? because the King putteth his trust in the Lord', and of 'no,

---

[28] The 'band of violins' evidently consisted of three trebles, one tenor (i.e. viola), and one bass violin, this last descending to low *B* flat. The 'consort' is written in the autograph (Oxford, Bod. Lib., MS Mus. c. 23) on staves allotted to the first choir in the treble, treble, alto, and bass clefs (see facsimile of first page in Dearnley, *English Church Music*, pl. 8).

no, he shall not miscarry', the negative particles here being an addition by the composer (Ex. 188).

Locke's motets are, on balance, even finer than the anthems. As with Child, but in a more controlled and yet vividly imaginative way, the very spirit of the early Italian baroque is recreated and assimilated to Locke's personal and in other respects English-derived idiom. Of those published, 'Audi, Domine' (no. 2) and 'Super flumina Babylonis' (no. 6), at least, are masterpieces of the first order. In the declamation of the texts, the expressiveness and integration of the themes, and the subtlety of their instrumental writing (here as normally for two violins with bass viol and organ), they exhibit a high level of the purest artistry. The culture that could support and sustain such music, whether in the chapel of a Roman Catholic queen or in the Music School at Oxford, was a rich one indeed.

While Locke was unquestionably the major figure of his generation at work in the decade and a half following the Restoration, the London musical scene was being enlivened by the presence of a prodigiously gifted and much younger composer, Pelham Humfrey. Born in 1647, he became one of the Children of the Chapel Royal on the Restoration, and in 1664 was awarded a substantial grant (£450) to study in France and Italy for two years. He left early in 1665, returning in October 1667 to become a Gentleman of the Chapel. In 1672, on the death of Henry Cooke, he became Master of the Children and took other posts including those of director of, and composer for, the King's band of violins. But two years later he was dead, claimed by an unidentified illness on 14 July 1674.[29]

Humfrey wrote odes, theatre music, and songs, but the bulk of his output consists of church music, mainly verse anthems accompanied by strings, written for the Chapel Royal.[30] He had begun to write verse anthems even before going abroad, for he had by then contributed to the so-called *Club Anthem*, 'I will always give thanks', written with two of his fellow-choristers, William Turner and John Blow. One or two others of the extant anthems appear to belong to the same period. They demonstrate not only his precociousness but also the predominance of French idioms in his artistic make-up. This would have been encouraged by the King's own preferences and by the availability in London of authentic models;[31] no English

---

[29] P. Dennison, *Pelham Humfrey* (Oxford, 1986), 1–9.

[30] *Complete Church Music*, ed. P. Dennison, 2 vols. (MB, xxxiv, xxxv). The numbering in the text refers to this edition.

[31] Louis Grabu, a pupil of Robert Cambert, entered the service of Charles II no later than 31 Mar. 1665. (*Records of English Court Music*, ed. Ashbee (Snodland, 1986–), i. 221). A year later he became Master of the King's Musick. Humfrey thought very little of him (Pepys, *Diary*, 15 Nov. 1667), but this is not incompatible with earlier influence. A vogue for French keyboard and lute music was of longer standing.

Ex. 188

composer of the time, Locke not excepted, could remain aloof, but it was the generation of Humfrey and Blow that became most strongly influenced. The course of Humfrey's peregrinations is uncharted, but there is little in his music to suggest a deep involvement with the current Italian style. The non-French element in it is predominantly native, with the admixture of older French and Italian that that implies; the distinguishing factor is the addition of directly derived and contemporary French characteristics. The likelihood that Humfrey spent a good deal of his time abroad at the French court is confirmed both by its political appropriateness and by the music itself.

Humfrey normally wrote for strings in four parts (unlike Lully and his successors, who wrote in five), occasionally in three. One example of the latter is in 'By the waters of Babylon' (no. 2), which is perhaps an early work on that account, though a very fine one nevertheless. It makes an interesting comparison with Locke's 'Super flumina', which it resembles in its scoring though differing in its rejection of Italianate declamation. It exploits the potential of the text for picturesque word-setting, as in the verse 'Sing us one of the songs of Sion', where the extraordinary progressions of the response 'How shall we sing the Lord's song in a strange land?' do seem to owe a good deal to the tutelage (formal or otherwise) of someone such as Locke himself (Ex. 189). 'The King shall rejoice' (no. 17) is based on the same psalm as Locke's 'Be thou exalted'; and while it lacks Locke's boldness, it opens with an intensely expressive passage for the upper strings alone, perhaps the earliest use by an English composer of this useful orchestral texture.

Humfrey was always ready to experiment harmonically, even with little expressive justification, as may be shown by the passage quoted in Ex. 190 from the opening symphony of one of his most assured works, 'O praise the Lord' (no. 15). His youthful enthusiasm led him into paths which Locke trod with more discretion, and along which Blow and Purcell followed eagerly behind, profiting from the experience of their precursors (p. 522).

The service 'in E la mi' (i.e. E minor, no. 19) shows what the plain a cappella style might mean to such a composer: it is a splendidly resourceful setting of all the musical items, except for the 'Venite', of Matins, Holy Communion, and Evensong, varied in its texture (the old tradition of harmonically complete vocal verse sections being put to good use), and thematically well integrated by its ingenious use of scalic motives. It is indeed Humfrey's refusal to resort to melodic cliché that marks him out as a major figure of the Restoration epoch, distinguishing him from the multitude of lesser men that now thronged the city and court.

Humfrey was in fact the eldest of a particularly promising group of Chapel Royal Children at the Restoration, the others being Michael Wise (c.1648–87), John Blow (1649–1708), Thomas Tudway (c.1650–1726), and William

Ex. 189

Turner (1651–1740).[32] John Blow was to prove by far the finest of this group, to be rivalled in his maturity by Purcell alone. Though by 1675 he had written extensively for the Church in a variety of styles, his music should be looked at as a whole in the context of the later seventeenth century. At the close of the period covered by this chapter, the music of the Chapel Royal, fostered as it was by the enthusiasm of a pleasure-loving but not entirely frivolous monarch, appeared to be destined for a brilliant and long-lasting future, secure in the hands of Blow and the young Purcell. That this was not to be was of course due in large part to the predilections of Charles's successors on the throne—his austere brother and Roman Catholic James II, and later the staunchly Protestant William and his meekly subservient wife—but it can also be attributed to a certain extent to the

---

[32] For these, and some lesser contemporaries, see Ch. 10, pp. 563 seqq.

Ex. 190

swift decay that inevitably follows the sudden explosion of a cultural phenomenon. The real future lay, not in the unceasing renewal of a self-consuming
brilliance, but in the cultivation of the deeper strata of the English idiom
and in the resolution of the conflicting elements as they rose to the surface.

One of these strata was the secular vocal idiom that had flourished unabated
through the changes and chances of monarchy, Commonwealth, and
monarchy again. The origins of continuo-song have been discussed in
Chapter 7. The principal figures there were Alfonso Ferrabosco and Robert
Johnson, to whom may now be added the younger Nicholas Lanier (1588–
1666), John Wilson (1595–1674), Henry Lawes (1596–1662), and John Hilton
(1599–1657). There were many others, but these four in particular dominate
the Caroline and Commonwealth lyric. A welcome feature of the new
epoch, already foreshadowed in the Jacobean period, is the regular association between musical settings and good (if sometimes limited) verse. The
songs of this period are meant to be a musico-literary experience. Too
often the Elizabethans and Jacobeans had bestowed fine music upon literary
trivia. But the consequence of the new literary awareness was that less
attention was paid to the music in its own right. The melodic contours,
as to both pitches and durations, were contrived above all with a view
to their appropriateness for the words to be set. 'Contrivance' does not
seem too harsh a term for this process. Harmony, however, became more
fortuitous. A simple bass-line, in Renaissance music, might unequivocally
imply the appropriate harmony. But in the seventeenth century a good
deal was left to chance. The melodies themselves often do not suggest

clear progressions, while the basses that are actually supplied, mostly with few or no figures, may not seem to be organically linked with them. The very simple rules then current for filling in the harmonies[33] do not always appear to meet the necessary requirements.

The appreciation of this kind of song, therefore, is heavily dependent on the listener's literary awareness. It is not the subject-matter, stereotyped as it inevitably is, that will detain him, but the manner of its treatment: the handling of metaphor, of rhyme and metre, and so on. The music, with these latter, is the medium through which the 'conceit', metaphor or simile, is to be expressed. If at first sight the conceptual ingenuity of the verse seems too weighty for musical setting, it should be remembered that rhyme and metre are in themselves a sonorous element, providing a framework within which the 'conceptual' aspect must be contained but at the same time restricted by the need for the verse to 'make sense'. Herein lies the appeal of verse: a musical setting should in theory reinforce it. Unfortunately the composers were sometimes led astray by metrical variation between one stanza and another; so that, as in the period of Morley and Dowland, the musical setting of the first stanza may be difficult to adapt to the others. It is sometimes hard to resist the conclusion that the musical setting is a superfluous gloss that can only detract from the poet's own balance between sound and sense.

On the whole, two main kinds of song were cultivated, the declamatory and the merely 'tuneful'. The former, without necessarily approaching true recitative, endeavoured to respond to every inflection of the verse to be set. It was extremely difficult to write good *strophic* declamatory song, and sometimes the verse made it impossible. In such cases only the first stanza would be singable. But sometimes (and as time went on more frequently), such songs were through-composed, or at least partly so. The 'tuneful' lyric, often in triple time, attempted less and was more likely to be successful as a whole. Ensemble vocal music tended to adopt the idiom of the tuneful solo song, using such combinations as two trebles and bass, or alto, tenor, and bass (always with *basso continuo* expressed or implied); the writing of catches, rounds, canons, and other pieces for three or four equal voices was also popular. The Renaissance tradition of the dramatic dialogue was maintained and extended; such works usually ended with a 'chorus' for two or three singers in the contrapuntally undemanding idiom of the day.

It was Nicholas Lanier who did as much as anyone to give the English declamatory song its definitive shape. Of French extraction but English birth, he travelled widely in Italy between 1625 and 1628, having become

---

[33] These are enshrined in Locke's *Melothesia* (1673), though they must have been generally understood, particularly as regards unfigured basses, for several decades before that.

Master of the King's Musick in 1625 on the accession of Charles I.[34] Officially he went abroad to buy pictures for the King—he was himself a painter—but it cannot be doubted that he picked up a good deal of knowledge of the latest musical fashions while there. Already in 1614 he had contributed (rather feebly) to the Earl of Somerset's masque with the mildly declamatory song 'Bring away this sacred tree'. More seriously, he wrote the music for Ben Jonson's masques *Lovers made men* (1617) and *Vision of Delight* (1618), described in the posthumous edition of Jonson's stage works (1637–40) as having been sung 'stylo recitativo', in the former case throughout. There is no reason to doubt the evidence of this authoritative text, but it may be, of course, that the music did not really resemble the Italian *stile rappresentativo* of the day; and it may be, too, that the actual expression 'stylo recitativo' was not in use in England as early as 1617.[35] This is to a certain extent confirmed by the survival, in highly decorated form, of one song from *Vision of Delight*, which when stripped of its ornament resembles fairly ordinary declamatory song of the type then current.[36]

A certain expansion of the declamatory idiom may be seen in Lanier's setting of Ralegh's 'Like hermit poor' (no. 7),[37] where however the constant use of repeated-note figures becomes wearisome and appears to stifle melodic expression. The second and third stanzas, moreover, provide a good illustration of the almost comic effect of repeating carefully controlled declamatory music to words which, while metrically identical, do not permit distortion in the same places (Ex. 191).

Lanier's famous dramatic monologue 'Nor com'st thou yet, my slothful love' (no. 10), portraying Hero's emotions as she awaits Leander on the shores of the Hellespont, is a tremendous advance, though as it belongs to a different genre the comparison is not entirely a fair one.[38] This is more than mere 'rhetorical' declamation: it is truly dramatic music. Roger North, who greatly admired the work, thought that it was written soon after Lanier's return from Italy,[39] and it does manage successfully to trans-

---

[34] He is first called 'master of the music' in a document of 13 June 1626 (*King's Musick*, 61); but he had already become Master of the Musick to Prince Charles in 1618 and may be presumed to have retained his responsibilities from Charles's accession. In this way was established one of the more colourful eminences of the profession.

[35] The matter has been discussed by McD. Emslie, 'Nicholas Lanier's Innovations in English Song', *ML*, 41 (1960), 13–27, and by P. Walls, 'The Origins of English Recitative', *PRMA*, 110 (1983–4), 25–40. In a supplementary note to Dr Walls's paper, F. W. Sternfeld traces the term *recitativo* itself back to Agazzari's *Del sonar sopra'l basso*, published in 1607. Sigismondo d'India had used the expression 'stile recitativo' in his collection of 1609; but it was not at all common, even in Italy, until the 1630s and 1640s, largely under the influence of G. B. Doni.

[36] I. Spink, *English Song, Dowland to Purcell* (London, 1974; repr. 1986), 46–8 (including transcription). Professor Spink's book is an admirable guide to the subject, and one to which I am greatly indebted.

[37] This discussion is based on *English Songs 1625–1660*, ed. I. Spink (MB, xxxiii), to which the numbers in the text refer.

[38] The story was made familiar by Marlowe's famous poem, but the author of Lanier's text is unknown.

[39] *Roger North on Music*, p. 294; *The Musicall Grammarian*, 205–6.

Ex. 191

plant the idioms of Italian recitative into English soil. The variety of pace
to suit the different moods is worthy of Monteverdi himself; but what
is especially remarkable is the control of tonality to lend a musical shape
to what could easily have become an amorphous mass. Lanier's skill is
shown in his opening away from the main key in order to give it a more
subtle role as a focus of dramatic resolution; a technique that finds its fulfilment in the closing bars where an even greater tonal terrain is traversed
before the final resting-place is reached (Ex. 192, overleaf).[40]

[40] None of the sources is earlier than 1670: the figuring, here supplemented, is unlikely to be original.

Ex. 192

Lanier's subtle set of strophic variations in triple time, 'No more shall meads be deck'd with flow'rs' (no. 4), to words by Thomas Carew (or Carey) shows another aspect of his art, though still of Italian inspiration. Here a 28-bar ground supports a melodic line that in the final stanza covers an amazing expressive range.[41] Lanier was also at home with the simplest tunes, which in his case are still very Jacobean in manner. Though he cannot be shown to have developed artistically beyond his middle years, he remains a highly influential and rewarding innovator in English song.

Wilson and Hilton were lesser figures by comparison. Wilson's career exhibits a curious dichotomy. In his younger days he had been associated with the theatre, especially the 'King's Men' under James I, and many of his theatre songs survive. He became a lutenist to Charles I in 1635 and, after a doubtless dispiriting interlude in the aftermath of the Rebellion, Professor of Music (or 'Choragus') at Oxford from 1656 to 1661. At the Restoration he returned to the royal service, and became a Gentleman of the Chapel Royal in 1662. His music is a reflection of his personal volatility. The 'academic' side is illustrated by his collection of fantasias for the lute in all the major and minor keys. But his many light songs and catches are more typical of his personality. His *Cheerfull Ayres* (1660),[42] scored for two sopranos and bass with *basso continuo*, consists entirely of arrangements of solo songs, as the full title makes clear. Most of his songs are simple, rather four-square, strophic efforts; the occasional through-composed example (such as his setting of Davenant's refrain-song 'Awake awake')[43] seems to have occasioned him a good deal of trouble while scarcely warranting the care bestowed upon it. His best-known song, 'Take, O take those lips away' from Shakespeare's *Measure for Measure*, was probably composed for a performance of John Fletcher's *Rollo* in 1619, where it is found with a second stanza and some textual variants that coincide with those in all the musical sources (see Plate XIII).

Hilton's fame rests largely on his *Ayres or Fa las* (1627) and *Catch as catch can* (1652), the latter an immensely popular anthology that ran into many editions thereafter. On the whole his songs are no more arresting than Wilson's, but mention should be made of the substantial dialogue 'Rise, princely shepherd' (no. 67) on the Judgement of Paris. With its four characters this is certainly one of the more ambitious pieces of its kind;

---

[41] The form of the ground is a a b a a c b. There is a curious similarity to the final duet, 'Pur ti miro', of Monteverdi's *L'Incoronazione di Poppea* (1642), though this may not be by Monteverdi himself (see Chiarelli in *Rivista italiana di musicologia*, 9 (1974), 117–51; *NGD*, s.v. Ferrari, Benedetto).

[42] 1660 is the date on the title-page. But a manuscript note in the British Library copy includes the date 20 Sept. 1659.

[43] *English Songs*, no. 28. John Wilson's songbook in the Bodleian Library, Mus. b. 1, copied by Edward Lowe, is an important collection and deserves a closer study than it has yet received. Several of the songs have an accompaniment in lute tablature as well as the usual bass. Towards the end are a number of settings of Latin texts, odes of Horace and the like.

but the idiom remains earthbound and the dramatic possibilities of the scene are exploited by neither the anonymous poet nor the composer.

Henry Lawes is in a quite different category, if only by virtue of his enormous output of nearly 450 songs of various kinds. With an autograph fair copy of over three-quarters of them and three collections published under his supervision, the editor of his secular vocal music could hardly be better placed. Like his younger brother William, Henry Lawes was a chorister at Salisbury Cathedral in the early years of the seventeenth century; like William he studied with John Coprario, and became a Gentleman of the Chapel Royal (1626) and a member of Charles I's 'Private Musick' (in 1631). Though he never possessed his brother's penchant for complex instrumental writing, he was a highly professional composer, much admired in his day. Milton's famous sonnet, first published in his highly Royalist *Choice Psalmes* (1648), of all places, perhaps overrates Lawes's sensitivity in the handling of English verse;[44] but it was written when the Renaissance idiom, itself so assured in that matter, had ceased to exercise the creative imagination, and should be thought of in the context of the search for a declamatory idiom that began with Ferrabosco and Johnson. In that light, it is a very fair assessment of his achievement.

Lawes was the Cavalier lyrist *par excellence*. It is not just that he set much 'Cavalier' verse (and a good deal else besides, not all of it of the highest calibre), but rather that his undemonstrative yet expressive idiom is perfectly suited to the refined sensibility of the courtly aesthetic, being neither too penetrating nor too shallow, so to speak. His songs achieved a wide popularity, and, like his contribution to the Caroline psalm-repertory, proved to have a more widespread appeal than the original context might have suggested. They were not the works by which he set the greatest store:

For my own part, I send not these abroad to get a Name; Were that my Designe, I have other *Compositions*, fitter for such as are Masters in our Art, when the Season calls for them. My poor talent never lay in a Napkin.[45]

That remark, it is true, prefaced a volume of ayres more than usually dominated by the lighter style. His best solo work is in the declamatory song, of which his setting of Herrick's 'Whither are all her false oaths blown?' is typical of his earlier, rather self-conscious manner (Ex. 193).[46] We note immediately the diminished fourth to illustrate 'false' (bar 2), and the picturesque settings of 'lightning', 'falling', and 'blast' towards the end. But there are also some less felicitous touches: the awkward high

---

[44] It begins: 'Harry, whose tuneful and well-measured song | First taught our English music how to span | Words with just note and accent, not to scan | With Midas' ears, committing short and long; | Thy worth and skill exempts thee from the throng...'.

[45] From the dedicatory epistle to his third collection (*Ayres and Dialogues... The Third Book*, 1658; cited from *The Treasury of Musick*, Book iii, 1669).

[46] No. 48; collated with the autograph (London, Brit. Lib., Add. 53723), fo. 46ʳ (see Plate XIV).

Ex. 193

continued

Ex. 193, continued

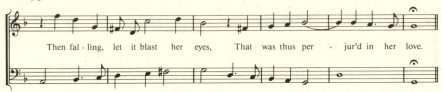

note on 'live', the rather pointless musical repetition in the next phrase, the false accentuation of 'My withered heart' and 'Until one of her oaths', the melodic cliché of 'There may they wrestle in the skies'. Lawes usually managed to achieve a more relaxed approach to word-setting in his mature songs, though he always remained subject to the pitfalls of the strophic declamatory form.

Lawes also cultivated the dramatic cantata, as we may call it, in which the expressive range is not limited by the requirements of strophic repetition. There are several fine examples in Playford's second collection,[47] including 'Help help, O help' (headed 'A Storm: Cloris at Sea, near the Land, is surprized by a Storm. Amintor on the Shore, expecting her Arrival, thus complains:');[48] A Tale out of Anacreon, 'At dead low ebb of night';[49] and the dramatic dialogue 'Charon, O Charon, draw near'. This, though belonging to a familiar genre, was 'occasioned by the Death of the young Lord Hastings, who dyed some few days before he was to have been Married to Sir Theodore Meihern's Daughter, in June, 1649'.[50] The most famous of Lawes's dramatic pieces, however, though not the best, was his Ariadne lament, 'Theseus, O Theseus'. Monteverdi's own 'Lasciatemi morire', the only surviving section of his opera Arianna (1608), may have been known to Lawes, though his music does not greatly resemble it. William Cartwright's verse was something of a handicap, and Lawes did not achieve even the freedom of dramatic expression shown in Lanier's Hero and Leander. The opening section will serve to illustrate his striving for expressive detail (Ex. 194).[51]

Lawes achieved early fame with his songs for Milton's Comus (1634),

[47] The Treasury of Musick, Book ii, 1669. This is not a reprint of Lawes's own second collection of 1655 but an independent anthology, possibly a reprint of a volume advertised in 1663 but no longer extant. Some of the attributions are unreliable.

[48] In the autograph MS, fos. 163^r–164^v; Treasury, ii. 1. In this song Amintor is Charles I and Cloris Henrietta Maria, who returned to England from the Netherlands in 1643. For the circumstances, and the whole genre of Cloris and Amintor laments, see M. Chan in The Well Enchanting Skill, 239.

[49] Ibid. 5 (not in autograph).

[50] Ibid. 109. It is followed (pp. 112–13) by a similar piece by William Lawes, 'Charon, O Charon! Hear a wretch oppressed' (English Songs, no. 86): this poem had earlier been set by Robert Ramsay. For an earlier example of the genre see Ch. 7, p. 458, and Ex. 173.

[51] Autograph MS, fo. 124^r: barring as in the MS. In the printing of Milton's sonnet (see n. 44 above) in the Choice Psalmes, the line 'That tun'st their happiest lines in hymn or story' is annotated: 'The story of Ariadne set by him to musick'.

Ex. 194

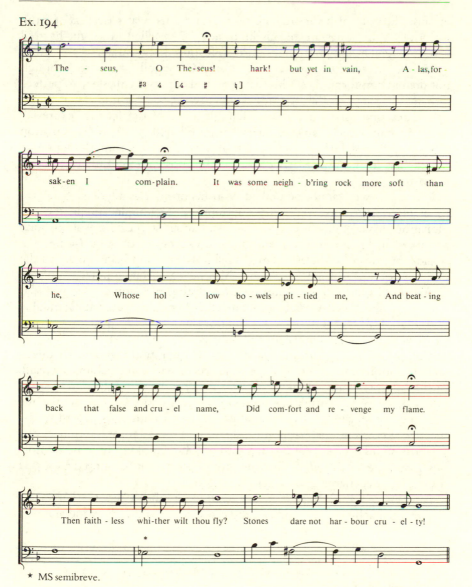

The - seus, O The-seus! hark! but yet in vain, A - las, for -

#3 4 [4 # ♮]

sak-en I com-plain. It was some neigh - b'ring rock more soft than

he, Whose hol - low bo-wels pit-tied me, And beat-ing

back that false and cru - el name, Did com-fort and re - venge my flame.

Then faith - less whi-ther wilt thou fly? Stones dare not har - bour cru - el-ty!

*

★ MS semibreve.

from which the poet's admiration doubtless stemmed. He achieved a more genuinely dramatic effect in his music for Cartwright's play *The Royal Slave* (1636),[52] and he was to be chosen to contribute to Sir William Davenant's *The Siege of Rhodes*, the music for which has not survived.[53] But his primary

[52] *English Songs*, nos. 43–6.
[53] See below, pp. 556–7.

impulse, in spite of his more ambitious aspirations, was lyrical. By far the majority of the songs are of this kind, and he excelled in a light-hearted vein as several examples from his third collection demonstrate.[54]

Lawes's affecting lament for his brother, 'Cease jolly shepherds', though not dramatic in form, shows his technical and expressive mastery to perfection. Madrigalian in the best and widest sense, it is as impressive for its artistic restraint as it is for the evident sincerity of the feelings expressed in it. Few composers of any period have inspired such a chorus of lamentation as William Lawes did by his patriotic death, and his own brother's memorial, placed first in the printed collection, is the most purely musicianly of all (Ex. 195).[55]

William Lawes cannot be ranked with his brother as a lyricist. Sensitive to dramatic situations, skilled in contrapuntal technique and in the exploitation of vocal effect, deeply serious as an artist yet (like Wilson) with a marked inclination towards the musical expression of good (sometimes ribald) fun, he nevertheless seemed unable to respond instinctively to the potential of well-turned lyric verse. Yet he has been somewhat unfairly treated until recent times,[56] and his own setting of Carew's 'Farewell fair Saint' in a shortened version, though it has been compared unfavourably with that of his brother,[57] has a declamatory subtlety within its limited span that reveals a strong potential for this kind of writing (Ex. 196, pp. 535–6).

Compression is a surprising characteristic in a composer whose instrumental conceptions could be on a large scale; yet Lawes could achieve a wealth of meaning, serious or humorous, in a tiny round or catch, in a glee for male voices, or in a drinking-song with a short chorus. His vocal writing is devised pragmatically for its aural effect, often with scant regard to the niceties of conventional harmony and counterpoint. The extraordinary dissonances in his own lament on the death of John Tomkins, or in his humorous part-song *The Catts*,[58] illustrate this tendency at its most fruitful; at times it can degenerate into a tiresome habit.

Lawes's twelve dialogues, including two on the 'Charon' theme, are a substantial achievement and an ample testimony of his dramatic ability.[59]

---

[54] One of these is the *Dialogue on a Kisse*, 'Among my Fancies tell me this' (p. 29: modern edition by R. McGrady, MC, lx). Apart from the good selection in *English Songs*, attention may be drawn to Lawes's *Hymns to the Holy Trinity* from his second collection (1655, pp. 44–6; modern edition by G. Beechey, MC, viii).

[55] *Choice Psalmes* (1648), at sigs. F, Q, Cc, and Ll respectively.

[56] *English Songs*, and Spink, *English Song* provide a selection and well-considered comment respectively. Lefkowitz, *William Lawes*, 164–5, is less complimentary about English declamatory song and about his hero's efforts in particular; but he prints what he considers William Lawes's finest song, 'Amarillis, tear thy hair', in full, pp. 162–3, with appreciative comments.

[57] Spink, *English Song*, 112–13. The song is in William's own autograph volume, Brit. Lib., Add. 31432, fos. 24ᵛ–25ᵗ: see Plate XV.

[58] Lefkowitz, *William Lawes*, 180–2.

[59] Cf. n. 50. There are several similar dialogues by William Lawes in vols. i and ii of the *Treasury*.

Ex. 195

continued

Ex. 195, continued

★ The *basso continuo* has minims *c d* in this bar.

Though two of them were actually prepared for theatrical performances ('What softer sounds are these' for Ben Jonson's *Entertainment at Welbeck*, 1633, and 'Come, my Daphne, come away' for Shirley's *The Cardinal*, 1641), it is a matter for regret that the social and historical conditions did not yet afford the opportunity for extended musical drama in the theatre. If they had done so, there can be little doubt that William Lawes would have become an opera composer of distinction. As it is, his very real genius for vocal writing was often frittered away on trivia.

Dramatic skill is sometimes manifested in surprising quarters. Robert Ramsey was but a minor figure as a song-writer, but his setting of Herrick's 'Howl not, you ghosts and furies, while I sing' is a powerful evocation of the Orpheus legend in a dramatic form,[60] comparable with William Lawes's 'Orpheus, O Orpheus, gently touch thy Lesbian lyre', while 'In guilty night' anticipates Purcell in its chilling representation of the raising of Samuel's ghost by the witch of Endor.[61] Hilton's classical effort has been referred to already; Lanier wrote several dramatic dialogues, and Simon

[60] *English Songs*, no. 15.
[61] Ramsey, *Sacred Music*, i (EECM, vii), no. 10.

Ex. 196

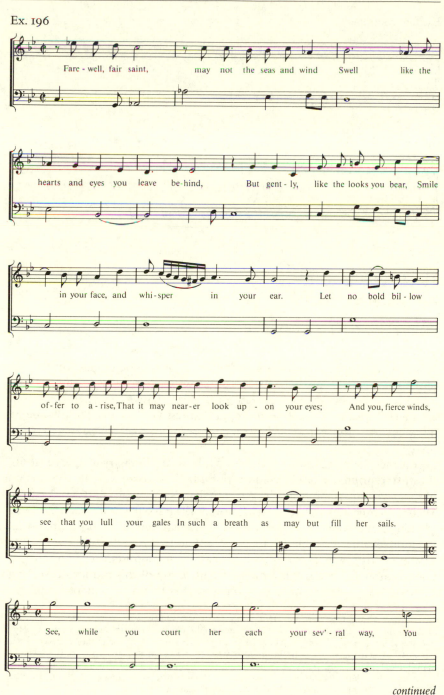

Fare-well, fair saint, may not the seas and wind Swell like the hearts and eyes you leave be-hind, But gent-ly, like the looks you bear, Smile in your face, and whi-sper in your ear. Let no bold bil-low of-fer to a-rise, That it may near-er look up-on your eyes; And you, fierce winds, see that you lull your gales In such a breath as may but fill her sails. See, while you court her each your sev'-ral way, You

continued

Ex. 196, continued

safe - ly   may   her to her port con - vey, And   loose her in a

no - ble   way   of   woo - ing   Whiles both   con - tri - bute

to   your own   un - do - ing.

Ives, George Jeffreys, and William Caesar (alias Smegergill) yet others. Jenkins, scarcely of any account as a song-writer, wrote two, one of them being his own lament on the death of William Lawes. Though the words are merely quaint, it is a fine piece, an expressive declamatory style being disciplined by the composer's strong sense of formal cohesion (Ex. 197, pp. 537–8).[62]

A glance at the first two volumes of Playford's *Treasury of Musick* (1669, the first reprinted from a volume published in 1659) reveals the wealth of song-writing talent available to him: Charles Coleman (d. 1664), William Webb, Thomas Brewer (b. 1611), Thomas Blagrave (d. 1688), Jeremy Savile (d. 1665), and John Goodgroome (d. 1704) are amongst those not so far mentioned. John Gamble (d. 1687) published two books of his own (1656, reprinted 1657, and 1659) as well as leaving an important commonplace-book,[63] though his was but a minor talent. Little of this music is deserving of extended consideration, but taken together it is an eloquent testimony

[62] *Choice Psalmes* (1648), sigs. Gɪᵛ, Ddɪᵛ, Llɜᵛ. There is a variant version, apparently in the hand of Jenkins himself, at the beginning of Lawes's autograph volume (see n. 57), starting on fo. 2ᵛ. After two pages, as a result of trying to compress the vocal parts on to one stave, the scribe confesses: 'Heare I was outt and now Ille begine another way.' The piece is then restarted, almost exactly as in the printed copy.

[63] See V. Duckles, 'The Gamble Manuscript as a Source of *continuo* song in England', *JAMS*, ɪ (1948), 23–40. The MS is in the New York Public Lib., Drexel 4257.

Ex. 197

continued

Ex. 197, continued

to the strength of English song-writing in the years before, during, and after the Commonwealth and Protectorate.[64]

Instrumental music in the Caroline epoch built upon and extended the advances made during the previous reign. A good deal of somewhat conventional music continued to be written, both by highly skilled practitioners working either for private use or for wider circulation, and by amateurs for their own amusement. Thomas Tomkins was far and away the most

[64] There is a good account in Spink, *English Song*, 161–71. Some minor transitional figures are listed below in Ch. 10, p. 591.

distinguished of those who confined themselves to conventional idioms;[65] but Michael East and Richard Mico were not far behind, while Christopher Gibbons, Simon Ives, George Jeffreys, John Okeover, Thomas Ford, Martin Peerson, and John Hilton all made substantial contributions. Much of this music is less intensely contrapuntal than the typical products of the preceding epoch, even those by minor masters: formally, it substitutes a kind of tuneful regularity for the severe logic of syntactic imitation,[66] while the textures are simplified and not infrequently reduced to three parts. But none of it embraces the formal and textural devices initiated by Coprario and carried to fruition by William Lawes and John Jenkins.

These two masters are unparalleled in the first half of the century for their versatility and capacity for innovation, at least in the sphere of instrumental music. William Lawes (1602–45), though the younger of the two, must be considered first in view of his early death at the siege of Chester. Brought up, like his elder brother Henry, as a chorister of Salisbury Cathedral, and apprenticed like him to John Coprario, he found his way into the Chapel Royal and the royal household, where he busied himself with the provision of music for masques and other court entertainments.[67] He must have been a delightful companion: he could toss off a catch or a glee for any occasion, and the sincere regret caused by his death—even if it were the result of impetuous folly—is evident from the chorus of lamentation which it provoked. As we have seen, Lawes's serious side did not find its happiest expression in vocal music, least of all the formally sacred. That was reserved for his instrumental compositions, in which a deeply introspective nature can be fathomed below the surface brilliance.

Lawes's dance music, particularly that collected together as *The Royal Consort*, gives a clear impression of the courtly composer at work; but a good deal of his other music fits less readily into a social framework, and we are left with a large body of it, for the most part carefully copied in autograph scores and parts, and revealing nothing but the innermost workings of a profoundly reflective mind. Such are the five- and six-part consort 'sets' (with organ), each containing one or two fantasias and one or two airs or dances. Outwardly conventional, they conceal a deep individuality, and, more than that, a capacity for the reconciliation of opposing forces. The skill with which contrasting forces are brought into a coherent relationship is remarkable. The composer bows to an ancient tradition in

---

[65] For Tomkins, see Ch. 8.

[66] Van den Borren's expression means, properly, 'imitation, by means of which the music is propelled forward in a logical fashion, just as verbal syntax binds words together and enables them to express continuous thought'. For the composers mentioned, see Meyer, *Early English Chamber Music*, 195–7 (2nd edn., 225–7); but a reassessment is long overdue.

[67] Lefkowitz, *William Lawes*, 4–6, 10–11. This account is much indebted to Lefkowitz's pioneering study.

the two In nomines and a piece 'On the Playnsong',[68] and to Dowland in the grave Pavan beginning as in Ex. 198.[69]

Ex. 198

At times he takes the listener by the scruff of his neck, as when in the second of the two six-part fantasias in F, the onward rush of the argument is suddenly halted with an extraordinary coda (Ex. 199).[70] There is no fixed plan for each 'set', and the ordering, both of the complete works and of the movements within them, is partly a rationalization by editors. Though the collection may have reached its final form only in the 1640s, its general character and instrumentation make it more closely bound up with earlier practice than any other work by this composer.

Lawes's most famous collection of instrumental works is the so-called *Royal Consort* for two violins, two bass viols, and two theorbos; but it has been conclusively shown that this was not its original title and that it was first composed for two 'trebles', a 'meane', and a 'Base'.[71] Lawes was apparently dissatisfied with the balance of this 'quartet' version and, taking sixty-six pieces from a larger total, arranged them into six 'sets' according to key.[72] The first two sets, in D minor and D major respectively, each consisted of three suites (as we should now call them), so that there are ten suites in all. Each consists of six or seven movements, the first being usually a pavan or 'fantazy', the others shorter airs.

The curious instrumentation of the work (in its final form) is characteristic of the period. The two bass viols alternate the bass and meane functions and from time to time indulge in rapid 'divisions' or passage-work. The resonance and flexibility of the instrument lend an extraordinarily rich yet luminous quality to the sonority, which is enhanced by the use of two

[68] *Consort Sets*, ed. D. Pinto (London, 1979), p. 5.
[69] Ibid. 30. (Additional notes from the organ part alone are placed in round brackets.)
[70] Ibid. 112 (organ part omitted).
[71] Lefkowitz, *William Lawes*, 74.
[72] Ibid. 75–6.

Ex. 199

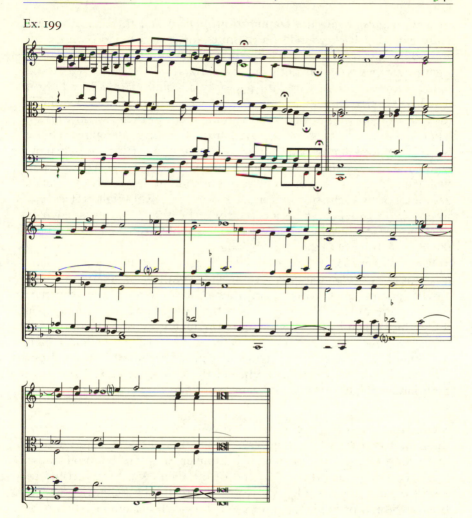

theorbo-lutes[73] to play the *basso continuo* part. The exact social function of this music may never be determined, but it is tempting to believe that it really was designed for courtly entertainment and even, in part, for the social dancing that invariably succeeded the formal presentation of a masque and doubtless predominated on occasions when no dramatic performance took place.

The so-called *Harp Consorts*, for violin, bass (or division) viol, theorbo, and harp, contain music that is even more finely wrought. The penchant for 'division', here entrusted both to the viol and to the violin, is carried

---

[73] The theorbo-lute was a lute with several free courses added (see Ch. 8, n. 9). The theorbo (Italian *tiorbo*) was a larger instrument similarly strung.

to new heights, while the combination of harp and theorbo provides a softly glittering background. Three suites for two bass viols with organ are also richly ornamented, while the three suites for three lyra viols provide a gorgeous tapestry of constantly shifting colours.

It is, however, in his works for one or two violins, bass viol, and organ, that Lawes's fiery genius is most in evidence. Formally they are similar to those of Coprario; but they are very different in their essential nature. Their nervous vitality is far removed from Coprario's serenity: at times we are reminded almost of a Carl Nielsen, so unpredictable and apparently random are the gestures (Ex. 200).[74] Their structure is rhetorical rather than logical: the stresses set up by extreme contrasts are resolved by grand gestures, not by thematic unification. Lawes had a well-nigh perfect sense of psychological length: he is a precursor of Beethoven in his deployment of sound-masses, but there is a waywardness about his manner that renders the ultimate balance all the more striking.

Lawes was one of the most completely developed musical personalities in a century that was unusually well provided with them. Tomkins, Henry Lawes, Jenkins, Locke, Blow, and Purcell are amongst those who stand out by virtue of their ability to project their own humanity in music. But there is in William Lawes a cavalier disregard for convention that is especially appealing. His art is the quintessence of the professionally pragmatic, judging its methods by results and totally disdainful of technical caution. But it also sounds depths which far transcend the courtly context in which it came into being, the product of a penetrating and visionary intelligence.

Mention has been made of the art of 'division' (or diminution), and something must now be said of this very characteristic mode of expression and of its chief theoretical exponent, Christopher Simpson. Simpson himself was a Yorkshireman who at the end of the Civil War, in which he had fought on the Royalist side, was received into the household of Sir John Bolles of Scampton in Lincolnshire. Quite how he had acquired his immense learning both in composition and in performance is uncertain; but he had by then become a highly respected musician. His theoretical writings include his contribution to Playford's *Introduction to the Skill of Musick* (1655); *The Division Violist*, first published in 1659; and *The Principles of Practical Musick* (1665).[75] There are also a number of chamber ensemble works in manuscript. Simpson tells us in *The Division-Viol* that a viol for the playing of divisions should be smaller than a consort bass, but with a bridge equally rounded

---

[74] *Select Consort Music*, ed. M. Lefkowitz (MB, xxi), no. 8a, bars 53–60.

[75] *The Division Violist* was reissued in 1665 with the bilingual title *Chelys/ The Division-Viol*: subsequent references are to this edition. *The Principles of Practical Musick* was reissued in 1667 as *A Compendium of Practical Musick*, running in this form to nine editions by 1775.

Ex. 200

(unlike that of a lyra viol) so that individual strings might be attacked with force. As for the practice of division, his own words cannot be bettered:

A *Ground, Subject,* or *Bass,* (call it which you please) is prick'd down in two several Papers; One for him who is to play the *Ground* upon an *Organ, Harpsechord,* or what other Instrument may be apt for that purpose; the Other, for him that plays upon the *Viol,* who, having the said *Ground* before his eyes, as his *Theme* or *Subject,* plays such variety of *Descant* or *Division* in Concordance thereto, as his skill and present invention do then suggest unto him.[76]

He goes on to explain that the player of divisions may either ornament the bass-line itself or descant freely above it; or else he may mix the two, either in single notes or in chords. At the end of his treatise he discusses extempore playing by two violists upon a ground, and the composition of divisions (or sets of variations) for one, two, or three viols, for one or two trebles upon a ground, and for various other combinations of treble and bass.

It is not clear how this art came to England. While one strand of development, the type of ground exemplified by the *passamezzo* and comparable series of harmonies, was derived in the first instance from Italy,[77] the evidence points to Spain as the ultimate origin of a practice that eventually spread throughout Europe. Cabezón and his contemporaries knew the ground later known as the *romanesca* and may have brought it to England. The *folia,* a dance of Spanish origin,[78] was based on a triple-time harmonic framework; it travelled to Italy, France, and England, and took various forms. One of these, on which Arcangelo Corelli was to write his famous sonata, had already reached England independently. The *passacaglia* originated from the strumming of Spanish guitarists as they 'walked the streets', and the *chaconne* was yet another ground-bass dance of Spanish origin. In Rome, in 1553, the Spaniard Diego Ortiz published his *Tratado de glosas sobre clausulas y otros generos de puntas en la musica de violones,* a close parallel to Simpson's own work. England was susceptible to all these influences at various times, both directly and through Italy and France; and in the first half of the seventeenth century the resumption of political contacts with Spain would surely have facilitated the channels of communication.

Wherever it came from, the practice of improvising and composing florid

---

[76] *The Division-Viol,* p. 27.

[77] See Ch. 5, n. 140, and Ex. 130(c), p. 343.

[78] On the *folia, passacaglia,* and *chaconne,* see the various articles in *NGD,* and the literature cited there. There is a copy of the *folia* in its later form in London, RCM MS 2093, under its usual English designation of 'Farranellas Ground' (referring to Michel Farinel, b. 1649): cf. *The Division Violin* (1684), no. 5 (fac. edn., London, 1982).

variations on a ground was widely popular at this time.[79] The bass viol was the most favoured for the purpose because of its range and versatility; but other instruments, and later especially the (treble) violin were also put to the same use. But this musical form had its limitations, even in the hands of so splendid a master as Simpson. A largely decorative treatment of a short bass theme could not rival in potential the contrapuntal type of ground that had been treated with such distinction by Byrd and his contemporaries; nor did it approach in emotional force the form as cultivated by Purcell and Blow, in which the *ostinato* is set off by the continuous flow of melody above it. Its significance, rather, lay in the other contexts in which the art of division could be practised. Simpson himself, in describing the composition of music for 'three basses' (perhaps lyra viols), writes:

In *Divisions* made for *three basses*, every *Viol* acts the *Treble*, *Bass*, or *Inward* Part, by turns. But here you are to take notice, that *Divisions* of Three Parts, are not usually made upon *Grounds*; but rather Composed in the manner of *Fancies*; beginning commonly with some *Fuge*, and then falling into Points of *Division*; answering one another; sometimes two against one, and sometimes all engaged at once in a contest of *Division*: But (after all) ending commonly in grave and harmonious Musick.[80]

He goes on to describe the composition of ayres or almains, in which the repetitions of the strains will call for variation in division. Simpson himself wrote a number of works in which division-writing plays a less formal role than in a set of variations on a ground. We have seen that it was practised in this way by Lawes; and it was also a feature of the work of Jenkins, the only one of his contemporaries whom Simpson cares to mention.[81]

The career of Jenkins strides like a colossus over the first three-quarters of the seventeenth century. Born in 1592, he obtained, perhaps during the 1620s, the patronage of two Norfolk families, the Derhams of West Dereham and the L'Estranges at Hunstanton. He participated—whether as player, composer, or both is uncertain—in the elaborate court masque, *The Triumph of Peace*, in February 1634; but he seems not to have been officially one of the court musicians, and his activities then and during

---

[79] One composer of such things was Daniel Norcombe, some of whose divisions for viol were published by Simpson: others remain in manuscript in the British Library and in the Bodleian. Norcombe was violist to the Archduke Albert in Brussels from 1602 to 1647 (not necessarily continuously: and the earlier reference could be to an older composer). His relationship to Daniel Norcombe the elder (b. 1576), lutenist and contributor to *The Triumphes of Oriana*, is unclear: the latter cannot be proved to have been Albert's violist in 1602.

[80] *The Division-Viol*, p. 60.

[81] Ibid. 61.

the Civil War are not altogether clear.[82] At the Restoration he became a theorbo-player in the King's Musick, but resided with the North family at Kirtling in Cambridgeshire. Roger North, youngest son of the fourth Lord North and brother of Francis the Lord Keeper, became his pupil and a warm though not uncritical admirer. Jenkins spent his last years at the home of Sir Philip Wodehouse at Kimberley, Norfolk, where he died towards the end of October 1678.

Jenkins was one of the last English composers to benefit at all thoroughly from the old system of private patronage by the country gentry. Until the Civil War, at any rate, this did not impede a close contact with fellow-professionals, most of whom were attached to the court; and during the Commonwealth period it proved to be a means of sustenance for many who had not relied on it hitherto. After the Restoration, as the Cavalier families gradually lost hold of their former dominance over English society, it ceased to provide the conditions under which an aspiring composer could hope to make his name. For the ageing Jenkins, such a change mattered little: his reputation was secure and his music widely known. New factors, such as the growth in music-publishing, provided new opportunities to younger men and in many ways dictated the type of music being written; the court and the London churches themselves enjoyed, at least temporarily, a brilliant revival; foreign musicians provided new excitements, and foreign travel brought new concepts of the musically desirable. Jenkins became old-fashioned, though still revered by the *cognoscenti*.

None of this is in the least surprising. The miracle is that Jenkins, and others similarly placed (Wilbye, Ward, and so on), had been able to build up their reputations while in private service. We must allow, of course, for periodic visits to London, even by far-flung families; but the main factor appears to have been their desire to keep up with rival establishments by obtaining copies of their music and securing the means to do it justice. Side by side with the enthusiasms of the cultivated country gentry were the focal points provided by the provincial cathedral organists (such as Tomkins at Worcester), and by the regular music meetings which took place in London and the provinces. Of the latter the most important was Oxford, where the Heather bequest had instituted regular weekly performances under the direction of the Choragus (later known as the Professor). The residence of the court in Oxford during the Civil War (1642–6) led to improved standards and a wider repertory; after a period of neglect during

---

[82] According to North, Jenkins lived during the Commonwealth 'in the country at gentlemen's houses'. *NGD*, ad loc. North gives the impression (*Roger North on Music*, 343–4) that Jenkins had a court appointment and lived with private families only after that had ceased; but this cannot be right.

the Commonwealth, they were revived first under John Wilson and then under the capable and energetic Edward Lowe.[83]

The evidence for the interaction between these centres of interest is provided by the sizeable quantity of surviving manuscripts, though these must be a fraction of what originally existed.[84] Many still belong to the Music School collection at Oxford for which they were first copied or bought. Jenkins is among the best-represented composers, and is also one of the most versatile. About 800 of his instrumental works—over 1000 separate movements—have come down to us, from short two-part ayres and lyra viol solos to large-scale fantasias for five or six viols with organ.

Jenkins was an adventurous composer, but not in the Italianate ways fashionable in the 1630s and 1640s. Though he was quite capable of writing declamatory song, he preferred to exercise his invention within a broadly contrapuntal framework. The five- and six-part consorts, like those of William Lawes (with which they offer an instructive comparison), are his most conservative works as to their outward form, though on closer inspection they prove to be as individual as any. It is probably in his deployment of tonality that Jenkins was at his most advanced. Far from relishing the sudden tonal shifts and bold dissonances of the Italian baroque, he always wrote suavely and without exaggeration. But unlike most earlier composers, and to a greater extent even than Lawes, he employed keys, and the processes of key-change, as a rhetorical device. The change to the tonic major or minor is a hallmark, all the more significant in that it is necessarily the direct expression of feeling rather than a mere structural device (Ex. 201, overleaf).[85]

But the denial of tonal change can be equally significant, as in the massive C minor six-part fantasia no. 3, where the predominance given to the lapidary main theme is reflected in a belated modulation to the relative major in association with the chief subsidiary idea. Rhythmic contrast is another favourite device, though in these works it is always kept within the bounds of polyphonic decorum.

Jenkins also wrote a number of fairly conventional works, mostly fantasias, for four and three viols with organ accompaniment. Again the sense of tonality is strong; occasionally there are wide-ranging modulations, as in no. 7 of the four-part works,[86] where a cycle of fifths drops the music quickly from C minor to D flat (C sharp) minor, and back almost as quickly to D minor, after which there is a more leisurely exploration of the tonal ground between there and the home key. Alternatively the music may make its effect through normality, as in a charming fantasia in B flat major.[87]

[83] Cf. D. Peart (ed.), John Jenkins, *Consort Music of Six Parts* (MB, xxxix), pp. xv–xvi.
[84] *Roger North on Music*, 296.
[85] Jenkins, *Consort Music of Six Parts*, no. 4, bars 51–65 (bar-lengths doubled in our example).
[86] *Consort Music of Four Parts* (MB, xxvi), no. 41.
[87] *Fancies and Ayres*, ed. H. J. Sleeper (Wellesley Edition, i), 46.

Ex. 201

About fifty of Jenkins's works are in suite or 'set' form; amongst the most interesting are those for two 'trebles', two 'basses', and organ (we are to understand treble violins and bass viols). Several of the movements have passages of more or less elaborate division, while his penchant for tonal planning is strongly evident in the fantasias. A different approach, the extension of binary form with its attendant possibilities, is found in the thirty-two ayres for the same forces.[88] Surprisingly, Jenkins chooses not to modulate widely, but his ayres are full of melodic and metrical surprises. 'Newark Siege' (no. 23) is pure descriptive music, the heat of

[88] *Consort Music of Four Parts*, nos. 1–32.

the battle being followed by a mournful conclusion that seems to prefigure the Battle and Defeat of Napoleon in Kodály's *Háry János*.

There are literally hundreds of shorter pieces by Jenkins, mostly ayres and the like for a variety of instruments. He was one of the first English composers to write a *basso continuo* in instrumental music instead of the two-stave (if often sketchy) keyboard part that had been customary. His sense of harmonic control made it an entirely feasible innovation in his case, even with the sparse or non-existent figuring that was usual at the time. He had bypassed the early baroque idiom in favour of the norms of the later seventeenth century, and it was his reward to be considered old-fashioned. But in his day, his was the most sought-after of all instrumental music; and we can, if we will, experience the rare satisfaction that comes of close contact with the mind of a fellow-musician, expressed through the medium that most directly represents his innermost self.

One could not say the same of Matthew Locke, whose extrovert temperament made him more the orator than the communer. His art is altogether more self-conscious, less self-effacing, than that of Jenkins. In this he heralds the Restoration aesthetic, whereby rhetorical points had to be more sharply defined for the sake of the listener. We become more vividly aware, for example, of the way in which an imitative point is presented in new guises on each appearance, or of pairs of themes in invertible counterpoint, than in earlier music. If anything it is Lawes, rather than Jenkins, who is the true precursor of Locke.

Roger North writes:

Mr Matthew Locke was the most considerable master of musick after Jenkins fell off ... In musick he had a robust vein, and many of his compositions went about. He set most of the psalmes to musick in parts, for the use of some *vertuoso* ladys in the citty; and he composed a magnifick consort of 4 parts, after the old style, which was the last of the kind that hath bin made, so wee may rank him with Cleomenes King of Sparta who was styled *ultimus herooum*.[89]

In saying this, North overlooks the fantasias of Purcell; but, more seriously, he underestimates Locke's significance in the indigenous development of an instrumental trio style that was to lead to Purcell's own trio sonatas. In fact, Locke's chamber music is of two kinds: that in which the parts, whatever their actual range, are equal partners in a contrapuntal dialogue, and that in which there is a polarity between one or more trebles and a bass that is usually supported by harmonic instruments. The duos for two bass viols, the *Flat Consort* 'for my cousin Kemble', and the *Consort of Four Parts*, are of the former kind, the consort of two parts 'for several friends', the *Little Consort*, and the *Broken Consort* of the latter. It is true

[89] *Roger North on Music*, 348–9.

that half of the *Little Consort* is for treble, tenor, and bass, but even here the texture is noticeably closer to that of the trio sonata than in the *Flat Consort*. Style and texture strongly suggest violins (trebles and/or tenor, i.e. viola) for the upper parts of the former, viols for the latter.[90]

Locke never wrote a fully written keyboard part for any of his instrumental music, and he seems to have regarded the support of an organ as an unnecessary encumbrance in his 'whole' consort music. For the 'polarized' trios, however, he specified (sometimes as optional) the use of the harpsichord and/or theorbos.[91] Though his autograph scores do not include *basso continuo* parts, there are three identical single-stave parts for theorbos for the *Broken Consort* in his own hand. Another singular feature of Locke's chamber music is that it is virtually all in suite or 'set' form. However, the plan of the Italian trio sonata is nowhere found: the movements are all fantasias or dances—the pavan, the ayre or almain, the corant, the saraband, and the jig. Usually the works begin with a fantasia, sometimes (as in Lawes and Jenkins) with a pavan. Two or three dances normally follow, with a slow 'conclusion' to round off the whole work. The *Flat Consort* alternates fantasias (two or three in each set) and dances. *The Consort of Four Parts* is arranged in pairs of works unified by key, every second work having a 'conclusion'.

The distinction between Locke's 'polarized' and 'homogeneous' chamber music must not be exaggerated. Through all of it shines his mastery of counterpoint as a medium of expression, his capacity for memorable tunefulness, and his penchant for dramatic gestures. The astonishing conclusion of the D major set from the *Broken Consort*, where the varied repeat of the second strain of the saraband is suddenly cut short, is an example of the last of these (Ex. 202, p. 551).

As for Locke's skill in counterpoint, the fantasias from the *Consort of Four Parts* are a never-failing marvel. In the fantasia from the second set, for example, we may note how a motive from the energetic main theme is transformed into a new subject which has its own counter-subject, with inversion at the twelfth and even, briefly, at the 21st, with re-inversion from the twelfth at the octave—all in combination with stretti, thematic transformations, and the like (Ex. 203, p. 552).[92]

Such things were an inspiration to Purcell in his own masterly essays in the genre. It is no wonder that North thought it a 'magnifick consort'; well-worn though the medium may have been, the music is timeless in its attention to the warp and weft of sonorous structure.

---

[90] Locke's chamber music has been edited in magisterial fashion by Michael Tilmouth (MB, xxxi–xxxii): reference in the text is to the numbers of this edition.

[91] There are no instructions for the consort duos 'for several friends', but a harmonic support seems essential.

[92] The 'counter-subject' shows of course the inversion of the intervallic *direction* of the subject. Ex. 203(c) extracts the four presentations of the combined subject and counter-subject in the order in which they occur.

Ex. 202

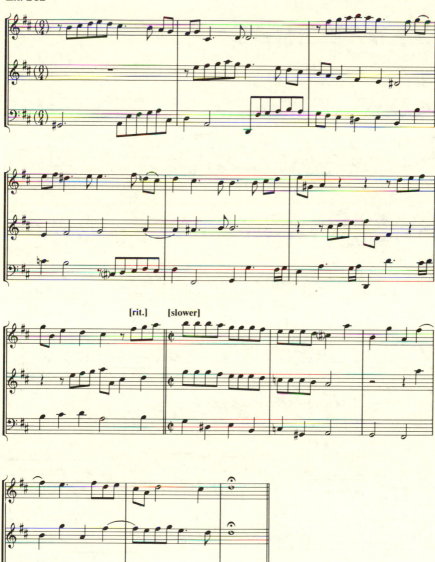

Ex. 203

Ex. 203, continued

In 1676 Thomas Mace, a singing clerk at Trinity College, Cambridge, lamented the passing of the old type of consort music in his quaintly written *Musick's Monument*.[93] He also did his best to popularize the lute, although the heyday of that instrument was now passing. The theorbo–lute, indeed, was still being used to provide harmonic support in consort and church music; but even that custom was not destined to last much longer. The golden age of solo lute and solo keyboard music had vanished with the end of the Jacobean epoch. Except for Tomkins and some minor figures, the old style no longer held any interest. The keyboard and lute books of the Caroline and Commonwealth periods are full of short pieces, mostly dances, for learners and amateurs. Playford's *Musicks Hand-maide*, first published in 1663, is of the same kind. But *Parthenia* continued to be reprinted, and in 1673 Locke's *Melothesia*, a treatise on figured bass with a large collection of suites and voluntaries appended, made no concessions to human frailty. The organ voluntaries are all by Locke himself, closely knit essays that lead beyond the skilful examples by John Lugge, organist of Exeter Cathedral in the 1630s and 1640s, into the world of Blow and Purcell. Similarly the suites, by Locke and a crowd of his lesser contemporaries, bridge the gap between the primitive specimens of the 1650s and the maturer examples of Purcell, Blow, and later Croft, Clarke, and Hart.

The lyra viol played solo or in groups of two or three (and in combination with other instruments), continued to be cultivated into Restoration times, while the violin increased in popularity as a result of the presence of foreign virtuosi such as the German Diesner and the Italian Nicola Matteis. As for the repertory of the lute itself, it relied heavily on importations from France. Jacques Gautier, a somewhat disreputable figure, settled in England and was enormously influential in furthering the fashion for the French

[93] pp. 233–4, 236.

style, with its penchant for arpeggiated chords (the so-called *style brisé*).[94]
John Wilson's fantasias in all the keys, probably composed in the 1650s,
are in marked contrast, the work of a tireless, if not very profound, experi-
mentalist, and lacking any trace of foreign influence whatsoever. And there
are hundreds of short, popular ayres which, like those in the keyboard
books, provide a valuable clue to the recreational aspect of music at this
period. Scottish manuscripts, with their curious mixture of fashionable
novelties and the age-old formulae of native origin, are especially rich in
this respect.[95] Back in England, Playford's *Dancing Master* and similar publications offer a wealth of material that has scarcely begun to be investigated.
Indeed it is with Playford's first publications in the 1650s that the continuous
documented history of English popular music can be said to begin.

Although opera on the Italian model failed to take root during this period,
considerable advances were made towards the establishment of a native
musico-dramatic idiom. The court masque became ever more elaborate,
culminating in the splendid trio of works for which William Lawes contributed much of the music: Shirley's *The Triumph of Peace* (1634), *The Triumphs
of the Prince d'Amour* (1636), and *Britannia Triumphans* (1638), the two latter
by Sir William Davenant. Lawes's set pieces for these reveal the kind of
organization that on the Continent had transformed opera from a succession
of dramatic monologues into a structure with the potential for genuine
musico-dramatic development. Shirley's and Davenant's efforts were not
equal to those of Jonson at his best, but another great poet, the youthful
John Milton, enhanced the literary status of the masque with his *Comus*,
acted before the Earl of Bridgewater at Ludlow in 1634. Milton's contribution was provided at the request of Henry Lawes, music tutor in the
Bridgewater household. Lawes wrote the music and performed the part
of the Attendant Spirit.

Neither the court masque nor the simpler type represented by *Comus*,
however, led directly to opera.[96] The former was too much occupied
with spectacle at the expense of drama, while the latter was close to being
an ordinary stage play with incidental music. It is true that as the calibre
of the spoken drama declined, its incidental music acquired a greater significance. Many songs from the plays of the Caroline epoch, by Henry and

[94] Jacques Gautier, whose name occurs in a wide variety of spellings, was apparently not related
to Denis and Ennemond Gaultier, nor to either of the two French musicians called Pierre Gautier.
He fled to England in 1617 after being involved in a murder, and was intermittently attached to the
English court from about 1620 onwards. *NGD*, ad loc.

[95] Scottish sources of lute music include the Wemyss, Balcarres, Skene, and Straloch books. The
Skene MS, strictly speaking for mandora, was edited by William Dauney, *Ancient Scotish Melodies*,
in 1838. The Straloch MS exists only in a 19th-cent. copy. See M. Spring, 'Lute Music in England
and Scotland after the Golden Age, 1620–1750', D. Phil. diss. (Oxford, 1987).

[96] The dramatic monologues and dialogues already discussed are far closer, as will have been the
earlier masques by Lanier and Jonson, if they were really sung 'stylo recitativo' throughout.

William Lawes in particular, can be identified in the songbooks of the period. Both composers contributed to the substantial musical requirements of Cartwright's *The Royal Slave*, acted before the court in Oxford in 1636.[97] In the drama of this age, however, can be seen in abundance the confusion as to the role of incidental music that was already in evidence in the preceding reign. At times it is conceived within the terms of spoken drama; but on other occasions it adopts a quasi-operatic role, and elsewhere again it seems to be included purely for the sake of entertainment. The quasi-operatic type of incursion, moreover, never attained the proportions that would justify the description of the representation as an opera with dialogue.

If one may summarize the position as regards the masques and plays of the Caroline epoch, it is this: the more elaborate and complete the music might be, the less probable was it that the libretto contained the potential for true opera. Thus *The Triumphs of the Prince d'Amour*, which was provided with music throughout, is devoid not merely of dramatic interest but of dramatic intention.[98] And this generalization remains largely true of theatre-music in the Commonwealth and Restoration periods, with a few notable exceptions. Another convention which hindered the growth of genuine musical drama was that of musical collaboration. But it would be wrong to perceive these efforts in an entirely negative light. The artistic confusions of the Caroline epoch led to the creation of that curious seventeenth-century hybrid the 'dramatick opera' or 'semi-opera' (the terms used respectively by Dryden, its most accomplished author, and by Roger North, its most discerning critic). Here there was usually little attempt at a unified dramatic structure, but rather a recognition of the two distinct roles that music and speech might play.

After the closing of the public theatres in 1642, and the cessation of masques at court, musical theatre survived in a number of ways. A few places of entertainment slipped through the net, and school masques and other kinds of musical presentation seem to have been tolerated.[99] Only one musical score has survived, but it is significant largely because it is just that: the complete performing score of a musico-dramatic work, Shirley's masque *Cupid and Death*. As such it is the first of its kind in England, and deserves full attention on that account alone.

James Shirley, the author of *The Triumph of Peace*, wrote several other masques not conceived as court entertainments, though apart from *Cupid and Death* hardly any of their music survives and the occasions of their

---

[97] For Henry's contribution see above, n. 52.

[98] Lefkowitz, *William Lawes*, 222. Cf. Lefkowitz's edition in *Trois masques à la cour de Charles I⁰ d'Angleterre* (Paris, 1970). The song 'Why do you dwell', from *The Triumph of Peace*, has been reconstructed by P. Walls in *ML*, 57 (1976), 58–61.

[99] The last court masque was Davenant's *Salmacida Spolia* (1639). Shirley's *Triumph of Beautie* was a school masque, first printed in 1646: William Lawes set the song 'Cease Warring Thoughts' from it.

first performances are unknown. *Cupid and Death*, based on a fable by Aesop in which the arrows of the two deities are mistakenly exchanged, was presented before the Portuguese Ambassador on 26 March 1653, and again 'att the Millitary Ground in Leicester Ffields' in 1659. The musical score is written in the hand of Matthew Locke and the music is by him and Christopher Gibbons.[100] Since the score mentions only the performance of 1659, it is reasonably concluded that it was prepared for it; and documentary proof of the identity of the composers for 1653 is lacking. It is generally believed, however, that Gibbons wrote the music for 1653, possibly with the assistance of Locke; and that Locke took charge of the music for 1659, adding at least the three long recitatives and accommodating Gibbons's music (much of it instrumental and superfluous to requirements) as best he could.

In *Cupid and Death*, even in the version of 1659, there is still a good deal of spoken dialogue, and much of the music is external to the plot. Each act or 'entry' begins with what in effect is a miniature suite, presumably to be danced to, and includes at least one song and chorus commenting upon rather than participating in the action. But Locke's music incorporates many delightful touches of description and characterization, and the long dialogue between Mercury, Cupid, Death, and Nature marks a further stage in the development of English dramatic recitative. Compared with (say) Lanier, we are conscious of a wider range of musical resource, particularly as to rhythm. It is indeed somewhat disfigured by roulades, sometimes on very weak syllables, and the whole thing has a rather experimental ring; but in some ways it does anticipate the manner of the great genius who first saw the light of day at around this time.

Of potentially still greater significance, though the music is entirely lost, was William Davenant's *The Siege of Rhodes*, first performed privately in his own home, Rutland House, in September 1656.[101] The audience had been primed by an 'Entertainment' given there earlier in the year, with speeches designed to justify the genre of opera: 'Think this your passage, and the narrow way|To our Elisian field, the *Opera*'.[102] Great attention was paid to the staging and scenery, which was by Inigo Jones's pupil John Webb, and the music was by Henry Lawes, Henry Cooke, Matthew Locke, Charles Coleman, and George Hudson. (The vocal music of the individual acts or entries was assigned to Lawes (2), Cooke (2), and Locke, while Coleman and Hudson supplied instrumental music.) We know that the dramatic action was advanced primarily through the medium of recitative;

---

[100] The score has been published (MB, ii).

[101] E. W. White, *A History of English Opera* (London, 1983), 68–9.

[102] Ibid. This passage affords interesting proof of the contemporary pronunciation of 'opera' (as of 'America' and even 'Sonnata', which as Purcell's spelling shows was, or could be, accented on the first syllable).

but while the loss of the music is regrettable it is doubtful if it would have cast much additional light on the capabilities of the contributors.

The immediate sequel to *The Siege of Rhodes* was Davenant's *The Cruelty of the Spaniards in Peru*; but in this there was no recitative and the dramatic action (such as it was) was carried on in speeches. Perhaps in view of its didactic quality, and because of the relaxed circumstances of the later Protectorate,[103] it was found possible to produce it in a public theatre, the Cockpit, Drury Lane, sometime in 1658. The real successor to *The Siege of Rhodes*, however, was *The History of Sir Francis Drake*, produced at the same theatre in the following year. In this it is all but certain that the music was continuous, with recitative to carry on the action. For neither work are the composers named, and all that survives is a fragment of instrumental music by Locke in the second work.[104]

The Siege of Rhodes was itself publicly revived in 1659, and, with a second part added, in 1661 (at the New Theatre in Lincoln's Inn Fields).[105] Davenant's other two efforts were combined, with other material, in a medley called *The Playhouse to be Let*, in 1663. Before he died in 1668 he had prepared revised versions of *Macbeth* and *The Tempest* on quasi-operatic lines. Though his vision of opera in English was clouded by his entrepreneurial opportunism, and though so much of the music written for his enterprises has disappeared from view, he deserves the credit for having, for the first time in England, contrived to present not one but two or three unified and serious dramatic actions conducted solely through the medium of song. That was no small achievement, and it was recognized as such by competent contemporary witnesses.[106]

The establishment of a permanent opera in London in the reign of Charles II was vitiated by commercial rivalries of various sorts. With the exception of Davenant's ventures, nothing worthy of the name was mounted during the 1660s. In the following decade several contradictory events occurred. The French composer Robert Cambert, tricked of his monopoly in France by Lully, came to London in 1673 with his pupil Louis Grabu, whose *Ariane, ou le Mariage de Bacchus* was performed at Drury Lane on 30 March 1674. Cambert's own opera *Pomone*, revised by Grabu, appeared a few months later. But that was all that came of the attempt to found a 'Royal

[103] G. Davies, *The Earlier Stuarts* (2nd edn., Oxford, 1959), 265. Richard Cromwell succeeded to the Protectorship in Sept. 1658.

[104] 'The Cimmerians' Dance', arranged for keyboard in *Musicks Hand-maide* (1663), no. 38. Evelyn saw 'a new Opera, after the Italian way, in recitative music and scaenes, much inferior to the Italian composure and magnificence' on 5 May 1659: this must have been *The History of Sir Francis Drake*. Cf. E. W. White, *A History of English Opera*, 74–8, 82–6.

[105] On 9 Jan. 1662, Evelyn saw 'The 3rd Part of The Siege of Rhodes... It was in recitativa musiq': nothing else is known of such a third part, and '3rd' is probably a mistake for '2nd'. Cf. White, p. 83.

[106] See Dryden's preface to *The Tempest* (1670), cited White, p. 88. Dryden had collaborated with Davenant on this reworking in 1667, but it was later recast as an 'opera' by Shadwell (see below).

Academy of Music' on French lines, although Lully's *Cadmus et Hermione* was to be heard in 1686.

English visitors to Italy such as Evelyn, who was there from 1643 to 1646, retained a vivid impression of Italian opera, with its spectacular scenery and staging, its 'eunuchs' and other magnificent vocalists; and there was doubtless an enthusiasm that could have supported the genre in the conditions of Restoration London. A contemporary score of Cavalli's *L'Erismena* with English text is evidently a symptom of this enthusiasm, though there is no evidence that it was ever performed.[107] But in the circumstances of the time this cultured taste succumbed to the prevailing apathy, and a species of semi-opera now became the most substantial fare offered to the public.

Locke's music for Davenant's *Macbeth*, produced by the Duke's Company at their new theatre in Dorset Garden in February 1673, is lost; but his surviving dramatic music from this period provides ample testimony to its calibre. The *Mask of Orpheus*, from Elkanah Settle's *The Empress of Morocco*, produced in the same year, illustrates this gift in miniature. Although the *Mask* is intrinsic to the plot of the play, it is in effect a tiny self-contained drama and well worthy of performance as such. For *The Tempest*, Davenant's text of 1667, written in collaboration with Dryden, was thoroughly revised by Shadwell for performance as an 'opera' in 1674. Locke wrote only the instrumental sections; the vocal music is by Banister, Humfrey, Reggio, Hart, and Draghi. Some of this may have descended from the less 'operatic' version of 1667, but in any case it is doubtful whether any definitive form of the work existed.[108]

Locke's musico-dramatic masterpiece is the *Psyche* of 1675, a preposterous farrago by Shadwell based remotely on Molière and Quinault. Draghi's dances have been lost, though the deficiency can be supplied from the abundance of unattached instrumental music left by Locke himself. Locke's published score, the first printed edition of any musico-dramatic work by an English composer, was a venture of which the composer was justly proud, though the quality of the printing left much to be desired.[109] But the vigour and boldness of the writing, placed at the service of deft characterization and dramatic effect, stand at the peak of his own remarkable achievement. It also marks the climax of this particular phase in the history of English opera; for the music of John Crowne's *Calisto*, by Nicholas Staggins, is lost. Crowne's play was a kind of court masque with a sung prologue, choruses between the acts, and so on; a huge orchestra of fifty-two players

---

[107] White, pp. 54–5, and his plate VIII.

[108] Locke's surviving dramatic music has been edited by Tilmouth (MB, li). Spink (*English Song*, 195) considers that Banister in particular provided the music for the version of 1667. An important collection of Locke's instrumental music, entitled *The Rare Theatrical* (New York, Pub. Lib., MS Drexel 3976), has been published in facsimile (MLE, A/4).

[109] The grandiloquent title reads: *The English Opera; or the Vocal Musick in Psyche, with the Instrumental Therein Intermix'd. To which is Adjoyned The Instrumental Musick in the Tempest* (1675).

was employed. But the ambience of the court was to harbour a far more significant production, Blow's *Venus and Adonis*, only a few years later.

Dramatic operas and masques were not the only large-scale forms of secular music in the early Restoration period. The earlier court custom of celebrating the New Year, or the King's birthday, or his return to London after an absence, with a song (in addition to whatever might have been planned by way of masques and other entertainments), was revived and extended at the Restoration. The result was the court ode, an inbred species that eventually succumbed to its genetic defects in the early nineteenth century.[110] But it would be wrong to think of the ode as purely a court genre, or of its progeny as being limited to its own kind. The interest of the form lies in its position as the ancestor of a number of non-operatic or semi-dramatic types that flourished in the eighteenth century and often had more life than the ode proper: the cantata, the serenata, the masque, and so on.

The definition of the ode and the identification of examples is made difficult by the casual English use of the word 'song' to denote anything from an eight-bar folk-tune to a 300-bar work with chorus, orchestra, and soloists. For the poets, the 'ode' was often a lengthy celebratory poem in stanzas of an unusual design, though it could be purely monostrophic. Such elaborate verse was rarely set to music before the Restoration, and even after that it was only occasionally that composers were called upon to set poetry of any distinction. The musical ode developed as an extended setting of purely occasional verse, often of the most mediocre nature. It also flourished outside the ambience of the court, for example at the annual 'Act' in Oxford, and in the annual celebrations of St Cecilia's day.

No music for any court ode, with the doubtful exception of Locke's short song 'Welcome, welcome, royal May', survives before Cooke's 'Good morrow to the Year' for 1666, though Jonson's text of Lanier's song 'Look, Shepherds, Look' (1664) is extant. Three such works by Cooke, and three by Humfrey, together with Locke's 'All things their certain periods have', remain for the period from 1666 to 1675. On the whole, these works closely resemble their composers' anthems, and except for Locke's have more or less elaborate instrumental introductions, interludes, and accompaniments. Cooke's contributions are decidedly limited in inventiveness and skill, as one might expect, but Humfrey brought a good deal of imagination to a task that he could hardly have found rewarding. Even with the advantages of his precocity, however, the form at this stage did not advance beyond infancy.

[110] R. McGuinness, *English Court Odes 1660–1820* (Oxford, 1971), offers a comprehensive account of the genre.

The readier availability of music to the wider public through the expanded music-printing industry was matched by a series of pedagogic works in which a comprehensive course of instruction was laid out. Charles Butler's *The Principles of Musik* (1636) was the first of these;[111] it was followed by Playford's *A Breefe Introduction to the Skill of Musick for Song and Violl* (1654), which in subsequent editions incorporated Campion's treatise on counterpoint until this was replaced by Purcell in the twelfth edition in 1694. Simpson's *The Principles of Practical Musick* was perhaps the best of all, clear, purposeful, concise.[112] A whole series of instrumental tutors, for example for cittern, lyra viol, (consort bass) viol, and violin, appeared from Playford's press; and in 1673 Locke's *Melothesia* contained the first English treatise on playing from figured bass, albeit at a very elementary level. More speculative, mathematical work appeared in Butler's treatise, in Descartes's youthful *Compendium musicae*, translated and annotated by William Brouncker (1653), and in John Birchensha's *Templum musicum* of 1664.[113] But the native tradition of speculative music was not strong—the attempt to teach it at Oxford was soon given up—except amongst classicists and mathematicians such as John Wallis, who edited the works of Ptolemy.[114]

The general health of the art is exemplified by its resilience in the face of political upheaval. For all its uncertainty, life in seventeenth-century England was easier in some respects than it had been previously. For much of it England was at peace with its neighbours, and even when it was not, foreign travel could be undertaken without undue hardship. An ever-increasing stream of foreign musicians came to settle here, and from now on their presence and their influence were a constant factor in English musical life. As the remnants of feudalism were dismantled, the scope for entrepreneurial activities and for the growth of a middle-class musical culture increased. The development of music-publishing and of opera, hesitant though the latter was at first, provide good examples of this. The availability of cheap music secured the involvement of a wide public just at the moment when the patronage of the nobility and gentry was becoming less broadly based. In its range and in its appeal, the beginnings of a pattern of musical life recognizable as that of our own day can be dimly discerned.

---

[111] Elway Bevin's *A brief and short instruction* (1631), a successor to Ravenscroft's *Briefe Discourse* (1614), is far from comprehensive.

[112] See above, n. 75.

[113] William Brouncker (1620–84), second Viscount Brouncker of Castle Lyons in Ireland, was a mathematician, and first president of the Royal Society at its inception in 1662. John Birchensha (or Birkenshaw) (d. 1681) was a composer and teacher of composition; the *Templum musicum*, however, was a translation of the musical section of J. H. Alsted's *Encyclopaedia* (Herborn, 1610), and his later work was devoted to the problems of temperament and tuning. See the article in *NGD*.

[114] See further on Wallis, and on the later development of speculative music in England, in Ch. 10, p. 612.

10

MUSIC UNDER THE LATER STUARTS

IN the middle years of the 1670s, the political and economic future of the nation might have seemed to be set on an uneventful course. The earlier troubles of the restored monarchy were over,[1] and while the newly consolidated character of Church and State might be threatened both from the Puritan or parliamentary side and from the Roman Catholic, the monarchy itself, at least in its public face, held a middle course, bowing occasionally to political pressures but losing neither its control nor its distinctiveness. But the seeds of disruption were already sown. Charles died without legitimate issue. Much attracted to Roman Catholicism, at least in its outward forms, the son and husband of Roman Catholic women, he was almost certainly a convert to their faith. His brother, an avowed Papist, succeeded to the throne as James II. His uneasy combination of private and public faith, whatever its moral justification, was doomed to failure in the current climate of opinion, and his conduct was unanimously regarded as a threat to the established Church. The loyalty that had enabled the crisis of Sedgemoor to be surmounted evaporated, and the ignominious flight of 1688 brought William of Orange and his wife Mary, James's daughter, to the English throne.

William's temper was markedly different from that of any Stuart. Coming in on the tide of revolution and retaining his Dutch interests and responsibilities, he was forced to accept a lesser personal role. Mary in her unique position as joint sovereign held the balance until her death in 1694; when William died in 1702 it was to another daughter of James, Anne, that the crown descended. Her Protestant upbringing ensured the continuance of the Anglican establishment, its character hardened into the mould ordained by opposition to the extremes on either side. Her own childless death in 1714 brought the legitimate Stuart monarchy to an end (legitimate, that

---

[1] The major ferment of the later 1670s was, of course, the pretended 'Popish Plot'; but the cumulative effect of this and other disorders was to strengthen the monarchy.

is, to the majority who accepted the Revolution of 1688, for James's second wife, Mary of Modena, had borne him an heir), and the crown was now offered to the remoter descendants of James I.

The period was thus one of marked, occasionally violent, change. The Revolution brought Britain to the brink of the modern world. The expansion in trade and industry, and in the financial organization which it necessitated, was enormous. Private capital and public borrowing laid the foundations for military and commercial greatness, while philanthropy helped to alleviate the hardships of those unable to compete in a competitive world. The first slow steps towards truly representative government were accompanied by the emergence of the Whig and Tory parties, representing different emphases but agreeing on much that would be controversial today. Slowly the reins of government were being eased from the hands of the monarch.

The year 1675 is a useful vantage-point from which to embark on the musical history of the later Stuart period. The deaths of several composers during the decade coincide with the early maturity of Henry Purcell. By far the youngest of them was Pelham Humfrey, whose significance for the future is of a different order for that reason. The combination of his precocity and his experience abroad led to substantial stylistic advances in the field of the anthem and the court ode.[2] His death at the age of 27 was a tragedy, though his potential for yet further development is questionable.

Humfrey was just one, possibly the eldest, of a group of musicians born in the late 1640s and early 1650s, and recruited by Henry Cooke for the revived Chapel Royal in 1660. Amongst the others were Michael Wise (c.1648–87), John Blow (1649–1708), and the long-lived William Turner (1651–1740).

John Blow's distinguished career is the best guide to the musical character of the age. Only four years after leaving the Chapel Royal in 1664, he became organist of Westminster Abbey, a post which he relinquished in favour of Henry Purcell in 1679 and which he resumed in 1695 when Purcell died. More importantly, perhaps, he was Master of the Children of the Chapel Royal from 1674 until his death in 1708; and he held a number of posts in the royal household music, amongst them 'musician for the virginals' (1669) and 'composer for voices' (1674). He also became Almoner and Master of the Choristers at St Paul's (1687–1703); he was one of the three Chapel Royal organists, and in 1699 was appointed to the new post of Composer to the Chapel Royal. His grip on the musical

---

[2] See Ch. 9, p. 559.

establishment was complete, and his career well demonstrates its institutional continuity during a period of great political turmoil.

Blow was a church musician first and foremost, and many a nonentity has filled such posts since his day. But he was also a composer of immense originality, and his career came at a time when the composition of church music was still a valid outlet for personal artistic expression. In any case, his contribution to other genres was substantial. There are twenty-four odes, much keyboard music and a little chamber music, many songs, and the masque *Venus and Adonis*, as well as ninety-six anthems and still other religious works. But he seems to have had no links with the public theatres, whether from choice or necessity is unclear, and as the prestige of church music and its artistic potential declined, so his star waned also. The festive sounds which had been a commonplace in Charles II's chapel, and which reached their acme at his brother's coronation, came to be reserved for odes and for religious works composed to celebrate special occasions. Even here, however, Blow rose to the challenge of expanded musical forms and lent them a distinction exceeded only by Purcell.

If Henry Purcell (1659–95) is the finer composer, it is because of his greater range and consistency. Though his apprenticeship was to John Hingston (keeper of the king's instruments) and to Blow himself, his early work also demonstrates the strong influence of Locke. The fantasias and other works for string consort are little more than an extension of Locke's own work, and his early anthems are a nice amalgam of Locke's idioms and the fashionable French style then current at court. In his trio sonatas Purcell strove to eliminate French influences in favour of Italian, though his very English personality comes through more strongly than either. In his church and dramatic music, too, French features gradually give place to Italian, partly in response to changing public taste, partly through inner conviction. It will always be a matter for regret that the prevailing mores did not favour true opera in England; but Purcell's contribution to musical theatre, with its associated genre of solo song, is one area in which he decisively outshone Blow and which ensured his posthumous reputation. Yet Blow had the last word even here, for his lament on Purcell's death is one of the most deeply moving examples of its genre; and it could be argued that *Venus* is a more perfect work of art than *Dido*.

The Chapel Royal anthem of the 1670s, though built on the foundations laid by Henry Cooke, was the creation of Humfrey, Wise, Blow, Turner, and the still more youthful Purcell. Wise returned from Salisbury in 1676; he thereupon became a Gentleman of the Chapel Royal, a post which he held until 1685, when he was suspended for some reason. He became Almoner and Master of the Choristers at St Paul's early in 1687 but died later that same year. Although his anthems (in their extant form) lack orchestral symphonies, his verse sections and solos employ the expressive and declamatory idioms then current. In Turner's anthems and odes, on the other hand, it is the instrumental sections that lend them what distinction they have, since his capacity for vocal expression was somewhat limited.[3]

While Blow's output of church music as a whole could only be described as markedly uneven, his twenty-eight orchestral anthems contain some of his boldest and most innovative writing.[4] 'Blessed is the man'[5] is characteristic of the works of the early 1680s, with its extended opening symphony in the manner of a French overture, its vigorous writing for alto and bass soloists, its occasional striking harmonic turns (for example in bars 220–3), and—let it be said—the monotony of nearly 200 bars of triple time out of a total of 262. His style reached its apogee in the masterly 'God spake sometime in visions' for the coronation of James II,[6] in which a series of vivid incidents is built up into a coherent structure through the careful control of the proportionate length and weight of the contrasting sections. His only orchestrally accompanied anthems after that were a modest affair for the coronation of William III and Mary, and three cantata-like works from the turn of the century, in which his deployment of unexpected and extravagant effects becomes almost overwhelming.

Purcell's progress as a composer of anthems followed a similar course to that of Blow, and those of his earliest period have similar faults: an over-indulgence in the jaunty triple rhythms of which Charles II was allegedly so fond, an undue liking for the merely picturesque, and an inclination towards a bewildering succession of minor incidents to the detriment of overall structure. But in his later work he could impart a more convincing sense of form by working out his ideas more thoroughly and at greater length. 'Unto thee will I cry', for instance,[7] moves effectively from minor to major at about the half-way point, and the rather skittish melody devised for the words 'Praised be the Lord' is turned into an imposing structure through the skilful deployment of contrasting forces and the overlapping of phrases. There are few more delightful movements in his anthems than the ground-bass setting of 'The Lord is great' from 'O sing unto the Lord a new song'.[8] The casual use of inversion (so exact as to transform major

---

[3] Other less noteworthy contemporaries included Thomas Tudway (c.1658–1726), more noteworthy for his substantial MS collection of church music, Harleian MSS 7337–42 in the British Library, than for his own compositions, Daniel Roseingrave (d. 1727), and Henry Hall (c.1656–1707). All are discussed in Dearnley, *English Church Music 1650–1750*.

[4] This discussion is based on two volumes of Musica Britannica: *Coronation Anthems/Anthems with Strings*, ed. A. Lewis and H. W. Shaw (MB, vii), and *Anthems with Orchestra*, ed. B. Wood (MB, l).

[5] *Anthems with Orchestra*, no. 1.

[6] *Coronation Anthems*, no. 1.

[7] *The Works of Henry Purcell* (Purcell Society), xvii, no. 2. Referred to subsequently as *PS*, the volumes of the revised edition being used wherever available.

[8] Ibid., no. 5.

into minor) in order to modulate to the dominant is almost impudently self-assured (Ex. 204, overleaf). 'My heart is inditing',[9] another work for James II's coronation, is perhaps altogether too grandiose, and certainly longer than it need be. But like Blow, Purcell was already exploring the medium of the ode and of drama to satisfy his need for self-expression on a larger scale; and unlike Blow, he found in the latter a truly congenial *métier*.

Although James II kept the Chapel Royal establishment going during his brief reign, his personal interest lay elsewhere; and his Roman Catholic chapel, staffed partly by Italians,[10] was opened in Whitehall on Christmas Day, 1686. The Chapel Royal itself became the preserve of Princess Anne, the future Queen, whose churchmanship was conservative and whose interest in music was slight. After the accession of William and Mary, the instrumental accompaniment of anthems was abandoned and the Chapel repertory became virtually indistinguishable from that of the cathedrals.

Much of the simpler church music of Blow and Purcell, including some at least of their canticle sets, will have been intended in the first instance for the Chapel of William and Mary. For Mary's funeral early in 1695, Purcell produced one of his masterpieces, his second setting of the words 'Thou knowest, Lord, the secrets of our hearts', as well as some solemn instrumental music. In William's later years interest declined and standards slipped, but Anne's reign coincided with a revival, when Clarke, Weldon, and Croft were all Gentlemen of the Chapel Royal and organists at one time or another. Westminster Abbey maintained high standards throughout the epoch,[11] and it was Croft who succeeded Blow as organist there in 1708.

William Croft (1678–1727) is indeed the outstanding figure in the period following the death of Purcell, and in many fields beyond that of church music. Though he attempted no opera, he was an active and versatile composer of theatre music, songs, and chamber and keyboard music. The aura of respectability that has always surrounded the name of 'Dr Croft', however well deserved on personal grounds, has detracted from his merits as a lively and imaginative composer. But he undoubtedly felt at home in the writing of Anglican church music, and did more than anyone to demonstrate how the liturgy might effectively be adorned in the Latitudinarian age. His writing has been undervalued because of a sobriety that disguises the skill with

---

[9] Ibid., no. 4.

[10] According to North (*Roger North on Music*, 52), the *maestro di capella* [sic] was Captain Prendcourt (or Prencourt, etc.), a musician of Saxon or French origin; but one Fede is elsewhere described as 'master'. Prendcourt must have been master of the children. The establishment consisted of six gentlemen including the master, ten 'gregorians' including an organist, nine instrumentalists, eight children and their master, and eight other functionaries including an organ blower (Ashbee, *Records of English Court Music*, ii. 16–17; *King's Musick*, 384).

[11] See Pine, *Westminster Abbey Singers*.

Ex. 204

which reduced resources have been deployed; a serious reappraisal is long overdue.[12]

Croft was one of the few major composers of the period to have contributed effectively to the parochial repertory. His four 'hymns' (or 'set pieces'),[13] though not published until *c.*1756, were probably composed for a London parish church around 1705. Their attractive mixture of solos and strophic choruses represents a peak of sophistication in a repertory that usually failed to rise to the level of basic musical literacy.

The staple musical diet in the parish churches was the metrical psalm. During the Commonwealth, the custom arose of having each line, or pair of lines, read out by the parish clerk before they were sung. This habit of 'lining out' became deeply ingrained; it disappeared in England during the eighteenth century but lasted longer in Scotland and survives even today in America.[14] It was associated with a painfully drawn-out performance of the tunes themselves; but the worst of the monotony came to be alleviated by strange embellishments which may have originated as a rationalization of involuntary congregational variants. When these embellished versions were harmonized by country musicians, the results could be exceedingly curious.

Parochial psalmody was the despair of serious-minded musicians, who constantly called for reform. One way in which this might be achieved was by installing an organ, an expensive project which only the wealthier urban parishes could afford. The earliest printed collection of psalm-tunes for organists were those of John Blow (1703) and Daniel Purcell (1718). In these, the tune was first 'given out' in ornamented form, followed by a plain harmonization with 'interludes' between each line. It has been suggested that these latter were meant to be played during the 'lining out', but it is perhaps more likely that they were intended to get each line off to a good start after the words had been read. Later, interludes were played between the stanzas only.[15]

Another medium for reform lay in the publication of harmonized psalm-

---

[12] Croft published a selection of his 75 or so anthems in score in two volumes in his *Musica Sacra*, 1724. There is a good appreciation of his music in *NGD*. His orchestral Te Deum and Jubilate is a fine work in the post-Purcellian tradition, and the Burial Service is austere and dignified (it actually incorporates Purcell's 'Thou knowest, Lord').

[13] See N. Temperley, *The Music of the English Parish Church*, 2 vols. (Cambridge, 1979), i. 167. 'Set pieces' are non-strophic, or partially strophic, settings of strophic poems or 'hymns'. One of those by Croft printed ibid., ii, no. 24; another, 'To thee O Lord of Hosts', ed. Temperley, has been published by Novello & Co. (1978).

[14] Temperley, *The Music of the English Parish Church*, i. 89. This account of parochial music is much indebted to Temperley's book. Some examples of psalm tunes, 'broken for the violin', may be seen in the 14th edn. of Playford's *Introduction*: see pp. 219–22 of the fac. edn.

[15] The manuscripts of John Reading, copied in the early 18th cent., contain similar material: Dulwich College, MSS 92a, pp. 1–33; 92b, pp. 1–41 (of which pp. 39–41 contain 'chanting tunes'); Manchester, Henry Watson Library, MS BR. m. 7105, Rf. 31, 156–87; Tokyo, Nanki Lib., MS n. 4. 31, pp. 21–47.

tunes, which might serve for either parochial or domestic use. The old four-part formula never lost favour—Ravenscroft's collection of 1621 was several times reprinted, and collections like John Playford's *Psalms & hymns in solemn musick of foure parts* (1671) continued the tradition—but its renewed cultivation in the eighteenth century became the preserve of country musicians. The more sophisticated usage is illustrated by Playford's *The whole book of psalms . . . compos'd in three parts, cantus, medius & bassus* (1677), and the same forces are adopted in Henry Playford's *The Divine Companion* (1701), which ran into several editions. This latter also included short 'anthems' by such composers as Clarke, Croft, Turner, and Weldon.[16] Many other collections, however, were for treble and bass only. Urban parochial choirs were formed from the children of charity schools, joined sometimes by the young men of the religious societies that were fashionable in the 'high church' environment of the early eighteenth century. Some churches even aspired to cathedral-like music, at least on an intermittent basis; and a small number of mostly provincial churches had in fact retained their ancient collegiate status, and in some cases these preserved fully choral services into the eighteenth and even the nineteenth century.[17] But except for the performances of the charity children, who became an established feature and who in London from 1704 enjoyed their own annual combined festival, the adoption of sophisticated art-music in parish churches remained a rarity.

As for the country parishes, little that was ambitious was attempted in this period; yet the first hints of an extraordinary flourishing of naïve art that lasted throughout the eighteenth century and well into the nineteenth are already in evidence. Starting on the basis of Playford's *Divine Companion* and its successors, the early eighteenth-century trickle of provincial collections of psalms and anthems rapidly became a flood. For the most part they endeavoured to provide music that could be sung without the support of an organ, though at a later date other instruments, fostered by the same enthusiasm that gave rise to the formation of voluntary choirs, were added to the vocal ensemble. In spite of much clerical opposition, and without the benefit of conventional training, a fascinating musical subculture arose in the far corners of rural England.

Some of the forms of parochial music were equally suited to domestic use, in particular the three-part psalms and anthems published by John and Henry Playford. They represent the simplest kind of vocal chamber music available, but the medium of one, two, or three voices and keyboard

---

[16] Temperley, *The Music of the English Parish Church*, ii, no. 27 (Clarke, 'Praise the Lord, O my soul').

[17] They are listed in Temperley, i. 349–52: they include Manchester, Ripon, Southwell, and Wimborne.

accompaniment was capable of infinitely greater things. The study of domestic sacred music becomes part of the history of solo song with its concomitants, the vocal duet and trio. If the word 'domestic' sounds unduly restricting, it should be remembered that once music in the theatre and the church is excluded, and remembering that indoor public concerts were in their infancy, 'domestic' music is what is left. It should be borne in mind, however, that the 'domestic' or 'private' music of royalty and the nobility might frequently assume the character of a public performance.

It is in this rather widely drawn social context, therefore, that one must consider the numerous sacred solo songs and dialogues of the later seventeenth century. In no case is any particular novelty involved, but one cannot fail to be struck by their potential for musical expansion. As in the earlier decades of the century, sacred and secular songs rub shoulders in the manuscript and printed collections of the day. Masterpieces such as Purcell's dialogue 'In guilty night' and his *Evening Hymn* are the culmination of a long development, not so much of sacred music as of vocal chamber music in all its diverse manifestations. It will be convenient to deal with this tradition at a later stage in this chapter; for the moment it suffices to record that sacred music of this kind is not in any sense liturgical, and only secondarily public, in character.

Roman Catholic chapels formed another outlet for sacred music of a semi-public nature and usually in Latin. Of course, some Latin sacred music will have been primarily 'domestic', but there were plenty of opportunities in the reigns of Charles II and James II for the public presentation of Roman Catholic church music. James II's own chapel has already been mentioned, though with its short life of only two years and its use of mainly Italian musicians its influence was restricted. Queen Catherine of Braganza, who had taken over Henrietta Maria's chapel in Somerset House on the latter's death in 1669, provided another outlet until her return to Portugal on the accession of William and Mary.[18] While James II was king, there was little obstacle in the way of those who wished publicly to emulate his religion. Embassy chapels and religious orders flourished in London, and two or three Oxford college chapels became effectively Roman Catholic.

It is nevertheless difficult to pin down any of the extant music to a specific context. Purcell's setting of Psalm iii, 'Jehovah quam multi sunt hostes mei', a masterpiece of the Italianate style if ever there was one, is a case in point. Setting an unidentified Latin version, it fulfils no ascertainable function; yet its grandeur of conception would have fitted it admirably for public worship. As it is, we are left with an inexplicable artefact,

---

[18] Her organist was Giovanni Battista Draghi, who remained in England after 1689 and became an established figure in English musical life. Her chapel was transferred to St James's Palace in 1671.

remarkable for its austere concision and declamatory fervour but unrepresentative of a continuing tradition.[19]

At the opposite end of the spectrum from the domestic and the otherwise unattached lie the large-scale works for special occasions. We have seen how Blow and Purcell rose to the occasion of the 1685 coronation, but at that stage the notion of a cantata-like sequence of movements was hardly formed. But as the occasion for regular performances of elaborate anthems diminished, so the capacity to provide for the grandeur of a national ceremony increased. Blow's 'I was glad'[20] was composed for the consecration of the chancel of Wren's St Paul's Cathedral in 1697: it is a brilliant and extravagantly effective work, relying on the boldness of its contrasts and a good deal of solo vocal virtuosity. 'O sing unto the Lord ... sing unto the Lord',[21] composed for a charitable concert in 1701, is if anything even bolder: it is the apogee of Blow's grand manner, but even here the notion of self-standing movements is only partly realized. Even a self-contained section like 'Ascribe unto the Lord', brilliantly written for countertenor, two violins, and bass, lacks the ritornelli that would lend it the status of a truly independent aria.

The grand manner could become rather tiresome, and both Purcell's Te Deum and Jubilate for St Cecilia's day, 1694, and that of Blow for the following year, are somewhat monotonous in their totality. Their manner is curiously reflected in Handel's 'Utrecht' Te Deum and Jubilate of 1713. So great a national triumph as the Peace of Utrecht called for rejoicing on the grandest scale, and by now Handel was available to give it musical expression. The work, like his Birthday Ode for Queen Anne in the same year,[22] shows how cleverly he was able to assimilate English expectations with his own more directly Italianate idiom. But we do not look for the essence of either Purcell or Handel in that style.

The tradition of the orchestrally accompanied ode developed in a similar fashion, though the opportunities for its cultivation were considerably greater.[23] After Humfrey's death, Purcell and Blow contributed in approximately equal measure to the regular series of court odes, to which was added an occasional contribution from Turner or Staggins. After Purcell's

---

[19] Purcell's other major Latin work, 'Beati omnes qui timent Dominum' (Ps. cxxvii), deserves mention here; and there are a number by Blow of which the well-known 'Salvator mundi' is the most considerable.

[20] Blow, *Anthems With Orchestra*, no. 2.

[21] Ibid., no. 5. The editor has quite unnecessarily recomposed whole sections of this work, relegating the readings of his source to an appendix.

[22] The rapt opening of this ode, a duet between countertenor and trumpet ('Eternal source of light divine'), is a striking inspiration, even though its roots lie in the English tradition of elaborate improvisatory writing for this voice.

[23] See McGuinness, *English Court Odes*; in particular, for the period covered by this chapter, the listing on pp. 15–29.

death, his brother Daniel, Eccles, Clarke, and Tudway joined Blow and Staggins up to the time of Handel's work just mentioned. Apart from the normal New Year and birthday odes (the latter being doubled in number during the joint reign of William and Mary), there were welcome odes to be composed, and occasional works for the birthdays and marriages of other members of the royal family.[24] Outside the sphere of the court there were the annual celebrations of St Cecilia's day by the 'Musical Society' and an annual celebration by the 'Society of Yorkshiremen' (for which Purcell's *Yorkshire Feast Song* was composed); and outside London altogether the academic odes of Oxford and Dublin;[25] and doubtless there were still other occasions in London and the provinces of which records have been lost and for which no music survives.

The ode is a difficult form to define, but there seems to be a valid musical distinction between the orchestrally accompanied type with chorus, and the much simpler continuo-accompanied song, dialogue, or chamber cantata (with or without obbligato instruments) which might on occasion serve a similar purpose. Of course, individual movements of orchestrally accompanied odes may correspond to the idiom of one of these latter types, and may even be published or copied separately as such; but it is as a whole that the form deserves to be considered. On the other hand there is little point in restricting usage to the courtly ode or to works with English texts.

Purcell wrote odes for a variety of purposes, and except for a few by Blow and Handel they are unequalled by those of any other composer. The quality of the texts (mostly by such poetasters as Tate, Shadwell, or the appropriately named Flatman) does sometimes appear to have acted as a depressant, but the general level is astonishingly high, even in works in which the sole motivation was courtly flattery unsubtly expressed.

Purcell's 'Welcome to all the pleasures', to words by Fishburn, was written in 1683 for the first of the St Cecilia celebrations on 22 November in that year, and is rightly considered as a model of its kind.[26] The pomposity of some later odes is entirely absent; instead there is a sort of wistful charm that in its own way is far more compelling (Ex. 205, p. 573). Blow's contribution for the following year, 'Begin the song' (Oldham), is a striking work, perhaps less coherent than Purcell's but more questing in its originality.

---

[24] Purcell's 'From hardy climes' (*PS*, xxvii. 1–28), for example, was written for the marriage of Princess Anne (the future Queen) to George of Denmark in 1683. This volume has a useful chronological list of all Purcell's known odes and welcome songs.

[25] Purcell's *Yorkshire Feast Song*, 'Of old when heroes', comprises *PS*, i; his ode for the jubilee, or centenary of the foundation of Trinity College, Dublin ('Great parent, hail', 1694), is in *PS*, xxvii. 59–92.

[26] *PS*, x. 1 seqq. The work enjoyed the distinction of being published in score (1683).

Towards the end the bass soloist has a rapt arioso (Ex. 206).[27] Writing of this kind, even though it lacks the confidence of later examples, is a remarkable achievement for its period: it has genuine dramatic potential of a sort that was to remain largely unfulfilled. A similar but much more controlled section, 'Music, celestial music', occurs in the massive ode for 1691, 'The glorious day is come' to words by d'Urfey. This is probably Blow's masterpiece, a huge cantata for chorus, four soloists (SATB), and an orchestra of recorders, oboes (including the 'tenor oboe'), trumpets, drums, and strings, exactly the forces (so far as the orchestra is concerned) required for Purcell's *Dioclesian*, published that year.[28] To 1692 belongs Purcell's 'Hail, bright Cecilia', a supremely self-confident display of musical imagery. The Te Deum and Jubilate provided by Purcell and Blow for 1694 and 1695 respectively have already been mentioned.

The Oxford 'Act', a public ceremony involving speeches and disputations in association with the annual feast known as the Encaenia, regularly called for musical odes. Blow's charming 'Awake my lyre' (Cowley) was written for the 1679 Act,[29] but the majority of the surviving works were provided by Richard Goodson, Professor from 1682 to 1718, and are of dispiritingly poor quality.[30] The two odes written by Croft as exercises for the degree of Doctor of Music, on the other hand, are surprisingly good and would merit revival.

The court ode proper maintained remarkably high standards in the later seventeenth century considering the routine nature of the task and the banalities of the texts served up for musical setting. One of the best, and still deservedly popular, is Purcell's 'Come ye sons of Art away' for Queen Mary's birthday (her last, as it turned out) in 1694. Here the simple images of the quaint text are translated into agreeably straightforward but beautifully crafted music. In these works of the 1690s, each segment of the text has become the basis of a fully independent movement expressing an individual *Affekt* (as German theory was later to have it). This is the raw material of opera, and of opera far transcending the conventions of the current Italian model; but it was only in that latter form that opera was able to flourish for long in this country, and almost invariably as an import from abroad.[31]

---

[27] From the original edition (1684), pp. 54–6. This section was reprinted in Blow's *Amphion Anglicus* (1700); there is a modern edition of the whole work by H. W. Shaw (London: Hinrichsen, 1950).

[28] There is a good modern edition by Maurice Bevan (London: Eulenburg, 1981).

[29] Ed. H. W. Shaw (2nd edn., London: Hinrichsen, 1968). According to Shaw's article in *NGD*, however, the work was composed around 1676.

[30] He was succeeded as Professor by his son (d. 1741). I am indebted for my estimate of the elder Goodson's calibre to transcriptions made by Mr A. Trowles. Another contributor to the 'Act' music was Henry Aldrich (see n. 122 below).

[31] A tradition of courtly ode was also established at Dublin Castle (information supplied by Mr Trowles). More will be said of Dublin's musical life at this period in Volume II.

Ex. 205

Ex. 206

Opera was so central a concern of the art in most of Europe during the seventeenth century that the historian of English music is inevitably drawn to the defensive when considering it. It is only with ballad opera and its successors in the eighteenth century—not true opera at all in seventeenth-century terms—that a genuine national tradition emerges. In the seventeenth and early eighteenth centuries the contribution amounts to two tiny master-pieces, a few experimental failures, and a considerable number of those hybrid works that were often described as operas but were in fact stage plays with substantial musico-dramatic interludes.

English usage at this period tended to distinguish between ordinary plays, with or without incidental music, on the one hand, and masques and (dramatic) operas on the other. Only occasionally, as in Purcell's *Dido*, was the term 'opera' applied exactly in our sense. More often it implied an entertainment with elaborate scenery and music—'the works', so to speak, that created such an impression on English visitors to Italy. The adjective 'dramatic' helped to make the point that there was a 'proper' spoken play as the backbone of the production.

A 'masque', on the other hand, might be a true opera, or else a complete musico-dramatic action inserted into a play. Such insertions are not to be disregarded in assessing the English contribution to opera, and occasionally, as in the masque from *Dioclesian*, they are masterpieces of the highest order.

After the high point of Locke's *Psyche* in 1675,[32] little of value was achieved until Purcell's *Dido* was produced in 1689. Banister's music for Charles Davenant's *Circe*, and that of Eccles for Shadwell's *The Lancashire Witches*, is lost, though in neither case is the musical contribution likely to have been extensive.[33] The only fully fledged opera in English at this period is Grabu's setting of *Albion and Albanius*, a patriotic effusion by Dryden produced early in the reign of James II.[34] It is doubtful whether any com-poser could have made much of this libretto, but the choice of Grabu, who had been dismissed as Master of the King's Music in 1674 and had spent some of the intervening years back in Paris, was an additional handicap. The opera was a failure, partly because its production coincided with Mon-mouth's invasion, but also no doubt because of its inept treatment of the English language. But Grabu had it published in the following year, and in his preface excused its poor showing by blaming the singers. This may not have been entirely frivolous: the tradition of great singing actors and actresses had not been established in England, the vocal parts in semi-operas

---

[32] See Ch. 9. For the date see Locke, *Dramatic Music*, p. xviii.

[33] Purcell wrote music for a later production of *Circe*, possibly in 1685 (*PS*, xvi).

[34] *Albion and Albanius* was originally conceived as an allegorical prologue to *King Arthur*, written in 1684, but was subsequently 'detached and inflated into an all-sung three-act opera'. It was privately performed before the Duchess of Portsmouth on 1 Jan. 1685, and 'received several other private perform-ances, or at least rehearsals', before the death of Charles II. See M. Laurie's preface to the revised edition of *King Arthur* (*PS*, xxvi).

being subsidiary to the main action. The effort of sustaining a full-scale opera may well have been too much for the vocal talent then available.

Albion and Albanius is in the French manner through and through: the string orchestra (wind instruments are added only occasionally for colouristic purposes) is scored in five parts with 'the bass continued' (an over-literal translation of 'la basse continüe'), and the principles of declamation follow those adopted by Cambert and Lully for use with the French language. The effect of this when applied to English may be sampled in Hermes' opening *récit* (as it would have been called in France) (Ex. 207).[35]

In the aggregate, however, the impression gained is not so much of incompetence as of unbearable tediousness, the consequences of the libretto and its setting alike. But the English taste for French-style opera was not yet sated. Lully's own *Cadmus et Hermione* was given at Dorset Gardens in 1686 with some success. No doubt it made a considerable impression on Purcell and his contemporaries, but as regards technical detail it was as good as ignored by them. Purcell would have to tackle the problems of English musical theatre afresh, initially in the context of true opera with *Dido*, subsequently in the sphere of 'semi-opera'.[36] It was his own success rather than foreign models that inspired his contemporaries to pursue a similar path, and it was his solutions that they adopted; for the 1680s had proved too barren a soil for the propagation of an international tradition.

One survival from the early 1680s, however, not merely deserves mention but must occupy a place of primacy in the annals of English opera. This is Blow's *Venus and Adonis*, a tiny and isolated masterpiece of courtly art. Its extreme compression is part of its charm: it plays for scarcely 50 minutes, yet the composer has managed to write a prologue and three acts, including plenty of instrumental music. The plot is of the slenderest, and much of the action is purely incidental. But at the end one feels that one has run through the whole gamut of emotions, such is the composer's expressive power. His art was squandered on one of Charles II's mistresses and her daughter of eight or nine years, who played the role of Cupid; the work was soon forgotten, though the sources indicate that a revised and bowdlerized form of it had some currency.[37]

Purcell's *Dido*, written in 1689 as an informal celebration of the coronation

---

[35] From the full score, p. 14; the figures are distributed above or below the bass as in the score. *Récit*, a term used in contemporary French operas (though not here) does not mean recitative in the Italian sense, but a kind of declamatory arioso, distinguished from the *air* proper.

[36] This is Roger North's useful term. His own judgement is as follows: 'But ... there is a fatall objection to all these ambigue enterteinements: they break with unity, and distract the audience.' *Roger North on Music*, 307. The whole passage is well worth reading.

[37] There is an edition, too much overlaid with marks of expression, by Anthony Lewis (Paris, 1939). On the recently discovered printed libretto see R. Luckett, 'A New Source for "Venus and Adonis"', *MT*, 130 (1989), 76–9.

Ex. 207

continued

Ex. 207, continued

la - tion, Mourn-ful   si - lence reigns   a - round.

of William and Mary,[38] has outwardly similar features: a prologue and
three acts, and a similar disposition of material for orchestra, chorus, and
soloists. But it is rather longer, the second and third acts having two scenes
each. Each scene is, at least in apparent intention, a tonal unity. As is so
often the case with seventeenth-century opera, the surviving musical sources
preserve the work only imperfectly. The Prologue, and the final chorus
of Act II, are entirely missing even from the two best sources, which it
is conjectured may derive from the work's revival as an afterpiece in 1704.
(An earlier revival, in which the opera appeared as a masque within a
performance of *Measure for Measure* given in 1700, had retained the missing
items.) If the fine detached G minor overture to 'Mr P.'s Opera' really
belonged to the Prologue, then the whole work would have been governed
by unity of key; but this is mere speculation.[39]

   Purcell's music has often proved its power on the modern stage; but
his opera is hampered by a feeble libretto in which platitudinous rhetoric
serves in place of genuine emotion, and in which the lofty symbolism
of Virgil's 'machinery' is devalued by the introduction of the Sorceress
and her brood. Perhaps the decision to include the latter was influenced
by the opera's destination as a piece for a company of 'young gentlewomen'.
This was as cloistered a context as that of Blow's earlier work (more so,
indeed: 'Rome may allow strange tricks to please her sons, | But we are
Protestants and English nuns', as D'Urfey's awkwardly phrased Epilogue
puts it); and it was a happy accident that led to its recovery for the public
stage in the early eighteenth century. But for that, we should be almost
entirely ignorant of an opera which, for all its naïvety, captures the essence
of human despair in its closing section.

   [38] So Laurie in her edition (*PS*, iii), which should be consulted for details of all the sources and
versions. See also the editions by Harris and Price listed in the Bibliography.
   [39] This overture, with an adaptation of the prologue to other music by Purcell and other suggestions
for fulfilling the instructions of the original libretto, are given in the performing edition by M. Laurie
and R. T. Dart (rev. edn., London, 1966). The musical sources divide the five scenes into the three
acts as 2, 1, 2, while the libretto (though it does not number the scenes and only implies, rather
than specifies, a change of scene in Act III) has 1, 2, 2. Harris in her recent study (*Henry Purcell's
Dido and Aeneas* (Oxford, 1987), p. 71) divides the first scene into two, the first in C minor and
the second in C major; but there is no musical need for this, and the change to the major mode
at 'Fear no danger' does not coincide with the dramatic division at the entrance of Aeneas. Harris's
book is most useful on the sources of the libretto and on the 18th-cent. performing tradition.

It was not with *Dido*, however, but with *Dioclesian* that Purcell made his reputation as a composer for the stage. The play was Thomas Betterton's much altered and adapted version of John Fletcher's *The Prophetess*; it was first produced at the Dorset Garden Theatre in 1690, and Purcell had the music published in full score in the following year.[40] The work was an immediate success, and it inaugurated not only the series of Purcell's four masterpieces in this form but a new wave of such productions that lasted until the early 1720s. It is worth looking at this prototype in some detail, for it laid down criteria rather different from those that had affected *Psyche*.

The principal change was that the music now tended to be less integral to the main action than before. The choruses and dances of *Dioclesian*, it is true, fulfil a dramatic role, but the songs are assigned to men and women who can only be regarded at the most as representatives of the bystanders. We find here too the device of the 'surrogate' song: the long-popular 'What shall I do to show how much I love her' is sung by a soprano, but it represents the emotions of Maximinian, who 'stands gazing on the Princess all the time of the song'. Only in the masque in Act V are the soloists assigned individual characters; and here the action is entirely subsidiary.

Purcell's score begins with the 'First Music' and 'Second Music' that had long been the traditional accompaniment to the arrival of the audience and their settling down in their seats. It is typical of Purcell's care as a craftsman that he should take this purely functional requirement with the utmost seriousness, even to the extent of using keys (C minor and C major) that would ensure the tonal unity of the entire work. The G minor overture, one of his most Lullian (the fast section is in dotted rhythm throughout), would have directly introduced the first act; but after that there is no music until the first act tune which separates the first and second acts. In Act II Diocles kills Aper, 'the boar', whom Delphia has prophesied he will overpower before becoming emperor. The extensive music to this act includes rejoicing at the death of Aper and on Diocles' investiture as emperor; but the dramatic intervention of a monster to stop his marriage calls for no music except for a brief dance of Furies. Act III is remarkable for its chaconne 'two in one upon a Ground', a dance of the spirits raised by Delphia, and for the song 'What shall I do' just mentioned. Act IV includes the delightfully pompous countertenor air 'Sound fame', with its jaunty trumpet solo and based like so many of Purcell's songs on an ostinato

---

[40] The play was first produced in 1622 and printed in 1647; Fletcher's collaborator was not Beaumont but Philip Massinger. The full title of Betterton's adaptation is *The Prophetess; or, the History of Dioclesian ... with Alterations and Additions, after the manner of an Opera*. Purcell's score has substantially the same title, but has generally been referred to simply as *Dioclesian*. The modern edition, by J. F. Bridge and J. Pointer, rev. M. Laurie, is *PS*, ix. The libretto is unfortunately given only in an abbreviated form.

figure. But these are merely incidental. Act V is occupied very largely by the supernatural masque raised by Delphia to celebrate Diocles' victory over Maximinian and his clemency towards him.

This masque is wholly unrelated to the main dramatic action; it is introduced on the flimsiest of pretexts, and is only minimally dramatic in itself. The outward structure is little developed from the traditional type of masque, with a prelude and five 'entries' (or dances followed by vocal music). The drama is rather one of atmosphere: the sense of expectancy created by the opening 'Call the nymphs and the fauns from the woods', the deft handling of the decorative vignettes that follow, the splendidly climactic effect of the concluding chorus on a ground, 'Triumph victorious love'. The whole feeling is that of an operatic finale; yet at the end speech must intervene to bring us down to earth and restore the equilibrium of the 'real' play.

The music of *King Arthur*, produced in the following year (1691), is much more fully integrated into the dramatic action: uniquely so, in fact, for a semi-opera by Purcell.[41] Dryden's play had originally been intended as a sequel to *Albion and Albanius*, but after the failure of the latter it was abandoned, and revived only after Purcell's success with *Dioclesian* persuaded Dryden that there was, after all, an English composer capable of doing justice to his poetic inspiration. It is doubtful whether the quality of Dryden's operatic libretti merited his concern for their musical setting, but the combination of Purcell's music and some impressive theatrical spectacle ensured the success of the piece. The most extended section of music is the celebrated 'Frost Scene' in Act III, but this is entirely self-contained, a vision conjured up by a touch of Osmond's wand.

1692 saw the production of Purcell's most extended semi-opera, *The Fairy Queen*. It was repeated in 1693 and seemed to be as popular as any of Purcell's stage works, but the complete version of the score was lost on his death and not recovered until early in this century. In this piece we are back to semi-opera at its most flippant: Shakespeare's play (*A Midsummer Night's Dream*) is barely recognizable in its anonymous adaptation, and the music is entirely incidental to it. Nevertheless it contains some masterly writing and two magnificent set pieces: the masque of the four seasons in Act IV and the 'Chinese' masque which brings the work to an end.[42] A passage from the stage directions introducing the latter will make it clear what it was the audience had really come to see:

While the Scene is darken'd, a single Entry is danced; Then a Symphony is play'd; after that the Scene is suddenly Illuminated, and discovers a transparent Prospect

---

[41] Ed. D. Arundell, rev. M. Laurie (*PS*, xxvi); for *Albion* see above and n. 34. The libretto is given in abbreviated form.

[42] Except, that is, for the inevitable epilogue, spoken by Oberon and Titania. The modern edition, with abbreviated libretto, is by J. S. Shedlock, rev. A. Lewis (*PS*, xii).

of a Chinese Garden, the Architecture, the Trees, the Plants, the Fruits, the Birds, the Beasts quite different to what we have in this part of the World.

But there is nothing Chinese about Purcell's music;[43] he simply responds in his natural manner to the situations prescribed by the libretto, never forgetting his sense of overall structure and timing.

Purcell's dramatic power was extended still further in *The Indian Queen* (Drury Lane, 1695)[44] and, as it was once thought, in *The Tempest*.[45] The latter is something of a mystery. There is no documentary evidence for a revival of Shadwell's adaptation at this period, but the publication in 1696 of Purcell's song 'Dear pretty youth' with the inscription 'A New Song in *The Tempest*' suggests that one did in fact take place. Since *The Tempest* was revived in 1712 with music by Weldon, the remaining incidental music, which is preserved anonymously, has more recently been attributed to him;[46] but suspicions remain, chiefly on account of the high quality of the music. Weldon was by no means a contemptible composer, but it is hard to imagine his being responsible for the entire range of inspiration to be found in this score. Possibly he added to a body of music already left by Purcell and accepted the credit for the whole work (though he is not named in the surviving copy).[47] This would account for the presence of certain numbers in a tangibly later style, such as the well-known soprano solo 'Halcyon days'. In any case, the whole score reflects a move towards a still greater Italianization of English music than had been reached by Purcell or anyone else before 1695 at the earliest. It is a pity that the Restoration taste for 'operatic' adaptations of literary masterpieces (as also of the second-rate and worse) should make it virtually impossible to hear such music in the context for which it was designed.

Some of Purcell's incidental music for ordinary plays rivals that of the 'operas' in its extent and sophistication. Into this category falls his music for *Timon of Athens* (Shakespeare, adapted by Shadwell, 1694) and *Bonduca* (adapted from Beaumont and Fletcher, 1695).[48] Indeed the music for *Bonduca* approaches that for *The Indian Queen* in its expressive depth. *The Tempest* itself, for which the disputed score just discussed was merely the latest in a series of Restoration adaptations going back to that of Davenant and Dryden in 1667, falls on the borderline between the two categories. But other plays are represented by a couple of songs only, together with the usual instrumental music between the acts. Purcell's contributions, as one

---

[43] Even Xansi becomes Daphne in Purcell's score!

[44] This was an anonymous adaptation of a play by Sir Robert Howard and John Dryden (*PS*, xix).

[45] *PS*, xix.

[46] See M. Laurie, 'Did Purcell set *The Tempest*?', in *PRMA*, 90 (1964–5), 43–57.

[47] It may, however, be significant that none of the instrumental music was included in *Ayres for the Theatre* (1696).

[48] The music for these is in *PS*, xvi and ii respectively.

would expect, are unusually sophisticated in their general level. It is convenient at this point to consider some of them in relation to the prevailing conditions of the theatre and its music.[49]

The first point to bear in mind is that, unlike some at least of the masques and operas of the period, there are hardly any formal full scores of incidental music to plays.[50] Research in this field begins by considering what is known of theatrical productions and then by identifying probable settings of the songs in contemporary (or later) manuscripts and printed collections. Sometimes the inferences are obvious enough, but at other times they may well be doubtful. Instrumental music may be lacking altogether; or it may be recovered, if recognized for what it is, from quite different sources. The composer of the instrumental music might be different from that (or those) of the songs: one recalls the multiple responsibilities for the 1674 production of *The Tempest*. Many of Purcell's instrumental movements survive only (or at least primarily) in the posthumously printed collection of *Ayres . . . for the Theatre* put out in 1696 by his widow Frances; and it is by no means always obvious what function each movement played in the production. A typical 'suite' of theatre movements would consist of one or two pieces at the beginning (possibly including a true overture), and an 'act tune' between each act (of which the usual number was five); but the original order of the movements was not always preserved in the sources.

In the circumstances one should not expect very much of incidental music as an art-form; and its individual components, song and instrumental music, belong to their own larger generic categories. In many ways, moreover, music played a less crucial role than it had done in the Elizabethan and Jacobean theatre. The weakening of its impact that began in the Caroline period was resumed after the Restoration. That partly reflects the general state of the drama at the time, and partly the fact that music had become so regular and necessary a part of the entertainment that it was apt to be introduced with little or no dramatic justification. The social context of a comedy of the period readily permitted the entrance of a 'musick-master' to 'oblige us with the last new Song',[51] and the playwright did not have

---

[49] The fundamental source of information about the theatrical productions of this epoch is *The London Stage 1660–1800*, i, ed. W. van Lennep (Carbondale, Ill., 1965). See also P. H. Highfill and others, *A Biographical Dictionary* (Carbondale, Ill., 1973–). There is a readable narrative account in A. Nicoll, *A History of English Drama*, i, ii, with vi (alphabetical index) (Cambridge, 1952–9). Some important materials have appeared in facsimile in the series Music for London Entertainment 1660–1800 (MLE). The musical side has been comprehensively dealt with by C. A. Price, *Music in the Restoration Theatre* (Ann Arbor, Mich., 1975), and in his *Henry Purcell and the London Stage* (Cambridge, 1984). For the early 18th cent., consult R. Fiske, *English Theatre Music in the Eighteenth Century* (London, 1973; 2nd edn., 1986).

[50] Exceptions are provided by some of the larger works (such as *The Tempest*), in so far as they belong to this category at all. The music for all three parts of D'Urfey's *Don Quixote* was published in score (Parts I and II, 1694); Part III, 1696: facsimile in MLE, A/2).

[51] Congreve, *The Old Bachelor*, II. ix. The song is 'Thus to a ripe, consenting maid', set by Purcell.

to be even as specific as that: any producer could think of a dramatically plausible peg on which to hang the simple direction 'Song'.[52]

The Restoration playwrights nevertheless often assigned their songs to principal characters, and their texts are normally apposite enough, either adding an agreeable piquancy to the sexual mores underlying comedy or emphasizing, in tragedy especially, an atmosphere of grief or doom.[53] But the extent to which music was employed in the Restoration theatre—in song, dance, and instrumental entr'actes—has tended to obscure the lack of a consistent aesthetic in its application. There was a confusion between the 'realistic' and the 'operatic' modes (the latter being that in which song usurps the role of speech); the dramatic appropriateness of a song might well be nullified by the intrusion of a musically essential accompaniment— there being little to choose in this respect between the adventitious arrival of 'musicians' on stage and the discreeter support of a harpsichord in the pit.[54] The 'operatic' use of song, though not subject to this problem and usually justified by its application to supernatural scenes, was not always clearly identifiable as such and often rubbed shoulders with 'realistic' song in a dramatically unsatisfactory way.

Purcell's predecessors in this field included Humfrey, Banister, Staggins, Thomas Farmer, and Simon Pack. Purcell himself joined the fray in 1680 with his music for Nathaniel Lee's tragedy *Theodosius*; amongst his contemporaries and successors were Robert King, John Eccles, his brother Daniel, Croft, and Weldon. But from 1685 until his death Purcell was the acknowledged master.[55] The list of plays to which he contributed songs and other music, over forty of them, epitomizes the English drama in the fifteen years from 1680 to 1695. Nearly half are tragedies, either adaptations from the Jacobeans (including Shakespeare) or original works by Dryden, Lee, and others. The remainder are either hybrid works or pure comedies. Many of them contain biting social and political comment; but it is a mistake to think of Purcell himself as consciously making political or social statements. He was the complete professional, enhancing every rhetorical gesture of the songs by his perfectly fitted settings, and interlarding the dialogue

[52] Ibid. III. x. The song, Purcell's 'As Amoret and Thyrsis lay', is followed by 'a Dance of the Anticks' (stage direction, 1710 edn.).

[53] Spink, *English Song*, 186.

[54] e.g., in Wycherley's *Love in a Wood* (1671, printed 1672), I. ii, Mrs Flippant says: 'Stay, Sir, because you hate marriage, I'll sing you a new song against it'; she sings 'A spouse I do hate', set by Humfrey and published in *Choice Ayres*, v (1684), 38–9. The scene is 'the *French* house'; are instrumentalists expected to be on hand? A dancing-lesson might provide an opportunity (Wycherley, *The Gentleman Dancing-Master*, II. i); but the 'Gentlewoman o' the next house' who arrives to sing 'the new Song against delays in Love' is indeed a thin device to cover the vocal inadequacy of the actress who played the heroine. The song is 'Since we poor slavish women know', set by Banister and published in *Choice Songs*, i (1673), 22. The devices used to justify the presence of instrumentalists on stage are retailed by Price, *Music in the Restoration Theatre*, 72–81, 106–9.

[55] For his miscellaneous dramatic music see *PS*, vols. xvi, xx, xxi.

with the pure entertainment that is his instrumental music. His contribution
to Congreve's *The Old Bachelor* (1693) illustrates these qualities to perfection:
the contrapuntal craftsmanship of the dances is immaculate, the taste and
restraint of the songs impeccable. But his songs as a whole cover a huge
range, from the bawdy suggestiveness of 'Man is for the woman made'
for Thomas Scott's *The Mock Marriage* (1695) to the passionate intensity
of 'Music for a while' for Dryden's and Lee's tragedy *Oedipus* (?1692).
The latter, it has been pointed out, is 'one of the few playsongs of the
time which manages to convey the inner, psychological impulse of its dramatic role; in this case, as part of a supernatural ritual in which the ghost
of Laius—the father of Oedipus—is raised in order to discover the reason
for the curse which hangs over the city of Thebes'.[56] It is a striking testimony
to Purcell's artistry that one of his most dramatically apposite pieces should
also become an anthology favourite, its context wholly forgotten.

Purcell had lent the music of the Restoration theatre a distinction not
justified by its aesthetic context. Others could not sound his depths, but
his younger (or longer-lived) contemporaries sometimes compensated for
this by an agreeable piquancy of expression. The music for D'Urfey's *The
Comical History of Don Quixote*, produced in three parts at the Dorset Garden
Theatre in 1694 (parts I and II) and 1696, was provided by Purcell, Eccles,
and several lesser musicians.[57] Eccles's elaborate setting of the dirge 'Sleep,
poor youth', from the second act of part I is a picturesque evocation of
the world of pastoral elegy (Ex. 208). The whole scene is expertly constructed, and a good example of the incursion of the operatic mode into
a stage play that, for all its musical elaboration, falls well short of being
a 'semi-opera'. But for the most part the music of the early eighteenth-
century theatre, notwithstanding the stylish contributions of Daniel Purcell,
Clarke, Croft, Finger, Weldon, and Eccles himself, sank, like the drama
whichit supported, into the realm of the superficially entertaining.

The semi-opera and masque did not die with Purcell. Daniel Purcell and
John Eccles each wrote several semi-operas in the decade 1696–1706,[58]
while the masque, considered as a short, self-contained dramatic action
set to music throughout, was still more widely cultivated, and forms a
not inconsiderable chapter in the history of opera in English.[59] *Dido* itself

---

[56] Spink, *English Song*, 230.

[57] See above, n. 50.

[58] The most interesting of the semi-operas of the period is *The Island Princess*, by John Fletcher,
adapted by Peter Motteux, with music by Clarke, Leveridge, and D. Purcell (Drury Lane, 1698).
The MS score has survived (Brit. Lib., Add. 15318) and has been published in facsimile (MLE, C/2).

[59] See Fiske, *English Theatre Music*, 7–62, and Dean and Knapp, *Handel's Operas 1704–1726* (Oxford,
1987), 140–67, for excellent accounts of the competing fortunes of masque, semi-opera and true opera,
in the first two decades of the 18th cent.

Ex. 208

continued

Ex. 208, continued

was revived in 1704 as *The Masque of Aeneas and Dido*, but the most note-worthy early eighteenth-century examples were four settings of Congreve's *The Judgment of Paris*—by Eccles, Daniel Purcell, Weldon, and Gottfried Finger.[60] Eccles also set Gay's *Acis and Galatea* (1701) and Congreve's *Semele*; but this (although the score survives) never received a performance.[61] The genre saw a new lease of life in the second decade of the century, with

---

[60] These were entries in a competition for the best setting of Congreve's libretto, the prize money being subscribed by the nobility. The settings of Eccles and Purcell were published (facsimile of Eccles in MLE, C/1); that of Weldon survives in MS (Washington, Folger Shakespeare Library); and Finger's is lost, as is a fifth setting by another German expatriate, Johann Franck. Of the competitors Weldon came first and Finger fourth, whereupon he returned to his native country in disgust. See Fiske, *English Theatre Music*, 14–24.

[61] See S. Lincoln, 'The First Setting of Congreve's "Semele"', *ML*, 44 (1963), 103–17.

such works as Pepusch's *Venus and Adonis* (1715), *Myrtillo* (1715), *Apollo and Daphne* (1716), and *The Death of Dido* (1716), Leveridge's *Pyramus and Thisbe* (1716), and J. E. Galliard's *Pan and Syrinx* (1718) and *Decius and Pauline* (1718). The crowning achievement here was of course Handel's own *Acis and Galatea*, composed in the spring of 1718 for the Duke of Chandos's establishment at Cannons.[62] There were also revivals of *Macbeth* (Leveridge, 1702)[63] and *The Tempest* (Weldon: see above), and of Purcell's *The Indian Queen*, *Bonduca*, and *Dioclesian*, the last of these receiving 32 performances between 1715 and 1718.

All these works, and others like them, belonged to the long-established tradition of English 'opera'. But at the same time the country was experiencing a new enthusiasm for things Italian, not least in the sphere of real opera, where it took the form both of English works on the Italian model and of Italian compositions, almost invariably adapted and sung wholly or partly in English. There was a great deal of rivalry amongst the impresarios of the day in pursuing these potentially highly profitable ventures. Christopher Rich, manager of the Drury Lane Theatre, was first in the field with Thomas Clayton's *Arsinoe, Queen of Cyprus*, produced on 16 January 1705. Clayton was a second-rater and his opera (an afterpiece merely) a pasticcio from Italian sources; but the transference of such material to the English stage was well received and it launched, not a new era of English opera as might have been hoped for, but the beginning of the fashion for Italian opera in this country.

Most of the new operas put on in the five or six years before the arrival of Handel were Italian in conception or origin. Rich's rival Sir John Vanbrugh opened his new Queen's Theatre in the Haymarket with Jakob Greber's pastoral *Gli amori d'Ergasto*, sung entirely in Italian; in the following year he introduced a new semi-opera, *The British Enchanters* by Eccles and Corbett, *The Temple of Love* by Saggione and Motteux, and *The Wonders of the Sun*, a sort of ballad opera by Tom D'Urfey. None of these was at all successful, and in the meantime Rich had launched the tremendously popular *Camilla* (produced 30 March 1706), adapted by Nicola Francesco Haym from an opera by Giovanni Bononcini.[64] The translation of the libretto was by Northman and Motteux, but in the following year a new principal, the castrato Valentino Urbani (known as Valentini) sang his part in Italian. This device of bilingual performance was repeated in more than one subsequent production. But Rich was also to taste failure: Clayton's *Rosamond* (produced 3 March 1707), an attempt (with a libretto by Addison) to write an entirely indigenous opera on the Italian model, had to be taken off after only three performances. Rich was more successful with *Thomyris,*

---

[62] For the date, see Dean and Knapp, 166.
[63] For Leveridge's version of *Macbeth* see Fiske, 'The "Macbeth" Music', *ML*, 45 (1964), 114–25.
[64] First produced in Naples, 1696.

Queen of Scythia, a pasticcio based on music by Scarlatti and Bononcini (1 April 1707), in which Valentini again sang in Italian in some of the performances.

By an edict of the Lord Chamberlain the Queen's Theatre became the sole venue for opera from early in 1708; under a variety of different managements (Vanbrugh having failed to keep afloat in these tempestuous waters) a series of pasticcios was performed, the music being adapted by such figures as Haym, Heidegger and Pepusch from music by Scarlatti, Bononcini, and Mancini. All were either bilingual or wholly Italian. Their absurdities did not escape the censure of the critics, of whom the most intelligent was the anonymous author of *A Critical Discourse upon Operas and Musick in England* (1709). Much other such writing was merely pettifogging, the product of prejudice against the aesthetic of opera itself.

The objection to opera in a foreign language, on the other hand, had considerable force; but the trend of the times was in the opposite direction. The bilingual problem was to be resolved in the direction of wholly Italianate performances. English opera on the Italian model had been a failure; perhaps because of this, Eccles's *Semele* had not even had the chance of a performance. *Semele* was technically a masque, a genre that by this date implied a complete musico-dramatic action; but the masque (or later sometimes the serenata) was generally a small-scale, intimate form, lacking the popular appeal of full-scale opera. But the inability of opera in English to establish itself cannot be explained by a terminological quirk; in the last resort it was only Italian singers who could command the attention of the public in a large theatre (despite some prima-donnaish behaviour by English singers),[65] and, language apart, no native-born composer seemed to have the knack of providing the vehicle in which they could best express themselves. London was full of foreigners busying themselves in the musical theatre—John Christopher Pepusch was one of the most intelligent and lively of these—but still the vital spark was lacking. An attempt to bring over Bononcini himself had failed. Something more was required.

It is not clear whose idea it was to invite Handel to London. Handel,[66] returning from his outstandingly successful Italian sojourn early in 1710, was appointed as Kapellmeister to the Elector of Hanover in June of that year. The conditions of his appointment allowed him to take extended leave. The opportunity was seized by Aaron Hill, then manager of the Haymarket Theatre, who prepared the scenario of *Rinaldo* and gave it to

---

[65] Mrs Tofts, for example, helped to ruin Vanbrugh by demanding 20 guineas a night—three times as much as Valentini. (Dean and Knapp, 145).

[66] Handel, properly Georg Friedrich Händel, was often referred to as Hendel during his early sojourn in England; later he used the form George Frideric Handel. He was naturalized by Act of Parliament in 1727.

one Giacomo Rossi to put into Italian verse.[67] It is not known when Handel himself arrived in London, but when he did so he prepared the score in some haste, borrowing much of the music from his earlier operas. The production, on 24 February 1711, was highly successful, and the opera was revived in 1712, 1713, 1714/15, 1717, and 1731.[68] It decisively marks the acceptance of Italian opera as an English institution, notwithstanding the sour reaction of Addison and Steele. Italian opera would always have its detractors, but it fulfilled a need for genuine musico-dramatic excitement of a kind which only Purcell with his semi-operas had achieved hitherto.

Handel's next operas were *Il Pastor Fido* (1712), *Teseo* (1713), *Silla* (1713, in a private production at Burlington House),[69] and *Amadigi di Gaula* (1715). He had returned to Hanover in June 1711, but was again in London in the late autumn of 1712. On this occasion he outstayed his leave, only to be confronted with the accession of the Elector of Hanover as George I in 1714. The story of his reconciliation with his former employer is well known,[70] but for Handel the period was one of a constant battle for commercial success. In the end opera ceased at the King's Theatre (as it now was), and Handel took employment with the Duke of Chandos. The seven seasons from 1710/11 to 1716/17 had embraced not only Handel's operas but adaptations of works by Mancini, Scarlatti, Bononcini, Gasparini, and others, together with the inevitable pasticcios. There was also one further attempt at Italianate opera in English. This was J. E. Galliard's *Calypso and Telemachus*, produced on 17 May 1712, with a libretto by John Hughes. It received only five performances at this theatre, and its later revival at Lincoln's Inn Fields only three.

The Lincoln's Inn Fields venture was due to Pepusch, who had been engaged in a number of attempts to put a genuine native musical drama on a securer footing. The first of these was his *Venus and Adonis*, a masque in the form of interludes between the acts of spoken plays. The libretto was by Colley Cibber and the piece was produced on 12 March 1715 at Drury Lane. Late in 1716 he transferred his company to the recently rebuilt Lincoln's Inn Fields Theatre and revived *Camilla*, *Calypso*, and *Thomyris*; but only the first of these enjoyed reasonable success. Drury Lane and Lincoln's Inn Fields between them offered an unstable diet of revivals and novelties ranging from the still popular semi-operas of Purcell and others, through the shorter masques and similar pieces by Pepusch, Leveridge, and Galliard mentioned above, to the most flippant of burlesques. This

---

[67] The Italian libretto was then put into English verse by Hill, and both versions were published.

[68] There were 53 London performances during Handel's lifetime (Dean and Knapp, 183).

[69] Dean and Knapp, 269.

[70] According to Mainwaring it was effected by Baron Kielmansegg, who arranged for Handel to escort a royal water party on the Thames with a band of musicians in a second barge. But the tale may well be apocryphal: see *NGD*, ad loc.

was the condition of affairs until the end of the 1718/ 19 season. The following one, that of 1719/ 20, saw the start of a new era with the inauguration of the Royal Academy of Musick at the King's Theatre, Haymarket.

Although it was Handel's original visit in 1711 that signalled a really decisive change in the direction of English music, it has been necessary to carry the story of English opera and its satellite forms to this point in order to set his early achievement in its proper context of theatrical experiment and reaction. From about 1705 to 1720, fashion oscillated between the traditional English forms of semi-opera and masque and the new Italian genre. The possibility of full-scale opera in English occupied many minds but attracted no composer of distinction. In the end, Italian opera was bound to prevail. It did so because its music was more immediately appealing than that of any English (or Anglicized) composer except Purcell, and because its singers were able to dominate the stage and conquer the affections. The inability of English musicians to capitalize on the new public acceptance of genuine musical drama was to set the pattern for the next two-and-a-half centuries.

Behind the dramatic and other large-scale forms that we have been considering lie their constituent genres, foremost among which is song. Here it is possible to be much more positive about the English achievement, for it was only the challenge of the expanded forms and emotional intensity of Italianate opera that English composers failed to meet. In other respects their heritage is a rich and complex one, to which a brief account such as this can hope to do but scant justice.

As far as the seventeenth century is concerned, in fact, it is hardly possible to separate the song of the theatre from its counterpart of the chamber. The genre is a potentially dramatic one from the outset, and its range, from the simplest of ditties to the larger forms of chamber cantata and ode, is comparable to that found on the stage itself. If it is difficult to decide when a song ceases to be a song by virtue of its formal complexity or its instrumental elaboration, or both (and contemporary usage favoured the use of the term to describe the largest genres), it is equally hard to separate the secular variety from its sacred counterpart. The only recourse must be to pragmatism. Many types of anthem, hymn, and ode have already been discussed. Our concern here is with those types of vocal music for one or more solo voices, accompanied by continuo alone or at the most by a small instrumental ensemble, that were susceptible of private performance in intimate surroundings, even if originally intended for the church or the theatre.

The range is best illustrated, as usual, by Purcell. A study of his songs would embrace all the separate solo (or duet, etc.) numbers from his stage works (well over 150), and all the separate songs (getting on for 100), together with a number of chamber cantatas and comparable works, and the sacred songs and ensemble music—more than 300 items altogether. Much of this material was published posthumously in the two volumes of *Orpheus Britannicus* in their various editions,[71] but it is also scattered in dozens of manuscripts and prints from both during and after Purcell's lifetime.

Song-publication in England entered a new phase with John Playford's *Choice Songs and Ayres for one voyce to sing to a theorbo-lute, or bass viol* (1673).[72] This was described as containing the latest 'songs sung at Court, and at the Publick Theatres'; the older repertory dominated by Henry Lawes and comprehensively reissued in 1669 as *The Treasury of Musick* was replaced by one in which the principal figures included Pelham Humfrey, William Gregory, William King, John Banister, Mathew Locke, Alfonso Marsh, Robert Smith, Thomas Farmer, James Hart, Robert King, William Turner, Isaac Blackwell, Nicholas Staggins, and Francis Forcer, as well as, in due course, Blow, Purcell, and their younger contemporaries. The first six of these were older men (Gregory died in 1663, only one year after Lawes); their music had nevertheless been more 'advanced' than that of Lawes and was still popular in the 1670s (Gregory was also represented in Locke's *Melothesia*, published in 1673). In general, the style is more four-square in rhythm and more controlled in harmonic tonality than in Lawes; the declamatory idiom is less in evidence, although there are some examples, and the two styles, declamatory and tuneful, may enjoy an uneasy coexistence in the same piece.

The conventions of contemporary lyric verse were such as to encourage the proliferation of strophic song in a simple, homely style. With their metrical regularity and stanzaic structure, such poems offered little challenge to the creative imagination but provided a suitable medium for a musical style that was developing independently along similar lines. (William Gregory even wrote a song cycle in the form of a four-movement suite.)[73] Dryden was the most popular poet, with Shadwell and Settle not far behind. Many of their songs originated in the theatre, but were instantly transferable to the published anthology and, one assumes, to the private gathering. Another poet, Abraham Cowley, inspired several collections devoted entirely to settings of his verse, those of William King (1668), Henry Bowman (1677), and Pietro Reggio (1680). His manner tended to promote a more serious, reflective type of musical setting, while at the opposite extreme Thomas D'Urfey provided the material for a great quantity of lighter song,

---

[71] Vol. i, 1698, repr. 1702; vol. ii, 1702, repr. 1711; 3rd edn. of both, 1721 (facsimile, Gregg). There is a useful survey of Purcell sources in *PS*, xxv.

[72] For a convenient list of printed sources of the period to 1703, and comment on both the major and minor figures of the period, see Spink, *English Song*. Much of the primary source-material is published, or due to be published, in facsimile in MLE, Series A.

[73] Spink, *English Song*, 155–6. The four movements are Alman, Coranto, Saraband, Jig.

Ex. 209

much of it of a somewhat bawdy nature. Many of his poems were written to pre-existent melodies, yielding the so-called 'mock songs' of the period. Much of this sort of thing is irredeemably trivial, but it is hard not to yield to the charm of a trifle like Purcell's 'When first Amintas sued for a kiss'.[74]

[74] PS, xxv, no. B1. The words, by D'Urfey, were set to an instrumental jig by Purcell; the song was published with a bass in *The Theater of Musick*, iv (1687) and *Comes Amoris*, i (1687).

Ex. 210

Go, tell A-min-tor,* gen - tle swain, I would not die, nor

dare com-plain; Thy tune - ful voice with num - bers join, Thy

voice will more pre - vail than mine: For souls op - press'd, and

drown'd with grief, The gods or - dain'd this kind re - lief: That

Mu - sic should in sounds con - vey What dy - ing lov - ers dare not say.

* 'Amynta' in Dryden's *Sylvae* (1685).

Robert Smith's 'The day you wish'd arriv'd at last', from Dryden's *Amboyna* (1673), illustrates the more thoughtful type of semi-declamatory ayre of the period, in spite of its almost comically direct text; it was certainly new enough to satisfy the most demanding purchaser when printed in Playford's 1673 collection. The verse is sufficiently regular, in spite of an eight-line stanza, to permit strophic performance without any problem arising, though in fact it is Dryden's second stanza that is underlaid in the edition (Ex. 209, p. 592 above).[75]

The period saw an immense amount of lyric verse in that jigging dactylic rhythm for which triple-time settings were almost invariably supplied. Some of these, like Smith's 'Farewell fair Armida, my Joy and my Grief' (from Dryden's *Marriage A-la-Mode*, 1673, and again published in the *Choice Songs and Ayres* of that year) are of considerable merit;[76] but the majority, especially of the later examples, are inevitably somewhat trivial in character. Short-lined iambic or trochaic stanzas began to generate straightforward tunes in 'common' time, of which the well-turned example in Ex. 210 by Robert King is fairly typical (p. 593).[77]

Some of Purcell's early songs, such as 'Amintas, to my grief I see' (no. 2, 1678),[78] 'Pastora's Beauties when unblown' (no. 7, 1680/1), or 'She, who my poor heart possesses' (no. 13, 1682/3), are closely analogous, though he cultivated from the outset triple-time, declamatory, multipartite (e.g. duple/triple), and ground-bass songs. The earliest independent example by Purcell of this last genre, for which there was no shortage of precedents, was his setting of Cowley's 'She loves and she confesses too' (no. 12), written in 1680 in response to a similar setting of the same text, and using the same ground, published by Pietro Reggio in that year. Purcell's effort is somewhat forced; at that date even a minor composer like John Abell could outshine him with this exquisitely crafted setting of Dryden's 'High state and honours to others impart'. A single emendation to the published score of 1683 reveals a subtle eleven-bar scheme, extended at the close to sixteen bars by a *petite reprise* (Ex. 211, pp. 595–6).[79]

But Purcell's command of the form quickly improved, and there are many striking examples in the collected edition. In his setting of George Etherege's 'Cease, anxious world' (no. 36, composed in late 1684), the rather grotesque four-bar unit is transformed towards the close from a gentle triple metre to a furious presto in ϕ time. 'O solitude' (no. 38, composed 1684/5), to a text by Katherine Phillips, anticipates the full flowering of the elegiac type in which he excelled; a good example occurs in the elegy for Thomas Farmer, 'Young Thirsis' fate' (no. 59, composed early in 1689). *Dido* itself, of course, enshrines two outstanding instances. A slightly different

---

[75] The poem begins 'The day is come'; Dryden, *Songs*, ed. C. L. Day (Cambridge, Mass., 1932), no. 29.

[76] Printed in Spink, *English Song*, 163.

[77] *The Theater of Musick*, i (1685), 30; fac. in MLE, A/1.

[78] The numbers are those of *PS*, xxv; the dates are those of first publication unless otherwise stated.

[79] *Choice Ayres and Songs ... The Fourth Book*, p. 21. The emendation is supported by Brit. Lib., Add. 19759, fo. 32ᵛ, and Add. 29397, fos. 8ᵛ–9ʳ, where the song is in D minor. These sources, with the literary MS Add. 30303, fo. 5ᵛ, offer an amusing series of variants on the last line, 'so give up my game'; they read respectively 'or give up my game', 'or give up your game', and 'so give up your game'. For Abell see Spink, *English Song*, 257–8.

Ex. 211

High state and ho - nour To o - thers im - part, But give me your

heart; That trea - sure, that trea - sure a - lone, I beg for my

own: So gen - tle a love, So fre - quent a fire, My soul does in -

spire; That trea - sure, that trea - sure a - lone, I beg for my own.

Your love let me crave, Give me in pos - ses - sing So

match - less a bles - sing, That Em - pire is all I would have;

continued

Ex. 211, continued

[4]

Love's   my   pe - ti - tion,   And   all   my   am - bi - tion.   If   e'er   you   dis -

co - ver   So   faith - ful,   so   faith - ful   a   lov - er,   So   re - al   a

[petite reprise]

flame,   I'll   die,   I'll   die,   I'll   die,   so   give   up   my   game.

Note. The copy used for reproduction in MLE, A/ 5b (London, Royal College of Music), has 'fervent' substituted for 'frequent' (bar 14) in an early hand.

★ ♩. ♩ in both parts in 1683 print.

type, the short ostinato, is used twice in one of his loveliest works, the elegy on the death of the publisher John Playford, 'Gentle shepherds' (no. 50, composed 1686/7).[80] The second, to the words 'Muses, bring your roses hither', uses a nine-beat scalic ostinato in quavers. The first is an ingenious combination of a binary melodic structure against an unchanging six-beat ostinato; the resulting dichotomy expresses to perfection that bittersweetness with which the pagan poets strove to purge their losses, their now threadbare imagery miraculously restored by a composer able to penetrate the conventions of the modern poetaster (Ex. 212).

Most elegies, whether by Purcell or others, are multipartite in form; but of course they do not all by any means hinge on the ground bass or short ostinato. An early example by Purcell is his elegy on the death of Locke in 1677, 'What hope for us remains' (no. 5), in which a lengthy declamatory section is followed by a rather too jaunty triple-time 'chorus' for treble and bass (the concluding sections of the Playford and Farmer

[80] The words, by Tate, are unexpectedly good. A suggestion that the elegy was intended for Playford's nephew John, who died in the previous year (1685) at the age of about 30, has not found general favour.

Ex. 212

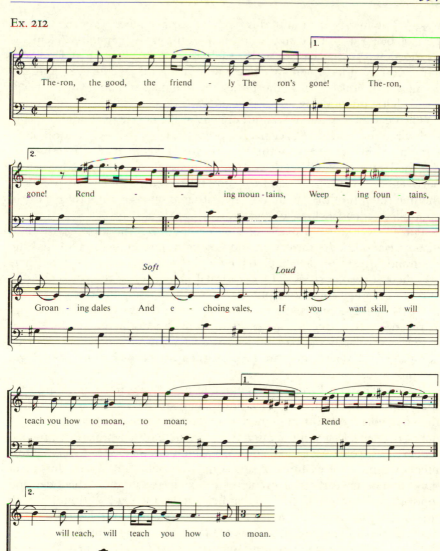

elegies are much more sensitively handled). The lament for Charles II, 'If pray'rs and tears' (no. 44) is a complex multipartite monody with both declamatory and lyrical sections, a form he used also for the setting of serious verse by Cowley and others. The supreme example of this type is his setting of George Herbert's *The Queen's Epicedium*, 'Incassum, Lesbia, rogas' (no. 79), written after the death of Queen Mary on 28 December

1694.[81] The middle section of this richly expressive piece gives the impression of being a ground but, apart from some freely repetitive elements in the slow-moving bass, it is no such thing. The Latin text lends the expression of grief a certain detachment that further enhances Purcell's strongly emotional setting: the result is a hieratic, formalized woe that is deeply felt without being unduly personal.

The declamatory idiom was not only available for elegy; it could equally well serve for comedy ('Bacchus is a power divine', no. 81) or for ecstatic fervour, as in the second setting of Henry Heveningham's 'If music be the food of love' (no. 80) (Ex. 213). In passages like this the distinction between the declamatory and the tuneful becomes somewhat pointless, the free rhythm of the opening being gathered up, as it were, into a finely controlled cadential phrase of great power.

Purcell's genius was capable of transforming even the most trivial kinds of popular song by a turn of melody or harmony. He also cultivated the catch and other forms of light part-song in the tradition of the Lawes brothers and their contemporaries. The occasional indelicacy of their texts was an affront to earlier commentators, but the robust tenor of Restoration life permitted a freedom of expression that would not have seemed outrageous at the time. It is true, however, that there is a distinction to be drawn between the catch and part-song for equal voices, intended for all-male company, and other genres, in the performance of which both sexes might be employed.

The cantatas are hardly distinguishable generically from the songs: for the purposes of the Collected Edition they are those that employ more than one voice (other than in mere concluding 'choruses') and an independent *basso continuo*; and more often than not there is a chamber instrumental ensemble as well.[82] (The dramatic works and odes incorporate many intermediate genres, for example of solo song with obbligato instruments.) But they do not have the full orchestra or choir required by the odes and 'operas': the 'chorus' of the songs and cantatas is merely a section in which the soloists join forces in a moral or explanatory conclusion, shedding their dramatic role (if any) for the purpose. The cantatas may exploit and extend the dramatic potential inherent in much solo song (in which the poet speaks not for himself but in the guise of an imagined character), as in the exquisite 'Hark, Damon, Hark' and the more rumbustious 'Hark, how the wild musicians sing';[83] or it may be moral and reflective, as in the two Cowley settings, 'If ever I more riches did desire', and *The Complaint*, 'In a deep

---

[81] An English version of this poem, 'No, Lesbia, no, you ask in vain', was set by Blow and published in *Three Elegies upon . . . Queen Mary* (1695).

[82] *PS*, xxvii; for simple duets, trios, and catches, see vol. xxii, as yet unrevised.

[83] *PS*, xxvii, 93, 100; cf. the sacred dialogue 'In guilty night', mentioned above, p. 569.

Ex. 213

If mu - sic, if mu - sic be the food

of love, Sing on, sing on, sing on, sing on, sing, sing

on till I am fill'd with joy;

till I am fill'd with joy;

Vision's intellectual scene'.[84] This latter is one of Purcell's most original and introspective conceptions.

John Blow was certainly Purcell's inferior as a song-writer, though perhaps by not so considerable a margin as has been imagined.[85] His response to Purcell's *Orpheus Britannicus* was an anthology entitled *Amphion Anglicus* (1700), drawn from existing work in many genres, much of it previously published. He was fortunate in not having to trust to posthumous piety for its appearance, and the volume was never reprinted.[86] Blow did nevertheless manage to amass no fewer than fifteen commendatory poems with which to grace his publication, and its fifty items are a far from negligible collection. Its opening item, the *Prologue* 'Welcome, welcome ev'ry Guest',

[84] Ibid. 118, 140.
[85] Cf. Spink, *English Song*, 241–52, where much of the comment is unenthusiastic.
[86] There are facsimiles by Gregg Press and in MMMLF, I/ii (1965).

is all that remains of a St Cecilia's day ode, the year of its performance unknown; part of the 1684 ode, 'Begin the song', is also given,[87] and the *Epilogue*, 'Sing, sing, ye Muses' is described as 'A Song for Four Voices and Two Violins, at an Entertainment of Musick in York Buildings'.[88]

Blow's gifts did not lie in the direction of the strophic lyric, even though his efforts were by no means contemptible in the light of the conventions within which he wrote. The sometimes tortured lines of songs like those by Smith and King quoted above, and such as are found even in Purcell from time to time, could become almost grotesque in his hands. His real talent was in the longer, cantata-like song, of which *Amphion Anglicus* contains several impressive specimens. Here, as in *Sappho to the Goddess of Love* ('O Venus! Daughter of the Mighty Jove') we can see the potential of the frustrated dramatist, while in 'When artists hit on lucky thoughts' (*On the Excellency of Mrs Hunt's Voice, and Manner of Singing*), or 'Employ'd all the day still in public affairs' (*A Song for the Musick Society*) we have examples of vocal virtuosity pressed into the service of a compliment to a fellow professional or to a society of gentlemen of congenial tastes. There is something curiously jocular and uninhibited about Blow's art, typified perhaps by those jovial trios for male voices which, even more than in Purcell, permeate his output. The rapid technical advances of the later seventeenth century were not yet checked by anything so mundane as good taste. Yet something like control is achieved in 'Why weeps Asteria', a tripartite song for solo voice and continuo,[89] or in the beautiful 'Poor Celadon' (*Loving above Himself*), for two violins, alto voice, and bass, of which the opening may be given (Ex. 214). We are close here to the spirit of Blow's masterpiece in cantata form, his Ode on the death of Purcell, 'Mark how the lark and linnet sing', to words by Dryden.[90] The poem, less pessimistic than some, was an open invitation to Blow's penchant for the elaborately picturesque. The tone is set by the opening duet (Ex. 215, pp. 603–4).

Of those who outlived Purcell, his brother Daniel, John Eccles, and John Weldon were the most considerable song-writers; Weldon in particular showed a liking for extended cantata-like pieces that are in many ways as ambitious as Blow's and in some respects more technically assured.[91] German, French, and Italian émigrés who contributed to the repertory

---

[87] This is the bass solo, 'Music's the Cordial', quoted above as Ex. 206.

[88] For York Buildings, an early home of professional concert-giving, see below, p. 613.

[89] *Amphion Anglicus*, 164.

[90] Published in 1696 as *An Ode on the Death of Mr Henry Purcell*: modern edition by W. Bergmann, 1962. Jeremiah Clarke's ode on the same occasion, 'Come, come along for a dance and a song', was edited by Bergmann in 1961.

[91] Most of Weldon's songs appeared in his *A Collection of New Songs* (1702), and *Third Book of Songs* (1703), the nomenclature of which suggests that a first book has not survived. There is also a lengthy cantata-like work in Playford's *Harmonia Sacra* (2nd edn., 1703), and upwards of 50 miscellaneous short songs.

Ex. 214

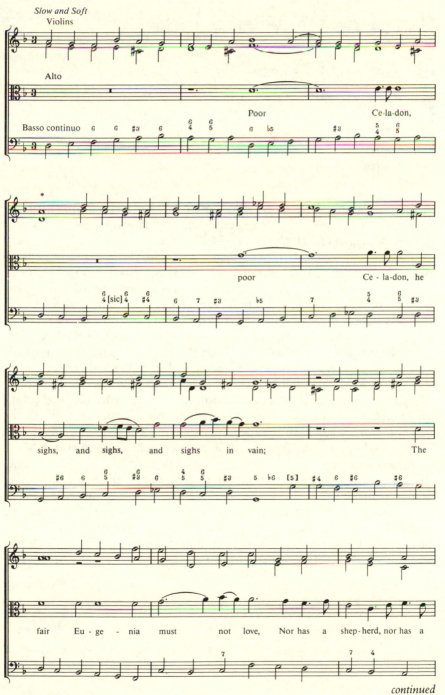

continued

Ex. 214, continued

shep-herd rea - son to   com-plain:

* But direct shows *f'* in 2nd violin.

included Gottfried Finger (the disgruntled winner of the fourth prize for his setting of Congreve's *Judgment of Paris*), the Hamburg opera composer Johann Wolfgang Franck (*Remedium Melancholiae*, 1690), Jean Claude Gillier (*A Collection of New Songs*, 1698), Rafael Courteville, and the Italian violinist Nicola Matteis (*A Collection of New Songs*, 2 books, 1696 and 1699).[92] Collectively their grasp of the appropriate idiom for English word-setting is surprisingly secure. Meanwhile the number of native-born contributors by no means declined. Richard Leveridge (well known for his music for a revival of *Macbeth* in 1702, and composer of 'The Roast Beef of Old England'), John Lenton, Jeremiah Clarke, and John Barrett were in no sense insignificant composers, whose songs were published in individual collections, in serial anthologies and single sheets.[93] At a lower level we find Thomas Morgan (1697), William Pearson (1699), and Vaughan Richardson (1701); while Robert King (*c.*1692, *c.*1695) and John Abell (1701, 1701, 1703), the latter newly returned from an exile forced on him by his Roman Catholicism, are amongst the figures from an earlier epoch still active in this.[94] Much of their music was conceived for the theatre, and much of it is either trivial or pretentious. Yet amongst the huge output of the first two decades of the eighteenth century are signs of a new orientation in the approach to art-song: a growing distinction between the merely popular and the artistically elevated, and a growing separation between the idioms of the theatre and those of the private home or concert-room. In this development William Croft and John Christopher Pepusch, the successors of Weldon

---

[92] To these may be added G. B. Draghi (*c.*1640–1708), mentioned above in connection with James II's Roman Catholic Chapel; about 26 songs survive.

[93] Much of their output was intended for the stage: see for example the list of Clarke's songs in *NGD*.

[94] Dates are those of their published collections. For a summary account, see Spink, *English Song*, 252–9.

Ex. 215

continued

Ex. 215, continued

and the predecessors of Greene, Boyce, and Stanley, played an important role.[95]

The period which we are now considering cannot be considered a major one for the composition of instrumental music. It saw some remarkable technical advances, but on the whole the quality of what was produced did not match that of the preceding age. Purcell, as always, provides the exceptions; but his unique combination of *pietas* and innovation went largely unheeded by his successors. Were this period of experiment the prelude to a rich flowering of native achievement in the eighteenth century, it would be easier to justify its historical significance; but, even more than in the sphere of song and music for the stage, the labourings of the mountain yielded only a negligible posterity.[96]

Purcell's earliest instrumental works were written under the direct influence of Matthew Locke, though he did not emulate his revered master's cultivation of the suite or 'set' form. His three- and four-part fantasias challenge the older man's skill in motivic working and in the exploitation of contrapuntal devices. The two In nomines, in six and seven parts respectively, are the last examples of the tradition that began with the sixteenth-century use of Taverner's famous Benedictus. (The model here cannot have been Locke, but may perhaps have been William Lawes.)[97] These

---

[95] Their work in this sphere, with other aspects of the period dealt with only cursorily here, will be considered in Vol. II.

[96] This is not to deny the solid worth of Greene, Boyce, Arne, Stanley, and others in the next epoch; but in the era of Bach and Handel a sense of proportion must be observed.

[97] Or perhaps Jenkins: see *Roger North on Music*, 287. On the origins of the In nomine, see Ch. 5.

works had no successors, and could have appealed only to the dwindling body of conservative amateurs who still cultivated the viol consort. Somewhat different is the famous Chacony in G minor (the spelling probably reflects the normal English pronunciation of *chaconne*); this is usually played nowadays by string orchestras, and indeed there is nothing to contradict the assumption that it is orchestral in conception. At any rate it seems to call for performance by the violin rather than the viol family; it could indeed be a theatre piece, a companion perhaps to the otherwise unattached 'Overture to Mr P.'s Opera'.[98]

Although Purcell's two sets of trio sonatas were published at widely differing dates, it is quite likely that the majority of them were written in the early 1680s. The same autograph manuscript that contains much of his early sacred music and (reversing the volume) his fantasias, pavans, chacony, and other instrumental works also includes several of the sonatas first published in 1697. It is possible that it once contained some or all of the 1683 sonatas, too, together with the remainder of the 1697 works.[99] At all events, Purcell in 1683 made a selection of what he presumably considered to be his twelve best sonatas to date and arranged them according to a definite key-scheme in which the first eight works were in keys rising by a third each time (G minor, B flat, D minor, F, A minor, C, E minor, G), and the last four in keys falling a third each time (C minor, A, F minor, D).[100] Those not published in 1683 were subsequently revised by the composer, it is clear, although no autograph of the revisions is extant. But they did not make up the total of twelve which he probably considered *de rigueur* for a published collection, and it was left to his widow to bring them into the world shortly after his death.

Although the 1683 sonatas were described on publication as being in three parts and the 1697 works as being in four, the two sets are for exactly the same combination of two violins, bass (violoncello or viol), and 'thorough bass' (i.e. *basso continuo*, figured, for performance on the organ, harpsichord, or even, still, a plucked stringed instrument such as the theorbo). Purcell claimed in 1683 that the printing of a separate thorough-bass part was 'a thing quite besides his first resolution'; and from the extant autographs of the 1697 works one can see what is meant: the thorough bass hovers uncertainly between independence and a literal following of the string bass part, sometimes on its own staff, sometimes not, and is only sparsely figured at best. Between composition and publication the composer opted for the most unambiguous method of expressing his intentions, unless indeed it

---

[98] See n. 39 above for the possible link between this overture and *Dido*.

[99] For the full details see Tilmouth's preface to his edition of the second set, *PS*, vii, p. ix.

[100] Tilmouth, ibid. It has been conjectured that the scheme originally included the sonatas in E flat (1697/2) and B minor (1697/1) after no. 8 and at the end respectively, making a tonal pyramid of which no. 8 would represent the apex; but a set of 14 would have been most unusual.

was his publisher, drafting the preface, who sought to excuse himself thus for the delay in publication.[101] But the relatively large degree of independence in the thorough bass part is an old-fashioned, not a forward-looking, feature. Purcell would have come across it in the Italian works that he claimed to be imitating,[102] in the nomenclature of which, incidentally, the *basso continuo* was not usually counted amongst the numbered parts; and it is a feature of the more advanced type of chamber music cultivated by his immediate predecessors such as Jenkins and Young.[103] But after Purcell's day, although the practice of publishing the thorough bass separately was almost invariably maintained in trio sonatas and in works for larger ensembles, its independence gradually lessened until the point where it became practically non-existent.

Purcell's trio sonatas, though avowedly based on Italian models, exemplified a very personal interpretation of the style.[104] They are contrapuntally ingenious, harmonically rich, and melodically graceful. Formally they lie somewhere between the sectional chamber *canzoni* or sonatas of earlier Italian composers (whether 'da chiesa' or 'da camera') and the regular four-movement pattern (slow–fast–slow–fast) of the eighteenth century. Most have more than four movements (in so far as the single movement can be regarded as a formal entity), though one (1697, no. 6) is an astonishing ground bass composition on an unvarying five-bar phrase. It is hard to select material with which to illustrate a repertory of such incomparable sophistication, and a mere recital of its ingenious features would become tedious. But the second sonata of the second collection, in E flat, does represent to perfection the qualities enumerated above. The second movement, a fugal 'canzona',[105] combines its main theme, both 'recto' and inverted, with a semiquaver figure first introduced *en passant* earlier in the movement (Ex. 216). For Purcell's ability to suggest remote harmonic vistas we might point to the first and third movements of this sonata; or, as an illustration of his ability to combine harmonic introspection with an appealing melodiousness, to the fourth movement, marked 'Largo' (Ex.

---

[101] J. A. Westrup, *Purcell* (London, 1937; 1980), 230. The Preface is quoted in full, 47–8, as well as in *PS*, v.

[102] Westrup (ibid. 231) refers to a collection of 22 Italian sonatas in the Brit. Lib., Add. MS 31413. But Purcell may well have had access to published materials: Cazzati and Legrenzi are possible models.

[103] William Young's sonatas were published in Innsbruck in 1653; the composer returned to England and the royal service in 1660. Comparable works by Jenkins were published in a now lost edition of 1660.

[104] Roger North's well-known comment bears repetition: 'And the masters here began to imitate them [the Italians], witness M[r] H. Purcell in his noble set of sonnatas, which however clog'd with somewhat of an English vein, for which they are unworthily despised, are very artificiall and good music.' *Roger North on Music*, 310 n. The passage is from *An Essay of Musicall Ayre*, Brit. Lib., Add. MS 32536, fos. 78[v]–79[r].

[105] Purcell favoured this term for a lively fugal movement. In this he probably followed the precedent set by William Young (see n. 103), who in turn had adopted current German usage.

Ex. 216

★ The natural is confirmed by MS Oxford, Bod. Lib., Mus. Sch. e. 400–3.

217, overleaf).[106] The fifth movement is again fugal, with perfect triple counterpoint, inversion of the theme, and stretto; but all in so dance-like a fashion that not a hint of academicism is present.

The Purcellian tradition of chamber music for strings with thorough bass was carried forward by Blow, whose contribution amounts to one trio sonata and a fine ground for two violins and bass, and by Croft, whose

[106] In the 1683 preface Purcell defined Largo as 'a middle movement'—meaning by that, of course, a moderate speed.

Ex. 217

trio sonatas and larger ensemble works have recently been brought to public notice.[107] But with these exceptions Purcell's example was not followed with any great success, and the eighteenth century inherited a form that would have seemed moribund had not Handel arrived to breathe new life into it. Far more vigorous was the growth of accompanied solo string music, nurtured as it was by an influx of foreign artists. At a somewhat earlier date, the German Gerhard Diesner and the Swede Thomas Baltzar had introduced new standards of violin-playing to England; now the most important figure was the Italian, Nicola Matteis, who published two books of 'Ayres' and became an immensely popular public figure.[108] The divide between professional and amateur was growing ever wider as technical expectations rose, but it could still be bridged by a collection such as Playford's *The Division-Violin*, first published in 1684 and often reprinted.[109]

---

[107] See the edition by H. D. Johnstone (forthcoming). For sources and editions of Blow see *NGD*. See also the trumpet repertory discussed below.

[108] We have already met Matteis as a songster. His ayres were published in 1677 (first and second parts) and 1685 (third and fourth parts); a second treble was added to the two latter on their republication in 1687. For a sample of his work see MC, xcvi, and Holman's prefatory remarks. See also P. Walls, 'The Influence of the Italian Violin School in 17th-century England', *Early Music*, 18 (1990), 575–87.

[109] There is a facsimile edition based on the 6th edn. of 1705 but retaining only the items printed in 1684 (ed. M. Gilmore, Oxford, 1982).

Here the various sets of divisions are mostly by older English and Continental violinists such as John Banister, Christopher Simpson, Davis Mell, and Thomas Baltzar; Solomon Eccles (father of the composer John Eccles), a player who turned Quaker and burnt his instruments around 1660, is represented in the enlarged second edition of 1685. It is fascinating to see the ancient grounds still in active use: the 'quadran pavan' or *passamezzo moderno* in Davis Mell's variations on 'John come kiss me now', the *folia* in 'Faronells Division on a Ground'. Michel Farinel's humble composition does not compare with the great set which forms Corelli's last violin sonata (itself but one of many sets of variations on this theme from the late seventeenth and early eighteenth centuries),[110] though it was popular enough to cause the composer's name to be attached to the ground itself.[111]

Divisions on a ground were also composed for recorder,[112] and it might be thought, with the growth of instrumental virtuosity and an increasing demand from the amateur performer, that the serious solo sonata would also have flourished. But on the whole it was less in evidence at this period than even the trio sonata. Henry Purcell himself wrote only one such work, and that in an incomplete form; those of his brother Daniel (1698: three for recorder and three for violin) are singularly unadventurous,[113] but there is more interest in the published sonatas of Croft (for violin, 1700) and William Babell (for violin or oboe, published *c*.1725). Amongst the many foreigners who swarmed to London in the early eighteenth century, the most important from this point of view was Jean-Baptiste Loeillet, a Belgian flautist who came over in about 1705. He introduced the then largely unknown transverse flute (which the English, taking their cue from current French nomenclature, dubbed the 'German flute') and published a set of twelve sonatas (six for flute and six for recorder) as well as trio sonatas and keyboard works.[114] His straightforward, clear-cut style and standardized formal procedures were extremely influential on English composers of the following epoch.

The domestic keyboard instrument—called virginal(s), spinet, or harpsic(h)ord, though the different names do not accurately reflect differences of size or shape—inherited the mantle of the lute and its cognates. The

---

[110] e.g. by Matteis (Oxford, Bod. Lib., Mus. Sch. c. 61, pp. 18–21, signed 'N.M.': I owe this reference to Miss Gilmore's notes), and for keyboard by d'Anglebert (1689) and Alessandro Scarlatti. See the article 'Folia' in *NGD*.

[111] The 1684 table of contents calls it 'A Division on Mr Farinell's Ground'. This is to put the cart before the horse. Michel Farinel, an obscure French musician, is of course not to be confused with the famous castrato Giuseppe Farinelli (1705–82), who enjoyed so great a success in London in the 1730s.

[112] See *The Division Recorder*, ed. P. Holman, 2 vols. (New York, 1979).

[113] Modern edition by P. Everett (London, 1980).

[114] He is not to be confused with his cousin, J. B. Loeillet 'de Gant' (1688–*c*.1720); both, in fact, were born in Ghent. The latter published four sets of twelve recorder sonatas, and a set of six trio sonatas, in Amsterdam and London.

experimental publications of the 1660s and 1670s were succeeded by a numerous progeny of popular anthologies of ever-broadening appeal: *The Second Part of Musick's Handmaid* (1689); *The Harpsicord Master* (1697) and its many successors, of which latter only the second and third books (1700, 1702) contained original compositions for keyboard; *A Choice Collection of Ayres* (1700); *A Collection of Lessons* (1702); the individual publications of Purcell (1696), Blow (1698), Jeremiah Clarke (1711), and Anthony Young (1719); and the popular series known as *The Ladys Banquet* (1704 seqq.) and, rather confusingly, *The Ladys Entertainment or Banquet of Musick* (1708 seqq.). Purcell's suites lent weight to a form that in England was always inclined to be insubstantial; his example was followed by Blow and Croft, whose suites and other pieces are amongst the most powerful examples of English keyboard writing between the Restoration and the arrival of Handel. But much of Blow's work and most of Croft's remained unpublished in their lifetime, and it had little influence on others. The demand for popular tunes and operatic transcriptions was one that could be more profitably met; it is typified by the activities of William Babell, a violinist and harpsichordist who cashed in on the success of *Rinaldo* by publishing his transcriptions of the overture and several arias.[115]

Organ music survives almost exclusively in manuscripts. The compilers of the period preserve the older repertory of Christopher Gibbons and his contemporaries, adding the miscellaneous productions of Purcell, Blow, Reading, Barrett, Hart, Croft, and the like. Blow, with thirty or more voluntaries to his credit, emerges as the dominating figure here. The five large manuscripts[116] of John Reading (1677–1764), who was organist of Dulwich College and of several London churches, illustrate the taste of the time; they include a wide selection of voluntaries including those of the youthful Greene and Stanley as well as popular tunes and operatic transcriptions for the harpsichord.

The distinction between chamber and orchestral music was emerging only gradually at this period, and many kinds of music seem to fall into both camps. An orchestral idiom was fostered above all by the King's Band of Violins, used primarily in anthems and odes, and by the development of an orchestral ensemble in theatre music. The essence of an 'orchestra' lies in the multiplication of the string parts, but it is not always easy to say to what extent this was aimed for or achieved in individual instances. The inclusion of the viola ('tenor violin') in the string ensemble is a guide,

---

[115] For modern editions of most of the composers and collections mentioned, see the Bibliography. Some of William Babell's harpsichord arrangements were given by Chrysander in vol. xlviii of his Handel edition.

[116] Three are still kept at Dulwich College (MSS 92a, 92b, 92d); the other two are in Manchester (Henry Watson Library, BR. m. 7105. Rf. 31) and Tokyo (Nanki Music Library, n. 4. 31). They date from between 1717 and 1737.

though not an infallible one; and paradoxically the viola part itself was often left as the weakest of all, while much of the bass doubling was entrusted to bassoons and keyboard instruments rather than to additional cellos ('bass violins'). But from about 1675 onwards, if not earlier, it is probably legitimate to think of the instrumental music of the theatre as almost invariably 'orchestral' in conception;[117] and there were, to begin with at least, few if any other outlets for the medium except for the occasional detachable movement from the anthems and odes of the court. The posthumous publication of Purcell's *Ayres for the Theatre* symbolizes their potential as independent suites. Croft was a vigorous composer in the same tradition: his 'Ayres in the Comedy call'd the Funeral, or Grief Allamode' (by Richard Steele, produced 1701) were published in the third part of a collection entitled *Harmonia Anglicana* (1702) together with similar music by Paisible, Barrett, Lenton, Lord Byron, and Daniel Purcell.[118]

Other sources show evidence of more independent repertories. Music for trumpets (or oboes) and strings by James Paisible and others (including John Eccles, Daniel Purcell, and Gottfried Finger) is found in a set of seven part-books of the early eighteenth century;[119] a somewhat similar set of four contains French-style orchestral suites and a few trumpet works by Corelli, Paisible, and others.[120] Henry Purcell himself had cultivated the form of 'trumpet sonata', the model for which was to be found in the Bolognese school of Torelli and others; but he and Daniel Purcell (who included three in his score for *The Judgment of Paris*), followed by Paisible and Croft, gave it a decidedly English accent. It was not necessarily heard in isolation from the stage or the larger secular vocal work, but it had the potential for independence and contributed effectively to the growing repertory of concert orchestral music in the period.[121] Together with a quantity of native and foreign music for strings alone, it illustrates the condition of the art on the eve of the publication of Corelli's concerti grossi and the impact of Handel's operatic orchestral manner. These two were to have a decisive influence on later developments in England.

[117] For the composition of Handel's orchestra at the Haymarket Theatre see Dean and Knapp, *Handel's Operas 1704–1726*, 154.

[118] Croft's instrumental music for *The Funeral*, ed. R. Platt, is published by Oxford University Press (MC, xlv, 1976). The complete contents of *Harmonia Anglicana*, amounting to nine collections published between about 1701 and 1706, together with the instrumental music for ten plays for the Haymarket Theatre, published by Walsh between 1705 and 1710, are listed in C. Price, *Music in the Restoration Theatre*, 238–43. His Appendix I, pp. 135–236, is a complete catalogue of instrumental music in Restoration plays, 1665–1713.

[119] London, Brit. Lib., Add. 49599: a sonata by Paisible (*c*.1650–1721), the tenth in this MS, ed. R. Platt, is published by Oxford University Press (MC, xliii, 1978). Paisible, of French birth, lived in England from 1685.

[120] Add. 39565–7 with 30839, dating from *c*.1700. Paisible's Trumpet Sonata, ed. P. Holman, is published as MC, xlii (1981).

[121] See further P. Holman, 'The trumpet sonata in England', *Early Music*, 4 (1976), 424–9.

The foregoing sketch will have given some idea of the frenetic activities of English musicians in this period. It was no less an age of intellectual curiosity. There was a renewed interest in the mathematical basis of aural phenomena, an interest kindled not only by the rediscovery of the ancient Greek theorists whose writings lay behind the familiar Latin text of Boethius, but by its relevance to contemporary problems such as those of tuning and temperament. John Wallis (1616–1703), Savilian Professor of Astronomy at Oxford, and a not unworthy predecessor of the formidable Newton, edited the *Harmonics* of Ptolemy and discussed systems of temperament, including what seems to have been equal temperament.[122] In the sphere of practical instruction the popular handbooks of Simpson and Playford continued to be reprinted, in the latter case with appropriate revisions; and no important substitutes for them appeared in this period.[123] The major new publication of the epoch, Thomas Mace's *Musick's Monument*, came out in 1676 and reflects the musings of an introverted, though learned, conservative. His chief enthusiasm was for the lute, an instrument which even his advocacy was unable to rescue from its decline in popularity; but he also had valuable things to say about church (parochial) music and about the viol as a consort instrument. His earnest exhortations are delivered in an extraordinary style reminiscent of dissident religious polemic (though he was himself a good Anglican), and reinforced by the over-liberal use of italics, brackets, and other visual distractions.

If Mace's style is a barrier to comprehension, it is with relief that one turns to Roger North,[124] a gracious writer whose easy way with the language recalls that of Simpson. North was the youngest son of Sir Dudley North, the fourth Lord North of Kirtling in Cambridgeshire. He trained as a lawyer and kept company in London with his elder brother Francis, who rose to become Lord Keeper. When Francis died in 1685, Roger gradually withdrew from London society; he bought the estate of Rougham in Norfolk, married and eventually settled there permanently, living on until 1734. He published comparatively little, and his voluminous writings can have had

---

[122] Others who contributed to the scientific study of music in the late 17th and early 18th centuries include John Birchensha (or Birkenshaw, d. 1681), William Holder (1616–96), Thomas Salmon (1648–1706), and James Talbot (1665–1708, Regius Professor of Hebrew at Cambridge, 1689–1704). Birchensha and Holder were also composers of a sort. Talbot's musical writings are preserved in Oxford, Christ Church, Mus. 1187: his information about musical instruments is mostly published in *GSJ*, vols. 1, 3, 5, 14, 15, 16, and 21. The manuscript also contains an account of ancient Greek music by Henry Aldrich (1648–1710), Dean of Christ Church from 1689 until his death. For a comprehensive general account of English musical science at this period see P. Gouk, 'Music in the Natural Philosophy of the Early Royal Society', Ph.D. diss. (London, Warburg Inst., 1982). See also L. E. Miller, 'John Birchensha and the Early Royal Society: Grand Scales and Scientific Composition', *JRMA*, 115 (1990), 63–79.

[123] Purcell's contribution to Playford's *Introduction* appeared in the 12th edn. (1694): fac. edn. by F. B. Zimmerman (New York, 1972). For a summary of English writings on 'practical' music see B. Cooper, 'Englische Musiktheorie im 17. und 18. Jahrhundert', in *Geschichte der Musiktheorie*, ix (Darmstadt, 1986), 141–314.

[124] For modern editions of Mace and North, see Bibliography.

no influence; but they mirror the age in a way that is scarcely approached by his contemporaries. His autobiography ('Notes of Me') and his lives of his brothers offer a charming glimpse into a distinguished and affluent family; and his musical opinions, though the work of an amateur whose technical accomplishment was probably never more than slight, are notable for their robust common sense and historical perception.

North casts interesting light on the growth of public concerts in the later seventeenth century.

The first attempt was low: a project of Old Banister, who was a good violin, and a theatricall composer. He opened an obscure room in a public house in White fryars; filled it with tables and seats, and made a side box with curtaines for the musick, I.^{s} a peice, call for what you please, pay the reckoning, and *Welcome gentlemen.*[125]

This was in 1672. A more professional effort was later mounted in York Buildings:

It was called the Musick Meeting; and all the Quality and *beau mond* repaired to it. But the plan of this project was not so well layd as ought to have bin, for the time of their beginning was inconsistent with the park and the playhouses, which had a stronger attraction ... Besides the whole was without designe or order; for one master brings a consort with fuges, another shews his guifts in a solo upon the violin, another sings, and then a famous lutinist comes foreward, and in this manner changes followed each other, with a full cessation of the musick between every one, and a gable and a bustle while they changed places.[126]

However, the concerts survived until well into the eighteenth century. Another successful venture was that of Thomas Britton, the 'small-coal' man (seller of charcoal), who held concerts in a room over his shop in Clerkenwell. The repertory included the latest Continental masterpieces, which in those free-and-easy days might be copied by hand and performed without profit to the composer. Britton was a remarkable man. In Westrup's words, 'He witnessed the rise of Purcell's genius and its sudden extinction, and lived to welcome Handel to his meetings.'[127]

Church and court, playhouse and tavern, domestic hearth and place of public resort—all called for the music of professionals or amateurs or both.[128]

---

[125] *Roger North on Music*, 302–4. But public concerts had begun somewhat earlier: ibid. 352–3, and Pepys, *Diary*, 5 Oct. 1664: 'To the Musique-meeting at the Post-office, where I was once before' (though this may have been a private meeting).

[126] *Roger North on Music*, 353.

[127] *Purcell* (3rd edn.), 101. MS Mus. Sch. c. 75 in the Bodleian Library is a copy in Britton's hand of Corelli's trio sonatas, Op. 1.

[128] Amateurism at its best can be seen in the career of Henry Aldrich (see n. 122 above). Both before and after his appointment as Dean of Christ Church he organized weekly music meetings in his rooms; he collected a large musical library which he bequeathed to the College and which forms the bulk of its present collection; and he was a competent composer, mainly of sacred music, and an indefatigable copyist and adapter of other composers' works.

No composer yet made a living purely out of composition, but his professional status was considerably enhanced by the growth of music-publishing, of the musical theatre, and of public concerts. These outlets were beginning to replace those of the Church and of private musical establishments as the means whereby composers might earn their living and come to public notice. The potential audience was now much wider than it had ever been before, and the gratification of the popular taste became a more pressing concern. In a period of some confusion of aims, we can nevertheless detect the beginnings of a distinction between popular music and a more 'patrician' style (to adopt an inadequate expression). Purcell, and perhaps Blow and even Croft—and of course Handel—were still able to bridge the gap, if not to satisfy the extremes of vulgarity; but many composers now concentrated entirely on the light, the trivial, and the ephemeral. The institutions of the monarchy—the court, the Chapel Royal, and other 'royal peculiars'—were to provide dignified patronage for another century; and the same period was to be one in which the highest artistic canons might still be satisfied in the context of the unsubsidized market. But the lines of demarcation were set out well before Purcell's untimely death.

With these developments came, not a decline in amateur music-making, but a sharper differentiation between it and the professional article. In the sixteenth century, and earlier in the seventeenth, there was much interaction. Now the tendency was either towards a more exclusive professionalism or else (for example in the choir-stalls of the provincial cathedrals) towards amateurism as the value of the endowed stipends decreased. The local organist became a more commanding and a more isolated figure. Formerly the finest composers, such as Tomkins, Locke, or Jenkins, might perform in consort-music of their own or of others, in the company of country gentlemen, or at city music-meetings. Now, although these activities continued, there was a growing tendency towards a lowering of standards amongst amateurs and towards the professionalizing of music-meetings if the standards were high enough to attract the public. In whichever direction the outcome might fall, the danger to traditional forms of chamber music-making was severe.

Church and chamber music had never been widely available in print before the later seventeenth century; and when music-publishing grew into a thriving trade, it tended to encourage the growth of professional exclusivism and the lowering of amateur ambitions at one and the same time. There was a lively domestic market for straightforward instrumental and vocal music, and indeed for parochial church music. But it was satisfied, at least in part, by the publication of 'professional' music: the violin 'ayres' of a Matteis, songs from the operas, and so on. The amateur gained pleasure from this spurious contact with virtuosity but no longer aspired to participation at the highest artistic levels. Current technical standards were beyond him (and her); and the finest artistic productions could be recreated in the home only in pale imitations. The professionals themselves achieved much of their effect through improvisation, and their most ambitious projects remained in manuscript.

These distinctions—between popular and patrician, amateur and professional—became more marked in the later seventeenth century but did not yet adversely affect the general health of English musical culture. The period was one of remarkable ebullience: its sheer appetite for life is reflected in the vigour of its music at all levels. But it took a particular kind of genius to accommodate the conflicting pressures; and the bustling activity of London music after Purcell's death could not compensate for his removal. The arrival of Handel heralded a renaissance; and Handel almost, but not quite, became a truly English composer. He was to dominate English music in the next epoch, and his own death revealed a more substantial void. This is not to prejudge the status of the native achievement in the eighteenth century; but it is to warn that it must be seen in a context other than that of innovation and individuality.

Bibliography

THE following is not intended to be an exhaustive list. It has two functions, the first of which is to give the full details of publications cited in shorter form in the notes. For that reason subdivision has been kept to a minimum. Its second function is to record those items that I have found to be of value, though they are not cited, and which I believe may be of continuing usefulness to others. It goes without saying that many potentially useful items will have escaped my notice. The 'General' section includes only those books and articles which incorporate a substantial overlap between the two volumes of this *History*. Items listed with the Abbreviations on p. 00 are not repeated here. The arrangement is as follows:

I. GENERAL

A. Works of Reference

ARKWRIGHT, G. E. P., *Catalogue of Music in the Library of Christ Church Oxford*, 2 vols. (London, 1915–23).

CROSBY, B., *A Catalogue of Durham Cathedral Music Manuscripts* (Oxford, 1986).

DAWE, D., *Organists of the City of London 1666–1850: A Record of One Thousand Organists with an Annotated Index* (for the Author, 1983).

DIXON, W. E., *A Catalogue of Ancient Choral Services and Anthems . . . in the Cathedral Church of Ely* (Cambridge, 1861).

EITNER, R., *Biographisch-Bibliographisches Quellen-Lexicon*, 10 vols. (Leipzig, 1900–4).

FELLOWES, E. H., *The Catalogue of Manuscripts in the Library of St. Michael's College, Tenbury* (Paris, 1934).

FENLON, I., *Catalogue of the Printed Music and Music Manuscripts before 1801 in the Music Library of the University of Birmingham Barber Institute of Fine Arts* (London, 1976).

FORD, W. K., *Music in England Before 1800: A Select Bibliography* (London, 1967).

FULLER-MAITLAND, J. A., and MANN, A. H., *Catalogue of Music in the Fitzwilliam Museum, Cambridge* (London, 1893).

GRIFFITHS, D., *A Catalogue of the Music Manuscripts in York Minster Library* (York, 1981).

—— 'The Music in York Minster', *MT*, 123 (1982), 633–7.

Handbook of British Chronology, ed. E. B. Fryde, D. E. Greenway, S. Porter, and I. Roy (3rd edn., London, 1986). Royal Historical Society Guides and Handbooks, no. 2.

HARMAN, A., *A Catalogue of the Printed Music and Books on Music in Durham Cathedral Library* (London, 1968).

HAYES, G., *King's Music* (London, 1937).

HIGHFILL, P. H., and others, *A Biographical Dictionary of Actors, Actresses, Musicians, Dancers, Managers, and Other Stage Personnel in London, 1600–1800* (Carbondale, Ill., 1973–).

HUGHES, Dom A., *Catalogue of the Musical Manuscripts at Peterhouse* (Cambridge, 1953).

HUGHES-HUGHES, A., *A Catalogue of Manuscript Music in the British Museum*, 3 vols. (London, 1906–9).

JAMES, M. R., *A Descriptive Catalogue of the Manuscripts in the Library of Corpus Christi College, Cambridge*, 2 vols. (Cambridge, 1912).

JULIAN, J., *A Dictionary of Hymnology* (2nd edn., London, 1907).

KING, A. H., *Printed Music in the British Museum* (London, 1979).

LOEWENBERG, A., *Annals of Opera 1597–1940* (Cambridge, 1943).

The London Stage 1660–1800: A Calendar of Plays, Entertainments and Afterpieces, ed. W. Van Lennep, E. L. Avery, A. H. Scouten, G. W. Stone, and C. B. Hogan, 5 pts. in 11 vols. (Carbondale, Ill., 1960–8).

MOULD, C., *The Musical Manuscripts of St. George's Chapel, Windsor Castle* (Windsor, 1973).

The Old Cheque-Book or Book of Remembrance, of the Chapel Royal, from 1561 to 1744, ed. E. F. Rimbault (London, 1872).

SQUIRE, W. B., *Catalogue of Printed Music in the Library of the Royal College of Music, London* (London and Leipzig, 1909).

—— *Catalogue of Printed Music published between 1487 and 1800 and now in the British Museum*, 2 vols. (London and Leipzig, 1912).

—— *Catalogue of the King's Music Library*, 3 vols. (London, 1927–9).

WILLETTS, P. J., *Handlist of Music Manuscripts Acquired* [by the British Museum] *1908–1967* (London, 1970).

B. Historical and Critical Works

ATKINS, Sir I., *The Early Occupants of the Office of Organist and Master of the Choristers of the Cathedral Church of Christ and the Blessed Virgin Mary, Worcester* (London, 1918).

BLOM, E., *Music in England* (Harmondsworth, 1942; 2nd edn., 1948).

BUKOFZER, M. F., *Music in the Baroque Era* (New York, 1947).

BUMPUS, J. S., *The Organists and Composers of St Paul's Cathedral* (London, 1891).

BURNEY, C., *A General History of Music*, 4 vols. (London, 1776–89, repr. 1789; ed. F. Mercer, 2 vols., New York, 1935, repr. 1957).

CALDWELL, J., *English Keyboard Music Before the Nineteenth Century* (Oxford, 1973).

CHAPPELL, W., *Popular Music of the Olden Time*, 17 parts or 2 vols. (London [1855–9]; reissued as *The Ballad Literature and Popular Music of the Olden Time*, 2 vols., London [1859]; 2nd edn. by H. E. Wooldridge, *Old English Popular Music*, 2 vols., London and New York, 1893; repr. of 1st edn. with Introduction by F. W. Sternfeld, New York, 1965; repr. of 2nd edn. in 1 vol., with Suppl. by F. Kidson [first publ. 1891], New York, 1961).

CLUTTON, C., and NILAND, A., *The British Organ* (London, 1963).

COLLES, H. C., *Voice and Verse: A Study in English Song* (London, 1928).

COOPER, B., 'Englische Musiktheorie im 17. und 18. Jahrhundert', *Geschichte der Musiktheorie*, ix (Darmstadt, 1986), 141–314.

DAVEY, H., *History of English Music* (London, 1895; 2nd edn., 1921).

FELLOWES, E. H., *Organists and Masters of the Choristers of St George's Chapel in Windsor Castle* (London [1939]).

—— *English Cathedral Music* (London, 1941; 5th edn., rev. J. A. Westrup, 1969).

FISKE, R., *Scotland in Music* (Cambridge, 1983).

GALPIN, F. W., *Old English Instruments of Music* (London, 1910; 4th edn., rev. R. T. Dart, New York, 1965).

HARRISON, F., 'Celtic Musics: Characteristics and Chronology', *Geschichte und Kultur der Kelten*, ed. K. H. Schmidt (Heidelberg, 1986), 252–63.

HAWKINS, Sir J., *A General History of the Science and Practice of Music*, 5 vols. (London, 1776).

HUMPHRIES, C., and SMITH, W. C., *Music Publishing in the British Isles from the Beginning until the Middle of the Nineteenth Century* (Oxford, 1970).

KIDSON, F., *British Music Publishers, Printers and Engravers . . . from Queen Elizabeth's Reign to George the Fourth's* (London [1900]).

KNIGHT, F., *Cambridge Music* (Cambridge, 1980).

LASOCKI, D., 'Professional Recorder Playing in England 1500–1740, I. 1500–1640', *Early Music*, 10 (1982), 23–9; 'II. 1640–1740', *Early Music*, 10 (1982), 183–91.

McGUINNESS, R., *English Court Odes 1660–1820* (Oxford, 1971).

MACKERNESS, E. D., *A Social History of English Music* (London, 1964).

MELLERS, W., *Harmonious Meeting: A Study of the Relationship between English Music, Poetry and Theatre, c. 1600–1900* (London, 1965).

Modern Musical Scholarship, ed. E. Olleson (Boston, Henley and London, 1978).

Music Survey: New Series 1949–52, ed. D. Mitchell and H. Keller, 3 vols. in 1 (London, 1981).

PINE, E., *The Westminster Abbey Singers* (London, 1953).

PROCTER, F., and FRERE, W. H., *A New History of the Book of Common Prayer* (London, 1908).

ROBERTSON, D. H., *Sarum Close* (London, 1938; 2nd edn., Bath, 1969).

TEMPERLEY, N., *The Music of the English Parish Church*, 2 vols. (Cambridge, 1979).

WALKER, E., *A History of Music in England* (Oxford, 1907; 3rd edn., rev. J. A. Westrup, 1952).

WHITE, E. W., *The Rise of English Opera* (London, 1951).

—— *A History of English Opera* (London, 1983).

WILSON, M., *The English Chamber Organ* (Oxford, 1968).

II. FOR VOLUME I

A. Modern Editions of Music

ADSON, JOHN, *Courtly Masquing Ayres*, ed. M. L. Born (London: Musica Rara, 1975). Also ed. P. Walls (London: London Pro Musica, 1975–6).

ALISON, RICHARD, *An Hour's Recreation in Music (1606)*, ed. E. H. Fellowes (London: Stainer and Bell, 1924; rev. R. T. Dart, 1961). EM, xxxiii.

—— *The psalmes of David in meter 1599* (fac.), ed. I. Harwood (Menston: Scolar Press, 1968). ELS (fac.), i (1).

—— CAMPIAN, MORLEY, ROBINSON, GILES, HUME, LANIER, LUPO, ANON.: *Twenty Songs from Printed Sources*, ed. D. Greer (London: Stainer and Bell, 1969). ELS, II/xxi

Anglo-French Sequelae, ed. Dom A. Hughes (London: PMMS, 1934; repr. Farnborough: Gregg, 1966).

Anne Cromwell's Virginal Book, 1638, ed. H. Ferguson (London: OUP, 1974).

ANON. [attrib. 'Leonel'], *Messa super Fuit homo missus* [ed. L. Feininger] (Rome: Soc. Univ. S. Ceciliae, 1950). DPL, I/ix

ANON., *Missa O Quam Suavis*, ed. H. B. Collins (Burnham: PMMS, 1927).

ANON., *Sanctus [and] Magnificat (Anonymous, 14th Century)*, ed. P. Doe (University of Exeter, 1973).

ANON., *Voluntary in D minor for Double Organ*, ed. H. W. Shaw (London: Novello, 1960). Early Organ Music, iv.

Anthems for Men's Voices, ed. P. Le Huray, N. Temperley, P. Tranchell, and D. Willcocks, 2 vols. (London: OUP, 1965).

An Anthology of English Church Music, ed. D. Wulstan (London: Chester/Hansen, 1971).

An Anthology of English Lute Music, ed. D. Lumsden (London: Schott, 1954).

Antiphonaire monastique (XIIIᵉ siècle): Codex F. 160 de la bibliothèque de la cathédrale de Worcester, 2 vols. (Tournai: Desclée, 1922–5). Paléographie musicale, I/xii.

ASTON, HUGH, MARBECK, JOHN, and PARSLEY, OSBERT, [Church Music] (London: OUP, 1929). TCM, x.

ATTEY, JOHN, *The First Booke of Ayres 1622* (fac.), ed. D. Greer (Menston: Scolar Press, 1967). ELS (fac.), i (2).

BACHELER, DANIEL, *Selected Works for Lute*, ed. M. Long (London: OUP, 1972). *Music for the Lute*, v.

BARLEY, WILLIAM, *A new Booke of Tabliture, 1596*, ed. W. W. Newcomb (University Park and London: The Pennsylvania State University Press, 1966) = *Lute Music of Shakespeare's Time.*

BARTLET, JOHN, *A Booke of Ayres 1606* (fac.), ed. D. Greer (Menston: Scolar Press, 1967). ELS (fac.), i (3).

BATESON, THOMAS, *First Set of Madrigals (1604)*, ed. E. H. Fellowes (London: Stainer and Bell, 1922; rev. R. T. Dart, 1958). EM, xxi.

—— *Second Set of Madrigals to 3, 4, 5 and 6 Parts (1618)*, ed. E. H. Fellowes (London: Stainer and Bell, 1922; rev. R. T. Dart, 1960). EM, xxii.

BENNETT, JOHN, *Madrigals to Four Voices (1599)*, ed. E. H. Fellowes (London: Stainer and Bell, 1922; rev. D. Moroney, 1979). EM, xxiii. With his madrigal from *The Triumphes of Oriana*, and two pieces from Ravenscroft's *Briefe Discourse*.

BLOW, JOHN, *Anthems II: Anthems with Orchestra*, ed. B. Wood (London: Stainer and Bell, 1984). MB, i.

—— *Coronation Anthems; Anthems with Strings*, ed. A. Lewis and H. W. Shaw (London: Stainer and Bell, 1953). MB, vii.

—— *Six Suites*, ed. H. Ferguson (London: Stainer and Bell, 1965). SBK, v.

—— *Thirty Voluntaries and Verses*, ed. H. W. Shaw (London: Schott, 1958; 2nd edn., 1972).

—— *Two Voluntaries from the Nanki Manuscript*, ed. H. McLean (London: Novello, 1971). Early Organ Music, xxiii.

—— *Venus and Adonis*, ed. A. Lewis (Paris: Éditions de l'Oiseau-Lyre, 1939).

The British Museum Manuscript Egerton 3307, ed. G. S. McPeek (London: OUP, 1963). Omitting the carols.

BROWNE, WILLIAM, *Works by William Browne*, ed. R. Vendome and C. Good (Oxford: John Brennan, 1983). Spanish Netherlands Keyboard Music, ii. Christ Church Music MS 89; Berlin Staatsbibliothek MS 40316.

BULL, JOHN, *Keyboard Music,* i, ed. J. Steele and F. Cameron (London: Stainer and Bell, 1960; 2nd rev. edn., 1967). MB, xiv.

—— *Keyboard Music*, ii, ed. R. T. Dart (London: Stainer and Bell, 1963). MB, xix.

BYRD, WILLIAM, [Arrangements for lute of music by] ed. N. North (London: OUP, 1976). Music for the Lute, vi.

—— *The Byrd Edition*, ed. P. Brett, 17 vols. (London: Stainer and Bell, 1970–). This supersedes *The Collected Works*, ed. E. H. Fellows (1937–50, rev. R. T. Dart and others, 1962–71).

—— *English Church Music: Part I* (London: OUP, 1922). TCM, ii.

—— *Gradualia, Books I and II* (London: OUP, 1927). TCM, vii.

—— *Keyboard Music*, ed. A. Brown, 2 vols. (London: Stainer and Bell, 1969–71). MB, xxvii–xxviii.

—— *Masses, Cantiones* [1575] *and Motets* (London: OUP, 1928). TCM, ix.

—— *Psalms, Sonnets and Songs (1588)*, ed. E. H. Fellowes, rev. P. Brett and R. T. Dart (London: Stainer and Bell, 1965). EM, xiv.

—— *Psalms, Songs and Sonnets (1611)*, ed. E. H. Fellows, rev. R. T. Dart (London: Stainer and Bell, 1964). EM, xvi.

—— *Songs of Sundry Natures (1589)*, ed. E. H. Fellowes, rev. R. T. Dart and P. Brett (London: Stainer and Bell, 1962). EM, xv.

CAMPION, THOMAS, *The Description of a Maske presented at the Mariage of The Earle of Somerset 1614* (fac.), ed. D. Greer (Menston: Scolar Press, 1970). ELS (fac.), ii (7).

—— *The Discription of a Maske in Honour of the Lord Hayes 1607* (fac.), ed. D. Greer (Menston: Scolar Press, 1970). ELS (fac.), ii (6).

—— *First Book of Ayres; Second Book of Ayres*, ed. D. Scott, 2 vols. (London: Stainer and Bell, 1979).

—— *Fourth Booke of Ayres*, ed. E. H. Fellowes (London: Stainer and Bell, 1926). ESLS, II/xi.

—— *The Songs from Rosseter's Book of Airs*, ed. E. H. Fellowes, 2 vols. (London: Stainer and Bell, 1922–4; 3rd edn., rev. R. T. Dart, in 1 vol., 1969). ELS, I/iv and xiii (in 1 vol.).

—— *Third Booke of Ayres*, ed. E. H. Fellowes (London: Stainer and Bell, 1926; 2nd rev. edn. by R. T. Dart, 1969). ELS, II/x.

—— *The Third and Fourth Booke of Ayres [ca. 1618]* (fac.), ed. D. Greer (Menston: Scolar Press, 1969). ELS (fac.), ii (5).

—— *Two bookes of ayres ca. 1613* (fac.), ed. D. Greer (Menston: Scolar Press, 1967). ELS (fac.), ii (4).

—— see also ALISON [etc.], *Twenty Songs*.

Canons in the Trent Codices, ed. R. Loyan (AIM, 1976). CMM, xxxviii.

CARLETON, NICHOLAS (the younger), see *Two Elizabethan Keyboard Duets*.

CARLTON, RICHARD, *Madrigals to Five Voices (1601)*, ed. E. H. Fellowes (London: Stainer and Bell, 1923; rev. R. T. Dart, 1960). EM, xxvii. With his madrigal from *The Triumphes of Oriana*.

CARVER, ROBERT, *Collected Works*, ed. D. Stevens, 1 vol. to date (AIM, 1959). CMM, xvi.

—— see also *Music of Scotland*.

CAVENDISH, MICHAEL, *Madrigals to Five Voices (1598, 1601)* [with works by T. Greaves, W. Holborne, and R. Edwards], ed. E. H. Fellowes (London: Stainer and Bell, 1924; rev. R. T. Dart and P. Brett, 1961). In EM, xxxvi.

Choice Ayres, Songs and Dialogues. Originally Published by John Playford, London, 1673–1684 (fac.), ed. I. Spink (London: Stainer and Bell, 1989). MLE, A/5a, 5b.

CLARKE, JEREMIAH, *Miscellaneous Keyboard Pieces*, ed. J. Harley (London: Stainer and Bell, 1988). SBK, xl.

—— *Seven Suites*, ed. J. Harley (London: Stainer and Bell, 1984). SBK, xxxix.

—— LEVERIDGE, RICHARD, and PURCELL, DANIEL, *The Island Princess (British Library Add. MS 15318)*, ed. C. A. Price and R. D. Hume (Tunbridge Wells: Richard Macnutt, 1985). MLE, C/2.

Clement Matchett's Virginal Book (1612), ed. R. T. Dart (London: Stainer and Bell, 1957). SBK, ix.

Collected English Lutenist Partsongs, ed. D. Greer, 2 vols. (London: Stainer and Bell, 1987–9). MB, liii–liv.

The Complete Country Dance Tunes from Playford's Dancing Master, ed. J. Barlow (London: Faber, 1985).

Consort Songs, ed. P. Brett (London: Stainer and Bell, 1967). MB, xxii.

COPRARIO, JOHN, *Fantasia-Suites*, ed. R. Charteris (London: Stainer and Bell, 1980). MB, xlvi.

—— *The Five-Part Pieces*, ed. R. Charteris (Neuhausen: AIM, 1981). CMM, xcii.

—— *Funeral Teares (1606); Songs of Mourning (1613); The Masque of Squires (1614)*, ed. G. Hendrie and R. T. Dart (London: Stainer and Bell, 1959). ELS, I/xvii.

—— *The Six-Part Consorts and Madrigals*, ed. R. Charteris (Clarabricken: Boethius Press, 1982), score and parts.

COSYN, BENJAMIN, *Three Voluntaries*, ed. J. Steele (London: Novello, 1959). Early Organ Music, xiv.

—— see also *Twenty-five pieces for keyed instruments*.

Cranmer's First Litany, 1544, and Merbecke's Book of Common Prayer Noted, 1550 (fac.), ed. J. E. Hunt (London: Society for Promoting Christian Knowledge, 1939).

CROFT, WILLIAM, *Complete Harpsichord Works*, ed. H. Ferguson and C. Hogwood, 2 vols. (London: Stainer and Bell, 1974; 2nd rev. edn., 1982). SBK, xxx, xxxi.

—— *Complete Organ Works*, ed. R. Platt, 2 vols. (London: OUP, 1976, rev. edn. in 1 vol., 1982).

—— *Overture: Laurus Cruentas*, ed. M. Bevan (London: OUP, 1977). MC, xliv.

—— *Suite: The Comedy Call'd The Funeral*, ed. R. Platt (London: OUP, 1976). MC, xlv.

—— *Te Deum* (vocal score), ed. H. W. Shaw (London: OUP [1979]).

CUTTING, FRANCIS, *Selected Works for Lute*, ed. M. Long (London: OUP, 1968). Music for the Lute, ii.

DANYEL, JOHN, *Songs for the Lute, Viol and Voice (1606)*, ed. E. H. Fellowes (London: Stainer and Bell, 1970; rev. D. Scott, 1970). ELS, II/viii.

DERING, RICHARD, *Cantica sacra, 1618*, ed. P. Platt (London: Stainer and Bell, 1974). EECM, xv.

—— *Secular Vocal Music*, ed. P. Platt (London: Stainer and Bell, 1969). MB, xxv.

The Division Recorder, ed. P. Holman, 2 vols. (New York: Shattinger International Music Corp., 1979).

The Division-Violin (fac.), ed. M. Gilmore (London: OUP, 1982).

DOWLAND, JOHN, *Ayres for four voices*, ed. R. T. Dart and N. Fortune (London: Stainer and Bell, 1953; 2nd rev. edn., 1963). MB, vi.

—— *The Collected Lute Music*, ed. D. Poulton and B. Lam (London: Faber, 1974; 3rd edn., 1981).

—— *Complete Consort Music*, ed. E. Hunt (London: Schott, n.d.).

—— *The First Book of Ayres*, ed. E. H. Fellowes, 2 vols. (London: Stainer and Bell, 1920–1; rev. edn. in 1 vol., based on 1606 versions, by R. T. Dart, 1965). ELS, I/i–ii.

—— *Lachrimae* (fac.), ed. W. Edwards (Leeds: Boethius Press, 1974).

—— *Lachrimae oder Sieben Tränen*, ed. F. J. Giesbert (Kassel etc.: Nagel, 1953). Seven pavans only, with tablature.

—— *Lachrimae or Seven Tears... Transcribed from the original edition of 1605 by Peter Warlock* (London: OUP, 1927) (without tablature).

—— *A Pilgrimes Solace; Three Songs from A Musicall Banquet*, ed. E. H. Fellowes, 2 vols. (London: Stainer and Bell, 1922–4; rev. edn. by R. T. Dart, 1960; 1969, 2 vols. in 1). ELS, I/xii, xiv.

—— *Second Book of Songs (1600)*, ed. E. H. Fellowes, 2 vols. (London: Stainer and Bell, 1921–2; rev. edn. by R. T. Dart and D. Scott, 1969, repr. 1977). ELS, I/v–vi.

—— *The Third Booke of Songs (1603)*, ed. E. H. Fellowes, 2 vols. (London: Stainer and Bell, 1923; rev. edn. by R. T. Dart, 1961–2; further rev. by D. Scott in 1 vol., 1970, repr. 1978). ELS, I/x–xi.

DOWLAND, ROBERT, *A Musicall Banquet (1610)*, ed. P. Stroud (London: Stainer and Bell, 1968). ELS, II/xx.

—— *Varietie of Lute Lessons* [1610] (fac.), ed. E. Hunt (London: Schott, 1958).

DRAGHI, GIOVANNI BATTISTA, *Harpsichord Music*, ed. R. Klakowich (Madison, Wis.: A-R Editions, 1986). RRMBE, lvi.

The Dublin Virginal Manuscript, ed. J. Ward (Wellesley College, Mass., 1954; 2nd edn., 1964; new [3rd] edn., London etc.: Schott, 1983).

DUNSTABLE, JOHN, *Complete Works*, ed. M. F. Bukofzer (London: Stainer and Bell, 1953; 2nd rev. edn., 1970). MB, viii.

—— *Gloria & Credo (Jesu Christe Fili Dei Vivi)* [ed. L. Feininger] (Rome: Soc. Univ. S. Ceciliae, 1950). DPL, I/viii.

Dutch Keyboard Music of the Sixteenth and Seventeenth Centuries, ed. A. Curtis (Amsterdam, 1961). Monumenta Musica Neerlandica, iii.

Early Bodleian Music, 3 vols., ed. Sir J. Stainer (vols. i–ii) and E. W. B. Nicholson (vol. iii) (London: Novello, 1901–13).

Early English Keyboard Music, ed. H. Ferguson, 2 vols. (London: OUP, 1971).

Early English Organ Music: An Anthology from Tudor and Stuart times in two volumes, ed. R. Langley (Oxford: OUP, 1986).

Early Scottish Keyboard Music, ed. K. Elliot (London: Stainer and Bell, 1958). SBK, xv.

Early Tudor Magnificats, i, ed. P. Doe (London: Stainer and Bell, 1964). EECM, iv.

Early Tudor Masses, ed. J. D. Bergsagel, 2 vols. (London: Stainer and Bell, 1963–76). EECM, i, xvi.

Early Tudor Organ Music, i. *Music for the Office*, ed. J. Caldwell (London: Stainer and Bell, 1966). EECM, vi.

Early Tudor Organ Music, ii. *Music for the Mass*, ed. D. Stevens (London: Stainer and Bell, 1969). EECM, x.

Early Tudor Songs and Carols, ed. J. Stevens (London: Stainer and Bell, 1975). MB, xxxvi.

EAST, MICHAEL, *(First Set of) Madrigals to 3, 4, and 5 Parts (1604)*, ed. E. H. Fellowes (London: Stainer and Bell, 1923; rev. R. T. Dart, 1960). EM, xxix.

—— *Fourth Set of Books (1618)*, ed. E. H. Fellowes (London: Stainer and Bell, 1923, in 1 vol. with the *Third Set*; rev. R. T. Dart and P. Brett, 1962, in 1 vol.). EM, xxxib: with a song from the *Sixth Set* (1624), and complete in the rev. edn. with verse anthems, etc.

—— *Second Set of Madrigals (1606)*, ed. E. H. Fellowes (London: Stainer and Bell, 1923; rev. R. T. Dart and P. Brett, 1961). EM, xxx. With his madrigal from *The Triumphes of Oriana*.

—— *Third Set of Books (1610)*, ed. E. H. Fellowes (London: Stainer and Bell, 1923, in 1 vol. with the *Fourth Set*; rev. R. T. Dart, 1962, as a single vol.). EM, xxxia. Revised version includes the instrumental music.

ECCLES, JOHN, *Eight Songs by John Eccles*, ed. M. Pilkington (London: Stainer and Bell, 1978).

—— *The Judgment of Paris* (fac.), ed. R. Platt (Tunbridge Wells: Richard Macnutt, 1984). MLE, C/1.

EDWARDS, RICHARD [ascr.], 'In going to my naked bed', ed. E. H. Fellowes [with words by M. Cavendish, T. Greaves and W. Holborne] (London: Stainer and Bell, 1924; rev. R. T. Dart and P. Brett, 1961). In EM, xxxvi.

Elizabeth Rogers' Virginal Book 1656, ed. G. Sargent (Neuhausen: AIM, 1982). CEKM, xix.

Elizabethan Consort Music, ed. P. Doe, 2 vols. (London: Stainer and Bell, 1979–88). MB, xliv–xlv.

Elizabethan Keyboard Music, ed. A. Brown (London: Stainer and Bell, 1989). MB, lv.

Elizabethan Popular Music for the Lute, ed. B. Jeffery (London: OUP, 1968). Music for the Lute, i.

Englische Fantasien aus dem 17. Jahrhundert, ed. E. H. Mayer (Kassel, 1949).

English Court & Country Dances of the Early Baroque from MS Drexel 5612, ed. H. Gervers (Neuhausen: AIM, 1982). CEKM, xliv.

English Fourteenth-Century Polyphony: Facsimile Edition of Sources Notated in Score, ed. W. J. Summers (Tutzing: Schneider, 1983).

English Lute Songs, 1597–1632: A Collection of Facsimile Reprints, ed. F. W. Sternfeld (Menston: Scolar Press, 1967–9).

English Music for Mass and Offices, ed. F. Ll. Harrison, E. H. Sanders, and P. M. Lefferts, 2 vols. (Monaco: Éditions de l'Oiseau-Lyre, 1983). PMFC, xvi–xvii.

English Music of the Thirteenth and Early Fourteenth Centuries, ed. E. H. Sanders (Monaco: Éditions de l'Oiseau-Lyre, 1979). PMFC, xiv.

English Songs 1625–1660, ed. I. Spink (London: Stainer and Bell, 1971). MB, xxxiii.

The Eton Choirbook, ed. F. Ll. Harrison, 3 vols. (London: Stainer and Bell, 1956–61). MB, x–xii. 2nd edn. of vol. i, 1967.

FARMER, JOHN, *The First Set of English Madrigals . . . 1599* (fac.), (Amsterdam: Theatrum Orbis Terrarum, and New York: Da Capo Press, 1973). The English Experience, no. 512.

—— *Madrigals to four voices (1599)*, ed. E. H. Fellowes (London: Stainer and Bell, 1914; rev. D. Moroney, 1978). EM, viii. With his madrigal from *The Triumphes of Oriana*.

FARNABY, GILES, *Canzonets to Four Voices (1598)*, ed. E. H. Fellowes (London: Stainer and Bell, 1922; rev. R. T. Dart, 1963). EM, xx.

—— and RICHARD: *Keyboard Music*, ed. R. Marlow (London: Stainer and Bell, 1965). MB, xxiv.

FARRANT, RICHARD: for 'Call to remembrance', 'Hide not thou thy face' and 'Lord for thy tender mercy's sake', see *The Oxford Book of Tudor Anthems*, 50–6, 94–8, 152–6 (all ed. A. Greening); the first and the third also in *The Treasury of English Church Music*, ii. 46–9, ed. P. Le Huray ['Lord for thy tender mercy's sake' is also ascr. to J. Hilton the elder].

FAYRFAX, ROBERT, *Collected Works*, ed. E. B. Warren, 3 vols. (AIM, 1959–66). CMM, xvii.

—— *Sacred Music from the Lambeth Choirbook*, ed. M. Lyon (Madison, Wis.: A-R Editions, 1985). RRMR, lxix.

FERRABOSCO, ALFONSO (I), *Collected Works for Lute and Bandora*, ed. N. North, 2 vols. (Oxford: OUP, 1979). Music for the Lute, viii/ 1–2.

FERRABOSCO, ALFONSO (II), *Manuscript Songs*, ed. I. Spink (London: Stainer and Bell, 1966). ELS, II/ xix.

A Fifteenth-Century Song Book (fac. of Cambridge, Univ. Lib., Add. MS 5943), ed. R. Rastall (Leeds: Boethius Press, 1973).

Fifteenth-Century Liturgical Music, i, ed. A. Hughes (London: Stainer and Bell, 1968); ii. *Four Anonymous Masses*, ed. M. Bent (ibid., 1979); iii. *The Brussels Masses*, ed. G. Curtis (ibid., 1989). EECM, vii, xxii, xxxiv.

FINGER, GODFREY, *Suite in E minor and Suite in D minor*, ed. A. Marshall (Ottawa: Dovehouse Editions, 1981). Viola da gamba Series, xxiv.

The Fitzwilliam Virginal Book, ed. J. A. Fuller-Maitland and W. B. Squire, 2 vols. (Leipzig: Breitkopf and Härtel, 1899).

FORD, THOMAS, *Ten Airs from* Musicke of Sundrie Kindes *(1607)*, ed. E. H. Fellowes (London: Stainer and Bell, 1921, rev. R. T. Dart, 1966). ESLS (ELS), I/iii.

The Fountains Fragments, ed. E. Kershaw (Newton Abbot: Antico Edition, 1989).

The Fountains Fragments (fac. of London, Brit. Lib., Add. 62132A and Add. 40011B), with intro. by M. Bent (Clarabricken: Boethius Press, 1987).

Four French Songs from an English Song-book; Six 15th-Century English Songs; Four Songs in Latin from an English Song-book; Four 15th-Century Religious Songs in English, ed. R. Rastall and A.-M. Seaman, 4 vols. (Newton Abbot: Antico Edition, 1976–9).

Four Hundred Songs and Dances from the Stuart Masque, ed. A. Sabol (Providence, RI: Brown University Press, 1978).

Four Italian Songs . . . by Galfridus and Robertus de Anglia, ed. D. Fallows (Newton Abbot: Antico Edition, 1977).

FRYE, WALTER, *Collected Works*, ed. S. W. Kenny (AIM, 1960). CMM, xix.

GIBBONS, CHRISTOPHER, *Keyboard Compositions*, ed. C. G. Rayner (2nd edn., Neuhausen: AIM, 1989). CEKM, xviii.

GIBBONS, ORLANDO, *Consort Music*, ed. J. Harper (London: Stainer and Bell, 1982). MB, xlviii.

——'Do not repine, fair sun', ed. P. Brett (London: Stainer and Bell, 1961).

—— [English Church Music] (London: OUP, 1925). TCM, iv.

—— *First Set of Madrigals and Motets (1612)*, ed. E. H. Fellowes (London: Stainer and Bell, 1914; rev. R. T. Dart, 1964). EM, v.

—— *Full Anthems, Hymns and Fragmentary Verse Anthems*, ed. D. Wulstan (London: Stainer and Bell, 1978). EECM, xxi.

—— *Keyboard Music*, ed. G. Hendrie (London: Stainer and Bell, 1962; 2nd rev. edn., 1967). MB, xx.

—— *Six Fantasias for Viols in six parts*, ed. M. Hobbs (London: Faber Music, 1982).

—— *Verse Anthems*, ed. D. Wulstan (London: Stainer and Bell, 1964). EECM, iii.

GILES, NATHANIEL, *Anthems*, ed. J. B. Clark (London: Stainer and Bell, 1979). EECM, xxiii.

GREAVES, THOMAS, *Madrigals and Songs in Five Parts (1604)* (with works by M. Cavendish, W. Holborne, and R. Edwards), ed. E. H. Fellowes (London: Stainer and Bell, 1924; rev. R. T. Dart and P. Brett, 1961). EM, xxxvi.

HANDFORD, GEORGE, *Ayres*, ed. A. Rooley with F. Steele, 2 vols. (London: Stainer and Bell, 1988).

The Harpsichord Master: Containing instructions for learners by Henry Purcell, with a collection of pieces by Purcell, Jeremiah Clarke, and others, ed. R. Petre (Wellington: Price Milburn; London: Faber; and New York: Schirmer, 1980). With a facsimile of the original edn. of 1697 (*The Harpsicord Master*) in a separate vol.

The Harpsicord Master, Book 1, ed. C. Hogwood (London: OUP, 1980).

The Harpsicord Master II and III (fac.) (Clarabricken: Boethius Press, 1980).

HOLBORNE, ANTHONY, *Complete Works*, ed. M. Kanazawa (Cambridge, Mass.: Harvard University Press, 1967–). Harvard Publications in Music, i, v.

—— *Pavans, Galliards, Almains, 1599* [ed. B. Thomas] (London: London Pro Musica Edition, 1980), score and 5 parts.

HOLBORNE, WILLIAM, *Airs to Three Voices (1597)* (with works by M. Cavendish, T. Greaves and R. Edwards), ed. E. H. Fellowes (London: Stainer and Bell, 1924; rev. R. T. Dart and P. Brett, 1961). In EM, xxxvi.

HOTHBY, JOHN, *The Musical Works of John Hothby*, ed. A. Seay (AIM, 1964). CMM, xxxiii.

HUMFREY, PELHAM, *Complete Church Music*, ed. P. Dennison, 2 vols. (London: Stainer and Bell, 1972). MB, xxxiv–xxxv.

Invitation to Medieval Music, ed. R. T. Dart (vols. i–ii) and B. Trowell (vols. iii–iv), 4 vols. (London: Stainer and Bell, 1967–78).

Jacobean Consort Music, ed. R. T. Dart and W. Coates (London: Stainer and Bell, 1955; 2nd rev. edn., 1962). MB, ix.

JENKINS, JOHN, *Consort Music in Five Parts*, ed. R. Nicholson (London: Faber, 1971), score, 5 parts, and organ.

—— *Consort Music of Four Parts*, ed. A. Ashbee (London: Stainer and Bell, 1969). MB, xxvi.

—— *Consort Music of Six Parts*, ed. D. Peart (London: Stainer and Bell, 1977). MB, xxxix.

—— *Consort Music for Viols in Four Parts*, ed. A. Ashbee (London: Faber, 1978), score and parts.

—— *Consort Music for Viols in Six Parts*, ed. R. Nicholson and A. Ashbee (London: Faber, 1976), score, 6 parts, organ.

—— *Fancies and Ayres*, ed. H. J. Sleeper (Wellesley College, Mass., 1950). The Wellesley Edition, no. 1.

—— *Fancy and Ayre Divisions*, ed. R. A. Warner (Wellesley College, Mass., 1966). The Wellesley Edition, no. 10.

—— *Fantasia-Suite 5*, ed. C. Field (London: OUP, 1976). MC, xxxvii.

—— *Three Suites for two viols and continuo*, ed. M. Bishop (Miami, Fla.: Ogni Sorte Editions, 1983). Viola da Gamba Series, ii.

John Blow's Anthology: Froberger, Strungk, Fischer, Blow, ed. R. T. Dart, rev. D. Moroney (London: Stainer and Bell, 1978). SBK, xxxvii.

JOHNSON, ROBERT (II), *Ayres, Songs and Dialogues*, ed. I. Spink (London: Stainer and Bell, 1961; 2nd edn., 1974). ELS, II/ xvii.

—— *Complete Works for Solo Lute*, ed. A. Sundermann (London: OUP, 1972). Music for the Lute, iv.

JONES, ROBERT, *First Booke of Songes and Ayres (1600)*; *Second Booke of Ayres (1601)*; *Ultimum Vale: Third Booke of Ayres (1608)*, ed. E. H. Fellowes (London: Stainer and Bell, 1926). ESLS, II/ iv–vi.

—— *The First Book of Songes and Ayres 1600*; *The Second Booke of Songs and Ayres 1601*; *Ultimum Vale 1605*; *A Musicall Dreame 1609*; *The Muses Gardin 1610* (fac.), ed. D. Greer (Menston: Scolar Press, 1970). ELS (fac.), vii (nos. 26–30).

—— *First Set of Madrigals (1607)*, ed. E. H. Fellowes (London: Stainer and Bell, 1924 (in 1 vol. with Mundy, *Songs and Psalms*); rev. R. T. Dart, 1961). EM, xxxva.

Keyboard Music of the Fourteenth and Fifteenth Centuries, ed. W. Apel (AIM, 1963). CEKM, i.

KIRBYE, GEORGE, *First Set of Madrigals (1597)*, ed. E. H. Fellowes (London: Stainer and Bell, 1922; rev. R. T. Dart and P. Brett, 1961). EM, xxiv. With his madrigal from *The Triumphes of Oriana*.

—— *Madrigals from Manuscript Sources*, ed. I. Payne (London: Stainer and Bell, 1988). EM, xxxix.

LAWES, HENRY, *A Dialogue on a Kiss* ['Among thy fancies tell me this'], ed. R. McGrady (London: OUP, 1978). MC, lx.

—— *Hymns to the Holy Trinity*, ed. G. Beechey (London: OUP, 1973). MC, viii.

LAWES, WILLIAM, *Consort Sets in Five and Six Parts*, ed. D. Pinto (London: Faber, 1979), score and parts.

—— *Select Consort Music*, ed. M. Lefkowitz (London: Stainer and Bell, 1963). MB, xxi.

—— *Trois Masques à la Cour de Charles Ier d'Angleterre*, ed. M. Lefkowitz (Paris: CNRS, 1970).

LEIGHTON, Sir WILLIAM, *The Tears or Lamentations of a Sorrowful Soul*, ed. C. Hall (London: Stainer and Bell, 1970). EECM, xi.

LE ROY, ADRIAN, *Fantaisies et danses, extraites de* A briefe and easye Instruction *(1568)*, ed. P. Jansen (with *Études des Concordances* by D. Heartz) (Paris: CNRS, 1962).

—— *Psaumes: Tiers Livre de Tablature de Luth, 1552; Instruction, 1574*, ed. R. de Morcourt (Paris: CNRS, 1962).

LICHFILD, HENRY, *Madrigals of 5 parts . . . (1613)* (fac.) (Amsterdam: Theatrum Orbis Terrarum, and New York: Da Capo Press, 1972). The English Experience, no. 472a–e.

—— *Madrigals of Five Parts (1613)*, ed. E. H. Fellowes (London: Stainer and Bell, 1922; rev. R. T. Dart and D. Scott, 1970). EM, xvii.

LOCKE, MATTHEW, *Anthems and Motets*, ed. P. Le Huray (London: Stainer and Bell, 1976). MB, xxxviii.

—— *Chamber Music*, ed. M. Tilmouth, 2 vols. (London: Stainer and Bell, 1971–2). MB, xxxi–xxxii.

—— *Dramatic Music*, ed. M. Tilmouth (London: Stainer and Bell, 1986). MB, li.

—— *Incidental Music*: The Tempest, ed. P. Dennison (London: OUP, 1977). MC, xli.

—— *Keyboard Suites*, ed. R. T. Dart (London: Stainer and Bell, 1959). SBK, vi.

—— *Melothesia*, ed. C. Hogwood (Oxford: OUP, 1987).

—— *Organ Voluntaries*, ed. R. T. Dart (London: Stainer and Bell, 1957). SBK, vii.

—— *The Rare Theatrical: New York Public Library, Drexel MS 3976* (fac.), ed. P. Holman (London: Stainer and Bell, 1989). MLE, A/4.

—— and GIBBONS, CHRISTOPHER, *Cupid and Death*, ed. E. J. Dent (London: Stainer and Bell, 1951). MB, ii.

London, British Library MS Egerton 3665 ('The Tregian Manuscript'), ed. F. A. D'Accone, 2 vols. (New York and London: Garland, 1988). Renaissance Music in Facsimile, vii.

LUDFORD, NICHOLAS, *Collected Works*, ed. J. D. Bergsagel, 2 vols. (AIM, 1963–77). CMM, xxvii.

LUGGE, JOHN, *Three Voluntaries*, ed. S. Jeans and J. Steele (London: Novello, 1956).

—— *Two Toys and a Jigg*, ed. S. Jeans and J. Steele (London: Schott, 1958).

LUPO, THOMAS, *The Complete Vocal Music*, ed. R. Charteris (Clarabricken: Boethius Press, 1982).

—— *The Four-Part Consort Music*, ed. R. Charteris and J. M. Jennings (Clarabricken: Boethius Press, 1983).

—— *The Two- and Three-Part Consort Music*, ed. R. Charteris (Clarabricken: Boethius Press, 1987).

Lute Music of Shakespeare's Time: see BARLEY, WILLIAM.

Manuscripts of Fourteenth-Century English Polyphony: Facsimiles, ed. F. Ll. Harrison and R. Wibberley (London: Stainer and Bell, 1981). EECM, xxvi.

MARBECK (or MERBECKE), JOHN, see ASTON, HUGH; *Cranmer's First Litany*.

The Maske of Flowers 1614 (fac.) (Leeds: Boethius Press, n.d.).

MAYNARD, JOHN, *The XII Wonders of the World*, ed. A. Rooley (London: Stainer and Bell, 1985).

Medieval Carols, ed. J. Stevens (London: Stainer and Bell, 1952; 2nd edn., 1958). MB, iv.

Medieval English Songs, ed. E. J. Dobson and F. Ll. Harrison (London and Boston: Faber, 1979).

Melothesia (fac.), [ed.] M. Locke (New York: Broude Bros., 1975). MMMLF, II/xxx.

MORGAN, THOMAS, *Suite: Love and Honour*, ed. R. Platt (London: OUP, 1974). MC, xix.

MORLEY, THOMAS, *Canzonets to five and six voices (1597)*, ed. E. H. Fellowes (London: Stainer and Bell, 1913; rev. S. Dunkley, 1977). EM, iii.

—— *Canzonets for Two and Three Voices*, ed. E. H. Fellowes (London: Stainer and Bell, 1913; rev. R. T. Dart, 1956). EM, i. With a 3-pt. canzonet from *A Plaine and Easie Introduction* (1597).

—— *Collected Motets*, ed. H. K. Andrews and R. T. Dart (London: Stainer and Bell, 1959).

—— *The First Booke of Ayres (1600)*, ed. E. H. Fellowes (London: Stainer and Bell, 1932; rev. edn. by R. T. Dart, 1958; repr. with addns., 1965, repr. 1969). ELS, I/xvi.

—— *First Book of Balletts (1595: 2/1600)*, ed. E. H. Fellowes (London: Stainer and Bell, 1913; rev. R. T. Dart, 1965). EM, iv.

—— *The first book of consort lessons 1599 and 1611*, ed. S. Beck (New York, 1959). For notice of two missing lute parts see *LSJ*, 4 (1962), 31.

—— *First Book of Madrigals (1594)*, ed. E. H. Fellowes (London: Stainer and Bell, 1913, rev. R. T. Dart, 1963). EM, ii. With 2 canzonets (English texts) from *A Plaine and Easie Introduction*, also in his Italian collection of 1597.

—— *Keyboard Works*, ed. R. T. Dart, 2 vols. (London: Stainer and Bell, 1959; 2nd edn., 1964). SBK, xii–xiii.

—— (ed.), *The Triumphs of Oriana (1601)*, ed. E. H. Fellowes (London: Stainer and Bell, 1923; rev. R. T. Dart, 1962). EM, xxxii.

—— *Two Part Canzonets for voices and Instruments*, ed. D. H. Boalch (Oxford: George Ronald, 1950).

—— see also ALISON [etc.], *Twenty Songs*.

MORTON, ROBERT, *Collected Works*, ed. A. Atlas (New York: Broude Bros., 1981). Masters and Monuments of the Renaissance, ii.

Motets of English Provenance, ed. F. Ll. Harrison (Monaco: L'Oiseau-Lyre, 1980). PMFC, xv.

The Mulliner Book, ed. D. Stevens (London: Stainer and Bell, 1951; 2nd edn., 1954). MB, i.

MUNDY, JOHN, Songs and Psalms Composed into 3, 4 and 5 Parts (1594), ed. E. H. Fellowes (London: Stainer and Bell, 1924, in 1 vol. with Jones's *First Set of Madrigals*, rev. as a separate vol. by R. T. Dart and P. Brett, 1961). EM, xxxvb.

MUNDY, WILLIAM, *Latin Antiphons and Psalms*, ed. F. Ll. Harrison (London: Stainer and Bell, 1963). EECM, ii.

—— see also *Anthems for Men's Voices*, i. 10–21 ('He that hath my commandments', 'Let us now laud'); *The Oxford Book of Tudor Anthems*, 240–7 ('O Lord the maker of all thing'); *The Treasury of English Church Music*, ii, 22–32 ('O Lord the maker of all thing', 'Ah helpless wretch').

Music at the Court of Henry VIII, ed. J. Stevens (London: Stainer and Bell, 1962). MB, xviii.

Music for Mixed Consort, ed. and reconstructed by W. Edwards (London: Stainer and Bell, 1977). MB, xl.

The Music of the Pepys MS 1236, ed. S. R. Charles (Rome: AIM, 1967). CMM, xl.

Music of Scotland 1500–1700, ed. K. Elliott (London: Stainer and Bell, 1957; 2nd edn., 1964). MB, xv.

Musica Antiqua, ed. J. S. Smith, 2 vols. (London, 1812).

Musick's Hand-Maid, ed. R. T. Dart (London: Stainer and Bell, 1969). SBK, xxviii. See also *The Second Part of Musick's Hand-Maid*.

Musik und Musiker am Gottorfer Hofe, i. *Die Zeit der englischen Komödianten (1590–1627)*, ed. B. Engelke (Breslau, 1930). Includes reprint of W. Brade, *Newe auserlesene Paduanen, Galliarden . . .* (Hamburg, 1610).

La Musique de scène de la troupe de Shakespeare, ed. J. P. Cutts (Paris: CNRS, 1959).

My Ladye Nevells Booke [music by William Byrd], ed. H. Andrews (London: J. Curwen and Sons, 1926; repr. New York: Broude Bros., n.d.; repr. ibid., Dover Publications, 1969, with new intro. by B. Winogron).

Narcissus Marsh's Lyra Viol Book (fac.) (Clarabricken: Boethius Press, 1978).

NICOLSON, RICHARD, *Collected Madrigals*, ed. J. Morehen (London: Stainer and Bell, 1976). EM, xxxvii.

Nine Dances from the Court of Elizabeth, ed. P. Holman (Corby: Earlham Press, 1983).

The Old Hall Manuscript, ed. A. Hughes and M. Bent, 4 vols. (i/1, 2, ii, iii) (AIM, 1969–73). CMM, xlvi. This replaces the older edn. by A. Ramsbotham, H. B. Collins, and Dom A. Hughes (Burnham and London: PMMS, 1933–8), save for some useful plates and an interesting intro. to vol. iii by Collins.

An Old St. Andrews Music Book (Cod. Helmst. 628) (fac. of Wolfenbüttel, Herzog August-Bibl., Helmst. 628), ed. J. H. Baxter (London and Paris: Humphrey Milford for St Andrews University, 1931).

Organ Music in Restoration England: Eight Anonymous Pieces, ed. R. Langley (London: OUP, 1981).

The Oxford Anthology of Music: Medieval Music, ed. W. T. Marrocco and N. Sandon (London and New York: OUP, 1977).

Oxford, Bodleian Library, MSS Music School e. 376–381 (fac.), ed. J. Milsom (New York and London: Garland, 1988). Renaissance Music in Facsimile, xv.

The Oxford Book of Tudor Anthems, comp. C. Morris; Preface by D. Willcocks (London: OUP, 1978).

Oxford Latin Liturgical D20, London, Add. MS. 25031, Chicago, MS. 654 App (fac.), ed. L. A. Dittmer (New York: Institute of Medieval Music, 1960). Publications of Medieval Musical Manuscripts, vi.

PAISIBLE, JAMES, *Sonata in D, for trumpet/ oboe, two violins, and basso continuo*, ed. P. Holman (London: OUP, 1981). MC, xlii.

—— *Sonata 10 in D major, for two trumpets (or oboes), strings, and continuo*, ed. R. Platt (London: OUP, 1978). MC, xliii.

PARSLEY, OSBERT, see ASTON, HUGH.

PARSONS, ROBERT, for the Nunc Dimittis from his First Service, see *The Treasury of English Church Music*, ii. 33–44; for his consort music, see *Elizabethan Consort Music*, i.

Parthenia (music by Byrd, Bull, and Gibbons):
   (*a*) ed. E. F. Rimbault (London: Chappell, 1847);
   (*b*) ed. M. Glyn (London: Reeves, 1927);
   (*c*) ed. O. E. Deutsch (London: Chiswick Press, 1942 (fac.)). Harrow Replicas, no. 3;
   (*d*) ed. K. Stone (New York: Broude Bros., 1951);
   (*e*) ed. R. T. Dart (London: Stainer and Bell, 1960; 2nd edn., 1962). SBK, xix.

Parthenia In-Violata, ed. R. T. Dart (New York: C. F. Peters Corporation, 1961). Also fac. edn. edited with historical intro. by R. T. Dart and bibliographical note by R. J. Wolfe (New York Public Library, 1961).

PHILIPS, PETER, 'Christus resurgens a mortuis' (from *Cantiones Sacrae... quinis vocibus*, 1612), ed. J. Cannell (n.p., 1979). Mapa Mundi, ser. C, no. 9.

—— 'In splendenti nube' (from *Cantiones Sacrae... quinis vocibus*, 1612), ed. J. Cannell (n.p., 1979). Mapa Mundi, ser. C, no. 8.

—— *Select Italian Madrigals*, ed. J. Steele (London: Stainer and Bell, 1970). MB, xxix.

—— 'Tu es petrus' (from *Cantiones Sacrae, octonis vocibus*, 1613), ed. P. Phillips (n.p., 1978). Mapa Mundi, ser. C, no. 3.

—— and CORNET, PIETER, *Works by Peter Philips and Pieter Cornet*, ed. R. Vendome (Oxford: John Brennan, 1983). Spanish Netherlands Keyboard Music, i. Christ Church Music MS 89.

PILKINGTON, FRANCIS, *Complete Works for Solo Lute*, ed. B. Jeffery (London: OUP, 1970). Music for the Lute, iii.

—— *First Set of Madrigals and Pastorals of 3, 4 and 5 Parts (1613)*, ed. E. H. Fellowes (London: Stainer and Bell, 1923; rev. R. T. Dart, 1959). EM, xxv.

—— *Second Set of Madrigals and Pastorals of 3, 4, 5 and 6 Parts (1624)*, ed. E. H. Fellowes (London: Stainer and Bell, 1923; rev. R. T. Dart, 1958). EM, xxvi. Rev. edn. is complete except for no. 27, 'A Pavin for the Orpharion'.

PLAYFORD, JOHN, *The Division Violin . . . Facsimile edition with introductory notes and a realisation of the ground basses by Margaret Gilmore* (Oxford, 1982). Title page and contents from 1st edn., 1684; actual music taken from 6th edn. (1705), though only to the extent of reproducing the 1684 contents.

PLUMMER, JOHN, *Four Motets*, ed. B. Trowell ([Banbury]: Piers Press for PMMS, 1968).

POWER, LIONEL, *Complete Works*, ed. C. Hamm (AIM, 1969). CMM, 1 (1 vol. only to date).

—— *Mass: Alma Redemptoris Mater*, ed. G. Curtis (Newton Abbot: Antico Edition, 1982).

Priscilla Bunbury's Virginal Book, Sixteen Pieces, ed. J. L. Boston (London: Stainer and Bell, 1962).

Processionale ad Usum Sarum (Pynson, 1502; fac. ed. G. R. Rastall) (Clarabricken: Boethius Press, 1980).

PURCELL, DANIEL, *Six Sonatas (1698)* (3 for recorder and BC, 3 for violin and BC), ed. P. Everett, 2 vols. (London: European Music Archive, 1980).

PURCELL, HENRY, *Dido and Aeneas*, ed. E. T. Harris (Oxford and New York: OUP, 1987).

—— *Dido and Aeneas: An Opera*, ed. C. Price (New York and London: Norton, 1986).

—— *Eight Suites*, ed. H. Ferguson (London, Stainer and Bell, 1964). SBK, xxi.

—— *Miscellaneous Keyboard Pieces*, ed. H. Ferguson (London: Stainer and Bell, 1964). SBK, xxii.

—— *The Organ Works*, ed. H. McLean (London: Novello, 1957; 2nd rev. edn., 1967).

—— *The Works of Henry Purcell* (London: Novello, Ewer and Co., 1878–1965). Reissued in revised or replaced editions (London and Sevenoaks: Novello, 1961–).

RAMSEY, ROBERT, *English Sacred Music*, ed. E. Thompson (London: Stainer and Bell, 1967). EECM, vii.

—— *Latin Sacred Music*, ed. E. Thompson (London: Stainer and Bell, 1986). EECM, xxxi.

RAVENSCROFT, THOMAS, *Deuteromelia . . . 1609, Melismata . . . 1611* and *Pammelia . . . 1609* (fac.) (Amsterdam: Theatrum Orbis Terrarum, and New York: Da Capo Press, 1971). The English Experience, nos. 410–12.

ROBINSON, THOMAS, *The Schoole of Musicke (1603)*, ed. D. Lumsden (Paris: CNRS, 1971).

—— see also ALISON [etc.], *Twenty Songs*.

ROGERS, BENJAMIN, *Complete Keyboard Works*, ed. R. Rastall (London: Stainer and Bell [1973]). SBK, xxix.

—— *Voluntary for the Organ*, ed. S. Jeans (London: Novello, 1962). Early Organ Music, xi.

The Scottish Metrical Psalter of A.D. 1635, ed. N. Livingstone (Glasgow, 1864).

Sechs [later *Sieben*] *Trienter Codices*, ed. G. Adler and others, 8 vols. (Vienna and Graz: Artaria, 1900–70). DTO, xiv–xv (= vii/1–2), xxii (= xi/1), xxxviii (= xix/1), liii (= xxvii/1), lxi (= xxxi), lxxvi (= xl), cxx.

The Second Part of Musick's Hand-Maid, ed. R. T. Dart (London: Stainer and Bell, 1958; 2nd rev. edn., 1962). SBK, x.

Seven Dances from the Court of Henry VIII, ed. P. Holman (Corby: Earlham Press, 1983).

SHEPPARD, JOHN, *Collected Works*, i. *Office Responds and Varia*, ed. D. Wulstan (Oxford: Oxenford Imprint, 1978); ii. *Hymns*, ed. R. Bray (ibid., 1981).

—— *Masses*, ed. N. Sandon (London: Stainer and Bell, 1976). EECM, xviii.

—— *Responsorial Music*, ed. D. Chadd (London: Stainer and Bell, 1977). EECM, xvii.

—— see also *An Anthology of English Church Music*, 56–88, 149–53 ('Christ our Paschal Lamb', Second Service, The Lord's Prayer); *Anthems for Men's Voices*, i. 5–7 ('Submit yourselves one to another'), ii. 5–11 ('Christ rising again').

Songs and Dances for the Stuart Masque, ed. A. J. Sabol (Providence, RI: Brown University Press, 1959); rev. and enlarged as *Four Hundred Songs . . .* (ibid., 1978).

Songs from Manuscript Sources (for voice and lute), ed. D. Greer, 2 vols. (London: Stainer and Bell, 1979).

STANDLEY, *Missa ad fugam reservatam* (ed. L. Feininger) (Rome: Soc. Univ. S. Ceciliae, 1949). DPL, I/vi.

—— *Quae est ista (Fuga reservata)* (ed. L. Feininger) (Rome: Soc. Univ. S. Ceciliae, 1950). DPL, IV/i.

TALLIS, THOMAS, *Complete Keyboard Works*, ed. D. Stevens (London: Hinrichsen, 1953).

—— *English Sacred Music*, ed. L. Ellinwood, 2 vols. (London: Stainer and Bell, 1971; 2nd edn., rev. P. Doe, 1974). EECM, xii–xiii.

—— *The Lamentations of Jeremiah*, ed. P. Brett (London: Stainer and Bell, 1969).

—— [Latin Church Music] (London: OUP, 1928). TCM, vi.

—— *Mass 'Puer natus est nobis'*, ed. S. Dunkley and D. Wulstan (Oxford: Oxenford Imprint, 1977; 2nd edn., 1980).

—— *Spem in alium numquam habui*, ed. P. Brett (London, 1966).

—— and BYRD, WILLIAM, *Cantiones Sacrae* (fac.) (Leeds: Boethius Press, 1976).

TAVERNER, JOHN, *Five-part Masses*, ed. H. Benham (London: Stainer and Bell, 1990). EECM, xxxvi.

—— *Four- and Five-part Masses*, ed. H. Benham (London: Stainer and Bell, 1989). EECM, xxxv.

—— *Part I: Masses* (London: OUP, 1923). TCM, i.

—— *Part II* [Miscellaneous Church Music] (London: OUP, 1924). TCM, iii.

—— *Ritual Music and Secular Songs*, ed. H. Benham (London: Stainer and Bell, 1984). EECM, xxx.

—— *Six-part Masses*, ed. H. Benham (London: Stainer and Bell, 1978). EECM, xx.

—— *Votive Antiphons*, ed. H. Benham (London: Stainer and Bell, 1981). EECM, xxv.

—— *The Western Wind: Mass for Unaccompanied Choir*, ed. P. Brett (London: Stainer and Bell, 1962).

Ten Pieces by Hugh Aston and Others [London, British Library, Roy. App. 58], ed. F. Dawes (London: Schott, 1951).

The Theater of Music (fac.), ed. R. Spencer (Tunbridge Wells: Richard Macnutt, 1983). MLE, A/1.

Three Anonymous Keyboard Pieces attributed to William Byrd, ed. O. Neighbour (Sevenoaks: Novello, 1973).

Three Caput Masses, ed. A. Planchart (New Haven, Conn.: Yale University Press, 1964). Collegium musicum, v.

Tisdale's Virginal Book, ed. A. Brown (London: Stainer and Bell, 1966). SBK, xxiv.

TISDALL, WILLIAM, *Complete Keyboard Works*, ed. H. Ferguson (London: Stainer and Bell, 1958; 2nd edn., 1970). SBK, xiv.

TOMKINS, THOMAS, *Keyboard Music*, ed. S. D. Tuttle (London: Stainer and Bell, 1955; 2nd edn., 1964). MB, v.

—— *Musica Deo Sacra*, ed. B. Rose, 4 vols. (London, 1965–82). EECM, v, ix, xiv, xxvii.

—— *Part I: Services* (London: OUP, 1928). TCM, viii.

—— *Songs of 3, 4, 5 and 6 Parts (1622)*, ed. E. H. Fellowes (London: Stainer and Bell, 1922; rev. R. T. Dart, 1960). EM, xviii. With his madrigal from *The Triumphes of Oriana*.

The Treasury of English Church Music, ed. G. H. Knight and W. L. Reed, 5 vols. (London: Blandford Press, 1965), i. *1100–1545*, ed. D. Stevens; ii. *1545–1650*, ed. P. Le Huray; iii. *1650–1760*, ed. C. Dearnley.

Trois masques à la cour de Charles Ier d'Angleterre, ed. M. Lefkowitz (Paris: CNRS, 1970).

Le Tropaire-prosaire de Dublin: Manuscrit Add 710 de l'Université de Cambridge (fac.), ed. R.-J. Hesbert (Rouen: Imprimerie rouennaise, 1966). Monumenta Musicae Sacrae, iv.

The Tudor Church Music of the Lumley Books, ed. J. Blezzard (Madison, Wis.: A-R Editions, 1985). RRMR, lxv.

The Turpyn Book of Lute Songs (fac.) ed. R. Rastall (Leeds: Boethius Press, 1973); also ed. P. Oboussier (London: Early Music Centre, 1981). Lute Series, iii.

Twenty-five pieces for keyed instruments from Cosyn's Virginal Book, ed. J. A. Fuller-Maitland and W. B. Squire (London: Chester, 1923). Music by Bull, Byrd, Cosyn, O. Gibbons, anon.

Two Coventry Carols, ed. R. Rastall (Newton Abbot: Antico Edition, 1973).

Two Elizabethan Keyboard Duets, ed. F. Dawes (London: Schott, 1949). The composers are T. Tomkins and N. Carleton (the younger).

TYE, CHRISTOPHER, *English Sacred Music*, ed. J. Morchen (London: Stainer and Bell, 1977). EECM, xix.

—— *The Instrumental Music*, ed. R. Weidner (New Haven, Conn.: A-R Editions, 1967). RRMR, iii.

—— *The Latin Church Music*, ed. J. Satterfield, 2 vols. (Madison, Wis.: A-R Editions, 1972). RRMR, xii–xiv.

—— *Masses*, ed. P. Doe (London: Stainer and Bell, 1980). EECM, xxiv.

—— *Ritual Music and Motets*, ed. N. Davison (London: Stainer and Bell, 1987).

The Use of Salisbury, ed. N. Sandon (Newton Abbot: Antico Edition, 1984–).

VAUTOR, THOMAS, *Songs of Divers Airs and Natures (1619)*, ed. E. H. Fellowes (London: Stainer and Bell, 1924; rev. R. T. Dart, 1958). EM, xxxiv.

WARD, JOHN, *First Set of Madrigals (1613)*, ed. E. H. Fellowes (London: Stainer and Bell, 1922; rev. R. T. Dart, 1968). EM, xix.

—— *Madrigals and Elegies from Manuscript Sources*, ed. I. Payne (London: Stainer and Bell, 1988). EM, xxxviii.

WEELKES, THOMAS, *Airs or Fantastic Spirits (1608)*, ed. E. H. Fellowes (London: Stainer and Bell, 1916; rev. R. T. Dart, 1965). EM, xiii. With his madrigal from *The Triumphes of Oriana*.

—— *Balletts and Madrigals to five voices (1598, 1608)*, ed. E. H. Fellowes (London: Stainer and Bell, 1916; rev. R. T. Dart, 1968). EM, x.

—— *Collected Anthems*, ed. D. Brown, W. Collins, and P. Le Huray (London: Stainer and Bell, 1966). MB, xxiii.

—— *Evening Service for Trebles*, ed. P. Le Huray (London: Stainer and Bell, 1962).

—— *Keyboard Music in facsimile . . . with introduction and transcriptions by Desmond Hunter* (Clifden: Boethius Press, 1985).

—— *Madrigals of Five and Six Parts (1600)*, ed. E. H. Fellowes, 2 vols. (London: Stainer and Bell, 1916; rev. R. T. Dart, 1 vol., 1968). EM, xi–xii.

—— *Madrigals to 3, 4, 5, and 6 Voices (1597)*, ed. E. H. Fellowes (London: Stainer and Bell, 1916; rev. R. T. Dart, 1967). EM, ix.

—— *Magnificat and Nunc Dimittis (the Ninth Service)*, reconstructed and ed. D. Wulstan (Oxford: Oxenford Imprint, 1979).

WHITE, ROBERT, *Five-Part Latin Psalms*, ed. D. Mateer (London: Stainer and Bell, 1983). EECM, xxviii.

—— *Ritual Music and Lamentations*, ed. D. Mateer (London: Stainer and Bell, 1986). EECM, xxxii.

—— [Sacred Music] (London: OUP, 1926). TCM, v.

—— *Six-Part Latin Psalms; Votive Antiphons*, ed. D. Mateer (London: Stainer and Bell, 1983). EECM, xxix.

WHYTHORNE, THOMAS, [3] *Graces [a 4]*, from *Songes of three, fower, and five voyces*, ed. J. Blezzard (London: Oecumuse, 1982).

—— [11 Songs from *Songes of three, fower, and fiue voyces*, 1571], ed. P. Warlock (London: OUP, 1927). Oxford Choral Songs, nos. 354–64.

—— 'What makes young folks simple in show' [from *Duos, or Songs for two voices*, 1590], ed. P. Warlock (London: OUP, 1927). Oxford Choral Songs, no. 365.

WILBYE, JOHN, *The First Set of English Madrigals . . . 1598* (fac.) (Amsterdam: Theatrum Orbis Terrarum, and New York: Da Capo Press, 1972). The English Experience, no. 493.

—— *First Set of Madrigals (1598)*, ed. E. H. Fellowes (London: Stainer and Bell, 1914; rev. R. T. Dart, 1966). EM, vi. With his madrigal from *The Triumphes of Oriana*, and two anthems from Leighton's *Teares*.

—— *Second Set of Madrigals (1609)*, ed. E. H. Fellowes (London: Stainer and Bell, 1914; rev. R. T. Dart, 1966). EM, vii.

WILDER, PHILIP VAN, *Fantasia con Pause et senza Pause*, ed. P. Holman (Corby: Earlham Press, 1983).

The Winchester Anthology (B.L. Add. Ms. 60577) (fac.), ed. E. Wilson and I. Fenlon (Cambridge: D. S. Brewer, 1981).

Worcester Add. 68, Westminster Abbey 33327, Madrid, Bib. Nac. 192 (fac.), ed. L. A. Dittmer (New York: Institute of Medieval Music, 1959). Publications of Medieval Musical Manuscripts, v.

The Worcester Fragments: A Catalogue Raisonné and Transcription, ed. L. A. Dittmer (AIM, 1957). MSD, ii.

Worcester Medieval Harmony, ed. Dom A. Hughes (London: PMMS, 1928).

YONGE, NICOLAS (ed.), *Musica transalpina* (London, 1588 and 1597) (fac.), ed. D. Stevens (Farnborough: Gregg, 1972).

YOULL, HENRY, *Canzonets to Three Voices (1608)*, ed. E. H. Fellowes (London: Stainer and Bell, 1923; rev. R. T. Dart, 1968). EM, xxviii.

YOUNG, WILLIAM, *Two Sonatas for violin, Viola da gamba, and continuo*, ed. D. Beecher and B. Gillingham (Ottawa: Dove House Editions, 1983). Baroque Chamber Music Series, x.

B. Modern Editions of Texts

ADELARD OF BATH, *De eodem et diverso*, ed. H. Willner (Münster i. W., 1903). *BGPM*, IV/i.

AMERUS [or ALFREDUS], *Practica artis musice*, ed. C. Ruini (AIM, 1977). CSM, xxv. (Previously ed. J. Kromolicki, Berlin–Rixdorf, 1909).

Ancient Songs and Ballads from the reign of Henry II to the Revolution, collected by Joseph Ritson (London [?], 1790; 2nd edn., 1829 (2 vols.); 3rd edn., rev. W. C. Hazlitt, London, 1877).

ANONYMUS, *Tractatus de figuris sive notis*, ed. G. Reaney in CSM, xii (AIM, 1966), 33–51. Previously ed. in CS, i. 369–77, as Anon. VI.

ANON. CISTERCIENSIS, *Johannis Wylde Musica Manualis cum Tonale*, ed. C. Sweeney (AIM, 1982). CSM, xxviii.

ANONYMUS IV, *Der Musiktraktat des Anonymus IV*, ed. F. Reckow, 2 vols. (Wiesbaden, 1967). Beihefte zur Archiv für Musikwissenschaft, iv–v. With German translation and Commentary. Previously edited in CS, i. 327–65.

—— *The Music Treatise of Anonymous IV*, trans. J. Yudkin (Neuhausen–Stuttgart: Hänssler-Verlag for AIM, 1985). MSD, xli.

Anonymous treatises on descant and faburden: see Bukofzer, *Geschichte* (1936), Georgiades, Meech, and Trowell (1959), in section C.

BACON, ROGER, *Opus majus*, ed. J. H. Bridges, 2 vols. (Oxford, 1897). A 3rd, suppl. vol. was issued in 1900.

—— *Opus tertium* [etc.], ed. J. S. Brewer (London, 1859). RBMAS, xv.

BARTHOLOMAEUS ANGLICUS, see Müller (in list C); TREVISA (below).

BATHE, WILLIAM, *A Briefe Introduction to the Skill of Song* (fac.), ed. B. Rainbow (Kilkenny, 1982). Classic Texts in Music Education, iii.

BEDE, *Historia ecclesiastica*, ed. B. Colegrave and R. A. B. Mynors (Oxford, 1969). Text and translation. Note also the translation by L. Sherley-Price, rev. R. E. Latham (Penguin Classics).

—— *Opera historica*, ed. C. Plummer, 2 vols. (Oxford, 1896; repr., 1 vol., 1946 etc.).

Book of Masques in Honour of Allardyce Nicoll (Cambridge, 1970).

Breviarium ad usum insignis ecclesiae Sarum, ed. F. Procter and C. Wordsworth, 3 vols. (Cambridge, 1879–86).

The Bridgettine Breviary of Syon Abbey, ed. A. J. Collins (Worcester, 1969). HBS, xcvi.

The Cambridge Songs: A Goliard's Song Book of the XIth Century (with fac.), ed. K. Breul (Cambridge, 1915; repr. New York, 1973).

CAMPION, THOMAS, *Campion's Works*, ed. P. Vivian (Oxford, 1909, repr. 1966).

—— *The Works of Thomas Campion*, ed. W. R. Davis (London, 1969).

Caxton's Mirrour of the World, ed. O. H. Prior (London, 1913). EETS, ES, cx.

Chronicon abbatiae Rameseiensis, a saec. x usque ad an. circiter 1200: in quatuor partibus, ed. W. D. Macray (London, 1886). RBMAS, lxxxiii.

Chronicon monasterii de Abingdon, ed. J. Stevenson, 2 vols. (London, 1858). RBMAS, ii.

Codex Oxoniensis Bibl. Bodl. Rawl. C. 270, 2 vols. *Pars A, 'De vocum consonantiis' ac 'De re musica' (Osberni Cantuarensis?)*; *Pars B, XVII Tractatuli a quodam studioso peregrino ad annum MC collecti* [ed. J. Smits van Waesberghe], 2 vols. (Buren, 1979–80). Divitiae Musicae Artis, A, x.

DRYDEN, JOHN, *The Songs of John Dryden*, ed. C. L. Day (Cambridge, Mass., 1932).

D'URFEY, THOMAS, *The Songs of Thomas D'Urfey*, ed. C. L. Day (Cambridge, Mass., 1933).

Durham Account Rolls, ed. J. T. Fowler, 3 vols. (Durham, 1898). SS, xcix, c, ci.

The Early English Carols, ed. R. L. Greene (Oxford, 1935; 2nd edn., rev. and enlarged, 1977).

EDWARDS, RICHARD (ed.), *The Paradyse of daintie Deuises (London, 1576)*, ed. H. E. Rollins (Cambridge, Mass., 1927).

English Lyrics of the XIIIth Century, ed. C. Brown (Oxford, 1932).

English Madrigal Verse, ed. E. H. Fellowes (Oxford, 1920; 3rd edn., rev. and enlarged by F. W. Sternfeld and D. Greer, 1967).

English Psalmody Prefaces: Popular Methods of Teaching, 1562–1835 (fac.), ed. B. Rainbow (Kilkenny: Boethius Press, 1982). Classic Texts in Music Education, ii.

Expositiones in Micrologum Guidonis Aretini, ed. J. Smits van Waesberghe (Amsterdam, 1957). Musicologica Medii Aevi, i.

Giraldi Cambrensis Opera, 8 vols., ed. J. S. Brewer, J. F. Dimock, and G. F. Warner (London, 1861–91). RBMAS, xxi.

GROSSETESTE, ROBERT, *Die philosophische Werke des Robert Grosseteste*, ed. L. Baur (Münster i. W., 1912). BGPM, ix.

HIGDEN, RANULPH, *Polychronicon Ranulphi Higden Monachi Cestrensis; together with the English Translations of John Trevisa and of an Unknown Writer of the Fifteenth Century*, ed. C. Babington and J. R. Lumby, 9 vols. (London, 1865–86). RBMAS, xli.

The Historians of the Church of York and its Archbishops, ed. J. Raine, 2 vols. (London, 1879). RBMAS, lxxi.

HOTHBY, JOHN, *Calliopea legale*, ed. E. de Coussemaker, *Histoire de l'harmonie au moyen âge* (Paris, 1852, repr. Hildesheim, 1966), 295–349.

—— *De arte contrapuncti*, ed. G. Reaney (Neuhausen, 1977). CSM, xxvi.

—— *Johannis Octobi Tres Tractatuli contra Bartholomeum Ramum*, ed. A. Seay (Rome, 1964). CSM, x.

—— *Regulae super proportiones* and *De cantu figurato*: in CS, iii. 328–30, 330–2.

JOHANNES [COTTO or AFFLIGEMENSIS], *De Musica*, ed. (1) M. Gerbert, *Scriptores*, ii. 230–65; (2) J. Smits van Waesberghe (Rome, 1950 (= CSM, i)); (3) trans. W. Babb in *Hucbald, Guido and John on Music*, ed. C. V. Palisca (New Haven, Conn., and London, 1978).

KILWARDBY, ROBERT, *De ortu scientiarum*, ed. A. G. Judy (Toronto, 1976). Auctores Britannici medii aevi, iv.

The King's Musick: A Transcript of Records Relating to Music and Musicians (1460–1700), ed. H. C. de Lafontaine (London, 1909).

Liber Pontificalis Chr. Bainbridge Archiepiscopi Eboracensis, ed. W. G. Henderson (Durham, London, and Edinburgh, 1875). SS, lxi (1873).

List of Payments to the King's Musick in the Reign of Charles II (1660–1685), ed. A. Ashbee (Editor, 1981).

LOCKE, MATTHEW, *Melothesia*: for the facsimile edn. see sect. II. A s.v. *Melothesia*.

Lyrics from English Airs 1596–1622, ed. E. Doughtie (Cambridge, Mass., 1970). For the texts of airs by Campion see the editions cited s.v. CAMPION.

MACE, THOMAS, *Musick's Monument*, i. *Reproduction en fac-similé* (Paris, 1958).

The Manner of the Coronation of King Charles The First of England, ed. C. Wordsworth (London, 1892). HBS, ii.

The Medieval Records of a London City Church [St Mary-at-Hill], ed. H. Littlehales (London, 1904–5). EETS, OS, cxxv, cxxviii.

Memorials of Saint Dunstan Archbishop of Canterbury, ed. W. Stubbs (London, 1874). RBMAS, lxiii.

Missale ad usum Ecclesie Westmonasteriensis, ed. J. W. Legg, 3 vols. (London, 1891, 1893, 1897). HBS, i, v, xii.

Missale ad usum Insignis et Praeclarae Ecclesiae Sarum, ed. F. H. Dickinson (Burntisland; Oxford and London: 1861–83).

Missale ad usum percelebris ecclesiae Herfordensis [ed. W. G. Henderson] (n.p., 1874; repr. Farnborough, 1969).

MORLEY, THOMAS, *A Plain and Easy Introduction to Practical Music*, ed. R. A. Harman (London, 1952). Also fac. of 1597 edn. (Farnborough, 1971).

NORTH, ROGER, *Autobiography*, ed. A. Jessop (London, 1887).

—— *Memoirs of Musick*, ed. E. F. Rimbault (London, 1846).

—— *The Musicall Grammarian 1728*, ed. M. Chan and J. C. Kassler (Cambridge, 1990).

—— *Roger North on Music*, ed. J. Wilson (London, 1959).

—— *Roger North's Cursory Notes of Musicke (c.1698–c.1703)*, ed. M. Chan and J. C. Kassler (Kensington, NSW, 1986).

ODINGTON, WALTER, *Walteri Odington Summa de Speculatione Musicae*, ed. F. F. Hammond (AIM, 1970). CSM, xiv. Previously ed. CS, i. 182–250.

The Ordinale and Customary of the Benedictine Nuns of Barking Abbey (University College, Oxford, MS 169), ed. J. B. L. Tolhurst, 2 vols. (London, 1927–8). HBS, lxv–lxvi (1927).

Ordinale Exon., ed. J. N. Dalton and G. H. Doble, 4 vols. (London, 1909–40). HBS, xxxvii, xxxviii, lxiii, lxxix.

OSBERN OF CANTERBURY, attrib., see *Codex Oxoniensis Bibl. Bodl. Rawl. C. 270*, i (Divitiae Musicae Artis, A/ xa, ed. J. Smits van Waesberghe).

PLAYFORD, JOHN, *An Introduction to the Skill of Musick: The Twelfth Edition, Corrected and Amended by Henry Purcell. With Selected Chapters from the Thirteenth and Fourteenth Editions* (fac.), ed. F. B. Zimmerman (New York, 1972).

Political Poems and Songs from Edward III to Richard III, ed. T. Wright (London, 1859, 1861). RBMAS, xiv.

Political Songs of England from the reign of John to that of Edward II, ed. T. Wright (London, 1839).

The Pontifical of Egbert, Archbishop of York, ed. W. Greenwell (Durham, London, and Edinburgh, 1853). SS, xxvii.

The Pontifical of Magdalen College, ed. H. A. Wilson ([London], 1901). HBS, xxxix.

The Processional of the Nuns of Chester, ed. from a manuscript in the possession of the Earl of Ellesmere at Bridgewater House by J. W. Legg (London, 1899). HBS, xviii.

RAVENSCROFT, THOMAS, *A Briefe Discourse* (fac.), ed. I. Payne (Clarabricken, 1984).

Records of English Court Music, calendered and ed. A. Ashbee, vols. i– (Snodland, 1986–).

Regularis Concordia Anglicae Nationis Monachorum Sanctimonialiumque, ed. and trans. Dom T. Symons (London etc., 1953).

Rites of Durham (1593). The following editions have appeared:
  Ancient Rites and Monuments of the Monastical and Cathedral Church of Durham (12mo, 1672. 2nd edn., 1733).
  A Description or Briefe Declaration of all the Ancient Monuments, Rites and Customes belonginge or beinge within the Monastical Church of Durham before the Suppression (London and Edinburgh: SS, 1842 [vol. xv], ed. J. T. Fowler, repr. 1903).

Rituale Ecclesiae Dunelmensis, ed. J. Stevenson (London and Edinburgh, 1840). SS, x.

ROBERTUS DE HANDLO: for the *Regula Magistri Franconis*, see CS, i. 383–403. English trans. by L. A. Dittmer (New York, 1959).

Songs and Carols now first printed from a MS. of the xvth Century, ed. T. Wright (London, 1847).

Three Coronation Orders, ed. J. W. Legg ([London], 1900). HBS, xix.

TORKESEY, JOHANNES, *Declaratio Trianguli et Scuti*, ed. A. Gilles and G. Reaney in CSM, xii (AIM, 1966), 53–63.

TREVISA, JOHN, *On the Properties of Things: John Trevisa's translation of Bartholomaeus Anglicus*, De Proprietatibus Rerum: *A Critical Text*, ed. M. C. Seymour, 2 vols. (Oxford, 1975).

—— *see also* HIGDEN.

The Use of Sarum, ed. W. H. Frere, 2 vols. (Cambridge, 1898–1901).

Vice-Chamberlain Coke's Theatrical Papers 1706–1715, ed. J. Bilhous and R. D. Hume (Carbondale and Edwardsville, Ill., 1982).

WHYTHORNE, THOMAS, *Autobiography* (*c*.1576), ed. J. M. Osborn (Oxford, 1961).

WILLELMUS, *Breviarium Regulare Musicae*, ed. G. Reaney in CSM, xii (AIM, 1966), 5–31.

WILLIAM OF MALMESBURY, *Vita Sancti Dunstani*. See *Memorials of Saint Dunstan*.

—— *Willelmi Malmesbiriensis Monachi De gestis Pontificum Anglorum Libri Quinque*, ed. N. E. S. A. Hamilton (London, 1870). RBMAS, lii.

—— *Willelmi Malmesbiriensis Monachi Gesta regum Anglorum atque historia novella*, ed. T. D. Hardy, 2 vols. (London, 1840).

—— *Willelmi Malmesbiriensis Monachi Gesta regum Anglorum Libri Quinque; Historiae Novellae Libri tres*, ed. W. Stubbs, 2 vols. (London, 1887–9). RBMAS, xc.

The Winchester Troper, ed. W. H. Frere (London, 1894). HBS, viii.

WYLDE, JOHN, see ANON. CISTERCIENSIS.

The York Plays, ed. R. Beadle (London, 1982).

C. Books and Articles

ADANK, T., 'Roger Bacons Auffassung der Musica', *Archiv für Musikwissenschaft*, 35 (1978), 33–56.

ALLENSON, S., 'The Inverness Fragments: Music from a Pre-Reformation Scottish Parish Church', *ML*, 70 (1989), 1–45.

ANDREWS, H. K., 'Transposition of Byrd's Vocal Polyphony', *ML*, 43 (1962), 25–37.

—— 'Printed Sources of William Byrd's "Psalmes, Sonets and Songs"', *ML*, 44 (1963), 5–20.

—— and DART, R. T., 'Fourteenth-Century Polyphony in a Fountains Abbey MS Book', *ML*, 39 (1958), 1–12.

APFEL, E., *Studien zur Satztechnik der mittelalterlichen englischen Musik*, 2 vols. (Heidelberg, 1959).

APLIN, J., 'A Group of English Magnificats "Upon the Faburden"', *Soundings*, 7 (1978), 85–100.

—— 'The Survival of Plainsong in Anglican Music: Some Early English Te-Deum Settings', *JAMS*, 32 (1979), 247–75.

—— '"The Fourth Kind of Faburden": The Identity of an English Four-Part Style', *ML*, 61 (1980), 245–65.

—— 'The Origins of John Day's "Certaine Notes"', *ML*, 62 (1981), 295–9.

ARKWRIGHT, G. E. P., 'Robert Douland's *Musicall Banquet*, 1610', *The Musical Antiquary*, 1 (1909–10), 45–55.

—— 'Early Elizabethan Stage Music', *The Musical Antiquary*, 1 (1909–10), 30–40; 4 (1912–13), 112–17.

—— 'Notes on the Ferrabosco Family', *The Musical Antiquary*, 3 (1911–12), 220–8, and 4 (1912–13), 42–54.

—— 'Elizabethan Choirboy Plays and their Music', *PMA*, 40 (1913–14), 117–38.

ARNOLD, D., 'Croce and the English Madrigal', *ML*, 35 (1954), 308–19.

—— 'Gastoldi and the English Ballett', *Monthly Musical Record*, 86 (1956), 44–52.

ASHBEE, A., *Records of English Court Music* (Snodland, 1986–).

ASTON, P., 'Tradition and Experiment in the Music of George Jeffreys', *PRMA*, 99 (1972–3), 105–15.

AUSTERN, L. P., 'Musical Parody in the Jacobean City Comedy', *ML*, 66 (1985), 355–66.

BAILLIE, H., 'A London Church in Early Tudor Times', *ML*, 36 (1955), 55–64.

—— 'A London Gild of Musicians, 1460–1530', *PRMA*, 83 (1956–7), 15–28.

—— 'Les Musiciens de la chapelle royale d'Henri VIII au Camp du Drap d'Or', *Fêtes et Cérémonies au temps du Charles Quint*, ed. J. Jacquot (Paris, 1960), 147–59.

—— 'Squares', *AcM*, 32 (1960), 178–93.

—— 'Some Biographical Notes on English Church Musicians, Chiefly Working in London (1485–1569)', *RMARC*, 2 (1962), 18–57.

—— and OBOUSSIER, P., 'The York Masses', *ML*, 35 (1954), 19–30.

BARLOW, G. F., 'Vanbrugh's Queen's Theatre in the Haymarket, 1703–9', *Early Music*, 17 (1989), 515–21.

BASKERVILL, C. R., *The Elizabethan Jig and related Song Drama* (Chicago, 1929, repr. New York, 1965).

BENHAM, H., 'Latin Church Music under Edward VI', *MT*, 116 (1975), 477–9.

—— *Latin Church Music in England c.1460–1575* (London, 1977).

—— '"Salve Regina" (Power or Dunstable): A Simplified Version', *ML*, 59 (1978), 28–32.

—— 'Prince Arthur (1486–1502), a Carol and a *cantus firmus*', *Early Music*, 15 (1987), 463–7.

BENT, I., 'The English Chapel Royal before 1300', *PRMA*, 90 (1963–4), 77–95.

BENT, M., 'Initial Letters in the Old Hall Manuscript', *ML*, 47 (1966), 225–38.

—— 'Sources of the Old Hall Music', *PRMA*, 94 (1967–8), 19–35.

—— 'New and Little-known Fragments of English Medieval Polyphony', *JAMS*, 21 (1968), 137–56, 4 plates.

—— 'The Transmission of English Music 1300–1500: Some Aspects of Repertory and Presentation', *Studien zur Tradition in der Musick: Kurt von Fischer zum 60. Geburtstag*, ed. H. H. Eggebrecht and M. Lütolf (Munich, 1973), 65–83.

—— 'The Old Hall Manuscript', *Early Music*, 2 (1974), 2–14.

—— *Dunstable* (London, 1981).

—— 'Rota versatilis—Towards a Reconstruction', *Source Materials and the Interpretation of Music*, ed. I. Bent (London, 1981), 65–98 (incl. 4 plates and transcription).

—— 'The Yoxford Credo', *Essays in Musicology: A Tribute to Alvin Johnson*, ed. L. Lockwood and E. Roesner (AMS, 1990), 26–51.

—— and BENT, I., 'Dufay, Dunstable, Plummer—A New Source', *JAMS*, 22 (1969), 394–424.

—— and BOWERS, R., 'The Saxilby Fragment', *EMH*, i (Cambridge, 1981), 1–27.

BERGSAGEL, J. D., 'An Introduction to Ludford', *MD*, 14 (1960), 105–30. 2 plates.

—— 'On the Performance of Ludford's *Alternatim* Masses', *MD*, 16 (1962), 35–55. 7 plates.

—— 'The Date and Provenance of the Forrest–Heyther Collection of Tudor Masses', *ML*, 44 (1963), 240–8.

BINNS, J. W., 'John Case and *The Praise of Musick*', *ML*, 55 (1974), 444–53.

BLAIR, P. H., *An Introduction to Anglo-Saxon England* (Cambridge, 1956, 2nd edn., 1976).

BLEZZARD, J., 'The Lumley Books', *MT*, 112 (1971), 128–30.

—— 'A New Source of Tudor Secular Music', *MT*, 122 (1981), 532–5.

BOLTE, J., *Die Singspiele der englischen Komödianten* (Leipzig, 1893).

BOSTON, J. L., 'Priscilla Bunbury's Virginal Book', *ML*, 36 (1955), 365–73.

BOWDEN, W. R., *English Dramatic Lyric, 1603–1642* (New Haven, Conn., 1951).

BOWERS, R. D., 'Some Observations on the Life and Career of Lionel Power', *PRMA*, 102 (1975–6), 103–27.

—— 'Choral Establishments within the English Church: Their Constitution and Development, 1340–1542', Ph.D. thesis (East Anglia, 1976).

—— 'The Performing Pitch of English 15th-Century Church Polyphony', *Early Music*, 8 (1980), 21–8.

—— 'Obligation, Agency, and *laissez-faire*: The promotion of Polyphonic Composition for the Church in Fifteenth-Century England', *Music in Medieval and Early Modern England*, ed. I. Fenlon (Cambridge, 1981), 1–19.

—— 'The Vocal Scoring, Choral Balance and Performing Pitch of Latin Church Polyphony in England, c.1500–58', *JRMA*, 112 (1987), 38–76.

—— 'Fixed Points in the Chronology of English Fourteenth-Century Polyphony', *ML*, 71 (1990), 313–35.

—— and WATHEY, A. (comps.), 'New Sources of English Fourteenth- and Fifteenth-Century Polyphony', *EMH*, iii (Cambridge, 1983), 123–73.

—— —— 'New Sources of English Fifteenth- and Sixteenth-century Polyphony', *EMH*, iv (Cambridge, 1984), 297–346.

BOYD, M., 'Music Manuscripts in the Mackworth Collection at Cardiff', *ML*, 54 (1973), 133–41.

—— and RAYSON, J., 'The Gentleman's Diversion: John Lenton and the First Violin Tutor', *Early Music*, 10 (1982), 329–32.

BOYD, M. C., *Elizabethan Music and Musical Criticism* (Philadelphia, Pa., 1940; 2nd rev. edn., 1962, repr. 1967).

BRAUN, W., *Britannia abundans: Deutsche-Englische Musikbeziehungen zur Shakespeare-zeit* (Tutzing, 1977).

BRAY, R. W., 'British Museum Add. MSS. 17802–5 (The Gyffard Part-Books): An Index and Commentary', *RMARC*, 7 (1969), 31–50.

—— 'The Part-Books Oxford, Christ Church, MSS 979–983: An Index and Commentary', *MD*, 25 (1971), 179–97.

—— 'British Museum MS Royal 24 d 2 (John Baldwin's Commonplace Book): An Index and Commentary', *RMARC*, 11 (1974), 137–51.

—— 'More Light on Early Tudor Pitch', *Early Music*, 8 (1980), 35–42.

BREIG, W., 'Die Lübbenauer Tabulaturen Lynar A1 und A2. Eine quellenkundliche Studie', *AMw*, 25 (1968), 96–117, 223–36.

BRENNECKE, E., *John Milton the Elder and his Music* (New York, 1938).

BRETT, P., 'The English Consort Song, 1570–1625', *PRMA*, 87 (1961–2), 73–88.

—— 'Edward Paston (1550–1630): A Norfolk Gentleman and his Musical Collection', *Transactions of the Cambridge Bibliographical Society*, 4 (1964–8), 51–69.

—— '*Musicae modernae laus*: Geoffrey Whitney's Tributes to the Lute and its Players', *LSJ*, 7 (1965), 40–4.

—— 'Homage to Taverner in Byrd's Masses', *Early Music*, 9 (1981), 169–76.

—— and DART, R. T., 'Songs by William Byrd in Manuscripts at Harvard', *Harvard Library Bulletin*, 14 (1960), 343–65.

BROTHERS, L. D., 'Avery Burton and his Hexachord Mass', *MD*, 28 (1974), 153–76.

BROWN, A., '"My Lady Nevell's Book" as a Source of Byrd's Keyboard Music', *PRMA*, 95 (1968–9), 29–39.

BROWN, D., 'William Byrd's 1588 Volume', *ML*, 38 (1957), 371–7.

—— 'Thomas Morley and the Catholics: Some Speculations', *Monthly Musical Record*, 89 (1959), 53–61.

—— 'The Styles and Chronology of Thomas Morley's Motets', *ML*, 41 (1960), 216–22. See further letters from F. Ll. Harrison in *ML*, 42 (1961), 97–8 and from D. Brown, ibid., 198.

—— 'The Anthems of Thomas Weelkes', *PRMA*, 91 (1964–5), 61–72.

—— *Thomas Weelkes: A Biographical and Critical Study* (London, 1969).

BROWN, J., PATTERSON, S., and HILEY, D., 'Further observations on W1', *JPMMS*, 4 (1981), 53–80.

BROWNING, A., 'Purcell's "Stairre Case Overture"', *MT*, 121 (1980), 768–9.

BRUCE-MITFORD, R. and M., 'The Sutton Hoo Lyre, *Beowulf*, and the Origins of the Frame Harp', *Antiquity*, 44 (1970), 7–13.

BUKOFZER, M. F., 'Gymel, the Earliest Form of English Polyphony', *ML*, 16 (1935), 77–84.

—— 'The First Motet with English Words', *ML*, 17 (1936), 225–33.

—— *Geschichte des englischen Diskants nach den theoretischen Quellen* (Strasburg, 1936).

—— '"Sumer is icumen in": A Revision', *University of California Publications in Music*, 2 (1944), 79–114.

—— *Studies in Medieval and Renaissance Music* (New York, 1950, and London, 1951).

—— '*Caput Redivivum*: A New Source for Dufay's *Missa Caput*', *JAMS*, 4 (1951), 98–102.

—— 'Fauxbourdon Revisited', *MQ*, 38 (1952), 22–47.

—— 'Changing Aspects of Medieval and Renaissance Music', *MQ*, 45 (1958), 1–18.

—— 'Popular and Secular Music in England (to *c*.1470), *NOHM*, iii (1960), 107–33.

—— 'English Church Music of the Fifteenth Century', *NOHM*, iii (1960), 165–213.

BURLING, W. J., 'Four more "lost" Restoration plays "found" in musical sources', *ML*, 65 (1984), 45–7.

BURSTYN, S., 'Early 15th-Century Polyphonic Settings of Song of Songs Antiphons', *AcM*, 49 (1977), 200–27.

BUTCHART, D. S., 'A Musical Journey of 1567: Alessandro Striggio in Vienna, Munich, Paris and London', *ML*, 63 (1982), 1–16.

BUTTREY, J., 'William Smith of Durham', *ML*, 43 (1962), 248–54.

BUXTON, J., *Elizabethan Taste* (London, 1963).

CALDWELL, J., 'Keyboard Plainsong Settings in England, 1500–1660', *MD*, 19 (1965), 129–53. Addenda et Corrigenda, ibid., 34 (1980), 215–19.

—— 'The Pitch of Early Tudor Organ Music', *ML*, 51 (1970), 156–63.

—— 'The "Te Deum" in Late Medieval England', *Early Music*, 6 (1978), 188–94.

—— 'The Influence of German Composers on English Keyboard Music in the Seventeenth Century', *Deutsch-englische Musikbeziehungen* (Musik ohne Grenzen, i, ed. W. Konold, Munich and Salzburg, 1985), 39–50.

The Cambridge Guide to the Arts in Britain, ed. B. Ford, vols. ii–iv (Cambridge, 1988–9).

CARPENTER, N. C., 'Music in the Chester Plays', *Papers on English Language and Literature*, 1 (1965), 195–216.

—— 'Music in the English Mystery Plays', *Music in English Renaissance Drama*, ed. J. H. Long (Lexington, Ky, 1968), 1–31.

—— 'Music in the *Secunda Pastorum*', *Medieval English Drama: Essays Critical and Contextual*, ed. J. Taylor and A. H. Nelson (Chicago, 1972), 212–17.

CHAMBERS, Sir E. K., *The Elizabethan Stage*, 4 vols. (Oxford, 1923).

CHAN, M., 'Edward Lowe's Manuscript British Library Add. MS 29396: The Case for Redating', *ML*, 59 (1978), 440–54.

—— 'John Hilton's Manuscript British Library Add. MS 11608', *ML*, 60 (1979), 440–9.

—— *Music in the Theatre of Ben Jonson* (Oxford, 1980).

—— 'A Mid-Seventeenth-Century Music Meeting and Playford's Publishing', *The Well Enchanting Skill* (Oxford, 1990), 231–44.

—— and KASSLER, J. C., *Roger North's The Musicall Grammarian and Theory of Sounds: Digests of the Manuscripts* (Kensington, NSW, 1988).

CHARLES, S. R., 'The Provenance and Date of the Pepys MS 1236', *MD*, xvi (1962), 57–71.

CHARLTON, D., '"King Arthur": Dramatick Opera', *ML*, 64 (1983), 183–92.

CHARTERIS, R., *John Coprario: A Thematic Catalogue of his Music* (New York, 1977).

—— 'Music Manuscripts and Books Missing from Archbishop Marsh's Library, Dublin', *ML*, 61 (1980), 310–17.

—— 'New Information about the Life of Alfonso Ferrabosco the Elder (1543–1588)', *RMARC*, 17 (1981), 97–114.

—— 'Autographs of Alfonso Ferrabosco I–III', *Early Music*, 10 (1982), 208–11.

—— 'Newly Identified Italian Madrigals Englished', *ML*, 63 (1982), 276–80.

—— *Alfonso Ferrabosco the Elder (1543–1588): A Thematic Catalogue of his Music with a Biographical Calendar* (New York, 1984). Thematic Catalogue Series, xi.

CHEVERTON, I., 'Captain Henry Cooke (c.1616–72): The Beginnings of a Reappraisal', *Soundings*, 9 (1982), 74–86.

CHEW, G., 'The Provenance and Date of the Caius and Lambeth Choir-Books', *ML*, 51 (1970), 107–17.

—— 'The Early Cyclic Mass as an Expression of Royal and Papal Supremacy', *ML*, 53 (1972), 254–69.

CLARK, J. B., *Transposition in Seventeenth Century English Organ Accompaniments and the Transposing Organ* (Detroit, 1974). Detroit Monographs in Musicology, iv.

CLULOW, P., 'Publication Dates for Byrd's Latin Masses', *ML*, 47 (1966), 1–9.

COATES, W., 'English Two-Part Viol Music 1590–1640', *ML*, 33 (1952), 141–50.

COLE, E., 'L'Anthologie de madrigaux et de musique instrumentale pour ensembles de Francis Tregian', *La Musique instrumentale de la Renaissance* (Paris, 1955), 115–26.

CONGLETON, J., 'The False Consonances of Music', *Early Music*, 9 (1981), 463–9.

COOPER, B., 'Albertus Bryne's Keyboard Music', *MT*, 113 (1972), 142–3.

—— 'Keyboard Sources in Hereford', *RMARC*, 16 (1980), 135–9.

CORAL, L., 'A John Playford Advertisement', *RMARC*, 5 (1965), 1–12. See also *RMARC*, 6 (1966), 1–2.

COWDREY, H. E. J., 'The Anglo-Norman Laudes Regiae', *Viator*, 12 (1981), 37–78.

CUNNINGHAM, W., *The Keyboard Music of John Bull* (Ann Arbor, Mich., 1984).

CURTIS, A., *Sweelinck's Keyboard Music: A Study of English Elements in Seventeenth-Century Dutch Composition* (Leiden and London, 1969).

CURTIS, G. R. K., 'Stylistic Layers in the English Mass Repertory, c.1400–1450', *PRMA*, 109 (1982–3), 23–38.

CUTTS, J. P., 'A Bodleian Song-Book: Don. c. 57', *ML*, 34 (1953), 192–211.

—— 'Jacobean Masque and Stage Music', *ML*, 35 (1954), 185–200.

—— 'Early Seventeenth-Century Lyrics at St. Michael's College, Tenbury', *ML*, 37 (1956), 221–33.

—— 'The Second Coventry Carol: And a Note on *The Maydes Metamorphosis*', *Renaissance News*, 10/1 (1957), 3–8.

—— *Seventeenth-Century Songs and Lyrics* (Columbia, Mo., 1959).

—— 'Robert Johnson and the Court Masque', *ML*, 41 (1960), 111–26.

—— '"Songs Vnto the Violl and Lute"—Drexel MS. 4175', *MD*, 16 (1962), 73–92.

DANIEL, R. T., and LE HURAY, P., *The Sources of English Church Music 1549–1660*, 2 vols. (London, 1972). EECM, suppl. vol. I.
DART, R. T., 'Morley's Consort Lessons of 1599', *PRMA*, 74 (1947–8), 1–9.
—— 'The Cittern and its English Music', *GSJ*, I (1948), 46–63.
—— 'New Sources of Virginal Music', *ML*, 35 (1954), 93–106.
—— 'The Printed Fantasies of Orlando Gibbons', *ML*, 37 (1956), 342–9.
—— 'Lord Herbert of Cherbury's Lute-Book', *ML*, 38 (1957), 136–48.
—— 'Morley and the Catholics: Some Further Speculations', *Monthly Musical Record*, 89 (1959), 89–92.
—— 'Henry Loosemore's Organ Book', *Transactions of the Cambridge Bibliographical Society*, 3 (1959–63), 143–51.
—— 'Music and Musicians at Chichester Cathedral, 1545–1642', *ML*, 42 (1961), 221–6.
—— 'Two New Documents Relating to the Royal Music, 1584–1605', *ML*, 45 (1964), 16–21.
—— 'Elizabeth Edgeworth's Keyboard Book', *ML*, 50 (1969), 470–4.
—— 'An Early Seventeenth-Century Book of English Organ Music for the Roman Rite', *ML*, 52 (1971), 27–38.
DAVIS, W. R., *Thomas Campion* (Boston, Mass., 1987).
DAVISON, N., 'Tye's Mass "Euge bone"', *MT*, 122 (1980), 727–30.
DAWES, F., 'The Music of Philip Hart (ca. 1676–1749)', *PRMA*, 94 (1967–8), 63–75.
DEAN, W., and KNAPP, J. M., *Handel's Operas 1704–1726* (Oxford, 1987).
DEARNLEY, C., *English Church Music 1650–1750 in Royal Chapel, Cathedral and Parish Church* (London, 1970).
DENNISON, P., 'The Sacred Music of Matthew Locke', *ML*, 60 (1979), 60–75.
—— *Pelham Humphrey* (Oxford, 1986).
DITTMER, L. A., 'An English Discantuum Volumen', *MD*, 8 (1954), 20–58, 6 plates.
—— 'The Dating and Notation of the Worcester Fragments', *MD*, 11 (1957), 5–11.
DOE, P., *Tallis* (London, 1968; 2nd edn., 1976).
—— 'Tallis's "Spem in alium" and the Elizabethan Respond-Motet', *ML*, 51 (1970), 1–14.
—— 'The Emergence of the In Nomine: Some Notes and Queries on the Work of Tudor Church Musicians', *Modern Musical Scholarship*, ed. E. Olleson (Boston, Henley, and London, 1978), 79–92.
DOUGHTIE, E., *English Renaissance Song* (Boston and London, 1986).
DOWLING, M., 'The Printing of John Dowland's *Second Booke of Songs or Ayres*', *The Library*, 4th ser., 12 (1932–3), 365–80.
DUCKLES, V., 'The Gamble Manuscript as a Source of *continuo* song in England', *JAMS*, I (1948), no. 2, pp. 23–40.
—— 'John Gamble's Commonplace Book', Ph.D. diss. (California, 1953).
—— 'The "Curious" Art of John Wilson (1595–1674): An Introduction to the Songs and Lute Music', *JAMS*, 7 (1954), 93–112.
—— 'Florid Embellishment in English Song of the Late 16th and Early 17th Centuries', *AnnM*, 5 (1957), 329–45.

—— 'The Lyrics of John Donne as Set by his Contempories', *Kongressbericht Cologne 1958* (Kassel, 1959), 91–3.

DUFFY, J., *The Songs and Motets of Alfonso Ferrabosco, the Younger (1575–1628)* (Ann Arbor, Mich., 1980). Studies in Musicology, xx.

EGAN-BUFFET, M., and FLETCHER, A. J., 'The Dublin Visitatio Sepulcri Play', *Proceedings of the Royal Irish Academy*, C/ 90 (1990), no. 7 (pp. 159–214).

EINSTEIN, A., 'The Elizabethan Madrigal and "Musica Transalpina"', *ML*, 25 (1944), 66–77.

ELLINWOOD, L., 'Tallis' Tunes and Tudor Psalmody', *MD*, 2 (1948), 189–203.

ELLIOTT, K., 'The Carver Choir-Book', *ML*, 41 (1960), 349–57.

EMSLIE, McD., 'Nicholas Lanier's Innovations in English Song', *ML*, 41 (1960), 13–27.

ENGELKE, B., *Musik und Musiker am Gottorfer Hofe I: Die Zeit der Englischen Komödianten* (Breslau, 1930).

EVANS, D. R., 'Blow's Court Odes: A New Discovery', *MT*, 125 (1984), 567–9.

FALLOWS, D., 'English Song Repertories of the Mid-Fifteenth Century', *PRMA*, 103 (1976–7), 61–79.

—— 'Robertus de Anglia and the Oporto Song Collection', *Source Materials and the Interpretation of Music*, ed. I. Bent (London, 1981), 99–128.

—— 'The Contenance Angloise: English Influence on Continental Composers of the Fifteenth Century', *Renaissance Studies*, 1 (1987), 189–208.

FELLOWES, E. H., *William Byrd* (London, 1936; 2nd edn., 1948).

FENLON, I., 'Instrumental Music, Songs and Verse from Sixteenth-Century Winchester: British Library Additional MS 60577', *Music in Medieval and Early Modern Europe*, ed. idem (Cambridge, 1981), 93–116.

—— (ed.), *Cambridge Music Manuscripts 900–1700* (Cambridge, 1982).

FINCHAM, K., 'Contemporary Opinions of Thomas Weelkes', *ML*, 62 (1981), 352–3.

FISKE, R., 'The "Macbeth" Music', *ML*, 45 (1964), 114–25.

—— *English Theatre Music in the Eighteenth Century* (London, 1973; 2nd edn., 1986).

FORD, A., 'A Purcell Service and its Sources', *MT*, 124 (1983), 121–2.

FORD, R., 'A Sacred Song not by Purcell', *MT*, 125 (1984), 45–7.

FORTUNE, N., 'A New Purcell Source', *MR*, 25 (1964), 109–13.

—— 'Philip Rosseter and his Songs', *LSJ*, 7 (1965), 7–14.

—— (in collaboration with I. Fenlon): 'Music Manuscripts of John Browne (1608–91) and from Stanford Hall, Leicestershire', *Source Materials and the Interpretation of Music*, ed. I. Bent (London, 1981), 155–68.

FRANK, P., 'A New Dowland Document', *MT*, 124 (1983), 15–16.

FRERE, W. H., 'Edwardine Vernacular Services before the First Prayer Book', *Walter Howard Frere: A Collection of his Papers* (London, 1940), 5–21.

FUGLER, P., 'The Lambeth and Caius Choirbooks', *JPMMS*, 6 (1983), 15–25.

FULLER, S., 'Discant and the Theory of Fifthing', *AcM*, 50 (1978), 241–78.

GEE, H., *The Elizabethan Prayer Book and Ornaments* (London, 1902).

GEORGIADES, T., *Englische Diskanttraktate aus der ersten Hälfte des XV. Jahrhunderts* (Munich, 1937).

GIBSON, M. T., LAPIDGE, M., and PAGE, C., 'Neumed Boethian *metra* from Canterbury: A Newly Recovered Leaf of Cambridge, University Library, Gg.

5.35 (the "Cambridge Songs" Manuscript)', *Anglo-Saxon England*, 12 (1983), 141–52.

GILL, D., 'The Sources of English Solo Bandora Music', *LSJ*, 4 (1962), 23–7.

GILLINGHAM, B., 'Lambeth Palace MS 457: A Reassessment', *ML*, 68 (1987), 213–21.

GODT, I., 'Prince Henry as Absalom in David's Lamentations', *ML*, 62 (1981), 318–30.

GODWIN, J., 'Robert Fludd on the Lute and Pandora', *LSJ*, 15 (1973), 11–19.

GOUK, P., 'Music in the Natural Philosophy of the Early Royal Society', Ph.D. diss. (London, Warburg Institute, 1982).

GREENE, R. L., 'Two Medieval Musical Manuscripts: Egerton 3307 and some University of Chicago Fragments', *JAMS*, 7 (1954), 1–34.

GREER, D., '"What if a Day"—an Examination of Words and Music', *ML*, 43 (1962), 304–19.

—— 'An Early Setting of Lines from "Venus and Adonis"', *ML*, 45 (1964), 126–9.

—— 'The Lute Songs of Thomas Morley', *LSJ*, 8 (1966), 25–37.

—— 'Campion the Musician', *LSJ*, 9 (1967), 7–16.

—— 'Two Songs by William Corkine', *Early Music*, 11 (1983), 346–9.

HAMM, C., 'A Group of Anonymous English Pieces in Trent 87', *ML*, 41 (1960), 211–15.

HAND, C., *John Taverner: His Life and Music* (London, 1978).

HANKEY, S., 'The Compleat Gentleman's Music', *ML*, 62 (1981), 146–54.

HANNAS, R., 'Concerning Deletions in the Polyphonic Mass Credo', *JAMS*, 5 (1952), 155–86.

HARDING, R. E. H., *A Thematic Catalogue of the Works of Matthew Locke: With a Calendar of the main events of his life* (Oxford, 1971).

HARLEY, J., *Music in Purcell's London* (London, 1968).

—— 'Ornaments in English Keyboard Music of the Seventeenth and Early Eighteenth Centuries', *MR*, 31 (1970), 177–200.

HARPER, J., 'Orlando Gibbons: The Domestic Context of his Music and Christ Church MS 21', *MT*, 124 (1983), 767–70.

HARRIS, E. T., *Henry Purcell's* Dido and Aeneas (Oxford, 1987).

HARRISON, F. LL., 'The Eton College Choirbook', *Kongressbericht Utrecht 1952* (Amsterdam, 1953), 224–32.

—— *Music in Medieval Britain* (London, 1958; 4th edn., Buren, 1980).

—— 'Music for the Sarum Rite: MS 1236 in the Pepys Library, Magdalen College, Cambridge', *AnnM*, 6 (1958–63), 99–144.

—— 'English Church Music in the Fourteenth Century', *NOHM*, iii (1960), 82–106.

—— 'English Polyphony (*c.* 1470–1540)', *NOHM*, iii (1960), 303–48.

—— 'Faburden in Practice', *MD*, 16 (1962), 11–34.

—— 'Polyphonic Music for a Chapel of Edward III', *ML*, 59 (1978), 420–8.

—— 'Faburden Compositions in Early Tudor Organ Music', *Visitatio Organorum* (Buren, 1980), 287–329.

HARTZELL, K. D., 'An Unknown English Benedictine Gradual of the Eleventh Century', *Anglo-Saxon England*, 4 (1975), 131–44.

HARWOOD, I., 'John Maynard and *The XII Wonders of the World*', *LSJ*, 4 (1962), 7–16.

—— 'The Origins of the Cambridge Lute Manuscripts', *LSJ*, 5 (1963), 32–48.

—— 'Rosseter's *Lessons for Consort* of 1609', *LSJ*, 7 (1965), 15–23.

—— 'On the Publication of Adrian Le Roy's Lute Instructions', *LSJ*, 18 (1976), 30–6.

—— 'A Case of Double Standards? Instrumental Pitch in England c.1600', *Early Music*, 9 (1981), 470–81.

—— 'Instrumental Pitch in England, c.1600', *Early Music*, 11 (1983), 76–7.

HEARTZ, D., 'The Basse Dance: Its Evolution circa 1450 to 1550', *AnnM*, 6 (1958–63), 287–340.

HELM, E., 'Italian Traits in the English Madrigal', *MR*, 7 (1946), 26–34.

HENDRIE, G., 'The Keyboard Music of Orlando Gibbons (1583–1625)', *PRMA*, 89 (1962–3), 1–15.

HINE, J. D., *Roger North's Writings on Music to c.1703: A Set of Analytical Indexes* (Kensington, NSW, 1986).

HOFMAN, M., and MOREHEN, J., *Latin Music in British Sources c.1485–c.1610* (London, 1987). EECM Suppl., ii.

HOLLANDER, J., *Ideas of Music in English Poetry, 1500–1700* (Princeton, NJ, 1961; repr. New York, 1970).

HOLMAN, P., 'The English Royal Violin Consort in the Sixteenth Century', *PRMA*, 109 (1982–3), 39–59.

—— 'Thomas Baltzar (?1631–1663), the "Incomparable *Luciber* on the Violin"', *Chelys*, 13 (1984), 3–38.

—— 'A New Source of Restoration Keyboard Music', *RMARC*, 20 (1986/7), 53–7.

—— 'The Harp in Stuart England: New Light on William Lawes's Harp Consorts', *Early Music*, 15 (1987), 188–203.

HOLSCHNEIDER, A., *Die Organa von Winchester: Studien zum ältesten Repertoire polyphoner Musik* (Hildesheim, 1968).

HOWLETT, D. R., 'A Possible Date for a Dunstable Motet', *MR*, 36 (1975), 81–4.

HUGHES, Dom A., *Medieval Polyphony in the Bodleian Library* (Oxford, 1951).

HUGHES, A., 'English Sacred Music (excluding carols) in Insular Sources, 1400–c.1450', D.Phil. diss. (Oxford, 1964).

—— 'Fifteenth-Century Polyphony Discovered in Norwich and Arundel', *ML*, 59 (1978), 148–9.

—— and BENT, M., 'The Old Hall Manuscript: A Reappraisal by Andrew Hughes; an Inventory by Andrew Hughes and Margaret Bent', *MD*, 21 (1967), 97–147.

ILLING, R., 'Barley's Pocket Edition of Est's Metrical Psalter', *ML*, 49 (1968), 219–23.

IRVING, J., 'Consort Playing in Mid-17th-Century Worcester: Thomas Tomkins and the Bodleian Partbooks Mus. Sch. E. 415–18', *Early Music*, 12 (1984), 337–44.

—— 'Oxford, Christ Church MSS. 1018–1020: A Valuable Source of Tomkins's Consort Music', *The Consort*, 40 (1984), 1–12.

—— *The Instrumental Music of Thomas Tomkins (1572–1656)* (New York, 1989).

JACKMAN, J. L., 'Liturgical Aspects of Byrd's *Gradualia*', *MQ*, 49 (1963), 17–37.

JEANS, S., 'Geschichte und Entwicklung des Voluntary for Double Organ in der englischen Orgelmusik des 17. Jahrhunderts', *Bericht der Internationalen Musikwissenschaftlichen Kongress, Hamburg 1956* (Kassel, 1957), 123–6.

JOHNSON, P., *Form and Transformation in Music and Poetry of the English Renaissance* (New Haven, Conn., and London, 1972).

JOINER, M., 'British Museum Add. MS. 15117: A Commentary, Index, and Bibliography', *RMARC*, 7 (1969), 51–109.

JORGENS, E. B., *The Well-Tun'd word: Musical Interpretations of English Poetry 1597–1651* (Minneapolis, Minn., 1982).

JOSEPHSON, D. S., *John Taverner: Tudor Composer* (Ann Arbor, Mich., 1979). Studies in Musicology, v.

KASTENDIECK, M. M., *England's Musical Poet, Thomas Campion* (New York, 1962).

KEMP, W. H., '"Votre trey douce": A Duo for Dancing', *ML*, 60 (1979), 37–44.

KENNEY, S. W., '"English Discant" and Discant in England', *MQ*, 45 (1959), 26–48.

—— 'Ely Cathedral and the "Contenance Angloise"', *Musik und Geschichte: Leo Schrade zum sechztigen Geburtstag* (Cologne, 1963), 35–49.

—— *Walter Frye and the Contenance Angloise* (New Haven, Conn., and London, 1964).

KEPHART, C., 'An Unnoticed Forerunner of "The Beggar's Opera"', *ML*, 61 (1980), 266–71.

KERMAN, J., 'Elizabethan Anthologies of Italian Madrigals', *JAMS*, 4 (1951), 122–38.

—— 'Master Alfonso and the English Madrigal', *MQ*, 38 (1952), 222–44.

—— 'Morley and the "Triumphs of Oriana"', *ML*, 34 (1953), 185–91.

—— 'An Elizabethan Edition of Lassus', *AcM*, 27 (1955), 71–6.

—— 'Byrd's Motets: Chronology and Canon', *JAMS*, 14 (1961), 359–82.

—— *The Elizabethan Madrigal* (New York, 1962).

—— 'The Elizabethan Motet: A Study of the Texts for Music', *Studies in the Renaissance*, 9 (1962), 273–305.

—— *The Masses and Motets of William Byrd* (London and Boston, 1981).

KING, A. H., 'The Significance of John Rastell in Early Music Printing', *The Library*, 5th ser., 26 (1971), 197–214.

—— 'An English Broadside of the 1520s', *Essays . . . in Honour of Sir Jack Westrup* (Oxford, 1975).

KNOWLES, Dom D., *The Religious Orders in England*, 3 vols. (Cambridge, 1948–59).

KOVANIK, E., 'A Newly-Discovered Dunstable Fragment', *JAMS*, 21 (1968), 21–33.

KRUMMEL, D. W., *English Music Printing 1553–1700* (London, 1975).

LASOCKI, D., 'The French Hautboy in England, 1673–1730', *Early Music*, 16 (1988), 339–57.

LAURIE, M., 'Did Purcell set *The Tempest*?', *PRMA*, 90 (1964–5), 43–57.

—— 'Purcell's Extended Solo Songs', *MT*, 125 (1984), 19–25.

LEFFERTS, P. M., 'Two English Motets on Simon de Montfort', *EMH*, i (Cambridge, 1981), 203–25.

—— *The Motet in England in the Fourteenth Century* (Ann Arbor, Mich., 1986).

—— and BENT, M. (comps.), 'New Sources of English Thirteenth and Fourteenth-Century Polyphony', *EMH*, 2 (Cambridge, 1982), 273–362.

LEFKOWITZ, M., *William Lawes* (London, 1960).

—— 'Shadwell and Lockes' *Psyche*: The French Connection', *PRMA*, 106 (1979–80), 42–55.

LE HURAY, P., 'The English Anthem 1580–1640', *PRMA*, 86 (1959–60), 1–13.

—— 'Towards a Definitive Study of Pre-Restoration Anglican Service Music', *MD*, 14 (1960), 167–95.

—— *Music and the Reformation in England, 1549–1660* (London, 1967; 2nd edn., Cambridge, 1978).

—— 'The Chirk Castle Partbooks', *EMH*, 2 (Cambridge, 1982), 17–42.

LEPPERT, R., 'Imagery, Musical Confrontation, and Cultural Difference in Early 18th-Century London', *Early Music*, 14 (1986), 323–45.

LESURE, F., and THIBAULT, G., *Bibliographie des éditions d'Adrian Le Roy et Robert Ballard* (Paris, 1955). Publications de la Société Française de Musicologie, II/ix.

LEVY, K. J., 'New Material on the Early Motet in England', *JAMS*, 4 (1951), 220–39.

LINCOLN, S., 'The First Setting of Congreve's "Semele"', *ML*, 44 (1963), 103–17.

LINDLEY, D., *Thomas Campion* (Leiden, 1986).

LIVI, G., 'The Ferrabosco Family', *The Musical Antiquary*, 4 (1912–13), 121–42.

LONG, J. M., *Shakespeare's Use of Music: Comedies*, 2 vols. (Gainsville, Fla., 1955–61).

—— 'Music for a Song in "Damon and Pithias"', *ML*, 48 (1967), 247–50.

LUCKETT, R., 'A New Source for "Venus and Adonis"', *MT*, 130 (1989), 76–9.

LUMSDEN, D., 'The Sources of English Lute Music (1540–1620)', 3 vols., Ph.D. diss. (Cambridge, 1957).

MCCOY, S., 'Edward Paston and the Textless Lute-song', *Early Music*, 15 (1987), 221–7.

MCGEE, T. J., 'The Liturgical Placements of the *Quem quaeritis* Dialogue', *JAMS*, 29 (1976), 1–29.

MANIFOLD, J., 'Theatre Music in the Sixteenth and Seventeenth Centuries', *ML*, 29 (1948), 366–97.

—— *The Music in English Drama from Shakespeare to Purcell* (London, 1956).

MARLOW, R., 'The Keyboard Music of Giles Farnaby', *PRMA*, 92 (1965–6), 107–20.

—— 'Sir Ferdinando Heyborne alias Richardson', *MT*, 105 (1974), 736–9.

MATEER, D., 'Further Light on Preston and Whyte', *MT*, 105 (1974), 1074–7.

—— 'John Sadler and Oxford Bodleian MSS Mus. e. 1–5', *ML*, 60 (1979), 281–95.

—— 'Oxford, Christ Church Music MSS 984–8: An Index and Commentary', *RMARC*, 20 (1986/7), 1–18.

MAYNARD, W., *Elizabethan Lyric Poetry and its Music* (Oxford, 1986).

MEECH, S. B., 'Three Musical Treatises in English from a Fifteenth-Century Manuscript', *Speculum*, 10 (1935), 235–69.

MEYER, E. H., *Die mehrstimmige Spielmusik des 17. Jahrhunderts in Nord- und Mittel-europa* (Kassel, 1934).

—— *Early English Chamber Music from the Middle Ages to Purcell*, 2nd edn., rev. by the author and D. Poulton (London, 1982).

MIES, O. H., 'Elizabethan Music Prints in an East-Prussian Castle', *MD*, 3 (1949), 171–2.

MILHOUS, J., 'Opera Finances in London, 1674–1738', *JAMS*, 37 (1984), 567–92.

—— and HUME, R. D., 'The Haymarket Opera in 1711', *Early Music*, 17 (1989), 523–37.

MILLER, L. E., 'John Birchensha and the Early Royal Society: Grand Scales and Scientific Composition', *JRMA*, 115 (1990), 63–79.

MILSOM, J., 'Songs, Carols and *Contrafacta* in the Early History of the Tudor Anthem', *PRMA*, 107 (1980–1), 34–45.

—— 'A New Tallis Contrafactum', *MT*, 123 (1982), 429–31.

—— 'English Polyphonic Style in Transition: A Study of the Sacred Music of Thomas Tallis', 2 vols., D.Phil. diss. (Oxford, 1983).

—— 'The Date of Ludford's Lady Masses: A Cautionary Note', *ML*, 66 (1985), 367–8.

—— 'A Tallis Fantasia', *MT*, 126 (1985), 658–62.

—— 'Tallis's First and Second Thoughts', *JRMA*, 113 (1988), 203–22.

—— 'Cries of Durham', *Early Music*, 18 (1989), 147–60.

MONSON, C., 'George Kirbye and the English Madrigal', *ML*, 59 (1978), 290–315.

—— *Voices and Viols in England, 1600–1650* (Ann Arbor, Mich., 1982).

MOREHEN, J., 'The Sources of English Cathedral Music *c*.1617–1644', Ph.D. diss. (Cambridge, 1969).

—— 'The Gloucester Cathedral Bassus Part-Book MS 93', *ML*, 62 (1981), 189–96.

MÜLLER, H., 'Der Musiktraktat in dem Werke des Bartholomaeus Anglicus *De proprietatibus rerum*', *Riemann-Festschrift*, ed. C. Mennicke (Leipzig, 1909), 241–55.

Music in English Renaissance Drama, ed. J. H. Long (Lexington, Ky., 1968).

NAGEL, W., *Annalen der englischen Hofmusik 1509–1649* (Leipzig, 1894).

—— *Geschichte der Musik in England*, 2 vols. (Strasburg, 1894–7).

NEIGHBOUR, O., *The Consort and Keyboard Music of William Byrd* (London, 1978).

—— 'Orlando Gibbons (1583–1625): The Consort Music', *Early Music*, 11 (1983), 351–7.

NEWCOMB, W. W.: *Studien zur englischen Lautenpraxis im elisabethanischen Zeitalter* (Kassel etc., 1968).

NIXON, H. M., 'The Book of XX Songs', *British Museum Quarterly*, 16 (1951), 33–5.

NIXON, P. J., 'William Bathe and his Times', *MT*, 124 (1983), 101–2.

NOBLE, J., 'Le Répertoire instrumental anglais (1550–1585)', *La Musique instrumentale de la Renaissance* (Paris, 1955), 91–114. A study of Add. 31390.

NOSKE, F., 'John Bull's Dutch Carol', *ML*, 44 (1963), 326–33.

OBERST, G., *Englische Orchestersuiten um 1600* (Wolfenbüttel, 1929).

OBERTELLO, A., *Madrigali italiani in Inghilterra* (Milan, 1949). Includes texts of the major publications.

OBOUSSIER, P., 'Turpyn's Book of Lute-Songs', *ML*, 34 (1953), 145–9.

OBST, W., '"Sumer is icumen in": A Contrafactum?', *ML*, 64 (1983), 151–61. Qualified by letter from R. Wibberly, ibid., 65 (1984), 332–3.

ORME, N., 'The Early Musicians of Exeter Cathedral', *ML*, 59 (1978), 395–410.

OTTERSTEDT, A., *Die englische Lyra-Viol: Instrument und Technik* (Kassel etc., 1989).

OWEN, E. A. B., 'Giles and Richard Farnaby in Lincolnshire', *ML*, 62 (1981), 151–4.

PACEY, R., 'Byrd's Keyboard Music: A Lincolnshire Source', *ML*, 66 (1985), 123–6.

PAGE, C., 'A Catalogue and Bibliography of English Song from its Beginnings to *c*.1300', *RMARC*, 13 (1976), 67–83.

—— 'Anglo-Saxon Hearpan: Their Terminology, Technique, Tuning and Repertory of Verse, 850–1066', D.Phil. diss. (York, 1981).

PALMER, F., 'Musical Instrumental from the *Mary Rose*', *Early Music*, 11 (1983), 53–9.

PATTISON, B., 'Philip Rosseter, Poet and Musician', *MT*, 72 (1931), 986–90.

—— 'Sir Philip Sidney and Music', *ML*, 15 (1934), 75–81.

—— *Music and Poetry of the English Renaissance* (2nd edn., London, 1970).

PAYNE, I., 'The Sacred Music of Thomas Ravenscroft', *Early Music*, 10 (1982), 309–15.

—— 'The Handwriting of John Ward', *ML*, 65 (1984), 176–88.

—— 'Instrumental Music at Trinity College, Cambridge, *c.*1594–*c.*1615: Archival and Biographical Evidence', *ML*, 68 (1987), 128–40.

PEARSON, D., *Old English and Middle English Poetry* (London, 1977).

PETTI, A. G., 'New Light on Peter Philips', *Monthly Musical Record*, 87 (1957), 58–63.

—— 'Peter Philips, Composer and Organist: 1561–1628', *Recusant History*, 4 (1957–8), 48–60.

PHILLIPS, P., '"Laboravi in gemitu meo": Morley or Rogier?', *ML*, 63 (1982), 85–90.

PINNOCK, A., 'Play into Opera: Purcell's *The Indian Queen*', *Early Music*, 18 (1990), 3–21.

PINTO, D., 'William Lawes at the Siege of York', *MT*, 127 (1986), 579–83.

PISTOR, J. C., 'Nicholas Strogers (Tudor Composer) and his Circle', 2 vols., B.Litt. diss. (Oxford, 1970). The 2nd vol. is a transcription of the extant works.

PLANCHART, A. E., *The Repertory of Tropes at Winchester*, 2 vols. (Princeton, NJ, 1977).

PLATT, P., 'Dering's Life and Training', *ML*, 33 (1952), 41–9.

POLIN, C., *The ap Huw Manuscript* (Henryville, Pa., 1982). IMM Musicological Studies, xxxiv.

POOLE, H. E., 'The Printing of William Holder's "Principles of Harmony"', *PRMA*, 101 (1974–5), 31–43.

POPE, J. C., *The Rhythm of Beowulf: An Interpretation of the Normal and Hypermetric Verse-Forms in Old English Poetry* (New Haven, Conn., and London, 1942; 2nd edn., 1966).

POULTON, D., 'Some Corrections of the Three Spanish Songs in "A Musicall Banquet"', *LSJ*, 3 (1961), 22–6.

—— *John Dowland* (London, 1972; 2nd edn., 1982).

—— 'The black-letter broadside and its music', *Early Music*, 9 (1981), 427–37.

POWELL, J., *Restoration Theatre Production* (London, 1984).

PRICE, C. A., 'An Organizational Peculiarity of Lord Herbert of Cherbury's Lute-Book', *LSJ*, 11 (1969), 5–27.

—— *Music in the Restoration Theatre* (Ann Arbor, Mich., 1975). Studies in Musicology, iv.

—— 'Restoration Theatre Music Restored', *MT*, 124 (1983), 344–7.

—— *Henry Purcell and the London Stage* (Cambridge, 1984).

PRICE, D. C., *Patrons and Musicians of the English Renaissance* (Cambridge, 1981).

RAINBOW, B., 'Bathe and his Introductions to Musicke', *MT*, 123 (1982), 243–7. See also C. Hill, Letter, ibid., 530–1.

RANKIN, S., 'Shrewsbury School, Manuscript VI: A Medieval Part-Book?', *PRMA*, 102 (1975–6), 129–44.

—— 'A New English Source of the Visitatio Sepulchri', *JPMMS*, 4 (1981), 1–11.

RANKIN, S., 'From Memory to Record: Musical Notations in Manuscripts from Exeter', *Anglo-Saxon England*, 13 (1984), 97–112.

RASTALL, R., 'The Minstrels of the English Royal Households, 25 Edward I–1 Henry VIII: An Inventory', *RMARC*, 4 (1964 [pub. 1966]), 1–41.

—— 'Benjamin Rogers (1614–98): Some Notes on his Instrumental Music', *ML*, 46 (1965), 237–42.

—— 'Music in the Cycle', in R. M. Lumiansky and D. Mills, *The Chester Mystery Cycle: Essays and Documents* (Chapel Hill, NC, and London, 1983), 111–64.

REANEY, G., 'The *Breviarium regulare musice* of MS Oxford, Bodley 842', *MD*, 11 (1957), 31–7.

REESE, G., *Music in the Middle Ages* (New York, 1940).

—— 'The Origin of the English *In Nomine*', *JAMS*, 2 (1949), 7–22.

—— *Music in the Renaissance* (New York, 1954; 2nd edn., 1959).

REMNANT, M., *English Bowed Instruments from Anglo-Saxon to Tudor Times* (Oxford, 1986).

RIGG, A. R., and WIELAND, G. R., 'A Canterbury Classbook of the Mid-Eleventh Century (the "Cambridge Songs" Manuscript)', *Anglo-Saxon England*, 4 (1975), 113–30.

ROESNER, E. H., 'The Origins of W1', *JAMS*, 27 (1976), 337–80.

ROGERS, C., *History of the Chapel Royal of Scotland* (Edinburgh, 1882).

ROOLEY, A., 'The Lute Solos and Duets of John Danyel', *LSJ*, 13 (1971), 18–27. With musical supplement.

—— 'New Light on Dowland's Songs of Darkness', *Early Music*, 11 (1983), 6–21.

ROPER, S. E., 'Medieval English Benedictine Liturgy: Studies in the Formation, Structure, and Content of the Monastic Votive Office, *c*.950–1540', D.Phil. thesis (Oxford, 1989).

SAMUEL, H. E., 'John Sigismond Cousser in London and Dublin', *ML*, 61 (1980), 158–71.

SANDERS, E. H., 'Duple Rhythm and Alternate Third Mode in the 13th Century', *JAMS*, 15 (1962), 249–91.

—— 'Cantilena and Discant in 14th-Century England', *MD*, 19 (1965), 7–52.

—— 'English Polyphony in the Morgan Library Manuscript', *ML*, 61 (1980), 172–6.

SANDON, N., 'The Henrician Partbooks at Peterhouse, Cambridge', *PRMA*, 103 (1976–7), 106–40.

—— 'Another Mass by Hugh Aston?', *Early Music*, 9 (1981), 184–91. See comments by J. Blezzard, ibid., 519–20; and by O. Neighbour, ibid., 10 (1982), 215–16.

—— 'Mary, Meditations, Monks, and Music: Poetry, Prose, Processions and Plagues in a Durham Cathedral Manuscript', *Early Music*, 10 (1982), 43–55.

—— 'The Henrician Partbooks belonging to Peterhouse, Cambridge . . . A Study, with Restoration of the Incomplete Compositions contained in them', Ph.D. diss. (Exeter, 1983).

—— 'F G A B flat A: Thoughts on a Tudor Motif', *Early Music*, 12 (1984), 56–63.

SCHOFIELD, B., 'The Provenance and Date of "Sumer is Icumen in"', *MR*, 9 (1948), 81–6.

—— 'The Manuscripts of Tallis's Forty-Part Motet', *MQ*, 37 (1951), 176–83.

—— and BUKOFZER, M. F., 'A Newly Discovered Fifteenth-Century Manuscript of the Chapel Royal', *MQ*, 32 (1946), 509–36 (Schofield), and 33 (1947), 38–51 (Bukofzer).

—— and DART, R. T., 'Tregian's Anthology', *ML*, 32 (1951), 205–16.

SCHUMANN, O., 'Die jungere Cambridger Liedersammlung', *Studi medievali*, NS, 16 (1943–50), 48–85.

SCOTT, A. B., 'English Music in Modena, Biblioteca Estense, α X. I. 11 and Other Italian Manuscripts', *MD*, 26 (1972), 145–60.

SCOTT, D., 'John Danyel: His Life and Songs', *LSJ*, 13 (1971), 7–17. With musical supplement.

SELFRIDGE-FIELD, E., 'Venetian Instrumentalists in England: A Bassano Chronicle (1536–1660)', *Studi musicali*, 8 (1979), 173–221.

Shakespeare in Music: Essays by John Stevens, Charles Cudworth, Winton Dean, Roger Fiske, ed. P. Hartnoll (London, 1964).

SHAW, W., 'A Cambridge Manuscript from the English Chapel Royal', *ML*, 42 (1961), 263–7.

—— 'Thomas Morley of Norwich', *MT*, 106 (1965), 669–73.

—— 'William Byrd of Lincoln', *ML*, 48 (1967), 52–9.

SIMPSON, A., 'Richard Mathew and *The Lute's Apology*', *LSJ*, 8 (1966), 41–7.

SMITH, A., 'Parish Church Musicians in England in the Reign of Elizabeth I (1558–1603): An Annotated Register', *RMARC*, 4 (1964), 42–92.

—— 'The Gentlemen and Children of the Chapel Royal of Elizabeth I: An Annotated Register', *RMARC*, 5 (1965), 13–46.

—— 'The Cultivation of Music in English Cathedrals in the Reign of Elizabeth I', *PRMA*, 94 (1967–8), 37–49.

—— 'Elizabethan Church Music at Ludlow', *ML*, 49 (1968), 108–21.

SMITH, D. A., 'The Ebenthal Lute and Viol Tablatures', *Early Music*, 10 (1982), 462–7.

SMITH, W. C., *A Bibliography of the Musical Works Published by John Walsh during the Years 1695–1720* (London, 1948).

SMOLDON, W. L., 'The Easter Sepulchre Music Drama', *ML*, 27 (1946), 1–17.

—— *The Music of the Medieval Church Dramas*, ed. C. Bourgeault (London, 1980).

SNYDER, J. L., 'A Road Not Taken: Theinred of Dover's Theory of Species', *JRMA*, 115 (1990), 145–81.

SPENCER, R., 'The Tollemache Lute Manuscript', *LSJ*, 7 (1965), 38–9.

SPINK, I., 'Angelo Notari and his "Prime Musiche Nuove"', *Monthly Musical Record*, 87 (1957), 168–77.

—— 'The Musicians of Queen Henrietta-Maria: Some Notes and References in the English State Papers', *AcM*, 36 (1964), 177–82.

—— *English Song: Dowland to Purcell* (London, 1974; repr. with corrections, 1986).

SPRING, M., 'Lute Music in England and Scotland after the Golden Age, 1620–1750', D.Phil. diss. (Oxford, 1987).

STEELE, H. J., 'English Organs and Organ Music from 1500 to 1650', Ph.D. thesis (Cambridge, 1958).

STEELE, R., *The Earliest English Music Printing: A Description and Bibliography of English Printed Music to the Close of the Sixteenth Century* (London, 1903).

STELL, J., and WATHEY, A., 'New Light on the Biography of John Dunstable?', *ML*, 62 (1981), 60–3.

STERNFELD, F. W., 'Music in the Schools of the Reformation', *MD*, 2 (1948), 99–122.

—— '*Troilus and Cressida*: Music for the Play', *English Institute Essays, 1952* (New York, 1954), 107–37.

—— 'Dramatic and Allegorical Function of Music in Shakespeare's Tragedies', *AnnM*, 3 (1955), 265–82.

—— 'Vautrollier's Printing of Lasso's *Recueil du Mellange* (London: 1570)', *AnnM*, 5 (1957), 199–227.

—— 'Shakespeare's Use of Popular Song', *Elizabethan and Jacobean Studies* (Oxford, 1959), 150–66.

—— 'Song in Jonson's Comedy', *Studies in English Renaissance Drama* (New York, 1959), 310–21.

—— *Music in Shakespearean Tragedy* (London, 1963; 2nd edn., 1967).

—— 'Ophelia's Version of the Walsingham Song', *ML*, 45 (1964), 108–13.

STEVENS, D., 'A Part Book in the Public Record Office', *Music Survey*, 2 (1950), 161–70.

—— *The Mulliner Book: A Commentary* (London, 1952).

—— 'A Recently Discovered English Source of the Fourteenth Century', *MQ*, 41 (1955), 26–40.

—— 'Tudor Part-Songs', *MT*, 96 (1955), 360–2.

—— *Thomas Tomkins, 1572–1656* (London, 1957).

—— 'The Manuscript Edinburgh, National Library of Scotland, Adv. MS. 5.1.15', *MD*, 13 (1959), 155–67.

—— 'A songe of fortie partes, made by Mr. Tallys', *Early Music*, 10 (1982), 171–81.

STEVENS, J., 'Music in Medieval Drama', *PRMA*, 84 (1957–8), 81–95.

—— *Music and Poetry in the Early Tudor Court* (London, 1961; repr. with corrections, Cambridge, etc., 1979).

—— *Words and Music in the Middle Ages: Song, Narrative, Dance and Drama, 1050–1350* (Cambridge, 1986).

STEVENSON, R., 'John Marbeck's "Noted Booke" of 1550', *MQ*, 37 (1951), 220–33.

SUMMERS, W., 'A New Source of Medieval English Polyphonic Music', *ML*, 63 (1977), 403–14.

—— 'Unknown and Unidentified English Polyphonic Music from the Fourteenth Century', *RMARC*, 19 (1983–5), 57–67.

THOMPSON, E., 'Robert Ramsey', *MQ*, 49 (1963), 210–24.

THOMPSON, R., 'George Jeffreys and the "Stile Nuovo" in English Sacred Music: A New Date for his Autograph Score, British Library, Add. MS 10338', *ML*, 70 (1989), 317–41.

THOMSON, R. M., 'The Music for the Office of St Edmund King and Martyr', *ML*, 65 (1984), 189–93.

TOFT, R., 'Musicke a Sister to Poetrie': Rhetorical Artifice in the Passionate Airs of John Dowland', *Early Music*, 12 (1984), 190–9.

TREND, J. B., 'The First English Songs', *ML*, 9 (1928), 111–28.

TROWELL, B., 'A Fourteenth-Century Ceremonial Motet and its Composer', *AcM*, 29 (1957), 65–75.

—— 'Faburden and Fauxbourdon', *MD*, 13 (1959), 43–78.

—— 'Faburden—New Sources, New Evidence: A Preliminary Survey', *Modern Musical Scholarship*, ed. E. Olleson (Boston, Henley, and London, 1978), 28–78.

—— 'Proportion in the Music of Dunstable', *PRMA*, 105 (1978/9), 100–41.

—— and WATHEY, A., 'John Benet's "Lux fulget ex Anglia—O pater pietatis—Salve Thoma": The Reconstruction of a Fragmentary Fifteenth-Century Motet in Honour of St Thomas Cantilupe', *St Thomas Cantilupe, Bishop of Hereford*, ed. M. Jancey (Hereford, 1982), 159–80.

TUTTLE, S. D., 'Watermarks in Certain Manuscript Collections of English Keyboard Music', *Essays Presented to Archibald Thompson Davison*, ed. R. Thompson and others (Cambridge, Mass., 1957), 147–58.

UNDERWOOD, P. J., 'Melodic Traditions in Medieval English Antiphoners', *JPMMS*, 5 (1982), 1–12.

VAN, G. DE, 'A Recently Discovered Source of Early Fifteenth Century Polyphonic Music', *MD*, 2 (1948), 5–74.

—— 'Inventory of Manuscript Bologna, Liceo Musicale Q 15 (*olim* 37), *MD*, 2 (1948), 231–57.

VAN DER MEER, J. H., 'The Keyboard Works in the Vienna Bull Manuscript', *TVNM*, 18 (1957), 72–105.

VINING, P., 'Gibbons and his Patrons', *MT*, 124 (1983), 707–9.

WAILES, M., 'Martin Peerson', *PRMA*, 80 (1953–4), 59–71.

WAITE, W. G., 'Johannes de Garlandia, Poet and Musician', *Speculum*, 35 (1960), 179–95.

WALKER, E., 'An Oxford Book of Fancies', *Musical Antiquary*, 3 (1911–12), 65–73.

WALLS, P., 'New Light on Songs by William Lawes and John Wilson', *ML*, 57 (1976), 55–64.

—— 'The Origins of English Recitative', *PRMA*, 110 (1983–4), 25–40. Followed by F. W. Sternfeld, 'A Note on *Stile Recitativo*', 41–4.

—— '"Music and Sweet Poetry"? Verse for English Lute Song and Continuo Song', *ML*, 65 (1984), 237–54.

—— 'The Influence of the Italian Violin School in 17th-Century England', *Early Music*, 18 (1990), 575–87.

WARD, J. M., 'The "Dolfull Domps"', *JAMS*, 4 (1951), 111–21.

—— 'Music for *A Handefull of pleasant delites*', *JAMS*, 10 (1957), 151–80.

—— 'The Lute Music of MS Royal Appendix 58', *JAMS*, 13 (1960), 117–25.

—— '*Joan qd John* and Other Fragments at Western Reserve University', *Aspects of Medieval and Renaissance Music: A Birthday Offering to Gustave Reese*, ed. J. LaRue (New York, 1966), 832–55.

—— 'The Lute Books of Trinity College, Dublin: Preface' and 'I: MS D. 3. 30/I: The so-called Dallis Lute Book', *LSJ*, 9 (1967), 17–40.

—— 'The Lute Books of Trinity College, Dublin, II: Ms. D. 1. 21: The so-called Ballet Lute Book', *LSJ*, 10 (1968), 15–32. 4 plates.

—— 'The Fourth Dublin Lute Book', *LSJ*, 11 (1969), 28–46 (incl. 4 plates).

—— 'Barley's Songs without Words', *LSJ*, 12 (1970), 5–22.

—— 'The Hunt's Up', *PRMA*, 106 (1979–80), 1–25.

—— *Sprightly and Cheerful Musick: Notes on the Cittern, Gittern & Guitar in 16th- and 17th-Century England* (London, 1983) = *LSJ*, 21 (1979–81).

—— 'The English Measure', *Early Music*, 14 (1986), 15–21.

—— 'Newly Devis'd Measures for Jacobean Masques', *AcM*, 60 (1988), 111–42.

—— '"And Who But Ladie Greensleeues?"', *The Well Enchanting Skill* (Oxford, 1990), 181–211.

WARLOCK, P., *The English Ayre* (London, 1926).

—— *Thomas Whythorne: An Unknown Elizabethan Composer* (London, 1927).

WARREN, E. B., 'The Life and Works of Robert Fayrfax', *MD*, 11 (1957), 134–52.

—— 'The Masses of Robert Fayrfax', *MD*, 12 (1958), 145–76.

WATHEY, A., 'Newly Discovered Fifteenth-Century Polyphony at Oxford', *ML*, 64 (1983), 58–66.

—— 'Dunstable in France', *ML*, 67 (1986), 1–36.

—— 'Lost Books of Polyphony in England: A List to 1500', *RMARC*, 21 (1988), 1–20.

—— *Music in the Royal and Noble Households in Late Medieval England: Studies of Sources and Patronage* (New York, 1989).

WEGMAN, R. C., 'Concerning Tempo in the English Polyphonic Mass, *c.*1420–70', *AcM*, 61 (1989), 40–65.

WEIDNER, R. W., 'New Insight on the Early "In nomine"', *Revue Belge de Musicologie*, 15 (1961), 29–46.

The Well Enchanting Skill: Music, Poetry and Drama in the Culture of the Renaissance. Essays in Honour of F. W. Sternfeld, ed. J. Caldwell, E. Olleson, and S. Wollenberg (Oxford, 1990).

WELLS, R. H., 'The Orpharion: Symbol of a Humanist Ideal', *Early Music*, 10 (1982), 427–40.

—— 'The Ladder of Love: Verbal and Musical Rhetoric in the Elizabethan Lute-Song', *Early Music*, 12 (1984), 173–89.

—— 'John Dowland and Elizabethan Melancholy', *Early Music*, 13 (1985), 514–28.

—— 'Ars amatoria: Philip Rosseter and the Tudor Court Lyric', *ML*, 70 (1989), 58–71.

WESTRUP, J. A., *Purcell* (London, 1937; rev. N. Fortune, 1980).

—— 'Foreign Musicians in Stuart England', *MQ*, 27 (1941), 70–89.

—— 'Domestic Music under the Stuarts', *PMA*, 68 (1941–2), 19–53.

WILCOX, H., '"My Mournful Style": Poetry and Music in the Madrigals of John Ward', *ML*, 61 (1980), 60–70.

WILKINS, N., *Music in the Age of Chaucer* (Cambridge, 1979). Chaucer Studies, i.
—— 'Music and Poetry at Court: England and France in the Late Middle Ages', in *English Court Culture in the Later Middle Ages*, ed. V. J. Scattergood and J. W. Sherborne (London, 1982).

WILLETTS, P. J., 'A Neglected Source of Monody and Madrigal', *ML*, 43 (1962), 329–39.

—— 'Musical Connections of Thomas Myriell', *ML*, 49 (1968), 36–42.

—— 'Autographs of Angelo Notari', *ML*, 50 (1969), 124–6.

—— *The Henry Lawes Manuscript* (London, 1969).

—— 'Silvanus Stirrop's Book', *RMARC*, 10 (1972), 101–7; and 12 (1974), 156.

WILLIAMS, R., 'Manuscript Organ Books in Eton College Library', *ML*, 41 (1960), 358–9.

WILSON, C., *Words and Notes Coupled Lovingly Together: Thomas Campion, a Critical Study* (New York, 1989).

WILSON, E., 'Some New Texts of Early Tudor Songs', *Notes and Queries*, 27 (1980), 293–5.

WILSON, H. A., 'The English Coronation Orders', *Journal of Theological Studies*, 2 (1901), 481–504.

WING, D., *A Short-title Catalogue of Books Printed in England . . . 1641–1700* (Cambridge, Mass., 1945–51).

WOOD, B., 'A Newly Identified Purcell Autograph', *ML*, 59 (1978), 329–32.

WOODFIELD, I., *The Early History of the Viol* (Cambridge, 1984).

WOODFILL, W. L., *Musicians in English Society* (Princeton, NJ, 1953).

WOODS, I., 'A Note on "Scottish Anonymous"', *RMARC*, 21 (1988), 37–9.

——'Towards a Biography of Robert Carvor', *MR*, 49 (1988), 83–101.

WRIGHT, C., 'The Coronation of Henry VI of England at Notre Dame of Paris', *La Musique et le rite sacré et profane: Actes du XIIIe Congrès . . . Strasbourg . . . 1982* (Strasburg, 1986), i. 433–8.

WULSTAN, D., *Tudor Music* (London, 1985).

YOUNG, A. R., 'Henry Peacham, Ben Jonson and the Cult of Elizabeth-Oriana', *ML*, 60 (1979), 305–11.

YOUNG, K., *The Drama of the Medieval Church*, 2 vols. (Oxford, 1933; repr. 1951, 1962).

ZIM, R., *English Metrical Psalm Poetry: Praise and Prayer, 1535–1601* (Cambridge, 1987).

ZIMMERMAN, F. B., *Henry Purcell, 1659–1695: An Analytical Catalogue of his Music* (London and New York, 1963).

——*Henry Purcell, 1659–1695: His Life and Times* (London, 1967; 2nd rev. edn., Philadelphia, Pa., 1983).

——Henry Purcell: *A Guide to Research* (New York, 1989).

Index